BENJAMIN BRITTEN

BENJAMIN BRITTEN

A Biography

Humphrey Carpenter

faber and faber

First published in 1992
by Faber and Faber Limited
3 Queen Square London WC1N 3AU
This paperback edition first published in 1993

Photoset by Parker Typesetting Service, Leicester
Printed in England by Clays Ltd, St Ives plc

A CIP record for this book is available from the British Library

ISBN 0-571-14325-3

2 4 6 8 10 9 7 5 3 1

Especially I would like to know whether your purpose is to give a comfortable or an uncomfortable picture, the true or the fictitious. This sounds terribly threatening, but truly it is not meant to be. I just feel most strongly that BB can survive the truth and still come through as one of the most supreme and lovable persons that ever lived, but if the whole truth is not told this image will in fact be impaired and will limp into history.

Stephen Reiss to the author, 5 February 1991

Contents

Preface

Benjamin Britten's music was part of my upbringing. At school, at university, and in a parish choir I played and sang in many of his works. When very young I was taken to *Let's Make an Opera*. Much later I stood in the Albert Hall and watched Britten conduct a Prom performance of the *War Requiem*. He and Peter Pears gave a recital at my school. They were a familiar feature of my cultural background.

I never met Britten, but in 1981, a little over four years after his death, I went to the Red House at Aldeburgh to interview Pears for a radio documentary on 'Britten country'. I also spoke to Imogen Holst. Already, I suppose, I was half-consciously hoping to write a life of Britten, though it was widely known that Donald Mitchell had been chosen by the composer as his biographer.

In the summer of 1988, during a lunch to mark the publication by Faber and Faber of my life of Ezra Pound, Matthew Evans, the firm's chairman, made several suggestions as to whose biography I might write next for them. Suddenly he came up with the name of Britten. I immediately realized that, if this were possible, it would be a biography I would want to write more than any I had previously undertaken. Next day, Matthew Evans approached Donald Mitchell, who to my great delight said yes.

Though he had intended to write Britten's life himself, Mitchell was at that time too deeply involved in editing Britten's letters and diaries to undertake a biography. Indeed, now that his and Philip Reed's edition of the letters has begun to appear, it may be judged that Mitchell *is* writing Britten's life in his extensive annotations to them. At all events, he made it clear from the outset that I was to have *carte blanche* access to all written material, and since the beginning of my work in May 1989 he has given me every possible form of help, generously sharing his huge knowledge of Britten with me, and putting no obstacle in the way of what I believe to be a candid and fully truthful biography. Equal generosity and candour has been shown, without exception, by all Britten's surviving friends and colleagues.

The Trustees of the Britten–Pears Foundation have kindly given me permission to quote extensively from Britten's correspondence and diaries, of which they are the copyright owners. I should, however, emphasize that this portrait of Britten and interpretation of his music represent solely my own viewpoint.

H.C.
Oxford, Christmas 1991

PART ONE

1913–37

No place like home

1: Once upon a time there was a prep-school boy

Benjamin Britten's mother was *'determined* that he should be a great musician,' recalls his childhood friend Basil Reeve. 'Quite often we would talk about the 3 B's ... Bach, Beethoven and Brahms, and the fourth B was Britten.' Yet Mrs Britten hinted to her daughter-in-law Marjorie that she and her husband had not meant to have a fourth child at all.

Three children to feed, clothe and educate must indeed have seemed enough to the father, Robert Victor Britten, who in the early 1900s was working hard to establish himself as a dental surgeon in Lowestoft, on the coast of East Anglia – the most easterly town in England. His was not a job with much social status. Though the town was already on the way down from its heyday as a grand nineteenth-century seaside resort, the Victorian boom years had left the place clique-ridden and snobbish, dominated by the 'county' set who patronized the yacht club. 'The county wouldn't recognize a doctor's wife. I think dentists would have been hardly noticed at all. They'd have hardly been considered to live,' recalls Mrs Marian Walker, born in 1897, who knew Lowestoft and the Brittens in her childhood.

By 1913, the year of Benjamin's birth, Robert Britten had built up a substantial practice at 21 Kirkley Cliff Road, a double-fronted, semi-detached villa overlooking the sea at the south end of the town. He had even been admitted to membership of the yacht club, just down the road, where he would walk for a drink.

He had wanted to be a farmer, but there was no money in his family, so he had trained in dentistry at Charing Cross Hospital and worked first in Ipswich before setting up in Lowestoft. His patients liked him – Marian Walker says he was a 'nice friendly dentist' – but he hated his job. Marjorie, his daughter-in-law, remembers that 'he used to come up from his surgery at eleven o'clock in the morning, to "Heaven", which was his name for the upstairs drawing-room, and drink a neat whisky. He'd sit there, with his leg up – he had a bad leg – and look sideways at you. I decided he drank more than he should, though I never saw him the worse for it.'

'I come from a very ordinary middle-class family,' said Benjamin Britten in 1968. The name 'Britten' means exactly what it appears to, a British person, and Beth Britten, Benjamin's younger sister, said that her father's family were reputed to have been by origin 'yeoman farmers'. Certainly there were Britten ancestors living in the prosperous farming countryside of Herefordshire during the seventeenth century. John Britten, Benjamin's great-grandfather, was born in the small village of Stoke Bliss, to the north-east of Hereford, in 1798. In the nineteenth century the family drifted to towns. One of John's sons, Thomas, Benjamin's grandfather, became a draper in Birkenhead and later a dairy owner in Maidenhead, but died young, and though his daughters did well enough (one became a headmistress in Barbados and the other married a missionary), the eldest boy died of drink and the second ruined the family business. The third was Robert, Benjamin's father. 'I think my mother probably saved him,' Beth Britten has said. 'He didn't go off the rails as his brothers did ... She was quite a lot older than he was, you know.' (There was a four-year gap in their ages.) She certainly seems to have been determined that her children should not go down the path to alcoholism. Bobby, the eldest son, pledged his mother that he would not drink before he was twenty-one, and went through Cambridge on orange juice. When Bobby became engaged to Marjorie Goldson, Mr Britten fetched up a bottle from the cellar, but everyone else had to sit and watch while he alone drank it.

On Benjamin Britten's mother's side, the ancestry was more mysterious. Beth once found a family Bible with some genealogical entries at the front, but this was promptly whisked out of the way, and when she found it again the crucial page had been cut out. Marjorie, too, noticed Mrs Britten skimming over certain bits of family background. Eventually, under Beth's questioning, Mrs Britten admitted that her own father had been illegitimate. As often in such instances, there was talk of an innocent girl being seduced by an aristocrat, maybe even a duke – Marjorie was half-promised ducal heirlooms on her marriage, though they never materialized. The plain facts were that a boy named William Henry Hockey was born in Exeter in 1842 to one Fanny Hockey, taking his mother's surname because no father had been identified. He eventually landed up in London, where according to Beth he became a Queen's Messenger and was given 'a beautiful flat in the Home Office'. On the certificate of his marriage in 1871 his job is given as 'office keeper' so his status was probably that of caretaker; hence the flat. He and his wife had seven children of whom Edith, Benjamin Britten's mother, was the eldest, but Beth says that the wife turned out to be 'a drunk' and 'spent half her life in homes'. Possibly this is why the daughters were sent away to the school in Maidenhead also attended by Thomas Britten's girls; hence eventually the marriage between Edith Hockey and Robert Britten.

The Britten ancestors do not seem to have had artistic talent, but there was plenty in the Hockeys. Edith's younger sister Queenie was a good painter, and two of her brothers became church organists. One was killed in the First World War, but the other could be found during Benjamin Britten's childhood at the Tower Church in Ipswich – though he too had a drink problem. Yet another brother went to sea at fourteen, but kept up his music, and many years later Peter Pears, singing in a concert at Southend, discovered him in the orchestra. Edith herself, Benjamin's mother, was a good amateur singer, an enthusiastic member of the Lowestoft Musical Society, for which she sang mezzo-soprano and con-tralto, and was sometimes given solos. The Society's concerts were con-ducted by the organist of St John's, an ugly early-Victorian parish church of Evangelical persuasion, which she attended regularly. Marjorie says she was 'very religious', but noticed that Mr Britten 'never went near a church'.

The social life of the Britten household revolved around music. Marian Walker would receive invitations to Mrs Britten's musical evenings in the drawing-room, and describes her hostess as 'an interesting amateur' who 'had a perfect ear but absolutely no training'. In 1953 Benjamin Britten wrote: 'My mother was never a professional singer, only a keen amateur one with a sweet voice.' Her favourites included Roger Quilter's 'Now Sleeps the Crimson Petal' and such Schubert popular pieces as 'Who is Sylvia?' and 'Hark! Hark! the Lark!' She was delighted that Benjamin's birth in 1913 had been on 22 November, feast-day of St Cecilia, patron saint of music. He was named Edward Benjamin, the first after his father's younger brother, the second to signify that he would be the last child. 'Edward' was soon dropped, and within the family he became known during early childhood as 'Beni'.

When he was three months old, he developed pneumonia, and was thought likely to die. His sister Beth writes that his survival was 'prob-ably due to the fact that my mother was breast-feeding him, as she did us all. She expressed the milk, and fed him with a fountain-pen filler, he was too weak to suck.' The baby's nanny and the doctor who lived next door (Marian Walker's uncle) both claimed, in later years, credit for his survival. According to Beth, the illness left him with a heart murmur, and the Brittens were told to treat him with great care, but Mr Britten, who had had some medical training, felt strongly that he would be miserable if prevented from leading a normal life, and after his recovery he was given no special treatment.

With his blue eyes and mass of golden curls, 'Beni' seemed especially designed for the role of youngest child. 'He looked so beautiful,' says Beth, 'wonderful hair and blue eyes and pink cheeks. He was a very, very fetching little boy.' She alleges that people called him 'Dear' so often that he came to believe it was his name. 'After the war started', she writes, 'one day he was in his pram asleep in the garden. He woke up crying, and when asked what was the matter he said "Bomb drop on Dear's head."' The First World War broke out when he was eight months old, and since Lowestoft was a naval base it became a target during the 1916 Zeppelin attacks. The Britten family often had to shelter in the cellar. Imogen Holst, who wrote one of the first biographies of Britten, was told by him that the first sound he could remember was a wartime explosion, though Beth says it was a hissing gas-light or gas fire. To Donald Mitchell, Britten alleged he remembered being born, and hearing 'the sound of rushing water' as the birth took place.

One sound was so constantly audible at 21 Kirkley Cliff Road that a small child would scarcely notice it at first: the sea breaking on the long sands of Lowestoft's South Beach, a hundred yards away. A mile or so to the south, the waves were eating into the soft coastline of pebbles and sandy cliffs. For afternoon walks the Britten nanny, who was a girl from a Suffolk village, would often take the children to see how many more houses had fallen off the cliff in the nearby village of Pakefield. If it was too wet for a walk, they would watch from the nursery window as a tug pulled a fleet of fishing smacks with broad tan-coloured sails out to sea. In the autumn they might accompany their mother down to the canteen she ran in the town for the Scots herring girls, who gutted and packed the fish and spoke only Gaelic, and would disappear north again after the three-month herring season. 'Very few local people went near the fish-markets,' writes Beth; 'they despised them as being smelly, but we felt it was the most interesting part of the town.'

The three elder children had proved a disappointment to Mrs Britten as musicians. Barbara, who was eleven when Benjamin was born, had no musical talent, and though Bobby, six years older than Benjamin, was musically quite gifted and had learnt the violin, he was more interested in picking out ragtime tunes on the piano. Beth, aged four at Benjamin's birth, was no more musical than her sister, so when Benjamin, like any other child, began to make experimental noises on the piano, his mother encouraged him so much that he decided the instrument was his private territory. Soon, he was elbowing Bobby from the keys on the pretext that he 'had a thought' and wished to try it out. 'We used to fight for the piano,' recalls his brother, 'and Mother used to come in and say, "Let Beni have it, he's the little one." So he usually got it.'

Britten himself, in adult life, did not regard these early attempts as significant: 'I believe I started strumming like any other kid as soon as I could walk.' Nevertheless when professional soloists came from London to perform with the Musical Society, he would be shown off to them as a child with musical promise. If he was sent to bed while music-making was going on in the drawing-room, he would cry until he was brought downstairs again. Barbara Britten says of their mother's treatment of him: 'Oh, he was always allowed to do everything ... He was her baby, and everything he did was always perfect.' By contrast, 'Pop' Britten was strict with Benjamin. 'I think he used to counteract my mother probably spoiling him,' Beth remarks. 'He never beat him or anything like that, [but] he was strict with all of us. We were all ... a bit afraid of him.'

At Christmas 1916, just after his third birthday, Benjamin was dressed up as an elf and allowed to speak a few lines in a family production of *Cinderella*, organized by the nanny. Two and a half years later he was given the part of Tom, the little sweep, in a dramatization of Charles Kingsley's *The Water-Babies*, performed in a local hall. He recalled being dressed 'in skin-coloured tights, with madly curly hair' – his natural curls were augmented by a wig – and 'trying desperately to remember the lines'. His mother played Mrs Do-as-you-would-be-done-by, the good fairy. He was soon writing his own plays. 'The Royal Falily' (*sic*) probably dates from the spring of 1920, since it contains a scene in which Britten's Aunt Florence, headmistress of a girls' school in Barbados, meets the Prince of Wales, who visited the island in March that year. There is a snatch of music in it, a four-bar setting of some nonsense words, though it looks more like a childish doodle than the real thing. Britten himself recalled that his earliest compositions were on visual rather than musical principles:

> I remember the first time I tried, the result looked rather like the Forth Bridge, in other words hundreds of dots all over the page connected by long lines all joined together in beautiful curves. I am afraid it was the pattern on the paper which I was interested in and when I asked my mother to play it, her look of horror upset me considerably.

He said much the same in a 1960 interview: 'it was really not much more than dots and dashes on a bit of paper . . . It was . . . the *look* of the thing on the paper which fascinated me.' At this stage, members of his family were more impressed by his drawings. Beth calls them 'beautiful . . . very detailed and expressive', and says that 'everyone thought he would be an artist'.

He began piano lessons at the age of seven, when he was sent to 'Southolme', a dame-school at 52 Kirkley Cliff Road, run by two Miss Astles and their mother. The younger daughter, Miss Ethel, was the music teacher. She advertised in the *Lowestoft Journal* as 'Miss E. K. M. Astle, ARCM . . . Singing, Pianoforte, Harmony. Modern Methods of Teaching.' These included the Sepping System, a wooden apparatus with adjustable pieces for teaching notation. Benjamin got on well in his piano lessons with her, and Imogen Holst says he was 'soon able to accompany his mother's songs and to play exciting duets with Mr Coleman, who was the organist of St John's Church where the family went every Sunday'. Beth, however, specifies that while their mother went to church, their father would make a car trip which began with visits to patients but ended 'at Sotterly which was a farm and public house combined'.

Beth stresses that 'we had a secure home and loving parents', and Benjamin's first cousin Elsie Hockey describes the atmosphere at 21 Kirkley Cliff Road as 'always rather like a party . . . such a peaceful, very happy household'. However, Marjorie Goldson noticed that the party atmosphere was carefully contrived when visitors were about to arrive. They would be greeted by a relaxed family group, with Bobby (never Benjamin) tinkling a popular tune on the piano, but Marjorie knew that he had been put up to it a moment earlier by Mrs Britten – 'Bobby, they're coming, do go and play something.' When Marjorie herself first came to the house, she sat down in a chair in the drawing-room, and faces fell: 'Oh, not *there*, that's Pop's chair.' She also remembers that, when she slept in the spare room on the top floor, voices could be heard raised in argument in the parents' bedroom beneath her. In 1970 Britten told Rosamund Strode, who was then working for him, that the scene in his opera *Owen Wingrave* in which Sir Philip ferociously rebukes Owen in his off-stage study, with the horn representing angry words we cannot hear, was a recollection of hearing his parents having a disagreement and not being able to make out what was said.

Elsie Hockey was the daughter of Benjamin's Uncle Willie, the Ipswich organist who drank too much, and around the age of eight Benjamin began to go to stay by himself with the Hockeys. He liked these trips for the steam trains as much as the music. A letter written home from

Ipswich describes seeing 'about 20 L & Ner Engines'. Beth describes him at home, lounging in the bath and reading a railway time-table, while the nanny, reluctant to admit that her youngest charge was no longer a baby and her time with the Brittens was coming to an end, carefully sponged him: 'Lift your leg, dear; now the other. Now get out and I will dry you.' At the age of eight he was sent to South Lodge Preparatory School, just down the hill from Kirkley Cliff Road. His brother Bobby had been a pupil there, when the school was run by an ancient clergyman named Phillips, who retired almost as soon as Benjamin arrived, handing over South Lodge to his mathematics master, Thomas Jackson Elliott Sewell.

*

Sewell was in his mid-thirties, a Cambridge graduate who had won the MC in the war and was referred to by parents as Captain Sewell. The boys called him The Beak, a common nickname for schoolmasters, but also a reference to his aquiline nose. Until he took over the school he was unmarried. For a while he courted Barbara Britten, who was turning twenty, but then he jilted her and married someone else. Barbara, crushed by this, went to London, trained as a health visitor, and took up with an older woman, a social worker named Helen Hurst, who shocked the Britten family with her Eton crop and mannish ways.

South Lodge was a very small school, with about thirty boys and a handful of staff. Most of the pupils were boarders, some of them abandoned there for holidays as well as term-time by parents who had gone abroad. Benjamin Britten was unusual in not merely being a day-boy but living just up the road. This must have helped him to settle in, and looking back in 1955 he suggested that everything had gone well from the start:

> Once upon a time there was a prep-school boy. He was called Britten mi., his initials were E. B., his age was nine, and his locker was number seventeen. He was quite an ordinary little boy; he took his snake-belt to bed with him; he loved cricket, only quite liked football (although he kicked a pretty 'corner'); he adored mathematics, got on all right with history, was scared by Latin Unseen; he behaved fairly well, only ragged the recognised amount, so that his contacts with the cane or the slipper were happily rare (although one nocturnal expedition to stalk ghosts left its marks behind); he worked his way up the school slowly and steadily.

In fact the school list for Christmas 1923, his fourth term, shows him in bottom (ninth) place in Form III. On the other hand, beneath this list in the school magazine appears the following paragraph:

As we go to press, we are very pleased to hear that Britten, who is just ten years old, has passed well in the Higher Division of the Associated Board of the Royal College of Music. We understand that he got good marks and just missed a distinction.

Captain Sewell, struggling (as his son Donald recalls) to keep his school off the financial rocks, evidently regarded any kind of success by a pupil as useful for impressing the parents. South Lodge had no music teacher, and Benjamin was still being taught by Ethel Astle.

The fact that he 'adored mathematics' made life easier for him, since Sewell himself taught that subject. 'If you were good at maths, then you couldn't go wrong,' says Britten's schoolfriend John Pounder. 'If you weren't, as I wasn't, you weren't quite so favoured.' Being out of favour with Sewell was a serious matter. Pounder describes the previous head-master, Phillips, as 'a dear old man', but recalls Sewell and his method of inflicting discipline very differently:

> You got beaten on the slightest pretext, with a hell of a palaver. For really extra special beatings the whole school was assembled, and the criminal was brought out before them, and then was led away to a dormitory above the school room. We always said that Sewell liked beating boys, but we were much too frightened to complain.

In 1971 Britten told a newspaper interviewer:

> I can remember the first time – I think it was the very first day that I was in a school – that I heard a boy being beaten, and I can remember my absolute astonishment that people didn't immediately rush to help him. And to find that it was sort of condoned and accepted was something that shocked me very much. Whether or not it all grew from that I don't know.

By 'it', he meant his pacifism. Peter Pears, too, believed that it had its origins here: 'There was some protest that he organized at his prep school, about some beating or other, some old-fashioned attitude that he didn't agree with, and he got into a certain amount of trouble over that.'

Donald Sewell remarks of the school in his father's day: 'It's rather horrifying to realize just how much punishment went on.' He says he and his brother and sister found their father a somewhat awe-inspiring figure, but defends him against the charge of sadism: 'He wasn't a vindictive person at all. It was just that this was how discipline was exerted in those days.' John Pounder says that the other staff were 'very pleasant' by comparison, and emphasizes that, unlike many boys, Britten was rarely punished, since he seemed to be Sewell's favourite, 'more than one noticed with anybody else'. In the next issue of the school magazine, Christmas 1924, Sewell wrote:

> We have to congratulate E. B. Britten on a remarkable achievement during the term. At the age of barely eleven years he has taken and passed the Intermediate Examination of the Associated Board of the R.A.M. and R.C.M. In the three-hour paper on the Theory of Music, the only written paper that lay before him, he obtained 95 marks out of 99. On this extremely creditable result we heartily congratulate him and all concerned.

Meanwhile Britten's school work was only mediocre. This term he came sixth out of eleven in Form III.

Sewell's praise of Britten's musical achievement made no mention of Ethel Astle (who looked the classic spinster music teacher, with pince-nez and hair in a bun). At her death in 1952 Britten said he owed her 'a tremendous debt'. His Uncle Willie in Ipswich played a part in his musical education too. Marian Walker once asked Britten, 'Where did your music come from?', because she was 'so aware of the extremely uncultured background that he'd come from. And Ben said to me – I clearly remember – "I had rather a reprobate old uncle, but he was intensely musical, and I think it was he who originally told me that he preferred to *read* a score rather than hear anything played."'

It was Uncle Willie who in November 1922 gave Britten on his ninth birthday *A Dictionary of Musical Terms* (1889) by Sir John Stainer and W. A. Barrett. Since beginning piano lessons with Miss Ethel, he had been writing music which he describes as 'much more conscious of *sound*'. The earliest of these pieces were 'elaborate tone poems usually lasting about twenty seconds, inspired by terrific events in my home life'. One which has survived is 'DO YOU NO THAT MY DADDY HAS GONE TO LONDON TODAY', which Britten himself dated '1919'; this would mean that it was written at the age of five or six. More sophisticated than the fragment in 'The Royal Falily', it is scored for piano and vocal duet, and has a simple melody plainly harmonized. A little later he began to set poetry to music. A fragment dated '1922', when he was eight or nine, is a spirited setting of Kipling's 'Oh, where are you going to, all you big steamers', perhaps intended to be sung by his mother – its vocal range would have suited her. A year or two later he put together a manuscript volume of songs which he entitled 'Twelve Songs for the Mezzo-Soprano and Contralto Voice'. When he acquired Stainer and Barrett's book, he began to use the Italian terms for tempi and dynamics which he found in it. The book also introduced him to the principles of composition, set out under such entries as canon, counterpoint, fugue, ground bass and modulation, all profusely illustrated with musical examples. Under its tuition he began to imitate rich Victorian harmonies such as are found in Stainer's own *Crucifixion*. His twelve-bar setting for voice and piano of a Longfellow poem, 'Beware!', probably dating from 1922–3, begins fairly simply, but concludes with four surprising bars of Stainer-like chromatic progression, a precocious achievement for a child who had not reached his tenth birthday.

It seems an oddly dated musical style for a schoolboy who was writing a decade after the first performance of *The Rite of Spring* and five years after the death of Debussy, but 'Pop' Britten refused to buy a gramophone or a wireless. Beth says he was 'afraid that if it came easily to us, we (or rather my brothers) would stop making our own music', but maybe he thought there was enough noise in the house already. Consequently, Benjamin had to acquire most of his early knowledge of the great composers not from records or broadcasts, but by what he describes as 'ploughing through the great symphonies' in arrangements for piano duet, played with friends or relatives.

By the age of ten he was pouring out what he calls 'reams and reams' of musical compositions, despite the long school day – lessons began at 7.30 a.m. and he was not free to go home until 8 p.m. 'His friends bore with it,' he writes of this, 'his enemies kicked a bit but not for long (he was quite tough), the staff couldn't object if his work and games didn't suffer.' Games were important to him. He says he was 'passionately keen' on them, and his sister Barbara says: 'He was just like all little boys, he loved sport, he loved games, he was very good at everything he did – the wretch!' John Nicholson, his best friend at South Lodge, greatly admired him as a sportsman: 'We all knew he played the piano, but ... we thought it would be far better if he played cricket, which he did very well indeed.' By the summer term of 1927, Britten, aged thirteen, had reached the position of vice-captain of the school's Cricket XI. 'A distinctly useful bowler with a leg swerve,' observed the school magazine. His reputation as a games-player saved him from the mockery his composing might otherwise have attracted. 'He could stand up for himself,' says Barbara. 'He never was bullied at school, as far as one can make out, because he was quite good with his fists.' She picks on an apparent contradiction which was to remain for the rest of his life: 'He was always a very sensitive little boy. He always worried about things. And yet in some ways he wasn't, he was very tough.'

*

In 1955 Britten wrote this wryly comic description of his juvenilia:

> they are still lying in an old cupboard to this day – string quartets (six
> of them); twelve piano sonatas; dozens of songs; sonatas for violin,
> sonatas for viola and 'cello too; suites, waltzes, rondos, fantasies,
> variations; a tone poem *Chaos and Cosmos*; a tremendous sym-
> phony, for gigantic orchestra including eight horns and oboe d'amore
> (started on January 17 and finished February 28); an oratorio called
> *Samuel*; and all the opus numbers from 1 to 100 were filled (and
> catalogued) by the time Britten mi. was fourteen.

All these items, and the list of opus numbers, can indeed be found
among his early manuscripts, though they were written over quite a
long period – about nine to fourteen. He composed on Sundays and
half-holidays, even snatching 'odd moments in bed' to take out his
manuscript paper. He acquired the habit of working under pressure. At
sixteen he observed: 'I can never write [music] when I've got time, I
have always to hurry.'

His mother, determined that school life should not interfere with his
progress, went to Sewell to ask that he should have time not merely to
practise the piano but compose. Sewell made sympathetic noises. Meanwhile Benjamin showed no sign of resenting her involvement. Indeed he
reciprocated her attention, playing up to the role of mother's darling. A
letter written just before his tenth birthday begins 'My Mummie darling' and ends

> With tons and cwts. and lbs. and
> ozs. of pakages of Love,
> Your own tiny little (sick-for-Muvver)
> BENI

Mrs Britten had become acquainted with a clergyman's wife, Audrey
Alston, who had been a professional viola player before her marriage.
At the age of eight, her son John was already playing the organ publicly
in his father's church at Framingham Earl, between Norwich and
Lowestoft. Beth Britten describes Benjamin and John being set to play
duets together, 'each mother thinking her son the better'. John Alston
dissents: 'I was never conscious of a talent contest with Ben – he was so
obviously a better pianist than I!' If there was rivalry, Mrs Britten
decided to side-step it, arranging for Benjamin to begin viola lessons
with Mrs Alston, which he did when he was ten. Pleased with his
progress, Mrs Alston encouraged him to attend concerts in Norwich,
where she played in a string quartet. During October 1924 the Norwich

Triennial Festival took place, and Benjamin 'heard Frank Bridge conduct his suite *The Sea* and was knocked sideways'.

Bridge was an outsider in English music. Born in 1879, the son of a Brighton violin teacher and music-hall conductor, he studied at the Royal College of Music and became a free-lance string player and teacher, and a conductor. Howard Ferguson, who knew him well in the late twenties, when he was studying under Bridge's friend, the pianist Harold Samuel, describes him as 'an extraordinary technician. And I think the only reason that he wasn't a success as a conductor was that orchestras disliked him, because he told them in no uncertain terms that they weren't playing very well.' Bridge had composed since childhood, and during his early years as a professional musician had churned out drawing-room ballads, chamber music and miscellaneous orchestral pieces. Some of it was memorable, some not, but all was technically excellent. Again, Ferguson suggests that his failure to make a solid reputation was due to acerbity. 'Frank did give one the impression always of being very superior musically. He did give one the feeling that he felt everyone else was rather a fool.' By 1928 his only work from the pre-1914 period to have remained in the repertoire was *The Sea*, which had become such a Prom 'lollipop' that Bridge would say to Sir Henry Wood, 'Oh, that, it's such an old work, why do you play it?' His recent music was far more adventurous than this 'English pastoral' tone poem describing the shifting moods of the seascape, but for the ten-year-old Benjamin Britten, who had heard very little modern music, it was a revelation, not least because of its lush orchestration. The Norwich audience liked it so much that Bridge, who was staying with Audrey Alston at Framingham Earl, went away with a commission for a new piece for the next Triennial in 1927.

A few weeks after the Bridge concert, Benjamin passed his Associated Board Intermediate Certificate in Pianoforte. His musical reputation had spread through South Lowestoft. Neighbours would stop on the pavement to hear him play, and (according to one resident's recollections) would admonish their own piano-playing children: 'Little Benjamin practises *properly*.' But 'Pop' Britten was unenthusiastic; he remarked to a patient that Benjamin 'spends far too much time at it for my liking', and Captain Sewell told the Brittens that the boy could be 'developed into a mathematical scholar', which could provide a more secure living than being a 'genius' at music. Mrs Britten, however, was determined that he should concentrate on music, and in January 1927, aged thirteen, he sailed through the Advanced Certificate in Pianoforte, still under the tuition of Miss Ethel. Sewell was delighted. 'We think that none will blame us for being proud,' he wrote in the school magazine that summer. 'E. B. Britten . . . will be head-boy next term.'

Britten took up this position in the autumn term of 1927, when he was almost fourteen and beginning his last year at South Lodge. The same term brought the next Norwich Triennial Festival, and Bridge returned to conduct the first performance of his commissioned piece, *Enter Spring*. Britten and his mother were in the audience. Once again Bridge was staying with the Alstons, and Audrey invited Benjamin to meet him. Beth believes that at first Bridge did not want to see the boy, 'complaining that he was always being asked to interview young people who were supposed to show musical promise, which they rarely had. However, Audrey was insistent, and as her guest, he could hardly refuse.'

Mrs Britten had already been trying to draw the attention of the musical world to her son's compositions. In June 1926 she had persuaded 'Pop' to send an 'Ouverture' by him, consisting of ninety-one pages of orchestral full score, to the BBC for their Autumn Musical Festival Prize. No reply from them survives. A few months later some of his music was submitted to Charles Macpherson, Organist of St Paul's Cathedral, London. Returning the manuscripts, Macpherson wrote:

> The outlook is founded on the simpler classical; there is no counter-point, or feeling in that direction. The work is of course remarkable for one so young, but there is as yet not much sign of individual outlook, or certainty in treatment. If unduly flattered I should say the spark would be quenched. It must grow undisturbed into flame; and for that reason let the boy develop naturally. If he wants to write he will still find the means of doing so. Let everyone be natural with him. If he is spoilt everything will go the wrong way. The next few years will be the real test.

Bridge was of a different opinion. According to Beth, he 'had not talked to Ben for more than a few minutes when he realized that here was something quite remarkable'. Certainly he was sufficiently interested to ask the boy to come back next day with specimens of his work. 'I spent the next morning with him,' writes Britten, 'going over some of my music.'

Bridge may have been impressed by Benjamin's obvious determination to write modern music, despite very limited access to the work of con-temporary composers. 'By the time I was 13 or 14 I was beginning to get more adventurous,' writes Britten. 'Before then, what I'd been writing had been sort of early 19th century in style; and then I heard Holst's *Planets* and Ravel's string quartet and was excited by them. I started

writing in a much freer harmonic idiom.' In 1953 he and Imogen Holst
were listening to a recording of *A Ceremony of Carols*. She wrote in her
diary: 'When I said how lovely the chord on "The Prince himself" was,
he said "That's one of the things I learnt from your father; the enhar-
monic change and the extraordinary effect it has on the note that is
changed." This was *terribly* exciting, and I could hardly eat the meal
because it was just what I'd guessed and hoped.'

At the end of his morning with Britten in 1927, Frank Bridge decided
that the boy deserved professional musical tuition. Bridge's friend Harold
Samuel, a notable exponent of Bach, was currently teaching Howard
Ferguson, whose family lived in Belfast and who lodged at Samuel's
home in London and so could have lessons every day. Bridge suggested
that Britten should become a Samuel pupil and join the household too,
and that he, Bridge, should provide some composition lessons as well – a
striking suggestion, since, as Britten himself points out, Bridge 'had no
other pupils' in composition.

Mrs Britten and 'Pop' were taken aback at the idea. Beth writes that
Bridge 'was the popular idea of the artist in those days. He had long hair,
was very excitable, and talked a lot. Our father was very conservative
and could not stand anyone who talked as much, thinking it showed an
empty mind.' A compromise was agreed: Benjamin would remain at
home for the present, and would go next year to public school as
planned, but would make day-trips to London at regular intervals for
piano and composition lessons with Samuel and Bridge. The first session
with Bridge would be during the coming Christmas holiday. Meanwhile
his fourteenth birthday, on 22 November 1927, was marked with a gift
of the full score of *Fidelio*. 'It was a red letter day,' he says of this.
'Between the ages of thirteen and sixteen I knew every note of Beethoven
and Brahms.'

Bridge and his Australian wife Ethel lived off Kensington Church
Street, in Bedford Gardens, and Benjamin's first lesson took place there
on 12 January 1928. 'Saw Frank Bridge in his London House,' he wrote
in his new *School Boy's Pocket Diary and Note Book for 1928*. 'Had an
absolutely wonderful lesson. Peter Pan in evening wonderful.' There was
another lesson the next morning before he and his mother returned to
Lowestoft. The sessions with Bridge may have been wonderful, but he
also found them challenging, even gruelling. 'Even though I was barely in
my teens,' he writes, 'this was immensely serious and professional study;
and the lessons were mammoth. I remember one that started at half past
ten, and at tea-time Mrs Bridge came in and said, "Really, you must give
the boy a break."' Britten's diary entries for 26–30 April 1928, his

second visit to Bridge, record lessons of about two and a half hours on three consecutive days, and another after a one-day break. Bridge's method was to take pieces that Benjamin had written since their last meeting and go through them on the piano. 'I used to get sent to the other side of the room. Bridge would play what I'd written and demand if it was what I'd really meant.' In a 1960 interview, Britten recalled how Bridge

> used to perform the most terrible operations on the music I would rather confidently show him. He would play every passage slowly on the piano and say, 'Now listen to this – is this what you meant?' And of course I would start by defending it, but then one would realize ... as he went on playing this passage over and over again – that one hadn't really thought enough about it. And he really taught me to take as much trouble as I possibly could over every passage, over every progression, over every line.

Britten gradually realized that there were 'two cardinal principles' in Bridge's teaching. 'One was that you should find yourself and be true to what you found. The other – obviously connected with the first – was his scrupulous attention to good technique, the business of saying clearly what was in one's mind.'

Bridge required that everything should be suited to the instrument for which it was written. 'At one point I came up with a series of major sevenths on the violin. Bridge was against this, saying that the instrument didn't vibrate properly with this interval: it should be divided between two instruments.' He also widened the boy's harmonic horizons. 'I also learnt about bitonality,' writes Britten, recalling that one of Bridge's favourite devices in his own later music was 'to harmonize with two common chords simultaneously'. This was advanced for a boy who a few months earlier had not even been writing simple counterpoint. 'I was perhaps too young to take in so much at the time, but I found later that a good deal of it had stuck firmly.'

He would emerge from the lessons looking worn out. Beth says her mother described him 'blinking and twitching nervously, and white with exhaustion'. Britten himself admits that 'often I used to end these marathons in tears; not that he was beastly to me, but the concentrated strain was too much for me'. His ego took a knocking. 'I, who thought I was already on the verge of immortality, saw my illusions shattered ... I felt I was very small fry.' Consequently his vast output of compositions began to diminish, as he responded to Bridge's demand for disciplined writing. There were no more ninety-page scores, and he began to write chiefly for small forces, such as voice and piano. 'Work Hard on string quartet,' he noted across five days of his diary at the end of January 1928. Occasionally, though, he still let himself loose on a big piece: on 6 March, 'Finish orchestral work which is called Humoureske.' This was an elaborate but short work for full orchestra, with touches of *Enter Spring*, though it slips exuberantly from one idiom to another. Simon Rattle, who conducted it in 1985, describes it as 'very strange . . . musically it seems very gauche, but on even our first sight-reading-through, it *sounded* wonderful, because of his mastery of the orchestra'. Britten's skill at orchestration is the more remarkable considering that he had had no training in it. Not until September 1929 did he begin to study Forsyth's *Orchestration*, the authoritative work on the subject, and it was impossible for him to hear performances of his orchestral compositions. Besides 'Humoureske', there was a song-cycle for high voice and orchestra, a setting of two poems by Victor Hugo and two by Verlaine (found by Britten in *The Oxford Book of French Verse*) which he wrote during the summer of 1928, half a year after he had begun lessons with Bridge.

Quatre Chansons Françaises displays a thorough understanding of late romantic and early twentieth-century music. It draws on Wagner, Debussy, Ravel and – remarkably – Berg, whose music Bridge admired. None of these is copied slavishly, and Britten displays a mastery of orchestral colour. It is an astonishing achievement for a fourteen-year-old, and Bridge does not seem to have had much hand in it. The dates in the manuscript score indicate that it was written during a period between composition lessons – at a time, incidentally, when Britten was supposed to have been preparing for the entrance examination to his public school. Though Bridge may have suggested improvements, the ideas are clearly all Britten's own.

The first song, 'Nuits de Juin', evokes a summer evening as sensuously as might Debussy or Ravel, and something more seductive than the words' literal description of the summer night is suggested. 'Sagesse', with words by Verlaine, continues this mood, but as the orchestra rises to a climax the singer asks: 'Qu'as tu fait, ô toi que voilà / Pleurant sans cesse, / Dis, qu'as tu fait, toi que voilà, / De ta jeunesse' – 'What have you done, you there, endlessly weeping? Tell me, what have you done with your youth?' Then comes the most remarkable of the four songs, 'L'Enfance', a setting of a Hugo poem describing a child singing innocently in a courtyard while, in the house, its mother is dying of consumption. Britten's setting juxtaposes the child's nursery rhyme, on the flute, with the singer's and orchestra's depiction of the dying mother. Indoors, the mother coughs in agony, while through the window comes the child's chirpy tune. Christopher Palmer, in a study of Britten's song-cycles, judges it remarkable that 'the fourteen-year-old Britten is already pre-occupied with the theme of the vulnerability of innocence which is to pervade his whole life's work'.

There is nothing in any contemporary document relating to Britten's childhood to suggest that this preoccupation might have had an external cause. It could easily have arisen spontaneously, maybe as a consequence of puberty. However, two of Britten's librettists have stated that, much later in his life, he made assertions to them about his school-days and family which, if true, might provide explanations for the recurrence in his operas of the subject of innocence violated. These assertions need to be treated with the utmost caution, and can only lead, at most, to specul-ation rather than certainty of fact.

*

In the spring of 1966, Eric Crozier, who had worked closely with Britten from 1944 to 1951 but had then become estranged from him, was disappointed to find that his name had been excluded from a newly published biography of Britten for children, written by Imogen Holst, then the composer's music assistant. Crozier had been the original pro-ducer of *Peter Grimes* and *The Rape of Lucretia*. He had then written the libretti of *Albert Herring, Saint Nicolas* and *The Little Sweep*, and had collaborated with E. M. Forster on that of *Billy Budd*. Along with Britten and Peter Pears, he had founded the Aldeburgh Festival. Imogen Holst's book quoted from his libretti, and even from two articles he had written, but nowhere was his existence alluded to.

Crozier suspected that she had 'suppressed all mention of my name in order to please Britten, even without such a wish having been consciously expressed by him'. In response, he wrote a thirty-seven page document, entitled 'Notes on Benjamin Britten', which he headed 'Confidential' and locked away without showing it to anyone, even his wife, the singer Nancy Evans, who had worked closely with Britten.

For an epigraph to the 'Notes', Crozier chose Samuel Johnson's words to Lord Chesterfield: 'I had done all that I could, and no man is well pleased to have his all neglected, be it ever so little.' In a Foreword to the 'Notes', Crozier described the document as 'notes on Britten as I knew him in the golden days of our collaboration. They may have a certain intrinsic interest, since they are based on first-hand observation or the witness of reliable friends, and perhaps they may serve to correct errors in other published material.'

There was nothing in the early part of the 'Notes' to have caused more than mildly raised eyebrows, had the document become public. Crozier alluded to Britten's tendency to drop collaborators and even friends after a while, but he discussed this with puzzlement rather than bitterness. Britten was generally presented in affectionate terms. Then, on page thirty-three, Crozier turned to the subject of Britten and Pears's homosexuality. After discussing whether Pears 'was or was not a homosexual by nature', Crozier went on: 'No doubt is possible, however, in Britten's own case. He told me he had been raped by a master at his school, as if his sexual deviation had stemmed from that one incident – but nobody who knew him well could doubt that he was inherently and undeniably homosexual.'

Questioned in 1990, for this biography, Crozier said that Britten made this remark to him some time in the late forties, when Crozier was living in Britten's household and working on his operas. He did not recall that Britten mentioned details: 'I wasn't given a date. And I can't pin it down to a particular school. That's simply what he told me.'

Britten's other surviving friends are, with one exception, inclined to treat the story with the greatest possible scepticism, since they never heard it or any hint of it from him. Nor is anyone who was at school with him able to confirm it. The general tendency is to agree with Joan Cross, the original Ellen Orford in *Peter Grimes* and creator of other Britten operatic roles, who remarks: 'I think Ben was just born homosexual.' Indeed it will be noted that in the 'Notes' Crozier himself is sceptical about the story as an explanation of Britten's homosexuality.

The exception is Beata Sauerlander, formerly Beata Mayer, whose mother Elizabeth Mayer gave Britten and Peter Pears a home at Amityville, Long Island, from the autumn of 1939. Questioned for this book half a century later, when in her late seventies, she recalled Britten's illness early in 1940:

> Peter and Mother looked after him during the day, and I nursed him at night. And he had a fairly high temperature, and he talked a lot. He was very uncomfortable. And although he was very reticent usually, he did talk about his schooldays, about his childhood. And although I can't remember exactly what he said, I remember that he had very traumatic experiences, sexual experiences. And it bothered him.

When told of Crozier's story, she said: 'I think you can take it as true. It comes as no surprise.'

After South Lodge, Britten attended Gresham's, the boys' public school in Norfolk. While he was there he kept a daily diary, and though it contains many grumbles about school life there is no hint of any sexual experience. No one who was at Gresham's with him knows of any schoolmaster who was under suspicion of sexually abusing boys. Those who were at South Lodge with Britten are on the whole less inclined to deny that such a thing could have happened there. John Pounder, who knew Britten well until long after their prep-school days, says: 'I think if it had happened there, at South Lodge, I might have known something about it, or we might have talked about it, or something like that.' But can he rule it out absolutely? 'No, no.' Another South Lodge old boy and friend of Britten's, Eric Reeve (brother of Basil), whose father was Vicar of St John's Church which Mrs Britten attended, comments: 'I don't know of anything having happened to Benjamin at South Lodge, though it wouldn't surprise me if it did.' Yet another contemporary of Britten's at prep school recalls that Sewell, the headmaster, removed boys' trousers and underpants before beating them: 'Sewell said [it was] "to enable me to see what I am doing", i.e. so that he could lay off if he was, say, drawing blood.' He emphasizes that 'Sewell was a God-fearing man and I do not consider he would ever have indulged in sexual assault on his pupils.' But he adds: 'He did occasionally indulge in a "friendly pat on the b-t-m" as Betjeman's poem [puts it] and once felt my bare bottom after beating to comfort me.'

It may be imagined that serious sexual abuse, as opposed to a moment's fondling, could not take place without risk of interruption and discovery, but Britten's diary records one occasion on which there would have been an opportunity. His first surviving diary was kept from January 1928, just before the start of his penultimate term at South Lodge, and on 13 June that year he writes: 'Set off to play Match against Taverham, but I only get ½ way and I go back to School in Capt. Sewell's car as I am not well. Lie down at school and come home after and go to bed.' He was unwell for three days afterwards, and it was on the second of these that he began to write the first song in *Quatre Chansons Françaises*, 'Nuits de Juin'.

In fairness to T. J. E. Sewell, it should be emphasized that the general impression he gave his pupils was of rectitude. John Pounder says 'he could be extremely pleasant – he had a great deal of charm, apart from his darker side', and Marian Walker, who knew him socially, recalls: 'We all liked him, and got to know him very well.' Sewell's son Donald, who was born while Britten was at the school and eventually succeeded his father as headmaster, allows that it is 'quite possible' that Britten could have been sexually assaulted by a member of the teaching staff, given 'the sort of school that South Lodge was in the twenties', but does not know of any such incident occurring in Britten's time. Being asked to consider the possibility of his father having committed an assault on Britten, he writes:

> The more I think about it, the more doubtful I am about there having been any possibility of some form of sexual assault in which my father was implicated. I cannot believe that my father would in such circumstances have spoken so openly and proudly about Ben's time in the school and his subsequent career, nor that Ben himself would have wanted to return to the school after he had left.

It is true that Britten revisited South Lodge and its successor Old Buckenham Hall School, during the years when T. J. E. Sewell was still headmaster – he remained in office until 1967, when he was nearly eighty – and wrote a setting of Psalm 150 for the school's centenary in 1962, coming to conduct it himself. But Donald Sewell allows that Britten's feelings about his old headmaster were mixed: 'Talking to him afterwards, at the time of Psalm 150, he had a sort of mixed respect and fear of my father . . . a sort of mix, contradiction.'

There were, of course, other teaching staff at South Lodge, and Crozier's recollection is that Britten said 'a master' rather than 'headmaster'. School group photographs from Britten's years at South Lodge – the only record of staff to have survived two fires which destroyed school buildings in the fifties – show that various young men came and went as the terms passed. On the face of it, it seems more likely that one of them would feel less constraint on his behaviour than the headmaster. However, in the sixties Britten remarked to John Nicholson, whose own son was approaching school age, 'You won't send him there?' meaning their old school, and this suggests that whatever he felt had been wrong about the school in the twenties was still wrong. The only staff then still teaching there who had been at South Lodge in his day were T. J. E. Sewell and William Hall, the senior master. Donald Sewell thinks it impossible that Hall could have been the sexual abuser – 'he wasn't that way inclined' – and John Pounder agrees.

It seems unlikely that, if Britten did experience sexual abuse as a child, it would have been enough by itself to make him homosexual. Present-day psychiatric opinion regards it as impossible to identify a simple set of causes for homosexuality. There can apparently be many factors, including an exceptionally close relationship with the mother, but possibly also a genetic disposition, so that Joan Cross may be right that Britten was 'born homosexual'. On the other hand child sexual abuse is now known to be highly traumatic for the victim, especially if perpetrated by an individual whom the child has trusted and respected. Although the abuse was not their fault, many victims blame themselves, even when they reach adult life, for supposedly allowing it to happen. 'You see,' sings Miles in *The Turn of the Screw*, 'I am bad, aren't I?'

Donald Mitchell, who was Britten's publisher for the last twelve years of his life, and was chosen by him as his executor and biographer, says of the 'rape' story:

> Was Ben fantasizing, perhaps? We shall never know, I guess; never know what he meant by 'rape', if he used the word. Nor can we summon back to life the inflection of tone or voice in which the claim was uttered. The greatest danger in all this, it seems to me, would be to build some enormous superstructure of speculation on such a flimsy basis. We should certainly take note of it, but it would be wise not to throw caution to the winds, above all to desist from thinking – even if the 'rape' proved to be well founded – that it would provide us with a key to, a readymade 'explanation' of, the music. It doesn't.

Myfanwy Piper, who wrote the libretti of *The Turn of the Screw, Owen Wingrave* and *Death in Venice*, never heard from Britten any suggestion that he had been abused by a schoolmaster, but towards the end of his life he made another assertion to her about his childhood:

> I can't remember [says Mrs Piper] when it was, or what the occasion was, or why he told me. I think it was at Fawley Bottom [the Pipers' Oxfordshire home]. He did say that his father was homosexual and that he used to send him out to find boys.
>
> It didn't sound a bit untrue. I don't see how you send your child out to find boys, but I didn't pursue it. I don't think he invented it. It was in the course of a general conversation about his family. What he may have said was possibly, 'Oh yes, he used to send me out to find boys,' not meaning to go to the street corners and see a pretty errand boy, but 'Why don't you bring your pals home from school?' But he did say it. I was quite surprised at his telling me. But not very surprised, in a way, because he never made any secret of his homosexuality.

Did she have any sense that he was offering an explanation for his own sexual orientation? 'No, he wasn't; there was nothing apologetic about it.' Was there any suggestion that his father had taken a sexual interest in Benjamin himself, or had interfered with him? 'No, not the faintest. That, I think, if it was so, would have come later' – that is, would have been raised in a later conversation. In fact they never spoke of the matter again.

Those who knew Britten's father are unanimous that there was no such rumour about him. John Pounder says there was no hint of it, and Alan Reeve, another of the sons of the Vicar of St John's, is 'sure something would have been said'. Marian Walker, who knew the family well, 'never heard a whisper'. Rita Thomson, to whom Britten talked candidly about his family at the end of his life, says she gathered that 'Pop' had 'a couple of flirtations' with young ladies in Lowestoft, but that was all. Britten never mentioned his father to Beata Mayer (Beata Sauerlander) when he spoke of childhood sexual trauma, nor in this context to Eric Crozier. On the other hand Crozier says Britten communicated 'a feeling of pretty strong dislike and disapproval' if the subject of his father came up, 'not in any sexual way, but of his father's drinking habits. The feeling of *very* strong disapproval of that.'

After Britten's death, Peter Pears talked candidly to several young male friends about his and Britten's homosexuality. To none of these did he mention the rape or Britten's father's supposed pederasty, matters which they believe he would have brought up if he had known about them. It seems almost inconceivable that, if they were true, Britten would not have divulged them to Pears.

In Tony Palmer's 1980 TV documentary about Britten, *A Time There Was*, Pears (interviewed by Donald Mitchell) said of Britten's childhood: 'The point is, everything seemed so simple when he was a boy, so simple and delightful for the most part.' Tony Palmer claims that while the film was being made he found some evidence to the contrary. Before being told of Myfanwy Piper's story about Britten's father, Palmer recalled how, in an off-the-record conversation,

> Beth had let slip that it was not actually a terribly happy family atmosphere, so that was the point of my question to Robert, before we started filming. We were just chatting away, and I said, 'You obviously had a very happy childhood.' And he said, 'Oh, no, it wasn't. We liked our mother, but we were a bit afraid of our father.' And I said, 'Afraid in what way?', imagining he'd clipped him round the ear. And all he said was, 'My sisters and I thought my father had funny habits.'

Palmer says he did not obtain any more information. Robert's widow Marjorie knows nothing about the 'funny habits' – Robert may have been referring to his father's fondness for drink – but, before being told of the allegation and hints about 'Pop', she gave this description of her feelings about him when she first went to 21 Kirkley Cliff Road in 1928: 'I took an instantaneous dislike to him, partly because he frightened me. It was his eyes – they were sort of hooded – that made me think there was something funny about him. I can't explain it, but here was this extraordinary father who gave me the creeps.'

Though Britten's remarks to Eric Crozier and Myfanwy Piper were separated by about twenty-five years, the manner of them is strikingly similar. Each was made to a librettist, and apparently to no one else. Could they both have been fantasies on Britten's part, sparked off while his imagination was at work on his operas?

2: Utter loneliness

On the evening of 20 September 1928, Benjamin arrived at his public school. 'I like this place quite', he wrote to his parents, 'but I feel horribly strange and small.' They had chosen Gresham's School in the small market town of Holt in Norfolk, about fifty miles from Lowestoft, because it offered musical scholarships worth £30 a year, and Benjamin had won one. At South Lodge he had been a hero-figure in his last year – head boy, admired cricketer, victor ludorum in the school sports, not to mention his music – but at Gresham's he was just a small boy whose head of golden curls attracted ridicule. 'I feel rather an ass here,' he told his parents, 'everyone stares, it is very nasty, but still it might be a lot worse.' In his diary he was more candid: 'I am in a study [with] 3 boys, who might be worse, but might be better. They are full of swearing and vulgarity ... I do not like the outlook of 13 weeks of this!' And two days later: 'In my study I have a ghastly time in the evening, Corner and 3 other boys, Meiklejohn, Savory, Briant, are positively vulgar. It makes me feel sick to think of it.' The full unpleasantness was not revealed until he had a chance to describe it to Beth. 'His mother', she writes, 'would have had a fit if she had known ... From what Ben told me later, he was thrown in a blanket and then into water. Luckily for him he fainted, so the senior boys who were the tormentors stopped in fright and thereafter he was left in peace.'

Such initiation rites were common in public schools, and Gresham's was comparatively civilized. Originally a small grammar school serving the locality, it had expanded since 1900 into a boarding establishment specializing, unusually, in the teaching of science. There were no dormitories – each boy slept in his own cubicle – and studies (small rooms for relaxation and homework) were provided for all pupils, however young. The Officers' Training Corps was voluntary (Britten did not join it) and, most unusually of all, the intellect was rated higher than sports, and boys were discouraged from cheering at football matches. Nevertheless for Britten it was barbarous enough. He was on the look-out for other boys from South Lodge, but 'they don't seem to try and find me'. On the first night he lay sleepless in bed, feeling 'horrible', though a booklet of daily Bible texts provided by his mother gave him some comfort. He had been confirmed in March, and at the front of his 1928 diary wrote, 'My duty towards God is to believe in him, to fear him, and to love him, with all my heart.'

He was pleasantly surprised when his voice was judged good enough for the Gresham's chapel choir, but when he had his first piano lesson with the director of music, Walter Greatorex, he was told that he had only a 'very flimsy' technique. 'He as good as said I had none at all,' Britten reported miserably to his parents. W. H. Auden, who had been at Gresham's a few years earlier, had found Greatorex one of the few civilized teachers, but Auden was a match for tough, domineering schoolmasters, and Greatorex resented the fact that his own teaching was not thought good enough for Britten, who had been given permission to leave school several times each term for lessons with Harold Samuel and Frank Bridge in London. On the first day he remarked sarcastically: 'So *you* are the little boy who likes Stravinsky!' As yet, Britten had not encountered Stravinsky, but Greatorex seemed determined to discourage in every possible way. When Britten played him some late Beethoven, Greatorex said it was 'hopeless for a boy of my age' even to attempt it – and anyway, Greatorex added, his love of Beethoven would 'soon die, as it does with everyone'. In his diary this term, Britten called Beethoven 'first . . . in my list of Composers . . . and I think will always be'. A few months later, after listening to the Kreisler recording of the Violin Concerto: 'Oh! Beethoven, thou art immortal; has anything ever been written like the pathos of the 1st & 2nd movements, and the joy of the last?'

Next in the lesson with Greatorex he tried a Chopin polonaise, playing from memory, but was ticked off for playing *forte* a passage Greatorex alleged was supposed to be *pianissimo*. Greatorex concluded by implying that 'it would be no good whatsoever for me to go into the musical profession'. (It was apparently his usual technique with pupils; Stephen Spender, who was also taught by him, remembers his 'domed, bald head, Beethoven's patent sour expression', and his growl of 'You will never learn to play the piano.') Reporting all this to his mother, Benjamin affected contempt for Greatorex; when the man had tried to demonstrate Chopin himself, he had played 'with no two notes together, and a gripping touch, and terrible tone'. Benjamin concluded: 'Music in this school is now finished for me!'

It was a grave disappointment. 'I am longing for November' – the month when he would have London lessons with Bridge and Samuel. He had been having dreams about his family falling ill and dying. 'Mummy darling, *please, please*, if you or any one of the family in the house are ill, *do* send Bobby or Pop over in the car to fetch me. Please do, Darling, promise that; oh! Darling *do*.'

At last November came and his mother took him to London. 'Wonderful lesson,' he wrote in his diary after working with Harold Samuel. Some years later he described Samuel as 'a great little man who was always so grand to me'. He and his mother heard the Hallé Orchestra at the Queen's Hall ('wonderful'), and the next morning he had his lesson with Bridge ('very nice'). All too soon it was back to school, and he was 'absolutely miserable' to be there again. It was just the same the next term. After a jolly family Christmas, he deplored the return to Gresham's and the 'utter loneliness at school'. He started going for walks in the surrounding countryside, and there was a gramophone he could use. Records included 'Stravinsky's "L'oiseau de feu", in which I'm very interested'. But the bleakness of school life soon drove him into the sick-room, and he spent much of the term ill with flu. 'All the time I am writing on odd sheets of writing-paper etc., scraps of new quartets and things. All that is possible.' The illness persisted, and he was allowed to go back to Lowestoft. 'It is ripping to be home!' When the doctor sent him back to school he was 'yearning for home and everybody there'.

While in bed at Gresham's he poured out passionate letters to his mother: 'I still think of you, every second of my life ... So farewell, angel of my heart, Your adoring son, BENJAMIN.' He asked her about the health of Francis Barton, a South Lodge friend two years his junior who was still at the school. On his last day there he had written in his diary: 'Go and see some boys off. I am frightfully sorry to say good-bye to them, Francis Barton especially, he has been a ripping boy.' He often saw Francis when he was at home. In May 1929, 'FRANCIS comes to tea. I fetch him to go for a walk (at 3.0) along the Beach. He has to go (worst luck!) about 5.45. So we don't really see much of him. He looks so young (he is 13), about 11, but when he talks he might be 15!!! All the same he is a marvellous kid!' In the summer holidays that year Francis came to stay. 'It's been topping having him, & I miss him dreadfully.' Years later, Britten wrote to Francis's sister: 'He meant a great deal to me in those very early days – His affection softened many blows.'

It was risky to form close attachments at Gresham's. The school was supposedly controlled by an 'Honour System' which demanded that boys promise not to indulge in smoking, swearing or indecency, and should attempt to dissuade others – and if that failed, should report them to the authorities. Auden said it made the school like a Fascist state. Britten was in Auden's old house, Farfield, and though the bachelor housemaster of Auden's time soon gave way to a genial married man who led the second violins in the school orchestra, and sometimes let Britten listen to concerts on his wireless, the atmosphere was much the same. 'Originality (oh! that blessed thing) is completely discouraged,' Britten wrote in his diary during his fourth term. 'If you are original, well you are considered a lunatic, & consequently become unpopular.' Nor could any amount of repression suppress romantic feelings among the boys. After three terms Britten had become the object of attentions by a sixth-former named Berthoud, two years older than him. 'The only reason why I don't want the end of term is because Berthoud is leaving . . . He has been marvellous to me, in spite of being a house-pre . . .'

During his third term he wrote a setting of Belloc's poem 'The Birds', with music reflecting the childlike quality of the words ('When Jesus Christ was four years old / The angels brought him toys of gold'), though the unresolved last bar – which Britten has recalled was the direct result of Bridge's teaching – seems to cast doubt on the efficacy of the singer's naïve prayers, an effect not unlike the ironic contrast between innocence and experience in *Quatre Chansons Françaises*. Britten could see how useless it was to be merely innocent. 'The day ends with some atrocious bullying in our Study, Marshall & Savory v. Williams (the small new boy) who ends in tears. Unfortunately I was out of the room. And this a school of the honour system!' A few months later:

> I think that the 'Honour System' is a positive failure in Farfield. If [J. R.] Eccles [the headmaster] new [*sic*] what happens he would either disbelieve it or have 10 blue fits. Atrocious bullying on all sides, vulgarity & swearing. It is no good trying the Honour System on boys who have no honour. Boys, small & rather weak are turned into sour & bitter boys, & ruined for life. The boy I am thinking of is Wood. Absolute bullying is not the word for it.

At the start of his second year he still disliked Gresham's as much as ever, and was back in the sanatorium, this time with a gastric complaint. But he was now making an impression on the school's musical life. Greatorex allowed him to take part in 'Saturday Music' recitals not as a pianist, but playing the viola in trios by Mozart and Brahms. The school magazine called him 'a very reliable musician in ensemble playing'.

Meanwhile one of his friends thought it 'positively miraculous' that he could sit down at the piano and sight-read the miniature score of a Schubert quintet.

He was beginning to become conscious of modernism as a movement. 'I am thinking much about modernism in art. Debating whether Impressionism, Expressionism, Classicism etc. are right. I have half-decided on Schönberg. I adore Picasso's pictures.' His discovery of Schoenberg may have been due to Bridge, who was fully aware of modern European music. A few months later, Britten listened to 'a marvellous Schönberg concert' on the wireless – 'Including "Chamber-Symp.", Suite of 25 (pft.) & Pierrot Luniare [*sic*]. I liked the last the most, & I thought it most beautiful.' He bought Schoenberg's *Six Little Pieces* for piano (1911) and performed them at a 'modern music' evening at Lowestoft in April 1930. As to modern literature, 'Read quite a lot of Swann's Way, which I love. It is absolutely fascinating.' On the whole, though, he preferred comic novels and thrillers, because 'I find that if I have to think about my books I can do less in writing [music].'

In December 1929, Greatorex finally allowed him to play the piano in a school concert – a Chopin nocturne and waltz, and two studies by Roger Quilter. 'E. B. Britten's performance was of a very high standard,' reported the school magazine, commending 'just the right delicacy of touch and quiet feeling' in the Chopin. He was very nervous before the concert – 'neither the piano or my head or my fingers will work'. After his success he observed: 'Sat. night seems to have softened many people towards me!!!' He hoped to use his increasing popularity to organize an 'effort against Bullying', but after a 'marvellous lesson' with Bridge in January 1930 he went back to Gresham's in a worse state of mind than ever: 'How I loathe this abominable hole . . . I simply cannot see how I can bare [*sic*] up through it, & suicide is so cowardly. Running away's as bad; so I suppose I've got to stick it. But 83 days!' As usual he retreated into illness, this time a severe sore throat.

Greatorex now unbent so far as to offer Britten a performance of one of his own pieces, 'Bagatelle' for violin, viola and piano. Britten himself took the viola part, and Greatorex and Miss Chapman, the string teacher, were the other performers. 'We knew that Britten was a composer,' said the school magazine for the 1930 spring term, 'but this was our first opportunity of hearing any of his work . . . Written in a modern idiom, the Trio shows that Britten has already advanced a considerable distance in the technique of composition. He should go far and we take this opportunity of wishing him every success in the future.' Britten's own comment was 'It goes very badly! My thing is quite well appreciated but not understood.'

Meanwhile in Lowestoft his mother was keeping him before the public eye. She is said to have lent his manuscripts to Miss Ethel Astle, who tried to play them to the girls in her school, with the announcement that it was 'what Benjamin has written this week'. Britten showed no sign of resenting his mother's efforts at publicity, and still basked in her encouragement. In his sixth term at Gresham's, when he was sixteen, he wrote in his diary after returning to school from several days in London with her: 'Quite a successful day considering it is the first away from my darling.'

Basil Reeve had become friends with him in Lowestoft, but says he was only allowed to spend time with Benjamin because Mrs Britten approved of him. 'She arranged his life ... Everything was absolutely controlled ... the length of time that we could be together, what we could do together – absolutely controlled ... she was a very formidable woman ... I could only see him with her permission.' It is Reeve who recalls her determination that he should become 'the fourth B' after Bach, Beethoven and Brahms. (On the other hand Benjamin's cousin Elsie Hockey says that when she remarked, 'When Ben becomes famous', Mrs Britten interrupted her with, 'Elsie, we don't know, it may have gone by the time he's fifteen.') Reeve suggests that her passionate devotion was imprisoning him emotionally: 'She didn't release all that enormous warmth that was in him, I think.' He adds that she organized things so that he was always 'the centre of everything ... and so it became, I'm sure, later, very easy for him to be at the centre of things, because this was how he'd been brought up'.

*

Nobody who was at Gresham's with Britten remembers him as anything other than a brilliant musician. If he showed skill at cricket, mathematics, or any of the other things which had made him a reputation at South Lodge, it was eclipsed by the musical reputation which, in spite of early discouragement by Greatorex, he achieved in his second year. 'The apex of the Concert', wrote the school chaplain in the *Gresham* for 7 June 1930, describing a performance at the end of the Easter term,

> was the playing of Britten. We have had fine pianists in the School; to this day I can remember the thrill of listening to [Heathcote] Statham, now Organist of Norwich Cathedral, and that was 24 years ago; but it is no slight to any of them to place Britten above them all. The interpretation of Raff's *Fileuse* alone was enough to establish him as a past-master of delicate workmanship, but the *Polichinelle* of

Rachmaninoff held one bewildered, spellbound. Two thoughts arose: 1. How on earth could anyone have written it? 2. How on earth could anyone play it? The effect was devastating. The more the fire and fury, or the leaping and plunging increased, the more rapturously I could have shouted for joy . . . of course Britten was encored.

Britten himself noted that 'my pieces seem to go down quite well'. The encore was Brahms' Waltz in A flat.

Naturally his parents were in the audience to witness his triumph, and after a holiday largely spent studying Ravel's *Miroirs* (for piano), Britten reported delightedly in his diary: 'Letter from Pop, saying I have to leave [school] this term, whether I pass my S[chool] C[ertificate] or no.' According to Beth, Benjamin had never wanted to go to public school, but had wanted to begin musical training in London right away. After a family council it had been agreed that 'he should go to a public school long enough to pass the School Certificate . . . and then the situation should be reviewed'. He was due to take School Certificate in the summer of 1930, his sixth term at Gresham's, at the age of sixteen. While pupils were normally expected to stay and study for the Higher Certificate, it was clear that Britten could no longer tolerate Gresham's. 'If I have to return next term (having failed my School Cert.)', he had written in his diary before Pop's decision, 'it will be all I can do to prevent me committing suicide.'

As to the future, there was one slight chance of getting to London to study music professionally. The Royal College of Music was holding its annual composition scholarship examination in mid-June, and his name was put down for it. For the first round candidates were required to submit a selection of their work by post. Those shortlisted would be invited to London for a written and an oral examination. At the end of May, Britten sent off *A Wealden Trio* (a setting of a Ford Madox Ford poem for women's voices), *The Birds*, and several instrumental compositions. Frank Bridge had not been consulted; it was a last-minute scheme with little hope of success. (Bridge expected that Britten would 'try for a musical scholarship at Oxford some time or other'.) For a long while, no reply came from the examiners, and Britten was dejected. 'I have given up what little hope I had (not that I really expected anything) . . .' Then a postcard arrived in Lowestoft summoning him to London the next day, 19 June. Mrs Britten telephoned Gresham's and made hasty arrangements. The two of them travelled to London that night, and next morning Britten was at the Royal College at ten o'clock.

The written paper came first. Candidates were set various exercises in composition – 'Pt. song, Scherzo, modulations', noted Benjamin in his diary. This was supposed to occupy them from 10 a.m. until 3 p.m. with a break for lunch, which he ate with his mother at Barker's department store in Kensington High Street. According to Beth, he completed the exercises in a mere twenty minutes, and then 'took his paper up to the invigilator, who could not believe that it was finished . . . there was quite a little scene and the invigilator insisted that Ben went back and checked the answers. This he did for another five minutes or so and left.' This is surely a considerable exaggeration. In his diary, Britten gives no indication of having left the examination early. But it seems probable that he completed the paper in much less time than was allotted. At three o'clock the oral session began, and he spent half an hour with the three examiners, John Ireland, Ralph Vaughan Williams, and S. P. Waddington, who taught harmony and counterpoint at the Royal College. 'After that', Britten wrote in his diary, 'I have surprise of winning . . .'

There were four other candidates, two of them, according to his diary, 'brilliant'. One was Alec Templeton, four years older than Britten, and blind, later the composer of *Bach Goes to Town*. But it was Britten to whom the sole scholarship was awarded, and he, his mother and his sister Barbara celebrated that evening with a hotel dinner and a performance of Coleridge Taylor's *Hiawatha* at the Albert Hall. 'That's a splendid piece of news!' wrote Frank Bridge when he heard. '*Congratulations.*'

*

Rather to his own surprise, Britten passed his School Certificate at the end of the summer term, earning credits in five subjects. J. R. Eccles, his headmaster, had already sent congratulations to Mrs Britten on the Royal College scholarship. 'We are *delighted* . . . he is such a dear boy & so modest about all his brilliant performances!' Now, his successes were marked with an armful of school prizes. He chose *The Oxford Book of English Verse*, the plays of the Georgian poet John Drinkwater, and a great deal of music: Strauss's *Don Quixote* and five orchestral songs, Rimsky-Korsakov's suite from *The Golden Cockerel*, and Schoenberg's *Pierrot lunaire*. On page eight of *The Oxford Book* he found 'A Hymn to the Virgin', a carol dating from about 1300, and one day towards the end of term he set this as an anthem for choir and semi-chorus. It took him only a few hours, even though he had to rule the staves himself on a plain writing-pad because he was ill again and had been forbidden music paper. 'Write . . . "Hymn to the Virgin", & a set of variations (¼ of it) for organ, which are rather rubbish – I rather like the Hymn tho'.'

In the end he was almost sad to be leaving Gresham's, where he had made warm friendships: 'I spend all the afternoon with David Layton in music rooms, & walk. Walk with Willcock after tea. I am terribly sorry to leave such boys as these . . .' (Later in the summer he began a 'sketch for strings describing David'.) And when he got back to Lowestoft: 'It is marvellous to be home, but I didn't think I should be so sorry to leave.'

3: What an institution

English music colleges have their origin in the Italian boarding schools in which orphans were taught to play and sing, in order to give them a trade. In 1930 the Royal College of Music (RCM), standing behind the Albert Hall in Kensington, still had much about it of school. Its prospectus contained an impressive list of composers and performers on the teaching staff, but these were often away from London for weeks at a stretch, leaving their pupils to fend for themselves, while the more basic instruction was in the hands of a largely mediocre and unimaginative team. In a 1941 article, Britten asserted that the RCM was not really concerned with professionalism. Sir Hubert Parry, who had been director from 1894 until 1918, had (he wrote) 'stressed the amateur idea', admiring 'the English Gentleman (who generally thinks it rather vulgar to take too much trouble)', while his followers, who were still much in evidence when Britten himself arrived at the RCM, were 'inclined to suspect technical brilliance of being superficial and insincere'. In 1959 he was even more blunt about the place: 'The attitude of most of the RCM students was amateurish and folksy. That made me feel highly intolerant.'

He had a room in a boarding-house at 51 Prince's Square, Bayswater, a few minutes' walk from the RCM, across Kensington Gardens. 'This is a topping place to live in,' he told his parents during the first week. As at school, his diary was more candid. 'It is rather a nice place but rather full of old ladies. A respectable boarding house.' He was desolate when his mother left him there and returned to Lowestoft. 'Oh, God, I wish she were here.' However, his sister Barbara, working in south London, rang up at frequent intervals to see if he was all right, and he was befriended by the twenty-two-year-old Howard Ferguson, Harold Samuel's pupil, who took him to a Prom at the Queen's Hall. Ferguson says he found the young Britten 'rather a cold fish', with 'a sort of withheld quality about him, a curtain between him and oneself'. They sat through a Humperdinck overture, a Mozart piano concerto, and Mahler's Fourth Symphony, and then, because the second half was going to be 'all Elgar', left in the interval. Ben told his parents that Mahler had been '*very* long', and in his diary he judged it 'Much too long but [?   ] in parts' (the illegible word may be 'beautiful'). It may have been this concert which he recalled when, in 1942, he described his awakening to Mahler:

I . . . saw from the programme that I had . . . to hear a symphony by Mahler. I naturally groaned in anticipation of forty-five minutes of boredom. But what I heard was not what I had expected to hear. First of all, in spite of a slack, under-rehearsed and rather apologetic performance, the scoring startled me. It was mainly 'soloistic' and entirely clean and transparent. The colouring seemed calculated to the smallest shade, and the result was wonderfully resonant. I wasn't bored for one of its forty-five minutes . . . The form was so cunningly contrived; every development surprised one and yet sounded inevitable. Above all, the material was remarkable, and the melodic shapes highly original, with such rhythmic and harmonic tension from beginning to end. After that concert, I made every effort to hear Mahler's music.

The day before the Prom, he began his studies at the RCM. Arthur Benjamin was to be his piano teacher. 'Mr Benjamin is very nice', he reported to Lowestoft, 'but says that if I wish to take Pft. seriously I must practise 4 hrs. a day.' Benjamin, a jovial thirty-seven-year-old Australian who thought *Rhapsody in Blue* the summit of modern piano-writing and was fond of Latin American dance music (he eventually made a huge success with his *Jamaican Rhumba*), was not the obvious person to get on with the young Britten, but he was enthusiastic and encouraging, and they made friends from the start. The diary for 8 October reports 'a marvellous lesson from Mr Benjamin. I don't touch the piano, but he goes thro' my concerto [his current composition, a rondo-concertante for piano and strings], & says he likes it, & when it is finished will try [?] it.' Britten had no great wish to become a concert pianist, but there was the question of supporting himself after leaving the RCM. At a tennis party in Lowestoft that summer he had been asked what career he meant to choose, and when he answered 'composer' was asked, 'Yes, but what else?' Though Gresham's had judged him a star pianist, Arthur Benjamin's opinion continued cautious. Towards the end of the term, Britten recorded that his piano teacher 'says that I am not built for a solo pianist – how I am going to make my pennies Heaven only knows'. A month later, his own judgement was 'Lor', I'm bad at the piano!'

Meanwhile the classroom part of the RCM syllabus proved to be absurdly easy – the 'music class with Dr. Buck' was 'so petty (Mus. dictation) that I asked to be moved up, & am eventually in a set 2 higher'. From his second term he was exempted from this class altogether, as it was 'so easy'. There remained his instruction in composition. Frank Bridge had warmly recommended him to study with John Ireland, who taught at the RCM, on the grounds that, unlike some of the teaching staff, he was 'a live composer whose activities are part of the present-day outlook with a heavy leaning towards tomorrow's'. Britten had read through an Ireland sonata for violin and piano and described it as 'positively ripping fun'. But Ireland failed to turn up for their first lesson together, and next day he kept Britten waiting outside his door for half an hour before giving him a very short session. He also proved to be 'terribly strict', even more severe than Bridge. He failed to turn up again for the third lesson, being involved in a Prom rehearsal of his own Piano Concerto. Britten heard it that night and described it as 'very beautiful'; he also admired Ireland's piano pieces *Spring Will Not Wait* and *Merry Andrew*, which he bought a few weeks later – 'marvellous'. But when he had his first full-length lesson with Ireland on 16 October, Britten wrote in his diary: 'He is *terribly* critical and enough to take the heart out of any one!'

Ireland was then in his early fifties, withdrawn and with a gloomy expression. In his early days he had formed attachments to boys in the choir he conducted in Chelsea; then he abruptly married a girl music student, who had swiftly left him. Now he lived alone in an untidy house in Gunter Grove between the Fulham and King's Roads, where, in defiance of RCM regulations, he sometimes taught. Beth Britten remembers Benjamin's descriptions of going there and finding Ireland 'still in bed, often with a hangover, and the place ... in a mess, with dirty milk bottles piled up outside. That disgusted Ben, who was always extremely neat and tidy.'

With hindsight, when Britten had become famous, Ireland spoke of him with pride, claiming to have given him the RCM scholarship single-handed: 'The other two adjudicators were against it, and one of them even went so far as to say, "What is an English public school boy doing writing music of this kind?" But eventually I managed to convince them ...' Ireland's biographer ascribes the 'public school boy' remark to Vaughan Williams, and takes the story further, alleging that Ireland asserted: 'This is the finest musical brain that has entered this building for generations.' In fact Ireland himself, telling the story on another occasion, stated that it was '*not* Vaughan Williams' but 'one of the examiners, who is now dead', that is, Waddington. Michael Kennedy, in his study of Britten, writes:

> Everything one knows of Vaughan Williams sustains the conviction that he would never have made the 'English public schoolboy' remark. He used to recall that Britten went into the room for his examination with a bundle of compositions under his arm. 'Is that all?' Vaughan Williams asked, with a twinkle. Britten blinked and replied: 'Oh no, I've got two suitcases full outside.'

Whatever Ireland had said or done during the examination, he showed no great enthusiasm at the prospect of teaching Britten. Perhaps, like Greatorex, he was resentful that Britten had already gone for lessons to Bridge. Ireland asserted that Bridge had 'not given him lessons' at all, but had simply encouraged and advised him. Now he set Britten to work to do some 'real' study. 'With me', Ireland writes, 'he spent a good deal of time over counterpoint, fugue & allied subjects before I let him loose, so to speak, to go his own way.' Consequently Britten reported to his parents: 'I am plodding through Counterpoint & Palestrina at the moment ...' Between October 1930 and January 1931 he wrote a mass for four voices in the Palestrina style. When he handed it in to Ireland, 'the Palestrina things I had written weren't much to his liking'. Next, Ireland set him to compose 'a choral piece for 8-voices on a bit of Psalm. It's jolly hard to write, & I am certain to find hundreds of consecutives [consecutive fifths] when revising.' By his third term, Ireland was 'quite pleased' with the fugues he was writing. He wrote a report praising Britten's 'grasp of form & technique', and called his music 'very able and interesting'. Many years later, Britten told Murray Perahia that he considered counterpoint the most important training in composition: 'That's what makes harmony; if you think of harmony as an entity in itself, it becomes too structural and you are not aware of the voices interrelating.'

Meanwhile he was filling his diary with musical discoveries and judgements, reactions to records, wireless programmes and London concerts. At present he was still very excited by Brahms. At a concert, someone observed to him that Brahms was 'fit only for the seventeenth century', and he replied that it would be 'fit for the thirtieth'. He put up a picture of Brahms in his bed-sitting-room, and would have framed it if he had had enough money. He was also still devoted to Beethoven. He spent hours one holiday playing 'innumerable Beethoven Sonatas', and on his writing table in his Lowestoft bedroom he had a small Beethoven plaster bust. During his second term at the RCM, in January 1931, he heard Schoenberg conduct two of his own early works, *Friede auf Erden* and

Erwartung, from the BBC's orchestral studio. He 'quite liked' the first, but 'could not make head or tail' of the second. His current attitude to Schoenberg was 'Heaven only knows!!' Three weeks later the BBC Symphony Orchestra under Ernest Ansermet broadcast a Stravinsky concert, which Britten summed up as 'Remarkable, puzzling'. He 'quite enjoyed' the Piano Concerto with Stravinsky himself as soloist, and wrote of the concluding item, *Le sacre de printemps*, 'Sacre – bewildering and terrifying. I didn't really enjoy it, but I think it's incredibly marvellous & arresting.'

He found much recent English music disappointing. In February 1931 he listened briefly to a broadcast of Elgar, '1 min of Elgar Symphony 2 but can stand no more.' In May he condemned the *Enigma Variations* for their 'sonorous orchestration' which 'cloys very soon', greatly preferring Mahler's *Lieder eines fahrenden Gesellen*, heard at the same concert. In November that year, Elgar's *Introduction and Allegro* reminded him of an Italian popular song; the performance was under Boult's baton, and Britten judged him a *'terrible execrable* conductor'. His comment on a typical 'English pastoral' piece, Bax's *November Woods* (1917), heard at a 1931 concert, was 'Didn't like Bax – bored with it – not much November about it.' However, Delius's *Brigg Fair*, which was on the same programme, was 'delicious'. At present Vaughan Williams won his approval. He found the *Fantasia on Christmas Carols* 'thrilling to sing' when he took part in an amateur performance, and he judged the *Fantasia on a Theme by Thomas Tallis* 'v. beautiful (wonderfully scored)', though 'over long', when he heard it in May 1931. But it was Frank Bridge whom he loyally named as 'England's premier composer'.

In June 1931, during his third term at the RCM, he was invited down to the Bridges' weekend cottage at Friston on the Sussex Downs near Eastbourne. 'The country round here is too superb for words,' he wrote in his diary. The cottage had its own tennis court, and Britten, who considered himself 'rather good and stylish' at the game, was amused by Bridge's 'wild and unconventional' style. Bridge was also a wild car driver. Britten found their motor trips hair-raising. Nevertheless he wrote many years later that these 'opened my eyes to the beauty of the Downs with their tucked-away little villages, and to the magnificence of English ecclesiastical architecture'. Always present during these weekends was Marjorie Fass, a cheerful amateur musician and painter who had the cottage next door and was in and out of the Bridges' house all the time. She gave nicknames to everyone (Bridge was 'Franco', 'Mr Brit', or 'Duddles'), and Britten quickly became 'Benjy'. (Howard Ferguson judges that she was in love with Bridge, and that it was a contented

ménage à trois.) Others of the Bridges' artistic friends would often stay
the weekend, and the conversation would, as Britten recalls, centre round
'the latest poems, and the latest trends in painting and sculpture'. Ferguson says that Bridge's own talk was garrulous rather than sophisticated, but it made an enormous impression on Britten. 'It was the first
time I had seen how an artist lived,' he writes.

Relations with John Ireland were getting worse. One evening in the
autumn term of 1931, Britten went to Gunter Grove for a lesson, postponed from earlier that day, and found him 'quite drunk . . . foully so'.
Eric Crozier says Britten told him that Ireland was not merely drunk but
incontinent – 'He peed on the floor, and Ben thought that was filthy and
was really shocked by it.' Another friend says that Britten told him that
Ireland, on at least one occasion, made a sexual pass at him: 'He was
most indignant about it and harped on it many times, usually referring to
him as a dirty old man.' (Peter Pears told the same story to a member of
the English Opera Group.) Quite apart from this behaviour, Ireland often
cancelled lessons at short notice. Though in retrospect he described
Britten as 'the most highly talented and brilliant pupil I've ever had', at
the time he paid more attention to Helen Perkin, a student pianist and
composer whom Britten referred to in his diary as 'Ireland's star & best
comp. pupil'. She was the dedicatee of his Piano Concerto (1931), and
there was much gossip about his relationship with her. Britten judged her
Ballade which she played in an RCM concert to be 'V. competant [*sic*]
with only about 1 bit of original work'. But he did not like to criticize
Ireland to others. When a friend described Ireland as 'a moaning misery'
he found himself 'sharply taken to task' by Britten for lack of sympathy.
Many years later, when questioned by Joseph Cooper about his tutors at
the RCM, Britten would only say that Ireland had been 'very kind to me'
and had 'nursed me very gently through a very, very difficult musical
adolescence'. Fortunately he also had Bridge, though he had now started
to disagree with him. 'At about 18 or 19 I began to rebel. When Bridge
played questionable chords across the room at me and asked if that was
what I'd meant, I would retort, "Yes it is," and he'd grunt back, "Well it
oughtn't to be."'

*

In the RCM end of term examination in July 1931, Britten was awarded
the Farrar Composition Prize for the year (Vaughan Williams was again
an adjudicator, and this time is supposed to have described Britten's
music as 'very clever but beastly'). Britten thought the exam an 'absolute
Farce', with the adjudicators looking at and asking him to play 'the
wrong things out of the hundreds of things I take them'. Now that he had

finished his Palestrina, counterpoint and fugue exercises for Ireland, he was again writing his own music prolifically. Many of his 1931 pieces were for voice and piano, among them a setting of W. H. Davies's poem 'Sport', which compares fox-hunting to 'rats that bite / Babies in cradle'. In South Lodge days he had got into trouble by writing an essay protesting against bloodsports and all forms of organized cruelty, including war – it was marked 'nought'. Now he found himself discussing pacifism with Frank Bridge. 'He had written a piano sonata in memory of a friend killed in France', writes Britten, 'and though he didn't encourage me to take a stand for the sake of a stand, he did make me argue and argue and argue. His own pacifism was not aggressive, but typically gentle.'

In September 1931, at the start of his second year at the RCM, Britten moved to new lodgings at 173 Cromwell Road, not far from the Royal College. His sister Beth came to London to study dress-making and joined him there, in a room adjacent to his on the top floor. Britten had a piano installed and began to practise with a young Italian violinist studying at the RCM, Remo Lauricella. They also formed a trio with a student cellist, Bernard Richards. Apart from this, most of Britten's music-making was still done with amateurs. Beth notes that at the end of each term he would hurry back to Lowestoft, not spending a day more than necessary in London. 'It's jolly nice to be home', he wrote in his diary during a long weekend in Lowestoft; 'no place like home, for all the Londons in the world.' He participated as willingly as ever in his mother's amateur events. '*Musical Evening* at 8.0,' he noted in January 1932. It was attended by the Miss Astles and other musical acquaintances; Britten played Ravel, Debussy and César Franck, his mother sang John Ireland and Armstrong Gibbs, and the entire company attempted part-songs, including Britten's own brand-new 'Variations on a French Carol'. (Marian Walker sang in this, and recalls that at the first rehearsal 'We made the most horrible noise and Ben ... disappeared up to his bedroom and stayed there.') Meanwhile more ambitious works had to lie in the drawer unheard. In the summer and autumn of 1931 he wrote a 132-page orchestral score for a ballet, 'Plymouth Town', to a scenario by Violet Alford, an associate of Cecil Sharp whom he had met in London, but nothing came of it.

He made a breakthrough when a set of three songs for two-part women's or boys' voices, settings of poems by Walter de la Mare, were performed by the Carlyle Singers, a London amateur group of which he was the accompanist, and then were published by Oxford University Press during 1932 – the first of his compositions to get into print. A year later he received his first royalty cheque for the sale of about a thousand copies: fifteen shillings.

He had now decided that *Le sacre de printemps* was 'the World's Wonder', and called Stravinsky's *Symphony of Psalms* 'great', whereas he wrote of Strauss's *Ein Heldenleben*: 'It contains some marvellous things, & some great scoring, but the common-place harmony of alot [*sic*] of it kills me.' A British discovery was William Walton's Viola Concerto. Before hearing it at the Proms in September 1931, Britten bought the score, and on reading it through thought it 'a fine work but difficult'. After the concert, a 'British Composers' Night' which also featured Constant Lambert, Holst, Peter Warlock, Rutland Boughton and Ethel Smyth, he judged the Walton to have 'stood out as a work of genius'. Walton, then turning thirty, was generally regarded as the most exciting young English composer. *Façade* had seemed to bring a much-needed breath of modernism into a musical scene dominated on the one hand by Elgar and the Brahms imitators (the Parry–Stanford school) and on the other by the 'English pastoral' composers led by Vaughan Williams and Holst, with Delius, Bax and John Ireland following closely behind. Sir Michael Tippett recalls that 'Elgar was already an older figure, and the general critical view at that time was that Vaughan Williams was the way English music should go – it was backed by the whole establishment, especially *The Times*.' Walton seemed a distinct improvement on this outlook. After hearing Ireland's Piano Concerto and Holst's *The Planets* in a Prom broadcast in September 1931, Britten wrote in his diary: 'I feel no music of that generation can be compared to works like Walton's Viola Concerto.' Thirty-two years later he wrote to Walton that the Viola Concerto 'showed me the way of being relaxed & fresh, & intensely personal'.

Frank Bridge had dissented from the general admiration of *Façade*, calling it 'high class cabaret and not much – if anything – to do with music itself', and Britten's admiration for Walton quickly became a little uncertain. In 1932 he judged *Façade* 'delightful and attractive', but was disappointed by the overture *Portsmouth Point* (1925) – 'apparently bad & careless workmanship'. He reacted to the London première (November 1931) of *Belshazzar's Feast* with mixed feelings: 'very moving & brilliant (especially 1st half) – but over long – & too continuously loud'.

John Ireland gave him little help or support with his entry for the Cobbett Chamber Music prize, an award which Bridge had won many years earlier with his *Phantasy* in C minor for piano trio (Ireland had been a runner-up). Entries had to be a single continuous movement of no longer than twelve minutes. Britten's piece, also entitled *Phantasy*, was a gentle, rather Edwardian-sounding string quintet, probably planned with the conservative character of the competition in mind. He composed it early in 1932 and at the beginning of May heard that it had won the Cobbett Prize. He spent the thirteen guineas on a new suit and the score of De Falla's *El Amor brujo*. A student quintet performed the *Phantasy* at the RCM at the end of the summer term – 'bad – but I expected worse'. Encouraged by this success he entered for the Mendelssohn Scholarship, which would be worth £150. He submitted the *Phantasy*, settings of Psalms 130 and 150 for chorus and orchestra, and 'Three Small Songs', with words by Samuel Daniel and John Fletcher, for soprano and small orchestra. There were forty candidates and the result was supposed to be announced in July. But Britten's diary records a 'complete fiasco': owing to a muddle among the adjudicators, who included Malcolm Sargent, 'the proceedings have to start from begginning [*sic*] again, so we won't hear until September'. In the meantime his work in the end-of-term composition exam won him the Sullivan Prize (£10). The pieces submitted included a *Sinfonietta* for chamber orchestra which he had just finished.

He had modelled it on Schoenberg's *Chamber Symphony No 1* (1906), which he had first heard in his school-days, using a similar ensemble of strings and wind. It was a hard piece to play, and when at the beginning of the 1932 autumn term some members of the RCM chamber music class began to rehearse it under his direction, he wrote in his diary: 'I have never heard such an appalling row!' It was scheduled for performance in a college concert, but as the weeks advanced rehearsals got worse, with players missing or replaced by others who did not know the parts. 'What an institution,' moaned Britten.

Not until November did the Mendelssohn Scholarship committee make up its mind, choosing Ivor Walsworth, four years older than Britten, to receive the £150. They felt that Britten showed originality of thought, but had not yet acquired the technical expertise necessary to make the best use of his talent. However, they decided to award him £50, 'so as not to discourage me in composing!!!!!!'

He had now spent more than two years at the RCM, and had made few friends in London. He saw a great deal of the Bridges, but besides his practice sessions with Remo Lauricella and Bernard Richards he did not fraternize with other students. His social life revolved around his sisters. He would meet one or other of them for tea in the West End, would go for walks and play tennis with Beth, and did much of his concert-going in their company. Eric Crozier, who got to know Beth and Barbara fifteen years later, describes them:

In many ways Ben and Beth seemed to me alike, even though she lacked his conviction and his strong personal ambition. She was over middle height, with a loose and gangling physical framework: she smoked a lot, was ugly in a not unattractive manner, and she gave me the impression of having a strong masculine element in her character. Ben used to address her as 'old thing' ... Barbara ... was a small, extremely tense, worried little woman. Her speech was quick and intense: she mostly dressed in a dark two-piece suit, a mannish-looking hat, and solid lace-up shoes: and her attitude to Ben was that of an agitated mother-hen fussing over a single, irresponsible chick ... Ben was half-amused, half-irritated by her over-solicitousness, and would sometimes lash out angrily, although in general his attitude to her was one of grateful and affectionate tolerance.

By 1932 Beth had her own circle of London friends, and soon took up with a young man studying medicine, Kit Welford. Barbara was living with Helen Hurst – much later, Britten remarked that his elder sister had spent her adult years in 'the lesbian twilight of the nursing world'. But he himself was as dependent as ever on his family, and was still finding it 'beastly' to return to London from Lowestoft.

He took to reading school stories from Boots' lending library, among them Hugh Walpole's *Jeremy at Crale* and H. A. Vachell's *The Hill*, set at Harrow, which describes how a young pupil develops 'a wild and unreasonable yearning' for an older boy. Britten judged it 'v. good, if too full of Harrow & Sentimentality'. He was unreservedly enthusiastic about J. M. Barrie's *The Little White Bird*, a forerunner of *Peter Pan*, in which the narrator writes lovingly of a small boy, and takes him into his bed, though there is no suggestion of sex. Britten called the book 'Barrie's little wonder'. Later he read another Barrie novel, *Tommy and Grizel*, an account of a marriage that fails through the husband's boyishness: 'He was a boy who could not grow up.'

Some of Britten's own tastes were still those of a small boy. He loved jig-saws, and at Easter 1931, when he was seventeen, wrote in his diary: 'It's good to get back to sweets after six long weeks of Lent!' At Lowestoft he sometimes had to attend dances given by local families, 'much against my will & principles'. (One of his closest friends, Marion Thorpe, danced with him at English Opera Group fund-raising balls in the fifties and says he was 'a hopeless dancer – he just hadn't got any rhythm!') He described his brother Bobby's behaviour with his fiancée Marjorie as 'positively unhealthy', and complained that Marjorie 'spends all her time "darling"ing him'. He enjoyed Mickey Mouse cartoons but judged one of Garbo's films to be 'slop', and another as 'violently & sickeningly sentimental'. He was highly excited by the film of *Emil and the Detectives*, in which a small boy and his friends outwit a professional criminal – 'the most perfect & satisfying film I have ever seen or hope to see . . . a colossal achievement'. He bought the book in its original German, gumming into it some photographs from the film, and was soon thinking of writing 'a Suite on "Emil"'. A lively *Alla Marcia* for string quartet, already written, was considered for inclusion; it begins with pizzicato strings emerging gradually out of silence. The suite as such was never composed. Some months later he was similarly affected by *Poil de Carotte*, the French film about a small boy driven to attempted suicide by the cruelty of his mother. He went to see it twice and was 'impressed, harrowed & thrilled'. Again it inspired him to begin a composition, 'a sketch "Poil de Carotte"', though nothing came of this.

One afternoon, returning on foot from a Thames river-steamer trip with Beth, he walked into the Tate Gallery and saw a painting he thought worthy of note in his diary, 'a marvellous picture of a "Dead Boy" by Alfred Stevens'. It depicted a curly-headed boy with eyes closed, lips apart, his head resting on a pillow. When he heard a broadcast of *Tannhauser* in June 1932 he was disappointed by the soprano who sang the role of the shepherd lad – 'Why not a boy for this?' And he was sufficiently attracted by Robert Graves's poem 'Lift-Boy', with its evocation of boyish carelessness ('nothing in my pockets but a jack-knife and a button'), to make it one of a pair of part-songs he composed during 1932. The other was the wistful 'I loved a lass' by the seventeenth-century poet George Wither. Was it the contrasting musical styles or the subject matter that led him initially to give the songs the odd title 'Two Antithetical Part-Songs'?

One new friendship did begin in the autumn of 1932. 'New Bass in Madrigals,' Britten wrote after a rehearsal of the English Madrigal Choir. 'Paul Wright – very nice.' Aged seventeen, Wright had just left Westminster. He recalls evenings in Britten's Cromwell Road digs: 'I would hunch myself in one of the uncomfortable, rickety armchairs while he sat at an upright piano pouring out inspired improvisations on popular themes, musical jokes, pianistic pyrotechnics and, after a sudden hush that presaged a change of mood, some of the loveliest, most original sounds I had ever heard.' Yet Britten was not altogether an easy companion. Wright discovered that he could be chillingly disapproving 'if one put a foot wrong', and describes him as essentially 'formidable'.

Wright had fallen in love with another boy at school, and had had sexual advances made to him, but had also been attracted by girls, and now had lost his heart to Iris Lemare, conductor of the Carlyle Singers. She was one of a group of young women who were determined to get an audience for contemporary British music. She explains that

> Elisabeth Lutyens couldn't break through as a composer on account of being a woman, and she knew I was having the same problem myself – trying to break through as a woman conductor. Anne Macnaghten had a string quartet and was herself having the same battle. Betty [Lutyens] really had thought it all out but did not want her name included as she naturally intended – and hoped – that her works would be played, and it would then have looked bad in the eyes of other composers.

So during 1931 the venture began as the Macnaghten–Lemare Concerts. They managed to get a venue, the tiny Ballet Club Theatre (later the Mercury) in Notting Hill Gate, where Marie Rambert ran her dance company. 'Financially the position was basically hopeless,' Iris Lemare remembers. 'The audience, in that tiny theatre, consisted largely of the critics, the publishers, and the composers. The "paying public" were largely Anne's relations, Betty's relations, and my aunt! We had no idea if the concerts would go down and we were literally staggered at the response and the press notices.' The Macnaghten–Lemare group came to Britten's rescue when he was in despair about the RCM.

By the end of 1932 there was no prospect of any more of his works being played publicly at the Royal College once the *Sinfonietta* had been performed, and it seemed impossible to find takers for them outside the RCM. He submitted the *Sinfonietta* and the *Phantasy* string quintet to the International Society for Contemporary Music (ISCM) for their 1933 Festival in Amsterdam, but both were rejected. At the instigation of John Ireland, Evelyn Howard-Jones, pianist and musical patron, arranged for the Stratton Quartet to give a private play-through of Britten's String Quartet in D Major, written in May 1931 (published in 1974 in a revised version), and he was 'v. pleased' with the result – 'it sounds more or less as I intended it'. But there was no public performance. Vaughan Williams made some attempt to get one of Britten's psalm settings done at the Three Choirs Festival at Gloucester, Hereford and Worcester, but was unsuccessful. In his letter to Sir Ivor Atkins, director of the Festival, Vaughan Williams wrote of the piece: 'I think it is rather good & well written for the voice. Of course it wd never have been written except for the "Symphonie de Psaumes" but is no worse for that.' The obvious place for Britten's music to be performed was the RCM, but Vaughan Williams said he thought the college choir could not cope with the psalm settings – to which Frank Bridge replied that Vaughan Williams 'ought to use his influence' to improve the choir's standard. Britten's modernity seems to have been the stumbling block. Imogen Holst, who studied at the RCM herself, points out that student compositions were frequently tried out there, and calls it 'incredible' that so little of Britten's music should have been heard while he was a student.

However, Vaughan Williams also mentioned Britten's name to Anne Macnaghten, in a letter some time during 1932 suggesting young composers she should consider for the Ballet Club concerts. They included Gerald Finzi, and his own composition pupils Dorothy Gow and Grace Williams. Seventh in the list came this suggestion: 'You ought to get in touch with Benjamin Britten – I believe he has a str quartet – I don't know it – but his orchestral & choral things are fine.' Anne Macnaghten telephoned Britten and arranged a meeting. She thought him 'very young, schoolboyish', but was sufficiently impressed to try his music. On 12 December 1932 a Macnaghten–Lemare Concert included the Carlyle Singers performing his Walter de la Mare part-songs, and the Macnaghten Quartet with an extra viola playing the *Phantasy*. Britten himself noted that the part-songs went 'v. well' with himself at the piano and Iris Lemare conducting, but the strings played 'v. badly ... Worse, by far, than the rehearsals'.

Reviewing the concert, *The Times* called the part-songs 'attractive' but felt that the *Phantasy* 'did not build up into a satisfying whole', while in the *Music Lover* a young composer named Christian Darnton (whose work had also been performed at the Macnaghten–Lemare Concerts) was condescending towards the songs – 'good for one who, I believe, is only 19, even though they were reminiscent in a quite peculiar degree of Walton's latest songs' – and utterly damning about the *Phantasy*: 'the licences in construction which the title implies only cover up a deficiency of technique'. When Britten wrote to Anne Macnaghten a week after the concert he had not yet seen Darnton's review, but the *Times* piece had evidently upset him: 'I saw the Times Criticism – upon which I pass no comment – & am slowly recovering. Needless to say, I shall continue to compose ...' When he did see Darnton's piece, he made no comment about it in his diary, or to anyone else. But twenty years later he spoke out about it in an article on critics and criticism:

> I can well remember my first contact with the critics ... The only written criticism [of the songs] damned them entirely – as being obvious copies of Walton's three *Façade* Songs. Now anyone who is interested can see for himself that this is silly nonsense. The Walton Songs are brilliant and sophisticated in the extreme – mine could

scarcely have been more childlike and naïve, without a trace of parody throughout. It is easy to imagine the damping effect of this first notice on a young composer. I was furious and dismayed because I could see there was not a word of truth in it. I was also considerably discouraged. No friendliness – no encouragement – no perception. Was this the critical treatment which one was to expect all one's life? A gloomy outlook.

He must therefore have approached the forthcoming performance of his *Sinfonietta* with particular apprehension. The student chamber orchestra at the RCM was not yet ready to play it in public, but Iris Lemare decided to conduct it at the Ballet Club on 31 January 1933, in a programme which also included works by Finzi, Gordon Jacob and Grace Williams. Britten noted that the performance had gone 'quite well' considering the very limited rehearsal time, though he added 'but oh!', indicating how much better it could have been. The *Daily Telegraph* review of the concert dismissed the *Sinfonietta* in a sentence: 'Mr Benjamin Britten in a Sinfonietta for ten instruments showed that he can be as provocative as any of the foreign exponents of the catch-as-catch-can style of composition.' But *The Times* was much more enthusiastic: 'Mr Benjamin Britten, after taking something from Hindemith, seems to be striking out on a path of his own . . . he possesses a power of invention apart from the efficiency with which he handles his material . . . He has already enough to say for himself to excuse his independence of tradition.' Britten described this review as 'very flattering'. Better still was to come from the *Music Lover*. Darnton, eight years his senior, wrote again that Britten was just a young composition student, but could not help admiring the speed of his development.

A Sinfonietta for ten instruments . . . by Benjamin Britten was a really outstanding work. When one is still nineteen events move fast. And this was a great advance on the other works heard at the last of these concerts. The Sinfonietta contained some exceedingly stimulating musical thought, considerable constructive power and surprising technical skill. Mr Britten is a credit to his teacher, John Ireland.

This praise from reviewers had immediate effect. The BBC had already begun to take notice of Britten – his *Phantasy* string quintet was booked for a broadcast in February 1933 – and now it accepted a new work, also entitled *Phantasy*, for oboe, violin, viola and cello. One of the Corporation's music staff, the composer Victor Hely-Hutchinson, invited Britten to come and play through new works to him, on 16 June 1933, and three days later circulated an internal memorandum: 'I do whole-heartedly subscribe to the general opinion that Mr Britten is the most interesting new arrival since Walton, and I feel we should watch his work very carefully.'

4: Depressed for English music

John Ireland came to the first Macnaghten–Lemare Concert at which Britten's music was performed, and pointedly said not a word to Britten all evening. Frank Bridge was so incensed by this, coming on top of all the missed and wasted lessons (Ireland's habits in this respect had worsened), that he complained to Sir Hugh Allen, head of the RCM, and telephoned Ireland, asking what he meant by his behaviour at the concert. Ireland replied with 'protestations of all kinds', but the call had the desired effect. 'Lesson with Ireland at 10.35,' Britten noted on 13 January 1933. 'Have it all out with him . . . it will probably clear the air abit.' The diary contains no further record of trouble with Ireland. In any case, Britten's growing success meant that he no longer paid much heed to his official teacher.

His letters home were full of excitement. 'Some good news,' he wrote on 22 June 1933.

> The broadcast [of his *Phantasy* quartet for oboe and strings] is all fixed up . . . Goossens is probably going to play . . . I have had a nice letter from Norman Stone of the English Singers, and my part-songs go along when copied out. Arthur Bliss is giving some chamber concerts in town next Winter (Grotrian or Wigmore Hall), & I hear from very reliable quarters that he is going to do my oboe quartet. Of course they are agitating for stuff for the Ballet Club concerts. And last – but definitely not least!! – Hermann Scherchen the very well known German conductor is going to do my Sinfonietta in Strasbourg in early August . . .

The *Phantasy* quartet was broadcast in August with Leon Goossens as oboist, and was repeated at a concert in Westminster, when *The Times* called the Britten work 'original . . . arresting . . . natural and unforced', adding that a 1917 piano trio by Ireland, also on the programme, sounded 'old-fashioned' by comparison. The New English Singers did not do anything with the part-songs, nor did Bliss organize a performance of the oboe quartet, and though the *Sinfonietta* was scheduled for broadcasting from Strasbourg, when the day came the programme seemed to have been altered. On the other hand 'a large choral work', as Britten described it, begun the previous autumn and completed in the spring, was tried out by the Wireless Singers in July 1933 and was accepted by the BBC for broadcasting in the near future. 'My dear Son Benjamin,' wrote 'Pop' Britten when he heard about this, 'Hearty congratulations! ... Oh! Ben my boy what does it feel like to hear your own creation? ... Go on my son. Your very loving & admiring Pop.' To Beth, 'Pop' wrote: 'Isn't old Ben a wonder? & so modest about it all.'

'Pop' had been unwell for some time, but Beth writes that 'no doctor could find out what was wrong with him'. Few doctors were given the chance. He grumbled about their fees and said he had 'seen too much of their ways' in his dental practice. He developed a debilitating cough, and took frequently to his bed. At the end of 1933 Ben wrote in his diary that the 'slur' on the whole year had been 'Pop's dreadful illness', and hoped that '1934 can give us back what seems to us the impossible – Pop's health'.

On 11 December 1933, at a Macnaghten–Lemare Concert, an unfinished string quartet by Britten was performed. Entitled *Alla Quartetto Serioso: 'Go play, boy, play'* (a quotation from *The Winter's Tale*), it had grown out of the *Alla Marcia* which he had considered making part of an *Emil and the Detectives* suite. The quartet was a highly personal project, an attempt both to portray certain friends from school-days and to give impressions of various forms of boyish fun and games. The *Alla Marcia*, which was the first movement of the new quartet, was subtitled 'P.T.' (Physical Training), and is referred to in Britten's diary as 'David's mov.' (David Layton from Gresham's). Another movement, 'Ragging', was dedicated to Francis Barton, his friend from South Lodge days. The quartet occupied him over a long period of time, and he kept finding it impossible to complete. Three movements were performed at the Macnaghten–Lemare Concert, and were liked by the audience and reviewers, though Britten himself was dissatisfied – so much that he walked off afterwards without thanking Anne Macnaghten and her quartet, which Iris Lemare thought 'rather rude and ungrateful'.

The 1933 autumn term was his last at the RCM. He passed his Associateship (ARCM) in December, taking a mere half-hour to complete the harmony paper, and was awarded a travelling scholarship worth £100 to be used for gaining wider musical experience abroad.

Bridge thought it an excellent idea that he should experience 'a different musical climate', and it may have been at his suggestion that Britten thought of going to Vienna and studying with Alban Berg. Britten's diary first mentions Berg's music on 14 February 1933: 'Listen to the Kolisch Quart. playing astoundingly, Berg's astounding Lyric Suite. The imagination & intense emotion of this work certainly amaze me if it not altogether pleases me.' The following month he listened to Sir Henry Wood conducting the *Three Fragments from 'Wozzeck'* (the opera had yet to be heard in its entirety in England). Britten called it 'thoroughly sincere & moving music', and wrote that Strauss's *Tod und Verklärung* 'seemed dull & banal after this'. A year later he listened to a broadcast of the entire *Wozzeck* conducted in London by Boult. The reception was poor and only parts were intelligible, but he judged much of the music 'extraordinarily striking', commenting: 'The hand of Tristan is over alot of the intense emotion, but Berg emerges a definite personality.'

He met Schoenberg, Berg's former teacher, in February 1933 when Bridge took him backstage at the Queen's Hall where the composer had been conducting his *Variations* (Op. 31). Britten wrote in his diary: 'What I could make of it, owing to a skin-of-its-teeth performance, was rather dull, but some good things in it. Meet Sch. in interval.' His attitude to Schoenberg had always fluctuated, and he was going through a period of intense admiration for the Beethoven of the *Choral Symphony* ('unapproachable genius & inspiration') and the Wagner of *Tristan und Isolde* ('what music!' he wrote after a performance at Covent Garden in May 1933 – 'He is the master of us all'). But he was acutely aware that Wagnerian late-romanticism was now dead, that it had faded away in the 'common-place' harmony of much of Richard Strauss. Mahler still seemed admirable; in April 1933 Britten praised the Fourth Symphony as 'a mix up of everything that one had ever heard, but it is definitely Mahler'. Imitation of Mahler was, however, out of the question, and he was now scathing about those British composers who were still working in the shadow of the late romantics. 'Ist, (& I hope, last) broadcast perf. of Bliss' Clar. Quintet,' he wrote in April 1933. 'V. unoriginal piffle.' As to the 'English pastoral' school, by the beginning of 1933 he was writing of Vaughan Williams: 'I am afraid that I don't like his music, however much I try.' He felt that much of it was 'technically inefficient' and 'didn't seem to hang together'. Many years later he said: 'My struggle all the time was to develop a consciously controlled professional technique. It was a struggle away from everything Vaughan Williams seemed to stand for.'

However uncertain he might feel about the contemporary Viennese school, it demanded technical excellence. Consequently he 'suggested to the RCM authorities that I'd like to study with Berg'. He met with resistance. 'I said at home during the holidays, "I *am* going to study with Berg, aren't I?" ... the answer was a firm, "No, dear." Pressed, my mother said, "He's not a good influence."' Looking back, Britten guessed that it was Sir Hugh Allen at the RCM who 'put a spoke in the wheel', though the precise objection to Berg was not altogether clear. In a 1963 interview Britten said he had 'discovered that it had been hinted to my parents that [Berg] was in some way "immoral", and they thought studying with him would do me harm'. It has been supposed that 'immoral' meant 'homosexual', but Berg was married, and at this date there was no reason why Britten's parents should have feared the temptation of homosexuality. The objection is more likely to have been musical. 'There was at that time', writes Britten in a 1963 article, 'an almost moral prejudice against serial music – which makes one laugh today!' He suggested that, while Sir Hugh Allen may have been suffering from such a prejudice, 'there was some confusion in my parents' minds – thinking that "not a good influence" meant morally, not musically.' (Even twenty-year-old Schoenberg was too much for the RCM, which turned down Britten's suggestion of buying *Pierrot lunaire* for the library.)

Britten was now in his twenty-first year, but he accepted the parental veto passively, as if he had been a schoolboy. No decision was made yet about how he would spend the travelling scholarship, but a foreign trip of sorts soon materialized. 'I *am* going to Italy,' he wrote to a friend at the end of February 1934. Again he had submitted work to the ISCM, and this time he had been successful. His *Phantasy* oboe quartet was accepted for their 1934 festival, to be held in Florence in April. His parents felt it was too far from him to travel on his own, so his South Lodge friend, John Pounder, son of a local bank manager, was enlisted as travelling companion.

In the weeks before departure, Britten was involved in the performance of two of his new works. The first was described by him in a letter to Grace Williams, the young Welsh composer, whom he knew through the Macnaghten–Lemare Concerts: 'I cannot write a single note of anything respectable at the moment, and so – on the off chance of making some money – I am dishing up some very old stuff (written, some of it, over ten years ago) as a dear little school suite for strings – You see what I have come to ...!' He had spent the Christmas holidays hunting through 'tons of old MS.' for material for the suite, and he took Bridge's advice with the work: 'F.B. looks over some of my Kid's pieces – telling me invaluable things abt. them.' The *Simple Symphony* was certainly intended as a money-making project – there was a large market for school music – but was also a way of keeping in touch with the child in himself. It was given its first performance in Norwich on 6 March 1934, with Britten himself conducting a string orchestra mostly drawn from local amateurs: 'my "Simple Symphony" ... doesn't go too badly'. It was published later in 1934 by Oxford University Press.

The other piece first performed shortly before the Italian trip was the 'large choral work' tried out the previous summer by the Wireless Singers, and already published by the Oxford University Press (OUP) in anticipation of the promised broadcast. The words were taken from ancient Christmas carols, and it was dedicated to 'Pop', perhaps because of his illness.

Entitled *A Boy Was Born*, it was structured with great ingenuity as a theme and variations, developed from the first four notes of the opening chorale, and Britten's diary shows that by his standards he took an unusually long time to write it – November 1932 to May 1933 – with many pauses and restarts and much rewriting. A semi-chorus of boys' voices played an important part in it, and when Britten first heard the choristers of St Mark's, North Audley Street working on it he wrote: 'They sing like angels – for this stage of rehearsal.' He was particularly concerned that they should not try to blend with the women's voices but be encouraged to keep their natural sound. He himself took their final rehearsal in February 1934 (the BBC had postponed the broadcast from Christmas).

At this period, the *Radio Times* devoted considerable space to contemporary serious music, and the composer Edmund Rubbra wrote a lengthy preview of *A Boy Was Born* in the issue dated 16 February 1934:

> Here in this striking choral work is yet another sign of the growing vitality of modern English music. In it are to be found the best elements of Elizabethan choral writing combined with a subtle rhythmic ingenuity ... In [Britten's] work there is no trace of fumbling, nor, which is even more remarkable, of outside influences. His statements are always direct and to the point, and his musical language is easily understandable.

A Boy Was Born was broadcast on 23 February 1934, the day of Elgar's death.

*

At the end of March 1934 Britten was off to Italy with John Pounder. In Florence, they put up in a *pensione* near the Arno. Allan Pearce, a friend of Pounder's who was visiting Florence too, observes that while Pounder was a 'great extrovert' who kept the party going, Britten was 'retiring' and made little impression, though at the *pensione* he improvised music on an upright piano in the lobby to describe Pounder's nimble descent down the staircase. He told Grace Williams that the festival was something of a disappointment – 'There was some pretty poor music played.' One concert consisted of pieces 'by Italian Parrys & Stanfords'. (It was around now that Britten began to turn against Brahms, Parry's and Stanford's model; in July he wrote in his diary: 'After dinner listen to Vaughan Williams' Benedicite – music which repulses me, as does most of Brahms (solid, dull).' The following spring he reiterated: 'I can't stand B[rahms] these days.')

The ISCM Festival performances took place under the 'patronage' of Mussolini's government. The German section of the ISCM had sent no representatives, but certain individual Germans antipathetical to the Nazis had managed to get there. Among these was Hermann Scherchen, who had intended to conduct Britten's *Sinfonietta*; he had recently taken up the directorship of the Zurich Radio Orchestra. His family were with him in Florence, staying in the same *pensione* as Britten, who made friends with the fourteen-year-old son, Wolfgang, known as Wulff. Following a successful performance of his oboe quartet – 'Goossens & the Grillers really play my Phant. very beautifully & it's quite well received' – Britten and the Scherchens went on a coach trip to Siena. 'Lunch given by the Mayor etc. – visits to Cathedral. Young Wulff Scherchen (son of Hermann) attaches himself to me, & I spend all the time with him.'

Wulff Scherchen suggests that the friendship began because

> we were the only two who were more or less of my age group ... All the rest were grown up ... people in their 30s and 40s and 50s ... performers and composers and what have you. I mean, it was an extraordinary collection at the *pensione* where we were staying ... Old Dent [Professor E. J. Dent, the Cambridge musicologist and President of the ISCM] was there, plus the composers whose pieces were being played, and as I say, Ben and I were the only people of roughly comparable ages.

In fact Britten had several companions of his own age – Pounder, Pearce, and Pearce's sister, who was also there – while there was a seven-year gap between him and Wulff. But the boy found him 'a marvellous companion ... He was full of fun ... He always had to play word games ... He used to drive me crazy at times with his puns and alliterations.'

It poured with rain in Siena, and since Wulff had no overcoat he shared

Britten's. 'It was ... a shower which made us shelter together in his mackintosh,' he remembers, 'one arm in each sleeeve.' He returns to this: 'And then we shared his mac. I mean, that was just – that was terrific.' The next morning, Saturday 7 April: 'Meet Wulff & have a short walk with him before lunch. At lunch get a telegram from home – come to-day, Pop not so well. Pack up at once – John [Pounder] marvellously sympathetically insists on coming too – see about things, leave score for Scherchen, & the Pearces come down to the station to see us off by 4.53.' When she sent the telegram, Mrs Britten concealed the truth. 'Pop' had died the previous day.

*

He was fifty-seven, and had been going downhill fast since Christmas. The doctors had prescribed morphia, and a nurse was in attendance at the house, though this was anathema to Mrs Britten, who, while still a practising member of the Church of England, had now become a believer in Christian Science. 'You know all this is contrary to my C.S.,' she wrote to Beth. 'I am only doing it as the family wants [it] and Pop himself!'

Britten's diary shows that he had been well aware for months of the gravity of the situation. Back in October 1933 it had been 'impossibly ghastly leaving home with Pop like this'. Beth says that the family were 'half expecting father to die' long before it happened. Indeed, 'the doctors gave my mother a definite date for him to die, one of them in January; then, as he lived on, another in February', and so on. His condition had deteriorated during the week before Britten's departure for Italy, but the possibility of his not making the journey seems not to have been discussed. On the day of his departure, 'Pop brightens a bit to say "good-bye" to me.' The end had come abruptly, ten days later. The immediate cause of death was a cerebral haemorrhage, but the mystery illness had been cancer of the lymph glands. 'Pop' had left a farewell note in an envelope addressed to 'the 4 B's' – Barbara, Bobby, Beth and Benjamin:

> Goodbye my four!
> My love to you all
> Its grand to have known you
> and have your love
>
> – –
>
> Comfort Mum

Leaving Florence on the Saturday afternoon, Britten had 'a pretty filthy journey – spending two nights travelling and not knowing what I was going to meet at the end of it'. His diary records the details:

Arr. Newhaven abt. 3.30 (English time) & at Victoria at abt. 6.0. Taxi across to Liverpool St. – hang about for an hour & then we catch 8.15 home – breakfasting on the way. When I arrive, I learn that Pop died on Friday – a stroke, hastened by general weakness. A great man – with one of the finest brains I have ever come across, & what a father! Bobby, Barbara and Beth are all here. Bobby & Beth came on Saturday, while Barb. has been here since Easter. Don't do much – except some walks with Bob. Fernande [wife of Mr Britten's partner in the dental practice] takes Mum, Barb. & Beth to Norwich in aft.

And the next day:

Don't do much all day – get up rather late – see Mr Coleman with Bobby abt. music for tomorrow [the funeral] (decide on last no. of Matt. Pass. and var. III of my 'boy' [*A Boy Was Born*]) – letters & read in aft.

His only comment on the death is: 'Mum is being marvellously brave.' On the day of the funeral: 'Mum is a perfect marvel, even when we go up to Kirkley Cemetery after, she has control of herself . . . Considering what Mum has been through – she is bearing up incredibly.' He makes no further reference to his own feelings about the bereavement, though to the diary entry for 6th April, the day of the visit to Siena and sharing the raincoat with Wulff, he added the words: 'Pop dies – see Monday.'

The *Lowestoft Journal* for 14 April 1934 reported that the music played before the funeral was 'written by Mr Benjamin Britten, younger son of the deceased'. A few weeks earlier another local newspaper, the *Eastern Daily Press*, had given him a highly complimentary notice, in a report of a lecture on contemporary English composers given in Norwich by Basil Maine, a leading music critic. After talking about John Ireland, Maine continued:

A pupil of John Ireland hails from these parts – from Lowestoft – of whom we shall hear something in these coming years, maybe of his great accomplishment. He is a boy of 19 [*sic*] at the Royal College of Music, and he has had a work chosen for the coming International Festival of Music in the spring. We have been up to now regarding as the most distinguished of our youngest composers William Walton and Constant Lambert, but there is now another relay on the way, and Benjamin Britten of Lowestoft, will, I think, be found to be foremost among them. I am not going to prophesy or to be too optimistic, but I think you will find that one of the lights of the future will come from these parts.

However, 'Pop's' death threw Britten's whole future into doubt. His student days were over, and the death (as he told the Mendelssohn Scholarship committee) had 'left us in somewhat straitened circumstances', so that unless financial help was forthcoming 'I shall be compelled to find a job.'

In fact Robert Britten had provided well for his family. Mrs Britten was left about £15,000, sufficient for her to live in some comfort on the interest. Each of the four children received only £100 in the will, but the elder three were now self-supporting, Barbara with her health-visitor job, Bobby by running a small preparatory school with Marjorie in Wales, and Beth as a dress-maker – she and a friend had opened their own small business in Hampstead. Only Benjamin had not, financially speaking, left home. The previous September he had received a further £50 from the Mendelssohn scholarship funds, but this was awarded grudgingly, and he had little hope of further help from that quarter. Yet, apart from his letter to the Mendelssohn committee, his correspondence immediately after his father's death was strikingly cheerful, giving no sense that a major blow, either financial or emotional, had just been dealt. 'Mum had had a very bad time, so I brought her here for a few weeks,' he wrote to Grace Williams from his brother's school, Clive House at Prestatyn, two weeks after the bereavement. 'She seems to be picking up a bit now.' The death had brought the two of them even closer together. 'My darling Mum,' he wrote to her when she left Prestatyn to visit her sister. 'I want . . . to tell you that you have my thoughts all the time – not that you need telling *that* I hope . . . I miss you most terribly, my dear . . . Much love to you, my sweet.'

He stayed at Prestatyn for a while, revising *A Hymn to the Virgin* for publication by OUP, and continuing work on a set of simple songs for schools, with witty piano accompaniments. He gave them the title *Friday Afternoons* because that was the day on which Robert took singing practice with the boys. 'Sketch a school song in morning & revise another,' he noted on Friday 4 May. 'Help Robert with a singing class, and at coaching the boys cricket . . .' Eric Crozier, who met Britten's brother in the forties gives this picture of him:

> Robert . . . was something of a misfit – he was never part of the tight little family group represented by Ben, Barbara and Beth, but . . . was treated more as a stranger. He was a nondescript and not specially intelligent teacher: I would hazard a guess that, of all the Britten children, he most closely resembled their father. He . . . gave the impression of being . . . anxious to please but out of place in the social and artistic world of his younger brother.

Britten was very happy at the school. 'I shall be sick to leave this place; & am so fond of the school & the kids that I dread going back to the void of Lowestoft.'

He had to leave towards the end of May, for important appointments in London. Leslie Woodgate, director of the BBC Singers (the Wireless Singers' new name), had agreed to try out 'I love a lass' and 'Lift Boy', and when Britten came down from Prestatyn to play the accompaniment at the run-through 'a man from Hawkes' was there to hear them. The OUP were sitting on the scores of the *Sinfonietta* and the oboe quartet, but neither had appeared in print, and Britten was anxious to stir up interest at Boosey & Hawkes. By the end of May, Hubert Foss, head of the OUP music department, had decided not to publish the oboe quartet, and Britten immediately spoke to other publishers: 'I see Ralph Hawkes about it (& Sinfonietta & two part-songs) at 12.30. I now await his decision.' He then rejoined his mother in Lowestoft – 'it is an effort coming here again with the empty space', and, 'Miss Astle comes in after dinner to cheer us up – which we (I esp.) need.' Britten took to going for 'long thinking walks' with the family dog, Caesar. In the past, he and his father had done most of their talking when out for walks together, and at Prestatyn a walk in a 'heavenly sunset' with Bobby had reminded him of 'those with Pop'. From now on he made a 'thinking walk' part of his routine when composing.

He passed some of the time playing cricket with the South Lodge boys, and, during the following months, singled out a particular boy for friendship, thirteen-year-old Piers Dunkerley, 'most disconcertingly witty'. Piers and his brother Tony were boarders at South Lodge; their mother, abandoned by her husband, was earning a living in London as a fashion buyer with Marshall & Snelgrove, and had sent the children away to school very young. A member of Piers' family describes him as 'certainly his mother's favourite – his letters to her begin "Darling Mummy" and so on', and calls him 'terribly good-looking'.

The BBC was due to broadcast the *Sinfonietta* on 20 June, and Britten went to London to attend the rehearsal and performance. Elisabeth Lutyens's husband Edward Clark was the conductor, ill-prepared in Britten's opinion, though the chamber ensemble played 'quite well considering all'. Britten wrote a note of thanks to Clark, and in another letter he mentioned his disappointment that *The Times* had not reviewed the broadcast. Many years later, he claimed that after Christian Darnton's harsh review of his de la Mare songs he had 'decided to avoid reading critics', but it is evident that at this stage in his career he was still scanning newspapers and journals for comments on his work. When a

review of the *Sinfonietta* broadcast did appear, in the *Musical Times* for
August, it was disappointing. 'Benjamin Britten's *Sinfonietta* brought the
concert to an end ... with comedy,' wrote William McNaught.

> This young spark is good company for as long as his persiflage remains
> fresh, which is not very long. To do him justice his Sinfonietta closed
> down in good time. One hopes earnestly that he is aware of the nature
> of his present phase – a kind of programme-music phase, of which the
> programme is 'See how knowing I am, how much wiser than my years'
> – and that he intends sooner or later to use his exceptional talent for
> the working out of a different story, the gist of which is, 'You will like
> this.'

This absurdly schoolmasterly tone predominated among British reviews
of contemporary music at this date – 'unobservant, if not actually inane',
wrote Britten many years later. He said he would have welcomed constructive criticism, comments on 'passages where I have not quite solved
problems', but he assumed the critics were too musically illiterate to
identify such weak spots, let alone suggest remedies.

Yet on the whole reactions to his work were encouraging. The OUP
decided to publish the *Simple Symphony*, and Britten suggested they
should get it into the catalogue in time 'to catch the beginning of the
school year'. They also accepted a *Te Deum* for choir and organ he had
written during the summer. Meanwhile Ralph Hawkes decided to publish not just the oboe quartet but also the *Sinfonietta* (taken over from
OUP), the two part-songs, and *Friday Afternoons*. He also commissioned a suite for piano, and Britten got to work at once. The result was
Holiday Tales (later retitled *Holiday Diary*), which Britten described as
'impressions of a boy's seaside holiday, in pre-war days', that is, pre-
1914.

He had still not spent his travelling scholarship money, and in October
1934 he set off on a European trip – accompanied by his mother. They
went first to Basle where Britten met the celebrated conductor Felix
Weingartner, who spared time for 'a very long talk' but 'was not
interested in modern music at all'. Weingartner was also 'very busy and
couldn't (or wouldn't) give me the introduction I wanted', though he
provided Britten with a pass for a rehearsal he was conducting. It was for
a Richard Strauss concert, and Britten was thrilled by the soprano
Elisabeth Schumann. He and his mother also went to the opera four
times, including 'a simply lovely show of Zauberflöte'. At the end of
October they moved on to Salzburg, staying three days and examining
'the Mozart relics', which 'thrilled' Britten, though there was no music to

be heard at that time of year. They then travelled to Vienna, where he had hoped to study.

Here Britten and his mother had 'quiet rooms – next to each other – and H & C water', Mrs Britten wrote to Beth, while 'Yesterday we went to a marvellous Opera to hear *The Bat* – Johann Strauss.' Britten was bowled over by the brilliance of the orchestral playing. 'Never such tone, & precision, & spirit,' he wrote to Grace Williams, 'the orchestra played as if it *wanted* to play ... those London orchestras [are] *nothing* like this'. He was able to feast himself at the opera – 'Meistersinger, Siegfried, last week & Götterdämmerung to-night!!!' Mrs Britten told Beth that, amid the fashionable clothes at the opera, 'Benjamin looks most remarkable in his grey flannel trousers – everyone stares at him!'

As to personal contacts, Britten had been apprehensive about having to 'go round introducing myself to crowds of people, who will never have heard of English music (don't blame them), and who don't speak English'. He had brought a letter of introduction from Hubert Foss to Hans Heinsheimer of Universal Edition, who allowed him to leave some of his scores for scrutiny. They were passed to an editor named Erwin Stein, whom Britten found 'very nice indeed', though for the present nothing came of the meeting. And it was a major disappointment to learn that Alban Berg was not in Vienna.

Britten had written to Beth that he was looking after their mother, who 'gets very dazed and dizzy at times, but that is to be expected, considering we are travelling so much and seeing so many new things. I have to be rather careful with her really, although she is being awfully sweet, and putting nothing in my way.' However, the impression given by his letters and those written by Mrs Britten is that she was firmly in charge, with Benjamin following obediently.

Mrs Britten had a fall in her bedroom and was 'a bit wobbly' for a few days, but they went on an exhaustive sightseeing trip. 'Personally I get bored with palace after palace,' Britten admitted in his diary, but added loyally that 'it was interesting seeing the town'. He consoled himself that he might 'come here again next year ... travelling 3rd [class], & living on nothing when I get here', providing some of the scholarship money was left over. The scholarship was intended to facilitate musical study – Britten said later that the £100 was 'enough to keep a youngster on the Continent for six months in those days' – but he was being taken on a social tour in which music played only an intermittent part.

Meanwhile Mrs Britten had found the Christian Science church. Benjamin refused to come to the service, but walked about outside. She believed she was receiving spirit messages from 'Pop'. 'I have a letter from him,' she wrote to Beth; 'he said: Give my love to Beth and tell her I expect her to be what all our kids are – "Perfect." '

Benjamin spent much of the time working in his hotel room. He began a suite for violin and piano with a strong Viennese flavour: there were touches of Schoenberg, and an entire movement in the form of a Viennese waltz. After a while he took to his bed with flu, but insisted on getting up for the five hours of *Die Meistersinger*. 'It cured him!' reported Mrs Britten. He was ecstatic about it: 'The five hours . . . didn't seem as many minutes; the incredible vitality, modernity, richness in lovely melody, humour, pathos in fact every favourable quality.' But all too soon Mrs Britten moved them on again. Britten told Grace Williams he was 'sick' at leaving Vienna so quickly. 'But I'm coming back – soon & oft.'

In Munich they saw Strauss's *Salome* – 'A great & epoch-making work,' judged Britten. They went on to Paris and from there flew home on Imperial Airways, which Britten found 'thrilling in the extreme'. They were back just in time for him to hear *Holiday Tales* performed at the Wigmore Hall on 30 November by Betty Humby. The suite had musical nudges in the direction of Arthur Benjamin, to whom it was dedicated, Stravinsky and Bartók, though a serene passage in the second piece, 'Sailing', was in a simple lyrical voice that was all Britten's own. This simplicity had not been achieved by sheer fluency. Gone were the days when he would compose profusely, rushing on to the next piece as soon as one was finished. 'To-day I make great effort,' he noted on 17 September while working on *Holiday Tales*. 'The result isn't satisfactory tho – & will all have to be scrapped.' A week later: 'Try in vain to continue these hellish pft pieces & walk frantically up & down the beach trying to think.'

The *Times* critic was pleased enough with the *Holiday Tales* pieces – 'they avoid formulae and yet have a sturdy unity and structure of their own' – but the secretary of the Mendelssohn Scholarship committee, who had been sent the new suite, said he found it outside his comprehension. Britten was made even more aware of a composer's precarious financial position when OUP refused to let him retain broadcasting and recording rights of his new works, explaining that his music was not selling well enough, and they needed to recoup the loss where they could. Replying in a hurt tone, he pointed out that the first public performance of *A Boy Was Born*, at a Macnaghten–Lemare concert in December 1934, had earned strong praise from A. H. Fox Strangways in the *Observer*: 'his music . . . has one mark of mastery – endless invention and facility . . . He rivets attention from the first note onwards: without knowing in the least what is coming, one feels instinctively that this is music it behoves one to listen to, and each successive moment strengthens that feeling. He inspires confidence . . .' Hubert Foss of OUP was equally enthusiastic about *A Boy Was Born* – in an internal memo he called it 'one of the most remarkable choral works I have ever heard' – but doubted whether his firm should bear responsibility for Britten's immediate future. He called the *Sinfonietta* and the oboe quartet 'uncommercial', and suggested that 'it may be worth while to let Boosey waste some money on him so long as we can keep his more remunerative efforts'.

Britten badly needed to find a job. 'Now I am waiting for Adrian Boult to return so I can be examined to see if I can be any use on the B.B.C.,' he told Grace Williams on 16 January 1935. At the end of that month he decided to abandon OUP and throw in his lot with Boosey & Hawkes. 'F[oss] has been for ages enthusiastic, then withdrawn by turns; besides there is always so much bother & hold-up about O.U.P. publications. My Simple Symphony has already been printed over 4 months & is not out yet!' He was depressed by the prospect of working for Boult, the BBC's musical director, who was one of his two least favourite conductors (the other was Beecham). Indeed, after Vienna he was altogether appalled by the English musical scene. 'It was *hopeless*,' he wrote to Grace Williams following a broadcast of contemporary music conducted by Vaughan Williams. 'R.V.W. I know is a very nice man, but he shouldn't conduct . . . oh, the ragged entries, the half-hearted & doubtful playing – & the beastly tone. I know I have heard the Vienna Phil; but I was also listening to the Basel Symphony to-night – under some quite unknown man – and it was streets ahead.' The music chosen to represent contemporary composers appalled him as much as the playing:

> I struggled for about three or four minutes with R. O. Morris & then switched off. I tried to be politely interested in Robin Milford, but failed utterly. The fifteen biblical songs of R.V.W. finished me entirely; that 'pi' and artificial mysticism combined with, what seems to me, technical incompetence, sends me crazy, I have never felt more depressed for English music than after that programme . . . especially when I felt that this is what the public – no, not the public, the critics love and praise . . . O for Wien!

As for English amateurs, he found them even more depressing than the professionals. At present he was conducting an amateur string orchestra at Bungay, not far from Lowestoft, but the players were hopeless. 'It is no use trying to rehearse them – the only advice worth giving them is "go away & learn to play your instruments." '

On 8 February 1935 he went to the BBC and was interviewed briefly by Boult and Leslie Woodgate. 'There is a probability of me going there for a whole time job! Ugh!' But a few weeks later a better prospect suddenly appeared. 'A most surprising day,' he wrote in his diary on Saturday 27 April 1935.

Edward Clark's secretary [at the BBC] 'phones at breakfast saying would I get into touch with a certain film impresario, M. Cavalcanti, which I do, with the result that I lunch with him (and another director Mr Coldstream) at Blackheath – where the G.P.O. Film studio is – and that I am booked to do the music to a film on the new Jubilee Stamp ...

5: The most amazing man

Alberto Cavalcanti, a Brazilian in his late thirties, and the painter William Coldstream were both working for John Grierson, who was making documentary films under the auspices of the General Post Office in a converted art school in Bennett Park, Blackheath. Cavalcanti was in charge of the soundtracks, hence his search for a composer. The GPO Film Unit worked on a tiny budget, but the mildly left-wing tone of its films made it an appealing place for young intellectuals. Coldstream, six years older than Britten, was directing *The King's Stamp*, a short film about the design and manufacture of a postage stamp commemorating George V's Jubilee, which was about to be celebrated. Britten was in two minds whether to undertake the music, but Coldstream and Cavalcanti assumed that he would do it, and he was soon frantically at work. 'Literal hell of a day,' he wrote on 1 May 1935.

> I spend the whole blessed day slogging at the film music in my room [he was back in his old lodgings in Cromwell Road] – with a watch in one hand and a pencil in the other – trying to make what little ideas I have (& they are precious few on this God-forsaken subject) syncronize with the Seconds. Have a short break for a walk after tea ... but otherwise I slog away until abt. 11.0 at night – trying to concoct *some* rubbish about a Jubilee Stamp.

There was no time for any creative block, such as he had been experiencing recently. On 24 January: 'I'm having a dreadfully blank time at writing – I can get on with nothing, much as I try.' The piece that had been giving most trouble was the still unfinished string quartet subtitled 'Go play, boy, play', with its portraits of boys at school. 'Usual day – usual unsuccess of work,' he wrote on 6 March 1935, after struggling with it. The film music may have seemed rubbish, but there was no time for hesitation. 'I had to work quickly,' he wrote some years later of his

Film Unit commissions, 'to force myself to work when I didn't want to, and to get used to working in all kinds of circumstances'. Because the Unit had so little money, large ensembles were out of the question. 'I had to write scores for not more than six or seven players, and to make these instruments make all the effects that each film demanded.' The music for *The King's Stamp* was for flute, clarinet, two pianos and percussion. Some years later he observed, 'I don't take film music seriously qua music,' and certainly much of the score in this and his later GPO films is merely onomatopœic in character – for example, the descending piano run which accompanies the stamp designer's brisk descent down a spiral staircase in *The King's Stamp* may be a reminiscence of that musical joke in Florence. Yet if they are closely analysed, his film scores prove to be as carefully constructed as anything he wrote during the thirties.

As soon as he had completed his hellish day's work, he had a taste of the unpredictability of the film business: 'At 10.30 I go to Soho Square to see Cavalcanti about the film & have all my plans changed – I now have until Tuesday to write the music & all yesterday's panic was for nothing.' Yet when he looked through what he had written, he decided he could not really improve on it, so he went back to Lowestoft for the celebration of the Jubilee on 6 May (he noted that the event was 'too nationalistic'). He was at Blackheath again two days later to play Cavalcanti and Coldstream the music. They liked it, but told him he would have to wait another week before working out the final version, which must be precisely matched to the completed footage. 'It was also extremely good practice for me as a young composer', he writes, 'to take exact instructions.'

The film commission came at a time when he was doing much cinema-going. He would tour the London news theatres in search of Walt Disneys – he called the best of them 'masterpieces' – and he enjoyed Hitchcock's *The Man Who Knew Too Much*, which had a score by Arthur Benjamin, though Britten was chiefly interested in the performance of *gamin* Nova Pilbeam, 'a little darling . . . so lovely to look at'. He went again to *Poil de Carotte*, noting that the boy actor Robert Lynen was 'glorious'. One evening while he was waiting to complete *The King's Stamp* he had dinner with his sister Barbara. 'Long talks about troubles of life – rather overwhelming at the moment – she is very good & nice on these matters.' He did not specify what they were.

When he was given the final timings for the film he produced the finished score at top speed – 'What a job!' – and conducted and played first piano for the recording at Blackheath. Howard Ferguson was the other pianist. 'It goes quite well – & is good fun to do,' Britten wrote in his diary. 'Cavalcanti is most charming & a marvellous director. Considering the hurry of everything, I think it is quite effective stuff & suits the film.' John Francis, a young professional flautist who had been at the RCM in Britten's time, played on the recording, and thought Britten 'a damn good musician who could not only write music but could conduct it extremely well, which is unusual'.

Britten now found himself being called to script conferences for a GPO film about coal miners. 'Spend morning & aft. with Coldstream hunting in Daily Herald offices, libraries & book shops for words for Mining film.' The subject had nothing to do with the Unit's sponsors, the Post Office, but Grierson and his staff were allowed to make films of general interest. The completed documentaries were shown in cinemas and hired to educational organizations. Britten's music for *Coal Face* was 'entirely experimental stuff – written for blocks of wood, chains, [film] rewinders, cups of water etc. etc.' He has described the scene at Blackheath during recording: 'I well remember the mess we made . . . We had pails of water which we slopped everywhere, drain pipes with coal slipping down them, model railways, whistles and every kind of paraphernalia.' (They could have used recordings of the real sounds, but the home-made variety was in keeping with the experimental character of the Unit.) The music was written and recorded in a few days, leaving Britten 'absolutely dead', but 'Everyone's very pleased with the stuff, & I must say that it comes off.'

His life now consisted of rushing about in taxis, writing, recording and cutting far into the night, and relaxing with the Film Unit crowd at Bertorelli's in Charlotte Sreet. On Friday 5 July 1935:

> Have a quick hair-cut before Basil Wright [another member of the Unit] calls for me in his car at 10.0 and takes me down to Colwall near Malvern. Very lovely journey via Maidenhead, Oxford, Tewkesbury. Arr. 1.45 – lunch at Park Hotel where we put up. We come here to talk over matters for films with Wystan Auden (who is a master at the Downs School here – incidentally Bobby [Britten] was a master at the Elms, another school in Colwall). Auden is the most amazing man . . .

Nearly seven years older than Britten, Wystan Hugh Auden had gone from Gresham's to Christ Church, Oxford, and thence into preparatory school teaching. His reputation as a poet, spokesman for the left-wing young, was already considerable. Among friends he made no secret of his homosexuality – though homosexual practices were illegal in Britain. Wanting a new job, he had written to Basil Wright (an old friend of C. Day Lewis, one of the Auden 'gang') and asked if he could work for the Film Unit. The result was an invitation to contribute words to the soundtracks of *Coal Face* and other projected films. Hence Wright's and Britten's journey to Colwall.

His pupils at the Downs School called him 'Uncle Wiz'. Magnetically charming, casually bohemian, intellectually a bully, he was able to mesmerize Britten from the first moments of their meeting. Britten sketched him in his diary as 'a very brilliant and attractive personality – he was at Farfield, Greshams, but before my time. Work with him in aft. & then tea in Malvern. After that, watch the boys have a rag – with remarkable freedom – & then eat at the Park. After that have a drinking party with most of the Downs masters (about 7) but very boring.' Though ordinary schoolmasters were bound to seem dull alongside Auden, the Downs was an unconventional school, and next day Britten succumbed to its spell:

> Walk about the village . . . in the morning. Also up to the Downs for
> 11's es with Auden. Have lunch with the school in the dining-room –
> they are a remarkably nice lot of boys – very free with the masters, but
> yet discipline is maintained – very sensibly stressed – most of them just
> in shirt & trousers. After lunch the Art Master (Mr Feild) shows us
> many of the boys' paintings (all in oils) & they are some of the most
> vital & thrilling things I have ever seen in modern art – so much that
> B.W. and I prevail on some of them to give us specimens, & we leave
> with 7 or 8 priceless ones each. In the aft. there is a match versus the
> masters. We stay on & watch, as it is such a heavenly day & the
> grounds look so lovely with the white-clad little figures prancing about
> on the green. One lad (David) makes a very fine century. After tea on
> the field, B.W. & I leave at 6.30 . . .

It seems that, before Britten and Wright's trip to Colwall, Auden had already written and sent to the Unit a verse to be sung on the soundtrack of *Coal Face* by women's chorus, representing the miners' women ('O lurcher-loving collier, black as night, / Follow your love across the smokeless hill'). When he heard Britten's setting of these and other lines he had provided for the Film Unit, Auden was struck by the young composer's 'extraordinary musical sensitivity in relation to the English language. One had always been told that English was an impossible tongue to set or sing . . . Here at last was a composer who set the language without undue distortion.'

Back in London, Britten was again caught up in the unpredictable demands of the Film Unit. The German artist Lotte Reineger had made them a silhouette film advertising the Post Office Savings Bank, and Britten was told to arrange 'fourteen small sections of about 8–20 sec. each', based on Rossini piano pieces. He went hunting in music shops for the Rossini, and learnt to work a Moviola viewing machine so as to measure film lengths himself. Ten days after he had begun this job, his ingenious orchestration of Rossini was recorded at Blackheath by a chamber ensemble and (in two pieces) a boys' choir. He was very pleased with the result, and the next year Boosey & Hawkes published a Rossini-Britten suite, *Soirées Musicales*, based on the film score (the score itself was re-recorded in its original form in 1988 as *Rossini Suite*). Other demands included arranging *I Dreamt that I Dwelt in Marble Halls* for a film about gas, and improvising a piano accompaniment when the Unit gave a showing of silent films – a task which froze Britten with nerves before the event. The Unit closed down for August, but at the beginning of September, 'Go straight to G.P.O. at Soho Sq. after lunch to work at Negro film with Auden (new recruit to G.P.O.), Coldstream etc.'

Auden had now left the Downs School and joined the Unit at a salary of three pounds a week, 'not princely' as he observed. He was living in Basil Wright's flat. Britten too felt underpaid. He was given only ten pounds for the music for *Telegrams* (one of the films), out of which he had to pay the copyist; 'seems rather ridiculous to me – & others'. Nevertheless during September he wrote title music and short sequences for *Men Behind the Meters, How the Dial Works, Conquering Space, The Savings Bank*, and other films. By the end of October he too was receiving a weekly wage from the Unit – two pounds more than Auden.

They and Coldstream were working on a proposed film about the West Indian slave trade. 'Work with Auden all morning first at Spender's (a friend of his) and then at [Frank] Bridge's.' Until recently, Britten had taken little interest in politics, but he was now developing left-wing opinions. One day earlier in 1935 he had spent several hours while in Lowestoft going along Kirkley Cliff Road 'delivering Peace Ballot papers. A foul job – but it may do a little good, and make a few people use their brains.' He found himself arguing pacifism to 'a road just packed with die-hards – Indian Colonels, army widows, typical old spinsters etc!' This may have had something to do with Frank Bridge. While staying at Friston in February 1935, Britten had a 'very serious & interesting argument' with Bridge and the others present about civilization, war and religion.

One day in August 1935 he tried 'to talk communism with Mum, but it is impossible to say anything to anyone brought up in the old order without severe ruptions. The trouble is that fundamentally she agrees with me but won't admit it.' The next month, when he was beginning to work regularly with Auden, he started to criticize music from a political standpoint. After a Prom, he commented of Elgar's First Symphony: 'I

swear that only in Imperialistic England could such a work be tolerated.'
However, in most respects he was thoroughly naïve compared to Auden
and his circle. 'Spend day with Coldstream & Auden,' he wrote on 17
September. 'I always feel very young & stupid when with these brains – I
mostly sit silent when they hold forth about subjects in general. What
brains!'

He was impatient to get out of the boarding-house in Cromwell Road,
but when he moved into a small flat in West Hampstead (in West Cottage
Road, off West End Lane) it was once again with his sister Beth, and
there was a bed kept for their mother – 'it is partly her flat', Britten
wrote.

*

Auden and Coldstream finished the draft script for *Negroes* and handed
it to John Grierson. Britten's initial exhilaration at being able to cope
with the film work had dissolved into self-doubts. 'I am hopelessly
inexperienced in such matters,' he wrote after an afternoon struggling to
synchronize music and film. Auden took the trouble to cheer him up. 'Go
to Soho Sq. feeling very depressed about the stuff & have tea with Auden
tho' who is cheering.' By 23 October, Britten felt able to sum Auden up,
in a letter to Marjorie Fass:

> I know you would like W.H.A. very much. He is a very startling
> personality – but absolutely sincere and very brilliant. He has a very
> wide knowledge, not only of course of literature but of every branch of
> art, and especially of politics; this last in the direction that I can't help
> feeling every serious person, and artists especially, must have. Strong
> opposition in every direction to Fascism, which of course restricts all
> freedom of thought.

Auden's knowledge was nothing like as extensive as Britten believed. His
dogmatic, didactic manner covered a good deal of ignorance, and he was
happy to be taken to concerts by Britten. They went to hear the BBC
Symphony Orchestra under Boult playing Berg's *Lyric Suite*, and it was
Auden's turn to listen to Britten's views – that Boult had only produced
'a Kensington drawing room apology' for what Berg meant.

Auden decided that Britten was *the* composer, a post previously
unfilled in his 'gang' of writers and artists, and he began to introduce him
to the rest of them. During September 1935 he took him to the Westminster Theatre where two of his plays, *The Dance of Death* and *The
Dog Beneath the Skin* (co-written with Christopher Isherwood), were
being rehearsed by the Group Theatre, the left-wing company which had
come into being largely to perform his work. Robert Medley, the Group's

designer, who had been at Gresham's with Auden, was busy with plans for a set when he was summoned into the auditorium:

> There was Wystan, highly animated, freely scattering ash from a succession of cigarettes, and talking with enthusiasm to Rupert [Doone, director of the Group Theatre] about a young new composer . . . In the semi-darkness I discerned a slim young man, unobtrusively dressed in sports jacket and grey flannel bags, with irregular features and crinkly hair, and wearing a pair of slightly owlish spectacles, which emphasised his watchful reticence.

(Britten had been suffering from eye strain and was currently wearing glasses.) Auden wanted Doone to commission Britten to write the music for *The Dog Beneath the Skin*, despite the fact that Herbert Murrill, the Group Theatre's musical director, expected to compose the score. Doone refused, but evidently agreed to consider Britten for future productions.

On 5 October, Britten was back at the Westminster to see a double bill of *The Dance of Death* and T. S. Eliot's *Sweeney Agonistes*. 'Both very exhilerating & interesting shows, splendidly put on (Décor & very lovely masks by Robert Medley) & acted. A's play is a very serious contribution to literature. I go back with Doone & Medley to their flat after the show & talk till 1.30 about possible music for Timon of Athens – very nice men.' Doone and Medley were probably the first homosexual couple he had met, though his diary gives no suggestion that he realized it. 'Over dinner and a bottle of inexpensive white wine', writes Medley, 'Ben lost his characteristic reserve, and something of the complexity that lay behind the deceptively conventional persona was revealed.'

Not much music was required for *Timon of Athens*, but when the play went into production Britten had to write one piece three times before Doone, by nature petulant and fussy, was satisfied. There was also the difficulty of hiring instrumentalists when the Group Theatre had almost nothing with which to pay them. A harpsichord, required by Britten, failed to materialize, and he and Herbert Murrill had to stick drawing-pins into the hammers of the theatre piano. The production opened on 19 November 1935 to chilly reviews, and the music was mostly ignored by the critics. Meanwhile, in the midst of the *Timon* preparations, Britten went to a BBC symphony concert which included the first complete performance of Walton's First Symphony (6 November 1935). 'A great tragedy for English music,' he wrote in his diary. 'Last hope of W. gone now – this is a conventional work, reactionary in the extreme & dull & depressing.'

While he was writing the *Timon* music the Film Unit almost closed –

there was 'absolutely no money' for shooting and 'Negroes seems definitely off', which Britten found 'Very depressing'. Fortunately Ralph Hawkes now raised the possibility of his firm paying Britten a retainer, and the sum of three pounds a week was agreed on as a 'guarantee of royalties'. With this and the Film Unit five pounds (which he was still receiving) he was at last earning his keep, 'with occasionally something to spare'.

Suddenly the Film Unit sprang to life again, and Britten was summoned to Tring to record 'railway sound' for a documentary about the 'Travelling Post Office', the mail train on which sorting took place as it journeyed through the night. 'Spend an interesting but very chilly day at the station,' he noted on 12 November 1935. Technical discussions for the film, which had the working title 'T.P.O.' gave him his usual 'pretty violent inferiority complex – these people know so much!' He and Cavalcanti passed an evening by a railway line at Harrow in pouring rain, listening to the exact sound made by trains, and Britten set about reproducing this at Blackheath to fit precisely with the rhythm of the visuals – using 'compressed steam, sand-paper, miniature rails, etc'. He described the results as 'Not very good as music – but I think that with the visuals they will be all right – one cannot write "music" to these minute instructions, when even the speed of the beat & number of bars is fixed.' Auden then spent many hours with him planning the commentary, and by 3 January 1936 had come up with what Britten called 'lovely verse' for the film, now called *Night Mail*, though the director, Harry Watt, was suspicious of intellectuals and could not at first see the point of the poem.

The music and verse-commentary were recorded at Blackheath on 11 January. 'A large orchestra for me,' noted Britten. 'Fl. Ob. Bsn. Trpt. Harp (Maria Korchinska – very good), Vln. Vla. Vlc. CB. Percussion & wind machine – a splendid team.' The percussionist was James Blades, who spent his nights playing drums in West End hotel bands and his days in recording studios. He remembers that he and the other 'somewhat blasé session men' found plenty to keep them occupied and interested in the score that was being conducted by the 'slim, shy young man' of whom none of them had heard. The verse had to be spoken in strict rhythm with the music ('This is the night mail crossing the border, / Carrying the cheque and the postal order . . .'), but no pauses had been allowed for the speaker, Stuart Legg, to take breath. 'There is too much to be spoken in a single breath by the one voice', Britten noted, 'so we have to record separately – me, having to conduct from an improvised visual metronome, – flashes on the screen – a very difficult job! Legg speaks the stuff splendidly tho'.' When he heard the rushes next day he judged them 'not at all bad'. *Night Mail* was the peak of his and Auden's achievement in the medium, and became the best-known documentary of the era. Britten, Auden, Cavalcanti and Basil Wright celebrated the completion of the soundtrack at a French restaurant in Soho – 'very good,' observed Britten.

*

Beginning his 1936 diary, he surveyed his present position and found it generally satisfying. He was earning his own living, had plenty of ideas for music (but little time to write it), was 'having alot of success but not a staggering amount of performances', still had 'a bad inferiority complex in company of brains like Basil Wright, Wystan Auden & William Coldstream', but was fortunate in friends such as the Bridges, Basil Reeve, '& young Piers Dunkerley – tell it not in Gath'. (Dunkerley, who had left South Lodge, had come to London the previous autumn, and Britten took him to the play of *1066 and All That*. They found it 'riotously funny'. Afterwards, 'We have tea at Strand Palace . . . Go most of the way back to Battersea with Piers – he is a very nice lad.')

In the early months of 1936, the number of performances of Britten's work increased dramatically. His *Te Deum*, written in the summer of 1934 and already premièred at a London church, was sung again at a Macnaghten–Lemare concert at the end of January under the baton of Reginald Goodall; Britten had arranged it for orchestra, and himself played the viola in the strings. The performance was 'quite competent', but the rest of the programme seemed to him 'a dismal concoction of odds & ends, played in an amateur way. This is the last year of my connection with these shows!' The *Sinfonietta* was on the programme at an Aeolian Hall concert in March, and he still felt pleased with it. 'It is absolutely genuine at any rate.' The *Te Deum* was broadcast at the end of February with the organist and composer Harold Darke conducting – 'it made some delicious sounds! Which I am not ashamed of – !' – and *A Boy Was Born* had been given a second BBC airing at the end of 1935. He managed to have some gramophone records made from this broadcast – the first discs he had ever had of his music – and he played them again and again. 'They are lovely . . . Terribly exciting,' though he feared that the piece was too difficult ever to become popular. *Holiday Tales* was broadcast by the pianist Millicent Silver in June 1936, and the *Simple Symphony* was taken on tour by the Boyd Neel Orchestra (a string ensemble specializing in baroque music) and broadcast by them in an April 1936 programme, which also included Schoenberg's new Suite for strings (1934), which Britten found 'delightful'.

He described the Schoenberg as 'a Hommage to Mahler both in matter & manner', and Mahler was still earning highly enthusiastic comments in his diary. The *Lied von der Erde* was music that 'makes one think furiously more than any other to-day'; the *Kindertotenlieder* made him 'feel it is worth having lived, if only for those little miracles'; the Fifth Symphony was music to 'revel' in – indeed 'I suppose there are more beautiful bits of music than Mahler's 5th – but I don't know them.' He played the Adagietto from it to Grace Williams, who 'surrenders completely to it – as I had hoped'. He could not get it out of his head; it left 'a nice (if erotic) taste in my mouth'.

A favourite recreation for him during spare hours in the summer of 1936 was 'playing Beethoven sonatas & reading Mahler scores'. Indeed, apart from his ever-increasing dislike of Brahms, Britten had not really changed his tastes since leaving the RCM. He still suffered from 'Wagner fever', and after hearing Beecham conduct the entire *Ring* at Covent Garden, felt an 'inferiority complex' when contemplating Wagner's achievement. It was no longer simply an emotional surrender. 'Now I more appreciate the colossal dramatic & musical skill, sheer invention in every direction.' He had been desolate when another hero, Alban Berg, died just before Christmas 1935. 'I feel it is a real & terrible tragedy', he wrote, 'one from which the world will take long to recover . . . The real musicians are so few & far between, arn't they? Apart from the Bergs, Stravinskys, Schönbergs & Bridges one is a bit stumped for names, isn't one . . . Shostakovich – perhaps – possibly.'

He had only heard a little Shostakovich. When the Suite from *The Nose* was broadcast in January 1934 it had left him doubtful. 'Very amusing & exhilerating – but I shouldn't be surprised if it were found to be uneventful & even conventional with all the glitter taken off.' But in March 1936 he attended a concert performance of *Lady Macbeth of the Mtsensk District*.

> Of course it is idle to pretend that this is great music throughout – it is stage music and as such must be considered. There is some terrific music in the entre'acts. But I will defend it through thick & thin against these charges of 'lack of style' . . . The satire is biting & brilliant. It is never boring for a second – even in this [concert] form.

The 'charges' against Shostakovich were evidently being made by British composers of the Vaughan Williams generation, since Britten added of this performance: 'The "eminent English Renaissance" composers sniggering in the stalls was typical. There is more music in a page of MacBeth than in the whole of their "elegant" output!'

The next day, lunching with a group of musician acquaintances who had heard the opera, he found himself the 'sole upholder' of Shostakovich. This argument took place after an audition at the BBC. Britten had gone there with a pianist named Adolph Hallis, offering items of two-piano music by various composers (including himself) for broadcasting. Somewhat against his inclination he was becoming more active as a performer, to add to his income. On 13 March 1936 he gave his first broadcast, as pianist in his own Suite for violin and piano, begun in Vienna late in 1934. The violinist was Frank Bridge's friend Antonio Brosa. Britten was very nervous during the rehearsal and balance test, but when the red light came on 'all nervousness forsakes me, thank heaven, & all goes as well as possible.' They also played a Beethoven sonata. (The Suite was billed in the *Radio Times* as his 'Op. 6'. He had now given his *Sinfonietta* the designation 'Op. 1', followed by the *Phantasy* oboe quartet, *A Boy Was Born*, the *Simple Symphony* and *Holiday Tales*.) However, he remained dissatisfied with his standard as a pianist. 'It isn't that I don't know what to do, but with so little time to practise, my fingers simply won't do what I want.'

At the Film Unit, Auden was helping to direct *Calendar of the Year*, a documentary about the work of the Post Office through the changing seasons. He had cast himself as a Father Christmas in a department store, and he enlisted Britten's help to provide children for a scene in which a 'typical respectable upper middle class family' holds a New Year party. The scene was filmed at Coldstream's house in Hampstead, and Britten brought fourteen-year-old Piers Dunkerley and his younger sister Daphne. He was taken aback to find that some of Auden's other 'extras' were 'definitely Bohemian'. They included twenty-year-old Giles Romilly, who with his brother Esmond had become infamous for the rebel magazine *Out of Bounds*, published while they were still at school. The magazine had taken a very relaxed attitude towards public school homosexuality, describing it as 'a consolation and amusement', and Britten became a little anxious that evening in Hampstead. 'Piers makes friends wth Giles Romilly – not too great, I hope, tho' Giles seems nice, & may broaden Piers mind a lot – which he needs – but he is a nice lad for all that,' remarks which indicate that Britten was in some confusion about his own attitude to the boy.

A week later he took Piers to a cinema and to tea, and noted anxiously: 'Giles Romilly isn't too good for him I fear . . . But what a boy to help! So splendid in brain & form – and delightful company.' Later this year he described himself as 'playing the step-father' to the fatherless Piers, and in a letter to John Pounder called him 'My foster child Piers D.' Yet he realized that he himself was in many respects still childlike. One snowy day in January 1936 he and two friends walked on Hampstead Heath, 'watch some tobogganing, enviously, & have a glorious snow-balling fight – still a child, I fear!' He still only needed to shave every other day, and struck most of his friends as more boy than man. The poet Ronald Duncan, who got to know him during 1936, writes that Britten was in his 'late teens' at this time. In fact he was twenty-two.

His 1936 diary, like its predecessors, was still kept in the *School Boy's Pocket Diary*, full of useful information for prep-school pupils. It records that in the early months of that year he took out of his drawer the uncompleted string quartet with the subtitle 'Go play, boy, play', and made efforts to improve its musical portraits of his friends from school-days. He also went to Cambridge to see David Layton, subject of the first movement, who was now a Trinity College athlete. 'He is a very good sort – clean, healthy thinking & balanced.' Three movements from the quartet, under the title *Three Divertimenti*, were performed by the Stratton Quartet at the Wigmore Hall in February, but were 'Received with sniggers & pretty cold silence. Why, I don't know.' In the *Daily Telegraph*, J. A. Westrup, a future Professor of Music at Oxford, described the pieces as 'depressing rather than diverting', and concluded: 'Mr Britten will have proved his worth as a composer when he succeeds in writing music that relies less on superficial effect.' Britten was so downcast by this review that work the next day – he was writing a commissioned piece for brass – proved almost impossible. 'I feel like a spanked school-boy – exactly as I used to feel after a jaw – I remember perfectly. It's all silly, as I don't usually care a jot for critics least of all J.A.W.' After this, the quartet was abandoned.

Despite Britten's admiration for the clean-living David Layton, his remark about his friendship with Piers Dunkerley – 'tell it not in Gath' (words from the biblical story of David's love for Jonathan) – suggests a sophistication in sexual matters which is confirmed by other diary entries. When attending a rehearsal of his *Te Deum* he noted that the solo chorister was bad. 'He is quite new on the job – apparently the good old one has been taken off by some man to live with him – for obvious reasons...' And the entry for 3 February 1936 makes it clear that he understood the ambiguity of his own feelings:

Arrive in town after a long & tedious journey at 5.55. Have some tea on the journey & some buns, but rather because of the very nice little restaurant-boy who brings it along & talks a bit. Quel horreur!! But I swear there's no harm in it. Dinner here ... & spend after in writing

letters (to Piers, (my protégé) & Francis Barton – this is getting bad!)
& telephoning.

He must have been aware of Auden's unashamed sexual interest in boys.
The entry for 14 February records 'lunch ... with Auden & one of his
young boy friends. A nice lad & a nice lunch.' But he was still wary of
any sort of sexuality. In the diary on 31 January he wrote: 'I am reading
(Auden's friend) Christopher Isherwood's Mr Norris Changes Trains. It
is splendidly done – & very exciting; I feel he over accentuates the
importance of the sex episodes – necessary as they are for atmosphere.'

6: The deluge and the earthquake

Auden had now known Britten for a year and a half, and in March 1936 he wrote and gave to him a poem encapsulating his observations on Britten's present character and predicament, and his recommendations for action:

> Underneath the abject willow,
>   Lover, sulk no more;
> Act from thought should quickly follow:
>   What is thinking for?
> Your unique and moping station
>   Proves you cold;
>   Stand up and fold
> Your map of desolation.
>
> Bells that toll across the meadows
>   From the sombre spire,
> Toll for those unloving shadows
>   Love does not require.
> All that lives may love; why longer
>   Bow to loss
>   With arms across?
> Strike and you shall conquer.
>
> Geese in flocks above you flying
>   Their direction know;
> Brooks beneath the thin ice flowing
>   To their oceans go;
> Coldest love will warm to action,
>   Walk then, come,
>   No longer numb,
> Into your satisfaction.

Everything that Britten's diary reveals about his friendship with Piers Dunkerley and his interest in other boys confirms the accuracy of Auden's portrait of a 'cold' and 'numb' individual who is restraining himself from full emotional commitment. Britten made no note of having received the poem, but towards the end of the year he composed a setting of it for two voices and piano – 'very light & Victorian in mood!' he observed in the diary. He was evidently determined (as Donald Mitchell has observed) that the music should not allow him to emerge as the subject of the poem.

He saw *Night Mail* at a London cinema early in March 1936 – 'it goes down excellently with the Audience'. Auden had now become impatient with the Film Unit and left the staff, but was determined to continue collaborating with Britten. At lunch one day they discussed 'at great length the psychology of teaching art in combination – & possibility of an Academy of Combined art'. Auden often floated schemes of this sort, and as usual it came to nothing. Early in January 1936, 'We talk amongst many other things of a new Song Cycle (probably on Animals) that I may write.' Britten here records the beginning of their collaboration on *Our Hunting Fathers*.

The idea was that the contemporary international political situation should be portrayed through a parable of man's relations to the animal kingdom. The cycle, to be scored for full orchestra, was planned just as the Italians were completing their subjugation of Ethiopia. In his diary, Britten protested at the British Government's 'quibbling about sanctions' (failing to take effective action against Mussolini) while 'being willing to spend £300,000,000 on men-slaughtering machines', that is, maintaining a vast armaments programme. But Auden never tackled a subject in the obvious way, and instead of presenting Britten with a set of words about man's inhumanity to the beasts he drew up a much more oblique scheme. The cycle was to open with his own short poem 'The Creatures'; then would come an anonymous invocation to rats to leave an infested dwelling, followed by another anonymous verse describing Messalina's lament for her dying monkey. The fourth song was to be a dance of death with seventeenth-century words by Thomas Ravenscroft, a warning to the partridge of the approach of the hawks, and the cycle would close with another Auden poem, 'Our hunting fathers told the story', which commented sardonically on the pre-Darwinian conviction that man was superior to the animals.

'Auden has done me some glorious words,' Britten told John Pounder. 'Real stunners.' He showed them to Frank Bridge, who was 'impressed', and also 'sympathetic towards my socialistic inclinations'. There was evidence of socialism in the closing lines of Auden's Epilogue to the cycle, 'To hunger, work illegally, / And be anonymous', which are a quotation from Lenin – though Britten may not have known this, for Auden was not in the habit of explicating his poems, even to friends.

By mid-February 1936, Britten had secured the agreement of the secretary of the Norwich Triennial Festival that *Our Hunting Fathers* would be performed there in September. Meanwhile he was 'getting ideas formulated for the Animal work', inspired a little by Stravinsky, whose *Duo Concertant* for violin and piano he was studying. At the end of February, Britten wrote a march for brass and percussion, *Russian Funeral*, to be performed at a concert given by the London Labour Choral Union, and he also provided the music for two left-wing plays, *Easter 1916* and *Stay Down Miner*, by a journalist named Montagu Slater. These were staged by Left Theatre, the first in December 1935 and the second in May 1936, at the Westminster Theatre, and Britten thought them '*very* good'. He was also delighted by Auden and Isherwood's *The Dog Beneath the Skin*, which he saw in January and again in March, and readily accepted Auden's invitation a few weeks later, 'to do music for his and Isherwood's new play'.

He had also written the music for a short film, *Peace of Britain*, commissioned from the documentary director Paul Rotha by the Trades Union Congress and the League of Nations Union. The film, lasting only three minutes, consisted of statistics about defence spending, culminating in an appeal to 'Demand peace by reason'. It was meant for showing in news cinemas, and so needed a certificate from the British Board of Film Censors, which was refused. According to the *Manchester Guardian*, 'the censor regards the film as controversial, but ... will license it if, after submitting it to the War Office, he does not find that parts of it (the shots of artillery and tanks, presumably) are the property of the War Office'. This assurance was evidently given, and *Peace of Britain* was released on 9 April. Britten went to a news cinema that day and saw 'the now "*famous*" Peace Film'. He was accompanied by David Layton, on vacation from Cambridge, who said that people there were 'mostly Communists'.

Later that month Britten went by plane to Barcelona, where his Suite for violin and piano had been chosen for this year's ISCM festival, with himself and Antonio Brosa playing. Musically it was far more exciting than the 1934 Florence Festival. Berg's last work, the Violin Concerto, was performed, and Britten thought it 'just shattering – very simple, & touching'. He was also taken with the beauty of a rural monastery, where he listened in semi-darkness to a choir singing Vittoria. 'It is difficult not to believe in the supernatural when in a place like this,' he wrote in his diary, suggesting that conventional Christian belief had now deserted him. Barcelona Cathedral appealed to him for 'the sensuous beauty of darkness & incense', and Spanish food excited him far more than British. After he had returned home he wrote longingly of a Barcelona restaurant 'where the food was taken seriously'. But his surrender to what Auden, in the Epilogue to *Our Hunting Fathers*, called 'southern gestures' was not complete.

Britten's diary records an evening spent with another British composer, the thirty-three-year-old Lennox Berkeley, and Berkeley's friend Peter Burra, in a night club in Barcelona's red-light district: 'my 1st & not particularly pleasant experience ... as a young harlot is very keen on picking my pockets tho I lose nothing. The dancing (mostly males – & dressed as females) is very lovely. But my god the sordidity – & the sexual temptations of every kind at each corner.'

Before the Barcelona trip he had taken Piers, who was home from public school, to the new Chaplin film *Modern Times*. 'Long walk in park after – he needs some help poor lad. Bloxham seems a queer [i.e. homosexual] school, & it makes one sick that they can't leave a nice lad like Piers alone – but it is understandable – good heavens!' A week later: 'meet Piers at 3.0 at Piccadilly & go to Tatler for Disney Season . . . & walk & ping-pong with the lad after. He is a nice thing and I am very fond of him – thank heaven not sexually, but I am getting to such a condition that I am lost without some children (of either sex) near me.' It was true that he found small girls almost as appealing as boys. When on holiday in the summer of 1936 he made friends with a family, he noted that 'Jennifer (aged 6)' was 'my especial friend', and he thought Daphne Dunkerley who was twelve 'very nice'. In January 1936 he read Lewis Carroll's *Sylvie and Bruno*, a sentimental portrait of a middle-aged man's friendship with a small brother and sister, and judged it a 'wonderful fantasy . . . which for sheer magical charm beats anything I know'. Yet his diary entry for 5 June 1936 shows he was not deluding himself that his feelings were entirely innocent:

> long thinking walk after tea, but not to much purpose. Life is a pretty hefty struggle these days – sexually as well. Decisions are so hard to make, & its difficult to look unprejudiced on apparently abnormal things.
>
> In the evening Mum & I go to see Shirley Temple in the Little Colonel in Walton with Mrs Forster. Very entertaining little star-vehicle. Certainly she's an attractive little girl – but then, children – – –!

*

Auden's text for *Our Hunting Fathers* may contain an allusion to
Britten's predicament. The opening poem, written for the cycle, speaks of
'A desire in which love and hatred so perfectly oppose themselves, that
we cannot voluntarily move; but await the extraordinary compulsion of
the deluge and the earthquake.' He was indeed imprisoned in emotional
immobility, because his feelings of sexual attraction were exactly
balanced by a fear of 'apparently abnormal things'. His anguished setting
of these words suggests that he perceived their personal relevance –
perceived that only a crisis could free him from the impasse.

On 22 May 1936 he noted that 'Wystan ... sent me another poem
apropos of nothing, yesterday.' Like 'Underneath the abject willow', this
poem was eventually published under the heading 'For Benjamin Britten'.
Unlike the earlier poem, it could be taken as a declaration that Auden
was in love with Britten:

> Night covers up the rigid land
>   And ocean's quaking moor,
> And shadows with a tolerant hand
>   The ugly and the poor.
>
> The wounded pride for which I weep
>   You cannot staunch, nor I
> Control the movements of your sleep,
>   Nor hear the name you cry,
>
> Whose life is lucky in your eyes,
>   And precious is the bed
> As to his utter fancy lies
>   The dark caressive head.
>
> For each love to its aim is true,
>   And all kinds seek their own;
> You love your life and I love you,
>   So I must lie alone.
>
> Oh hurry to the fêted spot
>   Of your deliberate fall;
> For now my dream of you cannot
>   Refer to you at all.

Possibly Auden had made approaches to Britten but had been rejected.
Many years later, Peter Pears described this poem and 'Underneath the
abject willow' as 'not poems, to my eyes, of a received lover, rather of a
rejected one'. However, Pears was far from certain that Auden had taken

a romantic interest in Britten, and there is no other evidence to suggest it. Auden did not usually indulge in declarations of unrequited passion. He sometimes invited his friends to go to bed with him but was not offended if they refused. If any such suggestion had been made, Britten would probably have hinted at it in his diary, as he did when Rupert Doone made a pass at him on 11 May 1936: 'I got to lunch with Rupert Doone (of Group Theatre) at his flat – to talk over new projects. A very good lunch, tho he is inclined to be too affectionate.' The poem 'Night covers up the rigid land', like 'Underneath the abject willow', was probably meant as an exhortation to erotic action, an encouragement to escape from the emotional prison. By dismissing it as 'apropos of nothing', Britten showed that he was unwilling to listen. (However, the musical setting he made of it eighteen months later treats it much more seriously than 'Underneath the abject willow'.)

He continued work on *Our Hunting Fathers* through the spring and early summer of 1936. In February his mother had moved from Lowestoft to the genteel Essex resort of Frinton-on-Sea, and Britten regarded the loss of his childhood home as significant: 'An era is passed. "In Lowestoft when I was young" etc.' When he stayed at Frinton (which happened frequently) his mother gave him 'lots of bother' over the attitudes he was developing. 'It is very difficult always to curb one's tongue!' he wrote. She was still combining Christian Science with Anglicanism, and on Saturday nights there would be 'the periodical row about going to Communion (for to-morrow). It is difficult for Mum to realise that one's opinions change at all . . .' By 11 June he was able to play her the second song from *Our Hunting Fathers*, 'Rats Away!' It calls upon 'All four Archangels' to expel the rodents, and ends with the Latin invocation to the Holy Trinity, organized (as Colin Matthews points out) as 'a manic parody of the prayer':

> *Et in nomine* (Rats!) *Patris et* (Rats!)
> *Filii* (Rats!) *et Sanc-* (Rats!) *-ti Spiriti* [*sic*],
> (Rats! Rats! Rats! Rats! Rats!) *Amen*!

On these last words, the voice and accompaniment rise to an excited climax. Mrs Britten's reaction was unequivocal. 'She disapproves very thoroughly of "Rats",' wrote Britten in his diary that evening, 'but that is almost an incentive – no actual insult to her tho'.'

His letters to her were as passionately devoted as ever. 'Now, ma cherie, take care of yourself . . . Much love, my darling.' And in another: 'Much love, my sweet, I think alot about you.' She responded with equal warmth. 'My darling Son,' she wrote to him just before his twenty-third birthday, in November 1936, 'I wish I could be with you & give you a big hug . . . Very much love & very many happy returns my darling precious son.' His diary gives occasional hints of the turmoil he was experiencing beneath the surface. On 8 June 1936, after a week at Frinton writing *Our Hunting Fathers* and talking to his mother: 'Beethoven's op. 110 to cool my troubled thoughts before bed . . .'

*

At the beginning of July he escaped to Cornwall, renting a chalet at Crantock from a Miss Ethel Nettleship, sister-in-law of Augustus John. He spent the first two weeks on his own, finishing *Our Hunting Fathers*, reading Marx ('Hard going though edifying'), and writing to Piers Dunkerley. (Another book read on holiday was E. M. Forster's *A Passage to India* – 'really great, simple, moving & biting'.) On 13 July he wrote in his diary: 'I find it engrossing playing the step-father to Piers – someday I must – – –'. He did not finish the sentence. There was a rocky shore nearby where he could 'undress and bathe stark naked. The sheer sensual exstasy [*sic*] of it! . . . Utter bliss!' At home he always took his baths cold. Hot water was 'luxury, but I don't like it; it makes one feel dead for hours.' So he was well prepared for the chill of the Cornish sea – 'pleasant – if cold, & cold because one musn't go in deeper than one's penis because of currents & what not (there have been umpteen tragedies round here)'.

The holiday was marred by the news of the outbreak of civil war in Spain. 'One thing is certain', Britten noted amid conflicting reports of atrocities on both sides, 'that the Fascists are executing hundreds (literally) of Popular Front or Communist members – including many boys of 14–16.' On the evening that he made this entry, 24 July, he sketched 'a funeral march to those youthful Spanish martyrs' (it was never completed). To his mother he wrote four days later: 'But what about the fascists lining up all the little Popular Front boys against a wall & putting the machine guns on them? Imagine English boys of 14 even knowing what Popular Front means – much less dying for it.'

The Swiss soprano Sophie Wyss, who was to sing *Our Hunting Fathers* at Norwich, came down with her husband later in the holiday, staying in rooms in the village, so that she and Britten could rehearse, using the village hall piano. She describes him as 'A boy with crisp curly fair hair', while Britten took warmly to her family: 'The small son aged 9 is a delightful lad – as full of animal spirits as 4 ft of person could be. Very intelligent too – & v. enthusiastic. His parents are charming & interesting of course.'

Another visitor to Crantock was Lennox Berkeley, whom Britten had got to know in Barcelona. 'He is a dear and we agree on most points & it is nice to discuss things we don't agree on!' ('A dear' was uncharacteristically warm for Britten, who rarely went beyond 'very nice' as a description of even close friends.) Berkeley stayed in the chalet with Britten and worked at his own music. Britten had heard some of it earlier in the year, and approved. 'To its advantage, it is under Stravinsky's influence, of course, but the harmony is extremely personal.' The friendship grew greatly during the holiday: 'we have a glorious bathe & then lie together on the beach partly naked – sun bathing', Britten noted on 28 July, describing it as 'Heavenly'. They also spent 'hysterical' evenings going through the scores of new symphonies by Vaughan Williams and Walton, laughing at 'the amateurishness & clumsiness of the Williams – the "gitters" of the fate-ridden Walton – & the over pretentiousness of both – & *abominable* scoring'. Britten admitted that both works were 'better than a tremendous amount of English music', but 'so much is pretended of them, & they are compared to the great Beethoven, Mozart, Mahler symphonies'. There was also conversation on more personal matters. 'Long talks before sleep – it is extraordinary how intimate one becomes when the lights are out!'

Though Berkeley had had homosexual relationships, he and Britten evidently did not advance to this stage during the holiday. On 30 July, when Berkeley left, with a parting vow that they would 'work a lot together', Britten recorded 'a very sorrowing farewell. He is an awful dear – very intelligent & kind – & I am very attached to him, even after this short time. In spite of his avowed sexual weakness for young men of my age & form – he is considerate & open, & we have come to an agreement on that subject.' He did not say what the agreement was.

The Britten family now arrived, followed by Beth, Bobby and his wife Marjorie. Britten commented on himself and his brother: 'we think differently on practically every subject (politics especially) & are both very keen on them [so] that arguments are liable to be extremely fierce!' Later in the month, he noted that he had been having 'long intimate talks' with Bobby last thing at night, which suggests that he alluded to his sexual impasse.

The holiday was curtailed abruptly when he was summoned to London to write the music for a feature film, *Love from a Stranger*, being made by Capitol Films. He had been back only a few days when he saw Piers Dunkerley, now aged fifteen. For the first time, Piers stayed the night at his flat. Also sleeping there was Beth's boyfriend Kit Welford. 'Kit & Piers both sleep here – Kit in the sitting room, & Piers shares my room – in my bed, & me on a camp bed.' Britten 'slept only periodically'.

*

The film job gave him a 'rosy' financial outlook, but his mind was 'entirely clouded by the continued disastrous news from Spain', and there was also the hurdle of *Our Hunting Fathers*, 'a work of which I admit I'm very proud', but which was 'very satirical' and therefore 'likely to cause a good amount of comment' at Norwich. On 19 September he went to Covent Garden to conduct a rehearsal, in the foyer, with Sophie Wyss and the London Philharmonic Orchestra. They did not get round to *Our Hunting Fathers* until 8.30 p.m., by which time the orchestra was tired and irritable, showing 'no discipline at all'. Britten became

> thoroughly het up & desperate – can't hear a thing in the wretched Foyer. I get a lot of the speeds wrong & very muddled – but I'm glad to say that in spite of the fooling in the orchestra & titters at the work – the 'Rats' especially brought shrieks of laughter – the rehearsal got better & better. But it was impossible . . . I'm feeling pretty suicidal . . . the most catastrophic evening of my life.

Sophie Wyss describes how

> the members of the orchestra were not used to that kind of music and played about disgracefully. When the reference to rats came in the score they ran about pretending they were chasing rats on the floor! They kept asking to leave the room, one after another. It was quite impossible to rehearse at all, the rehearsal broke up in disorder. Poor Benjamin, it was a terrible experience for him, there did not seem to be a chance of a performance at all in Norwich.

Next day, Britten went to Bridge's house and asked him to take over the conducting, 'but he won't consent & gradually talks me round till I reluctantly say I'll go on with it, but only if I get the extra rehearsal that [Heathcote] Statham [director of the Norwich Triennial Festival] half promised me. This I 'phone him about in the evening & get it settled.'

The extra rehearsal was in Norwich next day, and Britten went there after breakfast. 'Most of the orchestra are on the train & after Saturday's catastrophe I don't feel too inclined to meet them.' He had half an hour with them in the afternoon, and in the evening had to conduct an open rehearsal in front of an audience. 'I fear I don't take much notice of the audience & rehearse as hard as the one hour permits. It doesn't go perhaps so well as the aft[ernoon] but the orchestra were a bit more tired I suppose. Some people are very excited over the work.' Considering that his only previous conducting experience had been with the amateur string group in Bungay and the small ensembles at GPO Film Unit recordings, it was a major ordeal. Not surprisingly the performance, due to take place four days later, was now 'looming ahead like a thunder cloud'.

His mother had not attended the London concerts at which he had
begun to make his name, and though she had undoubtedly heard some of
his music on the wireless, his diary records no comment on it by her. She
arrived in Norwich the day before the performance, accompanied by
Beth. Britten did not join them. He stayed with Audrey Alston at Framingham Earl. Bridge and his wife were there too, eager to give support.
Next morning they set off early for St Andrew's Hall in Norwich, Britten
rigged out uncomfortably in morning dress. *Our Hunting Fathers* was to
come after lunch. During the morning performances, Britten sat with the
Bridges, 'Mum & Beth', he noted in his diary, 'sitting together elsewhere.' ('I always make a resolution never to attend any more first
performances'. Britten wrote in 1940, ' – it is terrifying, & I make
everyone all round me uncomfortable, by feeling sick, having diarrhoea,
& sweating like a pig!')

The concert began with Jelly d'Aranyi playing Brahms' Violin Concerto, after which 'V. Williams conducts a very successful show of his 5
Tudor Portraits (1st perf.) – not my music, but obviously the music for
the audience.' After this airing of two composers who represented everything Britten was struggling against, his party returned to Framingham
Earl for a hurried lunch – Mrs Britten did not accompany them – and
then 'We go back to the hall – & I conduct 1st. perf. of my Hunting
Fathers ...' The audience was already somewhat unsettled. The mildly
bawdy Skelton words to Vaughan Williams's suite are said to have
caused the elderly Lady Albermarle to walk out, exclaiming 'Disgusting!'
When *Our Hunting Fathers* began, they found themselves listening to
music which made the Vaughan Williams seem mild and conventional.

The composer Colin Matthews, who worked for Britten in the
seventies, has written that it is 'difficult to believe that this is the first
work of Britten's for full orchestra that he was to hear, such is the
confidence with which he organises the most hair-raising of instrumental
textures.' Elsewhere, Matthews has called *Our Hunting Fathers* 'dangerous, precarious' in its demands on soloist and orchestra, and these are
particularly appropriate adjectives for the fourth movement. Even the
ominous recitative of the Prologue, the grotesqueries of 'Rats Away!',
and the anguished hopelessness of Messalina's lament, mesmeric and
alarming as they are, scarcely prepare the listener for the nightmarish
'Dance of Death (Hawking for the Partridge)'. Britten provided a programme note for the Norwich audience, and in it he wrote of this
movement:

The soprano runs rapidly through the names of most of the birds . . . A sudden outburst from the trombones is the first indication that all is not as well as it might be. However with an effort the orchestra recovers, and the soloist launches into a hearty song . . . At a climax the roll-call is again called, but once more the trombones interrupt. Something depressing appears to have happened . . . perhaps a bird has been hurt. But after another bang the movement continues with additional energy, and a big climax follows . . . At this everyone falls to dancing a merry folk measure, but the trombones interrupt again and . . . eventually overwhelm everyone. The percussion maintains an exhausted roll; vain efforts are made to restart the movement: but the death is sounded by the muted brass.

It was a curious note; was the death a bird's, or something else's? The score supplies one answer. Among the hawks' names in Ravenscroft's poem are 'Jew' and 'German', and Donald Mitchell has pointed out that Britten has organized the words so that, when the dance fades away, the singer whispers them together – 'German, Jew'. This may have been Auden's idea, but Britten was fully aware of what was happening in Germany. He had been talking to a German *émigré*, whose 'account of present-day Germany is as depressing as possible'. No doubt he was also thinking of the Spanish Fascists and their machine guns. The 'Epilogue and Funeral March' which closes *Our Hunting Fathers* is dominated by a monotonously reiterated xylophone phrase suggesting humanity's inability to break out of its endless cycle of cruelty and despair.

'The orchestra plays better than I had dared to hope – tho' one or two slips,' wrote Britten afterwards. 'I am *very* pleased with it & it goes down well – most of the audience being interested if bewildered. A very complimentary & excited gathering in the artists' room afterwards – including F. Bridge & Mrs B. – Vaughan Williams . . . Ralph Hawkes, Basil Wright . . . Rupert Doone, Robert Medley, Alstons galore, Mum & Beth . . .' The diary entry gives the impression it was a success. A letter from Frank Bridge some months later tells a different story: 'the quintessence of disappointment on your young face was so marked that had I had a few minutes alone with you, I might have consoled you with the fact "that many a good work has begun its public life in much the same indifferent way"'. The audience was too well behaved to express disapproval vocally, but Beth, who had every reason to be partisan, felt that *Our Hunting Fathers* was 'not a very wise choice' for the occasion. It was apparent to Britten that even Bridge had disliked it: 'he was very sweet,' he wrote many years later, '[but] he didn't really like it . . . Later he gave me a long talking to about the scoring, which he thought didn't work . . . He was severe on the last movement as being too edgy.' As to Britten's mother, whose disapproval had been 'almost an incentive' to the composition of *Our Hunting Fathers*, Marian Walker, who was in the audience, remembers Mrs Britten saying to a Lowestoft friend after the performance: 'Oh, I do hope one day Ben will write something that somebody will like.'

Next day came the reviews. 'Notices of my work vary from flattering & slightly bewildered (D. Tel.) – to reprehension & disapproving (Times) – but I am pleased, because what would be the use of a work of this kind if the narrow-minded, prejudiced snobbish Colles (for instance) approved?' H. C. Colles, chief music critic of *The Times*, had written his review as if *in loco parentis* to the composer. He allowed that Britten, 'only now 23', knew 'exactly what sort of sound he wants to make at every moment', and that 'His earlier works have made their mark, and perhaps this one will,' but suggested that, whereas the Vaughan Williams was 'music for real people to sing and enjoy', it was doubtful whether 'young Britten's music is meant to be either'. He concluded of *Our Hunting Fathers*, 'if it is just a stage to get through, we wish him safely and quickly through it'.

Britten made no further comment about the reviews, which were mostly similar in tone, but it is evident from a letter to him from Bridge, after *Our Hunting Fathers* was broadcast by Sophie Wyss and the BBC Symphony Orchestra under Boult at the end of April 1937, that he felt the public rejection of the work acutely. 'It is extremely hard to bear', wrote Bridge, who had experienced many such rejections, 'but one *must* & I suppose *does*, anyway.' After this broadcast, the cycle received no further performances until 1960. Indeed, its importance was not recognized during Britten's lifetime. In a 1957 letter he refers to it as 'a very early work of mine . . . rather wild, but I think interesting.' Colin Matthews recalls that 'Ben was still diffident about the piece in 1976 – I remember him saying that he was slightly embarrassed by it, particularly "Messalina" which he described as "over the top".'

*

After the Norwich performance, he went back to London to make himself available for Capitol Films. *Love from a Stranger*, a reworking of the Bluebeard story, starring Basil Rathbone, kept him waiting around endlessly, and then he had to write the score at the last moment. Donald Mitchell has described the music he provided for the title sequence, depicting a stormy night in London, as 'a clear anticipation of the "Storm" interlude in *Peter Grimes*', but the remainder of the film makes little notable use of Britten's skill. He was paid £200 for it, but swore never to be involved with the commercial cinema again, unless (writes Beth) 'any of Arthur Ransome's books' were to be filmed.

He was pleased to have the film money, but affluence made him uncomfortable. Ralph Hawkes treated him to expensive theatre seats and Mayfair dinners, and Britten enjoyed whizzing through the streets in his host's Hispano Suiza, but thought it 'a bit ironicle to park this kind of car outside the houses that surround Sadler's Wells' – slum properties – and reckoned that the guinea Hawkes paid for their dinner at the Café de Paris would 'feed a poor family in comfort for a week'.

During November 1936 he provided incidental music for the Group Theatre *Agamemnon*, in a translation by Louis MacNeice, but he was now exasperated by Doone's fussy incompetence, and he handed over the musical direction to somebody else, though he still intended to write the score for the next Auden–Isherwood play. The script arrived early in October. 'Wystan Auden sends me a copy of his & Isherwoods latest – Ascent of F6 – on first glance it looks exciting & good.' The play portrays a hero who is driven to great feats by his mother. When he climbs the ultimate peak, he finds her waiting at the top. The same month, Britten, with his sister Beth, moved to a flat above her dress shop, 559 Finchley Road. 'Mum furnished one of the rooms', writes Beth, 'so that she could come and stay with us whenever she wanted to.'

There was also a lodger, but she went away occasionally, leaving room for guests. 'Piers comes back with me to spend the night', noted Britten on 19 December, 'as Beth's away to a dance with Kit & Kathleen's gone home.' Auden came to stay too, to work with Britten on a documentary, *The Way to the Sea*, for Paul Rotha at Strand Films. Britten was still suffering from an 'appalling inferiority complex ... with vital brains like his'. After dinner on the first evening 'he tells me he's decided to go to Spain after Xmas & fight – I try to dissuade him, because what the Spanish Gov. might gain by his joining is nothing compared with the world's gain by his continuing to write; but no one can make W.H.A. alter his mind.'

Beth found Auden a 'charming and entertaining' guest, though he had 'an enormous appetite'. Britten's diary that month records a meal in a restaurant with Louis MacNeice and Auden, the latter 'being slightly drunk & arguing hard with the waitress about 2nd helpings'. He took Auden down to see Mrs Britten at Frinton. 'Mum takes to W. alot & everything goes off well.' The same diary entry (6 December 1936) records that Britten had just read 'Byron verses in W's new Iceland book which are *great* & very, very amusing'. *Letters from Iceland* was then being finished by Auden and MacNeice. It concludes with the

authors' 'Last Will and Testament'. Among the mock bequests, such as
'To the Post Office Film Unit, a film on Sex', are these lines, by Auden:

> To my friend Benjamin Britten, composer, I beg
> That fortune send him soon a passionate affair.

Britten opened his 1937 diary with another survey of his position:

A happy New Year! – faint hope of that with the International Situation being as black as approaching thunder clouds. Being selfish (a
universal failing) I feel it cruel, as I have had a good year & think
that next year would be even better – with a very hopeful future,
given normal conditions. Ralph Hawkes is a splendid publisher &
general patron & I am getting not so bad a number of performances
& have lots of ideas for the future. No prospect & little inclination
for marriage, tho' unsettled by Beth's proposed change of state [she
was secretly engaged to Kit Welford]. But with plenty of friends old
& (mostly) young.

Two days later he spent a morning at a Lyons' Corner House with
Auden, who was about to go off to Spain. 'It is terribly sad & I feel
ghastly about it, tho' I feel it is perhaps the logical thing for him to do –
being such a direct person. Anyhow it's phenomenally brave.' As a
goodbye, Auden wrote out two of his poems, 'It's farewell to the drawing room's civilised cry' and 'Lay your sleeping head, my love' on the
fly-leaves of the miniature score of the *Sinfonietta* and the vocal score of
Our Hunting Fathers. Britten was deeply touched; he called them 'two
grand poems – a lullaby, & a big, simple, folky Farewell that is overwhelmingly tragic and moving. I've Lots to do with them.' This might
mean that he felt they demanded musical setting, or that he regarded
himself as having helped to inspire them. He and Auden parted, and
Britten, 'feeling very sore', went on to spend the evening with Francis
Barton, 'my paramour at South Lodge . . . He is still a grand person . . .'
Writing to thank John Pounder for a Christmas card expressing left-
wing sentiments, which he had dared to put on the mantelpiece at
Frinton ('Mum never objects, in fact silently acquiesces'), he dropped
hints about his sexual situation: 'even now I am capable of feeling quite
cheerful with a little drink or — to deaden one's brain. That reminds
me, I'm changing my views on Life (with a capital S) a bit.'

On 12 January he made a spur-of-the-moment visit to Paris with
Henry Boys, a friend from RCM days, and the young writer Ronald
Duncan, whom he had met in Cornwall the previous summer and who
shared his pacifist inclinations – they had been at work on a *Pacifist*

March, with words by Duncan, for a Peace Pledge Union concert. Duncan had stayed in Paris during school-days, and took them to a cheap hotel he knew. After discovering there was nothing on at the Opéra they headed for the Folies Bergère, but arriving early were recommended by 'a commissionaire to "try another little show"'. Britten's diary describes how

> we are taken to a large house a few yards away, & there are presented in the most sordid manner possible with about 20 nude females, fat, hairy, unprepossessing; smelling of vile cheap scent, & walking round the room in couples to a gramophone. It is revolting – appalling that such a noble thing as sex should be so degraded. We are given cheap champagne, but decide that we've had enough, & to the disgust of the fat proprietress, take a hasty departure – it cost us 100F too. After this disgusting little exhibition, we are in no mood for the Folies & as it turns out it is incredibly bad – just chocolate box pornography backstage, alternating with feeble comedy front stage. Besides Josephine Baker is as old as the hills, & can neither dance, sing nor act.

The next day they went to an excellent *Fidelio* at the Théâtre Champs-Elysées; the day after to see Oscar Wilde's grave, which they failed to find. While wandering around the shops, Duncan and Britten discovered illustrated editions of Rabelais' *Gargantua* and *Pantagruel* and, being impressed by a quick glance at the illustrations, bought both volumes,

> not examining them closely till we arrive back [at the hotel], when we do look at them – we are as appalled by the coarseness of it as we are impressed by the skill of it. Certainly we are having some experiences – what is one to make of an animal that can produce the hideous pornography of Tuesday evening, Notre Dame, Fidelio, & gives rise to these filthy & brilliant satires?

Early the next morning Britten and Boys saw Duncan off from the Gare de Lyon. He was heading for Marseilles, to sail to India in hopes of meeting Gandhi and Rabindranath Tagore. 'He is indeed a brave little man, & both Henry & I have become most fond of him.' The two returned overnight via the Dieppe–Newhaven ferry. Britten went to sleep on a bench near

> an attendant who is suspiciously attentive, but I wake apparently unharmed (!) ... London is dank & dark, & we feel furious at being back with realities again. This feeling is accentuated when I get back here [559 Finchley Road] at 8.0 & find Kathleen [the lodger] with the

bad Flu plague, & Beth sickening for it . . . Beth goes to bed with temp. of 101 . . . Phone Mum who's coming to-morrow to help nurse.

Mrs Britten arrived. 'It is a glorious relief to have her but I must see that she doesn't tire herself by running about too much.' She was sixty-three and apparently in excellent health. Beth was now 'pretty bad', and soon Britten himself was running a temperature and went to bed, missing a rehearsal of his *Sinfonietta* for a RCM concert under Malcolm Sargent. In bed he read Ronald Firbank's *Concerning the Eccentricities of Cardinal Pirelli*, with its coy references to Catholic clergy taking an erotic interest in choir-boys. He thought it 'brilliantly amusing . . . the stuffy sensual atmosphere of these Sanctuaries moves me a lot – I feel that it wouldn't take much to turn me R.C.'

His temperature went down after a day, but by now 'Mum's not feeling too well (terribly tired) & Beth's no better'. Next day, 20 January, 'Beth is much worse . . . Meanwhile Mum is down with the Plague, & so she moves into my room. I get up & dress after breakfast & stay in all day looking after them.' Barbara came at lunchtime, and with her professional knowledge as a health-visitor 'confirms our fears about Beth', and when the doctor arrived at tea-time he 'says it's pneumonia'. A live-in nurse was engaged, and Britten moved down the road to a friend of Barbara's to vacate a bed for her. The doctor did not seem too worried about Beth, but was 'prescribing the most drastic treatment – wide open windows – little or no heating'. The flat was in any case perilously cold; Britten afterwards called it 'the coldest in London, built on top of nothing, with nothing on either side of it'.

The next morning the doctor reported that Beth was 'holding her own'. Mrs Britten was now 'a good deal worse – accentuated by worrying for Beth of course. However we're hoping that it won't develop into anything worse.' Britten was soon back in bed with a recurrence of the flu, and Mrs Britten 'seems to be developing Bronchitis'. He passed the time reading Dorothy Sayers thrillers. By Monday 25 January 'Mum definitely has bronchial pneumonia & is completely wandering all the time. Beth no better . . . breathing is terribly fast & shallow. Poor dear, it's frightful to see her – indeed both of them.' On the Tuesday a Harley Street specialist was called in; he gave Beth oxygen and made 'reassuring comments'. Mrs Britten was still 'mostly incoherent', but on the Thursday the doctor judged that there was 'a fine chance for her'. Britten, who had recovered again, spent 'a lot of the day with her, but she mustn't talk much, much as she wants to'.

He was still sleeping down the road. Two more days passed, and on the night of Saturday 30 January he noted: 'Beth still slightly better, temp. coming down. Mum slightly better too – tho' completely delirious – still she says "good-night" to me & apparently recognises me.' The next morning: 'We get a 'phone call at 7.30 in the morning – Mum not so well – Barbara & I half run the distance – taking ¼ hr, there being no taxi. Then we find when we arrive that Mum had a heart attack at abt 7.0 & died in about ten minutes without being at all conscious or suffering – thank God. So I lose the grandest mother a person could possibly have – & I only hope she realised that I felt like it. Nothing one can do eases the terrible ache that one feels – O God Almighty –'

PART TWO

1937–42

Tell me the truth about love

1 : One's resistance . . . gradually weakening

'The undertakers come to take the coffin away to-night,' Britten wrote in his diary on 1 February 1937, the day after his mother had died, 'the darling little body but that has no relation to Mum herself. It is the most heartrending thought that I shall never set eyes on her again.' On the day of the funeral, 3 February, he and Barbara travelled to Lowestoft – Beth was still too ill – and he noted that the family of his school friend John Nicholson 'meet us & feed us before the show', the term he usually used for a concert. Charles Coleman, then organist at St John's, Lowestoft, played Britten's own *The Birds* (which he had dedicated to his mother) as a voluntary. 'It is a terrible strain – Barbara nearly faints, but we succeed in holding out.' He returned to London and, while Beth slowly recovered, got on briskly with work, writing the music for Auden and Isherwood's *The Ascent of F6*: '. . . helps one to forget the awful gap to do work again.' He was composing 'a little Mother's song', a lullaby for the domineering Mrs Ransom to sing to her son.

'O God, I wish something would ease this awful ache,' he wrote on 12 February. But the same day he noted that he had worked productively, and that he was pleased to get a BBC commission for a programme about King Arthur. Many years later he told Imogen Holst that he had felt 'responsible for his mother's death & it had taken ages to realize that he hadn't been'. But on the surface this guilt was not apparent. Basil Reeve observed the opposite: 'Certainly when the mother died, there was a great sense of release. I mean, Ben's personal life started.'

It took time to start. On 18 February he recorded that he felt 'defeatist & fatalistic about everything – art, politics, personal matters, sex'. He was disturbed that day by a conversation over tea with Peter Burra (whom he had met with Lennox Berkeley in Barcelona) – 'it is nice to see him, but it gives one contact with the world outside (mostly political) with its abominable intrigues'. And *The Ascent of F6* became a nightmare in rehearsals, with Rupert Doone making unreasonable demands for more music, then at the last minute cutting much of it, including parts of the Blues which Britten and Auden, who was back unharmed from Spain, had provided as a big set piece. But the first night went well, and the Group Theatre party afterwards restored Britten's spirits. They all sang the Blues and had 'a good & merry time (& me not far from being the centre of attraction strange as it may seem!)'.

The first glimmering of a new independence comes in his diary a few days later, 1 March, while he was visiting Frank Bridge at Friston. 'I feel that he has a rather precious & escapist view of art – but that is typical of his generation.' On the drive back to London he and the Bridges argued 'hotly' about politics, '& I fear their talent doesn't lie in that direction', though 'I curse myself for having done or said anything hurtful to the people who have helped & are helping me in every way possible'. Back in London he lunched with a school friend who was homosexual; he 'emphasises the point (very truly) that now is the time for me to decide something about my sexual life. O, for a little courage.' The next day, 6 March, he attended a rehearsal of his 'Lift-Boy' and 'I Loved a Lass' with the BBC Singers conducted by their assistant chorus-master, Trevor Harvey. 'Lunch with T.H., Peter Piers, & [Basil] Douglas – at their flat.' Britten had mis-spelt the surname of one of the Singers, who at this time was living with Harvey and Douglas.

Peter Neville Luard Pears was three years older than Britten. Most people found him rather remote and formidable. 'One really did get to know Ben over many years,' says Britten's childhood friend John Alston, who was at Lancing with Pears, 'but Peter – in some ways one never felt one knew him any better at the end than one had done at the beginning'. This comment is repeated in various forms by almost all Britten and Pears's friends and colleagues. Joan Cross says, 'You never knew what Peter was thinking, never'; the organist Ralph Downes feels that 'there was some sort of hidden element, something I couldn't explain'; and Basil Douglas calls him 'a far more opaque person than Ben was ... a mysterious sort of person'. Even Lord Harewood, who had a boundless admiration for Pears as an artist and was on the friendliest of terms with him for fifteen years, says: 'One always had a feeling of a close acquaintance, and not a friend.'

Pears's forebears were largely clergy and military officers, and he could have passed for a bishop or a general. Eric Crozier, who knew Pears's parents, describes them as 'rather stiff-necked people, conservative in their views, Edwardian in their manners, and haughty with social "inferiors". Peter inherited some of these attitudes.'

Peter's father, Arthur Pears, was a civil engineer who had usually worked abroad during Peter's childhood. His wife often went with him. Peter, the youngest of seven, has said that he loved his mother 'very dearly', but admitted that he only saw her rarely after nursery days. He was sent at the age of six to board at the Grange, a preparatory school at Crowborough in Sussex. Most school holidays were spent with relatives or friends. 'I never had a home, really,' he said of this. 'My home, when I was a young man, a child, was at school.' He did not remember having met his father properly until he was thirteen, when he felt jealous that he no longer had his mother's complete attention. His niece Sue Phipps emphasizes that his childhood, nevertheless, seems to have been entirely happy:

I had a similar experience as a child, and I found it terribly disturbing. I never really got settled at school, because I hadn't got a home. And according to today's psychologists, Peter ought to have been dreadfully unhappy. But he often said he didn't really want to go home for the holidays at all; he just couldn't wait for the next term to begin. And he seems to have been an incredibly contented small boy.

He became, in his own words, 'a well behaved little boy' at school who 'worked hard, and was no trouble'. He has said of being made to box at school that he was 'deeply shocked by a feeling that I had won and triumphed over another human being and reduced him to shame and pain'. Nevertheless he had a hot temper, perhaps inherited from his mother's family; one of her brothers was supposed to have been the worst-tempered officer in the British Navy. 'If Peter was roused', recalls Basil Douglas, 'his eyes flashed. He could be a very, very dominating figure.' He could seem vague or prevaricating when a firm decision was required, but this often turned out to be a technique for getting what he wanted.

From the Grange he won a scholarship to Lancing College, the Sussex public school. Again, he regarded it as his real home – it was now that his father came home and 'took my place with my mother' – and he was especially happy singing in the choir during the High Church services (Lancing was an Anglo-Catholic foundation). He experienced romantic feelings for younger boys, and has said that his 'amorous pursuits' occasionally got him into 'a little trouble'. John Evans, who knew Pears at the end of his life, recalls him saying that 'the wonderful thing about Lancing was the relaxed sexual atmosphere. He had lots of crushes on boys, and some assignations.' His strongest attachment was to Peter Burra, who was his own age, with whom Britten later became friends.

Pears and Burra founded an 'aesthetic' society and started a magazine. They also organized a chamber music group in which Burra played the violin and Pears the piano, and both sang tenor. But Pears's proudest memory from Lancing was of playing cricket at the Oval for the Young Amateurs of Sussex. 'I shall never forget . . . running up the steps of the pavilion at the Oval having made 81 not out . . . It's far more important than my debut at the Met, for instance.'

In 1928 he went up to Keble College, Oxford, to read music. He spent much of his time as 'temporary organist' at another college, Hertford, and after a year was sent down for failing Pass Moderations, the preliminary examination, 'and I hadn't enough money to go back, so I took up teaching'. Oxford life at this date was dominated by rich undergraduates, and by those who behaved as if they were rich, and Pears later told his niece Sue that 'it was a nightmarish existence there if you had no money'. It may be that lack of cash in his pocket, rather than shortage of parental funds to pay the fees, discouraged him from returning. In any case it was a period when many young men abandoned their university careers half-way, and drifted into some undemanding job, particularly prep-school teaching. Pears returned to the Grange to teach classics, music and games.

A flamboyantly homosexual manner was fashionable at Oxford during the twenties (though actual homosexual activity was rare), and Pears wrote in this style to a Keble friend:

> My dear . . . I suppose all other news-items shrink before the shattering fact that I have failed entirely in Pass Moderations. Weep on my shoulder . . . I am henceforth proceeding to plunge into the waters of life, alike homosexual and heterosexual, to indulge in all kinds of orgies, sadist and masserchistic [*sic*], and finally to end as a wreck, one of the very scum of the earth.

In fact he became a very conventional prep-school master who, though sometimes romantically attracted to his pupils, behaved himself, and seemed set for what a friend calls 'a rather drab destiny . . . He wasn't heading for professionalism . . . You see, he didn't have the stimulus at home. He was awfully lonely.'

These comments are by Peter Burra's sister Nell, who was studying to be a singer and persuaded Pears to audition for the Webber–Douglas School of Singing. The verdict was crushing – 'a marvellous *mezza voce*, but nothing much else to develop which would earn him a living' – but Nell Burra persuaded him to try again, and he won an operatic exhibition to the RCM to study with the singing teacher Dawson Freer, who had taught Joan Cross. He arrived there in 1934, at the age of twenty-three. Like Britten, he seems to have thought poorly of the tuition offered by the Royal College – 'I wanted many more lessons than one a week' – and in any case he had already managed to obtain virtually full-time musical employment outside its walls. The BBC Singers were being doubled in number to form a second choir, and Pears auditioned successfully. He began work at Broadcasting House during 1934. (He used to say that he sang in the first or second broadcast of Britten's *A Boy Was Born*, but he had not joined the BBC Singers on the first occasion and was performing elsewhere on the second.)

He gave up studying at the RCM and found himself rooms in Charlotte Street with two other members of the BBC Singers, Trevor Harvey, the assistant conductor, and Basil Douglas, tenor and chorus librarian. Douglas was struck by his restlessness; he would sit moodily at the piano for hours.

A cause of his gloom may have been uncertainty about his voice. Nell Burra says: 'He didn't trust himself, he didn't even know whether he was a baritone or a tenor.' He had studied at the RCM as a tenor and was singing that voice at the BBC, but she felt that 'in lots of ways he could have been a baritone, his build was a baritone build' – he was tall and broadly built. John Shirley-Quirk and Robert Tear, singers who both worked with Pears, believe he was really a baritone who extended his range upwards with falsetto, and his niece Sue says that Lucie Manén, the last singing teacher with whom he studied, was of much the same opinion. Basil Douglas recalls that in 1937 he still had 'a very small voice', and Anne Wood, who sang with him in the BBC Singers, agrees: 'It wasn't a big voice, and he needed more size. And he hadn't enough range: he was short of a couple of notes at the top.' On the other hand she remembers him as 'intensely sensitive to words, with the music coming out of the words', and possessing 'a very sweet quality ... and he was able to colour his voice without having to think much about it'. Yet he had given up regular singing lessons, and seemed to be making no effort to raise himself above the modest requirements of the BBC choral work. In 1953 Britten told Imogen Holst: 'I'm wiser about Peter than he is about himself. If it hadn't been for me, he'd never have been a singer, and although *he* might have been happier, lots of other people wouldn't have been.'

A diary Pears kept briefly in 1936 shows that he had an eye for handsome boys. On board ship he notes 'Two g-l [good-looking] bell boys: q [queer]?' And while reading Proust: 'All his love complex for the mother rings absolutely true. Will he turn homosexual?' But a nineteen-year-old friend with whom he went on holiday says that 'Peter's romantic friendships were platonic,' and he had plenty of women friends who found him attractive. 'Peter was the goal for a whole lot of women', says Joan Cross, 'who were absolutely *crazy* about him.' Eric Crozier writes: 'When I first knew him, he had a woman friend, Iris Holland Rogers, of whom he seemed fond and with whom he had at least once gone on holiday to Switzerland.' When he came to London he had continued his friendship with Peter Burra, who like him seems to have been dallying with the idea of homosexuality without committing himself. 'They had a very close friendship,' says Basil Douglas. 'I don't know whether it would have become closer had Ben not come on the scene.'

Burra was trying to make a name as a critic in the arts, and contributed music reviews to *The Times* (it was this which had taken him to Barcelona). He had been lent a cottage near Newbury by two wealthy patrons of the Bloomsbury circle, J. L. Behrend and his wife Mary, who lived nearby. In March 1937 he invited Britten down for a weekend. 'I catch 10.45 to Reading where Peter Burra meets me – he takes me to his lovely little cottage in Bucklebury Common. It is a heavenly day ... We go & look at a charming little cottage nearby – which I'm thinking of taking as it is in such a heavenly part of the country.' (Britten was about to inherit some money from his mother's estate.) 'After lunch ... Peter initiates me into the wonders of Squash which I find completely captivating ... After dinner play piano duets & talk till a late hour – I have a kindred spirit in thousands of ways (one way in particular) here.' He does not elaborate, but the shared attitude was undoubtedly sexual.

Britten's diary entry for the next day suggests a growing mutual attraction between him and Burra. They played squash again, and Britten sprained his ankle, hobbling about for the rest of the day with a stick – 'very pathetic, but secretly (I'm ashamed to say) pleased as it draws attention to my prowess at Squash, which Peter is proud of – & which I feel adds to my glamour!' They talked late again that night – 'Peter is one of the world's dears.' On the Monday morning, while Britten worked, Burra 'plays with his new toy, the Motor Bike which symbolises his craving for the normal or "Tough" at the moment.'

Back in London, Britten stayed a night with Lennox Berkeley. 'I am very fond of him – he is a charming creature & I feel a very good composer – but so far not more than "fond".' He now regarded himself as at least temporarily homosexual, though 'I have such a passion for sopranos that I may some time become "normal"', he wrote after an evening of listening to records of Flagstad and other great singers. He raised the subject of what he called his 'queerness' with his brother

Bobby while they were winding up their mother's affairs. Despite his 'obstinate conservatism in so many ways', Bobby 'hasn't been shocked', and had 'even helped with sympathy and advice'.

During April, Britten went to stay with Berkeley in Gloucestershire. Evidently Berkeley now wanted the relationship to go beyond friendship, but Britten held back. 'He is a dear & I am very, very fond of him, nevertheless, it is a comfort that we can arrange sexual matters at least to *my* satisfaction.' He was still seeing much of Piers Dunkerley, but the boy 'has suddenly become extremely mature – having turned 16 – & more adult than adults themselves!' which Britten evidently found disconcerting. Despite his flirtations with Burra and Berkeley, he was more attracted to pre-pubescents and pubescents than to young men. He noted that Sophie Wyss's elder son, then aged about twelve, was 'a special pet of mine', while the boy's infant brother was not yet 'really at an interesting age'. Meanwhile his scheme of taking a cottage near Burra was unsettled by a visit to his Hockey relatives in Suffolk, during which the sight of familiar countryside aroused 'sentimental memories' of 'deliriously happy summers' in childhood. He began to consider the idea of living there instead.

On the evening of 27 April, John Alston called at Britten's Finchley Road flat and told him he had seen a newspaper report of Peter Burra's death: 'killed in an Air smash near Reading – flying with one of his "tough" friends,' wrote Britten in his diary. He felt 'desperate', because 'in the short year & a bit that I've known him he has been very close & dear to me'. Peter Pears was even more distraught:

> I was on a visit – I was in [Peter Burra's] house in fact when the thing happened. It was brought to me – the news . . . an aeroplane smash quite near his cottage. It was an amateur pilot friend of his who took him up in a small (I suppose two-seater) plane, and they had a crash. Then his parents came down . . .

Britten travelled to Bucklebury for the funeral. The next day, back in London, he had 'dinner with Peter Piers & Basil Douglas – very nice, but sad as we have to discuss what is best about Peter Burra's things'. (This was the evening of the broadcast of *Our Hunting Fathers*. Britten attended it, and wrote in his diary 'it's my op. 1 alright'.)

It was agreed that Britten and Pears, whose surname Britten now began to spell correctly, should go down to Bucklebury and sort out Burra's things. They left London by train on 6 May, making the journey from Reading on Pears's motor bike, in pouring rain late at night. Britten arrived wet and sore from pillion riding, but after spending the next day sorting Burra's papers, he wrote: 'Peter Pears is a dear & a very sympathetic person – tho' I'll admit I am not too keen on travelling on his motor bike!' According to Pears's memory of that night at Bucklebury, 'the nightingales were singing all night, and I couldn't get to sleep because of it, and one's sorrow'.

They met again a few days later and went to a meeting of the Musicians' Circle of the Left Book Club. Two days afterwards, on 11 May, Pears came to dinner at Britten's flat and they listened to records. 'He is a dear,' wrote Britten. At the end of the month they had an 'exhilarating duel' at a London tennis club, and went to a Toscanini concert. Again, 'Peter is a dear.'

Britten's music for *King Arthur*, a dramatized radio feature scripted by the playwright and poet D. G. Bridson and produced by Val Gielgud of the BBC, occupied much of his time between the death of his mother and the beginning of his friendship with Pears. After the broadcast on 23 April 1937 he wrote that Bridson's script 'irritates me more than I can say', being 'a pale pastiche of Malory', but the music 'certainly comes off like hell & the orchestra . . . are enthusiastic about it'. Lennox Berkeley came to the broadcast. He and Britten were now working on a joint composition, an orchestral suite based on Catalan dance tunes that Britten had jotted down during a folk-dancing display in Barcelona. The suite was mostly written when Britten was staying with Berkeley in Gloucestershire in April 1937. 'Lennox . . . has sketched two movements which we discuss fully & alter accordingly, & then while I sketch a third (having settled form etc) he makes out a rough score of the first.' (The first two movements were Berkeley's, the third and fourth Britten's.) The *Mont Juic* suite, named after the park in Barcelona where they had heard the tunes, was dedicated by them to the memory of Peter Burra.

During the brief time that Britten had known him, Burra had taken over something of Auden's role as his intellectual and sexual mentor. Now he turned back to Auden. A few days after Burra's funeral he 'set a serious poem of Wystan's', lines beginning 'Now through night's caressing grip / Earth and all her oceans slip' from *The Dog Beneath the Skin*. In the play, the poem merely forms a rather casual link between scenes, but in the sombre Britten setting ('Nocturne') considerable emotional resonances are created, and the mood of the final bars suggests that he may have meant the piece as an elegy for Burra:

> May sleep's healing power extend
> Through these hours to our friend . . .
> Calmly till the morning break
> Let him lie, then gently wake.

The setting was written in a single morning. After lunch, and before a game of tennis, he dashed off another song, 'a light one for Hedli Anderson' (who had played the Singer in *The Ascent of F6* with great success), using words Auden had just written. The song was certainly light in verbal and musical style – the piano accompaniment slips through various pastiches (folk-song, polka, grand opera, Viennese waltz) – but again the words and music end sombrely:

> O last night I dreamed of you, Johnny, my lover,
> You'd the sun on one arm and the moon on the other . . .
> Ten thousand miles deep in a pit there I lay:
> But you frowned like thunder and you went away.

In the next few days Britten sketched further settings of what he called 'caberet [*sic*] songs' to words by Auden, observing after Hedli Anderson had tried them out, 'they are going to be hits I feel!' (From this burst of composition in May 1937 only 'Johnny' appears in Britten's posthumously published *Cabaret Songs* (1980); the remaining songs have not yet been discovered.) Then at the end of May he began to set more 'serious' Auden poems, with Sophie Wyss in mind as singer. The going proved tough; he rejected several attempts, and finished only one song for the present, 'Now the leaves are falling fast'. The *ostinato* accompaniment emphasizes the poem's tense preoccupation, the impossibility of (homo)-sexual fulfilment because of public disapproval:

> Whispering neighbours, left and right,
> Pluck us from the real delight;
> And the active hands must freeze
> Lonely on the separate knees.

Another Auden setting, 'Let the florid music praise', was begun during May but not finished for some months; 'it isn't there yet', Britten wrote in June. The subject was the same, the defeat of love by negative forces, inner and psychological this time rather than the prurient. The choice of these poems seems to have been entirely Britten's own. Evidently romantic and sexual non-fulfilment was a theme that currently held his attention. At the end of June, after an evening spent listening to Mahler's *Das Lied von der Erde*, he wrote to Henry Boys: 'It is cruel, you know, that music should be so beautiful. It has the beauty of loneliness & of pain: of strength & freedom. The beauty of disappointment & never-satisfied love.'

Early in June he went down to Colwall, where Auden had returned to the Downs School to teach for one term. They were planning a comic radio programme of bad music and bad verse, which they tried out on the boys, 'delighting their simple hearts with fireworks of the most superficial & Victorian manner (var. on Home Sweet Home – Polkas & Gallops etc). But they are splendid kids.' Britten found that Auden had staying with him Brian Howard, former gilded youth of the Evelyn Waugh set at Oxford in the twenties, and the most overtly homosexual member of that circle. Britten's diary describes him as 'very clever, intellectual but surprisingly foppish & affected. But definitely amusing ... As can be imagined the conversation (owing to the vicinity of the school) lies in rather specialised lines – but it is treated with such enthusiasm, with delicate synonyms and epithets, & with such genuine taste, that it doesn't aggravate.' Britten made another visit to Colwall ten days later, this time with Hedli Anderson and William Coldstream, he to paint Auden's portrait, she to work with Auden and Britten on the Blues from *The Ascent of F6*, which was to be rewritten as a solo song. They tried the new version on the boys, '& a great success it is too'. During this visit, Britten also played Auden the settings of his 'serious' poems. 'Wystan is terribly pleased with my straight songs for Sophie.' Then Britten was off to Peasenhall in Suffolk to stay with Beth's future in-laws, the Welfords, and look for 'suitable spots for our cottage'. He did not specify who the other half of the 'our' was. Mr Welford took them all sailing from Orford up river to Aldeburgh – 'simply lovely too'.

Back in London, Britten worked speedily at a commission from Boyd Neel, whose orchestra had just been invited to perform at the Salzburg Festival in August, with the stipulation that they must perform a brand-new work by an English composer. Neel writes that it seemed 'well-nigh hopeless' to find such a work in time,

> but suddenly I thought of Britten (till then hardly known outside inner musical circles) because I had noticed his extraordinary speed of composition during some film work in which we had been associated [*Love from a Stranger*, for which Neel had conducted Britten's score]. I immediately asked him whether he would take on the Salzburg commission, and in ten days' time he appeared at my house with the complete work sketched out. In another four weeks it was fully scored for strings as it stands today, but for the addition of one bar. This is one of the most astonishing feats of composition in my experience.

Britten's diary does not suggest that he found the time-scale particularly daunting. He began the piece while awaiting a summons for dangerous driving, following a collision in the car he and Beth owned (the case was eventually dismissed), and admitted that this 'is putting me off my stride in writing'. There was also the distraction of the visits to Colwall and Suffolk, and when he returned to London he began to suffer severe nose-bleeds, which kept him awake at night. Yet on 24 June, after only two hours' sleep, he wrote in his diary: 'The Variations are going quite well – a Waltz & Bourrée were finished to-day.'

Work was further interrupted by another visit to Suffolk, where he spent four days looking at cottages, eventually finding 'a Mill at Snape, which seems to have possibilities – but a lot of alterations to be made. The county is grand – none in England like it – & I feel I'm infinitely wise in choosing this place ... I do a certain amount of work but not as much as I should. I want to sleep all the time.' For the first time he left a few days blank in his diary. There was no time to write anything beyond a summary.

When he came back to London from Suffolk, Christopher Isherwood got him 'slightly drunk' at the Café Royal and took him at midnight to the Jermyn Street Turkish Bath, a well-known homosexual rendezvous of the day. 'Very pleasant sensation – completely sensuous, but very healthy,' wrote Britten, resuming his diary. 'It is extraordinary to find one's resistance to anything gradually weakening. The trouble was that we spent the night there – couldn't sleep a wink on the hard beds, in the perpetual restlessness of the surroundings.'

Isherwood, whom Britten described after a dinner with him in March 1937 as 'a grand person, unaffected, extremely amusing & devastatingly intelligent', said after Britten's death that he had never had a sexual relationship with him. In a 1980 letter, after writing that he did not believe there had been 'sex between Auden and Britten', he added 'Nothing between Britten and me, either.' Another member of the Auden–Isherwood circle, Sir Stephen Spender, wrote: 'I know nothing about Ben's sex life or how it was awakened or by whom.' On the other hand in the same letter Isherwood observed: 'No doubt both of us [Auden and himself] tried to bring him out, if he seemed to us to need it. We were extraordinarily interfering in this respect – as bossy as a pair of self-assured young psychiatrists – he wasn't a doctor's son and I wasn't an ex-medical student for nothing.' Basil Wright, who was homosexual too, has described a conversation between himself and Isherwood in which they asked each other, 'Well, have we convinced Ben he's queer, or haven't we?' The visit to the Jermyn Street Baths was evidently part of the process of bringing Britten out, and whether or not anything happened at the Baths that night, Britten seems to have felt more ready to become sexually active.

*

Next morning he did 'a little work – feeling like hell', then went down to Friston to stay with the Bridges. While there, 'I start to write out the score of the not yet completed Variations.' Most of the score was delivered to Boosey & Hawkes three days later, though the sketch for 'the end & fugue' was not written for another couple of days. On 11 July, Britten went back to Suffolk to take another look at Snape Mill, and while staying with the Welfords he managed to finish the score of the Fugue and Finale, writing 'straight in score in ink' without any pre-liminary pencil work. 'After a tremendous effort scarcely stopping for meals I get it off to copyist by 6.40 post.' So *Variations on a Theme of Frank Bridge* was completed.

It is an astonishing work, radiating energy and ideas, and reflecting all the conflicting states of mind Britten was experiencing while he com-posed it at tremendous speed: a residue of grief for his mother and Peter Burra, excitement at the new freedom her death offered him, delight in rediscovering the Suffolk countryside of his childhood, and the experi-ence of sexual liberation. The choice of Bridge for the theme was, of course, meant as a tribute to his 'musical father', but it was also a way of declaring his independence from his old teacher. He picked a motif not from one of Bridge's modern works, but from the 1906 *Idyll No. 2* for string quartet, a typical piece from the Elgar era, which represented much of what he was trying to reform in English music. (He had begun a set of piano variations on this same Bridge theme in 1932.) The Bridge motif is not stated at the outset of the Britten work, but only emerges gradually, stated delicately by a string quartet from behind powerful flourishes by the main orchestra, in which F major and E major are in unyielding opposition to each other. Bridge's pre-war idyll floats towards us on a stormy sea.

After the quartet has made its poignant little statement, the full strings take up the Bridge theme respectfully, but Britten's first variation then begins without a break, a restless Adagio, like a troubled dream, in which the violins make a series of passionate outbursts above the lower strings. The music fails to build towards the climax one expects, and instead resolves rather abruptly into an agreement (in C major) between the two conflicting sides, giving the impression that the real emotional issue, whatever it is, has not yet been faced. The mood now becomes playful, with a brisk March that recalls the *Simple Symphony*, and a movement entitled 'Romance', in which Bridge's theme is transmuted into an apparently untroubled melodic line which, however, becomes highly chromatic towards its conclusion, and seems to have difficulty resolving itself convincingly. Next – the whole thing is whizzing by at tremendous speed now, suggesting the haste with which it was composed – we are listening to a pastiche of Italian opera, 'Aria Italiana'. Private emotional struggles seem to have been banished by the sheer fun of life and all its possibilities. 'Bourrée Classique' and 'Wiener Walzer', the two movements completed after the night of nose-bleeding, continue the mood of escapism, though the element of parody is slight now, and the heady waltz contains hints of graver concerns waiting in the background. Then comes the furiously buzzing 'Moto Perpetuo', which seems like a self-portrait of a composer in a hurry, and suggests the huge energy necessary for writing a work like this against the clock. Then suddenly in 'Funeral March' we are back in the restless, self-questioning mood of the opening. 'Chant', which follows, hints at the return of Elgar-like romanticism, though nothing is resolved. At the beginning of the final movement a brisk fugue tries to return us to holiday mood. But cheerful abandon gradually breaks down into a sombre yet, at last, confident statement of serious purpose, in which there is no longer any attempt to banish emotional turmoil; private uncertainty is simply accepted for what it is. So we finally reach a state of mind which, in its very un-Elgarian way, is as tranquil as Bridge's innocence.

Britten himself greatly deplored this sort of critical 'reading' of his music. 'I ... cannot make out why it is that they have to hunt for programmes & "meanings" and all that rot!' he wrote in 1938. His own 'programme' for the *Variations* was quite different. On the composition sketch and in his own copy of the published score he indicated that each movement was meant to portray some characteristic of Bridge, 'His integrity ... energy ... charm ... wit ... gaiety', and so on. Bridge himself responded warmly to the work. 'I don't know how to express my appreciation in adequate terms,' he wrote to Britten. 'It is one of the few lovely things that has ever happened to me.'

'I have never been so busy in my life,' Britten told Nell Burra two days after finishing the *Variations on a Theme by Frank Bridge*.

> I think I have found a good spot to live in – it is an old Mill & house in a quaint old village called Snape ... It isn't exactly isolated, but it has a grand view and a lot of land to ensure its not being built round. But it will be ages before we can move in, as it has to be altered & enlarged, and generally improved.

He sometimes used the plural in his diary as well – 'our cottage' – but gave no indication with whom he intended to share it. Beth was about to get married and make her own home. Peter Pears was as yet only one of a circle of friends, with whom Britten sometimes played tennis (he still sometimes reverted to the spelling 'Piers'). The Mill was being bought by Britten alone, with £3,000 he had inherited from his mother. As soon as he had found it, he described it to Lennox Berkeley – 'I lunch with Lennox & tell him all about Snape & he seems pleased.'

On 15 July the Boyd Neel Orchestra played through the *Variations* with Britten conducting. 'Much time is spent in correcting parts & things but the work itself ... will be successful I think.' Neel himself was immensely enthusiastic: 'I saw at once that we had here, not just another string piece, but a work in which the resources of the string orchestra were exploited with a daring and invention never before known.' Frank Bridge came to the first rehearsal. Neel remembers that his principal viola had difficulty with a solo passage on harmonics in the 'Wiener Walzer' variation. 'First Britten, then Bridge, picked up the instrument and played the passage quite perfectly.'

A few days later, Britten lunched with William Walton, their first recorded meeting, though evidently there had been others. 'He is charming,' wrote Britten,

> but I feel always the school relationship with him – he is so obviously the head-prefect of English music, whereas I'm the promising young new boy. Soon of course he'll leave & return as a member of the staff – [Vaughan] Williams being of course the Headmaster. Elgar was never *that* – but a member of the Governing Board. Anyhow apart from a few slight reprimands (as to musical opinions) I am patronised in a very friendly manner. Perhaps the prefect is already regretting the lost freedom, & newly found authority!

That same day, 28 July 1937: 'Peter Pears comes – play songs for him, & also run thro the Variations for his benefit.' It was apparently the first time they had made music together. The entry for that day concludes: 'Dinner with Lennox at his Reform Club – much talk. He is a dear & I'm glad I'm going to live with him.'

*

Lennox Berkeley came from a wealthy upper-class English family, and had only taken seriously to music after leaving Oxford, spending five years in Paris studying with Nadia Boulanger. Britten, though ten years his junior, was far superior technically, and Berkeley gratefully accepted his advice. 'I was rather tied up in knots,' he has said; 'he was able to undo them for me and encourage me to be myself.' Britten often told him: 'If you want to do that, do it: don't think all the time about whether Nadia Boulanger would approve.'

Berkeley was slim and good-looking in a rather 'aesthetic' way. He had

had homosexual experiences in France, and seems to have developed the sort of feelings towards Britten that Britten, in turn, seems to have felt towards young boys. This may be reflected in his choice of two Auden poems which he set during 1937, 'Lay your sleeping head, my love' and 'Night covers up the rigid land'. His settings of both are dedicated 'To Benjamin'. Britten's diary gives the distinct impression of Berkeley as wooer and himself as being wooed, and in one entry there is a hint of discomfort. 'Lunch with Lennox at the Barcelona,' he wrote on 20 September 1937. 'I always feel better towards L.B. when I am with him.'

Berkeley was not the only pursuer. Isherwood has recalled how, at twenty-three, 'Ben ... always seemed very much younger in appearance than he actually was, with his curly hair ... always very boyish in his demeanour.' There were always plenty of men ready to take him out to a meal and a concert. He was flattered by such attentions but wary of getting involved. 'I decide to end this little friendship,' he wrote after one individual had taken him for a 'romantic' drive around the East End. He was still seeing Piers Dunkerley, but the diary gives the impression that, now that Piers was in his mid-teens, Britten was no longer physically attracted by him. Ironically, Dunkerley's own feelings for Britten had now been aroused. Writing to him from Bloxham School, he ended 'Much love', and in another letter, 'all the best, with love, hugs, and kisses'.

Britten seems to have been searching for a successor to Piers. Somebody introduced him to a young boy from a poor London family, 'a splendid little boy', Britten wrote, '& I hope I'll be able to do something for him'. He took him on holiday to Cornwall, with the consent of the parents, but without much enthusiasm from Britten's brother Robert who was there when they arrived. After two weeks even Britten had had a 'slight over-dose' of the lad. Undeterred, and at the suggestion of a friend of Peter Burra's who was working with Spanish refugees, he decided to 'adopt' a Basque boy, pay his keep for a year, and bring him to live at Snape.

The Mill had still been working when he bought it, and there was much conversion work to be done – Kit Welford's father, a professional architect, designed the alterations free of charge. For the time being there was no question of Britten and Berkeley moving in, and during the summer and early autumn of 1937 the Finchley Road flat remained Britten's home. Beth would soon be leaving it to marry Kit, and Britten began to make plans for somewhere else in London, and a flatmate. His diary for 8 September records 'lunch with Peter Pears in Kensington.

He's a dear – & I'm glad I'm going to live with him' – exactly the same words that he had used of Berkeley.

On the same day, 'Peter stays the night – talk till a late hour.' He was back the next night, and they had 'much talk before bed'. An opportunity now came up for a musical collaboration. Trevor Harvey had got Britten a BBC commission to write a score for a religious programme about Michaelmas Day. Britten sketched the music – which included a setting of Emily Brontë's poem 'A thousand gleaming fires' for tenor and strings – early in September 1937, and while Pears was staying at Finchley Road 'he runs thro' my Emily Brontë song (for Michaelmas programme) that he's going to sing – & he makes it sound charming. He is a good singer & a first-rate musician.'

Pears soon became aware that Britten was no ordinary pianist. He describes him as having 'an extraordinary connection between his brain and his heart and the tips of his fingers. You could watch Ben holding his hands over the piano preparatory to playing a slow movement, a soft, soft chord, and you could see his fingers alert, alive, really sometimes even quivering with the intensity of what was going to occur.' He observes that Britten 'could make lighter sounds than anyone else I can recall; he was anxious to imitate the timbre of early pianos rather than emphasizing that of a modern Steinway'. As to technique, 'He had his own method of fingering, which other, more regular players might find strange, but he worked out his own ideas very carefully . . . Although he was aware of the need to practise, there seemed to be no question of technique coming between his thoughts and their execution.' Others who worked with him in later years were struck by his extraordinary physical control over the instrument. The keyboard player Viola Tunnard used to say, 'Ben manages to make the hammers move in a way that other people don't,' while Sue Phipps remarks: 'Ben could create a crescendo on the keyboard even after he'd put the notes down!' Some of it was due to what he called his 'half-pedal technique', 'letting it up halfway', says Marion Thorpe, 'so as to get a slightly smudged sound, and clearing something, and catching something else – it was very subtle'. Altogether his command over the instrument was extraordinary. 'It was amazing what colours he could get,' Pears has remarked. 'He thought a colour and he could do it.' Meanwhile it seems to have been at these early private sessions together that Pears's voice began to develop into a remarkable instrument. As Lord Harewood puts it, 'Ben wanted, and found, imagination and sensitivity in Peter's singing and approach, and from this he conjured what he wanted for his music.'

Pears has said that by the time he knew him, 'Ben didn't go so often to church ... I am not sure that he would really have called himself a Christian.' Perhaps for this reason, he was soon 'bored' with working on *The Company of Heaven*, the religious radio programme. He listened to a Strauss Prom on the radio while scoring it, 'without slackening speed'. But he admitted that there were 'nice words' to set, and he had been allowed his choice of soloists. 'Peter Pears and Sophie Wyss both sing their songs beautifully,' he wrote after the broadcast. The orchestra told him it was 'the best incidental music they've ever played'.

Trevor Harvey, who conducted it, did not expect much of Pears's professional future. 'In those days I could never conceivably have imagined Peter as an opera singer, or even as a Lieder singer or anything, because he had a quite small voice. He was frankly pretty lazy, and I very seldom heard him practising or anything like that at home, and he didn't seem to have any great ambition.' Britten knew that Pears would have to work hard to realize his potential. '. . . if he studies he will be a very good singer,' he wrote in his diary soon after *The Company of Heaven*, when Pears had been singing through his Auden settings. 'He's certainly one of the nicest people I know, but frightfully reticent.' For his part, Pears found Britten invigorating. Writing from Salzburg, where he had gone during a European holiday to hear the première of *Variations on a Theme of Frank Bridge*, he commented that all the other English composers represented in the Boyd Neel concert lacked life, 'and that, the Almighty be praised, is what you have, Benjie ... Much Love to you – Peter.' A few weeks later, he set off for a tour of America (his second) with the New English Singers. Britten exhorted him not to oversleep and miss trains, indications of Pears's usual habits. As to his singing career, 'Next year must be the beginning of grand things ... All my love & Bon Voyage – Benjie.'

Britten was currently full of optimism about his own work. 'I'll have written you about four more vols. of music by the time you come back,' he told Pears. 'More songs, & with luck a piano concerto. I'm feeling on first-rate terms with the Muse at the moment.' Yet alongside this self-confidence he was searching for the security his mother's death had removed. In October 1937 he moved out of the Finchley Road flat, storing his possessions in an outbuilding at Snape until the Mill was ready. He wrote in his diary: 'The loss of Mum & Pop, instead of lessening, seems to be more & more apparent every day. Scarcely bearable. No where to look for help or comfort – & I am weak enough to want them very often.'

*

He spent the next few months leading a 'flying Dutchman existence', staying with friends, including Isherwood's family in London ('Christopher's one of the nicest people I know') and Auden and his parents in Birmingham ('I like his parents enormously, in fact things are very pleasant'). He and Auden played 'lots of Mozart (Viola & piano – & piano duet) at odd hours – Wystan's passion', and worked on a BBC radio documentary about Hadrian's Wall. Britten's music for the programme has disappeared, but it evidently included a setting of Auden's 'Roman Wall Blues'. Britten conducted the broadcast from Newcastle; it went 'fearfully badly, there's a big hitch which makes nonsense of the first part of the programme. But there's good stuff in it I know.' He had now completed a set of five Auden songs, *On This Island*, and he and Sophie Wyss broadcast them in November as one of the BBC's 'Contemporary Concerts'. Britten judged that, though the audience had enjoyed them, 'they are far too obvious & amenable for Contemporary music'.

The songs were the cause of conflict with Frank Bridge. Marjorie Fass, who lived with the Bridges at Friston, vividly portrays in a December 1937 letter the tension that had grown up in the household on account of Britten's affiliation to the Auden gang. 'I'm having a bit of fun with him by not being bowled over with everything that Auden & Christopher Isherwood do,' she wrote to a friend, and she described Bridge ('Mr Brit' in her parlance) emerging from a 'lesson' with Britten on the Auden songs:

> [He] muttered to me that never again wld he try & help Benjy over his work, as some of the things he pointed out, the boy simply wldn't alter, so why waste his time & energy . . . Benjy . . . said he's had to 'stick up for himself', a thing he'd never done before with Mr Brit – so I said that was allright, but surely it was of value to him to have Mr Brit's criticism & he said, 'Yes, but they're *my* songs' & I said 'certainly', but since Mr Brit knows so infinitely more about music than you do I shld have thought his wisdom & experience were worth your accepting' which left spoilt young Benjy in a silent temper . . . The thing that is bad for him is that he's meeting brilliant people who are not brilliant in *his* sphere, but their own, & so make a mutual admiration society . . .

It is remarkable that the twenty-four-year-old Britten was still willing to put up with this parental-style domination. But, as another passage from Miss Fass's letters shows, he badly wanted mothering:

> I know he is in a mental muddle abt a great deal & dreads the future, so I had to go & put my arms round him & give him a good hug & he said 'thank you, Marj, that was nice of you'. He really hates growing

up & away from a very happy childhood that ended only with his Mother's death last Christmas.

Auden and Isherwood were setting off for the Far East, to write a book about the Chinese–Japanese War, and on 19 January 1938 the Group Theatre gave them a send-off party at the Hammersmith studio of the painter Julian Trevelyan. Britten and Hedli Anderson performed a new cabaret song that he and Auden had just written:

> Some say that Love's a little boy,
>   And some say he's a bird,
> Some say he makes the world go round
>   And some say that's absurd . . .
>
> When it comes, will it come without warning
>   Just as I'm picking my nose,
> Will it knock on my door in the morning
>   Or tread in the bus on my toes,
> Will it come like a change in the weather,
>   Will its greeting be courteous or bluff?
> Will it alter my life altogether?
>   O tell me the truth about love.

Robert Medley describes this song as 'the *pièce de résistance*' of the evening, and Julian Trevelyan recalls Anderson and Britten performing 'very professionally', though 'the party ended in a bit of a rough-house' (Brian Howard picked a quarrel with Trevelyan and someone was punched on the nose). Britten described the party in his diary as 'Beastly crowd & unpleasant people'. Next day, 'Lunch with Peter Pears (back from America).'

When in London, Britten was now 'Sleeping with Peter P.', as one diary entry (9 February 1938) puts it, evidently meaning no more than that – sharing Pears's temporary accommodation in a friend's flat. Meanwhile Snape Mill was 'going marvellously & will be fine for us [presumably himself and Berkeley] to live in'. On 19 February: 'Lunch Peter & Lennox.'

Over Christmas he had been 'laid up under doctor's orders' on account of overwork. Marjorie Fass reported that the Bridges were 'so worried abt him being on the verge of a complete mental & physical breakdown – & as he'd been fainting about lately we thought his heart might be groggy'. The doctor found nothing wrong with his heart, but Miss Fass fretted at him staying up 'till 2 a.m. every night & get[ting] up at 8 & instead of decent meals fortifying himself with brandy, when he felt rotten'. After several weeks' enforced rest he was back to his usual pace. He had sent word to the BBC, via Boosey & Hawkes, that he would like to write a piano concerto for the next Prom season, with himself as soloist, and when they agreed he got to work at once – 'it dashes along full-speed', he wrote in his diary on 7 February while sketching the hectic first movement.

At the end of February he and Pears found a flat of their own at 4 Nevern Square, Earls Court. 'Probably a rash decision', wrote Britten, 'but we *must* get settled.' Before they could move in, the news of Hitler's entry into Austria made Britten suppose that war would soon bring an 'end to all this pleasure – end of Snape, end of Concerto, friends, work, love – oh, blast, blast, damn'. But the threat receded, and by mid-March they were both sleeping in the flat, 'unfurnished abit still, but going to be grand I think'. Pears soon became aware that Britten had no domestic skills, or did not care to develop any. 'He was no good in the kitchen. He could boil an egg, I think, but that was about as far as he could go. He could have watched a piece of toast, I suppose, being burnt slowly. But he was not very good domestically. If he made his bed, somebody probably had to come along and make it again.'

By mid-March the Piano Concerto was being difficult. 'Stuck in 2nd movement – which is poor stuff.' But on 6 April he told the BBC he was 'elated' about his progress. On 9 April 'the great move into Snape begins . . . Things are chaotic.'

Snape is a straggling village just off the road to Aldeburgh. The River Alde, broad and marshy in its lower reach, becomes a small stream above the sluice at Snape Bridge. In 1938 the Garrett family was still operating the big Maltings by the old bridge, and lorries, barges and railway goods wagons came and went. Britten's Mill stood about half a mile north of this activity, in Snape village proper, but in a few minutes he could be walking on the reed-fringed path that wound past the Maltings towards Iken Marshes, with only the wildlife of the estuary for company.

His first days in residence were all he could have hoped for. 'The country is heavenly & the view from the Mill superb . . . Mr Blowers, 20 years inn-keeper at Sotterley, which we knew so well when at Lowestoft, keeps the Pub here. He is a grand man & comes for a drink before dinner.' Britten had bought a second-hand Morris Eight 'for tootling about the place'. He went shopping in Saxmundham, and began to sort out the 'ton' of family crockery and cutlery he had acquired. 'Lennox's furniture arrives.' There was also the wildlife. 'As I go to bed, the noise of the birds is deafening – Cuckoo, Nightingale, Sand Piper, & Shell drake.'

Then the Basque refugee boy, Andoni Barrutia, arrived. A housekeeper, Mrs Hearn, had been engaged, but objected to serving Britten and the boy at meals, since the boy did chores with her and was therefore, in her eyes, a servant. Mrs Welford, Beth's mother-in-law, persuaded Britten that he was being taken advantage of by a local family – father, mother and son – who were helping in house and garden, and Britten dismissed them all. Andoni Barrutia objected to this because he was fond of them. The housekeeper said she could not manage without the extra help and gave notice. Consequently Britten got no work done, though the deadline was approaching for the Piano Concerto. 'It's been h–l,' he wrote to John Pounder.

Even the housekeeper, let alone the others, sounds like an extravagance in his financial position. He had become overdrawn at the bank while paying for the conversion of the Mill, and his income from music was entirely unpredictable. But wages were low for live-in staff, Lennox Berkeley was undoubtedly contributing, and the Mill after the conversion was a substantial house which required a lot of looking after. The circular mill building itself had been altered to form, on the ground floor, a round studio for Britten, with a grand piano. Stairs led up to his bedroom, also round, which had been given a long window with a balcony overlooking the Alde marshes. The remainder of the living quarters, which included a studio for Berkeley with his own piano, had been formed out of the old granary and miller's cottage, connected to the mill itself by a passage. 'Ben did not have enough furniture to fill the place,' writes Beth. As to Andoni the refugee boy, Beth says he was 'about twelve' and could speak no English. 'Ben expected too much of this child and gave him various jobs to do about the place as he had to be occupied while Ben was working, but like most young of that age he was lazy, he lost the key of the woodshed and did not cooperate at all. Poor child, he was probably very unhappy!'

Early in May, Britten wrote to John Pounder that domestic peace had been restored. 'Andoni is going – which bleeds my heart but it is better on the whole.' The boy was sent back to the refugee camp in Berkshire from which he had come. With the crisis over, Britten was able at last to spend a 'lovely day – in alone all the time – working hard, a little gardening and wireless. A real Snape day – the first of many I hope.'

On 21 May, Berkeley arrived to sleep at the Mill for the first time with José Raffaeli – 'José (Lennox's Paris Friend) & L. come down by mid-day train.' Britten left them to enjoy Snape by themselves and went up to London. 'Francis Barton (late of South Lodge) comes to flat to stay. He is a nice person.' Francis, aged twenty-two, was now an officer in the Royal Marines. Britten reported their time together to Peter Pears, who was singing in the chorus at Glyndebourne. 'Francis sounds quite fascinating', Pears replied, 'and just the sort of person I should hopelessly lose my heart to.' He mentioned that he had been 'running mildly after a sweet tough Stage Hand but as usual I can't come to the point! . . . Much love, Benjie darling.' Britten's diary suggests that he had not come to the point with Francis. 'He is a great contrast to most of my friends – being in the Marines, a Tory & conventional, but he is so charming & ingenuous, that he is decidedly bearable!' They went down to Snape for two days. Then on 27 May: 'Francis goes after an early lunch & I am desperately miserable after he goes.'

Auden was taking as keen an interest as ever in Britten's sexual progress. It may have been now that he sent him an undated letter consoling him after a failed attempt at seduction, and giving advice: 'The correct line is (a) To appear comparatively indifferent emotionally (b) To take not the slightest notice of a refusal . . . Did you play the piano. Most important . . . Quite friendly, but cold. And LOTS of music.' If it was Francis Barton that Britten had hoped to seduce, Barton's letters to him suggest that he stood little chance. They are jolly and hearty, with no whiff of anything other than cheery friendship. At the end of 1939 Barton got married. (He subsequently rose to the rank of Major-General; Britten remained on warm terms with him and his family.)

Besides his work on the Piano Concerto, Britten was writing incidental music for another BBC religious programme, *The World of the Spirit*. It was broadcast successfully at Whitsun, after which Britten had to 'get down in earnest to Concerto. Finish off 3rd movement.' Three days later, on 16 June, his diary, kept faithfully (apart from a few recent blanks) since he was fourteen, comes abruptly and without explanation to an end. Entries had been briefer of late, and he was under considerable pressure to complete work to deadlines, so that it is remarkable that he had continued it so long. It ceased just as he was hurrying to finish, and practise, the Piano Concerto. But its cessation may also have something to do with the beginning, shortly after the last entry, of a new relationship about which he must have wished to be discreet.

2: I daren't mutter the name

In June 1938 the ISCM music festival was being held in London. The *Variations on a Theme of Frank Bridge* were performed by the Boyd Neel Orchestra, and Britten and Frederick Grinke played his Suite for violin and piano. During the festival, Britten saw a good deal of Hermann Scherchen, and learnt that his son Wulff, with whom he had shared a raincoat in Siena four years earlier, was now, at the age of eighteen, living in Cambridge with his mother, who had separated from Hermann. Britten lost no time in writing to Wulff: 'I do not know whether you will remember me or not – but in 1934 ... we spent a long time together – especially one day in Siena ... I should very much like to see you again.' Wulff replied by return of post, recalling the day in Siena as vividly as Britten: 'We two went to the piazza something or other and explored the "guildhalla". Nein? I was in shorts and sandals (as I am now) and it started to rain. I got thoroughly wet, but it was worth it – "pleasant reminiscences of a glorious past!" (Excuse my poetic strain.)' Britten had suggested that Wulff come to stay in his 'windmill in Suffolk'. Wulff accepted enthusiastically, and arrived in mid-July.

Britten found that in appearance he had not changed much from the fourteen-year-old he had known in Italy. They had a happy weekend, though Britten was preoccupied with the Piano Concerto, still to be finished. Wulff was going abroad with his father and would not be able to attend the Prom performance, but hoped to hear it on the radio. 'Mind you listen in hard,' Britten wrote to him on 1 August; 'it is a thousand pities that you can't be there – at least I think it is!'

The Concerto was completed and the parts copied just in time for the first rehearsal on 5 August. A few months earlier, Britten had told Sophie Wyss that he felt it 'always a bit of an effort to play the piano ... I so seldom do it.' Now, he wrote to Ralph Hawkes that the rehearsal had gone well: 'The piano part wasn't as impossible to play as I feared, &

with a little practice this week ought to be O.K.' As to its character, 'It certainly sounds "*popular*" enough & people seem to like it all right.' On the day of the performance, 18 August, Auden sent a telegram from Brussels: 'VIVE LA MUSIQUE A BAS LES FEMMES.' Lennox Berkeley, to whom the Concerto was dedicated, had written to Britten: 'If music be indeed the food of love, I think you stand a very good chance.'

In the audience at the Queen's Hall were Frank and Ethel Bridge and Marjorie Fass. Britten had shown Bridge the first movement, and Bridge had suggested a small alteration to the orchestration, but apparently he had not seen the entire work. Also sitting expectantly were Beth and her husband Kit, who had lent his best shirt studs to Britten. The programme began with Rossini's *Barber of Seville* Overture and Schubert's *The Shepherd on the Rock*, and then Sir Henry Wood brought Britten on to the platform.

Advance information had emphasized the popular nature of the Concerto. The music critic Alan Frank had written in the *Radio Times* that Britten 'dislikes this business of dividing music up into light and serious compartments', and in the programme note at the Queen's Hall the Concerto was described by Britten himself as 'simple and direct in form'. The note also stated: 'This Pianoforte Concerto in D was written during the first half of this year and finished on the 27th of July.' It was 'not by any means a Symphony with pianoforte' – that is, a concerto on the strict classical model – 'but rather a bravura Concerto with orchestral accompaniment'.

The word 'bravura' must have seemed highly appropriate to the audience as they listened to the bold, almost brash opening of the Concerto, with brass and percussion heralding the piano's sparkling entry. Britten had written himself the most challenging of solos, full of hectic leaps and runs – during one of which a borrowed shirt stud flew out. He brought off the performance superbly. Constant Lambert in the *Listener* called his playing 'brilliant', and at the end there was prolonged applause for him, while Beth describes autograph hunters waiting at the artists' entrance – 'he was quite overcome'. As to the quality of the writing, Lambert called the first movement 'admirable throughout', and described the second as 'neither a "straight" valse nor a "cod" valse but hover[ing] cynically and convincingly between the two'. After this, however, he felt that 'the composer seems to lose his grip on the work. There are effective and brilliant things in both the last movements but they sound like essays in texture rather than a direct expression of musical thought.' Other critics reacted similarly. The third movement, as played in 1938, was entitled 'Recitative and Aria'; it began with the piano commenting sardonically, in the style of polka, Blues and other dance rhythms, on the woodwind's attempts to introduce a lyrical tune, but ended in full-blown romantic mood. The *Times* critic could not decide whether this conclusion was meant seriously, 'or is the composer's tongue still in his cheek . . . ?'

Auden regarded the Concerto as a potential aid to seduction. 'And what about its effect on a certain person of importance?' he wrote to Britten. Wulff Scherchen had managed to pick up the broadcast in Strasbourg. 'I'm glad to know that you recognised the work as mine,' Britten wrote to him, '& that quality about it which reminded you of the Mill. *That* certainly pleased me!'

Marjorie Fass felt the same as the critics. 'I expect you'll have been as disappointed . . . as we were,' she wrote to a friend, who had heard the broadcast. 'The orchestra & Wood liked the work very much – as it's amusing to play . . . but of *music* or originality there is no trace . . . If Benjy develops some day later on, he will see the insignificance of this work.' The letter describes Britten bringing records of the broadcast to the Bridges, who listened 'with shut faces'. But Britten affected to be indifferent to these reactions. He told Wulff he would be appearing again at the Proms, to conduct the *Variations on a Theme of Frank Bridge*, and then he might go to Brussels. (Auden was waiting there with a sixteen-year-old boy as bait: 'Shall I get a photo? Such eyes. O la, la.') Britten made it clear that his plans depended on Wulff: 'On when (& if!) you wish to come here.'

Wulff was not able to get to Snape, so Britten went to Cambridge to see him. When Auden got back from Brussels he was impatient to see Britten's new friend. 'Wystan was very naughty,' recalls Wulff.

> He arranged to meet Ben in order to meet me, at the Café Royal . . . Ben and I had . . . tea, nothing more than that; and then we met Wystan, and Wystan said, 'What are you drinking?' and they decided on brandies, and then he turned to me . . . And of course . . . I said, 'Well, I'll have the same as you.' . . . And of course I was made to drink mine up by Wystan . . . That was very naughty of him. He knew exactly what he was doing, I'm quite sure. There was a malicious glint in his eye.

Wulff was also introduced to Peter Pears, who late this year moved with Britten to a flat behind the BBC at 67 Hallam Street. 'I adored Peter,' Wulff has said.

> He was a wonderful father figure . . . to me . . . and I thought in a sense that he was the father to Benjamin at the same time . . . He would

restrain Benjamin when Ben was going off the rails, or threatening to
go off the rails in some way. He was the wise man in the background
... He had this air of stability that Ben didn't have. I mean, Ben was
ebullient, outgoing, and Peter was the quiet, steadying influence.

Wulff's perception of a parent–child element in the relationship is
echoed by one of Britten's friends from Lowestoft, Basil Reeve. When he
first heard Pears sing, Reeve noticed a 'strange thing' about his voice. He
recalls how Britten's mother 'used to sing a lot, and Ben used to accompany her. His mother's voice and Peter Pears's voice were fantastically
similar ... That's the first thing I noticed ... the same voice. [Britten]
couldn't miss it. And I told this to Beth, and she said, "My God, yes!" '

*

Meanwhile Lennox Berkeley was still a factor in Britten's complicated
private life. Though Berkeley spent much time in Paris, where he shared a
flat with José Rafaelli, he was often at Snape. A note he sent to Aaron
Copland shortly before Christmas 1938 may hint at jealousy of Wulff
Scherchen: 'Benjamin ... is being very successful in all departments of his
life and enjoying it all.'

In October 1938 Britten told Wulff he was writing him 'a bit of music'.
This may have been the Overture and Interlude to the new. Auden–
Isherwood play, *On the Frontier*, since Britten gave Wulff the composition sketches of these pieces. The play itself had been dedicated by its
authors 'To Benjamin Britten'. Britten called this 'a grand little dedication' and said the play was Auden and Isherwood's 'best so far'.

The Group Theatre had nearly collapsed in the summer of 1937, when
a rift had developed between Auden and Isherwood, who had their sights
on the West End, and Rupert Doone, who wanted the Group to have
exclusive rights to their plays. A peace congress was called at the
Oxfordshire farmhouse belonging to the artist John Piper, a member of
the Group Theatre, and Britten attended, meeting Piper and his second
wife Myfanwy. 'Rows – & more Rows,' he wrote gloomily in his diary
about the heated discussions, and the Pipers noticed him escaping into
the garden to smoke a cigarette – 'first since adolescent efforts at school',
he noted, 'with disastrous consequences ... Never again'. Myfanwy
Piper recalls that Britten was 'very much the unsophisticated schoolboy'
at this Group Theatre gathering, not participating in the rows but 'tag-
ging along under Auden and Isherwood's thumb – John and I used to call
them the Prefects'. She remembers Britten and Auden playing 'Night and
Day' and 'Stormy Weather' as piano duets.

Though Britten had liked *On the Frontier* when he first read it, the play was the fruit of its authors' West End ambitions and lacked most of the vigour of its predecessors. Britten directed the music, which he had written for piano, percussion and two trumpets, during a week's run at the Arts Theatre, Cambridge, and Peter Pears took part in the sung passages between scenes and played small spoken roles. The Cambridge run was not a great success, and the play was only seen in London for a single night the following February. The drama critic Ivor Brown, reviewing this performance, damned the Britten score as 'music which made one fear to be removed to hospital suffering from Percussion'. Wulff Scherchen, however, was delighted by the contrapuntal overlaying of the national anthems Britten had written for the countries of Ostnia and Westland – 'In my mind's ear', he said fifty years later, 'I can still hear clearly the two march tunes and their intermingling.' Britten was depressed by the week's run at the Arts, and by his twenty-fifth birthday which fell immediately afterwards. 'The strain of becoming a quarter of a century is bearing hard upon me,' he told Wulff. 'It's a horrible thing to feel one's youth slipping o-so surely away from one & I had such a damn good youth too. I wish you were here to comfort me!'

Also slipping away, at least in the Auden circle, were the left-wing certainties that had characterized the thirties. The failure of *On the Frontier* was largely the result of Auden's growing indifference to the anti-Fascist struggle, or at least his increasing feeling that art should stand apart from politics. Britten was still willing to lend his name and music to the old left-wing causes; he wrote a motet, *Advance Democracy*, for the Co-Operative movement, to words by the editor of *Left Review*, Randall Swingler, and he agreed to provide, for a 'Festival of Music for the People' (featuring choirs from the Co-Operative and Labour movements), a cantata for tenor soloist, massed choirs and orchestra, entitled *Ballad of Heroes*. It was intended to commemorate British members of the International Brigade who had fallen in Spain, and consisted of settings of appropriate poems by Swingler and Auden. Britten wrote the piece in a few days, and liked it enough to give it an opus number (14). Yet as the threat of war advanced and receded again with each European crisis and its aftermath, his predominant feelings were of fear that the world he knew might soon be destroyed, and relief when there was a temporary stay of execution. When Chamberlain came back from Munich with his piece of paper in September 1938, Britten announced to Ralph Hawkes that he was 'much more cheerful', and was going out blackberrying to celebrate – 'might even have a next year in which to eat the jam'. By the following spring he was experiencing 'jitters . . . over the International Situation', and on 16 March, as Hitler advanced through

Eastern Europe, he wrote to Pears: 'Isn't everything bloody . . . However, we're going away.'

*

The idea of going to America seems first to have occurred to Britten when Pears went there on tour in October 1937. 'I envy you,' he had written before Pears set off. 'In fact I must go myself before long.' In 1930 he had called it 'wicked' that Frank Bridge should have to go abroad to increase his reputation, but nine years later he was apparently eager to take that step himself.

Not that his reputation seemed to need enhancing. For a twenty-five-year-old, he had achieved a remarkable eminence. His new works now received widespread publicity and many repeat performances – he played the Piano Concerto at three more important British concert-halls during the weeks following the Prom. *Variations on a Theme of Frank Bridge* was recorded by the Boyd Neel Orchestra for Decca in July 1938, and of his other principal works only *Our Hunting Fathers* had failed to enter the repertoire. His speed and efficiency at executing commissions for film, radio and theatre meant that he was never short of work, and thanks to this and the enthusiastic support of Ralph Hawkes his income was becoming much more secure. Though the Piano Concerto had had mixed reviews, in general he enjoyed an esteem that must have been the envy of every other composer in the country. 'No composer of today has greater fluency or greater natural gifts,' wrote Constant Lambert in his review of the Concerto, and praise almost as high as this could be found in numerous other articles. His professional life could hardly have been going better. Why then, by October 1938, did he 'v. much want to go to U.S.A.', as he wrote to Ronald Duncan?

It was partly a desire to achieve the same success there as in England. He had been approached by a producer from Paramount in Hollywood to write the score for a projected Arthurian film, *The Knights of the Round Table*, and as he told Wulff 'that means [a] lot of money – & won't we have fun'. He had also begun to realize that America was rich in musical ideas. Aaron Copland had attended the 1938 ISCM festival in London, where his *El Salón México* was performed. Britten, who had first heard Copland's music in 1935, when he judged it 'really beautiful & exhilarating', thought *El Salón* the brightest piece in the festival. He invited Copland to Snape; the visit was a great success, and during it Copland played and sang through his 'play-opera' for high schools, *The Second Hurricane*, which delighted and impressed Britten. Six months later Montagu Slater and his wife gave him *The American Songbag*, the poet Carl Sandburg's compendium of several hundred folk-songs and ballads from all over the USA. Writing to thank the Slaters, Britten told them he was 'now definitely into my "American" period, & nothing can stop me. I hum the tunes & mutter the words all day, & all my ideas now seem to be that way too.'

To another friend, he gave as the principal reason for the journey his desire 'to do some really intensive thinking . . . to do some work to please *myself* & not necessarily the BBC or Basil Dean!' (Dean, the theatrical and film impresario, had recently commissioned a lengthy score from him for J. B. Priestley's West End extravaganza *Johnson Over Jordan*. Britten did the job superbly, but the play closed after a few weeks.)

The suggestion that he needed to go away and rethink his music would have met with agreement from many critics who had reviewed his recent work. Alan Frank, discussing the *Variations on a Theme of Frank Bridge* in the *Musical Times* in July 1938, had suggested that it was 'time that Britten, easily the brightest of the really young English composers, began to settle down again and to start writing music as good as his earliest works were'. Frank was among those who felt that Britten was giving in to the lure of popularity, or was in some fashion failing to measure up to the very considerable promise of the *Sinfonietta* and *A Boy Was Born*. A. H. Fox Strangways in the *Observer* ventured the opinion that Britten might 'never be a big composer because he [has] not quite enough character: he [can] be neither serious nor stupid with real intensity'. Britten himself wryly quoted Vaughan Williams's opinion that he was 'letting the side down' by moving away from the manner of *A Boy Was Born* and becoming 'too Continental & all that!' Even Constant Lambert, who unlike Alan Frank and presumably Vaughan Williams thought the *Variations on a Theme of Frank Bridge* as good as anything Britten had done, was disturbed by what he called the 'increasing brilliancy of technique but hardly an added maturity of thought'.

However, a journey to America and work in Hollywood would not necessarily provide a sabbatical; nor was Britten fair in blaming the BBC for keeping him on a treadmill. Their willingness to commission the Piano Concerto shows that they would now follow where he chose to lead. The obvious way to do some musical rethinking would be to stay exactly where he was and write what he wanted. Indeed, he had already begun a new project of his own devising, which gave evidence of an important change of direction.

Sophie Wyss describes how, some time in 1938, she and Britten

> were travelling back by train after having given a recital together, when he came over to me very excitedly . . . and said that he had just

read the most wonderful poetry by Rimbaud and was so eager to set it to music . . . He was so full of this poetry he just could not stop talking about it. I suspect he must have seen a copy of Rimbaud's works while he was recently staying with Auden in Birmingham.

Auden may have drawn Britten's attention to Rimbaud on account of the poet's homosexual relationship with the older Verlaine (two of whose poems Britten had set in *Quatre Chansons Françaises*). During March 1939, Britten told Wulff Scherchen that he had just written 'two good (!) songs . . . French words. Arthur Rimbaud – marvellous poems.' These were 'Being Beauteous' and 'Marine', and they were performed a month later by Sophie Wyss, accompanied by a string orchestra, in a BBC concert from Birmingham, greatly impressing the critic of the *Birmingham Post* – 'beautiful exercises in the exploitation of vocal technique'. So began a project which seemed to excite Britten much more than the Violin Concerto which he had started, with a somewhat dutiful air, the previous November.

There was at this stage no question of his settling in the USA. His sister Beth, recollecting long after the event, has claimed premonitions that it would not be a short trip – 'I did not know when I would see Ben again', 'We thought that he was going for ever' – but Britten's own letters before leaving give no indication of long-term American plans. He and Pears were to go first to Canada. Indeed, in a letter written shortly before departure, Canada was the only destination definitely envisaged: 'Peter'll be back at the end of the summer, but I have other ideas & may stay on a bit or go to U.S.A.'

There seemed no obvious reason for Pears to make the trip. He had been to America twice on tour with the New English Singers, and had made friends there, but stood little chance of achieving much during a short and scarcely planned visit. It is true that he and Britten were beginning to perform together; their first recital seems to have been on 17 February 1939 at the Master's Lodging in Balliol College, Oxford. But most of their friends were surprised that they were going together. Basil Douglas regarded both of them as homosexual but had not thought of them as a pair; however, 'I realized that if they were good enough friends to go to America together they must be pretty close.'

There is no evidence that they had yet begun a physical relationship. William Coldstream may have summed up the situation accurately when he wrote in his notebook an account of a party given by Britten at the Hallam Street flat on 17 January 1939. He referred to Pears as 'a singer who lives with Benjamin', and listed among the guests 'a German boy friend of Benjamin's'. Twenty years later, Britten himself described his pre-America relationship with Pears as a friendship based on the intellect: 'I liked him enormously, admired his way of thinking, found him stimulating.' With Lennox Berkeley, however, the situation was more complicated.

Berkeley now seems to have been pressing his attentions on Britten. He gave him the use of an AC sports car, hand-made to order. Wulff Scherchen describes Britten taking him for jaunts in it at terrifying speeds. A letter from Britten to Pears on 16 March 1939 indicates that Britten found Berkeley's adoration stifling, and sometimes showed it:

> Well, the car is a wonder . . . I managed her like a school-boy on Saturday – and even you wouldn't have been frightened. I let L.B. drive for a bit and it wasn't *too* bad. However, re. him we've had a bit of a crisis and I'm only too thankful to be going away. I had the most fearful feeling of revulsion the other day – conscience and all that – just like the old days. He's been very upset, poor dear – but that makes it worse! I wish you were here, old dear, because I want terribly to tell someone.

Jackie Hewitt, Christopher Isherwood's boyfriend at this date, had got to know Britten and Pears quite well – he looked after the Hallam Street flat when they left for America – and says he gathered that Berkeley and Britten were now having sexual relations, 'which Ben didn't care for'. John Evans, who knew Pears in the eighties, says that 'Peter always gave me the impression that Ben and Lennox had had a sexual relationship, and that Ben was happy to get out of it.' The fact that in 1939 Britten confided about it to Pears suggests that their own relationship, too, was extremely close. Certainly Pears was now deeply attached to Britten. 'Benjie my dear,' he wrote to him during 1938, 'I miss you very much, Benjie . . . I miss you v. v. much . . . Much Love. Benjie darling . . . Lots of love Peter.' Britten, on the other hand, tended to end his letters to Pears merely with 'Much love, Benjamin,' and did not go in for endearments of the same sort.

Pears's own recollections many years later give no hint of the complexities behind the journey to America. 'Somehow things weren't working awfully well in England,' he said in Tony Palmer's 1980 television documentary *A Time There Was*,

> at least [Ben] didn't think they were . . . and we were both pacifists, and we didn't much see what we were going to do [when war broke out]. Short of going to prison or something for a long time, which didn't

terribly appeal . . . And so we decided – as Auden had earlier – that the only thing to do was to go to America.

Pacifism was certainly a principal cause of their remaining in America after the outbreak of war, but when they set out across the Atlantic war was not a certainty, nor is it clear that at that date they thought of themselves as irrevocably pacifist. Certainly Britten had been through a pacifist phase earlier in the thirties, but the issue does not seem to have concerned him quite so much towards the end of the decade. Pears's reference to Auden, however, has very much the ring of truth.

Since 1935, Britten had been following Auden's lead in many aspects of his life, and the fact that Auden and Isherwood had left for New York in January 1939 undoubtedly encouraged him to go too a few weeks later. There is no evidence that the Britten–Pears trip was arranged before Auden had left. Auden's own motives for his journey were confused and largely indeterminate, but Britten would probably not have been aware of this, and once again he followed obediently.

Wulff Scherchen came to one of several farewell parties that were given for Britten and Pears, though he felt that 'I didn't fit into this crowd' – the homosexual circle that gathered around the departing musicians. Britten slipped away to take Wulff to Liverpool Street in a taxi, and put him on the last train to Cambridge. He was extremely discreet about his private life, but he confided in Enid Slater, for whose husband Montagu's Left Theatre plays he had written music. 'One relationship had got difficult before he went to America', Mrs Slater recalled many years later, 'and I used to go and try and sort things out a bit.' The need for a cooling-off period with regard to Wulff was another motive for the American journey; possibly the strongest of all.

There was another party at Hallam Street on the night before departure. 'I say "party",' Britten wrote to Wulff, 'but it was rather a sort of "drop-in" with a bottle of sherry on the floor.' Both his sisters were there, Beth with Kit and their new baby, and among the friends were Trevor Harvey and Antonio Brosa. The next morning, 29 April, Harvey, Ralph Hawkes and Barbara went with Britten and Pears in the train to Southampton, where they found Frank and Ethel Bridge, who had driven from Friston – 'darned nice of them', said Britten. Just as he and Pears were boarding the *Ausonia*, which would take them to Quebec, Frank Bridge, who may have suspected that they were going for more than a few weeks, and possibly feared that he would never see Britten again, stepped forward and gave him his viola.

*

'A thousand reasons – mostly "problems" – have brought me away,' Britten wrote to Aaron Copland a few days later, during the voyage. 'I got heavily tied up in a certain direction, which is partly why I'm crossing the ocean.' Already he was having second thoughts. 'What a fool one is to come away,' he wrote to Wulff; 'the more I think of Snape . . . the more I feel a fool to have left it all.' Wulff's photograph was on his cabin table.

At first the voyage was 'bloody boring'; there was a 'terrific gale' and even 'ice bumping against the ship', though towards the end of the journey 'Peter & I gave a recital.' They berthed briefly in Quebec on 9 May, then sailed on to Montreal, where Britten was welcomed by the music department of CBC (Canadian Broadcasting Corporation), who had intended to mark his arrival with a broadcast of *Variations on a Theme of Frank Bridge* – 'but the band wasn't big or good enough & anyhow, the boat was late'. A performance was, however, planned for a few weeks later, and Britten decided to remain in the area for it. He and Pears found a comfortable hotel in the hills, and Britten spent a week writing the incidental music for a BBC radio adaptation of one of his favourite books, T. H. White's *The Sword in the Stone*, about the boyhood of King Arthur. With this posted off to London he turned back to 'the Rimbaud suite' and the Violin Concerto. The plan was still for Pears to return to England after a few weeks, '& I stay on *if* money lasts', Britten wrote to Copland. Meanwhile Britten wrote to Beth: 'We are getting on well together & no fights . . . We are going for a picnic to-day . . . both our companions are of the fair sex & pretty fair at that! Don't be surprised if I've changed my state when I get back.'

During May a letter arrived from Auden, who was teaching for a few weeks in Massachusetts: 'I am mad with happiness, but will tell you all about it when we meet.' A later note explained that he had fallen in love with an eighteen-year-old New Yorker, Chester Kallman: 'I am so anxious for you to meet Chester, though a little frightened as he is extremely musical, and you do play so fast.' Britten told Auden he hoped to see him soon: 'The next time you write – *please* give me an outline of your plans for Autumn . . . Much love, old thing.' Auden sent him words for another cabaret song, a calypso inspired by his new love-affair:

> Driver, drive faster and make a good run
> Down the Springfield Line under the shining sun,
> Fly like an aeroplane, don't pull up short
> Till you brake for the Grand Central Station, New York.
> For there in the middle of that waiting hall
> Should be standing the one that I love best of all . . .

Britten was delighted with the words – 'Calypso is grand for Hedli' – but made no comment on the real events behind them. Discussing another cabaret lyric Auden had sent him, he suggested this couplet, his own composition:

> Most shout the names they think are fine
> But I daren't mutter the name of mine.

He wrote to Beth that he had had 'a letter from Wulff this morning by Air Mail', and to Enid Slater he referred to Wulff in terms which suggest that he had resolved to end the relationship, but was finding it difficult. She was to go to Snape 'as often as you can ... *And* Cambridge', where Wulff lived, because 'I've just had a very sweet letter – & nearly broken all my resolutions.'

On 7 June he and Pears paid a short visit to Toronto to arrange the broadcast of *Variations on a Theme of Frank Bridge* and a joint recital. They stayed at a hotel in University Avenue. According to Pears, it was there that their relationship underwent a significant change. Long afterwards he pointed out the hotel to the opera producer Basil Coleman, and said it was there that he and Britten realized that they were in love with each other. Pears's letters to Britten suggest that he had reached that state at least a year earlier. Perhaps Britten now began to respond. 'I wonder if you remember what happened at Toronto 19½ years ago?' Pears wrote to Britten when he was in that city in February 1959. 'It is a place which cannot help having a certain importance in my life.'

Four days later, they crossed the border into the USA and stayed for ten days, 9–19 June, in Grand Rapids, Michigan, with Harold Einecke, organist of Park (First) Congregational Church, and his wife, Mary, whom Pears had met on one of his American tours with the New English Singers. Here, the relationship went one stage further. Six months later, Pears wrote to Britten: 'I shall never forget a certain night in Grand Rapids.' Thirty-five years later he told him: 'it is *you* who have given *me* everything, right from the beginning, from yourself in Grand Rapids'.

While some form of physical relations may have begun between the two before they left England, it was evidently at Grand Rapids that what Pears regarded as a consummation took place. Pears's biographer Christopher Headington asked Walter Hussey, an Anglican clergyman who knew them both well, what Britten and Pears did together in bed, and was told that Britten liked to be the passive partner. Hussey's source was probably Pears, who seems to have liked to talk about it. Britten himself alluded to it to Rita Thomson. She says he told her that he was the more masculine of the couple in every respect except in bed: 'He said that he was really the male partner, except for making love.'

It was presumably in Grand Rapids that this full-scale sexual relationship began. Yet Britten's letters to Wulff Scherchen give only the faintest hint of any development between him and Pears. 'Peter sends his love, & says he's looking after me – as he certainly is – like a mother hen. He's a darling – .' If, like Pears, he regarded what had happened as a consummation or surrender, it did not affect his feelings for Wulff. In the same letter he wrote to the boy: 'How I wish I could get you out here . . .'

3 : Stuck here

Britten was delighted with the amount of publicity he was attracting in Canada and Michigan – 'interviews with press . . . & meeting conductors etc. In fact the more I get about here', he told Ralph Hawkes, 'the more I feel that – should I stay out [for] the autumn – lots of shows might be fixed . . . People are so friendly.' On 20 June 1939 he wrote from Toronto to Wulff Scherchen: 'I'm thinking hard about the future. This *may* be the Country. There's so much that is unknown about it – & it is tremendously large & beautiful. *And* it is enterprising & vital.' Five days later, he wrote to Beth:

> I might as well confess it now, that I am seriously considering staying over here permanently. I haven't decided yet of course and I'm terribly torn, but I admit that if a definite offer turned up (and there are several in the air) I might take it. Use your judgement as to whether you tell anyone. As it is so much in the air I suggest you don't . . . Canada is an extraordinary place. I am *certain* that N. America is the place of the future . . . & though certainly one is worried by a lack of culture, there is terrific energy & vitality in the place.

This mood had somewhat evaporated two days later, when he and Pears set off for New York. Britten wrote to Enid Slater that he was 'nervous' about coping with the big city – 'I can't do that sort of thing very well!' – and admitted that snapshots of friends sent from England made him homesick. He said that the political situation in Europe looked 'very black to us', though 'Here, I'm afraid, one is inclined to speak of Europe in the past tense' (it could have been Auden writing).

Arriving in New York, they booked into the George Washington Hotel on 23rd Street and Lexington Avenue, a cheap establishment recommended by Auden, and were taken on the town by Hans Heinsheimer, the music publisher whom Britten had met in Vienna in 1934, and who was now working for Boosey & Hawkes in New York. Pears already knew the city, so Heinsheimer, who loved the place, concentrated on showing it off to Britten. 'It was an absolute fiasco,' he recalls. 'The noise, the dirt ... and I'd said: "Isn't it marvellous?" ... I still remember this unbelievably polite smile Ben had ... but really it was a flop.' In fact initially Britten liked it more than Heinsheimer realized. 'New York is a staggering place', he wrote to Wulff, '*very* beautiful in some ways – intensely alive & doing – bewildering in some ways, but always interesting.'

Heinsheimer told him that the opportunities for a composer of his talents were 'immense'. Indeed, he was already attracting attention. When the New York Philharmonic Orchestra played *Variations on a Theme of Frank Bridge* to an audience of several thousand at an open-air concert on 12 July, Britten 'had to come on the stage & bow twice – !!', and there was considerable press coverage. With Heinsheimer, he discussed the possibility of writing an 'operetta for children', with words by Auden – an idea no doubt sparked off by Copland's *The Second Hurricane*. He and Pears went up to Woodstock in the Catskills to see Copland, who had a home there. They liked it so much that they decided to rent a studio for part of the summer.

In Woodstock, Britten worked at a commission for CBC Toronto, a 'fanfare' for piano and orchestra. Meanwhile Pears helped by copying out vocal scores of songs from the still unfinished Rimbaud cycle, now entitled *Les Illuminations*. Spare time was spent at Copland's house, swimming and sunbathing. Britten told Enid Slater that the 'fanfare' was 'rather inspired by such sunshine as I've never seen before'. Entitled *Young Apollo*, it was broadcast from Toronto on 27 August with Britten as piano soloist. He allotted it an opus number (16) but later withdrew it. He told Wulff Scherchen it was 'founded on last lines of Keats' Hyperion', which describe the young Apollo's 'golden tresses' and 'limbs / Celestial'. He also made it clear that Wulff himself was the subject of the piece: 'You know whom that's written about.'

At Woodstock, Britten and Pears talked to Copland about the prospect of war. Copland recalls that they 'worried constantly about whether to return to England'. After they had left he wrote to Britten: 'I think you absolutely owe it to England to stay here ... After all anyone can shoot a gun – but how many can write music like you?'

Britten had contemplated visiting California in the early autumn. The Hollywood job had faded, but Auden had arrived there, at the conclusion of a 'honeymoon' with Chester Kallman, and had issued an invitation. In the event, Britten changed his plan, and in late August he and Pears went to stay on Long Island with a family Pears had met on his 1936 journey to America with the New English Singers. Mrs Elizabeth Mayer had been travelling with two of her children on the same ship as Pears, to join her psychiatrist husband, who being Jewish had already fled from Munich. By 1939 he held a post at the Long Island Home, a psychiatric clinic in Amityville. There, Britten and Pears were made welcome by the Mayers.

From Amityville, Britten wrote to his sister Barbara, just after Britain had declared war on 3 September: 'You can't tell how glad I was to get your wire, & to know that you are well.' She had advised him to stay in America for the time being. 'So far I am taking your advice,' he wrote, 'because (a) I hear that we are not wanted back (b) if I come I should only be put in prison – which seems silly, just to do nothing & eat up food ... God, what a mess man has made of things. And force has never done any good.' The statement that British citizens living or staying in America at the outbreak of war were 'not wanted back' by their Government is corroborated by Auden's experience a few months later. 'I went to the British Embassy', he wrote to a friend in June 1940, 'to see if they had any suggestions and was told that only technically qualified people are wanted back.' Britten and Pears made similar approaches to the authorities during 1939 and 1940, with the same result. But Britten's 'if I come home I should be put in prison' begs more questions. Merely to identify oneself as a pacifist did not lead to a prison sentence. Many sorts of non-military war work were permitted by the conscientious objectors' tribunals. In any case, until now Britten had not made it clear that he would take up a pacifist stance to the war.

When in December 1936 Auden had told him that he was going to fight in the Spanish Civil War, Britten had tried to dissuade him not on pacifist grounds, but with the same argument that Copland used in 1939 – 'what the Spanish Gov. might gain ... is nothing compared with the world's gain by his continuing to write'. Certainly Britten's diaries are full of expressions of horror at the mass killings in Spain, but no unambiguous indication of pacifism is recorded after his door-to-door peace ballot leafleting in 1935. His score for the film *Peace of Britain* in the following year, and the writing of the *Pacifist March* for the Peace Pledge Union, indicate a continuing sympathy for the cause, and certainly his identification of himself as a pacifist in September 1939 was not a radical departure from his stance during the thirties; but it was not inevitable.

That he should declare himself pacifist at this juncture may have something to do with Auden's recent intellectual history. During his 'honeymoon', Auden had been writing a set of prose *pensées* in which he considered the implications of his recent revulsion from politics, and his conviction that the artist must stand aloof from the public fracas. By the time he returned to New York and saw Britten – for the first time since they had both left England – he had decided that 'my position forbids me to act as a combatant in any war'. He did not wish to be identified as a pacifist (it was always in his nature to create movements rather than join existing ones), but he announced that during the war he would perform only 'non-violent' actions. He commemorated this decision in his poem 'September 1, 1939', with its conclusion 'We must love one another or die.' It is unimaginable that the ever-didactic Auden should not have talked in these terms to Britten. (The precise date of their meeting in New York is not known, but it was before 3 September when war was declared.) Indeed, Britten's letter to his sister suggests that he was leaving decisions about his and Pears's future to Auden: 'I've seen & am seeing Auden a lot, & our immediate future is locked with his, it seems.'

Writing to Ralph Hawkes on or shortly after 3 September, Britten made no mention of pacifism, but simply stated: 'It looks as if I shall be out here for a bit still – I have lots of things to do.' And to Aaron Copland on 10 September, replying to Copland's counsel not to return to England and fight: 'Thank you so much for your letter – it was honestly a great comfort.' Again there was no mention of pacifism. He added: 'Peter is still here – I persuaded him to stay, so that *if* we had to go back we could at least go together.' (Pears had had a passage booked on the *Queen Mary* on 23 August, so it is evident that Britten persuaded him to stay before war was a certainty.) The letter continued: 'We are staying with a friend of his (a Psychiatrist – German refugee who has a job here) – & they couldn't be nicer or more opportune!'

Elizabeth Mayer, in whose home they were staying, had studied music in her youth in the hope of becoming a concert pianist. When marriage ruled that out, she transferred her hopes to her children – 'my mother had four children because she wanted a quartet', remarks her son Michael – and when they failed her musically, she looked elsewhere. In Munich she had held open house to musicians, and when Pears and Britten arrived on her doorstep in 1939 it was apparent to her family that, in her daughter Beata's words, 'Ben and Peter were in a way the children she had always wanted to have.'

'Mrs Mayer is such an angel,' Britten wrote to his sister Beth, '& looks after me like a mother.' Pears describes the relationship in similar terms, in a 1985 interview:

> She was – I was going to say, a sort of goddess, because she had a godlike quality. She was a very, very remarkable woman . . . She loved

us dearly, and we loved her dearly, and it was an extraordinary arrangement. She wanted to help Ben as much as she possibly could, and offered us both, in fact, this wonderful hospitality to (sometimes) the inconvenience, I think, of the family, because they were not over-housed. The house was quite a simple one, in the grounds of a mental home ... She couldn't have been kinder to us; indeed the children really were too. I think they must have felt sometimes supplanted. They were absolute dears.

Britten portrayed the Mayer household in a letter to Enid Slater, written two and a half months after he and Pears had moved in:

Peter & I have found some wonderful friends – who are (luckily) devoted to us – & on no account will let us depart. They are German émigrés (from Munich). He – is a Psychiatrist & an assistant at this mental Home. She – is one of those grand people who have been essential through the ages for the production of art; really sympathetic & enthusiastic, with instinctive good taste (in all the arts) & a great friend of thousands of those poor fish – artists. She is never happy unless she has them all around her – living here or round about at the moment are lots of them – many refugees ... I think she's one of the few really good people in the world – & I find her essential in these times when one has rather lost faith in human nature.

As Pears indicates, Stanton Cottage, the Mayers' residence in the grounds of the Long Island Home, was far from large. There were only two bedrooms and, according to family recollections, Britten and Pears were given one of these, displacing those of the Mayer sons and daughters who were still at home. However, by November 1939 they were sleeping in the house of the superintendent of the Home, Dr William Titley, an enthusiastic amateur pianist, 'tho' we eat chez Mayer'. The Mayer children believe their mother was utterly unaware that her guests were more than friends with each other.

Lennox Berkeley, besides being on the other side of the Atlantic, was now *persona non grata* with Britten. Writing to Enid Slater in November 1939, Britten observed of him:

re other little problems my mind is firmly made up. You cannot think what distance does! Things can be examined in the cold light of 3000 miles, & don't look so nice! Besides letters from the Mill have been dreadful. The only person who wrote to me about 'duty', 'conscience' – 'being a pacifist at heart, but this was a war, etc.' – (sic, sic, SIC!!!); was he of that noble ancestry.

Berkeley (to whose aristocratic connections Britten alludes) had written to Britten on the day that war was declared: 'I've always been a pacifist at heart, how can one be anything else? But I think if there ever was a case where force has got to be used, this is it.' Yet the letter continued: 'Ben dear, for heaven's sake don't come back ... You must be able to go on writing ... anyhow only you can decide what you think the right thing to do.' There was no trace in this letter of the jingoism imputed by Britten. (Berkeley himself was thirty-six, too old to be called up.) But Britten seemed determined to blacken Berkeley to his friends. Though he and Berkeley continued to correspond with every appearance of warmth on Britten's side, not long after war had broken out Britten wrote to Hedli Anderson: 'oh Hedli, what a bloody fool I was about that – one sees so much more clearly when one's away. He's just NO GOOD.'

Britten finished writing *Les Illuminations* during October 1939. The cycle uses only a fraction of the poems and prose-poems from Rimbaud's book of that name, in an order of Britten's devising. The Fanfare with which it opens, a setting of the words 'J'ai seul la clef de cette parade sauvage' ('I alone hold the key to this savage parade'), is a pointer to the highly personal nature of what is to follow.

After the fanfare comes 'Villes', in which Rimbaud describes the bustle of life in an industrial city – 'a very good impression of the chaotic modern city life', Britten wrote to Sophie Wyss, adding that he believed Rimbaud had London in mind. His music for this poem, written in October 1939, perhaps sketches the New York bustle, though the song is probably also meant to portray the lure of worldly success. Towards the end the pace relaxes and the singer, as Britten puts it in the letter to Wyss, utters 'a prayer for a little peace' – wishes to withdraw from these superficialities into the world of private emotion. Next, the dreamy and transitional 'Phrase' leads into 'Antique', written in March 1939 before Britten left England, and dedicated by him to 'K.H.W.S.', the initials of Wulff Scherchen: 'Oh, gracious son of Pan! Thine eyes – those precious globes – glance slowly; thy brow is crowned with little flowers and berries ... Thy heart beats in that womb where sleeps Hermaphrodite. Walk at night, softly moving this thigh, the other thigh, this left leg.' (This is the translation by Helen Rootham which Britten used and which is printed in the vocal score.) Britten's setting of these words to a languid dance rhythm is strikingly simple melodically – the 'tune' is chiefly made up of arpeggios of a major chord, like a child's piano practice, so that the music manages to be highly sensual while also suggesting juvenile innocence. The happy love-affair implied by 'Antique' is presumably the cause of the exuberance of the two songs that follow, 'Royauté', in which a loving couple think themselves king and queen, and 'Marine', an ecstatic vision of seascapes.

The second half of *Les Illuminations* opens with the singer again asserting 'J'ai seul la clef...', this time within a much more sombre orchestral meditation, which Britten told Sophie Wyss was 'a reproof for the exaggeratedly ecstatic mood of Marine'. This interlude is dedicated to an appropriately serious and parental figure, 'E.M.', Elizabeth Mayer. Following it comes a setting of Rimbaud's 'Being Beauteous' (he gave his prose-poem an English title). The Rimbaud text is orgiastically sexual: '... dying breaths ... cause this adored body to rise, to swell ... Scarlet and black wounds break out of the superb flesh ... Shudders rise and mutter ... Oh rapture! Our bones are covered anew with a body of love ... And there is the cannon upon which I must cast myself...' Britten's music sets these words graphically. The song, written in March 1939 (that is, before the visit to Grand Rapids), is dedicated 'To P.N.L.P.', Peter Neville Luard Pears.

The 'K.W.H.S.' song in the first part of *Les Illuminations* engendered cheerfully ecstatic reactions in the two following pieces. The 'P.N.L.P.' song in the second part has no such unclouded results. It is followed by 'Parade', in which Rimbaud describes 'very sturdy rogues' who 'have made use of you and your like', with their 'bestial poses and caresses'. (A line omitted by Britten specifies that these people are denizens of the homosexual underworld, 'catamites ... rigged out in revolting *luxury*', as the Penguin translation puts it.) Britten's vivid treatment of these words is based on the original version of the *Alla Marcia* incorporated into his string quartet subtitled '*Go play, boy, play*' in which he had attempted to portray Francis Barton and other schoolboy loves. This hell of grotesque sexuality, *Les Illuminations* seems to be saying, is where his adolescent crushes have finally brought him.

Beata Sauerlander (Mayer) confirms that this appeared to be Britten's mood during these months: 'Peter seemed to be at ease with his homosexuality. And I had the feeling that Ben felt guilty.'

*

'My Darling Ben,' Pears wrote on 9 January 1940 to Britten, who had left Amityville for a visit to the Midwest,

> It was marvellous to get your letter ... I was so sad that you were depressed and cold – I wanted to hop into a plane and come over and comfort you at once. I would have kissed you all over & then blown all over you there & then – & – & then you'd have been as warm as toast! ... I shall never forget a certain night in Grand Rapids – Ich liebe dich,

io t'amo, jeg elske dyg(?), je t'aime, in fact, my little white-thighed
beauty, I'm terribly in love with you –

P.

No reply from Britten survives, but a note from him to Elizabeth Mayer,
written during this trip, hints that he found Pears somewhat overwhelming: 'Do you know when I'm by myself I'm pretty efficient at arranging
matters – booking rooms, tickets etc, & getting about. It's only when
Peter's around that I become so shy & retiring – what – what! Don't tell
him tho' –'.

In another letter during this separation, Pears told Britten: 'I am worth
nothing without you.' He addressed him as 'my pussy-cat', and began
one letter to him 'My boy'.

In an interview after Britten's death, he remarked: 'I was aware, I
suppose, that I did dominate Ben.' William Servaes, who knew both men
well at the end of their lives, observes of the relationship: 'Peter wasn't
Svengali, but in a way – and this sounds like putting down Ben, which I
don't mean to – he was a sort of puppet-master. I think (and I'm going to
get on very thin ice, because I'm not a psychologist) that Ben needed to be
dominated, and that Peter did it.' The musicologist Deryck Cooke once
attended a dinner party given by the critic and Britten enthusiast Hans
Keller, at which Keller challenged Britten's pacificism in the light of the
1967 Israeli-Arab War. Eventually Britten and Pears walked out. Afterwards Cooke told Colin Matthews that

he could never forget the figure of Pears standing behind Ben, and
feeling that he was being Svengali. It was an argument about pacifism,
for which Ben couldn't provide an intellectual justification, and of
course against somebody like Keller he didn't have a chance. And
Cooke said he had a terribly strong feeling of this sinister figure
controlling Britten.

Pears was not the only person who wrote lovingly to Britten when he
was away from Amityville early in 1940.

My darling,
    ... How I miss you, dear boy, how I miss you! ... Everything here
awaits you patiently. Your table at the window, the little piece of red
blotting paper, which made me cry silently, the ruler ... Good night,
darling. I hope you'll have more rest in Ch[icago] than here ... I long
to see you again.

Elizabeth

This letter from Elizabeth Mayer, which received an equally affectionate reply from 'Your very loving Benjamin', shows how completely she had stepped into his mother's shoes.

He had gone to the Midwest to play his Piano Concerto in Chicago, and to give interviews and attend parties. Max Winkler of Belwin Music, Boosey & Hawkes's partners in New York, was getting him as much publicity as possible, with a view to establishing him in American music. Ralph Hawkes suggested that if he came back to Britain, he could 'get you made a Bandmaster or put you in a Band,' and understandably Britten preferred Winkler's offer to sign him up with a financial retainer. He was to write 'simple marketable works' of all kinds, the first major commission being the 'High School Operetta' with Auden as librettist. Work was well in progress by the end of 1939, with the mythical lumberjack Paul Bunyan as subject, and there was hope of a Broadway première.

Meanwhile the Violin Concerto was finished, and a New York performance scheduled, and Ralph Hawkes told Britten that the Japanese Government was commissioning orchestral works to celebrate the 2,600th anniversary of its empire. Britten decided to offer them 'a short Symphony – or Symphonic poem. Called Sinfonia da Requiem (rather topical, but not of course mentioning dates or places!) which sounds rather what they would like.' He told a newspaper that the Sinfonia would be dedicated 'to the memory of my parents', and would express 'my own anti-war conviction'. Lennox Berkeley observed that 'the Jap: Government' commissioning an anti-war work 'seems a piece of disconcerting irony', but the commission promised a good financial return, and by the end of 1939 Britten's worries about how he would survive financially in the USA had begun to evaporate. The British authorities still had no interest in his or Pears's return home, and the two began to consider renting their own house in Amityville. Meanwhile Pears's voice was improving spectacularly. As Pears himself wrote to a friend, it had become 'bigger, easier, brighter, more telling', the result of intensive practice and breathing exercises. 'Some wonderful friends of mine from Munich have put us up', Pears added, 'and we are staying indefinitely. We couldn't be happier . . .'

Yet Britten gave some evidence of not being so happy. He came back from Chicago with a 'vile cold & flu', and by mid-February 1940 was seriously ill. 'His temperature ran high up to 104° and a bit,' Pears reported to Beth Welford:

> you can guess it was a bit alarming . . . Dr Mayer who was in charge was confident about it, but when his temperature suddenly went up to

107° for a bit last Sunday night, he got a specialist . . . apparently, he's all right . . . (heart, lungs, chest, etc. in perfect condition) but . . . he has to take it very easy indeed . . . as . . . there are always possibilities of complications.

Beata Mayer had served as a nurse in Italy before coming to America, and she looked after Britten at night: 'I remember quite clearly many nights he was really, I think, delirious. He talked and talked . . . about his childhood, I remember, about his school-days constantly.' (It was now that he alluded to sexual trauma at school.)

Auden, who believed that illness was psychosomatic in origin, diagnosed Britten as suffering from indecision about staying in America. Certainly there seemed to be no physical reason why his ill health should persist, as it did, throughout the spring of 1940. (The last time he had been ill like this was at Gresham's, when the sick-room had provided a retreat from the harshness of school.) Britten himself eventually came to the conclusion that his condition had a psychological cause. 'Outwardly the ailment was infected tonsils,' he said in a 1959 interview. 'But the real cause was my mental perplexities.'

When Antonio Brosa came over to New York to give the first performance of the Britten Violin Concerto with John Barbirolli and the New York Philharmonic at Carnegie Hall on 28 March 1940, Britten only just managed to get to the performance – 'The bug hasn't completely left me yet,' he wrote to Kit Welford. 'Toni played marvellously,' he reported, and the Concerto had a 'wonderful reception' from the audience. 'The N.Y. Times old critic (who is the snarkyest & most coveted here) was won over, so that was fine.' This critic, Olin Downes, wrote in the *New York Times* with cautious approval, particularly praising the orchestration: 'There is modern employment of percussion instruments.' Indeed the Violin Concerto opens with a staccato figure stated by unaccompanied timpani and cymbals, a sinister repeating motto which is taken up by bassoon and horn before the solo violin's passionately melancholy entry. Undoubtedly the work, conceived during the first half of 1939 and sketched that summer, acquired some of its character from external events. '. . . just completed the score of my Violin Concerto,' Britten wrote to Wulff Scherchen on 29 September 1939, adding that 'it is at times like these that work is so important – that humans can think of other things than blowing each other up! . . . I try not to listen to the Radio more than I can help.' Yet the Concerto also gives the impression of a painful internal struggle which gradually resolves itself into resigned melancholy. It ends inconclusively.

'... in so many ways this country is such a terrible disappointment,' Britten wrote to Kit Welford after describing the Concerto's successful première. He was appalled by the political corruption, the paranoid fear of Communism 'in which anything vaguely liberal is labelled as Communist & treated as such', and the ignorant bigotry which had, for example, prevented Bertrand Russell from teaching at New York University. As to the city itself, his earlier delight had melted away. 'I hate New York ... Everything here is crazes – crazes – crazes. You see – I'm gradually realising that I'm English – & as a composer I suppose I feel I want more definite roots than other people.' Such a letter, written on 4 April 1940, might have been expected to announce his return home. 'But against all this,' he continued,

> one must put the facts that U.S.A. is *not* engaged solely with killing people ... enterprise *still* is rewarded in this country, & I'm sure there is a future for this country altho' the next decade or so may be very black ... Don't take my tirade too seriously, Kit, because I'm still feeling a bit (convalescently) down after my bug.

He urged Kit to consider emigrating to America himself. Three days later, writing to John Pounder, he gave a more honest account of his reasons for staying: 'Personally I'm crazily homesick, & if it were not that Peter looks after me like a lover, & the family Mayer were surely made in heaven, & that Wystan Auden's about the place & always coming down here, I should be home, war or no war, like a shot.'

*

Pears was now having singing lessons in New York with Thérèse Schnabel, the German alto, and Britten wrote to Sophie Wyss that 'the improvement in his voice after only a month is quite staggering'. (After a few months he changed to another teacher, Clytie Mundy.) He had been booked to sing *Les Illuminations* in Chicago (the performance did not take place because of financial complications; the entire work was given its première by Sophie Wyss with the Boyd Neel Orchestra in London on 30 January 1940), and he seemed likely to make a name for himself in America, whereas in London most work for singers had vanished with the war. As to Auden, he was as powerful an influence over Britten as ever, and he had decided to stay in America.

To Lennox Berkeley, Britten wrote in January 1940: 'I've seen Wystan – a very changed Wystan – a lot & it looks as if we shall be doing the same things for a period of time now ... more & more I am being pushed off my old materialistic beliefs.' This refers to the fact that Auden had now entered a 'philosophical' phase, with leanings towards religion. He demonstrated this in his long poem *New Year Letter*, written in January 1940 and addressed to Elizabeth Mayer. It was an elaborate justification of his decision to remain in the USA, on intellectual grounds. Yet Auden admitted to a friend in England that his chief reason for staying was that 'for the first time, I have a happy personal life' – his affair with Chester Kallman. Britten may not have realized it was as simple as that; to him, Auden was still Uncle Wiz, who must know best. In fact Britten's own hope at this date seems to have been that America would enter the war, providing him with a reason for returning to England. 'I suppose', he told John Pounder, 'America will be in this war within a year & then I'll be back.'

However, 'for the moment I am stuck here,' he wrote to Beth. Suddenly, he had to carry out the Japanese commission: 'I now find myself with the proposition of writing a Symphony in about 3 weeks!' he told her on 26 April 1940. 'Something went wrong with negotiations . . . & I only heard officially on Friday.' The *Sinfonia da Requiem* was written in 'a terrible hurry' and finished early in June, the composition sketch being in the form of a piano duet, so that it could be tried out at the keyboard with Pears assisting. The Japanese Government 'paid up on the dot', and Britten was asked to go to Tokyo to attend the festivities. 'So I may be leaving for the rising Sun in September,' he told Beth. Meanwhile he occupied himself writing a set of *Diversions* for piano (left hand) and orchestra, commissioned by the one-armed pianist Paul Wittgenstein, brother of the philosopher, and in trying to discover the whereabouts of Wulff Scherchen, who had been interned somewhere in England on account of his German nationality, and was being shipped to Canada. By August, Wulff had surfaced in a camp near Ottawa, and Britten wrote at once: 'I hope things aren't too bad, my dear. Although I haven't written I have thought about you constantly.' Censorship of mail made it impossible to say more.

Britten now had enough money to buy an elderly car, in which, during August, he and Pears travelled around New England, meeting Auden *en route* for work on *Paul Bunyan*. The weather was excellent but Pears reported: 'Ben caught an awful cold which he's still got.' Britten himself wrote that his temperature had risen to 'about 103°', and admitted in a letter to Beth that he was not altogether enthusiastic about returning to the Mayer household:

> one gets a bit tired of it – you see the Home is really a small village where everyone knows everyone & everyone's business, & the intrigues & scandals are unbelievable . . . Mrs Mayer, darling as she is, is inclined to put people's backs up by not being very tactful. Of course

she *is* very intelligent & has met lots of poets & writers & can speak six languages, but that doesn't excuse her in the eyes of the assistant-secretary who has been snubbed for talking of the new doctor's lady-friend – etc. etc. etc. So it's all a bit trying . . .

The same letter also contained a hint that he and Pears might not go on living together: 'Actually Peter ought to be more in New York next season, so we'll have to see whether we can afford a room for him somewhere & I'll go on living at Amityville.'

*

Plans worked out differently. 'Peter & I are going to take a flat with Wystan Auden for the winter in Brooklyn,' Britten told Beth on 18 September. 'We feel we have to be nearer the big city where things go on & jobs are born . . . But I loathe the idea of living in a town again . . . The flat . . . is . . . hideously expensive.' So why was he making the move? 'There are so many alternatives as to what to do, & what one *wants* to do too – that I, who never was good at decisions, don't know where I am.' Auden wanted a large apartment which he could share with Kallman, and needed to sub-let some of the rooms, while Pears would benefit from musical contacts in the city.

The apartment was not taken, and instead Auden, Pears and Britten joined an experiment in communal living set up by a bisexual New York littérateur, George Davis, at 7 Middagh Street, Brooklyn Heights, a big brownstone house. Britten had never lived anywhere remotely like it. 'The house in Brooklyn is still in a great deal of a mess,' he told Antonio Brosa in mid-December 1940, several weeks after moving in. There had been a house-warming party at which 'Gypsie Rose Lee was a feature and we played murder all over the house and you could not imagine a better setting for it.' The other residents were writer and composer Paul Bowles and his wife Jane, novelist Carson McCullers, Thomas Mann's son Golo, and Oliver Smith the theatre designer. Large numbers of other New York bohemians came and went. Auden appointed himself house-mother and announced rules and regulations which no one observed. He also made out bills for everyone: one of them survives among Britten's papers. It is headed 'Bengy and Peter' and itemizes 'food for two weeks . . . Service, laundry, coal etc.' Meanwhile George Davis wandered around naked with a cigarette in his mouth. Pears has called the ménage 'sordid beyond belief', but at the time he evidently enjoyed it. Britten's letter about the house-warming describes 'Peter and George Davis . . . doing a ballet to Petrushka, up the curtains and the hot water pipes – an impressive if destructive sight'. Britten himself saw the funny side of the place, but hated being back in New York. 'I am *not* enjoying . . . the city one likkle bit,' he told Elizabeth Mayer, and the tempo of life in Middagh Street did not suit his needs. 'I find it almost impossible to work', he wrote to Antonio Brosa, 'and retire to Amityville at least once a week.'

Word was now coming from England that his absence had had, as Ralph Hawkes put it, an 'unfortunate effect' on his reputation. Hawkes warned him that 'we are going to have difficulty in getting performances of your works'. Word had got around about his commission from the Japanese Government. 'So much for our leading young leftist composer,' remarked Humphrey Milford of the OUP's London office. Britten told Hawkes he was not really worried about what people were saying. 'I feel that one's real friends in England will be unselfishly pleased that one is being spared the horrors.' He emphasized that the British authorities had again told him to 'stay where you are until called back . . . get on with your work as artistic ambassadors etc. etc.' As to the Japanese commission, he had been advised by the British Consul in New York not to go to Tokyo, and during November he heard that the committee which had received the score of the *Sinfonia da Requiem* considered it unsuitable because it did not 'express felicitations for the 2,600th anniversary of our country', and was 'purely a religious music of Christian nature'. He was thereby saved from considerable embarrassment. The Tokyo concert for which the work had been intended was distinguished, according to a British observer, by the Axis representatives giving the Hitler salute during the Japanese national anthem, while the resident conductor of the orchestra was debarred from appearing because he was Jewish. The only music of note came from Germany and Italy – Richard Strauss's *Festmusik* and Jacques Ibert's *Festive Overture* (Ibert was living in Rome). No composers from Allied countries were represented.

Unaware of the political disaster he had just avoided, Britten was nonchalant about the rejection – 'after all', he told Ralph Hawkes, 'I have had the money and spent it . . . Anyhow, the publicity of having work rejected by the Japanese Consulate for being Christian is a wow.' But his spirits were low. Although his tonsils, supposedly the cause of his ill health, were removed in October 1940, he was still not well. Around Christmas he told Beata Mayer that he was 'just staggering out of an acute depression – probably into another one'.

*

He and Pears decided that they would both cross the border out of America and return as immigrants, so as to qualify them to work freely in the USA. Then they postponed the plan – 'feel this is the wrong moment to change our status,' Britten told Hawkes, '& anyway we may be called back.' America no longer seemed the land of infinite promise. Glamorous offers from conductors in the Midwest were always in the air, but 'So far none of these have materialized and frankly the outlook is not good,' Britten wrote to Hawkes in December 1940. He was reduced to taking on the conductorship of an amateur orchestra on Long Island. It was called – 'believe it or not' – the Suffolk Friends of Music Symphony Orchestra, after Suffolk County, and he was paid $10 a week for rehearsals, which required 'an infinite amount of tact' – the players were mostly music teachers and their best pupils. Meanwhile Pears became conductor of a local choral society, which paid $15 a week.

The orchestra's announcement that Britten had been engaged for the 1941 season mentioned that 'Mr Britten's new "Sinfonia da Requiem" will be played by the New York Philharmonic on March 29 and 30'. The première was at Carnegie Hall, with Barbirolli conducting. Britten supplied a programme note which confined itself to musical matters and made no mention of the work's purpose. However, in an interview with the *New York Sun* the previous April he had given some account of this:

> I'm making it just as anti-war as possible . . . I don't believe you can express social or political or economic theories in music, but by coupling new music with well known musical phrases, I think it's possible to get over certain ideas. I'm dedicating the symphony to the memory of my parents, and, since it is a kind of requiem, I'm quoting from the Dies Irae of the Requiem Mass. One's apt to get muddled discussing such things – all I'm sure of is my own anti-war conviction as I write it.

His programme note stated that there were three movements, Lacrymosa ('A slow marching lament'), Dies Irae ('A form of Dance of Death') and Requiem Aeternam.

Anyone in the audience who had read the newspaper interview would probably have assumed that the thunderous timpani strokes which open the Lacrymosa are meant to represent the guns of war. Yet the character of the first movement is oddly sinister for an anti-war tract. It is more like the beginning of a nightmare. Something appalling is approaching with relentless tread. As the Lacrymosa reaches its climax, it – whatever it is – lurches discordantly into view, and suddenly (without a break) we are in the Dies Irae, an excited scherzo in which somebody seems to be pursuing something. Its orgiastic character – particularly the climactic whoops and cries – seems to have little to do either with war or the death of Britten's parents, though Donald Mitchell draws attention to the morse-code-like character of the basic rhythm of the movement. We seem to be back in the guilty raptures of *Les Illuminations* or the wild hunt in *Our Hunting*

Fathers. Britten himself seems to have felt there was something dangerously revealing about the *Sinfonia da Requiem*. 'Personally, I think it is the
best so far', he wrote to Antonio Brosa's wife Peggy after the first
performance, 'although to me it is so personal & intimate a piece, that it is
rather like those awful dreams where one parades about the place naked –
slightly embarrassing!'

Only in the final movement, the Requiem Aeternam, does the *Sinfonia
da Requiem* assume the character suggested by its title. In what the
musicologist Peter Evans calls a 'mood of drained calm' – surely a reaction
to the frenzy of the Dies Irae – and with echoes of 'Sailing' from *Holiday
Tales*, we seem to be contemplating a calm seascape, with waves (audible
in the cymbal clashes) breaking evenly on what could be the sea-front
below Kirkley Cliff Road. There seem to be memories too of Bridge's *The
Sea*. Bridge was still alive when Britten composed the *Sinfonia da
Requiem*, but he died on 10 January 1941, shortly before it was performed.

*

In his letter to Peggy Brosa reporting the performance of the *Sinfonia da
Requiem*, Britten apologized for not writing before, 'but I have seriously
miscalculated the time it would take to score Paul Bunyan & every
moment of the day (& most nights!) is taken up with that'. The operetta,
written at intervals since the autumn of 1939, was scheduled for performance five weeks after the première of the *Sinfonia da Requiem*, not on
Broadway but on the campus of Columbia University, this evidently being
the best that Britten's publishers could arrange. After a play-through in the
apartment of Douglas Moore, head of the music deparment at Columbia,
with Britten at the keyboard and Pears singing, various theatre and music
groups within the university had teamed up for the production, with a few
young professional singers but a predominantly amateur cast. Dr Milton
Smith, who was to produce, thought the music 'tremendous', and was
determined to stage the operetta 'dead or alive'.

Paul Bunyan was certainly a challenge, requiring a large cast of solo
singers, a chorus, and a big orchestra, while Auden's libretto – as eccentric as anything he had written for the Group Theatre – demanded
imaginative staging. Britten himself had been puzzled how some of the
effects would be achieved. 'Wystan ... is coming down tomorrow', he
wrote to Ralph Hawkes in November 1939, 'and I will find out how he
has cast Paul Bunyan's feet ... I gather that Paul Bunyan never appears
on the stage ...' Although the operetta was supposedly finished by the
time it went into production, a good deal of extra material had to be
written during rehearsals, and it was only just ready in time for the

preview, on 4 May 1941, in the Brander Matthews Hall at Columbia. Elizabeth Mayer was in the audience. Afterwards she wrote to Britten praising his 'sweet melodies', and Britten himself told his sister Beth a few days later: 'The opera "Paul Bunyan" I think you'd like a lot – full of tunes that people even whistle!'

One can well imagine the audience coming away whistling the simple tunes sung by the country-and-western-style ballad singer who, to a strummed guitar, narrates those events in the operetta which cannot be feasibly presented on stage – such as the birth and early life of the gigantic Paul, super-lumberman, who (as Britten said) is never seen, merely heard as disembodied voice. Indeed, the entire opera is richly melodic, sometimes leaning towards Kurt Weill (whom Britten had met in August 1940) and the style of Broadway, as in the love-duet for Paul's daughter Tiny and Slim, the logging-camp cook; sometimes imitating Gilbert and Sullivan, as in the concluding Christmas party scene, where the pioneers leave the camp for the sophistications of modern society; and sometimes adopting the manner of *The Beggar's Opera*, as in the numbers for the camp's cats and dogs. Auden's libretto generally goes in for broad comedy – it is full of rather wearisome jokes about the bone-headedness of the Swedish lumberjacks – but Britten's score never descends to comparable banalities.

During the week's run at Columbia, *Paul Bunyan* was certainly a success with audiences, as is testified by a private recording of one of the performances, during which much laughter is caused by Auden's allusion to American advertising styles:

> Do you feel left out at parties,
> when it comes to promotion are you passed over,
> and does your wife talk in her sleep?
> Then ask our nearest agent
> to tell you about soups for success!

Yet the critics were unenthusiastic. Olin Downes in the *New York Times* praised Britten's skill but complained that the score failed to say 'something genuine', while he felt that Auden's libretto 'seems to wander from one to another idea, without conviction or cohesion'. The composer Virgil Thomson in the *New York Herald Tribune* called the libretto 'flaccid and spineless' and the music, at its best, 'sort of witty' but mostly 'undistinguished'. *Time* magazine dubbed it an 'anemic operetta put up by two British expatriates'. Most reviewers' feelings were summed up in Virgil Thomson's conclusion: 'I never did figure out the theme . . .'

Auden had provided plenty of information for those who wanted to work it out. In the *New York Times* on 4 May 1941 he observed that, for a mythical figure, Bunyan is remarkably ordinary: his feats are not superhuman but managerial – he organizes the logging camp and watches benevolently over his employees. As to the suggestion that Englishmen had no right to make an operetta out of American legend, Auden observed that the story's implications were 'not only American but universal'. The theme, he explained, was that modern man has almost boundless moral choice: 'Now that, in a material sense, we can do anything almost that we like, how are we to know what is right . . . ?'

It was rather an *outré* moral to draw from the Bunyan story, and Auden's libretto actually gives little evidence of being concerned with such matters until the end. However, in the last scene, in answer to the question 'What's to become of America now?', Paul intones this answer:

> Every day America's destroyed and re-created,
> America is what you do,
> American is I and you,
> America is what you choose to make it.

These words seem to be an answer to Britten's frequent complaints, in his letters to relatives and friends in England, and presumably also in conversation with Auden, that America was not living up to its promise. 'This country is dead,' he had written to Enid Slater in April 1940, when he was recovering from his illness, 'because it hasn't been lived in, because it hasn't been worked on. It may come in several hundred years but I doubt it, if the Americans go on as they are going at the moment. Everything comes too easily – success, wealth, luxury. They have no standards; no culture.' Auden had written to him in February 1940: 'I do hope, Ben dear, that your illness was the pangs of rebirth and not simply an outraged cry of homesickness.' He surely intended the conclusion of *Paul Bunyan* to change his collaborator's attitude to the New World, and to induce him to contemplate rebirth as an American.

On this personal level, the character of Johnny Inkslinger, Bunyan's book-keeper, could stand for Britten (though Donald Mitchell believes it to have been 'a self-portrait by Auden'). Arriving as an outsider, an intellectual or artist, among the rough pioneers, Inkslinger initially spurns Paul's offer of food in return for work (disdain for the American way of life), but eventually gives in, though for a long while he refuses to be on friendly terms with Bunyan. Finally he is rewarded with an invitation to work in Hollywood – the very thing Britten had been hoping for in 1939. Another personal detail is discernible in the chorus 'But once in a while the odd thing happens, / Once in a while the dream comes true, /

And the whole pattern of life is altered, / Once in a while the moon turns blue.' Britten once remarked to Donald Mitchell of these lines, 'That was Peter', and indeed a letter from Pears to Britten dated 9 January 1940 includes the words 'as long as I'm with you, you can stay away till the moon turns blue'.

Britten took the mixed reception of the operetta philosophically. 'The performance wasn't too good,' he wrote to Beth, 'but there are future productions in sight, which may be better.' The intention was to cut and revise, so as to make it more suitable for the high-school market. Auden and Britten decided on some drastic alterations, and a few weeks after the production Britten reported that 'in spite of the bangs it received there is a genuine interest being shown in it in various quarters'. Nothing materialized, and it was more than thirty years before *Paul Bunyan* was heard in public again. In 1941, Britten summed up the operetta in negative terms: 'I feel that I have learned lots about what not to write for the theatre.' The most obvious lesson he learnt from it was not to be dominated by his librettist.

Eric Crozier writes that in the late forties 'on several occasions I knew him to get the score from a cupboard after dinner and play right through it, with Peter acting and singing all the parts'. However in a letter to Eric Walter White of the Arts Council on 6 April 1951, replying to a suggestion that the operetta might be discussed in the forthcoming symposium on his music to be edited by Donald Mitchell and Hans Keller, Britten wrote:

> I've found it difficult to make up my mind about 'Paul Bunyan'. I have finally got hold of the score from B[oosey] & H[awkes] (before I had only the roughest sketches) & I must say the whole thing embarrasses me hugely. One trouble is that there are two unresolved versions – changes Auden & I started making, & then gave up. If ever the piece were to be brought out into the open, an enormous amount of work would have to be done by him & me – & I don't think that either of us are keen enough.

He suggested that the 'only possible' way of referring to the operetta in the book 'could be an eye witness account of the 1st performances', perhaps by Elizabeth Mayer. In the event *Paul Bunyan* received only two cursory mentions in the book.

*

Though Britten claimed not to be too downcast by the reviews of the operetta in May 1941, he was becoming sensitive about his reputation in America. '. . . the reaction of the intellectual composers has been bad,' he wrote to Beth *à propos* the operetta and the *Sinfonia da Requiem*. 'I am definitely disliked (a) because I am English ... (b) because I'm not American ... (c) because I get quite a lot of performances (d) because I wasn't educated in Paris.' This may sound a little paranoid, but Virgil Thomson, who had studied with Boulanger, had written sneeringly in his review of *Paul Bunyan*: 'Benjamin Britten's music ... is easily recognizable as that considered by the British Broadcasting Corporation to be at once modernistic and safe.' Also, Thomson's pupil Paul Bowles (who was living at Middagh Street), seems to have kept his distance – 'he and I had nothing memorable to say to one another', Bowles has written of Britten.

Britten had another taste of American chauvinism when he was told that he could only conduct *Les Illuminations* over the CBS radio network, with Pears singing, if he joined the American Musicians' Union. This was achieved, and the broadcast, on 18 May 1941, was described by him as 'splendid'. A recording of it survives, and shows that Pears had now developed his characteristic voice, not an Italian *bel canto* nor even an English 'cathedral tenor', but a strange and unique sound in which any technical limitations were lavishly compensated for by the strong personality it expressed. Britten was surely thinking of Pears when he said in a radio programme many years later: 'The only thing which moves me about singers ... is that the voice is something that comes naturally from their personality, and is a vocal expression of their personality. I *loathe* what is normally called "a beautiful voice", because to me it's like an over-ripe peach, which says nothing.'

Meanwhile in England the resentment at Britten's absence, which Ralph Hawkes had perceived the previous autumn, was coming to a head. Ernest Newman's favourable *Sunday Times* review of the first British performance of the Violin Concerto (given by Thomas Matthews and the London Philharmonic Orchestra conducted by Basil Cameron on 6 April 1941) sparked off some angry letters from readers, which Newman dubbed 'the battle of Britten'. The paper did not print these letters, and Newman continued to praise Britten as a 'thoroughbred' whose talent was 'beyond question'. This provoked a choleric letter to the editor from the honorary treasurer of the Royal Philharmonic Society, George Baker, a professional singer and organist who was doing war work for the BBC Overseas Service. Baker wrote of Britten:

> He is in America. He may have had perfectly good reasons for going there, and may decide to return to his native land some time or other. In the meantime I would like to remind Mr Newman that most of our

musical 'thoroughbreds' are stabled in or near London and are directing all their endeavours towards winning ... the Battle of Britain; a
programme in which Mr Britten has no part.

Baker's letter was published on 15 June 1941. In that month's issue of the
Musical Times, a letter from Pilot-Officer E. R. Lewis alluded to Britten
without naming him: 'The favour recently shown to a young English
composer now in America, has, to my knowledge, caused discontent
which calls for notice ... Why should special favour be given to works
which ... come from men who have avoided national service?'

Newman was not Britten's only defender. Another reader of the *Musical Times* asked whether the nation would prefer a repetition of the
destruction of composers such as Ivor Gurney and George Butterworth –
the latter had been killed on the Somme, and Gurney was gassed in
Passchendaele and became insane. Was it not better that such artists
should be 'alive and composing in America'? To which the editor of the
Musical Times, Harvey Grace, responded that such an absentee might be
experiencing 'the consciousness of having saved one's art and skin at the
cost of failure to do one's duty'.

There is no evidence that Britten saw the *Musical Times* while this
argument was going on. Letters to him from his family and friends – even
his conservative-minded brother Robert – continued to encourage him to
stay in America for the duration of the war. However, somebody sent
him Ernest Newman's *Sunday Times* remarks about 'the battle of
Britten', so he must have been at least partially aware of the climate of
feeling. His only comment on Newman's remarks, in a letter to Ralph
Hawkes in mid-July 1941, was: 'I feel really grateful to the old boy for
his support.'

During the spring of 1941, Britten and Pears were still planning to
leave and re-enter the USA as registered immigrants. With this in mind
they accepted an invitation to southern California. '. . . we want to go to
Mexico', Britten told Beth, 'so as to get on to the labour-quota (you have
to go out of the country & then come back, so as to be able to work
without hindrance).' The invitation was from Ethel Bartlett and her
husband Rae Robertson, a British piano duo who were staying for the
summer at Escondido, near San Diego. Britten had met them in New
York, and had already written for them an *Introduction and Rondo alla
Burlesca* for two pianos. He still hoped for film work in California – 'if
possible I want to land a Hollywood job', he told Beth in May.

He and Pears made the coast-to-coast journey in an old Ford V8 which
the Robertsons had left in the East, stopping early each evening so that

Britten could 'write the extra numbers for the Rossini ballet'. This was another Rossini–Britten suite, *Matinées Musicales*, required by Lincoln Kirstein's American Ballet Company (it was to be teamed up with *Soirées Musicales* for a Balanchine ballet, *Divertimento*, to be performed in Rio de Janeiro at the end of June). They had no sooner arrived in Escondido than Britten received a visit from Mrs Elizabeth Sprague Coolidge, distinguished elderly patron of music, whose Coolidge Foundation promoted concerts and administered prizes. Two years earlier Frank Bridge had sent Britten a letter of introduction to her, and she now commissioned a string quartet from him, to be performed in Los Angeles in three months' time. 'Short notice & a bit of a sweat', he commented, 'but I'll do it as the cash will be useful!'

On the whole, he had liked what he saw of America on the journey across. 'The people are *much* nicer when you get out of the Eastern cities,' he told his sister Barbara. He was particularly intrigued by hitchhikers,

> mostly young men or boys who make their way across the continent asking for lifts ... one aged 18, awfully nice person, had been doing it for 5 years ... One small boy aged scarcely more than 10 had hitch-hiked over 1000 miles to stay with his grand-mother, & we picked him up on his way back. As casual as anything!

Yet, having arrived in California, he made no further mention of the plan to re-enter the country on the labour quota. The idea now was to remain on the West coast until the end of the summer, '& then God knows what, with America just on the brink of war' – a hint of the possibility of a return to England. Maybe this change of heart had something to do with absence from Auden.

An article Britten had written for the New York journal *Modern Music* some months earlier shows the extent to which he was under Auden's thumb. (On at least one occasion Auden helped to write a letter for him; a draft of Britten's response to the Japanese Government's complaint about the *Sinfonia da Requiem* is in Auden's hand.) Concluding a discussion of 'England and the Folk-Art Problem', he declared in words which could be Auden's:

> The attempt to create a national music is only one symptom of a serious and universal malaise of our time – the refusal to accept the destruction of 'community' by the machine. [Here he quoted from Auden's still unpublished *New Year Letter*.] ... It is only those who accept their loneliness and refuse all the refuges, whether of tribal nationalism or airtight intellectual systems, who will carry on the human heritage.

Yet earlier in the same article he had wistfully recalled the Scottish fisher girls who came to Lowestoft in his childhood and sang 'their lovely, lilting Highland tunes', whereas nowadays their successors hummed hit-songs from the radio – a clear indication that he actually deplored the destruction of local communities by the machine age.

In California, out of reach of Auden, his real feelings could begin to emerge more strongly. A letter written to Enid Slater on 17 June begins by giving the impression that he will remain in the USA – 'I think I am pretty well established' – but eventually admits: 'I *am* homesick, & really only enjoy scenery that reminds me of England.' And then, on 29 July, to Elizabeth Mayer: 'We've just re-discovered the poetry of George Crabbe (all about Suffolk!) & are very excited – maybe an opera one day —!'

4: O weep away the stain

To someone on the look-out for 'scenery that reminds me of England', the issue of the *Listener* for 29 May 1941 was likely to have particular appeal. Alongside articles by John Piper on the Euston Road Group (which made much mention of Britten's old Film Unit colleague William Coldstream) and the critic Frank Howes on music and politics (a preview of Alan Bush's Piano Quartet) was the text of a talk which had just been given on the BBC Overseas Service by E. M. Forster, entitled 'George Crabbe: the Poet and the Man'. It began 'To talk about Crabbe is to talk about England,' and went on to describe the precise sights and sounds that Britten had lived among at Snape: 'an estuary, and here the scenery becomes melancholy and flat; expanses of mud, saltish commons, the marsh-birds crying'. Somehow Britten or Pears came across a copy of this issue – possibly it was being mailed to their hosts, the Robertsons – and, as Pears recalls, 'the reading of this article stirred Ben so deeply that he felt he couldn't stay in America any more'. (It is not impossible that the copy of the *Listener* was sent to Britten by Auden, who was a friend of Forster's and would have guessed that the article would particularly interest him.)

Forster, who had first written on Crabbe in 1932 in the introduction to the World's Classics edition of his poems, gave a brief account in the *Listener* piece of the poet's life and works. Crabbe was born at Aldeburgh, just along the estuary from Snape, in 1754, and many of his narrative poems depict the local scenery and the character and lives of the town's inhabitants. From *The Borough* (1810), Forster quoted Crabbe's description of the Alde estuary with its melancholy bird-calls, and he also mentioned one of the tales found in the poem: 'A famous one is "Peter Grimes": he was a savage fisherman who murdered his apprentices and was haunted by their ghosts; there was an actual original for Grimes.' All this seems to have been new to Britten. His letter to Elizabeth Mayer says

that he and Pears have just 're-discovered' Crabbe, but in 1945 he gave a
different account: 'I did not know any of the poems of Crabbe at that
time [1941], but reading about him [in the *Listener*] gave me such a
feeling of nostalgia for Suffolk ... that I searched for a copy of his
works.' On 5 July 1941 Pears mentioned to Elizabeth Mayer that he had
found 'a marvellous Rare Book shop' in Los Angeles, and it seems to
have been there that he bought *The Poetical Works of the Rev. George
Crabbe edited, with a life, by his son* (1851). Twenty-three years later
Britten recalled how

> it was in California in the unhappy summer of 1941, that, coming
> across a copy of the Poetical Works of George Crabbe in a Los Angeles
> bookshop, I first read his poem, *Peter Grimes*; and, at the same time,
> reading a most perceptive and revealing article about it by E. M.
> Forster, I suddenly realized where I belonged and what I lacked.

Elsewhere he said that, when he read the poem, 'in a flash I realized two
things: that I must write an opera, and where I belonged'.

The copy of Crabbe is among Britten and Pears's books at the Red
House, Aldeburgh. In it, Pears noted in 1981: 'I bought this book at a
Los Angeles book-seller in 1941 and from this we started work on the
plans for making an opera out of "Peter Grimes".' In 1982 he added
above 'Los Angeles' the words '? San Diego', unable to remember for
certain where the shop was.

Crabbe was an Augustan who survived into the Romantic Age. The
'Peter Grimes' section of *The Borough* is, in outline, a moral tale in the
manner of Samuel Johnson's contemporaries. Peter, the son of a God-
fearing fisherman, goes to the bad after his father's death, thieving as well
as fishing to pay for his drink. Out of sheer cruelty he decides to acquire a
pauper boy whom he can bully and beat, and the townsfolk connive at
this abuse:

> Some few in town observed in Peter's trap
> A boy, with jacket blue and woollen cap;
> But none enquired how Peter used the rope,
> Or what the bruise, that made the stripling stoop ...
> None reason'd thus – and some, on hearing cries,
> Said calmly, 'Grimes is at his exercise.'

After three years of this treatment the boy, Sam, dies. Grimes acquires
another, who falls to his death from the fishing-boat mast, and a third lad
dies at sea. Grimes is brought before a town court and forbidden to keep
any more apprentices. Eventually he goes mad, haunted by the ghosts of

the boys and his father, and expires before the eyes of the townsfolk.

Despite its general character, the poem is in several respects very un-Augustan. Grimes is not simply a stereotype drunkard and bully, but is portrayed with some psychological insight. His treatment of the boys is represented as what the twentieth century would call sadism – 'his cruel soul ... wish'd for one to trouble and control' – and his hatred of his father has, to modern ears, Freudian overtones; Grimes calls him 'this father-foe'. Peter Pears has written that Crabbe's Grimes is 'nothing more than a villainous fisherman ... Not a very glamorous figure for the operatic stage'; but it is easy to imagine Crabbe's sketch suggesting to Britten the possibility of incorporating another layer of meaning into the story.

According to Britten's recollections in 1945, as soon as he and Pears had read Forster's article and Crabbe's poem they 'began trying to construct the scenario of an opera'. For the moment, however, the project had to remain in the realm of day-dreams, since, as Britten writes in the same article, 'discussions with a librettist, planning the musical architecture, composing preliminary sketches, and writing nearly a thousand pages of orchestral score, demanded a freedom from other work which was an economic impossibility'. As to his decision to return to England, he may indeed have made up his mind as he read Forster and Crabbe, but there is no contemporary evidence of this. Certainly he indicated his keenness to get away from the Robertson ménage, where, as he told his sister Barbara, 'scraps' had broken out between him and the piano duo, with Pears having to act as peacemaker. Another letter mentions 'unnecessary emotional scenes'. The cause seems to have been Ethel Bartlett falling in love with Britten, the situation being complicated by her husband offering her to him. The Robertsons were both exceptionally small; a photograph shows Britten and Pears looming over their hosts like giants. Their private nickname for the couple was 'the little Owls'.

This emotional turmoil may be reflected in the string quartet which Britten wrote during July, to Mrs Coolidge's commission, though its tense and restless character may also have something to do with his working conditions. He had to shut himself in a tool shed and turn on a fan to drown the noise of the Robertsons practising their pianos.

Getting away from Escondido was urgently on the agenda, but leaving America was altogether another matter, and Britten's letter to Elizabeth Mayer on 29 July which mentions the possibility of a Crabbe opera suggests that, far from any intention of an immediate return to England, he and Pears were still considering taking up permanent residence in the

USA. The letter revives the plan of re-entering the country as immigrants: 'We haven't yet made any definite decision – but I think we'll emigrate from Canada (Peter has this friend, who is son-in-law of the Minister of Emigration of Canada (very useful!)) at the beginning of the Fall.'

*

Pears was probably in no hurry to return to England. He had formed his own vocal ensemble in New York, the Elizabethan Singers, and several performances were planned. Britten had now completed a song-cycle for him, though they were not yet ready for it to be heard publicly. 'One only does them for one's own pleasure,' Britten told Enid Slater. 'Still – one day –'

Britten's *Seven Sonnets of Michelangelo* for tenor and piano set a high standard for Pears's still developing vocal technique – they are full of copy-book vocal styles and challenges – and are a demonstration of Britten's own skill with Italian words; 'after Rimbaud in French I feel I can attack anything!' he remarked. The cycle has also been taken as a declaration of love between composer and singer. For example, the pianist Graham Johnson writes of it as 'a garland of songs to celebrate a marriage of minds and hearts'. Yet its 'storyline' does not celebrate a matrimonial bond. It portrays a restless and largely unsatisfied desire.

The first song, 'Si come nella penna' (Michelangelo's Sonnet XVI) describes the 'doubtful hope and certain miseries' of the lover, while the second (XXI) tells how 'intense desire' makes a 'captive and slave' of him (quotations are from the John Addington Symonds translation (1878) used by Britten while composing the cycle). The third (XXX) gives some suggestion that love needs to be requited – the lover is like the moon, and can only reflect the light of the beloved – but in the fourth (LV) the lover asks why he has been rejected, and the fifth (XXXVIII) is his complaint that he will never learn how to woo the beloved. In the sixth (XXXII) 'angry spite' has undone a seemingly indestructible love, and in the seventh (XXIV) the lover anticipates the eventual dissolution of the beloved's perfection in death. Only the third and seventh songs, then, contain any suggestion of a settled and happy relationship. There are many Michelangelo sonnets celebrating the joys of unclouded love, but Britten did not choose to set them.

Though the manuscripts of the songs are dated between April and October 1940, there is some evidence that the cycle was contemplated, and perhaps even begun, some time earlier. A letter from Auden to Britten dating from November 1937 has a note in Britten's hand about a biography of Michelangelo, and Wulff Scherchen has a memory from the late thirties of 'Ben complaining of a "mental block" over a Michel Angelo Sonnet & "putting it away". I'm sure I saw the Italian text.' If this is correct, the initial inspiration for the cycle – and this would fit the implied narrative of the sequence of poems – may not be Pears.

When Britten wrote to his brother Robert on 4 August 1941, some days after the forecast of 'an opera one day', he gave no hint of a return to England; quite the reverse. 'I've had quite a lot of success and a surprising lot of performances,' Britten wrote, 'and next season looks even better.' On 9 September he wrote to Wulff Scherchen that his plans for the winter were 'extremely vague'.

He and Pears visited Hollywood, which Britten found 'really horrible' and where he made no attempt to get film work. In Los Angeles they attended the première of his String Quartet No. 1, on a college campus on 21 September. Then they set off east again in the Robertsons' car, feeling like 'released prisoners' – and also rather guilty at having lived rent-free through the summer, though Britten hoped he had repaid the Robertsons by writing several pieces for them, including *Scottish Ballad*, a medley of traditional Scottish tunes for two pianos and orchestra. (After his return to England he gave recitals of his two-piano works with Clifford Curzon.) It was on his arrival in Amityville at the beginning of October that he mentioned to Albert Goldberg, a conductor in Chicago, 'our trip across that particularly nasty bit of ocean in December', this evidently being the month when he and Pears were expecting to leave for England. To Mrs Coolidge he wrote on the subject at some length:

> I have made up my mind to return to England, at anyrate for the duration of the war. I am not telling people because it sounds a little heroic, which it is far from being – it is really that I cannot be separated any longer from all my friends and family – going through all they are, and I'm afraid will be, in the future. I shall continue with my work over there, which is what I most want to do, of course. I don't actually know when I shall be sailing, since boats are scarce and heavily booked up – and anyhow I have so much to get finished here, so I may not be leaving much before Christmas.

This letter made no mention of his feeling that he belonged among English scenery, or his desire to write an opera. He said nothing to his family. (Later, he said this was because he did not want them to worry about his crossing the Atlantic at this time of U-boats and torpedoes.)

The timing of his decision may have had something to do with Auden's absence from New York. If things had followed their old pattern, Auden would probably have stepped in and made Britten suppress his feelings of homesickness. But Auden had just begun a year's teaching at Ann Arbor, Michigan, and was also feeling the double blow of his mother's death and Chester Kallman's sexual involvement with a sailor, so he was scarcely in a state of mind to write domineering letters, if indeed Britten told him of the decision. Another factor may have been Britten's recent lack of earnings. Though he had been in the USA for more than two years, his income was still well below what he had earned in England in the months just before the war. There had been plenty of commissions, but none of them paid more than a few hundred dollars. The largest ($400) had come from Mrs Coolidge for the String Quartet, and Britten still had to depend on his publisher's retainer for his survival. Certainly there were immense financial possibilities in the USA; Douglas Moore of Columbia University offered to recommend him for the headship of the music department in the University of New Mexico at Alberquerque, with amazing salary of $32,000. But a post of this sort held no appeal for Britten, and it was becoming apparent that he would not easily earn a good living as a freelance. As to his reputation, American critics were now making the sorts of remarks their British counterparts had voiced three years earlier. The *Chicago Daily Times* thought the *Sinfonia da Requiem* lacked 'content and substance', while Frederick Stock, conductor of the Chicago Symphony Orchestra, told Albert Goldberg that Britten's music had 'more manner than matter'. This may have played a part in the decision to return to England.

However, that decision may not yet have seemed irrevocable. A letter from Britten to Beth on 4 November implied that he was staying in the USA. He had been 'seeing my agent about things' in New York; there was '*possibly* a commission from Benny Goodman!' (a sketch of a first movement of a clarinet concerto is among his manuscripts); and he told Beth 'maybe I'll be so rich' from earnings in America that he could support her family if they joined him there after the war. Then, a few days after this letter, came some sort of personal crisis.

One of the members of the committee which ran the amateur orchestra Britten had conducted on Long Island was David Rothman, proprietor of a hardware store at Southold, near the island's north-eastern tip. 'You are such a delightful family,' Britten wrote to him, describing Rothman's son Bobby, who was in his early teens, as 'a grand kid'. On 6 November he went to stay with them for two nights, during which, according to Elizabeth Mayer's diary, he 'played at salesman in store'. According to David Rothman it was more serious than that: 'He wanted to stop writing music, and wanted to work in my store.'

Elsewhere in the same interview, made for Tony Palmer's Britten television documentary four decades later, Rothman tells the story again: 'He had the feeling that he would like to work in a store, and give up composing, which seemed to me most ridiculous. I don't know whether he was serious or not, but I had the idea he might have been.' Rothman says that in response to this extraordinary suggestion, 'I told him, "Look, you're only about twenty-six years old [actually 27]; you've already done well . . . they did [your] violin concerto with the New York Philharmonic. What do you want? Blood?"'

The cause of this near-breakdown could have been a sudden drying up of musical creativity. Ralph Hawkes had asked Britten to write a short overture for Arthur Rodzinski to conduct with the Cleveland Orchestra; it was wanted in a great hurry for a New York concert. The piece was completed but for some reason never performed. Originally entitled 'Occasional Overture', it was eventually played for the first time in 1983 under the title *An American Overture*. When the score came to light in the sixties, Britten had 'absolutely no recollection whatsoever' of having written it. He added: 'My recollection of that time was of complete incapacity to work . . . I was in quite a psychological state then . . .' Possibly the commission for the overture was the last straw after a long period of prolific composition (the *Sinfonia da Requiem*, *Paul Bunyan*, and the String Quartet No. 1, as well as slighter pieces), much of it done against the clock. Yet the 'Occasional Overture' seems too slight a piece to have caused Britten much trouble. His 'complete incapacity to work' may have been related to the fact that, as he admitted to Beata Mayer, he had fallen in love with young Bobby Rothman.

He had probably hoped that by committing himself to Pears he would be able to eliminate his powerful feelings for boys. In fact Bobby seems to have been the first boy he had the chance of befriending since the watershed of his relationship with Pears in Grand Rapids a little over two years earlier. David Rothman has recalled how 'Bobby was so fond of him, you could see. He played with Bobby, carried him on his shoulders . . .' Faced with the prospect of leaving the boy and crossing the Atlantic with Pears, he seems to have longed to abandon every commitment, musical and personal, and settle down in Bobby's household.

In the event, the Southold weekend passed quickly, and Britten was soon back at Amityville, writing to thank David Rothman:

> you, especially, David, I feel a real source of inspiration & encourage-
> ment, such as I have rarely met. I am very touched by your urgings on a
> certain important decision – please don't be injured if I seem to treat
> them lightly, that is only to cover how seriously I consider them. In

spite of my jocularity, I am a great believer in 'Fate' or 'God' or what-you-will, and I am for the moment going on with the work in hand (which is plenty, I can assure you!) and letting the future take care of itself . . .

from a grateful
Benjamin B

*

Two weeks after the visit to the Rothmans, he was in the Midwest, performing with Pears in Chicago (*Les Illuminations* and the *Sinfonia da Requiem*) and again in Grand Rapids, where once again their hosts were the Eineckes. At the Grand Rapids concert they repeated *Les Illuminations* with Britten playing the orchestral score on the piano. They also performed some settings of English folk-songs which Britten had been writing in recent months. Each bore a dedication to some American friend. One of them, 'The Trees They Grow So High', was dedicated to Bobby Rothman, but the words of the song, which narrates the tragedy of a boy who is married too young, could be read as a narrative about Britten himself:

O father, dearest father, you've done to me great wrong,
You've tied me to a boy when you know he is too young . . .
All because he was a young boy and growing,
All because he was a young boy and growing.

This setting was published in 1943 in Britten's first volume of folk-song arrangements. An article by him on folk-song arranging, published in an American magazine in 1941, gives little hint of why he was attracted to them. He writes of 'the weakness of the tunes, which seldom have any striking rhythms or memorable melodic features'. It is noticeable that, in this first volume, songs about lost innocence and early death predominate. The two exceptions, 'O Can Ye Sew Cushions?' and 'Oliver Cromwell' are, respectively, a cradle-song and a child's game, representations of the innocent state.

From Grand Rapids, Britten and Pears travelled to Ann Arbor, where Auden wanted to work with Britten on an oratorio. He had engaged a student, Charlie Miller, as house-sharer and cook. Though Miller was not homosexual he was alive to the nuances of relationships during that visit. Elizabeth Mayer had come west with Britten and Pears, and Miller describes her as 'handsome and stately, a European presence, her brown hair, silver-laced, braided and coiled into a crown; her queenly bosom shook with laughter as she chummed with us four raucous males'. Miller recalls '"Benjy" conduct[ing] Peter a cappella in the Britten–Rimbaud

"Illuminations", Peter's erotic tenor seeming to swell the room'. He also gives this description of the pair:

> Benjy smiled as soon as anyone looked at him, but I don't remember hearing a note of laughter from that pale, patient face. As he sat in Wystan's blue upholstered chair, I was impressed with his melancholy, his generally passive attitude, even while Peter and Elizabeth rocked with laughter ... Peter, handsome and irresponsible, loomed large over his Benjy, and I didn't need Wystan to tell me, as he did in a murmured aside, 'Now there's a happily married couple.'

On the last day of 1941, at the end of the month in which the United States had finally entered the war, Britten wrote to console Antonio Brosa's wife, Peggy, who like him had been suffering from depression. 'I think after a time', he told her, 'one gets into a routine of things, and just lives from day to day. That's what has happened to me ...'

*

He and Pears were now waiting for exit permits, 'and when we get them, we've got to wait for a boat'. Meanwhile he went to Boston to hear Serge Koussevitzky and the Boston Symphony Orchestra give a 'wonderful' performance of the *Sinfonia da Requiem* on 2 January 1942. Two weeks later Paul Wittgenstein, who had proved thoroughly tiresome about his *Diversions* for piano (left hand) and orchestra, gave the first performance with the Philadelphia Orchestra. The work took the form of a theme and variations. Wittgenstein was finally very pleased with it, and Britten himself described it as 'not deep – but quite pretty!'

On 6 January 1942 he was expecting to leave America 'in about a week's time'. On 20 January he wrote that they would be going 'any day now'. They were still in Amityville on 31 January, when Auden wrote Britten a long letter from Ann Arbor. He said he found it difficult to believe that they really were going. 'I need scarcely say, my dear, how much I shall miss you and Peter, or how much I love you both.' But the letter was not just an affectionate goodbye.

'I have been thinking a great deal about you and your work during the past year,' Auden told Britten. He said he regarded Britten as 'the white hope of music', and so was especially anxious about 'the dangers that beset you as a man and as an artist'. All great art, he declared, was the result of

> a perfect balance between Order and Chaos, Bohemianism and Bourgeois Convention. Bohemian chaos alone ends in a mad jumble of beautiful scraps. Bourgeois Convention alone ends in large unfeeling

corpses. Every artist except the supreme masters has a bias one way or the other ... Technical skill always comes from the bourgeois side of one's nature.

Britten's bias, he went on, was towards Bourgeois Conventions:

Your attraction to thin-as-a-board juveniles, i.e. to the sexless and innocent, is a symptom of this. And I am certain too that it is your denial and evasion of the demands of disorder that is responsible for your attacks of ill-health, i.e. sickness is your substitute for the Bohemian.

So far, this was merely one of Auden's standard lectures. Then came an acutely perceptive passage:

Wherever you go you are and probably always will be surrounded by people who adore you, nurse you, and praise everything you do, e.g. Elisabeth, Peter (Please show this to P to whom all this is addressed). Up to a certain point this is fine for you, but beware. You see, Bengy dear, you are always tempted to make things too easy for yourself in this way, i.e. to build yourself a warm nest of love (of course when you get it, you find it a little stifling) by playing the lovable talented little boy.

It is striking that Auden classes Pears as one of those who provided the 'warm nest' which could be 'a little stifling'. (Michael Tippett wonders whether his attitude may not have been partly motivated by jealousy of the stable Britten–Pears relationship, considering that he had been largely abandoned by his own lover.) Auden went on:

If you are really to develop to your full stature, you will have, I think, to suffer, and make others suffer, in ways which are totally strange to you at present, and against every conscious value that you have; i.e. you will have to be able to say what you never yet have had the right to say – God, I'm a shit ...

All my love to you both, and God bless you.
Wystan.

Britten evidently replied but, as usual, when he had read the letter Auden threw it away. We do, however, have Britten's letter to Kit Welford of 1 March 1942 in which he repeats Auden's observations rather sketchily, and adds: 'A carefully chosen discipline is the only possible course.'

From Auden's next letter to him, it is evident that Britten had misunderstood, or chosen to misunderstand, a crucial passage. 'Dearest Ben,' he wrote,

Of course I didn't mean to suggest that your relationship with Peter was on the school boy level. Its danger is quite the reverse, of you both letting the marriage be too caring. (The escape for the paederast is that a marriage is impossible.) You understand each other so well, that you will always be both tempted to identify yourselves with each other.

With which he abandoned the subject. He ended by expressing sympathy for the irritation of hanging about for the boat, but added: 'I, of course, hope that the migration will be finally cancelled.'

Britten does not seem to have replied.

*

He was still waiting for the boat in mid-February, and still unable to write music fluently, though he told Peggy Brosa he had 'started ... pushing a pen around'. There was some good news. In Boston he had mentioned the projected opera to Kousevitzky, whose wife had just died, and who was now offering $1000 to finance the writing of it, from a fund to be established in her memory. Yet Britten did not seem overjoyed. In his letter to Kit Welford on 1 March he complained, much as he had done when leaving England in 1939, that he needed time to 'think & think & work & work, completely undistracted'. It may be that he regarded the opera commission as yet more pressure on him. He and Pears had asked Christopher Isherwood to be the librettist, and Isherwood had politely declined. It was an odd choice of collaborator if Britten was about to leave America, where Isherwood was definitely remaining.

In the letter to Peggy Brosa he took a gloomy view of prospects in England: 'There seem to be only two possible courses – (1) that we get some official music jobs, connected with the service or organising music (2) or just become C.O.s [Conscientious Objectors]. I think the first will be easier for me because of my commissions.' Besides the opera and the possible piece for Benny Goodman, there was a request for a concerto from an American harpist.

Suddenly the date of departure was definite, Monday 16 March. 'The Ides of March', wrote Elizabeth Mayer miserably in her diary. Pears was overjoyed: 'we shall be arriving at such a heavenly time', he wrote to the Brosas; 'April is such a marvellous month – Think of seeing real spring again –'. In the same letter, Britten added a postscript: 'As Peter has told you it is soon now – & in some ways I'm glad, as this wait hasn't been fun. But now – how I wish I weren't going – there are so many people I love here and life in England isn't going to be fun.'

In the Mayers' visitors' book on 6 March he wrote, 'The end of the week-end (see Aug. 21st 1939)', this being the date on which they had arrived at Amityville, supposedly for the weekend. After all the drama of farewells, the ship, a Swedish cargo vessel named *Axel Johnson*, remained tied up at the pier in New York, undergoing repairs for several days. Then it crawled slowly up the coast to Boston. On 31 March, two weeks after they had said goodbye to her, Pears and Britten sent Beata Mayer a postcard from Halifax, Nova Scotia: 'God how slow & boring!' Twelve days later they were on the other side of the Atlantic, but the ship took a further five to reach Liverpool.

They found the company on the boat uncongenial – 'callow, foul mouthed, witless recruits', wrote Pears – and their cabin was small, miserable and airless. Britten had intended to work at the commission from Benny Goodman and at a *Hymn to St Cecilia* for which Auden had written the words, but his drafts for both pieces were confiscated by customs officials, on the look-out for anything that might be coded information, before the boat sailed. Undaunted, he wrote out the beginning of the *Hymn* again from memory, and finished it during the voyage, though Pears wrote that 'it was difficult for him as people seemed to whistle up and down the corridor all day!' He also drafted what Pears described as '7 Christmas carols for women's voices & Harp'. Pears thought them 'Very sweet & chockfull of charm!' Britten's only comment on all this work done on the voyage was: 'one had to alleviate the boredom!'

Paradoxically, in the confined and oppressive conditions aboard ship, with no certainty when or indeed if they would reach home – 'the U boat menace was at its height', writes Beth – Britten's creative block, and apparently also his deep depression, lifted with spectacular results. Both *A Hymn to St Cecilia* and the '7 Christmas carols', which were the first draft of *A Ceremony of Carols*, radiate a relaxed joyfulness. Perhaps it was simply relief at the ending of three years' indecision about where he should live and work. Yet it may be that the *Hymn* and the *Ceremony* were themselves the reason for the joyfulness.

Since Britten's birthday fell on St Cecilia's day, it is not surprising that as far back as 1935 he had contemplated writing a work in her honour. On 19 January that year he was 'having difficulty finding Latin words for it', and at that period nothing had been composed. Then in the summer of 1940 Auden had begun to supply him with English words, which Britten had started to set – two sections beginning 'In a garden shady' and 'I cannot grow'. The first of these portrays the saint with surprising *double entendre*: '. . . this innocent virgin / Constructed an organ to enlarge her prayer'. Auden seems to be pointing out that music does not just have a rarefied aesthetic and spiritual appeal. Its business is also with the erotic: 'Blonde Aphrodite rose up excited, / Moved to delight by the melody, / White as an orchid she rode quite naked . . .' (One recalls Auden's recommendation to Britten that he play the piano as an aid to seduction.)

In the second section, music itself speaks, first in a kind of Peter Pan voice, which perhaps reflects Auden's view of Britten – not so much innocent as ultra-naïve and therefore incapable of moral choice: 'I cannot grow; / I have no shadow / To run away from, / I only play'. Then it identifies itself, as John Fuller writes in his book on Auden, as 'a product of man's life at the point where emotion has exhausted any possibility of action', which was Britten's state of mind when he and Pears boarded the *Axel Johnson*: 'I am defeat / When it knows it / Can now do nothing / By suffering.' Auden's lines seem to be echoing Britten's 'one . . . just lives from day to day'. This was the point in the *Hymn* which Britten had reached some time in 1940 or 1941, and where, despite promising the piece to Pears's Elizabethan Singers in New York, he had stuck. Only when he was on board ship did the final section take shape.

For it, Auden had provided words quite unlike the first two sections of the poem. Possibly they had been written recently, for they seem to refer to Britten's creative block, and to be an exhortation to him to come to terms with its cause. (When Auden published the words of the *Hymn to St Cecilia* in his next collection of poetry he subtitled it 'For Benjamin Britten', just as he had done with his thirties poems about Britten's sexuality.) The first of the three stanzas in this final section praises music for its power to express all emotion without gaucheness or outworn images, and calls upon it to 're-arrange' our lives, restoring the innocence we feel ourselves to have lost. The second stanza portrays music as children playing casually among the 'ruined languages' of civilization's failure. Then suddenly the poem changes course, and Auden seems to be addressing Britten personally:

> O hang the head,
> Impetuous child with the tremendous brain,
> O weep, child, weep, O weep away the stain,
> Lost innocence who wished your lover dead,
> Weep for the lives your wishes never led.

It is noticeable that, in Britten's setting, on the words 'wished your lover dead' the tenor comes to the fore.

Now (Auden goes on to say in the final stanza), enough is enough. It is time to accept your loss of innocence and not go on punishing yourself for it. While the chorus define music's ability to portray the inner struggle of reason against passion – as Britten's major works seemed to have been doing since the *Variations on a Theme of Frank Bridge* – solo voices stand out from them with the exhortation to cease that struggle. Instead, urge the soloists, the loss of innocence must be *celebrated*, must itself become the subject of the music:

> O weep, child, weep, O weep away the stain
> That what has been may never be again,
> O bless the freedom that you never chose,
> O wear your tribulation like a rose.

The joyfulness in Britten's sparkling setting of the *Hymn to St Cecilia* showed that he understood this message, and was already acting on it. And, as further proof that he was coming to terms with his predicament and was able to celebrate rather than regret it, he went on at once to create, as the first stage of this new Auden-inspired task, an evocation of innocence before its loss, *A Ceremony of Carols*.

Though Britten's original intention was to use women's voices – early sketches are for sopranos and altos – the published score specifies that *A Ceremony of Carols* is to be sung by trebles, that is, boys. Britten's choice of harp as accompanying instrument was no doubt partly influenced by the fact that, intending to work on the proposed harp concerto, he had brought two harp manuals with him on the voyage. A similar stroke of luck was finding the book which contained most of the medieval poems in a shop in Halifax while the ship was berthed there.

A Ceremony of Carols is neither a medley of carols – something quite different from the Christmas story is being narrated – nor a ceremony, unless one regards the opening and closing procession and recession (*Hodie Christus natus est*) as ceremonial. Was Britten already thinking of Yeats's poem 'The Second Coming', which is quoted in *The Turn of the Screw*?

> Turning and turning in the widening gyre
> The falcon cannot hear the falconer;
> Things fall apart; the centre cannot hold;
> Mere anarchy is loosed upon the world,
> The blood-dimmed tide is loosed, and everywhere
> The ceremony of innocence is drowned . . .

A Ceremony of Carols is indeed a ceremony of innocence, a musical representation of life before the fall. (Yeats's poem concludes with a grotesque Nativity: '. . . what rough beast, its hour come round at last. / Slouches towards Bethlehem to be born?' Arguably *A Boy Was Born* and *A Ceremony of Carols* should have their titles interchanged, since the earlier work is unambiguously concerned with Christmas and the latter chiefly with boyhood.)

The opening procession of *A Ceremony of Carols*, in which the boys' voices gradually emerge out of nothing, recalls the similar opening of the 1933 *Alla marcia*, and the first half of the *Ceremony* has affinities with the abortive 'Go *play, boy, play*' string quartet in the mid-thirties. The *Ceremony* achieves what the quartet failed to manage to Britten's satisfaction – it portrays all aspects of boyhood. 'Wolcum Yole!', the first song, evokes the hurly-burly of the school playground, while 'There is no Rose' indulges in lush vocal beauty. 'That Yongë Child' introduces the mother ('With song she lulled him asleep: / That was so sweet a melody . . .'), and in 'Ballulalow' she sings her child a love-song. The vigorous 'As Dew in Aprille' again idealizes the mother-son relationship, and 'This Little Babe', which concludes the first half, could be subtitled – as was one of the movements of the quartet – 'Ragging', for the two-part setting demands to be sung with all the vigour of a dormitory pillow fight.

Now, as in another Britten work concerned with innocence and experience, *Les Illuminations*, comes an instrumental interlude in which Britten seems to be poised reflectively between the two states. The song which opens the second half, 'In Freezing Winter Night', has a plaintiveness which recalls parts of the *Hymn to St Cecilia*. The boys' voices no longer seem to represent the happy state before the fall, but suggest the tragedy of lost innocence. However, this is not to be another *Les Illuminations*. Britten has learnt the lesson which Auden taught him in the *Hymn to St Cecilia*, and the penultimate song, 'Spring Carol', shows how music can rescue even the most downcast spirit: 'Pleasure it is to hear iwis the Birdès sing, / The deer in the dale, the sheep in the vale, / the corn springing'. And in 'Adam lay i-bounden', the work's resounding finale, Britten's chosen words go even beyond Auden, and remind us that without the Fall of Man there would be nothing, no Christian story, no love, no life, no art:

> Blessèd be the time that appil takè was.
> Therefore we moun singen
> Deo gracias!

With this exuberant, delighted shout, over swirling harp glissandi, the cycle ends, and the boys' voices retreat again into silence.

It was in this exultant mood that, as soon as possible after the *Axel Johnson* docked at Liverpool on 17 April 1942, Britten rushed off to see Montagu Slater, for whose left-wing plays he had written music in 1936. He had decided that Slater should be the librettist for *Peter Grimes*. Before he left America the project had seemed almost like a threat, but on 4 May he wrote to Elizabeth Mayer: 'the opera is *leaping* ahead'.

PART THREE

1942–54

The ceremony of innocence

1: The invisible worm

Travelling down from Liverpool, Pears thought the English countryside 'dazzlingly green', and was impressed at the efficient tidying up of bomb damage in London. Britten, however, perceived only 'drab shabbiness' and was nostalgic for American energy – 'there is a provincialism & lack of vitality that makes one yearn for the other side'.

When they arrived in London, Pears went to stay with his parents, who lived in Barnes. Britten had sent a telegram to his sister Barbara to say he was back, asking to stay with her, and for some while he went 'backwards & forwards from Beth (Norwood) to Barbara (Chelsea)' until a permanent London home could be found again. Beth thought he looked 'much older'. Marjorie Fass, too, was struck by his changed appearance – 'very thin & looked ill – Already up to the eyes in work connected with his music.'

Only a matter of days after their arrival, he and Pears went to Boosey & Hawkes to play Ralph Hawkes the recently written works. (Pears played second piano in the orchestral and two-piano pieces, as well as singing.) Julian Herbage of the BBC was there, and was greatly struck by the *Sinfonia da Requiem* and the *Seven Sonnets of Michelangelo*. 'My whole impression', he wrote to his head of department, Sir Adrian Boult, 'is that during the last couple of years Britten has grown greatly in stature as a composer and has now found a simple individual and clear cut style. With his extraordinary mastery of technique one looks for most important if not great things from him in the future.' The BBC immediately commissioned him to write incidental music for a series of propaganda features being sent to America, while Pears's performance of the Michelangelo songs so impressed those present that he was engaged to sing Hoffman in Offenbach's opera at a West End theatre. He learnt the part in a week. But before long-term plans could be made, there loomed the problem of officialdom's attitude to Britten and Pears *vis-à-vis* the war.

'So far people have all been nice to me', Britten wrote to Elizabeth Mayer, 'and there has been no suggestion of vindictiveness. In one or two places, *over*-kindness, which makes one suspicious.' On 28 May 1942 he was called before a tribunal for the registration of Conscientious Objectors. He was accompanied by Canon Stuart Morris, general secretary of the Peace Pledge Union, who had probably helped to write the statement he had already sent to the tribunal. 'Since I believe' (it began)

> that there is in every man the spirit of God, I cannot destroy . . . human life . . . The whole of my life has been devoted to acts of creation (being by profession a composer) and I cannot take part in acts of destruction . . . I believe sincerely that I can help my fellow human beings best, by continuing . . . the creation or propagation of music. I have possibilities of writing music for M[inistry] O[f] I[nformation] films, and for B.B.C. productions . . .

When he came before the tribunal, he was questioned about this statement, and his answers were written up in a report. Evidently he was asked if he was a churchgoer. 'I was brought up in the Church of England,' answered Britten, but added, 'I have not attended for the last five years.' Did he believe in the divinity of Christ? No, he answered, though 'I think his teaching is sound and his example should be followed.' What would he do if Britain were invaded? 'I believe in letting an invader in and then setting him a good example.' Would he be willing to join some non-combatant service, such as the Royal Army Medical Corps? He said he would, but seems to have indicated that he felt it would be a waste of his abilities. What evidence was there that he was a convinced pacifist before the war? 'I have written music for a pacifist song, and a pacifist film.' With this, the proceedings terminated. A week later he received the tribunal's decision: he was to be called up for non-combatant duties.

This was not as bad as it might have been. 'I have passed my first hurdle,' he told Elizabeth Mayer. He could now submit an appeal, which would be heard in a few weeks. (Pears's tribunal had been postponed because he was away in Scotland, on tour with *The Tales of Hoffman*.) Meanwhile Britten began to pick up the threads of his pre-war life.

He went down to Snape, where Beth, Kit and their small son Sebastian had lived at intervals in the Mill. 'Snape is just heaven,' he told Elizabeth Mayer, though petrol rationing and the difficulties of wartime train travel made the journey arduous. Montagu and Enid Slater came down to 'get atmosphere for & discuss "Peter Grimes"', and Britten was delighted by his librettist's attitude to the story – 'full of respect for

Crabbe' – though Slater also had the benefit of 'real stage experience'. A journalist by profession, Slater had been found unfit for active service and was still working in Fleet Street. He was writing the libretto in the early hours of the morning before going to work. 'He has splendid ideas,' Britten told Elizabeth Mayer.

Wulff Scherchen was back in England, serving in the army. In September 1941 Britten had written to him full of hope that they would soon meet. But when they did, Britten found him 'rather altered, I am afraid'. His experience of internment followed by army life had left him 'rather vindictive, and hard'. (He was also twenty-two, significantly older than the eighteen-year-old who in 1938 had still closely resembled the boy with whom Britten had shared the raincoat in Siena.) After another meeting Britten described him, in a note to Pears, as 'impossible', and agreed with Barbara's advice that 'I shouldn't see him much.' He hoped that Wulff might find 'the right girl' and get married. (This eventually happened.)

When he was in London, Britten was still staying with Barbara – Beth had gone north to join Kit – and he told Elizabeth Mayer that he would continue to make temporary homes with her, the Slaters, and at Snape 'until I know my plans'. He assured her that in the long term he wanted to return to America – 'the greater part of my life *must* be spent with you all' – but this was perhaps part of his quasi-filial lavishing of affection on her rather than a serious intention. 'Peter . . . was such a ravishing personality on the stage,' he reported of *The Tales of Hoffman*, prophesying that 'he has a great time ahead on the opera stage', though there was no mention of *Peter Grimes* in this context, nor did he give any indication that they would set up home together.

Pears, however, was definitely on the lookout for a flat they could share. A note to Britten mentioned 'a lovely one in Manchester Square . . . What do you think? . . . my honey bee . . . I love you, I love you . . .' Britten wrote back with playful affection:

Boohoo – why don't you stick around instead of dashing up to Scotland – God, if you prefer the Scotch to me, I'd better pack up shop & go – but, perhaps, it's the Bally [ballet]-Boys. How are they? . . . I went down to Sophy [Wyss] . . . for the week-end . . . & we all motored over to Bradfield [the boys' public school] where Sophy sang . . . & there were some sweet things around (who are filling my mind now, because of course if one can't rely on – – one must have something – etc. you old she-deville). I'm too sleepy to go on with this diary – but . . . I love you very much, & I wish to God (reverently, this time), you were here in bed with me . . . All my love, you old so & so. B.

Pears came down from Scotland one weekend, and Britten walked across London in the early morning to meet him at King's Cross. Yet the letter from him reporting this to Beata Mayer makes no mention of any flat-sharing plan, and reiterates his hope of returning to America, observing of his decision to come to England: 'I still really don't know why I did it – except that I happened to feel it was the right thing.' He told her that 'when this mess is over (& Astrologers say hostilities will cease in Europe in the late fall!!) I'll come running.'

Meanwhile he was sending affectionate letters to young Bobby Rothman on Long Island:

My dear old Bobby,
    . . . The song I wrote for you is now being printed – I'll send you a copy when it's done – mind you sing it!!! . . . tell your father . . . to send me the photos he took of us – especially, the one when I was holding you up like a sack of coals! . . .

With much love,
Ben.

In another letter he told Bobby: 'I do think about you a lot, and anyhow how could I forget you when I have a large photo of you staring at me all the time when I'm working . . .'

By the beginning of August 1942, Pears was back in London, and he and Britten moved on a temporary basis into a house in Cheyne Walk owned by Ursula Nettleship, whom Britten had known since renting the Crantock chalet from her sister in 1936. She was heavily involved with the Council for the Encouragement of Music and the Arts (CEMA), wartime forerunner of the Arts Council. Britten described her as 'a dear person who runs a lot of these CEMA Concerts in Villages & small towns all over the East of England'. He and Pears began to give recitals for her, 'all over the place', wrote Britten, 'under the strangest conditions – playing on awful old pianos – singing easy, but always good, programmes'. They had 'the greatest successes with the simplest audiences'. Besides Britten's own music, including his folk-song arrangements, they performed works by Purcell, Handel, Schubert and Schumann.

This 'war-work' probably counted in Britten's favour when his appeal against the tribunal ruling came up on 18 August. He had written that he could 'not conscientiously' undertake non-combatant duties in the armed forces 'because by doing so I should be no less actively participating in the war than if I were a combatant'. He asked to be 'left free to follow that line of service to the community which my conscience approves & my training makes possible' – that is, music. The appeal was supported in writing by Lawrence Gilliam of the BBC, who stated that Britten's availability to work for radio programmes was in the national interest, and by Frank Bridge's widow, Ethel, who wrote that when still a school-boy he had shown revulsion for military uniform: 'he would ... say "I hate all of it & what it stands for.' Montagu Slater and, rather remark-ably, William Walton came to the appeal hearing as witnesses for Britten. As it happened, the chairman was Sir Francis Floud, father of a school friend of Britten's. Britten recalled that he had been 'good to me when I was at Gresham's', and now he proved 'a wise & sympathetic judge'. The decision was that Britten should be 'completely free to go on with [his] work'.

While delighted by the verdict, Britten was also 'guilty about the whole situation – why I was able to go on working while so many others – etc. etc. However, that was just reaction I suppose.' Pears was equally suc-cessful at his own tribunal.

On 23 September the two of them took part in a recital of new music published by Boosey & Hawkes, at the Wigmore Hall. The programme included *Seven Sonnets of Michelangelo*. Britten felt it 'cruel' to parade the song-cycle 'in the cold light' of a public recital, but the work proved 'a *grand* success'. Those in the audience who had heard Pears sing before the war were amazed at the transformation. 'I shall never forget', Basil Douglas has said, 'hearing Peter for the first time after they got back – this wonderful golden quality, you know, which was quite different to what I'd heard before.' Writing in the *New Statesman*, Edward Sackville-West called the Michelangelo cycle 'indescribably moving ... the finest chamber songs England has had to show since the seventeenth century'. John Ireland, who was present to play the piano in his Second Violin Sonata, had grown thoroughly jealous of Britten's success. 'There are *too many* composers whose names begin with B,' he wrote after the concert, 'Bach, Beethoven, Brahms – Bax, Bliss, BRITTEN.' Yet he allowed that the song-cycle was 'very effective'.

Britten and Pears were immediately invited to perform the cycle again in one of the celebrated wartime National Gallery concerts, on 22 October, and were signed up to record it for HMV. The discs were out in November (an odd-looking pair, one twelve-inch and one ten-inch), and a few months later Pears reported that they had 'sold enormously'. In consequence of the duo's widening reputation, Sophie Wyss lost her position as foremost interpreter of Britten's vocal music. Britten now thought poorly of her singing. In a letter to Pears he describes it as 'screaming'. When she proposed new performances, he side-stepped the suggestions. 'I'm too fond of her to be rude, & not interested enough to be critical. In other words, just weak, weak, weak.' He regretted that she was still singing *Les Illuminations*. Her performance was 'hopelessly inefficient, subjective & (of all things) so coy & whimsey!!!', whereas 'Peter has shown people now how it *really* goes.'

Besides announcing the arrival of a new musical partnership, the Wigmore Hall recital spread word of Britten's personal involvement with Pears. Britten wrote to Pears that an elderly stage hand at the hall, complimenting him on his partner's singing, added that he hadn't been aware of their 'particular (hm) friendship'. Several of Britten's old friends and acquaintances were similarly surprised when it dawned on them that he had a male lover. Nor did they all take to Pears when they met him. Basil Reeve thought him an 'absolute pain', lacking in 'human warmth'. Ronald Duncan had nothing against Pears personally, but suspected that Britten was not at ease with his sexuality. 'He remained a reluctant homosexual', writes Duncan, 'a man in flight from himself, who often punished others for the sin he felt he'd committed himself. He was a man on a rack.'

After Britten's death, Michael Kennedy, preparing a book about him, wrote to Pears making a similar suggestion about Britten's attitude to his sexual orientation, and its effect on his life and music. Pears wrote back:

> As to 'anguish through guilt'! Forget it! Ben never regarded his own passionate feelings for me or his earlier friends as anything but good, natural, and profoundly creative. In that direction there was never a moment of guilt. I do not believe that Ben's private life plays any role in 'the assessment of his artistry & personality'. He was a musical genius. Is one really interested in the sex life of the great musicians or the less great? In Bach, Mozart, Gounod, Stanford or Wm Walton? I don't think so.

Norman Del Mar, who knew Britten well in the fifties, observes: 'Of course Peter would say that; it stands to reason.' John Evans remarks that Pears himself was completely lacking in guilt about his sexuality: 'Peter was absolutely together about himself – he was far more together about it than most present-day gays.' Del Mar agrees entirely with Duncan: 'Ben really was tortured by homosexuality. You weren't aware of the guilt, of course, when you were with him – when I was working with him, it didn't come into my vision. It's only in retrospect that one realizes it.'

Donald Mitchell says: 'I think Peter was quite wrong in suggesting that Ben was a hundred per cent homosexual. There were other percentages otherwise directed, many other empathies and sympathies. Basically, of

Top 21 Kirkley Cliff Road, Lowestoft, Britten's birthplace and childhood home.
'I come from a very ordinary middle class family,' wrote Britten.

Left Edith Rhoda Britten, née Hockey, Benjamin's mother.

Right Robert Victor Britten, Benjamin's 'Pop'.

Benjamin, aged about six, on board ship with his father and a naval acquaintance, probably in Lowestoft harbour.

The four Britten children in the garden at Lowestoft. (Left to right) Barbara, Bobby, Beth and Benjamin.

Top Benjamin, aged six and a half, as Tom the Water-Baby, sitting on the lap of his mother (as Mrs Do-as-you-would-be-done-by), at the Sparrow's Nest Theatre, Lowestoft, June 1919. Leaning against her is John Pounder, afterwards a prep-school friend of Benjamin.

Above Benjamin and his mother on Lowestoft beach.

T. J. E. Sewell as Britten knew him. 'I can remember the first time . . . that I heard a boy being beaten . . .'

Captain T. J. E. Sewell, six years before he became Britten's headmaster.

Top Britten, aged nine, sits on the ground just to the left of his headmaster in this South Lodge School group photograph.

Above 'Pop' and Mrs Britten in the garden at Lowestoft. Mr Britten's daughter-in-law remembers how 'He'd sit there . . . and look sideways at you . . . His eyes . . . were sort of hooded.'

A studio portrait of Britten at the age of sixteen.

Top   Britten's parents, with 'Pop' in his dentist's coat.

Above   Britten with his sister Beth and the family dog Caesar, snapped by a street photographer on the Lowestoft sea-front.

Top   John Ireland, Britten's composition teacher at the Royal College of Music. 'He is *terribly* critical and enough to take the heart out of any one!'

Above   Frank Bridge, Britten's unofficial composition teacher, hosting a tennis party at his cottage on the Sussex Downs. Britten stands to the right of Bridge; Mrs Bridge kneels at their feet.

Right Frank Bridge and his wife photographed by Britten. Between them sits the third member of the Bridge ménage, Marjorie Fass.

A group of South Lodge boys photographed by Britten, when he was aged twenty. He had invited them to his home for tea in June 1924. Thirteen-year-old Piers Dunkerley, 'most disconcertingly witty' and 'terribly good-looking', is the second from the right. Mrs Britten sits under the awning.

Top left   Britten in 1934, aged twenty, with Francis Barton, who at the age of eighteen was about to become a Royal Marine. 'He meant a great deal to me in those early days,' said Britten.

Top right   W. H. Auden, photographed by Carl Van Vechten. On the day of their first meeting, Britten wrote in his diary: 'Wystan Auden . . . is the most amazing man.'

Left   A wartime photograph of Piers Dunkerley. In the thirties Britten referred to him as 'My foster child'.

Right A snapshot by Britten of a group of friends he made at a music festival in Barcelona in 1936. On the left stands Peter Burra, then a close friend of Peter Pears. Seated is Lennox Berkeley.

Below Britten on a Cornish beach with his mother and sister Barbara in the summer of 1936, while composing *Our Hunting Fathers*. He wrote in his diary that his mother disapproved very strongly of part of it, 'but that is almost an incentive'.

Left Britten sent Piers Dunkerley this photograph of himself outside the Old Mill, Snape, which he bought in 1937, at the age of twenty-three.

Below Peter Pears (back row, far right) with a group of fellow teachers at the Grange Preparatory School, Crowborough, during the academic year 1931–2. A friend feared he had consigned himself to 'a rather drab destiny' as a schoolmaster.

Top   A 1938 Howard Coster photograph of Britten with Lennox Berkeley. Britten wrote: 'He is a dear & I'm glad I'm going to live with him.' (*National Portrait Gallery*)

Right   Wulff Scherchen photographed by Britten at the Old Mill.

Elizabeth Mayer. 'How I miss you, dear boy!' she wrote to Britten when he was away from her Long Island home. 'Everything here awaits you patiently. Your table at the window, the little piece of red blotting paper . . .'

In upstate New York during the summer of 1939, Aaron Copland looks at the camera but Peter Pears seems unable to take his eyes off Britten. 'Ich liebe dich . . . je t'aime . . . I'm terribly in love with you,' Pears wrote to him.

Top   Britten conducts Pears in *Les Illuminations*, CBS studios,
New York, May 1941.

Above   Britten's photograph of Pears with 'the little Owls', Ethel Bartlett and
Rae Robertson, taken while staying with them in California during 'the
unhappy summer of 1941'.

Auden, photographed with Britten in America, looks as if he is delivering the lecture he gave Britten in his letter of 31 January 1942: 'If you are really to develop to your full stature, you will have, I think, to suffer, and make others suffer.'

Britten with David Rothman, Long Island music enthusiast and shopkeeper. Rothman has recalled how Britten 'wanted to stop writing music, and wanted to work in my store'.

On the same occasion, Britten was also photographed with Rothman's son Bobby. 'I do think about you a lot,' he wrote to Bobby after returning to England.

Top   Enid Slater, wife of the librettist of *Peter Grimes*, took this picture of Britten on the balcony outside his bedroom at the Old Mill, Snape, while he was writing the opera, premièred in June 1945.

Above   Britten and his piano at the Old Mill. (*George Rodger*) course, yes; but I resist the exclusivity that Peter was proposing, as I believe Ben would have done. Indeed, I recall him saying to me in Edinburgh in 1968, when we went out for a drive, that he objected to being categorized, "type-cast" (his word). And I think he was right in his attitude – and about himself.' Another close associate of Britten in the post-war years, Stephen Reiss, echoes this: 'I think it would be a mistake to see him as purely homosexual.' Eric Crozier writes: 'Britten once said to me that he "hoped Peter would get married one day" (just as Lennox Berkeley had done in middle age) and he even mentioned Kathleen Ferrier as a possible partner for him.' Imogen Holst's diary for 1953 records how, one day while out driving near Snape, Britten 'became more confidential than ever before & talked about Peter & how if he found the right girl to marry he supposed he'd have "to lump it" and that nothing would ever interfere with their relationship.'

*

A few days after the Wigmore Hall recital, which had been taken by many people as a public announcement of his involvement with Pears, Britten went down with influenza, and was still suffering from it two months later. A specialist could find nothing essentially wrong with him, but concluded that he had 'practically no resistance'.

During the autumn of 1942 he renewed his romantic friendship with 'young Piers Dunkerley' as he still described him, though Dunkerley was now twenty-one and an officer in the Royal Marines. They spent 'as much time as possible' together, some of it at Snape. Yet in the meantime his letters to Pears expressed total devotion. 'I just can't bear the thought of separation,' he wrote when Pears was setting off for a series of factory concerts. 'Never never have I or could I love anyone as I love my darling.' He had written to his mother in just the same manner in his school-days.

Early in 1943, he and Pears found rooms that suited them both, on three floors above the Home & Colonial Stores at 45a St John's Wood High Street. They moved in together. 'It was very exciting going round choosing curtain materials,' Pears told Elizabeth Mayer. 'You can imagine how I enjoyed it and Ben loathed it!' No sooner had they moved in than Britten became ill again, this time with an oddly childish ailment, an attack of measles – 'a very bad attack', reported Pears. He was admitted to a fever hospital in South London and told to undertake no work for two months.

Since his return from America eleven months earlier he had written no music other than BBC ephemera and revisions to *A Ceremony of Carols*. He was now grateful to the measles for getting him out of further 'boring jobs' such as writing the score for a film of Shaw's *Caesar and*

Cleopatra. According to a Boosey & Hawkes internal memorandum, he said that the film would do nothing 'towards the solution of his own problem as a composer'. From hospital, he wrote of his illness that 'the worst trouble is depression'.

Another letter from his sick-bed, to Ralph Hawkes, asked for the score of *Rosenkavalier.* Britten said he wanted to 'pick the old man's brains for my opera'. There are traces of Strauss in the ensemble for women's voices in Act II of *Peter Grimes.* He signed his next letter to Pears in German, 'Immer dein', ever thine.

Not a note of *Peter Grimes* was yet written. In the letter to Hawkes, Britten said he was glad to be released from the Shaw film because it 'would have held up the Ballet & the Opera too long – To say nothing about the Sonata!' This suggests that the opera was not necessarily more urgent than a projected ballet for Sadler's Wells on the Mark of Cain, and a sonata for orchestra which he had been contemplating for some while. In fact he was having serious doubts about the opera's viability, not musical but dramatic. Would anybody, he asked Enid Slater, 'be able to bear it on the stage?'

Until now he had seemed happy with Montagu Slater's libretto, which had been completed a few months earlier, but from hospital he wrote to Pears wondering whether another writer ought not to be co-opted. Auden was a possibility, but 'there are the old objections, & besides, he's not to hand'. (The objections were presumably to Auden's domineering personality.) Nobody else seemed suitable, so Britten began to reconsider the opera's story himself.

He concentrated on 'the character of Grimes himself which I find doesn't come across nearly clearly enough. At the moment he is just a pathological case – no reasons & not many symptoms! He's got to be changed alot.' Yet he was still convinced that 'it is right for me to do *this* opera. I am too interested in it for me to drop it now.' He sensed that there could be a whole string of future operas if this one came off – 'I mean to write a few in my time!'

Grimes had indeed become a rather motiveless psychopath. In the early days of planning, he had been supplied with a motive, but then deprived of it again. The earliest attempts at a synopsis, written by Britten and Pears while they were waiting for their boat home from America, include a passage in Pears's hand in which Grimes addresses the apprentice:

Admits his [the boy's] youth hurts him, his innocence galls him, his uselessness maddens him. He [Grimes] had no father to love him, why should he [deal kindly with the boy]? His father only beat him, why

should not he [beat the boy]? 'Prove yourself some use, not only pretty
– work – not only be innocent – work do not stare; would you rather I
loved you? you are sweet, young etc. – but you must love me, why do
you not love me? Love me darn you.'

In the next notes that they made for the opera, while on board ship,
Britten and Pears omitted any such homoerotic motivation. (Pears has
said that, at the beginning of work on *Peter Grimes*, when various people
were being considered as librettist, he 'wondered whether I couldn't have
done [it] myself, but . . . I hadn't the skill or the time really.')

In Slater's hands, *Peter Grimes* became a story about a community,
much like Slater's own left-wing plays of the thirties, with Grimes, the
poor working-class fisherman, being driven to violence by an iniquitous
class system – his cruelty to the apprentices was shown as the consequence of his effort to make himself rich and join the bourgeoisie.
Slater writes of his view of Grimes: 'Sooner or later there will be inten-
tional cruelty [to the boys] . . . Yet what else is a Peter Grimes to do?'

An advantage of Slater's approach was the expansion of the background characters. The early Britten–Pears drafts of the synopsis had
referred vaguely to 'villagers', but Slater drew on other parts of Crabbe's
The Borough to give the opera a splendid gallery of local inhabitants. In
May 1942, Britten wrote to Elizabeth Mayer: 'It is getting more and
more an opera about the community, whose life is "illuminated" for this
moment by the tragedy of the murders. Ellen [the schoolmistress] is
growing in importance, & there are fine minor characters, such as the
Parson, pub-keeper, "quack"-apothecary, & doctor.' Yet while this
opened out the story in one direction, it narrowed the character of
Grimes. Britten here talks of 'murders': Grimes's guilt in the apprentices'
death is assumed. Slater's concentration on the socio-political implications had robbed the central figure of psychological interest and
reduced him to a 'pathological case' or victim of the social system, whose
tragedy nobody might 'be able to bear . . . on the stage'. It also removed
the opera very far from the theme of innocence and its loss towards
which Auden, in the *Hymn to St Cecilia*, had directed Britten. It is
therefore understandable that Britten felt uneasy about the project. As to
Pears, the extent to which the opera had now drifted away from him is
indicated by a list of characters jotted down by Britten on the back of a
letter which he received on 1 June 1942, soon after Slater had become
involved. In this list, no major role is allocated to a tenor. Peter Grimes is
to be sung by a baritone.

This detail was noticed among Britten's papers by Philip Brett, who in

the book he has edited on *Peter Grimes* describes it as a 'rather ...
devastating' detail of the opera's history. Brett suggests that Britten may
not have believed that Pears, a young unknown in the opera world,
would be allowed to sing the role. Yet by June 1942, the earliest date at
which the list could have been written, Pears had already achieved a
breakthrough into opera in *The Tales of Hoffman*, and during the
following nine months, when there was still no indication that Britten
intended him to sing Grimes, he greatly strengthened his operatic reputation.

His performance as Hoffman was seen by the soprano Joan Cross,
artistic director of the Sadler's Wells Opera Company and Eric Crozier,
then a young member of the Wells production team. 'A week or two
later', writes Crozier, 'he came to sing for us and some of the musical
staff.' There were certain differences of opinion: Crozier thought him 'a
wonderful find – quite different from anyone we had in the company, the
average operatic tenor. He looked good, he was intelligent, he was
quick.' However, some of the music staff felt that he was 'not operatic
material', since his voice was very un-Italian and possibly too small to
carry. Joan Cross overruled these objections, largely because of Pears's
personal charm. 'I make no bones about that,' she says; 'I thought him
immensely charming.'

'Peter ... is permanently with Sadlers Wells Opera,' Britten wrote in
May 1943. Pears was plunged into a heavy schedule of touring dates –
the company's parent theatre in London was closed, and it mostly
appeared in the provinces – and had to learn major roles as he went
along. He was Tamino in *The Magic Flute* in January 1943 and the Duke
in *Rigoletto* in April, to name only the first two of a whole series of
principal parts. There was some resentment among the older tenors in the
company whom he displaced, and Joan Cross admits that his acting had
limitations – 'He took stage direction from people and did the right
things at the right time, but he was frightfully awkward'. (Noël Coward
described Pears on stage as 'the one who looks as if his legs don't belong
to him'.) However, a young army officer, George, Viscount Lascelles,
later the Earl of Harewood, was in the audience when Pears sang Alfredo
in *La Traviata* and was impressed by this very awkwardness, 'the slight
withdrawness, the slight shyness, the ability to stay within oneself and
not be over-forthcoming', which he found a refreshing change from the
usual operatic style of 'wearing your heart on your sleeve'.

As to Pears's voice, Harewood says: 'I think what struck one was its
strangeness, its non-operatic quality ... a sort of lightness of colour ... a
very un-Italian voice ... It took a lot of getting used to at that time.'

Another member of the Wells audience expected the worst of British tenors, and literally sat up in astonishment at Pears's first entry. This was the Austrian-born musician Hans Keller, then in his early twenties. 'For once,' Keller writes, recalling that night,

> a singer who isn't a poor substitute for an instrumentalist! A voice of character which carries farther and deeper than any voice thrice as strong! A musician who knows, lives, what Mozart and he are doing ... He does not merely act well. He instinctively acts the music. No movement, no fooling that contradicts it ... Within eleven bars, I have turned from a stern examiner into an admiring pupil.

Keller realized that Pears's voice was not in itself particularly fine – it 'would not be anything out of the ordinary if he were a mediocre musical personality'. But equipped with a greater voice (argues Keller) 'he would have found it more difficult to achieve the pronounced character of his timbres, the powerful tensions of his phrasings ... It is not easy to be the master of one's voice when it is easy to be its servant.' Murray Perahia, who often accompanied Pears in his later years, describes his voice in similar terms to Keller's: 'It didn't have this great singer's kind of polish to it, so you felt the person immediately from it ... You felt that everything was very sincere; the emotions came to you straight – a little bit understated, perhaps, and I loved that; I loved that they weren't in Technicolor.'

Britten must have been aware of the impression Pears was making on audiences. Eric Crozier says that he attended as many of Pears's Sadler's Wells performances as he could. 'Ben and I often sat together', writes Crozier, 'squashed together side by side in the cramped staff-box, and I shall always remember his rapt attention when Peter or Joan were singing and how he actually breathed each phrase with them.' Pears's apparent exclusion from *Peter Grimes* does not, therefore, seem explicable on professional grounds.

Britten, on the surface, seemed to be utterly contented with their 'marriage'. In a letter to Pears on 21 March 1943 he refers to it in that fashion: 'think of all the other married couples who are separated for everso much longer!!' After a 'tiff' in November 1942, he wrote abjectly that he was 'Worrying as to whether I am not good for you – not caring enough for your health & work. But, in humbleness I say it, give me a chance to reform, my dear. I swear in the future I will look after you.' Pears replied: 'You are so sweet taking all the blame for our miserable tiffs, our awful nagging heart-aches – but I know as well as I know anything that it is really *my* fault.' And in another letter Pears wrote: 'O my precious darling, parting from you is such agony – Just hearing your voice is joy . . . Your loving man P.'

Joan Cross observed the ups and downs in their relationship at this period: 'It was on, it was off, it was on, it was off! It was just the same as any young people who were in love, and who had rows. They had terrible rows.' Certainly they had differences much like any married couple. Sue Phipps says that her uncle was 'always changing pictures' around the house or flat, and 'Ben used to get quite worried, and say, "I know where I am in this house, please don't change it."' Another difference was over punctuality. Pears became notorious, at least when in Britten's company, for cutting it fine when catching trains. 'Really there did seem to be a sort of Jekyll and Hyde to Peter in this respect,' says Sue Phipps. 'On the one hand he liked to be beautifully organized, but he liked to defy that organization a lot of the time too. The thing about catching trains at the last minute wouldn't ever have got that far if Ben hadn't liked to be at the railway station the day before.'

Britten's intention of making Grimes a baritone role seems to have melted away while he was in hospital with leisure to consider the problems of the character. Only a few days after telling Pears that the opera had 'got to be changed a lot', he was writing to Ralph Hawkes that he had 'some new improvements in view'. He did not say what these were, but a letter to Elizabeth Mayer shortly afterwards, on 6 April 1943, revealed that a crucial decision had been made:

> Peter is with Sadlers Wells Opera company these two weeks – doing Magic Flute, Rigoletto, & rehearsing Traviata. He is singing so well, & acting with such abandon, that he is well on the way to becoming an operatic star. I wish you could see him, & we all could discuss his performances. *When* I write it, & *if* it is put on here, I hope he'll do the principal part in Peter Grimes.

*

Britten was out of hospital by 21 March 1943, convalescing at Snape and telling Pears he felt well enough 'to write things for you, – better than nothing'. Two weeks later he told Elizabeth Mayer: 'I've practically completed a new work (6 Nocturnes) for Peter and a lovely young horn player Dennis Brain, & Strings . . . It is not important stuff, but quite pleasant, I think.'

The *Serenade* for tenor, horn and strings, a breaking of the creative silence Britten had experienced since *A Ceremony of Carols*, owed its instrumentation to his admiration for the twenty-two-year-old principal horn player in the RAF Orchestra, which had broadcast his incidental music to a radio series, *An American in England*, the previous summer and autumn. After Britten had heard Brain's playing in the first pro-gramme, 'I took every opportunity to write elaborate horn solos into each subsequent score!' Norman Del Mar, playing in the horn section alongside Brain during these broadcasts, remembers Britten questioning Brain about the instrument's technical possibilities. The Prologue which opens the *Serenade* was a consequence of these discussions. The horn plays unaccompanied, entirely on its natural harmonics, without the use of valves. As Peter Evans has pointed out in *The Music of Benjamin Britten* (1989), this is music which evokes the natural order of things, a world in which the natural laws are being unquestioningly obeyed.

One of the non-musical inspirations of the *Serenade* may have been the landscape paintings of Britten's fellow Suffolk-native John Constable. Enid Slater had lent him a book about Constable, already one of his favourite artists, to read in hospital, and he told her he was 'lapping [it] up' – that he had 'an almost sexy love for his paintings'. He was attracted by the story of the young Constable's friendship with a local lad, Johnny Dunthorne, twenty-two years younger than him. Britten commented: 'Young Dunthorne was a pet!'

The 'Pastoral' which forms the first song in the *Serenade* is a setting of lines by the seventeenth-century poet Charles Cotton, which could be a description of a Constable landscape: 'The Day's grown old; the fainting Sun / Has but a little way to run . . . / The shadows now so long do grow, / That brambles like tall cedars show . . .' The BBC producer Richard Butt says Pears told him that Britten's wide-ranging knowledge of poetry, evident in his choice of texts for the *Serenade* and other song-cycles, was largely the result of his habit, when experiencing difficulties in his work, of wandering about the house and picking books from the shelves at random. Long afterwards he would remember poems encountered by chance on these occasions.

Throughout the 'Pastoral', the horn continues to play in simple dia-tonic phrases, while the tenor soloist is given an elegiac melody. Similarly in the second song, a setting of Tennyson's 'The splendour falls on castle walls', an equally 'natural' musical palette – this time major thirds – is used in voice and horn-calls to give an almost childlike impersonation of the bugle echoes described in this poem. However, the *Serenade* is not simply an exercise in musical landscape painting, as its dedicatee Edward Sackville-West fully realized. Cousin of Vita, original of the hypo-chondriac Uncle Davey in Nancy Mitford's *The Pursuit of Love*, dilet-tante writer and wartime member of the BBC, he had fallen in love with Britten, whom he addressed in letters as 'My dear White Child' – an allusion to the *Hymn to St Cecilia*. He helped to choose words for the

Serenade, so his description of it in a 1944 article on Britten's music in *Horizon* is probably close to Britten's own concept of the work:

> The subject is Night and its prestigia [conjuring tricks]: the lengthening shadow, the distant bugle at sunset, the Baroque panoply of the starry sky, the heavy angels of sleep; but also the cloak of evil – the worm in the heart of the rose, the sense of sin in the heart of man. The whole sequence forms an Elegy or Nocturnal (as Donne would have called it), resuming the thoughts and images suitable to evening.

The 'sense of sin' makes its presence chillingly felt in the third song. 'Elegy'. This begins wordlessly, with more 'natural' chords in the strings, but the horn, though still moving according to a 'natural' pattern (octaves and other perfect intervals), introduces chromaticism for the first time, and in a few bars has ranged through all twelve notes of the chromatic scale. The effect is of a pastoral landscape strangely disturbed. The voice now enters, with a recitative setting of a very short Blake poem which tells us what we already know from the music:

> O Rose, thou art sick;
> The invisible worm
> That flies in the night,
> In the howling storm,
> Has found out thy bed
> Of crimson joy;
> And his dark, secret love
> Does thy life destroy.

The horn then resumes its doleful peregrination around the twelve notes.

Nowhere before had Britten conveyed the 'sense of sin' so graphically. And now comes the equivalent of a *dies irae* or dance of death, a relentless funeral march in the strings, over which the tenor, at the very top of his range (increasing the sense of strain), intones the fifteenth-century Lyke Wake Dirge, with its dread-filled description of what awaits the soul after death ('This ae nighte, this ae nighte . . . / Fire and fleet and candle-lighte . . .'). Britten's setting, with the tenor's grotesque swoops up the octave, suggests no ordinary night fears experienced by a restless sleeper, but mortal terror of judgement – 'The fire will burn thee to the bare bane'. One remembers Ronald Duncan's words about Britten's attitude to homosexuality: 'the sin he felt he'd committed . . .'

There is now a startling change of mood in the *Serenade*, as if in attempt to banish the fear of hell-fire. Abruptly we are in the high-spirited baroque world of Ben Jonson's invocation to Diana in her role as moon goddess. Britten's exuberant music certainly evokes 'the Baroque panoply of the starry sky', but the gaiety seems rather forced. The last song, Keats' 'O soft embalmer of the still midnight', attempts to lull the restless mind into oblivion, but the 'natural' major triads in the strings are juxtaposed chromatically, so as to produce a mood that is at once soothing and disturbed, and the music makes it by no means certain that the singer's final plea, 'Save me from curious Conscience, that still lords / Its strength for darkness, burrowing like a mole', will be answered. The horn is silent during this song, as if it might tip the balance in the uneasy calm, and when it returns for the unaccompanied Epilogue it is off-stage, reiterating its 'natural' harmonics so far away that they no longer seem accessible, but merely a distant memory of innocence.

A seventh song was written for the *Serenade* but then discarded, a setting of Tennyson's 'Now sleeps the crimson petal, now the white', which was a favourite of Britten's mother (in the Roger Quilter version). The Britten setting begins languidly, with cradle-rocking strings, and the horn (as it never does in the *Serenade* proper) compliantly repeats the tenor's vocal phrases. However, this is no mere cradle-song, but an invitation to make love: 'So fold thyself, my dearest, thou, and slip / Into my bosom and be lost in me.' As tenor and horn both reach their climax, they move – not quite together rhythmically – in chromatic thirds which create a powerful discord against the strings. The love portrayed in this music is clearly at odds with the 'natural' world – is indeed that 'dark, secret love' which causes such agonies of conscience in the *Serenade*.

*

'I'm much better', Britten wrote to Enid Slater from Snape on 7 April 1943, just as he was finishing the *Serenade*, 'but it takes ages to get fit, & I get horrible attacks of depression (I've been down with it in the last four or five days.)' A work completed the following month suggests that the depression had not receded: the *Prelude and Fugue* for eighteen-part string orchestra, written for Boyd Neel, whose ensemble was celebrating its tenth anniversary. It opens so tensely, with violent tonal clashes between lower and upper strings, that it evokes the hell-fire fears of the *Serenade*. But then came a work which managed to dispel this mood.

A parish clergyman, the Revd Walter Hussey, was organizing the forthcoming Jubilee of his church, St Matthew's, Northampton, and wrote to William Walton asking if he would compose a piece for the occasion. Walton declined, and Hussey turned to Britten, emphasizing the excellence of his amateur choir. He apologized for what seemed an 'impertinent' request, but explained that he had a 'bee' about 'closer association between the arts and the Church'. Britten accepted, at first declining a fee and saying he would recoup his reward in royalties when the work was published. Pressed by Hussey, he asked for £25, which Hussey willingly paid. Britten suggested 'Something lively for such an occasion, don't you think?', came to Northampton to hear the choir, and got to work quickly. He chose as text parts of the Jubilate Agno of Christopher Smart, a rambling mid-eighteenth-century poem composed largely in a madhouse. It had only been published for the first time in 1939, as *Rejoice in the Lamb*, and Britten told Elizabeth Mayer that 'Wystan introduced me to [it] in the States.'

Finished in July 1943, Britten's festival cantata for soloists, choir and organ, *Rejoice in the Lamb*, stands in the same relation to the *Serenade* as does *A Ceremony of Carols* to the *Hymn to St Cecilia*. As in the earlier pair of works, Britten is turning from the (in this case despairing) contemplation of the loss of innocence to a re-creation of that innocence itself. The choice of a madman's semi-nonsensical ramblings may seem an odd one for this purpose, but as Peter Porter has observed, 'Smart captures in his poem an innocence known perhaps only to children and the benignly insane, and in so doing shows the rest of us ... that heaven does indeed lie about us.'

Rejoice in the Lamb – in which, Peter Evans points out, the influence of Purcell is perceptible for the first time in Britten's music – uses much the same devices as the *Serenade* to tell the same story, except that this time there is a happy ending. Once more, innocence is depicted by musical simplicity. In the opening section the choir, singing in unison, scarcely moves away from middle C, the note from which every child's knowledge of music begins, and the lyrical solo for boy treble, 'For I will consider my Cat Jeoffrey', is given an accompaniment suggesting juvenile piano exercises. Once again chromaticism, introduced in the tenor's lament that he is possessed with a devil portrays a mind struggling against itself. Yet, as in the *Hymn to St Cecilia*, music itself is embraced for its power to heal such anguish, and the cantata reaches a joyful climax with Smart's delighted catalogue of musical instruments, and the assurance that, when God the Father plays upon his harp, 'malignity ceases and the devils themselves are at peace'. Britten's serene setting of these words suggests that he believed them himself.

He conducted the final rehearsals and the performance at St Matthew's, Northampton, during a Jubilee service on 21 September 1943, and was delighted with the standard of the choir. The alto solo, a setting of Smart's lines about a mouse challenging a cat (which Britten handles in mock-operatic style, possibly recalling the melodramatic cat-and-mouse cartoon films he had loved in the thirties), was sung by the curate, the Revd Methuen Clark, who recalls: 'I did croak a bit on the lowest note, but . . . when I'd finished he winked, and gave the thumbs up sign to say that he was pleased.' Walter Hussey had managed to draw out the small boy in him. Urgently requiring answers to various questions about the cantata, Hussey had sent Britten a questionnaire in the form of a mock examination paper. Britten signed it 'E. B. Britten (minor)', adding: 'So now you know the stature of the composer you're dealing with – !'

2: The clue whose meaning we avoid

Processing alongside Britten as he walked into St Matthew's, Northampton, to conduct *Rejoice in the Lamb* in September 1943 was a man whom he described to Elizabeth Mayer as a 'great new friend Peter & I have made, an *excellent* composer, & most delightful & intelligent man, Michael Tippett'. Britten had shared his commission from Walter Hussey with Tippett, who had written a *Fanfare for Brass*. Hussey recalls how Britten 'wore surplice and cassock and processed with the choir, though he had slight hesitations about this. However, Michael Tippett encouraged him and they walked together and sat in choir in like style.'

Tippett had first become aware of Britten nine years earlier, at a Macnaghten–Lemare Concert on 17 December 1934 which included the first public performance of *A Boy Was Born*. 'I had no intuition then', Tippett writes, 'that the slim figure walking down the gangway to take his bow before the public would become so decisive and beloved a personality in my life.' In 1934, Britten had been twenty-one, Tippett nearly thirty, but while Britten had already broken through the barrier of public recognition, Tippett was still a musical unknown. Brought up in Suffolk by parents not unlike Britten's – his father was an entrepreneurial businessman with a lively sense of humour, his mother a former Suffragette who wrote novels – he had been encouraged to play the piano and to improvise wildly at the keyboard, 'which I called "composing", though I only had the vaguest notion of what that meant'. No Frank Bridge had appeared in his early life, and he was sent away to boarding-school at the age of nine. Fettes College, Edinburgh, which he attended in his early teens, was even more discouraging to a musician than Gresham's, while homosexuality was rife. Tippett says in his autobiography:

> Most alarming was the sexual side of things. My naïve confessions on the subject in a letter to my mother brought my parents immediately . . .

they threatened to publicise the goings-on unless the headmaster was removed. A new headmaster arrived, who persuaded my parents I should stay on. I was then pressurised by my housemaster into standing before the entire school and accounting for the sexual behaviour of every boy I knew. This was particularly difficult as I was myself 'involved' with a boy. I couldn't remain at Fettes much longer and decided the only way out was to reveal all to my parents. I geared myself up to face my mother to tell her I was no longer a virgin. It was the first time I stood up openly to her, and it resulted in my being taken away from Fettes – which indeed I desperately wanted. For decades afterwards I had such amnesia about the whole experience that I hardly acknowledged the existence of Fettes in any account of my early life.

Tippett's biographer Ian Kemp suggests that 'a certain moral toughness in his makeup' may be said to derive from this experience. This became evident at his next school, at Stamford in Lincolnshire, where he refused to join the army cadet corps and declared himself atheist. His parents were asked to remove him after he had boycotted house prayers for a fortnight. He was now determined to be a composer, and he remained in the town of Stamford, living in lodgings and studying the piano with a Mrs Tinkler, who had taught another Stamfordian, Malcolm Sargent. At the age of eighteen he was admitted to the Royal College of Music.

Though his relations with his composition teacher, Charles Wood, were much happier than Britten's with John Ireland, Tippett soon discovered that the RCM syllabus only provided very limited training, and he began his own systematic study of the history of music, by stages so slow and careful that he reckoned he would be forty before he reached the twentieth century. (His way of learning a work he considered important was to copy it out in full.) To compensate for the RCM's failure to provide practical experience of performing, he found a small choir to conduct at Oxted in Surrey, where after leaving the RCM in 1929 he made his home, earning a small amount from a preparatory school where he taught French and played the organ for services ('I never played the pedals properly'). In Oxted he conducted some of his own work, but was entirely discontented with his progress as a composer, and decided to study for a further two years (1930–2) with R. O. Morris at the RCM. Like Britten, he was attracted to left-wing politics, and he too came under a poet's influence, in this case T. S. Eliot. 'Eliot told him what to read', writes Ian Kemp, 'and having read the book recommended Tippett would return and ask what to read next.'

In 1932 he fell in love with a painter named Wilfred Franks. 'Meeting Wilf', he says in his autobiography,

> was quite the deepest, most shattering experience of falling in love: and I am quite certain that it was a major factor underlying the discovery of my own musical 'voice' – something that couldn't be analysed purely in technical terms: all that love flowed out in the slow movement of my First String Quartet, an unbroken span of lyrical music in which all four instruments sing ardently from start to finish.

The relationship with Franks came to a painful end in 1938, and to survive this upheaval Tippett turned to Jungian self-analysis, which left him much more confident and independent as an individual and a composer. Meanwhile his political sympathies led him to take various musical jobs in the Co-operative and Workers' educational movements, and in 1940 he was appointed director of music at Morley College in south London, where he had already conducted an orchestra of unemployed professional musicians. During 1942 he wanted a tenor soloist for an Orlando Gibbons anthem at the Morley, and Peter Pears was recommended by a friend who had heard him. 'I suppose I wrote to him,' says Tippett. 'He turned up, and he brought Ben with him.'

Tippett was soon listening to them both performing *Seven Sonnets of Michelangelo* at their National Gallery concert. Himself no pianist, he was astonished by Britten's playing – 'the music simply spurted out of his fingers' – and he thought the Michelangelo settings 'extraordinary, because they sounded almost Italian'. Asked whether he was attracted by Britten's music at this period, Tippett answers: 'No composer can be objective about another composer.'

By the end of 1942 a friendship had been established. 'I had been to supper with Ben & Peter last Saturday,' Tippett wrote to a mutual acquaintance on 4 December. 'Showed them my magnum opus, an oratorio called "A Child of Our Time". The text is my own, with advice from T. S. Eliot ... Ben has just written me a p.c. "What a grand work the Oratorio is & A performance *must* be arranged soon." Easier said than done!'

Several of Tippett's pieces, including his *Concerto for Double String Orchestra* (1939), had received performances, and the German music publisher Schott had accepted some of his work, but because of wartime conditions it was very slow in appearing. He depended on the encouragement of friends, and this was not always forthcoming. He had shown *A Child of Our Time* – a meditation on the assassination in 1938 of a Nazi official by a Jewish boy – to Walter Goehr, who had conducted some of his music. Goehr was enthusiastic but could offer no immediate hope; Tippett writes that he 'advised me ... to shut it up in a drawer, which, being rather patient and literal, I did. Ben had the manuscript out of the drawer at once ...'

Reading the score, Britten found a composer and librettist who was *sui generis*. In student days Tipett had had difficulty in assimilating classical harmony and tonality, and his contemporary style was a natural voice rather than the imitation of other moderns or, as in Britten's case, the product of a fluent technique. As to the libretto, Tippett had assembled *A Child of Our Time* from such sources as Jung and Wilfred Owen, but had narrated the story with childlike bareness – 'He shoots the official . . . / And see – he is dead' – and had included, at moments when Bach might have placed chorales, a number of Negro spirituals. Britten turned his attention to these, perhaps because they were the most conventional part of the score, and suggested that Tippett could improve one of them by raising the tenor solo an octave. 'This I entirely agreed with,' writes Tippett, 'and so this minute piece of Britten composition is in the score.'

Britten's encouragement was apparently effective with Tippett's publishers. 'Schotts are going to bring out a piano-vocal score as the first move,' Tippett wrote a few days after his meal with Britten and Pears. Certainly it was Britten who persuaded him to 'venture on a performance' of *A Child of Our Time*, though it was more than a year before it took place. Pears and Joan Cross were among the soloists at the première in March 1944.

'We were close, the three of us,' Tippett says of his friendship with Britten and Pears during wartime. 'Ben came with Peter, and stayed in my tiny bungalow-cottage – extremely uncomfortable; there was one bed for me and a sort of half double bed for them.' In his autobiography he recalls that 'Once, Peter had to go off to London to sing and Ben remained behind. He thought it would be nice if we slept together, which we did, though I drew back from sexual relations; Peter was nevertheless quite disturbed at our intimacy on that occasion.' Tippett seems to have felt no sexual attraction to Britten, but greatly valued the companionship of another composer: 'I'd gone deliberately away, out of London, to live in my own particular shell, and I didn't know a lot of musicians, so that the joy of talking to Ben in the early days was to talk as professional to professional, composer to composer. And that was how we did talk.' They each spoke of their ambitions, and Britten made some revealing remarks:

Ben and I discussed what we thought our futures were. And Ben said: 'I am possibly an anachronism. I am a composer of opera, and that is what

I am going to be, throughout.' And I said: 'No, I won't be like that; I certainly will write operas, but I want to go all over the field.' He then made a comment – whether it was that particular time or another, I don't remember. He said: 'I would be a Court composer, but for my pacifism and homosexuality.' I think he meant it. I don't see why he shouldn't. And I think that's what happened.

Donald Mitchell suggests that

> Britten – if he said it – did not mean *courtier* composer – a royal servant – but someone willing and, above all, able to provide music of character and quality for public occasions – even to find them a source of inspiration! That *would* have appealed to him. How any of Britten's operas – not excluding *Gloriana* – could be interpreted as the work of a *courtier*, God only knows. Even his arrangement of the National Anthem was conspicuously anti-jingoistic, anti-pomp and circumstance. It's all a total nonsense.

Early in 1943, Tippett wrote 'my first piece of music for Pears and Britten as a duo', *Boyhood's End*. He describes its origin: 'I had been looking at Purcell, independently of Ben, and thought I would like to write a Purcellian cantata for solo voice. The great problem was to find something that was in *oratia recta* [direct speech], and I suddenly realised that there it was, in one tiny paragraph of Hudson.' He found the words in the 'Boyhood's End' chapter of W. H. Hudson's autobiographical *Far Away and Long Ago* (1918), in which Hudson's adolescent self becomes painfully aware that he may lose his boyhood perceptions as he grows up: 'What, then, did I want? What did I ask to have? ... Only to keep what I have. To rise each morning and look out on the sky and grassy dew-wet earth ...' The choice of words might seem to reflect a perception of Britten's own determination to preserve the child in himself, but Tippett denies this: 'I was concerned with this particular feeling for nature, which occasionally I'd felt (perhaps Ben did too; I don't know). I was sorry in a way that it had to go back into somebody's childhood. I wasn't drawn that way.'

Boyhood's End was first performed by Britten and Pears in the Holst Room at Morley College on 5 June 1943. They next gave it at a concert in Leicester at the end of July. By that time Tippett was in prison. He had registered as a Conscientious Objector when his call-up came in 1940, but his case was not heard until February 1942 when, like Britten, he was ordered to undertake non-combatant duties. He appealed, but unlike Britten was then allocated to full-time work as an air raid warden, a fireman, or on the land. He refused to accept these conditions, but it was more than a year before a magistrate heard the case and sentenced him to three months' imprisonment. Britten was among those who had tried to prevent this happening – 'we're all fighting to keep him out', he told Elizabeth Mayer – and offers were made of jobs, such as choir trainer for the National Fire Service, which would comply with the tribunal's ruling but still allow Tippett to continue with his music. Tippett says of this:

> The question was whether I took an absolute line over it, or whether I took conditions. Ben took conditions. Nearly everybody did. And I was told that if I went and did virtually what I was doing at Morley College over the road in an ARP shelter I should be complying with conditions. But I thought that was idiotic, and I did feel quite genuinely that if there were the young ones who were going into prison and getting big sentences, I didn't feel I should get off because of my position. And there were other elements, to do with my view about being a scapegoat – *A Child of Our Time* was already written, you see.

He was grateful for Britten and Pears's support:

> The nice thing is that Ben was very worried – they were both very worried about me. *I* was curiously unworried. Because that's my nature to some degree. And I never gave it a moral connotation of any kind, because I thought they were both genuine pacifists. After all, there are many shades of this business.

Prison warders and inmates were likely to regard 'conchees' (Conscientious Objectors) as worse than criminals, but Tippett endured his three months in Wormwood Scrubs without complaint, and even managed to enjoy certain aspects: 'I went to the Sunday morning Church of England service because I'd never before heard a thousand men singing those hymns; they were glorious.' He organized an orchestra of prisoners and taught it Handel's *Largo* and a Bach chorale, and obtained permission for these to be performed during a recital to be given at the prison by Britten and Pears as part of their CEMA activities. 'Ben and Peter had already offered their services', he says of this, 'and once they realized I was in, I gather that they tried to arrange it that they came at the same time.'

Before the concert, which was on 11 July 1943, Tippett asked a friend to 'ring Peter & Ben ... & tell them not to be distressed by the "orchestra" ... It's for the sake of social progressiveness not to rival their artistry!' Years later, Britten told Rosamund Strode that the only thing which distressed him about the prison was the smell. He had brought a page-turner, a young man named John Amis who worked in the Boosey & Hawkes building, but meanwhile Tippett had told the prison staff that he would turn the music. He says this was to ensure he was at the recital. 'And what the prison service teaches you is to lie! So I said that nobody could turn the pages for Ben except me. Well, they believed it, for some extraordinary reason. What I didn't foresee, of course, was that Amis was going to be there! He went out, naturally, and there I was, sitting beside Ben.'

Amis later became a friend of Tippett, and was struck by his and Britten's different approaches to composition. It seemed to him that

> Ben corresponded with Mozart, Michael with Beethoven. Ben worked his compositions in his head; Michael laboriously with piano and paper. Ben always knew where he was going every bar of the piece in advance; Michael had the plan but wrestled with his material . . . Ben knew when he put a note on paper what finger would play it, on what string or with what technique . . . where the singer would breathe, how the choir would find the pitch . . . Michael has none of this . . . Britten once said to me that he thought that Tippett could have been just as distinguished if he had gone in for something other than music and that he wondered sometimes why he hadn't. And I know that Tippett did not particularly care for a lot of Britten's later music nor for his choice of subjects.

Tippett dismisses this Mozart–Beethoven analogy – 'We weren't Mozart and Beethoven, and I know exactly what I'm going to do before I do it' – but makes no pretence that he liked everything that Britten wrote. For example, he says of *A Ceremony of Carols*: 'It wasn't me – I'm not a carol person.' However, he emphasizes that composers find it impossible to be objective about each other's work – 'I've never made judgements about whether music is of any use, certainly not my colleagues'' – and points out that 'you learn a great deal from negatives', that is, from what you disagree with or dislike. He adds: 'I watched Ben, because he was the only one that was worth watching. The others didn't seem to know what they were doing at all.'

He admits that he envied Britten's technical fluency:

> What I admired, and what I would have liked to have had, was his wonderful facility. I remember his sitting with me in my little cottage, and the Walton Violin Concerto was being played on the radio. I only detected its derivation from Elgar or whatever, but Ben went straight to the piano and played it. I've never had that. I had certain other

things, though. Ben himself knew that; he once said he felt my creative energy, or whatever it is. That's as far as he'd go, and I didn't want him to make judgements. That's not the point.

I have to ask, did I lose out by not having his fluency? And one part of me says no, I gained. The most obvious example was the piano. I didn't perform. So I had to invent. It's possible that it became more interesting. Ben was gifted in a way which I certainly never had. Therefore I had to look at it in another way. I used to say, 'You have only one gift, perhaps. If you want to get the rest, you've got to learn it.' So I had to learn like hell. On the face of it, Ben didn't seem to have to learn. Of course he did, but he was there very, very much earlier, 'there' being a kind of facility of utterance.

William Walton said much the same in a 1962 interview: 'I do envy Ben Britten his – not facility, but being able to do it all in his head, like Mozart or Rossini ... It's hard work, for me ... The trouble is I wasn't properly trained.'

Tippett came out of prison in August 1943, on a day when his String Quartet No. 2 was being performed at the Wigmore Hall. 'England was a very curious, tolerant country then,' he says of this. 'Whether it is now, I wouldn't know.' Britten drew Walter Hussey's attention to Tippett as part of his effort to establish his reputation. Tippett recalls that 'he was trying to help, and he told me, "I've got this commission, and I'd like to give a part of it to you."' Tippett himself sang in the choir during *Rejoice in the Lamb*. 'I was not really very good,' he says of his singing voice.

A month after the Northampton service, in October 1943, *Boyhood's End* was on the programme of a recital which Britten and Pears gave at Dartington Hall in Devon. Teaching music there was Imogen Holst, whom Britten and Pears already knew from her work as CEMA organizer for the South West. After the concert she wrote to Britten, full of enthusiasm for his work, and said that she felt a musical renaissance was in the air. He wrote back that he entirely agreed: 'I feel terrifically conscious of it, so do Peter, & Clifford [Curzon], & Michael Tippett ... Whether we are the voices crying in the wilderness or the thing itself, it isn't for us to know ...' Tippett confirms that, despite their differences, he and Britten felt part of the same movement in British music:

Ben knew Mahler and all sorts of things that I didn't. But his feelings for Purcell, and Dowland and all that, brought us together. I was going away from the English folk-song world, from the intellectual nonsense of nationalist music, and had tried to express some of the concerns of central Europe in *A Child of Our Time*. And although Ben remained extremely rooted in England, he was looking to an international standard. We were instinctively together.

*

Though he had yet to discover Tippett, William Glock, reviewing the première of Britten's *Serenade* given by Pears, Dennis Brain, and an orchestra conducted by Walter Goehr at the Wigmore Hall on 15 October 1943, communicated the same sort of excitement as Britten's letter to Imogen Holst:

> I used to listen rather sadly to my predecessor [as *Observer* music critic], Fox-Strangways, while he told me of his good fortune as a young man in being able to hear Brahms's maturest works as they came out. Now I feel differently for in Benjamin Britten we have at last a composer who offers us visions as great as these. His new Serenade . . . surpasses everything else of his in strength and feeling.

Meanwhile *A Ceremony of Carols*, which had just been published and recorded (by the Morriston Boys' Choir and Maria Korchinska), with Britten conducting, was proving a sell-out. Britten had reason to pass his thirtieth birthday on 22 November 1943 with some confidence.

'I am quickly scribbling a short choral work for a prison camp in Germany where some friends of mine are,' he told Elizabeth Mayer three weeks after it. *The Ballad of Little Musgrave and Lady Barnard* was written at the request of Richard Wood, whose sister Anne had been in the BBC Singers with Pears and who was imprisoned at Eichstätt in Germany, where he had organized a male voice choir. The style of Britten's three-part setting resembled his folk-song arrangements; the subject matter was a page's betrayal to his lord of his lady's planned adultery. 'And THEN', continued Britten's letter to Elizabeth Mayer, 'I start the OPERA – for production next Summer! Isn't that exciting?'

Peter Grimes was scheduled to be performed at Koussevitzky's summer 1944 Berkshire Music Festival in Massachusetts, with an English première to follow. In a letter to Sir Henry Wood on 14 December 1943, Britten explained that because of the 'enormous commitment' to finish it on time, he could not accept Wood's invitation to write a new work for the fiftieth Prom season, though he might be able to offer 'an orchestral excerpt' from the opera. A postcard to a friend on 9 December announced that he was 'at Snape trying to get my spirits up after 'flu – & also starting the opera'. (The illness had caused the cancellation of his thirtieth-birthday celebration, planned as a large party in the St John's Wood flat.) But it was apparently not until after Christmas that he actually began the composition sketch of *Peter Grimes*. On 10 January 1944 he wrote to Pears:

> Well, at last I have broken the spell and got down to work on P.G. I have been at it for two days solidly and got the greater part of the Prologue done. It is *very* difficult to keep that amount of recitative moving, without going round & round in circles, I find – but I think I've managed it. It is also difficult to keep it going fast & yet paint moods & characters abit. I can't wait to show it to you. Actually in this scene there isn't much for you to do (I haven't got to the love duet yet); it is mostly for Swallow, who is turning out quite an amusing, pompous old thing! I don't know whether I shall ever be a good opera composer, but it's wonderful fun to try once in a way!

Meanwhile at Snape he had the company of Beth, to whom a daughter had now been born and who was living there for the present. The elder child, Sebastian, was nearly five, and Britten wrote to Pears that the boy 'gets more charming every day – in ten years' time he'll be a real menace, I'm afraid!'

At the end of February, Pears took a respite from a gruelling schedule of performances up and down the country and came to Snape. Britten played him what had been written so far. 'Ben my darling,' Pears wrote a few days later,

> Peter Grimes was quite madly exciting! Really tremendously thrilling. The only thing you must remember is to consider that the average singer hasn't much gift for intensity off his own bat, so make sure that the tempi etc make a tense delivery inevitable . . . the bit I was thinking of was Swallow in the Prologue – Can it sound pompous at that pace? Aggressive yes – & perhaps that's enough.

This is a glimpse of what seems to have been Pears's frequent involvement, not always of an encouraging sort, in Britten's compositions. When at work on the *Serenade* the previous year, Britten had played some of the songs to him, and had evidently had to listen to criticisms. 'I do hope I didn't damp your poor old enthusiasm too much about them,' Pears had written to him a few days later. 'Don't be discouraged. Don't forget, my darling, that I am only as critical as I am because I have high standards for you.'

Pears's letter about *Peter Grimes* also raised the question of the homosexual element in the opera: 'The more I hear of it, the more I feel that the queerness is unimportant & doesn't really exist in the music (or at any rate obtrude) so it mustn't do so in the words. P.G. is an introspective, an artist, a neurotic, his real problem is expression, self-expression. Nicht war? What a part! Wow!' It was around this time that Michael Tippett was shown the libretto. He gathered that Britten's view 'was that it was really somewhat left-wing, the individual against a wicked society. I didn't regard that as very accurate, and I don't think he seemed to understand that a problem would come over the question of Peter Grimes's relation to the boys.' However, Britten himself was moving confidently ahead. Before starting to write the music he had got Slater to make some alterations in the libretto, which he described as '*excellent* for Grimes now', and he was rewriting it further himself when necessary. A letter to Ralph Hawkes mentions that 'I am making enormous changes all the while in the libretto.'

He pressed on with the composition sketch during the spring and early summer of 1944, sending Pears reports which indicated that there were no more than temporary hitches. On 9 April: 'Grimes is being such a brute at the moment. Still, I am over the worst now, and I can at least see ahead.' On 12 June: 'My bloody opera stinks, & that's all there is to it. But I dare say that I shall be able to de-odourise it before too long.' The manuscript gives evidence that there were no more than occasional changes of mind or 'blocks'. RAF fighter planes from nearby airfields were a constant distraction at Snape, where most of the work was done – 'the aeroplanes are bloody, bloody, all the time' – but the company of Beth and her children amused Britten, and Pears was away on tour all this time, so he was left undisturbed by suggestions and criticisms.

In a broadcast interview later in his life, he said of his daily routine:

> I like working to an exact timetable. I often thank my stars that I had a rather conventional upbringing, that I went to a rather strict school, where one was made to work, and I can, without much difficulty, sit down at nine o'clock in the morning and work straight through the morning until lunchtime. I don't say I always *enjoy* the work at that time, but it isn't a great struggle ... In the afternoon ... I go for a walk, where I plan out what I am going to write in the next period at my desk.

In her memoir of her brother, Beth recalls Britten's working habits while he was writing *Peter Grimes* at Snape in 1944:

> Always an early riser he would be in his studio [on the ground floor of the circular mill itself] at least by 9.0 a.m., working through until 1 o'clock with a break for coffee, then a light lunch and some form of exercise ... He walked far and fast [and] did much of the planning ...

on these walks and sometimes sang as he went ... Sometimes, when I went to take him his coffee, I found Ben reading a 'who-dunnit'. When I looked surprised, he would look up guiltily and say that it relaxed him. After the afternoon walk and a cup of tea, Ben returned to his studio and worked again solidly for three more hours; then dinner, perhaps a read or a game, and bed.

In an interview in the early sixties he had something to say about the planning of his work:

Usually I have the music complete in my mind before putting pencil to paper. That doesn't mean that every note has been composed, perhaps not one has, but I have worked out questions of form, texture, character, and so forth, in a very precise way so that I know exactly what effects I want and how I am going to achieve them.

And in another interview at the same period:

I can only quote T. S. Eliot. Someone asked him how were *Four Quartets* getting on. He said, 'Oh, they're practically finished.' But he hadn't written a word. I mean, the words came later. [And] the actual thematic material is a very, very late stage. And it's almost dangerous if you do get thematic ideas in an early stage, in my experience.

Eric Crozier observed the importance of *form* in this planning stage of Britten's work:

All I knew of him suggested that he thought first of each new composition in terms of forms, that these notions of form gradually became clearer in his mind, and that it was prolonged consideration of the formal units and relationships among them that finally gave rise to the melodies and harmonies that would express them most vividly.

Crozier suggests that this formal planning went on partly while Britten was asleep: 'He had considerable faith in the ability of his subconscious mind to solve daytime problems while he slept: perhaps partly for that reason his favourite reading before going to sleep was poetry.' If he did rely on the subconscious, it may explain his dislike of having his music analysed. Christopher Headington writes that 'Peter Pears has told me that [Britten] rather resented analysis "as a kind of prying". Graham Johnson ... remembers him as very disinclined to be analytical ... as if there was a special secret about composition and creative flow which would somehow be spoiled by analysing it too much.'

On the other hand, as Crozier observes, there was no question of his waiting passively for inspiration: 'Writing music, in his view, was a process of hard, regular, sustained work.' Indeed, he found it hard to stop working. Crozier recalls a day in the late forties when Britten was being driven across Europe, and had fallen silent. 'Peter turned round from the front seat and asked what he was thinking about. "Nothing much," he answered. "I was just working out a wind quintet."' Twenty years after the composition of *Peter Grimes* he told an interviewer: 'I do the bulk of my work away from the paper, when travelling around, when walking, when driving cars, in trains, not in aeroplanes which I don't enjoy so much. I actually go to the paper at a very late stage in the creation.'

After the planning came what he called 'finding the right notes'. In a 1961 letter he wrote: 'My great aim as a composer is to find exactly the right notes to say what I have to say ... to express what is ... in [my] mind.' Crozier understood that Britten regarded this 'as the most important stage of all, and one not wholly under his control'. Britten himself described this part of the process in a 1962 interview:

> You get the sense of the whole work, and then you plan it, and you sit down and write it, and it takes charge, and it all goes to pieces, in my experience! ... You try and control it, and sometimes you succeed, but not always ... As E. M. Forster writes, very wisely, in *Aspects of the Novel*, the work has to take over. One doesn't like it taking over, because it does things quite often that you don't like. But there is ... an inner compulsion that one does one's best to control.

And in 1963: 'I think one can say that the actual process of *planning* the work comes to me fairly easily, that is, before I get to the paper and start thinking about the notes. That is where the agony ... starts.' He claimed to be detached from his subject matter when composing: 'One is curiously uninvolved ... It's all the result of previous experiences digested.'

With an opera or large orchestral work, his habit was to write the music initially in short score (the vocal parts and two or three staves of accompaniment), leaving the full orchestral score until this 'composition sketch' as musicologists call it – a misleading term, for in Britten's case there was nothing sketchy about it – had been completed. Ronald Duncan describes him writing a composition sketch:

> In Ben's converted windmill ... he had a circular music room ... It was here he composed ... He always composed at a desk, not at the piano as Stravinsky did, and with a pencil – there was always an india-rubber to hand. Musicologists, and the like, may at some time,

looking at Britten's manuscripts, conclude that he seldom made any revisions. They are mistaken: he erased or re-composed as he did his first sketch. It was only when he had this first sketch that he went to the piano and played it over. His revisions then were few.

Colin Matthews says of Britten's habit of not composing at the piano: 'It wasn't remotely an affectation – he just didn't need it! He said to me that once when he'd worked away from the piano for quite a long period, he'd got the proportions all wrong. It was never notes; he used to play through what he'd just written to hear the shape.'

*

After Britten had been at work on *Peter Grimes* for some while, he heard that Koussevitzky's 1944 festival had been postponed for the duration of the war. Koussevitzky had generously agreed that a British première of the opera could precede an American production. Discussions therefore began with the Sadler's Wells company. Meanwhile Britten was nearing the end of Act Two.

'Well, your scene with the apprentice is going on well,' he wrote to Pears on 16 July 1944. 'It is difficult to do, & I get terribly upset by what I'm creating, but it is nearly done, & I think will be good & effective.' Three days later he told Elizabeth Mayer: 'I've just finished Act II, & it is the next production after Così at the Wells. Isn't that thrilling! It is becoming a bigger affair than I expected and so topical as to be unbearable in spots!'

Having rejected both the explicitly homosexual and the pathological-villainous versions of his hero, he had to find a third alternative. As Pears had perceived from the parts of the opera he had seen and heard, in Britten's hands Grimes was becoming 'an introspective, an artist', a sensitive and gifted individual who is misunderstood and rejected by society. This had a good deal of topical relevance. Looking back on the composition of the opera two decades later, Britten had this to say about his and Pears's concept of the principal character:

> A central feeling for us was that of the individual against the crowd, with ironic overtones for our own situation. As conscientious objectors we were out of it. We couldn't say we suffered physically, but naturally we experienced tremendous tension. I think it was partly this feeling which led us to make Grimes a character of vision and conflict, the tortured idealist he is, rather than the villain he was in Crabbe.

However, as Tippett observes, this approach to Grimes created its own set of problems.

Peter Grimes opens without any orchestral prelude. The Prologue, beginning with the inquest in the Moot Hall into the death of Grimes's most recent apprentice, sets out the musical characteristics of the main participants more clearly than a purely instrumental overture could do. The Borough, led by Swallow, the mayor and coroner, is characterized by fussy, neo-baroque music which is superficially straightforward but full of harmonic clashes, hinting at the community's hypocrisy beneath its apparently good-natured surface. In contrast, when Grimes himself steps forward to give evidence his music, a series of triads, identifies him as (at this stage) an honest man. Even his account of the boy's death from thirst during a long sea journey is quite without discord in the accompaniment, clear confirmation that he is telling the truth. (Colin Graham, longest-serving producer of Britten's operas under the composer's supervision, writes that Britten 'held the theory ... that what goes on in the orchestra is neither a description nor an accompaniment to the action (as in film music) but is rather what is going on in the hearts of the characters'.)

Though Grimes is formally cleared by the court, the only citizen of the Borough to take his side is Ellen Orford, subject of a starkly tragic section of Crabbe's *The Borough* (her past life is considerably softened by Slater and Britten). However, in their duet which concludes the Prologue – the 'love duet' mentioned by Britten – she and he sing in different keys, and only come to a rather unsteady musical agreement at its close. Ellen seems to be trying to draw Grimes out of his element and into hers. What Grimes's element is, we now learn.

Britten had to provide orchestral interludes to cover changes of scene in each of the three acts, and from this necessity he created a set of Sea Interludes which are the best-known music from the opera. They portray the most fully developed character in *Peter Grimes*, the sea itself. In 'Dawn', which follows the Prologue, the strings and woodwind initially sound all the 'white' notes in the scale, while the brass play major triads. This is simplicity itself, 'naturalness' presented in the same musical language that Britten had used in the *Serenade*. As this Interlude progresses, discords seem to appear in the pedal-bass notes, but these dissonances are absorbed by the higher instruments. The Prologue has indicated that the Borough's apparently harmonious surface conceals profound discord, but Nature (the sea) is at peace with itself.

Christopher Palmer, in an essay in *The Britten Companion* (1984) on the role of the sea in the opera, identifies it as a kind of mother-figure to Britten (and Grimes). Palmer observes that the Sea Interludes owe much to Frank Bridge's *The Sea*, the work which introduced the young Britten both to modern music and to Bridge himself, his 'musical father', so 'father-figure' might be an even more appropriate image. Indeed, in an early version of the libretto Grimes has a soliloquy, addressed in his imagination to the apprentice, which contains these lines:

> I have a father in the sea
> Scolding from tides, and it was he
> Who made the laws that we shall disobey.

Slater seems to have regarded the sea as representing the paternalistic laws of Nature, which Grimes, in his relationship with the boy, deliberately flouts.

Though the Borough makes its living from the sea, it is incapable of understanding its 'naturalness'. So much is obvious from the opening of Act I scene 1, when the town's fisherfolk sing a kind of shanty which moves doggedly to its own measure, ignoring the sea swell which continues in the orchestra. There are a few 'natural' people in the Borough, but not in the obvious places: Auntie, the landlady of the Boar Inn and madame of the town's unofficial brothel, and Bob Boles the half-mad Methodist. Throughout the opera these two invariably perceive the truth, Auntie through her knowledge that everyone is motivated by sexual desire, Boles through his hell-fire conviction – which Britten possibly shares – that all are sinners. Boles is the only member of the Borough to get unashamedly drunk and openly demand a woman at the Boar. In other words, though half-crazed he is no hypocrite.

The best response to such a community is to keep out of its way, and in Act I scene 1 Grimes sits silently on his boat, cleaning nets. But the Borough will not let him alone. Against a disconcertingly chromatic version of 'Dawn', Ned Keene, the apothecary, tells him that he has got him another apprentice from the workhouse. Hobson, the carrier, identified musically as something of a 'natural' man, at first refuses to fetch the child, but Ellen Orford steps forward with an offer to chaperon the boy, in a reprise of Hobson's music into which discord has now been introduced. The Borough people warn her against 'fetching boys for Peter Grimes', and she responds with words and music that suggests a biblical oratorio – except that the words are a jumble of half-remembered tags from the Gospels and the music a similar patchwork of disconnected 'sacred' phrases. The same 'sacred' music accompanies the supposedly respectable widow Mrs Sedley as she asks Keene for the laudanum to which she is addicted, surely a barbed comment on Ellen's real motivation.

Why is Grimes drawn to her? Why indeed does he remain in the

Borough? The retired sea-captain Balstrode puts this second question to him as the townspeople scatter to protect their homes against an imminent storm. Grimes's answer, 'I am native, rooted here,' does not have the simplicity of his earlier musical statements, and his answer to Balstrode's 'Rooted by what?' is superficially attractive – he is accompanied by the almost self-parodying romantic sound of a solo violin – but highly chromatic, a sure signal that he is at war with himself. His tragic fault is that he will not ignore the Borough, but is determined to become a success in its eyes ('They listen to money, / These Borough gossips'). For the first time in the opera one is aware of Slater's influence. Britten's Grimes, or at least the Grimes whom Britten has shown us so far, would have more sense than to play the Borough's own game.

Left alone, Grimes asks himself 'What harbour shelters peace?' Though the music is yearningly beautiful, its key (A major) has so far been associated with the Borough, so it is not surprising that his answer to his own question is, Ellen: 'Her breast is harbour.' He has turned his back on his true element, the sea, which now bursts upon the town as if in vengeance. Built round the music of Grimes's question, the 'Storm' Interlude begins with ferocious chromaticism, yet at the height of the squall a very simple tune (in E flat, a key so far associated with Grimes's 'natural' state) maintains itself in spite of a clashing key (D major) in the lower instruments. The storm is a struggle between the natural man in Grimes (even the child, for the high tune is very childish) and his ambitions to join the 'adult' world. For a while, all resolves, but in A major, the Borough's key. The 'adult' ambitions seem to have won.

The second scene of Act I, set in the Boar Inn, further defines the Borough's shoddy mores. 'We live and let live, and look / We keep our hands to ourselves,' sings Balstrode, in lines recalling Auden's 'And the active hands must freeze / Lonely on the separate knees'. Grimes bursts in – his personal storm has been heard raging whenever the door is opened – with a vision that goes far beyond this petty-bourgeois outlook: 'Now the Great Bear and Pleiades . . . / Are drawing up the clouds / of human grief'. But in the third stanza he admits to finding the stars' horoscope 'bewildering' if taken as a guide to action. Natural man can no longer rely on Nature's wisdom once he has cut his roots.

The Borough now makes its own attempt to recover lost innocence. Tempers have risen in the pub, and Keene starts a round to restore social harmony. Though 'Old Joe has gone fishing' promotes a superficial 'togetherness', its 7/4 time-signature is disconcerting. Also, for a sea shanty or nursery rhyme the words are strikingly sinister: 'Old Joe has gone fishing and / Young Joe has gone fishing and / You Know has gone fishing . . .' The Devil himself is among them, and Grimes's interruption with his own version of the round, in which the fishing party catches a corpse, is no more than a recognition of the song's (and the Borough's) true character. Lost innocence, we learn in this scene, cannot be recaptured by resorting to such devices as poetry ('Now the Great Bear') or folk-song; and it is at this moment that the carrier arrives with Ellen and the boy, who is delivered into Grimes's hands as Act I ends.

*

In the early planning stages of the opera, Britten and Pears had intended that the boy should sing or speak, but at the beginning of Act II, in a scene set on the beach on Sunday morning, Ellen fails to cajole him into opening his mouth. However, he is not entirely silent. He answers her questions about his former life wordlessly, as he plays by the sea, by means of the flute, a device Britten had used to impersonate a child long ago in *Quatre Chansons Françaises*. The boy, then, is wordless innocence – and is contrasted by Britten with the Borough congregation in church off-stage, praying for the redemption of its sins (another way of trying to escape one's loss of innocence). At first the congregation's hypocrisy is suggested by the discord between the organ (A major) and a church bell (E flat), but eventually organ and congregation come together in the simplest of hymns, and it is Ellen who becomes discordant against them, with her claim to understand the boy's thoughts. When she discovers a tear in his coat and a bruise on his neck, it is with this same music, as if her own attempt to take over the boy, and Peter via him, has caused the damage to him. And it is she who, for the first time in the opera, suggests the threats inherent in sexual love: 'the treason of the waves', she sings, 'Glitters like love' (the reading 'Glitters like love's', found in drafts of the libretto, the composition sketch, and the manuscript full score, makes more sense). Does Britten mean us to wonder what are her own motives in trying to 'rescue' Grimes? Is she, despite appearances, really some sort of seducer, or representative of another threat?

When Peter arrives to demand the boy for a fishing trip, it is evident that he is torn between a determination to rid himself of Ellen and an utter dependence on her. In her company he is not his own man. His ambition to 'Buy us a home, buy us respect' is sung in phrases which parrot hers. At one moment he is goaded into shouting at her 'Take away your hand!', but an instant later he declares: 'My only hope depends on you. / If you take it away, what's left?' Two years before Britten began to write *Peter Grimes*, Auden had defined for him the twin poles of Bohemianism and Bourgeois Convention, and had warned him of the dangers of being drawn too closely to either. Grimes's predicament so far in the opera has been that of a man who is torn between the equal pull of both extremes. Ellen's hand is partly held out to help him enter acceptably into a conventional role in the Borough, but there is another possible meaning to her behaviour.

Auden's letter had particularly hinted that Britten was stifling himself in the 'warm nest of love' provided by Elizabeth Mayer and Pears, and in a sense Ellen is an amalgam of those two. But Mrs Mayer had been left behind in America, and Britten's letters to Pears had now assumed that air of utter dependence which Grimes expresses to Ellen. 'I only come alive when you're around,' he wrote to Pears while composing the opera. Grimes now makes the choice of which Britten seemed incapable in real life. He strikes Ellen, declares that their attempt to make a life together has failed, and, with the words 'God have mercy upon me!', goes off with the boy. For its remaining scenes, *Peter Grimes* becomes Britten's dream of what he might be like if he abandoned Pears – 'the freedom that you never chose', as Auden put it in the *Hymn to St Cecilia*.

In his early discussions with Slater about the opera, Britten evidently believed that Grimes murdered his apprentices. His letter to Elizabeth Mayer reporting progress with the libretto speaks of 'murders', and an early synopsis dating from the voyage home in 1942 describes one scene as 'P.G.s Hut. Murder.' Although actual murder disappeared from the drafts of the libretto as soon as they became detailed, the text as completed by Slater left open the question of how Grimes treated the boys – in particular the boy who appears in the opera. No violence is depicted in Act II scene 2, in which Grimes and the boy arrive at his cliff-top hut, but Britten intended that the Interlude which precedes it should fill the gap in the libretto's account of their relationship.

In a handwritten note in the margin of one of the libretto typescripts he described this Interlude as ' "Boy's suffering" fugato', then changed the last word to 'passacaglia', this being the musical form the Interlude takes. In a 1945 booklet about the opera, published for Sadler's Wells, with contributions by Britten and Slater which give it an official stamp, Edward Sackville-West wrote at length on the musical structure. Given that it was in this context, and that Sackville-West knew Britten well (he stayed with him at Snape in November 1944 while Britten was scoring *Peter Grimes*), it seems likely that his account of this crucial Passacaglia had Britten's approval. Indeed it reads like a composer's rather than a critic's summary. Sackville-West states that the Passacaglia

is intended to epitomize the tragedy of Grimes's ambivalent personality – his loneliness aggravated rather than assuaged by the constant

presence of a child too young to give him real companionship; his need
to give, as well as to receive, affection ... At the same time it would not
do to shirk the fact that Grimes is guilty of manslaughter: his wilful
and choleric nature contains an uncontrollable vein of real ferocity
which he is apt to visit on anybody in his power, and especially on the
helpless little creatures who, in his better moods, excite in him com-
passion and tenderness.

Already this has told us more than we know from the opera so far.
Grimes is 'guilty of manslaughter' (whereas the town court has found
him innocent), and has a tendency to be violent, especially towards his
apprentices. Moreover he wants to 'give affection' to the boy. Suddenly
we are back with the pathological monster, and perhaps also the 'queerness' which has been kept at bay by Britten in the first half of the opera.
Sackville-West continues of the Passacaglia:

the theme represents the obdurate mood of Grimes himself ... Inter-
woven is a desolate, wandering motif depicting the workhouse boy
who, accustomed no doubt to a steady lack of kindness, does not know
how to deal with Grimes's sudden changes of mood and so – as
children often do – takes refuge in silence. This theme (in which
Grimes sees, not only the solitary boy beside him, but also the innocent
child out of which he himself has grown) is heard first as a solo
viola ...

– Britten's own instrument, Sackville-West might have added.

Rather oddly, considering his willingness to discuss the other Interludes in narrative terms, Sackville-West does not go on to narrate the
actual story implied in the Passacaglia. But it is possible to guess it. The
endlessly repetitive bass line, which Sackville-West identifies as expressing Grimes's 'obdurate will', is recognizable from the previous scene as
his 'God have mercy upon me!', sung as he breaks free from Ellen
(though the audience will more probably recognize it as 'Grimes is at his
exercise', the Borough's only comment on Grimes's cruelty to the boy,
sung to the same musical phrase). But his prayer for mercy has not been
answered. At one time Britten intended that, at the moment of Grimes's
breaking away from Ellen, the church congregation off-stage, intoning
the Creed, should reach the words 'And he descended into hell.' The
Passacaglia shows him there.

Listening to it, one is reminded of another passage in Auden's 1942
letter: 'If you are really to develop to your full stature, you will have, I
think, to suffer and make others suffer, in ways which are totally strange

to you at present, and against every conscious value that you have . . .'
The first variation on the viola theme (scored for woodwind) is rather
like the music that accompanies the boy's games on the beach in Act II
scene 1. In the second variation, brass and strings suggest the games of
older boyhood, grand and heroic and a little wild. Woodwind, harp and
muted brass, in the third, introduce the first hint of uneasiness, and the
fourth (violins and woodwind, evoking the mood of the Blake Elegy in
the *Serenade*) could be a lament for lost innocence. The fifth (brass
arpeggios) has a bold confidence which suggests that manhood has been
reached. In the sixth, the violins play nervously *col legno* (the wood of
the bows tapping against the strings). In the seventh variation, the upper
strings have a melodic line which once again suggests youth and innocence, but the bass line (in the lower brass, reinforced by bass drum)
plods sinisterly nearer as if a youthful prey is being stalked. The entire
brass now sound unpleasantly triumphant chords (in the eighth variation), and a moment later a gong stroke indicates achievement (variation nine), while the upper strings (variation ten), joined by the brass
(variation eleven), swirl in ecstasy. And at this moment the curtain rises
and the boy stumbles, terrified, on to the stage – 'as if thrust from
behind', specifies the libretto.

'Go there!' sings Grimes as he pushes him through the door, in an
extraordinary vocal flourish ending in gasps – 'Go there! Go there!' We
are now in Grimes's hut, made from an upturned boat – an upside-down
world where everything is inverted out of its true nature. Grimes is
ordering the boy to get ready for their fishing trip: 'Take those bright /
And fancy buckles off your feet . . . / I'll tear the collar off your neck. / . . .
Don't take fright, boy . . . / Coat off! . . . / Stop moaning, boy.' His harsh
shouts are interrupted by his dreams of the respectability he has lost
through the rejection of Ellen – 'In dreams I've built myself some kindlier
home' – and by a vision of the boy who died before the beginning of the
opera: 'He's there now, I can see him, he is there!' This is not the
innocent sea creature of Act I, nor 'an introspective, an artist', but a
criminal momentarily tormented by guilt before he plunges into his next
crime. He is roused to his task by the sound of a posse of Borough folk
coming after him, and immediately suspects betrayal by his victim.
'You've been talking,' he snarls to the boy. 'You and that bitch were
gossiping.'

In an earlier version of the libretto for this scene, Slater tried to show
the audience much more of what was really happening. A fragment in his
handwriting gives these words to Peter to sing at the boy:

By God I'll beat it out of you. Stand up (*lash*) Straighten (*lash*). I'll count two. And then you'll jump to it. One —— Well? Two. (*The boy doesn't move. Then Peter lashes hard, twice. He runs. Peter follows.*)

> Your soul is mine
> Your body is the cat o' nine
> Tails' mincemeat, O! a pretty dish
> Smooth-skinned & young as she could wish.
> Come cat! Up whiplash! Jump my son
> Jump (*lash*) jump (*lash*) jump, the dance is on.

In another early fragment, after Grimes has chased the boy round the hut 'slashing with his rope', the child screams and falls, and Grimes, picking him up, tries to soothe him:

> We're seamen, rough, with little talk.
> Fists and whipknots do the work.
> O you'll cry I beat you till
> Body loses grip on soul.
> That's the sea, man, that's our life.
> When blood rises to your eyes
> Throbbing, red and blinding, when
> The whole world is your broken flesh – – –
> Leave clinging. Put your hand down. I
> Have no desire to beat you now.

All that remains of this in the final libretto is Grimes's threat: 'Will you move / Or must I make you dance?'

An early synopsis by Pears specifies that Grimes 'drives the boy back to the door over the cliff & in terror the boy opens it: dashes out – onto the rocks'. In the finished opera the boy is climbing down to the boat when he loses his footing accidentally. Yet the manner of his dying hints at Britten's real theme. Grimes's hut is said to be on a cliff some forty feet above the sea. There are no cliffs at or near Aldeburgh, original of Crabbe's Borough. The Grimes-style fishermen's huts at the north end of the town stand not on the edge of a precipice but on the shingle beach. This indeed is the landscape implied in Act I of the opera, when Grimes's boat is winched up the shingle, while in Act III the libretto specifies that the boat is pushed 'down the slope of the shore'. The introduction of the cliff in Act II scene 2 provides a means for the boy's death, but it would be easy to devise another. In Crabbe, one of the boys is killed by a fall from the mast and another is found 'lifeless in his bed'. The cliff must have been introduced so that the apprentice could *fall*, could experience a literal version of the fall from innocence which the Passacaglia implies. Britten emphasizes this in the score, specifying that as the boy hurtles down the cliff he sings, at last – no mere scream but a wordless cry beginning on a top C and descending into the depths. In a 1954 letter Britten remarks that it is 'for me an important matter' that the scream should start 'on the right note (i.e. top C)'. C major is the key in Britten's music which generally symbolizes purity and simplicity. Moreover after the boy has fallen, Grimes, instead of remaining in the hut to protest his innocence to the Borough people who are about to arrive, hurries after the boy, climbing down the cliff out of our sight. Whatever has happened to the boy involves his participation. He too has 'fallen'.

The Interlude which follows this scene and precedes Act III portrays, according to Sackville-West, 'the town and harbour lying tranquil under a moonlit sky'. Act III scene 1, set outside the Moot Hall where a dance is taking place, opens with Swallow pursuing one of the 'Nieces' from the pub, with the words 'Assign your prettiness to me'. Britten is making a bitter observation that some sorts of sexual pursuit are socially accep-table and some are not. Here is Grimes's judge, outside his court-room, engaged in the species of sexual predatoriness that society tolerates while condemning the homosexual equivalent. Mrs Sedley now arrives to warn everyone that she suspects Grimes of having murdered the boy. The boy's jersey is found, washed up by the tide, and Ellen, in an Aria recalling her own lost childhood, describes the garment as 'the clue whose meaning we avoid'. Balstrode suggests that Grimes must be suffering 'unearthly tor-ment', and Sackville-West's commentary, again with an air of authority that may emanate from Britten himself, confirms this in its description of the Interlude which precedes the final scene (and which is not included in the orchestral suite of Interludes from the opera): 'A thick fog creeps in from the sea and swathes the town; in the fuliginous blackness which matches that of his own soul Grimes, weary in body and half-demented, makes his way back to the harbour and his boat – the only refuge he has left from the torment of his guilt.' Why should Sackville-West (Britten) use the word 'guilt' if Grimes is innocent of any crime in the hut?

Peter Pears did not view Grimes as guilty. In a 1974 radio talk about the role he observed: 'I do not believe Grimes killed his apprentices . . . I don't think he is a sadist . . . I see him as an oversensitive being . . . but not a rough brute nor a hysterical maniac.' (It could be Ellen talking.) Even thirty years after the opera had been written the matter remained debatable to him. Grimes himself, in the opera, experiences no such doubts. As he lingers on the shore in the fog and darkness in Act III scene 2 he tells himself: 'The first one died, just died, / The other slipped, and died / And the third will ...' He mockingly repeats Swallow's verdict, 'Accidental circumstances', which he (and Britten) now knows to be untrue.

There has been much debate why, when Balstrode and Ellen find Grimes on the beach and Balstrode instructs him to commit suicide – 'Sail out till you lose sight of land, then sink the boat' – this is done in spoken dialogue, with the orchestra silent. Britten has perhaps identified so closely with Grimes that he cannot portray his death musically. Death means for Grimes what it would mean for Britten, the end of all music.

*

The composition sketch of *Peter Grimes* was completed in the early autumn of 1944, and Britten immediately began the orchestral full score, with the aid of an amanuensis to rule bar-lines and put in clefs, key-signatures and other repetitive details. This was an eighteen-year-old student from the Royal College of Music, Arthur Oldham. Orphaned at the age of fourteen and with no money beyond his RCM scholarship, Oldham had approached Britten and asked if he would look at his music. Britten liked it, and suggested that Oldham should come and work with him at Snape. 'People automatically jump to the conclusion,' says Oldham, 'that because I was a young man and he was a homosexual, therefore there must have been something. That I can tell you with utter honesty there never was, and there was never any approach. In fact it was quite a long time afterwards before I realized he was a homosexual.'

Britten intended to give Oldham some instruction in composition, and Oldham explains that he had 'a medieval attitude' to teaching.

> He felt that the right way to learn any art was the way that Michelangelo did, learning (and he quoted this) to 'mix the paint' first, working together with a master, and from that something would rub off. He proposed that I should do menial tasks for him, and we'd talk about composition. And the first job he gave me was ruling the bar-lines for *Peter Grimes*.

Whereas Oldham's composition teacher at the RCM, Herbert Howells, whom Oldham calls 'a vain little man', had always been referring Oldham to his own compositions, Britten never did this, but took examples from composers from whom he himself had learnt.

> He would score all the morning, and then we'd go for long walks in the afternoon, talking about music, and then in the evening he'd do some more scoring and then after dinner we'd relax and listen to music. He also gave me various more constructive jobs. I made a piano duet

arrangement of the *Simple Symphony*, because the publishers wanted
it.

Asked if Britten was not getting the best of the arrangement, Oldham
answers: 'I would say it was beneficial five per cent to him and ninety-five
per cent to me!' Eventually Britten got Oldham a commission from the
Boyd Neel String Orchestra. He also persuaded a Suffolk neighbour to
provide him with board, lodging and piano while he wrote the piece. 'He
was an immensely good man,' says Oldham.

While the full score of *Peter Grimes* was being written, negotiations
for the production were continuing with Sadler's Wells. Eric Crozier and
Joan Cross had heard rumours about the opera ever since Pears joined
the company. At first it was said to be about East Coast smugglers,
'which sounded unattractive and not even original', writes Crozier, 'for
an opera on a similar theme, Ethel Smyth's *The Wreckers*, had died a
swift death forty years earlier'. Then one day in 1943 'speculation about
"Ben's opera" turned to certainty when he came to a performance with a
typescript which he asked me to take home and read'. This was Slater's
libretto, and Britten wanted Crozier's opinion 'as a stage producer and
theatrical technician'. Crozier thought some of the words rather man-
nered, and had discussions with Britten and Slater – he found the librettist 'non-communicative' – to agree on improvements before Britten
began composition.

Crozier's involvement, and Britten's hope that Joan Cross would sing
Ellen, led to a general assumption that the Wells would stage the opera.
However, the proposal had to be put formally to the directors, and in
August 1944 Britten played through the Prologue and Act I to Cross,
Lawrance Collingwood the company's musical director, and probably
also Tyrone Guthrie, its administrator. 'Ben came and smashed it out on
the piano,' recalls Joan Cross. 'It was really exciting.' Nancy Evans, who
sang in later Britten operas, describes his skill as a performer on
occasions like this: 'Ben had an unmatchable gift for bringing the characters of an opera to life: even without a real singing voice, he was able to
convey how each part should be sung, and his piano playing seemed
positively orchestral.' ('Britten had one of the most appalling singing
voices of any composer I've ever come across,' says Oliver Knussen, who
heard him at rehearsals in the sixties. 'There was no pitch to speak of –
just a kind of *Sprechstimme* drone. It was a very strange sound indeed.')

Britten wrote that the play-through to the Wells directors 'went down
well', and Joan Cross says 'we realized it was a major work'. But what
was it about? 'I really didn't know myself,' she admits. 'I was awfully

dumb at the time.' However, she spotted the overtones of pacifism in Grimes the outsider, and thought this 'excellent – I was all for that'. Crozier says that Guthrie, hearing a summary of the libretto some months earlier, had remarked: 'I suppose it's a sort of love-murder really, isn't it?' Since Crozier 'had no idea what he meant', he gave no answer.

Guthrie decided he did not want to direct it himself, so he handed it over to Crozier, who was already staging *The Bartered Bride*, his first production for the company – until now his job had been re-staging other producers' work and coaching new singers in their stage movements. Crozier was a few months younger than Britten. He had struggled from an impoverished and bitterly unhappy London childhood into the professional theatre, training at the Royal Academy of Dramatic Art and in Paris. He then worked as one of Britain's first television producers at the BBC, before joining the Wells as Guthrie's assistant. He too was a Conscientious Objector. He was married with two children, but around the time of *Peter Grimes* was becoming estranged from his wife.

Even though the Wells definitely wanted to stage the opera, it was uncertain where and when this could be managed. The actual Sadler's Wells Theatre in the Islington district of London had been closed since the Blitz, and the company had been giving its London seasons in cramped West End theatres. *Peter Grimes* required more space, and though peace seemed near – in one letter Britten wondered which would be finished first, the full score of the opera or the war – the Wells company did not know whether they could go back to Islington. Various West End theatres were considered, among them the Covent Garden Opera House, then in use as a dance hall. Boosey & Hawkes were keen on a grand Britten première to reopen it. But now faint rumbles of discontent about *Peter Grimes* became detectable within the ranks of the Wells performers.

The company's two pre-war excursions into modern British opera, *Macbeth* by their own Lawrance Collingwood and *Greysteel* by Nicholas Gatty, had been flops, and though Britten's reputation was high there were some who argued that the regular Wells audience, used to Mozart, Verdi and Rossini, would stay away from contemporary music and a gruesome story. Someone suggested that a better work to celebrate the coming of peace would be *Merrie England*. According to one of Britten's letters, even Joan Cross began to suffer 'nerves' about it, while Pears was becoming anxious about the demands of the role – 'the part is so dramatic it needs a Chaliapin,' he told Elizabeth Mayer, '& my voice is still lyrical and not dramatic. However ... perhaps I shall reach Grimes by April – !' This was the month guessed at for the production.

Britten now needed other commissions to keep afloat financially. While still scoring the opera, he wrote an unremarkable *Te Deum* for a church in Swindon, and provided Edward Sackville-West with two choral pieces for a Christmas programme he was producing at the BBC. They had words by Auden, taken from the libretto of the oratorio which, since 1941, Auden had hoped Britten would write with him. Ostensibly on the subject of Christmas but really concerned with Auden's mother's death and Chester Kallman's infidelity, it was far too long to be set as it stood. For the radio programme, Britten used two short sections, one of which was a 'Shepherds' Carol' which Auden had dropped from the published text of the oratorio, *For the Time Being* (1944) – perhaps because his readers might misunderstand the refrain 'O lift your little pinkie and touch the winter sky', though he explained to friends that 'pinkie' only meant finger. Britten wrote to Pears that he thought the carol would 'make you smile'. He told Elizabeth Mayer he would certainly get around to the oratorio in its entirety 'one day'.

On 10 February 1945 he wrote to a friend: 'I have actually just this minute written "End" to the opera score.' During this month the Sadler's Wells singers were given vocal scores for the Prologue and Act I. These had been reduced from the full score, as it was being written, by Erwin Stein, the musicologist and publisher whom Britten had met in Vienna in 1934. He had fled to England with his family four years later, and was now on the staff of Boosey & Hawkes, where he looked after Britten's music; the *Serenade* seems to have been partly his idea. Lord Harewood has described him as 'someone with the whole of European culture behind him who yet lived and thought in the present and was able and prepared to impart this wisdom without preaching'. Donald Mitchell calls him

an impregnable musician of a calibre we rarely encounter nowadays. (Later, Imo [Imogen Holst] was to offer Ben some of those same incomparable qualities but in a much narrower, more insular perspective.) Erwin was a renowned Schoenberg pupil – with all that that implies – and it was to Erwin that Schoenberg entrusted the first theoretical 'explanation' of the twelve-note method, a justly famous essay. When a young man, he was also a Mahler disciple, attending many Mahler performances at the Vienna Opera and then – with Berg and Webern – moving on to the coffee house where he would listen to the irrepressible Schoenberg challenging Mahler's opinions. I've often thought that Erwin in a very real and musically rich way provided Ben with that experience of Vienna that he had been denied earlier, when his plans to study with Berg had been scotched.

John Amis, who describes Stein as an 'absent-minded professor turned publisher, never with the right spectacles on his nose', was rather surprised that he had fathered 'an exceedingly beautiful girl called Marion'. Britten described the Steins as 'almost second Mayers'.

Towards the end of February 1945 he went to Manchester to begin rehearsing the opera with the Wells company, which was on tour there. 'We are having a terrific time with Grimes – & Peter & I are pretty well re-writing his part.' While staying with Ronald Duncan in Devon, Britten had sought his help in improving the words of Grimes's 'mad' soliloquy in Act III scene 2. He told Duncan that Slater's lines were too pedestrian in this passage to give him any musical 'springboard', and Duncan rewrote the soliloquy, echoing phrases from earlier in the opera. (He recalls that Britten was writing the full score during this visit, and would hold a conversation or keep the Duncans' small daughter Briony amused while at work, so 'automatic and easy' did he seem to find it.) Now, Britten reported to Duncan that Slater had 'agreed to the new mad-scene, & I kept your part in it fairly quiet, altho' I murmured that you helped us a bit! Actually your work in that omens well for our future work together, I think.' He and Duncan were talking about collaborating on an opera based on Chaucer's *Canterbury Tales*. Meanwhile Slater had become deeply offended by all the changes made in the libretto during composition, and said he would publish his text separately, as he wished it to stand. It appeared in his *Peter Grimes and other poems* (1946).

During the final weeks of the war it was agreed that Sadler's Wells could return to its own theatre for the season which would include *Peter Grimes*, though the date of opening was put forward to June. Publicity material began to appear, giving Britten's opera rather a low billing beneath the announcements of *Madam Butterfly, La Bohème, The Bartered Bride, Così Fan Tutte* and *Rigoletto*. However, *Peter Grimes* had been chosen for the first performance of the season, the reopening night of the theatre, and grumbles began to be heard among the chorus about the difficulty of singing Britten's music. There was also a feeling that, as artistic director, Joan Cross should not have the part of Ellen but should give it to a younger singer. She herself was finding the part 'hard to memorize and technically hard to accomplish', but Britten and Crozier insisted that she retain it. To defuse the situation she resigned her directorship.

Rehearsals continued wherever the company happened to be: in Sheffield (where they laboured at *Peter Grimes* in a Methodist hall) and

Wolverhampton, where on VE Day, 9 May, they worked on (in a civic centre) because there was no time to join the victory celebrations. Britten attended many of the rehearsals, but the opera was being conducted by one of the company's music staff, Reginald Goodall, who had directed Britten's *Te Deum* in C Major for Iris Lemare in 1936. Like the chorus, the orchestra grumbled at some of Britten's demands, but at their first rehearsal they were (according to Beth Welford) 'bowled over' by the Sea Interludes.

In Wolverhampton the company was joined by the boy who was to play the apprentice, fourteen-year-old Leonard Thompson from Lambeth, who had been recommended to Crozier by a friend, a parish priest there, Paul Gedge, who produced plays with local youths. The boy's voice was breaking, so his top C scream was provided by one of the Nieces. He had never before heard or seen an opera, so Britten took his musical education in hand. 'It was one of Ben's many kindnesses,' Leonard Thompson has written,

> to walk with me around the town telling me the story of the opera we were about to hear [he took the boy to the Wells performances at Wolverhampton in the evening]. Every evening, usually after giving me tea, Ben and I would walk around and I learned about the lives of the composers concerned and the highlights to watch for ... He most certainly had this wonderful gift of communication ... Somehow he managed to retain all his enthusiasm without in any way talking down.

Thompson says he was 'completely unaware' that Britten was homosexual. There was 'no hint' of it in the friendship, nor any suggestion of a particular warmth towards him. 'He seemed to be the same with everyone as far as I was concerned.'

Two weeks after Wolverhampton, the company arrived at its own theatre in Islington for a final intensive fortnight of work before *Peter Grimes* opened. Tempers immediately became worse. At Britten's suggestion, Crozier had engaged as designer Kenneth Green, a painter then doing a wartime job as art master at Wellington College, the boys' public school. He had been brought up in Southwold, a few miles north of Aldeburgh, and got to know Britten and Pears via his son, an evacuee on Long Island. Crozier had decided that his and Green's job was to evoke the particular character of a Suffolk fishing town, and Green had based his Borough designs on the Aldeburgh originals, though he allowed the Southwold lighthouse to peep over the top of the Boar Inn. Space backstage was very cramped at the Wells, and Crozier found that there was not enough music in the 'Storm' Interlude to cover the difficult change from the beach to the Boar interior. He asked Britten to lengthen it, which Britten said was 'like someone who came to an architect when he had just finished building a cathedral, gave him a huge slab of stone, and said "Here, you *must* find room for this."' But finally he complied.

Unrest within the company now came to a head. The Welsh baritone who was to sing Balstrode had already resigned the part, declaring that he 'could not be bothered to learn such outlandish stuff', and only a matter of days before the first performance a deputation of singers met a representative of the Vic–Wells governing body, accompanied by two representatives of Equity. 'They announced,' writes Crozier, 'that they would not perform at all during the forthcoming season – for which they had already refused to sign contracts – unless the governors appointed them as an executive committee in charge of the company. One of their complaints was about the amount of publicity Benjamin Britten and his new opera were receiving.'

Certainly several newspapers carried interviews with him. 'At 31 Mr Britten, a tall, stooping young man with thick brown hair and none of the "Bohemian" appearance one usually expects in musicians,' wrote one reporter (in an unidentified cutting in Joan Cross's scrapbook), 'hopes that his opera will be sufficiently successful to encourage other young people to follow his example.' Another journalist called on Britten in St John's Wood High Street and

> found him speedily orchestrating the score of the opera from his original musical sketch, propped on the table before him. A slight, unassuming young man, with advancing nose and retreating chin, commanded by a worried forehead, he complained that the labour involved . . . was 'something colossal' . . . His only assistant is a student who rules the vertical bar lines for him . . . I asked if he liked singing himself. Britten confessed that last year he zestfully sang bass in a choir which performed his 'Hymn for St Cecilia'. But, he chuckled, the noise that came out hardly resembled what he intended!

The Sadler's Wells singers' complaint about the amount of pre-*Peter Grimes* publicity Britten was getting may seem ridiculous, but Crozier explains that they were really upset by the fact that Britten, Pears and Crozier himself were Conscientious Objectors. They also declared that it was a waste of time and money to stage 'such a piece of cacophony' as *Peter Grimes*. Exactly who was in the deputation is not clear. Joan Cross says she cannot remember, and Crozier writes that they were 'mostly those without parts in *Grimes*'. The rebellion quickly fizzled out when the self-appointed 'executive committee' found it could not face the administrative responsibilities it had demanded, but the unpleasantness simmered on. Leonard Thompson remembers an atmosphere of closed doors and whispers, much like the Borough in the opera.

Meanwhile the London musical world was agog to see and hear what Britten had created. On Thursday 31 May, a week before the opening night, the principal singers gave excerpts from the opera in a Boosey & Hawkes concert at the Wigmore Hall, with Crozier narrating the story and Britten at the piano. In *Horizon*, Edward Sackville-West announced that London was about to hear the English equivalent of *Wozzeck*.

A few of Britten's friends were allowed to attend rehearsals. Michael Tippett came to the Wells one day, and recalls 'this marvellous sound' welling up from the orchestra pit, though he says of the opera itself: 'I didn't like it personally, because it seemed to me a false statement. I thought, this is an English *verismo*, and I don't want to go down that road. I'm going into the world of magic.'

Eighteen months earlier, Britten had written to Elizabeth Mayer that his supporters seemed to outweigh his detractors, 'but for how long one can't say'. Pears observed that their association with Tippett had made them 'enemies' as well as friends. The music critic of the *News Chronicle* in the forties, Scott Goddard, has recalled the 'spiteful antagonism' and 'ethical bickering' that *Peter Grimes* aroused in the weeks before the première, hinting that homosexuality and Conscientious Objection were the chief issues. No one knew what might happen at the première of *Peter Grimes*. However, Britten wrote cheerfully to Walter Hussey to remind him of the date – 'Mind you keep June 7th!' – and backstage before the curtain went up on the opening night he seemed, to the young Leonard Thompson, dressed in the tattered costume of the Apprentice, to be 'completely nerveless, still with his grin – "Hello, Leonard, how are you?" – far more concerned with me than with his opera'.

3: Have a nice peach?

'A slim, curly-haired young man in evening dress stood for three hours at the back of the stalls in Sadler's Wells Theatre last night, too nervous to sit down,' reported the *Daily Express* on the morning after the first performance of *Peter Grimes*, Friday 8 June 1945. The *News Chronicle* alleged that Britten had 'stood at the back of the dress circle or paced up and down'. Nerves were still bad backstage. Just before the curtain went up Tyrone Guthrie wished Joan Cross good luck with the gloomy words 'Whatever happens, we were right to do this piece.' Quite apart from the strife in the company, the audience ranged from the country's most eminent musicians – the *Evening Standard* reporter spotted Vaughan Williams, Walton and Yehudi Menuhin in the stalls – to the 'gallery regulars', some of whom had been coming to the Wells for decades and had no knowledge of modern music. Some of them had camped outside the theatre overnight to be sure of places at the reopening performance. They settled in their seats as the curtain went up and Owen Brannigan as Swallow stepped forward: 'Peter Grimes, we are here to investigate the death of your apprentice . . .'

The performance was not faultless. Principals and chorus sometimes seemed under-rehearsed, and in the pit Reginald Goodall was not altogether happy about the playing – many of the best London musicians were still in the armed forces, and in any case British opera orchestras had not often been confronted with music of this difficulty. But the work triumphed over these limitations. Walter Hussey thought it 'stunning', and Imogen Holst (who was at the second performance) writes:

Actors and audience were aware all the time of the cold, grey sea of Crabbe's poem; when a door at the back of the stage suddenly blew open at the height of the storm, Suffolk listeners sitting in the stalls could feel the north-east draught round their ankles. The music stretched beyond the boxed-in sides of the stage, and when the hostile crowds in the wings called out 'Peter Grimes! – Peter *Grimes!*', their voices sounded as if they were coming from far along the coast. In the fog of the terrible man-hunt, the poor demented fisherman seeemd to grow in stature until he was ... bearing the burden of all those other outcasts who are rejected by their law-abiding neighbours because they are different from other people.

Demented was indeed how Pears looked. Kenneth Green had given him a lank, straggling wig and greasepaint stubble. As he stared wild-eyed at young Leonard Thompson he was scarcely recognizable as the debonair soloist of Wigmore Hall recitals and the romantic tenor of other Wells productions. As to his singing, Walter Hussey calls it 'unforgett-able', and Lord Harewood, who was also in the audience, says that Pears's performance was 'something much deeper' than other inter-preters of Grimes since 1945, 'because so filled with understanding'. Pears's own recollection of that evening is: 'I think I managed to get by.'

The approach of the final curtain caused some anxiety. Pears recalls that there had been 'threats of a demonstration' by those of the rebellious singers who were not in the cast. Leonard Thompson describes what happened as the last bars died away:

> When the curtain came down, for I imagine something like – well, it seemed like minutes, but it must have been about thirty seconds – there was *nothing*. Absolutely nothing. And then it broke out. And it went on and on. I think there were something like fourteen curtain calls. And Ben, of course, came on immaculate, in white tie and tails, looking like a matinee idol. And he just *folded* in the middle. That's the only way I can describe it – the deepest bow I've ever seen from anybody!

Amid the cheers, according to one reporter, 'a few timid and half-hearted boos', but these were 'quite drowned by enthusiastic applause. I lost count of the curtain calls.' Ronald Duncan had the impression that the boos were for Guthrie when he took a bow on behalf of the Wells administration. Imogen Holst reports only the ovation: 'They stood up and shouted and shouted.' Joan Cross – who confirms Thompson's recollection of the long silence before applause broke out – says: 'The stage crew were stunned: they thought it was a demonstration. Well, it was, but fortunately it was the right kind.'

Ronald Duncan found Britten backstage, wearing his usual first-night expression: 'Whatever his achievement had been that night, he looked like a schoolboy about to receive fifty lines.' Britten and Pears gave Joan

Cross a large bowl of waterlilies ('Everything Ben and Peter did was original,' she says) and they all went off to the Savoy where Ralph Hawkes was throwing a party for them, and where the film producer Gabriel Pascal mistakenly congratulated Ronald Duncan on his performance as the Apprentice. For the first time in the evening Britten smiled.

Despite the length of the performance, many papers carried reviews next morning. Eric Blom in the *Birmingham Post* called the opera 'gloomy, harrowing and depressing in the extreme', but did not hesitate to judge it 'a work of genius, an opera so impressive and original that only the most absurd prejudice will keep it out of the great foreign opera houses'. Scott Goddard in the *News Chronicle* found it 'astonishing', and called Pears's and Cross's performances 'profoundly sympathetic'. Beverley Baxter in the *Evening Standard* concluded his review: 'As for Benjamin Britten, young as he is, this opera will outlive him.'

In *The Times*, Frank Howes was more restrained, though there was no doubt that he admired the opera. He wrote of its 'sharp turns of the dramatic screw', described the orchestral music as having 'diabolical cunning', and felt that Pears was 'not completely convincing as a sadist'. William Glock in the *Observer* scarcely discussed the opera's subject matter, concluding his piece: 'it is a most thrilling work. Don't miss it.' Only Philip Hope-Wallace, in a lengthy and perceptive review in *Time & Tide*, hinted at the full implications of the story, and felt slightly cheated in this respect: '*Peter Grimes* . . . just fails to make explicit enough . . . its . . . "hidden" theme of its hero's divided nature . . . which is finally the sole claim on dramatic interest.'

John Ireland was not at the first night, but a week later he went to a London Philharmonic Orchestra concert at which Britten conducted the *Four Sea Interludes* from the opera, their first performance as a separate suite. 'I was very much impressed,' Ireland wrote to a friend. 'He really has achieved something very remarkable here – it is quite different from anything I have heard before from him. In some respects he could twist every other composer in this country round his little finger. It was not pleasant or uplifting – rather Satanic, I thought.'

*

There were eight further performances at the Wells, to full houses. 'We are all excited about the way it's going,' Britten wrote to Mary Behrend, Peter Burra's old patron. And to Basil Wright's mother: 'people are turning up so numerously to see it. It looks as if the old spell on British opera may be broken at last.' John Amis and the writer Eleanor Farjeon were among those who came back for every performance. Somebody boarding a bus for Sadler's Wells was told by the conductor: 'That'll be threepence for *Peter Grimes*,' and as they reached the theatre: 'Sadler's Wells! Any more for Peter Grimes, the sadistic fisherman!' Meanwhile *Picture Post* hazarded a guess that in years to come the opening night 'may well be remembered as the date of the reinstatement of opera in the musical life of this country'. (Among those in the audience on the first night was Eric Walter White, then an administrator with CEMA. He brought a Swiss publisher friend who was so impressed by *Peter Grimes* that he commissioned White to write a short book on Britten. It was published in German in 1948, and Boosey & Hawkes issued it in English the same year. Britten provided what White calls 'detailed and most considerate' replies to his questions, and he gave similar help when White enlarged the book in 1954 and again in 1970.)

On 26 June 1945, three weeks after the première, Britten wrote to Imogen Holst:

> I must confess that I am very pleased with the way that it seems to 'come over the foot-lights', and also with the way the audience takes it, & what is perhaps more, returns night after night to take it again! I think the occasion is actually a greater one than either Sadler's Wells or me, I feel. Perhaps it is an omen for English Opera in the future.

However, there was still unpleasantness backstage. On the last night the audience was cheering wildly for more curtain calls, but the stage management abruptly brought down the safety curtain. More seriously, Britten was told a few weeks later that a complete recording of the opera, which was to have been financed by the British Council, had had to be called off because many of the cast refused to take part. Faced with the attitude of 'those ludicrous fools', as he called them to Pears, he decided to withdraw the opera from the Wells repertoire as soon as possible, so that it could be performed elsewhere in Britain.

The outlook was not good for this. Covent Garden had not yet reopened, and when it did, there was little likelihood that contemporary British operas would be given much space in its repertoire. 'If more new operas were to be composed and performed', writes Crozier, '– and, having begun, Britten was immensely eager to continue – an independent company would have to be created for staging them.'

Indeed, the idea of forming such a company pre-dated the opening of *Peter Grimes*. Crozier again:

> Only a few weeks earlier, during a free day from rehearsals at Wolverhampton, Britten, Pears, Joan Cross and I had taken a boat up the river at Bridgnorth. Later we lay on the bank and discussed our predicament.

We knew that after *Grimes* we had to go on, we had to create and stage more English operas; but Sadler's Wells had turned against us. Covent Garden was still in use as a Mecca dance hall. Glyndebourne was closed 'for the duration' ... Twelve years earlier, while still at school, I had been enormously impressed by a group of French actors, La Compagnie des Quinze [directed by Michel Saint-Denis], brilliant young artists who had been trained to use not merely speech but also movement as a vital part of dramatic expression. Nobody who saw their *The Rape of Lucretia* [1931] could ever forget the tense, terrifying journey that Tarquinius made through the house to reach Lucretia's bedroom ... I was so thrilled that I ordered two of their plays, *Loire* and *Le Viol de Lucrèce*, from Paris and spent my summer holidays translating them. Twelve years later, lying on the river bank at Bridgnorth ... I suggested that we should form a small company of gifted singers on the French model, with ourselves as artistic directors, no chorus, and the smallest group of instrumentalists that Ben would find acceptable for chamber opera. André Obey's play on Lucretia would suit us admirably, not least because it offered splendid parts for our Peter Grimes and our Ellen Orford ... I lent Ben my text of the Obey play, and this he passed on to his friend Ronald Duncan, asking him to write the libretto.

Crozier knew that Britten had been discussing a *Canterbury Tales* opera with Duncan, but he was certain that Chaucer's bawdy 'Miller's Tale' could not be put on the operatic stage. However, Duncan's contribution to the *Peter Grimes* libretto made him seem a promising collaborator, and Britten was happy to provide music for Duncan's verse-play *This Way to the Tomb*, a satire on attitudes to religion, staged in London with much success in the autumn of 1945. When he heard Crozier's suggestion of *The Rape of Lucretia*, Duncan was willing to put aside the Chaucer project and begin discussions about the possibility of a 'chamber opera' on the Lucretia legend. Britten was happy to pare down vocal and instrumental resources, and not just for economic reasons. 'Music for me is clarification,' he said in an interview some years later. 'My technique is to tear all the waste away; to achieve perfect clarity of expression ... and there are many occasions when far smaller units – forms of chamber orchestra – seem nearer to one's ideas.' In 1946 he wrote: 'I am keen to develop a new art form (the chamber-opera, or what you will) which will stand beside the grand opera as the quartet stands beside the orchestra. I hope to write many works for it.' (As early as 1943 he had told Ralph Hawkes that he envisaged writing operas with smaller orchestral resources, for Sadler's Wells: 'It may mean cutting down means abit . . . but that doesn't hurt anyone . . . It's the ideas that count.')

A few weeks after the opening of *Peter Grimes*, he reported to Pears, from Snape: 'Plans are going ahead for the Opera Company – Dartington is fixed, Tennants are extremely interested, & Ronnie has a man with money.' Dartington Hall, where Imogen Holst was director of music, had offered, according to an internal memorandum that August, to give 'Benjamin Britten's opera company a start at Dartington next April'. H. M. Tennant, the theatrical production company, had been approached for financial backing for a tour. Duncan's 'man with money' slipped out of the picture, but the owners of Dartington, Dorothy and Leonard Elmhirst, offered a generous donation towards the project. 'We plan opening May or June, with the New Op. Co.,' Britten told Pears.

In the same letter he reported: 'Well, honey darling, I go off tomorrow at 3.0. Pray for me. I only hope Yehudi remains nice. How I wish it were you!' He had been introduced to Yehudi Menuhin at a Boosey & Hawkes party, and had gathered that the violinist was about to visit Germany and give recitals to survivors of the concentration camps. 'He urged me to take him,' writes Menuhin. Gerald Moore, who was to have been the accompanist, 'very gracefully gave way'. They met to rehearse – and abandoned the attempt after a few minutes because, according to Menuhin, 'our understanding of each other's approach seemed so intuitively sure'.

They arrived in Germany late in July and gave two or three recitals a day, over ten days. 'Yehudi was nice, & under the circumstances the music was as good as it could be,' Britten wrote to Pears.

> We travelled in a small car over bad roads . . . saw heavenly little German villages . . . & . . . completely destroyed towns . . . And . . . millions of D[isplaced] P[erson]s in, some of them, appalling states, who could scarcely sit still & listen, & yet were thrilled to be played to. We stayed the night in Belsen & saw over the hospital – & I needn't describe *that* to you.

Menuhin does describe it, in his autobiography: 'Men and women alike, our audience was dressed in blankets fashioned . . . into skirts and suits . . . they seemed desperately haggard, and many were still in hospital.' One member of that audience, Anita Lasker, who after the war became a professional cellist, wrote to a relative three days later describing the recital. She had the feeling that Menuhin had been saving his best for a more receptive audience, but she was struck by the accompanist, whose name she did not know: 'Somehow one never noticed that there was any accompanying going on at all, and yet I had to stare at this man like one transfixed as he sat seemingly suspended between chair and keyboard, playing so beautifully.'

Two days after he had returned from Germany, Britten began to compose a new song-cycle for Pears, with piano accompaniment. Pears writes that he had been planning it 'for some time'. Indeed, John Donne's 'Holy Sonnets' from which he chose the texts had been favourites of his and Pears's since at least 1943. They seem to have been led to them by Auden. Britten has recalled that 'Auden got us to take Donne seriously.' A letter from Britten to Pears on 2 August 1945, three days after the end of the German tour, gives the impression of desultory work on the cycle: 'I ... can't get down to much yet. But it's heaven to deal with Donne instead of Montagu [Slater]!' In fact he had already set two sonnets, and finished another that day. The letter is cheery but the music portrays black despair and, as in the *Serenade*, terror of hell-fire punishment.

The cycle, entitled *The Holy Sonnets of John Donne*, uses nine of the sequence of nineteen Holy Sonnets, probably written at different periods of Donne's life, in which Donne tries to convince himself (with only limited success) that despite his past sinning God loves him and will not commit him to the eternal fire. The order of poems in the cycle is Britten's, not Donne's. Britten's choice of opening sonnet, 'O my blacke Soule! / now thou art summoned / By sicknesse, death's herald', proved unpleasantly topical, for shortly after he had set it (and two others), he had to go to bed with a high temperature, apparently a delayed reaction to vaccination before the German tour. Though Pears's recollection that the entire song-cycle was composed 'on a bed of high fever' is not strictly accurate, the remaining six settings were indeed written before recovery, for the illness lingered all month.

The cycle is full of self-searching and feverish attempts to believe that, despite the apalling corruption of human nature, there is still some hope of salvation. *Peter Grimes* had given its central character no opportunity for repentance. The *Holy Sonnets*, written to be sung by the man who had played Grimes, provide an epilogue to the opera.

Some of the sonnets give hope, yet Britten's settings do not indicate that the terror of damnation has been overcome. Though the words are set to naturalistic speech patterns, contrasting strongly with the almost robot-like piano part, the vocal line is painfully chromatic, portraying the fears of someone who knows that damnation waits around the corner:

> I runne to death, and death meets me as fast,
> And all my pleasures are like yesterday ...

> Despaire behind, and death before doth cast
> Such terror, and my feeble flesh doth waste
> By sinne in it, which it t'wards Hell doth weigh . . .

The piano accompaniments consist of a series of hypnotically repetitive figures which sometimes, as in the first sonnet, 'O my blacke Soule!', suggest Death knocking at the door, and at other moments seem to portray an obsession that lurks at the back of the mind (they also recall the heavy tread of Grimes in the Passacaglia). Donne and Britten are both desperately praying to be saved from the consequences of their own weakness.

Britten chose to end the cycle with Donne's 'Death, be not proud', which asserts that Death has no special power – 'poppie, or charmes can make us sleepe as well'. (Britten himself was taking sleeping pills at this period of his life.) Even Donne makes the defiance of Death sound rather hollow, and Britten emphasizes this. For the first time in the cycle the piano's repetitive figure is shared by the singer, but the penultimate line, 'One short sleepe past, wee wake eternally', which, if felt to be true, ought (in the music) to suggest the transfiguration of eternal life, is merely accompanied by the same repetitive phrase.

That this is not the real ending to the cycle – that no ending is possible, save the continuing fear of death and damnation – is suggested by the fact that Britten originally intended to add an epilogue, a setting of Donne's famous prose meditation on sickness and death: 'Perchance he for whom this Bell tolls, may be so ill, as that he knowes not it tolls for him . . . And therefore never send to know for whom the bell tolls; it tolls for thee.' He completed this setting but then discarded it, and dedicated the finished song-cycle 'To Peter'.

In an interview in the sixties, Britten indicated that the cycle had been affected by his visit to Belsen, which 'was in many ways a terrifying experience'. Pears, who was aware of this, suggests that the cycle 'defies the nightmare horror with a strong love, the instinctive answer to Buchenwald from East Anglia'. The cycle offers no such message. Menuhin says that Britten 'never talked' about his reactions to Belsen. After Britten's death, Pears told Tony Palmer that he would not speak about it until near the end of his life, when he said 'how shocking it was, and that the experience had coloured everything he had written subsequently'.

*

The Holy Sonnets of John Donne was given its first performance by Pears and Britten at the Wigmore Hall on 22 November 1945, Britten's thirty-second birthday. The previous night, also at the Wigmore, the Zorian

String Quartet gave the première of his String Quartet No. 2, written a few weeks after the Donne cycle. Both concerts were to mark the two-hundred-and-fiftieth anniversary of the death of Purcell, whose influence was perceptible in both Britten works, and to whose music Britten and Pears were now devoting much attention. For the past six years they had been including Purcell in their recitals, with piano parts realized by Britten from Purcell's figured bass (some of these realizations were published by Boosey & Hawkes from 1946 onwards), while *Peter Grimes* demonstrated how much Britten had learnt from Purcell's handling of words. In the Sadler's Wells handbook accompanying the opera he explained that 'One of my chief aims is to try and restore to the musical setting of the English language a brilliance, freedom, and vitality that have been curiously rare since the death of Purcell.' Some years later he said: 'I had never realized, before I first met Purcell's music, that words could be set with such ingenuity, with such colour.' The Passacaglia is a form often found in Purcell's music (for example Dido's famous aria 'When I am laid in earth'), and Britten used it again in the closing song of the *Holy Sonnets*, 'Death be not proud', and in the final movement of String Quartet No. 2 (which is headed 'Chacony', the spelling used in Purcell's day for the Chaconne, another name for the Passacaglia).

Britten once remarked that as a boy he had identified with Beethoven so closely that he 'sometimes had the uncanny feeling that he had written some of the music'. He may have come to identify in a maturer but not dissimilar way with Purcell. There were certainly marked similarities in their careers: Purcell began composing in childhood, had made his name by the age of twenty, wrote much for the theatre, married young but seems from his music to have been a restless personality, and died on 21 November, the day before Britten's birthday. Britten's Purcell realizations are idiosyncratic rather than historically accurate, and make the music seem like the work of one man, Britten–Purcell. The critic William McNaught wrote of a Britten–Pears performance of Purcell's *Lord, What is Man?* in January 1946 that it communicated 'an intricate and unified whole, compounded of Purcell's mind, his fellow-composer's, and the mind and gifts of the singer'.

Britten's String Quartet No. 2, premièred at the Purcell celebrations, was commissioned by Mary Behrend, though Britten passed most of the fee to famine relief in India. He told Mrs Behrend that he had had a quartet 'at the back of my mind' while composing *Peter Grimes*, and after the performance he wrote to her that 'to my mind it is the greatest advance that I have yet made, & altho' it is far from perfect, it has given me encouragement to continue on new lines. People don't understand it as they do the Donne, but that is because those wonderful words help so.'

Much attention was paid to the Quartet by Hans Keller, who had walked into Sadler's Wells one night under the impression that he was about to hear *Così Fan Tutte* and found himself at *Peter Grimes* instead, becoming an instant convert to Britten's music. In *Tempo* (the house journal of Boosey & Hawkes) for March 1947 he published one of his first musical analyses in English, an enthusiastic study of the new quartet. (He had also formed the highest opinion of Britten as accompanist, observing of his playing of Schubert: 'It was almost as if he was composing the music there and then.') Erwin Stein introduced Keller to Britten, with whom he discussed sonata form in the quartet, Keller daring to voice one or two doubts about Britten's method. It was rather a stiff friendship; Britten seemed unwilling to engage in anything but small talk, and was reluctant to say much about his music. If Keller managed to prompt him into making some comment on it, it was usually (says Keller) 'vapid'. Keller judged that he 'felt in some way guilty about verbalizing'.

John Amis, then married to Olive Zorian whose quartet gave Britten's piece its first performance, found him equally reticent during rehearsals for it. Amis 'listened and would occasionally ask about some detail or comment with delight, "Oh, I see, this new tune is really the old one upside down," or something like that, at which Ben would look hard at his score and say, "Oh, is it? Fancy that?" Sometimes he would wink as he said it. At other times it was difficult to know whether he was fooling or not.' (In a 1963 interview Britten observed that he did not like making 'a big thing' of approaching music 'intellectually', adding: 'All that is important is that the composer should make his music sound inevitable and right; the system is unimportant.') His comment to Mrs Behrend that the String Quartet seemed to him his 'greatest advance' to date, and suggested 'new lines' on which to continue, is typical in that it contains no real information. Was he thinking of the structural innovations detected by Keller, or of the Quartet's intensely dramatic nature?

It opens with a drone of two sustained notes on the viola, probably modelled on Purcell's *Fantasia upon One Note*, throughout which a viola sustains a middle C. Britten chose this piece to fill up the final side of the Zorian Quartet's recording of his own String Quartet No. 2, and was persuaded to take out his viola and play the sustained C himself. Amis, who was there, says he was 'terribly nervous' about it. In Britten's harmonic language, the drone, which is on two notes, implying a C major chord, probably represents a state of naturalness. Above it is played a lyrical, slightly chromatic theme which seems to suggest the mind of the contemplative artist, much like Grimes in the early part of the opera. As the first movement progresses it alternates between feverish energy and exhaustion, and gradually introduces the same sort of 'obsessive' repetitive patterns as were heard in the *Holy Sonnets*. The second movement, a Scherzo played on muted instruments, has been variously described by critics as 'uncanny', 'eerie' and 'panic-stricken'. The Quartet concludes with a Chacony (that is, a Passacaglia). Any narrative interpretation of an instrumental work is subjective, yet Eric Walter White, one of Britten's more cautious biographer-critics, declares that the String Quartet No. 2 is 'an instrumental sequel to *Peter Grimes*'. If this is true, then Britten's discovery which he mentions to Mrs Behrend may have been the possibility of encompassing such huge subject matter within the confines of the string quartet.

'I have a small film to write for the Board of Education,' Britten told Mrs Behrend in the same letter. During the war the GPO Film Unit had become the Crown Film Unit. Basil Wright was now producer-in-charge, and had approached Britten to write the score for a film to be distributed by the Ministry of Education, which would demonstrate to school-children the instruments of the orchestra. Unusually, Britten allowed what he himself called a 'long wait of months' to elapse before he undertook the commission. He did not begin the composition sketch until mid-December 1945, finishing at midnight on New Year's Eve. Certainly it had been a busy year – besides all his other work he had been writing incidental music for Louis MacNeice's radio play *The Dark Tower*, broadcast on 21 January 1946 – but he was usually adept at squeezing commissions into his timetable. It may be that he did not feel ready to write the music for *Instruments of the Orchestra*, as the film was to be entitled, until *Peter Grimes* and its 'sequels', the Donne song-cycle and the string quartet, were out of his mind.

The film, with Malcolm Sargent as conductor-narrator, was first shown in November 1946. *The Young Person's Guide to the Orchestra*, as Britten called his soundtrack in the version for concert performance, was first played in public the previous month, with Sargent conducting the Liverpool Philharmonic Orchestra. Montagu Slater wrote the film script, and the concert version had a commentary by Eric Crozier. The music is linked to the Donne song-cycle and the string quartet by its debt to Purcell. Its subtitle is *Variations and Fugue on a Theme of Henry Purcell* (the BBC often infuriated Britten by giving this as the title, which Sargent preferred to the anti-pompous *Young Person's Guide*), and the theme in question is a hornpipe from *Abdelazar, or, the Moor's Revenge*. Britten had a particular young person in mind while writing it, Humphrey Maud, eleven-year-old son of John Maud, a senior civil servant, and his wife Jean Hamilton, a concert pianist. Britten and Pears met the family when Jean Maud invited them to give a recital at a Berkshire music society in 1944, and Britten became especially friendly with Humphrey, who played the cello. The published score of *The Young Person's Guide to the Orchestra* bears the names of all the Maud children as dedicatees, but the copy given to the Mauds has a more specific handwritten inscription: 'For Humphrey and his sisters with much love from Ben.' The passage for solo cellos, which has a Mahlerian melancholy and tenderness that stands out from the rest of the work, may be another mark of dedication.

'I am glad that the Min. of Ed. chaps approve,' Britten wrote to Basil Wright, who had reported enthusiasm for *The Young Person's Guide to the Orchestra* in Whitehall. 'I never really worried that it was too sophisticated for kids – it is difficult to be that for the little blighters!' Critics sometimes direct the opposite charge at the piece: that it is too simple-minded and cliché-ridden in its use of the various orchestral instruments. This usually elicits the response from Britten's defenders that cliché was required by the film. Yet, listening to the exuberant simplicities of *The Young Person's Guide* after the dark, disturbing *Holy Sonnets* and String Quartet No. 2, one has the impression that Britten is writing chiefly for himself. Just as *A Ceremony of Carols* followed the self-examination of the *Hymn to St Cecilia*, and *Rejoice in the Lamb* came after the anguish of the *Serenade*, so once more Britten seems to be coming out into the daylight after a period 'on the rack', to be restoring his faith in life by impersonating a lost innocence. The major chords at the end of the *Holy Sonnets* and the String Quartet seem to offer only precarious hope, but the brilliant fugal finale to *The Young Person's Guide* thunders to its exhilarating D major conclusion like one of the massive steam engines that Britten loved to watch in childhood, as if he has persuaded himself that life is good after all.

*

'Excuse brief scrawl,' Britten concluded his letter to Basil Wright about *The Young Person's Guide*, 'but Lucretia is patiently waiting to be raped – on my desk.' He had set himself the tightest of deadlines for the new opera. A summer 1946 première was planned, but on 19 December 1945 he told Ralph Hawkes: 'I haven't started the Rape of Lucretia yet ... Ronnie Duncan is half-way thro' the libretto which I think terrific.' Duncan had André Obey's play – which in turn was based on Livy, Shakespeare, and other retellers of the Lucretia legend – before him as he wrote, and he and Britten decided to retain Obey's pair of narrators as a Male and Female Chorus, commenting on the action. The casting of these parts was determined at the outset. 'I think we can make Lucretia into a lovely piece – with you & Joan as *such* commentators,' Britten wrote to Pears in August 1945. It was an ingenious way of making Pears a central figure without his having to be a protagonist in such an unambiguously heterosexual story.

The librettiest, on the other hand, must have seemed entirely suited to the sexuality of the opera. Duncan, an ex-pupil of F. R. Leavis and former protégé of Ezra Pound, was devoted to his glamorous blonde wife Rose Marie, who was ill with tuberculosis while the opera was being written – Duncan has claimed that this made him write of Lucretia's death with real feeling – but he had a roving eye. Erwin Stein and his family had been living in the Britten–Pears household in St John's Wood High Street since their own home was damaged in a fire, and Duncan describes how, while working there one morning, he was searching for words to describe Lucretia sleeping. He decided to take an early morning cup of tea to their daughter Marion, then in her late teens:

Her bedroom was next to the kitchen. Noiselessly I opened her door not unaware that I was enacting Tarquinius' stealthy walk through the sleeping house towards Lucretia's bed. Marion didn't wake. Unlike Tarquinius I put her tea down beside her. I sat down to watch Marion sleeping. I picked up a pencil and just described what I saw before me:

> She sleeps as a rose
> Upon the night
> And light as lily
> That floats on a lake ...
> Thus sleeps Lucretia ...

Then I tiptoed out of the room and put the lullaby on Ben's piano.

Though the much smaller vocal and instrumental forces in the new opera – eight singers and a chamber orchestra – combine with the classical setting to make it seem very different from its predecessor, *The Rape of Lucretia* is very close in subject matter to *Peter Grimes*. Once again it opens with the portrayal, in highly chromatic music, of a corrupt society, in this case a Rome where sexual infidelity is the *modus vivendi*. Once more an individual stands out from the crowd, displaying independence of mind which is rewarded with suspicion and hostility: Lucretia, mocked in the first scene for her loyalty to her husband Collatinus. Once again the natural world, in this case a sultry summer's night in Act I followed by bright morning sunshine in Act II, both depicted in the score as vividly as is the sea in *Peter Grimes*, forms a backdrop to the pursuit and destruction of this 'individual against the crowd'. Once again this central character is torn between bohemianism and bourgeois convention.

Lucretia appears to enjoy the happiest of marriages. When at the opening of the second scene she sings of her love for her absent soldier husband, the music emphasizes the genuineness of her feelings:

> Collatinus! Collatinus!
> Whenever we are made to part
> We live within each other's heart,
> Both waiting, each wanting.

It could be Pears writing to Britten. 'The days are going very quickly really and I shall soon be with you ... My whole being longs to be with you, my darling,' Pears told him while *The Rape of Lucretia* was being planned. Yet Lucretia's expression of longing is only one of a series of yearnings felt by the women of her household. Her old nursemaid Bianca mourns her lost youth and wishes she had been Lucretia's real mother, and the young maidservant Lucia longs for the day when somebody will love her. Moreover in the previous scene two of the men have indulged in similar yearnings. Tarquinius and Junius describe the ceaseless male search for a dream girl: 'A pilgrimage to a pair of eyes / In which there lies ... / perfection which is love's brief mirage'. The only character not to indulge in such day-dreaming is Collatinus, who makes some rather complacent utterances about the joys of monogamy: 'Those who love create / Fetters which liberate ...' Moreover the Male Chorus, who tells the truth throughout the opera, has just observed that 'Collatinus is politically astute to choose a virtuous wife. / Collatinus shines brighter from Lucretia's fame.' Collatinus would evidently feel at home in the Borough.

In contrast Tarquinius, Lucretia's ravisher, is portrayed in Act I as a mere child, whose taunts to Junius ('Junius is a cuckold') are set to the tune of a playground sneer. Britten seems to be contrasting this boyish enthusiasm with the depressing adult values of Collatinus. In Act II Tarquinius becomes something more splendid. He approaches Lucretia's bedroom through the darkened house not to the sinister music one might expect, but with the electrifying sound of unaccompanied percussion (untuned drums). This describes him so unmistakably that we scarcely need the Male Chorus's whispered words: 'Panther agile and panther virile, / ... with all the alacrity of thought ...' This superb creature has erupted into a bourgeois household, described in Obey's play as 'the best ordered in Rome', where the most exciting event of the evening is folding the linen – this occupies an entire and rather cloying musical number in Act I. No wonder Lucretia is drawn to him. (Janet Baker, who sang the title role in the sixties, agrees that Lucretia has an 'underlying fear' that she may yield to Tarquinius. 'If she weren't in danger from his sexuality she wouldn't be frightened. If she had been emotionally uninvolved, she wouldn't have felt guilty after the rape.')

When he awakens her with a kiss, she protests her immutable love for her husband, but this is contradicted by the first violin's frenzied reiteration above her voice of a musical figure based on the opera's 'Tarquinius motive'. Quite apart from this and other musical indications that Tarquinius is by no means a totally unwelcome intruder into Lucretia's marriage, there are a number of pointers in the libretto. Gazing at her, Tarquinius asserts that in truth she desires him: 'Yet the linnet in your eyes / Lifts with desire / And the cherries of your lips / Are wet with wanting.' She does not refute this. Indeed, she has already confessed his power over her imagination: 'In the forest of my dreams / You have always been the Tiger.' Certainly when, on the morning after the rape, she comes into the presence of her unsuspecting husband, Britten provides her with a haunting instrumental lament for cor anglais and strings, which powerfully expresses regret and sorrow at her predicament. Yet when she actually reports the rape to Collatinus, her halting narrative is broken up with musical recollections of Tarquinius which take the most extraordinary forms. 'Last night', she sings, 'Tarquinius – ', whereupon the strings break into a fragment of a Viennese waltz. A moment later, after the words 'ravished me', comes a little polka such as a café orchestra might play. Before she has finished her story another waltz is heard. These musical fragments, reworkings of what Tarquinius had sung to her before the rape, suggest a certain ambiguity in her attitude to the night's events. She is a Grimes who chose the safe path of marrying Ellen (just as Britten had chosen a closed relationship with Pears), but whose darker, Bohemian side has tragically emerged and triumphed. Like Grimes, she realizes that the only escape from this disaster is suicide. The outlook, then, seems to be equally bleak whichever path you choose. It is not an encouraging conclusion, and the surviving characters are left asking, in the Passacaglia which forms Lucretia's funeral march, if this is all the story has to teach. They answer themselves: 'It is all! It is all!'

Musically and dramatically this is the true end to the opera, and Ronald Duncan would happily have stopped it there. However, Britten was understandably uneasy about this harsh conclusion, and asked Duncan for a specifically Christian epilogue (possibly this was Pears's suggestion). Duncan complied, providing a suitable reassurance that fallen man can be sustained by Christ. Yet Britten seems to question this, in the accompaniment, by echoing the bleak 'It is all!' of the Passacaglia. Similarly Ernest Ansermet, who conducted the first production, pointed out to Duncan that the pious hymn sung by the Male and Female Chorus in the Interlude while the rape is actually happening – 'Nothing impure survives, / All passion perishes' – is clearly contradicted by the orchestra's depiction of 'the rhythm of copulation'.

*

Britten began the composition sketch of *The Rape of Lucretia* on 25 January 1946 and finished on 26 May. He then immediately began 'ploughing away at the score'. Plans for the production had changed. While producing a play at the Lyric, Hammersmith, Crozier met one of the directors of the company then resident there, Rudolf Bing. He was about to return to Glyndebourne, where he had been John Christie's manager before the war, and asked if there was any chance of the next Britten opera being staged there. Crozier went down to Glyndebourne, where there was so much to discuss that he found himself staying the night 'in a pair of Christie's green silk pyjamas', and the outcome was 'the setting up of the Glyndebourne English Opera Company, with Christie, Bing, Britten and myself as its four directors'. Dartington gracefully relinquished the opera group with the observation that 'Glyndebourne can obviously provide greater facilities and considerably more prestige'. In *Tempo* for March 1946, Crozier announced that the new company would provide a 'method by which singers of the first rank can devote five months of each year between June and October – slack months in the concert world – entirely to the rehearsal and performance of opera'. The plan was to rehearse each season's programme in June, perform it at Glyndebourne in July, then go on tour.

At the outset Christie, Eton schoolmaster and upper-class eccentric turned opera house proprietor, seemed to be the ideal patron. When the *Lucretia* company arrived at Glyndebourne on 10 June 1946 to begin rehearsals they found everything laid on, with accommodation in the Christies' mansion or in cottages on the estate. Pears and Joan Cross had just returned from singing *Peter Grimes* in German in Zurich. Britten went with them, and told Erwin Stein: 'I wish you could hear it if only for the Interludes, & the hut-scene which with Peter is most moving. The little boy is very pathetic, & a good actor, but not quite the figure that Leonard was.' He also went to see another *Peter Grimes* at Basle, where Grimes himself came across as '*far* too dotty, & not sympathetic enough'.

Rehearsals for *Lucretia* were complicated by the need for two casts, so that the opera could be given nightly for three months (it was to tour after Glyndebourne) without straining voices. Each had its own conductor, Reginald Goodall for the second team, in which the young mezzo-soprano Nancy Evans (then married to the impresario Walter Legge) would sing Lucretia, and Ansermet for the first, with Pears, Joan Cross as the Female Chorus, Owen Brannigan and Otakar Kraus as Collatinus and Tarquinius, and Kathleen Ferrier making her operatic début as Lucretia. She and Pears had sung together in a 1943 *Messiah* in Westminster Abbey, when Britten, who was in the audience, was 'very excited' by her voice, and they had often performed together since then. She was Pears's suggestion for Lucretia. Although she had no stage experience, Britten thought that the 'very grand personality' she displayed on the concert platform would suit the role admirably: 'I knew that for Lucretia you couldn't have a sexy dame, which Kathleen certainly wasn't!' When rehearsals began she found acting hard: 'I couldn't believe how difficult it was to do the simplest arm-movements without feeling like a broken-down windmill. And when I finally stabbed myself, I fell down like a hard-baked dinner-roll!' However, the good humour of 'this lively, mischievous Lancashire girl', as Pears calls her, 'who'd left school at fourteen to work in the Post Office', made her a willing learner. 'The beginning was always marvellous,' Britten recalls of her interpretation of Lucretia. 'She sang it beautifully; she didn't find the music as difficult as I think she felt she was going to find it ... And her natural beauty, sitting there on the stage – one realized that this *was* Lucretia. [But] it was only slowly, I think, that Kathleen developed the right kind of confidence for the later scenes.' Pears confirms that 'to begin with, she did have difficulty with the high, hysterical last scene before Lucretia kills herself ... Hysteria wasn't part of her make-up – she couldn't feel it easily; she was a very balanced person.' However, John Francis, flautist in the orchestra, recalls that he and his colleagues were biting back the tears as she sang this final scene.

After two weeks of rehearsal, Britten reported that Glyndebourne was 'an excellent place to work in'. The orchestra sounded 'most exciting' and Ansermet was doing a fine job. However, Ronnie Duncan noticed a 'growing tension between Ben and Crozier [who was producing] against Rudolf Bing', and also 'a marked coolness from Ben towards John Christie which was not reciprocated'. Part of the trouble was Christie's John Bullish manner. Duncan says that he was inclined to show more interest in a new lavatory he had installed in the foyer than in what was happening on stage. Such comments as he made about the opera were rarely encouraging. 'He was not an easy person to work with,' recalls

John Piper, who had been brought in by Crozier to design the costumes
and sets; these, says Pears, 'came in for some very ill-informed and
ill-timed criticism' from Christie. He also took a boorish attitude to the
score, and was heard to say that *Lucretia* had 'no music in it'. (Emanuel
Hurwitz, who was leading the orchestra, comments on Christie's lord-of-
the-manor way of running things: 'During the breaks, the singers would
eat with the Christies, but the orchestra were treated like servants and sent
round to the kitchen quarters for sandwiches.')

Something of Britten's growing hostility to Christie may be detected in a
letter to Ralph Hawkes ten days before the opening of *Lucretia*. This
stresses that the new opera group 'was Eric's, & my (& Joan's & Peter's)
scheme originally, & although Christie put the money up & Bing manages
it, it remains "our" company & its policy is directed by us'. Duncan
thought Britten's attitude to Christie rather a mistake: 'I myself liked John
Christie because he was an eccentric. Ben lacked that tolerance.'

Meanwhile Joan Cross, who had abandoned her artistic directorship at
Sadler's Wells for the sake of *Peter Grimes*, and had thrown in her lot with
Britten's group, began to feel that the triumvirate of Britten, Crozier and
Pears was running the new opera company to the exclusion of everyone
else. 'I felt I was simply there as a performer, nothing else. I was rather
bitter about it. Nobody knew what I'd done before.' She thought parts of
the opera, especially the spinning song for the women, 'absolutely
dazzling', but felt that Act II did not deliver the promise of the first half.

The first performance was on the evening of Friday 12 July 1946.
Ronnie Duncan says that Britten was 'alarmed' by the arrival of 'the
usual Glyndebourne white-tie brigade'. As at *Peter Grimes*, he stood at
the back of the auditorium during the performance, looking tense. It
went smoothly, but the audience's response, according to Duncan, was
'polite but unaware'. Next morning's reviews were favourable if a little
reserved. '*Lucretia* is a masterly work,' wrote Scott Goddard in the *News
Chronicle*. 'In Britten's music there is evidence of great talent, exquisite
touches of art in the use of the tiny orchestra and the handful of singers
... The decor, by John Piper, is a perpetual joy.' Frank Howes in *The
Times* praised Ferrier's 'splendid voice and great dignity of bearing', and
wrote of Britten's 'very sure touch'. But only Ferruccio Bonavia in the
New York Times felt that *Lucretia* was an advance on *Peter Grimes*.
Bonavia judged that 'the most striking feature in the new Britten opera is
the widening of range, the deepening of sympathy suggested by music
that is at times quite as fierce and robust as anything in *Grimes*, and also
more exquisite and more delicately beautiful than the finest page of the
earlier opera.'

Several critics expressed doubts about the libretto. Over two weekends it came under sustained attack from Ernest Newman in the *Sunday Times*, who complained of Duncan's determination to be 'literary', demonstrated in such lines as 'The oatmeal slippers of sleep / Creep through the city and drag / The sable shadows of night / Over the limbs of light'. 'Can slippers', asked Newman, 'drag anything over anything?' He also criticized the Christian epilogue, suggesting that Duncan's 'piety, or his love for easy effect, seems to me to have got the better of his dramatic sense'. Michael Tippett was equally dismayed by the libretto. He went to see *Lucretia* with William Walton, with whom he had now struck up a friendship, and

> went backstage to see Ben after it, and I said: 'Oh dear!' He said: 'What do you mean by "Oh dear"?' I may have said: 'I think it's more interesting than *Grimes*' – I'm not sure what I said. But I did say: 'If you're now going to write a comic opera' – as he'd already told me – 'for Christ's sake don't use this librettist.' Ben took it, but he withdrew. He was already in a touchy state.

Tippett adds an anecdote about a performance of *Lucretia* in Italy. The curtain is supposed to fall just as the rape begins, but on this occasion it stuck, leaving the singer playing Tarquinius utterly at a loss. 'And he didn't get on with the rape, and then suddenly there were shouts from the audience: *"Coraggio, coraggio!"* It was marvellous! But I would never have told Ben that.'

*

After the two-week run at Glyndebourne, *Lucretia* went on tour, with John Christie as financial guarantor. It opened in Edinburgh, where Britten and Duncan stayed at the Caledonian Hotel. Duncan alleges that, shortly after they arrived, he saw Britten going down the corridor in a peculiar manner: 'He seemed to be lame, moving slowly forward as though crippled on both feet ... "What I'm trying to do, Ronnie," he said, "is to see if I can get right down this corridor and back without touching any of the red lines on the carpet ... If I can ... it will mean that I am a composer."' This would seem like one of Duncan's wilder inventions were it not for a note by Donald Mitchell in his edition of Britten's letters:

> Many of Britten's friends – I among them – will remember a street game (the subject of a poem by A. A. Milne) he played while out walking ... he would hop from square to square of the paving-stones and if he could complete a stretch without his feet touching any of the

lines he would claim that this showed that after all he was a good composer – or going to be.

Whatever he felt about his achievement, he was now making a comfortable living from royalties and performance fees. During 1946 he bought an elderly Rolls Royce. Eric Crozier says that soon afterwards Vaughan Williams turned up at an orchestral rehearsal in a Rolls, countering the players' surprised comments with: 'Well, why shouldn't I? Ben Britten's got one!' Some years later, Britten told Rosamund Strode that, though he felt guilty about buying expensive cars, 'It's really the only thing I spend on myself.'

On the other hand the *Lucretia* tour was a financial disaster. The company played to half-empty theatres in Edinburgh, Glasgow, Liverpool, Manchester and Oxford, and Christie was hugely out of pocket. Had he not already advertised the return of Britten's opera company to Glyndebourne the next summer, with a revival of *Lucretia* and 'a new Contemporary Opera', the Glyndebourne English Opera Company would probably have come to an end there and then.

While *Lucretia* was still on tour, Britten left for a brief visit to America – his first transatlantic journey by air – where *Peter Grimes* was at last to be staged at Koussevitzky's Berkshire Festival at Tanglewood, a vast event involving hundreds of music students, past and present. Three performances were given in early August by a young and enormous cast – enormous in every sense, for Crozier, who had flown over to produce, recalls that in overfed America it was impossible to find a thin child to play the apprentice. The conductor was the twenty-eight-year-old Leonard Bernstein, a former pupil of Koussevitzky. Crozier was so depressed by the standard of performance that he telegraphed Britten not to come, but this was interpreted by Britten as a *cri de cœur*, and he duly arrived, finding that, after the first night, he had to share a bedroom with Auden, who had come up from New York to see the opera, and who infuriated him by smoking in bed.

To a reporter, Britten politely described the production as a 'lively student performance'. Auden was more candid: 'The performance was terrible but the work made an impression just the same.' He had already heard excerpts from the opera at the New York studio of Pears's former teacher Clytie Mundy, and wrote to Britten: 'I loved what I could hear.'

He had stayed briefly with Britten and Pears in London in the spring of 1945, on his way to Germany. For a long while he had continued to hope that Britten would set his oratorio *For the Time Being*, and his friend Charlie Miller says he was 'hurt' when he realized this would never happen. A letter he wrote to Britten in January 1946 assumes that Britten will write the music for a litany for St Matthew's Day, commissioned by Walter Hussey, and encloses the words – a great many of them. Britten complained good-humouredly to Hussey that no one had warned him about it, and 'Auden's stuff is desperately hard to set, & can't be done overnight.' Yet this was in February, and the patronal festival for which the piece was required was not until September. Moreover when the occasion came he had managed to find time to write a *Prelude and Fugue on a Theme of Vittoria* for organ, while Auden's words remained unset and had to be recited. (Another commission was an *Occasional Overture* for the opening of the BBC Third Programme on 29 September 1946. Britten did not think it worthy of publication or further performance, perhaps because he associated it with Boult, who conducted the broadcast.)

Peter Pears has suggested, of Britten's wish, now gradually becoming apparent, to collaborate no further with Auden, that 'Ben was on a different track now, and he was no longer prepared to be dominated – bullied – by Wystan.' In a Foreword to the libretto of *The Rape of Lucretia*, Britten says that a ' "working together" of the poet and composer . . . seems to be one of the secrets of writing a good opera', and he knew that this would never be possible with Auden, who always took the lead. But there was another side to it. 'Ben told me that Peter got him away from Auden,' writes Beth Welford, and it is clear that Pears had won a personal struggle against Auden just as, a few years earlier, he had managed to wrest Britten away from Lennox Berkeley. The question remains whether Pears himself was possibly now exercising a domination over him which was far more subtle than Auden's bullying but also far more effective.

Leonard Bernstein, who had met Britten in England and seen *Lucretia* before he conducted *Peter Grimes* at Tanglewood, felt that Pears had erected a barrier between Britten and other people: 'Peter Pears . . . represented for him all relationships put together . . . which . . . made it difficult for him to have other deep friendships.' At Tanglewood he was 'surprised to find how diffident he was . . . slightly mistrustful, very shy, but when he had a point to make . . . there was no question about it.' Bernstein soaked himself in *Peter Grimes* – 'in fact I strongly feel in some ways as though I've written it myself . . . I wish I had' (its mark can be perceived in *West Side Story*) – but he remained puzzled and disturbed by Britten himself: 'I remember talking with Aaron Copland . . . They had been very good friends . . . but . . . there was always something that placed a distance between them . . . Aaron . . . said . . . "There's something about Ben that prevents us from becoming friends." He could never put his finger on it.'

Ronnie Duncan now had occasion to become equally puzzled and disturbed. He had assumed that after *Lucretia* they would write other operas together. Indeed Britten had encouraged him to begin work on Jane Austen's *Mansfield Park*, suggested by Joan Cross. They also discussed writing an oratorio in reaction to the atomic bombing of Hiroshima and Nagasaki. Britten mentioned it in a letter to Victor Hely-Hutchinson at the BBC on 25 February 1946: '... the oratorio "Mea Culpa" ...' Duncan started on the Austen libretto, and only by chance heard that 'Ben was already working on another opera, *Albert Herring*, with Eric Crozier.'

Duncan confronted Britten with this. 'He admitted the position, looked sheepish but gave no explanation.' Duncan does not seem to have asked for one. Perhaps he felt the bad reviews of the *Lucretia* libretto were enough to explain it. What rankled was not so much being replaced as not being told about it; leaving him to hear from a third party. Duncan's comment in his memoir of Britten is: 'Ben could charm the skin off a coconut when he wanted something; when he didn't he was harder than its shell.'

Crozier was astonished to find himself appointed to replace Duncan. Like *Lucretia*, the new opera arose from his knowledge of French literature. He and Britten were discussing possible subjects for the next chamber opera, which would have to be written as quickly as *Lucretia*, and, writes Crozier,

> I suggested a comic opera based on Maupassant's short story, *Le Rosier de Madame Husson* ['Madame Husson's May-King']. Britten liked the idea, especially when he saw how easily the action could be translated from Maupassant's France to his own native coast of East Suffolk. We made a brief sketch of how the story might be adapted as an opera, and, before I quite understood what was happening, it was agreed that I should undertake the libretto.

There now began a period of what Crozier calls 'a close and genuine affection' between him and Britten.

> We talked about anything and everything: we met or spoke by telephone almost every day: we went on holiday together – holidays in which work and fun were marvellously blended: I was a constant visitor at Ben's home ... When Ben had to write an article (a task he hated), we would sit at either side of the fire with pencil and paper, and

by gradual questioning I would get from him what he wanted to say ... Even when he needed some publicity photographs, I fixed the appointment and took him to the studio and talked to him throughout the session ... Our friendship was so close and so enduring that some people took it for granted that I must be a homosexual, but I was not.

Montagu Slater and Ronald Duncan had in turn enjoyed similarly close friendships with him, and both had been bitterly hurt by abrupt rejections – 'frightfully disappointed' says Slater's widow of her husband's feelings when he was replaced as librettist by Duncan. Twenty years later, long after his own close friendship was over, Crozier felt that Britten had 'always had a particular favourite, somebody whose confidence mattered a great deal to him, and upon whom he would lavish affection and admiration in the most generous fashion, while at the same time foreseeing with a grim kind of enjoyment the day when that special friend would be cast off'. Crozier admits that this sounds 'like exaggeration', but he cites a specific incident:

Just before Christmas one year during that period [the late forties] a parcel arrived marked FRAGILE. Ben unpacked it eagerly and found inside a sixteenth- or seventeenth-century map of Suffolk in a frame – a very pleasant and generous present. 'Who is it from?' I asked. He handed the picture to me with a curious expression of distaste mixed with embarrassment. 'Monty Slater,' he replied. 'One of my "corpses".' Then, with a queer kind of pleasure, he went on: 'You'll be one, too, one day.'

Marion Thorpe (Marion Stein) comments: 'I don't think Ben himself would ever have said "corpses". *We* [his friends] invented it, I think, and used to say it to him.' Crozier, however, is emphatic that Britten used the word himself.

*

Following his financial loss on the tour of *Lucretia*, John Christie said he could not possibly support other tours. In any case Britten, still angry with Christie for his attitude to the opera, now wanted to have nothing more to do with Glyndebourne beyond keeping the agreement to present the new piece there next summer. The Glyndebourne English Opera Company was wound up, and into being came the English Opera Group, a title echoing the Group Theatre. This created an alarming timetable and agenda. As Crozier writes, 'it would be necessary to raise at least twelve thousand pounds ... Advance theatre bookings [for the tour of the new opera] also had to be secured – in itself a difficult task for a new and unknown opera-company – to enable [the English Opera Group] to offer contracts to singers, orchestral players, conductors and stage technicians.' Meanwhile the new opera had to be written, by the two people most heavily involved in setting up the company. Moreover *Lucretia* had been booked for six performances in Amsterdam early in October 1946, with Britten himself conducting. Crozier stayed in England to begin the new libretto, and Britten wrote to him from Holland that Peter Diamand, the lively administrator of the Netherland Opera, was 'very relieved that we've made our great decision, & very hopeful about the future here . . . I hope that Christie & Bing aren't being too vile . . . P.P.P.S. How's *Albert*?'

Maupassant's short story, set in a small Normandy town, describes the elderly do-gooder Madame Husson looking for a virtuous local girl to be crowned May Queen. Finding none, she picks on the greengrocer's son Isidore, a mother's boy and simpleton too timorous even to look at the local girls. At the celebrations, however, he develops a taste for wine, and afterwards goes on the rampage, remaining a drunkard for the rest of his life.

Crozier was well qualified to transfer the setting to Suffolk, for one of his grandfathers had kept a country shop there, and he had sometimes helped behind the counter. (Britten, too, had played storekeeper at the Rothmans' in Suffolk County, and had wanted to stay there.) The name Albert Herring was taken from the owner of a grocery at Tunstall, near Snape, and the surname of Lady Billows, the opera's version of Madame Husson, from Lionel Billows, British Council representative in Switzerland, who looked after the *Lucretia* company when it went on there from Holland. Lady Billows's character was modelled partly on Beth Welford's mother-in-law, self-appointed lady of the manor in her Suffolk village of Peasenhall – Beth writes that she 'liked to think herself Queen Bee of the village and was a terrible snob' – and perhaps also partly on Joan Cross, who was to play the part. Certainly Florence, Lady Billows's companion/housekeeper, was the name of Joan Cross's own housekeeper. The vicar, Mr Gedge, was named after the London priest who had provided Leonard Thompson for *Peter Grimes*. Harold Wood, one of the village children in the opera, is the name of a railway station on the Liverpool Street to Ipswich line, while another child in *Albert Herring*, Cissie Woodger, was named after a girl in Snape for whom Britten had once bought a ticket for a CEMA concert. ('When asked next day how she had enjoyed herself,' writes Crozier, 'she replied, "Oh, I didn't mind it at all!" ')

Loxford, the setting of the opera, is an adaptation of Yoxford, on the road from Snape to Peasenhall. 'Ben threatened to call the schoolmistress Miss Welford,' writes Beth (the character appears under that name in a typescript of the libretto), 'but I dissuaded him and he called her Miss Wordsworth instead.' Nancy the baker's daughter owed her name and character to Nancy Evans, Lucretia in the second cast, whom Crozier, separated from his wife, hoped to marry (her own marriage to Walter Legge had broken up). The part of Nancy was earmarked for her, and he sent her progress reports on the writing of the opera.

'Ben is being awfully nice about *Albert*,' he wrote to her on 20 November 1946. 'He is rather glum about life generally, and he says the only exciting thing at the moment is how well the libretto is shaping and that I must write more. Hooray!' And some time in December, from Snape: 'Ben . . . is going off on a long walk this afternoon to think, before actually sitting down to begin writing the music.' A few days later: 'I see now what Ben means about having me here to consult with. There are dozens of tiny points he comes to ask about while he is setting the text – minor problems keep cropping up. It is exciting to see some of it in score already – like seeing one's child in party clothes for the first time.' Many years later, Crozier recalled how Britten 'liked to have me within arm's reach' while composing the opera, 'so that he could come down the corridor or call across the room and say: "After the duet for Nancy and Sid, I shall need four more lines," or "When the vicar arrives, how does he greet Mum?"'

Like *Lucretia*, *Albert Herring* is a re-run of *Peter Grimes* with a different twist. A social misfit is faced with the choice between bourgeois convention and bohemianism, and opts for the latter. Just as Grimes was poised between the Borough and the sea, and Lucretia between respectable domesticity and the sexual magnetism of Tarquinius, so Albert is suspended between two social worlds, each with clearly defined musical language. Loxford society, headed by Lady Billows, is in many respects the Borough once again, stuffy, repressive and hidebound, musically characterized by a near-inability to express itself without cliché. Anything sung by its members is likely to lapse into pastiche, the choice of musical model depending on social class. Lady Billows makes her public pronouncements about morality and the May festivities in a style which is either Handelian or Imperial – she seems perpetually about to launch into *Rule, Britannia!* or *Land of Hope and Glory*. The vicar and Miss Wordsworth are drawn to nineteenth-century parlour music, and the Mayor and Police Superintendent hold forth in the fashion of, respectively, Italian popular opera and English brass bands.

Ranged opposite these prisoners of worn-out styles are two sets of 'free' people: the village children, whose music is in the form of traditional singing games and ball-bouncing rhythms, and the two lovers, Sid from the butcher's shop and Nancy, whose utterances resemble the children's in their lilting, swinging rhythms, but have more maturity and erotic overtones. Meanwhile Albert, poised between these two factions, is given no strong musical personality of his own. He acquires characteristics from whichever party is influencing his state of mind that moment. He is also bullied and henpecked by his mother, whose music resembles just that – the fussy pecking of a hen. Britten draws a scathing caricature of his own mother's treatment of him, though he also mocks Albert's folly (that is, his own) in remaining tied to the apron strings into adult life.

As well as these broad strokes of character painting, the two sides (Loxfordians and children-and-lovers) are identified by sound effects. Lady Billows's pompous utterances and the deliberations of her urban district May Day committee are constantly punctuated by the chime of a clock. Its two 'cuckoo' notes, which may be a private joke about Mrs Welford's family nickname, 'Cuckoo', help to create the major triad 'May King, May King' motif which dominates the opera. Britten is saying that the Loxfordians are driven by the clock. Similarly Sid, when urging Nancy to come love-making, equates the repressive world from which they must escape with the clock: 'Come along, darling, come follow me quick! / Time is racing us round the clock, / Ticking and tocking our evening away.' When Albert decides to break loose he tells himself: 'The clock begins its rusty whirr, / Catches its breath to strike the hour / And offers me a final choice.'

Just as the clock stands for repression, freedom is symbolized by whistling. In the Interlude between the first and second scenes the pomposities of Lady Billows's committee give place to the cheeky whistle of a street-urchin, which Britten depicts with uncanny realism in the harmonics of the upper strings. Later in the opera, Sid's sexy invitations to Nancy largely take the form of whistling under her window, and when Albert has decided to run away the first thing he does is imitate Sid's whistle. Just as the Loxfordians' clock chime provides the music for their public utterances, so the whistle, on an upward glissando, supplies the phrase for Sid's invitation to Nancy: 'Have a nice peach?' Britten fully exploits the erotic implications of fruit in the opera, not merely the peaches ('You can bring them tonight, and we'll each take a bite,' Sid sings to Nancy) but also the apples which the children steal from Albert's shop, imitating the Fall.

The Loxfordians and the children-and-lovers collide in Act II scene 1, the May Day celebrations, when Miss Wordsworth tries to force the children into the strait-jacket of Imperial music, with hilarious results. Until now Crozier and Britten have stuck fairly closely to Maupassant, but unlike Isidore in the short story Albert is no simpleton, nor is his decision to break loose the result of alcohol. Sid and Nancy lace his lemonade with rum, but what pushes him over the brink is overhearing one of their amorous encounters. Unlike Grimes or Lucretia, he has made a conscious choice to break loose, so one waits with particular keenness to discover the consequences.

What happens first is a manhunt, echoing the Borough's pursuit of Grimes. It ends when Albert's May King wreath is found crushed in the road and his death is assumed. The Loxfordians and lovers join forces in a magnificent Threnody, yet another passacaglia, in which each voice sings its individual variation in turn over a repeated ground: 'In the midst of life is Death. / Death awaits us one and all. / Death attends our smallest step, / Silent, swift and merciful.' Under the stress of grief the Loxfordians escape from musical cliché and are able to express real feelings. Then, abruptly, Albert reappears, and describes his naughty night out: drunkenness and, by implication, loss of virginity. The outraged Loxfordians storm out, Albert demonstrates that he is no longer under his mother's thumb, and he is left alone with the children and the lovers.

Several commentators have found this a disappointing end. Peter Evans suggests that Albert deserves 'a less contemptuous dismissal', Michael Kennedy calls it 'small change rather than pay-off', and Eric Walter White suspects that Albert will soon live down the scandal and return to being a respectable Loxfordian. Certainly the opera ends swiftly, possibly failing (as Joan Cross felt *Lucretia* had failed) to deliver all its promised goods. Yet both libretto and music indicate that Albert will never revert to Loxfordianism. His final action is to invite the children into the shop and give them the freedom of the fruit. The meaning of this is perfectly clear, and it suggests a change of attitude in Britten. Until now he has, as it were, sided with Lady Billows and identified innocence with sexual inexperience, virtue with virginity. *Albert Herring* mocks the folly of such an attitude. It is not merely on the side of the children but also of Sid and Nancy and their cheerful sexuality. Britten's music makes it clear that, though they may be 'fallen' in the eyes of Lady Billows, they have retained their essential innocence, while the stuffy Loxfordians have lost theirs in the cause of respectability. Albert's last solo words in the opera, sung to the children, are 'Have a nice peach?' They show that he and Britten now understand that there is nothing inherently virtuous in sheltering in the maternal 'warm nest'.

Some years after writing *Albert Herring*, Britten told the painter Sidney Nolan: 'Auden is in all my operas.'

4: A family affair

Much of *Albert Herring* was composed in Switzerland, where Britten and Pears spent a month early in 1947, giving recitals and taking a holiday. 'We've fallen (literally) for ski-ing, whch we do passionately & erratically,' Britten wrote to Jean Maud, 'but we work early mornings & late nights to keep the conscience clear.' Crozier joined them – he was still writing the libretto while Britten composed – and on 12 February he told Nancy Evans: 'The opera [i.e. the libretto] is all finished except for rewrites! ... We celebrated with a glass of Genever ... and Ben said would I devote the rest of my life to writing libretti for him?'

The English Opera Group (EOG) was now sufficiently organized to issue a prospectus, which named Britten, Crozier and John Piper as artistic directors; Ralph Hawkes, Erwin Stein, Tyrone Guthrie and Sir Kenneth Clark were on the board, which was chaired by Oliver Lyttelton. 'We believe the time has come', began the prospectus,

> when England ... can create its own operas ... We believe the best way to achieve the beginnings of a repertory of English operas is through the creation of a form of opera requiring small resources ... A first essay in this direction was ... Britten's *The Rape of Lucretia* ... The success of this experiment has encouraged the ... persons chiefly involved ... to continue their work as a group by establishing ... THE ENGLISH OPERA GROUP, incorporated on a non-profit-making basis. This Group will give annual seasons of contemporary opera in English and suitable classical works including those of Purcell.

The prospectus went on to describe the preparations for *Albert Herring*, and to appeal for funds: 'a total sum of £12,000 is urgently needed as working capital. Of this, the sum of £2,000 has already been generously given by a private subscriber.' This anonymous benefaction was from Leonard and Dorothy Elmhirst of Dartington. (Three years later Britten wrote his *Five Flower Songs* for their silver wedding, explaining: 'They were written about flowers because they are both amateur botanists.' The Arts Council had provided some money, and Pears's old friend from the BBC Singers, Anne Wood, was appointed general manager.

As to *Albert Herring*, it was intended that Carl Ebert, who had produced at Glyndebourne before the war and was booked to return there in the summer of 1947, should stage the opera. Britten wrote to Walter Süsskind, then directing the Scottish Orchestra, to ask whether he would conduct it. This proved impossible, and it was agreed that Britten should conduct *Albert Herring* himself.

Before the war, Frank Bridge had given him a few conducting lessons, but did not consider them successful. Marjorie Fass described him (in August 1938) as 'stiff & held in'. Yet when in 1937 he had conducted the music for *Hadrian's Wall* in the BBC studios in Newcastle, one of the members of the amateur male voice choir that was taking part was heard to ask: 'Who was that young man? He never swore at me but he frightened me out of myself.'

Britten never came to like conducting. Norman Del Mar says he 'hated' it, and Britten himself wrote in 1953: 'I wish I could say I enjoyed doing it.' Anne Wood recalls: 'Ben used to say of himself, "I can't conduct, I'm not a conductor, I've no technique." Yet the players would give just anything for Ben to be conducting rather than anyone else.' Emanuel Hurwitz, who led the Glyndebourne orchestra for *The Rape of Lucretia* and was leader of the English Chamber Orchestra when it played for Britten in the sixties, describes him as

> a quite wonderful conductor in the greatest sense of the word. He was a conductor who made the orchestra feel they wanted to play for him. His stick technique was unassuming, but so were Weingartner's and Richard Strauss's. The people of the old conducting school were not there to mime the piece to the audience, and you can say that the greater the conductor, the less they're bothered about stick technique. Ben had a small beat, and if it went a foot high, that meant a *forte*. An incredible difference from Beecham, who enjoyed doing things that looked like sword-fighting – and we had to decide which of his ninety-three movements was the actual beat! Twenty years ago, I wrote in the *Radio Times*: 'When you work for Ben, everything is an occasion.' There was no routine about it; you were making music in the highest sense.

The harpist Osian Ellis says that

Ben *liked* his players. He knew them by their names – he would remember your wife's name, even your kid's name, which is very unusual for a conductor . . . He was the one conductor who made you play your best – you couldn't do enough for him. I don't know another conductor who does that for you.

As for singers, Dietrich Fischer-Dieskau, who first performed for Britten in 1962, notes: 'Unlike so many conductors, he had no mannerisms at all. He was much too much of an original to seem like an actor, as is true for most of the lions of the podium. No one ever caught him playing a role.' Janet Baker remembers that 'one was upheld by his marvellous shaping of the phrase but at the same time given room, a sort of freedom, to yield to the inspiration of the moment. Only the very greatest conductors have this ability.' When he began to rehearse *Albert Herring*, Joan Cross found him 'a great inspiration'. She noticed that at performances when he was conducting, the opera would 'convulse the audience' with laughter as it did under nobody else's baton. John Francis makes a similar comment: 'Ansermet was a wonderful rehearser, meticulous and serious, but when Ben conducted he made you feel the emotion.'

When Carl Ebert listened to a play-through of *Albert Herring* he declined to produce it. Marion Thorpe believes that he 'disliked what he took to be the mockery of a mother's grief in the last act'. The choreographer Frederick Ashton was invited to take on the job, which he did enthusiastically, though tension soon arose between him and Britten, Crozier and Pears. 'Fred was excellent,' recalls Joan Cross, but when the cast ran through the first scene as directed by Ashton, 'Ben and Eric got lower in their chairs, because we were treating it as a farce'. She grew 'very cross' at Britten and Crozier's entrenched opposition to Ashton's burlesque production style, and disliked the way in which 'Eric and Peter and Ben sort of gathered together against us. I think that Peter did, but definitely Eric and Ben.' It seemed to her that Pears was an *éminence grise* in this disagreement. 'He was standing behind Ben, and if Ben didn't approve of anything, Peter put the words in his mouth.'

Elizabeth Sweeting, who was on the Glyndebourne staff during the production, says that while Pears could be 'a peacemaker' if trouble broke out, there was also a 'Machiavellian' streak in him. Years later, Ashton told Keith Grant, then manager of the EOG, that 'Ben and his friends behaved impossibly during *Albert Herring*, and that he (Fred) really felt quite vexed by their cliqueishness – he used to say, "I never liked coterie art." He also felt that the hushed reverence and intensity which Britten expected during rehearsals was overcooked. He used to say, "I can't stand much more of this. I'm going out for a cigarette."'

Besides the difference of opinion with Ashton, there was now something like open warfare between John Christie and Britten and his associates. On the opening night of *Albert Herring*, 20 June 1947, Christie greeted his friends with the words: 'This isn't *our* kind of thing, you know.' The audience did not agree with him; next morning's *News Chronicle* reported that, when the final curtain fell, 'There was great applause, and I have never heard so many bursts of laughter at Glyndebourne before. Britten, who conducted, took many curtain calls. His speech to the audience was the same as that of the tongue-tied Albert (before his swig of rum) at the feast – the one phrase, "Thank you."' However, Frank Howes in *The Times* judged that the opera was merely 'a charade', and Richard Capell in the *Daily Telegraph* was similarly sour, lamenting that 'all these talents have gone to no more purpose than the raising of a snigger'. William McNaught in the *Manchester Guardian* admitted to liking the music – 'Britten's phenomenal invention works at a great pace, and never fails of something spicy and witty and original, or lovely, or even thrilling' – but judged the opera 'only a diverting piece on the second plane'. Ernest Newman in the *Sunday Times* saw in Britten 'a first-rate opera talent going partly to waste because of a failure to find the right libretto', and though William Glock in *Time & Tide* thought *Albert Herring* 'a work of even more astonishing talent than *The Rape of Lucretia*', he judged it 'hardly an opera ... rather a play with an extremely animated musical surface'. Pears's performance as Albert and John Piper's designs were widely praised, but only Desmond Shawe-Taylor in the *New Statesman* appreciated the opera's depths:

> Throughout the three acts Britten's musical invention remains brilliantly resourceful. He can distil music out of anything – children playing ball, street corner whistling, an attack of the hiccups ... the total result is not only a smash hit with any audience, but a piece of music to which ... one could listen again and again with delight ... More remarkable still is the solemn threnody for the supposedly dead Albert ... reaching a high pitch of eloquence in its own right. It is such moments as these which make it a superficial judgement to write the work off as a farce or a charade.

(An equally perceptive review came from Neville Cardus in the *Manchester Guardian* in October, when the opera reached Covent Garden; he wrote that he was 'entirely engrossed in the way the work changes from almost parodistic origins to significant life capable of revealing sore wounds and pitiable humanity'.)

In a letter to Walter Hussey immediately after the first night, Britten appeared not to be downcast by the initial press response. '"Herring" went off splendidly,' he reported, '& audience reaction all we hoped for – wish we could say the same of the critics, but it is the old story.' However, Anne Wood remembers that on the morning after the first performance Peter Diamand, who had booked *Albert Herring* for his first Holland Festival, was so depressed by Frank Howes's *Times* review that he telephoned and suggested cancellation. 'We said no, it was a lovely work, and he'd got to go through with it. That was a nasty moment.'

The EOG duly travelled to the Hague and Amsterdam, and Britten reported to the Maud family: 'Albert was much to their taste (even to the critics' taste!!).' He, Pears, Crozier and Nancy Evans then set off south in the Rolls Royce, heading at a leisurely pace for Lucerne, where the EOG was to perform *The Rape of Lucretia* as well as the new opera. 'The rest of the artists were travelling by train,' writes Crozier,

> our scenery was on its way in three enormous lorries ... We were ... proud of the warm and appreciative response our new operas could draw from European audiences ... And yet – there was something absurd about travelling so far to win success with British operas that Manchester, Edinburgh and London would not support. The cost of transporting forty people and their scenery was enormously high; despite packed houses in Holland, despite financial support from the British Council in Switzerland, it looked as if we should lose at least three thousand pounds on twelve Continental performances. It was exciting to represent British music at international festivals, but we could not hope to repeat the experiment another year.
>
> 'Why not,' said Peters Pears, 'make our own Festival? A modest Festival with a few concerts given by friends? Why not have an Aldeburgh Festival?'

In Pears's own words, 'I remember quite well saying: "Why don't we have a festival in Aldeburgh? Why do we have to come abroad to Switzerland to perform *Albert Herring*? Why can't we perform it at Aldeburgh?"'

*

In 1947 festivals were springing up everywhere. In Britain that same month (August) the first Edinburgh Festival was about to open under the management of Rudolf Bing. Yet Aldeburgh seemed a highly eccentric location, a tiny town remotely situated in East Anglia, with poor railway and even worse road connections to London. When Joan Cross heard Pears's suggestion, 'I thought it was daft. I thought it was absolutely mad.'

Yet Pears had perceived the direction in which Britten was moving. Rebuffed first by the members of the Sadler's Wells company, then by John Christie, he had surrounded himself with his own coterie, the EOG. If the Aldeburgh suggestion proved feasible, he would largely achieve independence from the British musical world.

He had already decided to move house from Snape to Aldeburgh. He could afford a better home than the Mill, which was cramped and awkwardly laid out, and where the roof of his bedroom always leaked. For a time he had considered purchasing the dilapidated Victorian rectory at Iken, a lonely hamlet on the Alde estuary, but eventually he decided that the house (and maybe its isolation) was more than he could manage. In the summer of 1947 he purchased a big three-storey house on Crag Path, the Aldeburgh sea-front, overlooking the shingle and the waves. 'Snape . . . *is* a sweet place,' he wrote to Erwin Stein, '& one part of me regrets leaving it – but you know how I am about the sea, & really that Crag House is *pretty* nice I think.' He moved into Crag House on his return to England from Lucerne.

While they were in Switzerland, Britten, Pears and Crozier went thoroughly into the question of an Aldeburgh Festival. Its feasibility hung on the size of the town's Jubilee Hall, where Britten and Pears had given a recital the previous year – did it, as they believed, hold more than three hundred people? 'It was agreed', writes Crozier, 'that if the stage of the Jubilee Hall proved large enough to accommodate a simple form of opera, we would try to plan a Festival for 1948.' Britten was living in Crag House by the beginning of September. 'It is a heavenly day,' he wrote to Pears, who was singing in the Edinburgh Festival, '& the sea is as still as a mill-pond . . . Eric came last night, & its lovely having him here. We've already bathed twice – cold sea, but wonderfully clear & refreshing after those stuffy Swiss lakes.' As to 'the "Festival Idea"', they had not yet seen over the Jubilee Hall, 'but I'm full of hopes . . . Even if we have to cut it to 300, that isn't quite so hopeless economically as we feared.' Meanwhile he had seen the town clerk about changing the postal address of Crag House to '4 Crabbe Street', and told Pears: 'Everyone is all of a titter to have us here – & I think it's going to be fairly sick-making if we don't take a strong line about not seeing chaps & going out.' His housekeeper was already 'being pestered with invitations to bring Mr

Britten to tea to meet dear Mrs so-&-so who's *so* musical. But she's being very firm.' He concluded the letter: 'Come here quick, because I think you'll like it. Your devoted B.'

He and Crozier must have felt that they had stepped into *Albert Herring* as they paid calls on the mayor of Aldeburgh (Colonel Colbeck, MC., J.P.) and the vicar, to discuss the possibility of a festival. They also visited Great Glemham, a few miles inland from Aldeburgh, to invite the Countess of Cranbrook, an active supporter of the rural music movement, to accept the chairmanship of the Festival's executive committee. But Fidelity Cranbrook, young and pretty with five children, was no Lady Billows. She threw herself wholeheartedly into their project, despite blimpish objections to 'modern music' from the two reigning Aldeburgh cliques, the yacht club and the golf club, who (she says) 'thought that Aldeburgh was destined just to be a sporting centre'. She admits that the title of Lady Cranbrook was 'very useful' for persuading such people, whom she nicknamed 'the Antibodies', to support the Festival.

She chaired the first meeting of the executive committee on 27 October 1947. 'It was AGREED,' states the minute book, 'that the Festival be called "The Aldeburgh Festival", but the question as to whether the words "Music" and/or "Drama", and a reference to Mr Britten's name be included, was left open.' Britten himself was not present. He, Pears, Crozier and Nancy Evans had each offered £25 towards the £1,000 'local guarantee' they required to make the Festival possible. A further £150 was immediately subscribed by committee members, and the Arts Council soon made £500 available. It was agreed that the EOG would draw up a 'skeleton programme' for the Festival.

At first, opera performances seemed beyond financial possibility, but Britten and Pears offered to give a recital unpaid, so that the takings could be devoted to this. (Thereafter they always performed free at the Festival, a large if hidden contribution to the finances.) Many of their friends agreed to take part for less than their usual fees. Meanwhile Britten himself was doing much of the preparatory work. 'Peter & I have just been around measuring seats & placing imaginary people & pianos at the Church & Cinema,' he wrote to Crozier. A professional organizer was now deemed necessary, and Elizabeth Sweeting, who had recently left the Glyndebourne staff and joined the EOG as assistant to Anne Wood, was asked to take over the management of the Festival. (She was on secondment to Glyndebourne from a lectureship at London University, but in the event she never went back to it.) 'I confess', she writes, 'that I did not even know at that time exactly where Aldeburgh was.'

She went there for a first visit, and was 'captivated' by the windswept sea-front and the doll's house High Street behind it. Similarly Joan Cross, when she had her first sight of Aldeburgh, thought it 'lovely, absolute heaven', and banished her doubts about the Festival. This is how E. M. Forster, writing in 1948, describes Aldeburgh:

> What does the place look like? It is described in a gazetteer of the year 1844 as a 'sea-port, fishing town, and delightful bathing place, pleasantly situated on the site of a picturesque acclivity, rising boldly from the German Ocean'. Which as far as it goes is all right. The church stands on the summit of the acclivity, at its base runs a long High Street, parallel to the sea. Still nearer the sea runs a sort of parade, and by 'sort of' I mean the sort of parade I enjoy. There is a sense of space, of unfussiness, and in the midst of the gentle area, in the midst of the shingle and the windswept grasses, rises a tiny Elizabethan Moot Hall. North and south of the town stretch marshlands, which prevent it from expanding, and the southern lands are intersected by the river Alde. The conduct of the Alde is peculiar. It flows straight towards the sea, and when only a bank of shingle intervenes, it bends, and flows a course of many miles before it debouches. On this bank of shingle was built Slaughden Quay, where Crabbe used to roll barrels of butter as a boy.
>
> I have only to add that Aldeburgh is connected with our majestic British Railways by a local locomotive, locally known as the Aldeburgh Flier, and I have told you as much as an outsider can tell outsiders.

Forster's only significant omission is the town's social character. During the first half of the nineteenth century, the fishing port which Crabbe had known acquired a genteel overlay of prosperous visitors, many of whom built summer residences. The golf club was opened in 1880, and at Slaughden Quay the sea pilots and cargo boats began to give way to pleasure yachts. The fishermen did not vanish, but their Grimes-like huts became confined to the northern end of the shingle beach, while the men themselves gradually moved to the inland margin of the town, leaving the central and sea-front villas to the upper classes, many of them retired couples. Several boarding-schools for children of the well-off were opened. William Servaes, one of Elizabeth Sweeting's successors as general manager of the Aldeburgh Festival, was a pupil at a preparatory school on the sea-front shortly before the Second World War, and saw – and continues to see – Aldeburgh in a rather less pleasant light than Forster:

It's the most awful place, and always has been. The mix of people is wrong. There are masses of retired chairmen, generals, admirals. They're the top level. Then there's the 'real' Aldeburgh, which you don't normally meet – local working-people. They provide daily helps and other services for the top level, who move in from Woking or wherever. And the top lot, the retired people, haven't really got enough to think about. Even as a small boy, I hated the place. It's terribly cold and bleak, and I've always thought of it as a very cruel place.

Beginning to organize the first Festival early in 1948, Elizabeth Sweeting persuaded Lyn Pritt, owner of the Wentworth Hotel on the sea-front, to provide her with an office and a telephone, and she was soon issuing announcements of the 'first annual Festival of Music and Painting at Aldeburgh from June 5th–June 12th 1948' – exhibitions of East Anglian painters were to play a large part in it. *Albert Herring* was to be performed in the Jubilee Hall, and there was to be an important new Britten work, as well as a general emphasis on 'British music and the arts connected with the eastern part of England'. Meanwhile Elizabeth Sweeting observed Britten's delight with Crag House: 'Oh, he was so happy with it. Everybody said he'd turned into a different person.'

Downstairs, a big sitting-room ran the full length of the house, with bay windows looking across the small garden to the beach. Here, Britten's grand piano was installed, and here too were displayed the pictures which Pears was beginning to collect. 'At Snape I do not remember a single painting,' writes Crozier, but the walls of Crag House soon began to fill. A small pastoral by Constable formed the nucleus – 'They bought it in London,' says Crozier, '(what they paid, I do not know), and they were so excited that they showed it to everybody who came to the house.' Soon, Pears had acquired two Sickerts, and Crozier also lists among the early acquisitions 'a square canvas by Diana Cummings of some brutal-faced boys playing football'. With high earnings from his performances and few demands on them – for Crag House was Britten's, not jointly owned – Pears (writes Crozier) 'began to frequent art galleries and to cultivate the acquaintance of young artists, which provided him with an absorbing hobby and also proved to be a shrewd form of investment'. Over the next few years, letters between him and Britten excitedly mention several recent or potential purchases. 'The Blake & Cotman made sensations – as well they should,' wrote Britten in 1950. 'The former looks terrific over the fireplace. And Pears wrote, at about the same time, that he had seen '*the most gorgeous* Constable – "Boys fishing near Flatford Mill". Wow!'

On the first floor of Crag House, with a stunning view of the beach, was Britten's study. It contained another grand piano, and a comfortable armchair stood beside the fireplace. His desk was in the window, over-looking the shore; he sat at it on a hard stool. His bedroom was next door, and though Pears nominally occupied another bedroom, in practice the two men shared Britten's. Writing to Nancy Evans in September 1947, Crozier refers to it as 'Ben and Peter's bedroom'. It contained a large double bed. This surprised William Walton's wife Susana, who visited Crag House with her husband soon after their marriage in 1948. She remarks that 'Ben and Peter shared a double bed, a situation which I would now take in my stride, but which shocked me at the time.' Similarly, Michael Tippett recalls that 'they shared the same bed – it was quite open, though it was illegal. They ignored everybody, lived their private life as though the law hardly existed.'

It did exist. Homosexual acts between consenting adults in private – let alone other forms of homosexuality – were still illegal in Great Britain, and punishable by imprisonment. In particular, buggery carried a maximum sentence of life. Police prosecutions were generally confined to goings-on in public lavatories, and the seduction of juveniles, but Pears and Britten were at risk with their bed-sharing. In his account of his experiences as a homosexual in Britain in the late forties and early fifties, *Against the Law* (1955), Peter Wildeblood, diplomatic correspondent of the *Daily Mail*, writes:

> A man who feels an attraction towards other men is a social misfit only; once he gives way to that attraction, he becomes a criminal. This is not the case in most other countries, where the behaviour of consenting adults in private is considered a matter for themselves alone. Britain and America are almost the only countries in which such behaviour con-stitutes an offence, and in America the law is reduced to absurdity by the fact that it applies officially, also, to a variety of acts between men and women, whether married or not; it has been estimated that a strict application of the law would result in the imprisonment of two-thirds of the adult population, and as a result it is seldom invoked, even against homosexuals. In Britain, however, the law is very much alive, and heavy penalties are incurred by anyone who breaks it.

Wildeblood observes that a homosexual in Britain could 'never know the companionship that comes with marriage' – an indication that in this climate a relationship like Britten and Pears's seemed almost inconceiv-able – and added: 'One of the charges often levelled against homosexuals is that they tend to form a compact and exclusive group. They can hardly

be expected to do anything else, since they are legally excluded from the
rest of the community.' Pears and Britten were discreet in their
behaviour, but their relationship was an open secret in the musical world.
Christopher Headington remembers seeing, scrawled across a poster for
one of their London recitals in the forties, the word 'PANSY'.

When a photographer from the *Ladies' Journal* came to Crag House
some years after Britten had moved in, to take pictures for a feature on
the composer's home, his picture of Britten's bedroom with the double
bed was not published. A photograph with the caption 'Peter Pears's
bedroom' depicts a narrow single bed. This room may not have been
entirely for show. The top floor was at first occupied by Crozier, in the
expectation that he and Nancy Evans would make their home there when
they were married. A letter from Britten to Nancy Evans on 23 January
1948 announces the cancellation of this arrangement, and also gives a
hint of tensions between Britten and Pears:

> Eric has been here you know, & I have had to break some disappoint-
> ing news to him, which I am afraid has upset him a bit. That is
> this – – –
>
> Peter you know has spent his holiday here, & hasn't been at all
> happy that he couldn't work anywhere in the house without disturbing
> me (I'm silly about music being audible when I'm writing), and has
> said that in these kind of crazy working holidays, he *must* have
> somewhere to work, or else will have to go elsewhere for them, or have
> again some larger London establishment than we intended to have,
> after getting rid of Oxford Square. Now obviously that is wildly
> expensive & inconvenient. The only room possible is the top back
> room – your prospective kitchen – so he feels he must have a separate
> bedroom. I agree too, instead of crowding in with me. I think it is
> important, especially as we plan to have more time to work together in
> the future, that he has this *pied-à-terre* in Aldeburgh. So what I
> suggested to Eric was that when you were married we should try &
> buy a small cottage (there are two now for sale here) and let you have it
> all to yourselves, for whenever you want, the oftener the better! Of
> course, before that happy date (!), the position is the same as now –
> Eric lives here; and even after if he wants he can live (and/or eat) here,
> if he wants to.
>
> I do apologise most warmly for this change of plan . . .

The letter gives the impression that Pears had not altogether settled at
Crag House. Isador Caplan, Britten's solicitor from the mid-forties (they
were introduced by Erwin Stein), confirms this:

Peter did not put his roots down in Aldeburgh in the same overwhelming and total way that Ben did ... Peter, I think, was very much a
London man and wanting, among other things, to be able to meet
friends, attend ... art exhibitions and enjoy other aspects of London
life, whereas Ben was happiest in Aldeburgh; and these differences in
outlook and needs certainly troubled Ben from time to time.

Pears sometimes kept engagement books, and these indicate that at this
period he spent little time at Aldeburgh – for example during 1951 he
was there for only six visits of a few days each, including the Festival.

'Oxford Square', referred to in Britten's letter to Nancy Evans, was 3
Oxford Square, a house in the Bayswater district of London which Pears
bought in the spring of 1946, partly to accommodate his ageing parents.
Erwin Stein and his family moved there from the Britten–Pears flat in St
John's Wood, and Crozier had the use of a room on the top floor. He
describes the house:

It was in a district of huge early-Victorian houses ... In theory, the
plan was a good one. Peter had two elderly parents who needed
somewhere to live: so what could be better than for them to make their
home with him and Ben, plus, of course, the Erwin Stein family, and
for Sofie [Stein] to manage the housekeeping? ... But Sofie, a courageous and cheerful woman, was run off her feet trying to manage the
house and to conjure up three meals a day from the antediluvian
kitchen in the basement ... Mr and Mrs Pears, a stiff-necked and
rather arrogant couple, did not like the Steins. They objected to the
food, they criticized Sofie, and they went out of their way in general to
make mischief. They strongly objected, too, to Marion's piano playing.
She was now eighteen or nineteen, a pretty girl who had recently begun
studying the piano in earnest, and she had a basement room where she
used sometimes to practise four or five hours a day. The elderly Pears
hated it ... so did the old man who lived in the enormous house next
door ... He used to hammer violently on the party-wall ...

Pears's mother died in October 1947, and her husband a few months
later. In 1948 the Steins moved to 22 Melbury Road, a Victorian house
off Kensington High Street, where Pears and Britten sub-let two rooms
from them.

Pears could have provided himself with a small flat, ensuring privacy
when he and Britten were in London, but both men seemed disposed to
create a family atmosphere in their houses. Crag House, like Pears's
London homes, was never a simple *ménage à deux*. Britten engaged a

live-in housekeeper, whom Crozier describes as 'a middle-aged, pleasant, but highly-strung lady who suffered from severe alternations of mood and would sometimes seem almost distraught with anxieties'. Her social position caused problems, since she was 'too ladylike to be relegated to the kitchen'. She ate with Britten and his friends, but was not expected to take a lead in the conversation, and Crozier says that 'her awareness of not being wanted except as a servant' aggravated her instability. Elizabeth Sweeting describes her as 'possessive about Ben'; like all women, she 'wanted to take him over'. Why did he put up with this? Elizabeth Sweeting answers: 'He looked for a surrogate mother in every relationship.'

The housekeeper had to provide good plain cooking. 'Peter was a sort of gourmet,' says Elizabeth Sweeting, 'but Ben always said he liked nursery food.' This consisted of 'herrings, treacle puddings and apple puddings – and his guests got things like that'. The evening meal was served formally. Basil Coleman, a regular visitor from 1949 onwards, remembers that 'we always had to put ties on for supper'.

The herrings were bought fresh from the Aldeburgh fishermen, and in fine weather Britten's day began with a bathe. 'When he moved to Crag House', writes Crozier, 'he would swim four or five times a day in summer and quite often last thing at night.' Basil Coleman remembers late-night bathes 'with nothing on'. Crozier says: 'Always, if one stayed with them, one had to be perpetually plunging into the water, not only for the physical pleasure it was supposed to give, but as if it were a kind of moral code one had to obey.' In the winter, cold baths were substituted. Pears has recalled that 'it was Ben who introduced me first to the charms of cold baths ... I hadn't, until I met him, really realized what a charming occasion a cold bath is'.

*

Crozier observed that Britten revelled in the extra pressure put on him by the Aldeburgh Festival. 'He was never really satisfied unless the telephone was ringing, piles of letters arriving ... and people ... with queries needing his urgent attention ... My own impression is that he not only needed, but positively enjoyed, these demands ... however much he might pretend to grumble about them.' Elizabeth Sweeting says that Britten once told her that, if he had not been a composer, he might have become an accountant. She and everyone who worked for him in the Festival of the EOG was astonished by his grasp of figures. Basil Douglas, a later manager of the EOG, marvelled that 'somebody so sensitive, so in other worlds as Ben, was able to show me how to budget for an opera!' Elizabeth Sweeting says he could do elaborate calculations in his head, and Oliver Knussen feels that mathematical ability is a key to his musical genius: 'Britten could have been anything that involved the effective deployment of small components within big masses – he could have been a general, ironically enough, or at least a chess master.'

At Crag House, all work stopped in the evenings, when, says Crozier, 'nothing pleased him better than to have somebody to talk to'. Elizabeth Sweeting would receive a telephone call asking if she were free after supper, and knew that this was a summons. 'We'd play draughts, or Happy Families – "Mr Bun the Baker".' At first Elizabeth Sweeting was amused to find him devoted to the childish card game, but 'we had to play properly, because you know how fierce and ferocious it can be in a nursery!' (In Snape days a favourite relaxation, according to Wulff Scherchen, had been jig-saws.)

Although a large radiogram stood in the sitting-room at Crag House, and Crozier remembers Britten and Pears playing piano duets in the evenings, Elizabeth Sweeting recalls that in his spare time 'Ben didn't listen to music, unless there was someone special whom he wanted to hear broadcasting.' She sensed that the lightweight evening amusements were only occupying the surface of his mind, while the rest was planning his next day's work – though she was impressed by his 'mathematical acute memory' in the games. 'You couldn't beat him. And he would have hated being beaten.'

Some evenings, there would be no games, and she 'would just be there, and he might potter around, rehanging the pictures or something like that'. Perhaps she was partly supplying the place of his sister Beth, whose departure from Snape in September 1946 to live with Kit and the children in Woodbridge, a few miles to the south, may have been a cause of Britten's move into Aldeburgh. For the first time in his life he could no longer live with a member of his real family. Life at Crag House seems to have been planned largely to provide substitutes – the nursery food (before the war he had loved Spanish cooking and deplored the British fondness for plain gastronomy), the frequent swims (as in his Lowestoft childhood), the children's games in the evening. This mood seems to be perceptible in the first three musical works he composed after moving into Crag House.

'My Canticle goes nicely now & I'm in love with the form,' he wrote while at work on *Canticle*, later retitled *Canticle I*, for high voice and piano. He and Pears gave the first performance on 1 November 1947, at a memorial concert for the Revd Dick Sheppard, one of the founders of the Peace Pledge Union. The words, by the seventeenth-century poet Francis Quarles, are taken partly from *The Song of Solomon* (ii.16): 'My beloved is mine, and I am his . . .' The same chapter of the Bible contains words sung by the vicar and Miss Wordsworth in the first scene of *Albert Herring*, 'For lo, the winter is past, the rain is over and gone . . .', and *Canticle I* seems to be an epilogue to the opera. In our last glimpse of Albert he appeared content with his discovery of sexuality – 'Have a nice peach?' – and this relaxation of the old anxieties is confirmed by Britten's choice of the Quarles words (which he found in an American anthology) and his setting of them. *Canticle I* seems to be, as no other work had yet been, a happy celebration of his relationship with Pears. 'Ev'n like two little bank-divided brooks,' it begins,

> That wash the pebbles with their wanton streams,
> And having raged and searched a thousand nooks
> Meet both at length at silver-breasted Thames,
> Where in a greater current they conjoin,
> So I my best beloved's am,
> So he is mine!

The music portrays the gradual merging of the two streams into 'firm-united souls', and though as Graham Johnson has observed the scherzo section, with its restless accompaniment, suggests the relationship weathering a storm, *Canticle I* ends with the voice's reaffirmation of love backed by G major triads, a clear indication that all is well. Robert Tear says he has heard that the piece was a gesture of reconciliation by Britten after Pears had been unfaithful to him on a foreign trip. Sue Phipps, who lived in the Melbury Road household in the late forties, says: 'Ben did get jealous of Peter sometimes. But I don't see it as anything more serious than a couple who needed a little bit of outside diversion now and then.' John Evans believes that Pears's life as a musician on the road could have given him little chance for other relationships, 'but I think if the opportunity arose Peter would have taken it'.

A Charm of Lullabies was written for Nancy Evans soon after the completion of *Canticle I*. 'The title, thought up by Eric & me, is only provisional, do you like it?' Britten asked her in December 1947, enclosing the manuscript of five lullabies for voice and piano. Christopher Palmer, in his study of the song-cycles, has suggested that the choice of 'Highland Balou' for the second song was influenced by Britten's memory of the Scottish herring girls singing in Lowestoft in his childhood.

The third work written immediately after Britten's move to Crag House, *Saint Nicolas*, was to have its first performance on the opening day of the Aldeburgh Festival, though its official première was to take place six weeks later at Lancing College, Pears's old public school. One of the masters' wives there, Esther Neville-Smith, took a maternal interest in him and Britten, and when plans were discussed for the school's centenary celebrations in July 1947 she offered £100 to commission a Britten work for the occasion. The sixth form master, Basil Handford, knew the *Hymn to St Cecilia*, and suggested 'a hymn to St Nicolas', patron saint of children (and co-patron of Lancing itself). Handford writes:

'Tell me about St Nicolas,' said Ben. So I told him the legends. Almost immediately he saw it as a series of episodes: 'It will have to be a cantata, I think.' Esther suggested that I should write the libretto. That would have been a great honour, but rather, I fancy, to the relief of Ben I demurred. 'Never mind, Eric Crozier will do it.'

So Crozier began. 'Eric has started S. Nicholas & it looks good – I think he's developing well as a poet – & very settable,' Britten wrote to Pears in September 1947. 'I've given him the Creation as a model – a good one, I think.' The part of the saint was to be sung by Pears, who was about to appear at the recently reopened Covent Garden Opera House in a new production of *Peter Grimes*, directed by Tyrone Guthrie. The opera had now received a number of overseas productions, and its place in the repertoire seemed assured, but although the Covent Garden version, which opened on 6 November 1947, included Joan Cross and several other principals from the original cast, it was not very well received by the critics, who found Tanya Moiseiwitsch's sets too overpowering – nor by the composer. 'Really grand opera is too much of a strain,' Britten wrote to a friend during rehearsals; 'the organisation of the Garden is nil – our opera group is something of a rest-cure compared. Tony Guthrie has some fine ideas of production but on the whole, I'd rather have Eric.' Excerpts from this production were recorded by HMV in July 1948, but were not issued, apparently because William Walton, in his role as consultant to the British Council which was to distribute the records overseas, advised against public money being used for what he called so 'commercially viable' a project.

By December 1947, Crozier had finished the libretto of *Saint Nicolas*, for which he had read volumes of history and legends of the early church. On 18 December, Britten wrote to Pears: 'I am beginning St Nicholas, & enjoying it hugely. It'll be difficult to write, because that mixture of subtlety & simplicity is most extending, but very interesting.' It was his first big work intended for performance chiefly by amateurs. In an interview in the sixties he was asked if he ever felt scornful of the amateur or the child musician:

Oh, never! I want to write for people. I passionately believe in professionalism and I think the professional must know his business
thoroughly, but this shouldn't prevent him from writing for amateurs.
Just the reverse. After all they have always been an important force in
the shaping of our musical tradition ... There is something very fresh
and unrestrained in the quality of the music produced by amateurs.
What annoys me more is the ineptitude of some professionals who
don't know their stuff. I have no patience with that.

Saint Nicolas, of which the composition sketch was written in three
weeks, is designed to bring out that 'fresh and unrestrained quality' in the
voices of the young people who were to sing in it. 'The main choir would
be provided by Lancing College,' explains Crozier, 'but it was essential to
allow for the participation of representative smaller choirs from each of
the other Woodard schools' (Lancing was one of the Woodard Foundation boarding-schools). 'I think St Michaels will have to be relegated to
the galleries (where anyhow all girls should be in Church),' Britten wrote
to Pears while composing the cantata, 'because ... their breathy voices
are obviously most suited to the wind noises & so forth.' Basil Handford
recalls Britten, on a visit to Lancing, dreaming up some of the other
musical effects: 'During the gestation of the work Ben was observed in
Chapel walking round saying "how can I make a noise like bath water
running out?"'

The cantata opens with Nicolas addressing the audience 'Across the
tremendous bridge of sixteen hundred years', but the real time-travelling
in the work has been done by Britten, who has journeyed back to
childhood. The saint's life story begins with a waltz song for children's
voices depicting his birth and infancy (including the bath scene mentioned by Handford), and this ends with a vivid depiction of Nicolas
reaching puberty. The words 'God be glorified!', until now sung as a
refrain by a boy treble, are suddenly heard from the tenor soloist – that
is, in a 'broken' voice. However, the cantata reverts to its childlike
manner with an account of Nicolas miraculously quietening a storm,
with pianos and percussion for the waves, high voices for the lightning,
and other naïve effects. Though there are solo reflections by the adult
Nicolas, these chiefly take the form of regret for the corruption of man –
'O man! ... / You hug the rack of self, / Embrace the lash of sin' – and all
the dramatic weight lies in the children's contributions, supported by two
hymns which Britten includes for everyone to sing. As performers and
congregation join together for the Old Hundredth and 'God moves in a
mysterious way', the cantata allows its participants to re-experience

childhood church-going. John Culshaw, who produced the Decca recording of *Saint Nicolas* in 1955, has testified to the power of these hymns to 'shake normally impervious men to their foundations'.

The climax of *Saint Nicolas* comes in the seventh number, 'Nicolas and the Pickled Boys', which is not in the first draft of Crozier's libretto and seems to have been added at Britten's suggestion – a letter from Crozier to Nancy Evans on 19 December 1947 mentions that he is writing this 'new section' of the cantata. To the accompaniment of an *alla marcia*, a group of exhausted travellers mourns three boys who have gone missing in a time of famine: 'Timothy, Mark and John are gone, / Are gone! Are gone!' They sit down to eat at an inn, but Nicolas warns them not to touch the food that has been served; it is the flesh of the boys, 'slaughtered by the butcher's knife'. He sings an invocation on a rising A major triad, 'Come! Come! Come! Come!', whereupon the boys, restored to life, walk in, hand in hand, singing Alleluias. (The vocal score is specific about the boys actually walking in at this point: 'THREE SMALL BOYS (entering)'.) Is this miracle a metaphor for Britten's belief that he could resurrect or at least preserve his own childhood, as suggested by his way of life at Crag House? It is notable that the boys are brought back to life not with any magic spell or even a prayer, but simply through the power of the triad.

*

Britten's next task after *Saint Nicolas* was an adaptation. 'I . . . haven't started Beggar's Opera yet – altho' I'm off to the Continong in 2 weeks for 6 weeks! It's a bloody nightmare,' he wrote to Ronald Duncan in January 1948. He had promised to provide the EOG with a realization of *The Beggar's Opera* for their 1948 season, and the production, directed by Tyrone Guthrie, was due to open in Cambridge in May. (Some years later, Britten told Colin Graham that it was the music's affinity to both Purcell and folk-song that attracted him, 'as well as the ironies of the piece'.) Somehow he managed to write the score during two months spent giving recitals with Pears in Italy, Switzerland and Holland. It was a thorough 'Brittenization' of the eighteenth-century ballad music. While orchestrating the songs for the EOG chamber group (the same instrumentation as for *The Rape of Lucretia* and *Albert Herring*, including harp and percussion), he clothed them in startling new harmonic colours. He described the score as 'probably more entertaining to write than to listen to', but this was far from the case. 'Some of the tunes get lost in Britten's clever and elaborate settings,' wrote Frank Howes in *The Times* when the production opened, 'but on the whole he has preserved their character and . . . contrived some fascinating sounds.' Caryl Brahms in the *Evening Standard* complained that Pears played Macheath as 'a polite Palm Court tenor'. Tyrone Guthrie had said much the same in rehearsal; Norman Lumsden, who was in the cast, recalls Guthrie snapping at Pears: 'You look as if you're doing Stainer's *Crucifixion* on skates at Scunthorpe,' and Colin Graham says that Britten told him that Guthrie had described Pears as disqualified for Macheath 'as it was a part that could only be played by a real man'. Graham comments: 'You can imagine the traumas that this set up – also the division with Guthrie thenceforward.' Lumsden confirms this: 'After that production we never saw Guthrie again.'

Ten days after the opening of *The Beggar's Opera*, Britten wrote to Lennox Berkeley, now married with two children: 'We are just starting our crazy festival.' Four-fifths of the tickets were already sold, and the three performances of *Albert Herring* were entirely booked out. Britten had written to Pears that March that it looked liked 'a good beginning I think'.

E. M. Forster had been invited to give a lecture at the Festival, and to stay at Crag House, and he arrived several days in advance of the opening. Britten's gratitude to him for sowing the seed of *Peter Grimes* was reciprocated by Forster's admiration for Britten's music ever since he attended the opening of *The Ascent of F6* in 1937. They had met in October 1942, when Forster heard Britten and Pears perform the *Seven Sonnets of Michelangelo* at the National Gallery. Britten gave Forster a score of the cycle and a gramophone on which to play the records – Forster had bought them after the concert, but had no machine of his own. For his Aldeburgh lecture, he had decided to compare Crabbe's poem with the libretto of the opera, in which he had taken a close interest. 'It amuses me to think what an opera on Peter Grimes would have been like if I had written it,' he wrote in the lecture. 'I should certainly have starred the murdered apprentices. I should have introduced their ghosts in the last scene, rising out of the estuary ... blood and fire would have been thrown in the tenor's face, hell would have opened, and on a mixture of *Don Juan* and the *Freischütz* I should have lowered my final curtain.' He also reminded his audience that Aldeburgh had once contained an 'obscure and unattractive citizen' who was the model for Crabbe's villain; 'he is the first step in a series of creative events which has produced your Festival'.

Forster greatly enjoyed his stay at Crag House. Britten and Pears played and sang for him, improvising musical parodies, and he described them in a letter to his friend William Plomer as 'the sweetest people'. He had nothing but praise for the first performance of *Saint Nicolas*, the principal item in the opening concert at the parish church on the afternoon of Saturday 5 June. 'It was one of those triumphs outside the rules of art which only the great artist can achieve,' he wrote in his article on the Festival for the *Listener*. He particularly singled out, 'the miracle of the three little boys who had been pickled', where

the sudden contrast between elaborate singing and the rough breathy voices of three kids from a local 'co-op' [Co-operative Choir] made one swallow in the throat and water from the eyes ... Wonderful too was Britten's throwing about of a tune from the main choir in the church to the girls' choir up in the gallery under the tower. The church seemed alive, and at the end the whole congregation was drawn into a hymn.

This opening concert, which also included Ralph Downes playing a Handel organ concerto and the première of *God's Grandeur* by Martin Shaw, was conducted by Leslie Woodgate, who had directed the first broadcast of *A Boy Was Born* fourteen years earlier. Britten and Crozier sat outside in the churchyard, listening tensely. A photograph shows Britten flat on his back, eyes shut with anxiety.

There were no performances that night. The next day the pianist Noel Mewton-Wood, substituting for Clifford Curzon, gave a recital in the cinema. 'As he was going happily ahead,' writes Forster,

the cinema was shaken by two loud bangs. Most of the audience knew what they meant, but the visitors did not learn until the end of the concert. They were maroons. They signified that the Aldeburgh lifeboat was going out, and they summoned the 'floaters', the men who push the boat down the slips into the sea ... Next morning we heard the maroons again. The boat was back safely. The episode, coming in the midst of our pleasure-going, had allowed us to reflect on the life of the town.

Writing in the Festival's handsome programme book, Lord Harewood, who was now a twenty-five-year-old Cambridge undergraduate and had agreed to be president of the Festival, made much the same point: that while festivals were springing up everywhere, the one at Aldeburgh was intended to 'belong' to the locality 'in the sense that Mozart did to Salzburg'. Harewood hoped that visitors 'may feel that the hosts have at least not hired the entertainment for their guests, but have provided it themselves'.

Britten made his first Festival appearance as performer on the Monday evening, to conduct *Albert Herring* in the Jubilee Hall. Forster was amused by the ingenuity with which the production was crammed into the tiny building:

The harp had to be up in the auditorium with a screen in front, and the percussion on the opposite side was blanketed by gaily-coloured eiderdowns, to deaden the sound. The stage too was congested. The naughty children had to bounce with discretion, and Albert's sack of turnips to be dumped where no one would trip. I had seen the opera before in the immensities of Covent Garden, where the problem was not so much to avoid collisions as to get into touch. I preferred the Aldeburgh performance.

Forster was also entertained by the mixture of social types in the audience. Some were in evening dress, some 'dressed anyhow', and a man who went into the Cross Keys pub at the interval – there being no room for a bar in the hall – was heard to say: 'I took a ticket for this show because it is local and I felt I had to. I'd have sold it to anyone for sixpence earlier on. I wouldn't part with it now for ten pounds.'

Forster's enthusiastic report in the *Listener* drew a pained letter from the critic Scott Goddard, who complained that 'the London press' had been 'excluded from the whole of this festival'. Elizabeth Sweeting says that the national reviewers were not kept out, but no invitations were issued to them. She recalls that Britten was on his guard against one critic who had sometimes (but by no means always) given him hostile reviews: 'Ben kept open house for anybody – you could almost just walk into the door of Crag House during the Festival – but he said to me: 'You must never, but never, let Frank Howes come in.''

Local papers were made welcome, and carried lengthy and enthusiastic notices, and the actor Robert Speaight, who was giving a reading at the Festival, wrote a report in the *New English Review*, remarking that 'no one seemed able to explain where the large audiences came from. The Parish Church was equally full for a recital of verse and music at eleven in the morning as it was for a concert by Britten and Pears or the Zorian Quartet at six in the evening.' The Britten–Pears recital included *Canticle I* ('written at Aldeburgh', stated the programme book), and the Zorian Quartet played Tippett's String Quartet No. 2, Britten's realization of Purcell's *Golden Sonata*, and, with Britten at the piano, Bridge's *Phantasy Quartet*. Besides Forster, the lecturers (in the Baptist Chapel) included William Plomer on Edward Fitzgerald – another Suffolk writer – and Sir Kenneth Clark on 'Constable and Gainsborough as East Anglian Painters'. The exhibitions, mostly in private houses, included a display of paintings and watercolours by Constable. Speaight wrote that it all added up to 'more than an invitation to pleasure; it was a recall to integrity ... In Suffolk, at least, we had found an antidote to the Invisible Worm.'

The flautist for *Albert Herring* was once again John Francis. 'The whole Festival was absolutely delightful for the EOG orchestra,' he says, 'because we did everything. The strings, led by Olive Zorian, would give a quartet recital, and the wind would make up a quintet, and Ben would play a Mozart piano concerto. It was all like a family affair.'

*

The Festival closed on Sunday 13 June, with a chamber concert in the Jubilee Hall. Three days later Britten wrote to E. J. Dent, president of the ISCM: 'We have just come out from a most interesting experimental Festival here, in Aldeburgh; hundreds of people came – and Albert Herring was received with joy in the Jubilee Hall! What we seem to have proved without a doubt is that local people react strongly and encouragingly to this kind of local festival.'

According to the Festival executive committee minute book, there was now 'a universal desire that the Festival should be repeated from year to year', which seemed feasible, for thanks to prudent management of resources (especially the use of a few performers to create a large number of events) there was a credit balance in the Festival funds. Meanwhile Forster announced to Britten that he was coming back to stay at Crag House in August, bringing his policeman friend Bob Buckingham. 'My dear Morgan,' Britten wrote to him, 'It is lovely that yours and Bob's visit steadily gets nearer.'

Britten's diary was fuller then ever in the weeks following the Festival. During late June and early July he conducted the EOG at the Holland Festival and in France, then at the Cambridge Festival, making a hasty trip with Pears to Lancing for the official première of *Saint Nicolas* on 24 July. August was theoretically free. 'Peter & I collapsed down here last week,' Britten wrote to Eric Walter White from Crag House on 11 August, 'with nothing to do but swim, sail, tennis & read poetry for next new piece. It's bliss.' He told Erwin Stein he was 'reading possible poems for the Spring piece'. This was to be a choral symphony on the theme of Spring, commissioned some while earlier by Koussevitzky, to whom Britten had written in January 1947: 'I am keen not to do it in a hurry; I want it to be my biggest & best piece so far.' On top of this David Webster, administrator of Covent Garden, asked if he would consider writing a big new opera for the Festival of Britain in 1951. Britten replied: 'I certainly intend to write a big new one which should be ready, if everything goes to plan, by that year,' though he would not commit himself further. During Forster's visit to Crag House in August 1948, the idea came up that he might be a collaborator in this. Britten told Erwin Stein that it was 'possible that E. M. Forster (who's staying here now) will collaborate with Eric & me on the next opera – opera needs a great human being like him in it – which is a dazzling prospect'. (Forster's lecture at the Festival had broadly hinted that he would like to write a libretto for Britten.) Writing twenty years later, Britten recalled how they 'each suggested subjects', nearly settling on Richard Cobbold's 1845 novel *Margaret Catchpole*, about a servant-girl fatally involved with a smuggler. 'Who brought up the idea of *Billy Budd* no one can quite remember; it was probably telepathic and simultaneous.'

Immediately after the August break came an EOG tour of Britain, and then Pears set off for New York, partly to have lessons with his old teacher Clytie Mundy, but partly, it seems, for pleasure. Britten went back to Aldeburgh to begin the *Spring Symphony* for Koussevitzky. By early November he had sketched six movements, and wrote to Pears that he was pleased with the results: 'I'd got it all neatly planned, but it's coming out different, bigger (& I hope better!).' In another letter to Pears: 'I hope you'll be pleased, but you're so very severe a critic that I darn't hope!'

Pears was back in Aldeburgh in mid-November, and Britten felt obliged to apologize to Lesley Bedford (who as Lesley Duff sang in *The Rape of Lucretia* and *Albert Herring*), who had stayed at Crag House not long after Pears's return:

> I am sorry you got muddled up a bit in a purely domestic tiff (I gather over the week-end too – in telephone calls!) – it was really all my fault for being touchy & silly – caused largely by my tummy & general pregnancy [with the *Spring Symphony*] (the first, happily cured, the second – even worse to date!) I do hope it didn't leave a nasty taste in your mouth . . . Peter sends love – he is much less tired now, & we are working hard together, he singing like a civilised Siegfried – a tremendous din!

In early December they set off together for a recital tour of Holland, but Britten's stomach 'went *all* wrong again . . . I had to cancel one concert,' he told Lesley Bedford, '& only staggered thro' the others.' Back at Aldeburgh he was ordered to take 'three months absolute rest'. He explained that his condition had been diagnosed as 'nervous exhaustion', and commented: 'it is a good thing that . . . I'm no worse, because I have been leading rather a mad existence these last years!' His condition left him 'grumpy & nervy, & incapable of thought'. Pears was not often there. 'Peter is hard breadwinning . . . but gets here occasionally.'

Britten now gave Pears a hint that they might have to cease giving recitals together. 'I *do* adore working with you,' he wrote to him during December, '& think we really achieve something together. My only way of coming sane thro' this miserable time is to think that this [his enforced rest] will make it possible for us to continue working together in the future, & if I *didn't* rest we might have had to cut it out altogether.' Marion Thorpe recalls that around this time, 'when Ben wasn't prepared to travel as much with Peter to do concerts, Peter said, "Well, then I'm going to share a flat with Iris Holland Rogers [his friend from pre-war days]. If you don't want to come to London, I'll find somebody to share a flat with."'

Britten was suspected of having an ulcer, but an X-ray showed nothing. He remained exhausted and depressed, and a foreign trip was decided upon. 'Peter's taking me to Italy on Sunday for three weeks,' he wrote to Ronald Duncan on 19 January 1949, '& if that doesn't cure me I feel nothing else will!' From Venice he reported 'perfect sun & weather . . . & we're both feeling on top of the world!', and to Lord Harewood: 'Venice has cured me completely.' They went on to Portofino, then returned to England. 'When I got back I found I wasn't quite so much better as I thought I was,' Britten wrote to John Maud. He had started to work again, but was still experiencing depression. 'I am sorry I was so gloomy yesterday,' he wrote on 19 February to Pears, who had paid a visit to Aldeburgh, 'but it was the bottom of the well for me. Work was impossible, & I felt absolutely desperate.' He had spent the afternoon at Glemham with Fidelity Cranbrook and her family and then gone to bed early 'with lots of pills'. Pears kept in touch from London by telephone, not always with happy results. 'Perhaps after all we'd better NOT telephone,' Britten wrote to him, 'because we always get cross – ! But somehow even getting cross, or feeling you're cross with me, is better than silence, so perhaps after all we'd better keep it up !'

As always, their letters to each other were full of expressions of love. 'My memories of the three weeks grow lovelier & lovelier.' Britten wrote on 2 March, recollecting their Italian holiday.

> Lovely as Venice, Bellini, the little Carpaccio boys, Mimosa and the wine-dark sea off Portofino were, my happiest & most treasured memory is of the wonderful peace & contentment of your love & friendship. Love, such as I felt we had in those 3 weeks, is a rare thing – as beautiful and luminous as this sea outside, & with endless depths too. Thank you, my dearest . . .

Pears wrote to Britten:

> *don't* worry, and remember there are lovely things in the world still – children, boys, sunshine, the sea, Mozart, you and me – I love you my honey – my honey Bee – my pie – love you. P.

5: It is I whom the devil awaits

By the beginning of March 1949 Britten had recovered sufficiently from his depression to contemplate the concert tour he and Pears were to make of the United States in the autumn. 'I don't know why one does it,' he wrote to John Maud. 'I couldn't be more worried about anything, nor . . . more bored about going.' Three days later, to Leslie Boosey at Boosey & Hawkes: 'I have at last got back to work and hope to be able to write soon to Ralph Hawkes that the Spring Symphony will be ready for Koussevitzky to perform in Tanglewood this summer.' To Jean Maud he reported: 'I have at last completed the sketches of the Spring Symphony, & am most relieved & happy about it. I had a bad patch, when I thought I was quite recovered, & found I wasn't. But that's all finished now.' However, before the *Spring Symphony* could be scored, he had to turn aside and write a new work for the second Aldeburgh Festival, which was only a few weeks away.

For two years he and Crozier had contemplated a chamber opera for children. 'I can recall the exact spot,' says Crozier,

> where Ben and I first discussed writing a stage work for children to perform – an almost empty ski-lift coming down one afternoon from the slopes above Zermatt . . . At that time (early February 1947) we could not think of a story, but eighteen months or so later, after the success of the first Aldeburgh Festival, the idea came up again as a distinct possibility for next summer.

They considered various stories. Britten thought an opera could be made out of Arthur Ransome's *Swallows and Amazons*, and Crozier dreamt up a plot about a family of musical children who creep out at night to listen to the rehearsals of the local choral society. Then Britten remembered the child chimney-sweep who appears in two of Blake's lyrics in *Songs of Innocence* and *Songs of Experience*: 'When my mother died I was very young / And my father sold me . . . / So your chimneys I sweep, & in soot I sleep'. Crozier writes: 'Here was our subject, if ever there was one. By that evening we had planned the structure, the action and the characters.'

The subject had been treated at length in Charles Kingsley's *The Water-Babies* (1863), and though Crozier had never read the book Britten was steeped in it, 'brought up' on it, '& am still devoted', he wrote to Eric Walter White around this time – omitting to mention that he himself had played Tom, the little sweep, in early childhood. In Kingsley's book the boy sweep, whose master is named Grimes, loses his way in the chimneys of a great house and comes down into the bedroom of the squire's daughter Ellie. Panicking when she screams, he jumps out of the window, is pursued across the park by the household, and finds refuge in a river, beneath whose waters he is transformed into a tiny immortal 'water-baby'. Crozier and Britten retained the setting of the great house, the little sweep's unexpected descent into the presence of children, and the pursuit across the park. An early draft of the synopsis, headed 'Sweep, Sweep!', is set in the home of the Jordan family – no Suffolk location is mentioned – and there are two boy sweeps, the experienced Rob and the novice Tom. Otherwise the story is much the same as in the finished opera.

When they came to work on the libretto, Britten and Crozier located it, like *Albert Herring*, specifically in East Suffolk, at Iken Hall on the estuary near Snape, in reality the home of the Spring-Rice family, well known to composer and librettist. They decided to give the children in the opera the names of Fidelity Cranbrook's sons and daughters, the Gathorne-Hardys: Gathorne, Juliet, Sophia, Christina and Hugh, together with those of two cousins who had lived with them during the war, and whose parents now had a small house in Aldeburgh, Jonathan and Samuel Gathorne-Hardy. In the opera they are reorganized into two families, three 'home' children and three visiting cousins (the nursemaid, Rowan, was Crozier's invention; he does not recall why he chose this name for her), and in the 'home' family the ages were altered so that Juliet, Gay and Sophia come in the same order as Barbara, Robert and Beth Britten. Sam, the little sweep, fills Benjamin's place as youngest. The Britten family's rocking-horse was lent by him for the first production.

Britten wrote the composition sketch of *The Little Sweep* in two weeks. 'I am pushing on terrifically with the children's opera,' he told Pears on 8 April 1949 (it was due to be performed on 14 June),

> not stopping to think what I'm doing or how it is – because I have to deliver some of the score on Monday to Erwin! I think anyhow that it's

gay enough, altho' possibly not very distinguished – and also it's *easy*, which is something! It's funny writing an opera without you in it – don't really like it much, I confess, but I'll admit that it makes my vocal demands less extravagant.

Crozier noticed that, whereas Britten had had a long face while composing the *Spring Symphony*, he 'went about with a beaming smile' while racing through the children's opera. 'Time was short: so he composed all day and did the scoring each evening.'

The three scenes of *The Little Sweep* are framed by songs for the audience, a natural development from the congregational hymns in *Saint Nicolas* but a daring idea for the time. 'We take these "Audience Songs" for granted,' wrote Imogen Holst in 1966, 'but they caused a hubub of excited comment at the first performance in 1949, when hardened opera-goers anxiously clutched their song-sheets.' After the opening 'Sweep!' song in 5/4 time – a challenge to musical sophisticates who might regard communal singing as beneath them – the first scene, in which the brutal sweeps Black Bob and Clem force little Sam to climb the chimney, seems like a replay of the hut scene in *Peter Grimes*, with the child victim once again urged to strip off his clothes. The white innocent is duly blackened in the chimney, and though he escapes he seems likely, in the imaginings of Rowan, to suffer the same fate as Grimes's apprentice:

> Run, poor boy!
> O do not slacken, do not slacken!
> Black Bob follows swift behind!
> See his angry features blacken!
> Rage and fury make him blind!

But this is not *Peter Grimes*, and the story of lost innocence is now put into reverse by the children and – crucially – the audience.

The second audience song, 'Sammy's Bath', is, like the childhood song in *Saint Nicolas*, in waltz time. It presents bathing as a washing away of corruption, a baptism back into innocence. Britten and Crozier then allow Sammy and the children a momentary glance at the sorrows of adult life: 'Oh why do you weep through the working day? . . . / Father and mother are far away. / How shall I laugh and play? . . . / Home is a hundred miles away.' The process of regression then resumes with the number which is the opera's master-stroke, the audience's 'Night Song'.

If it was daring to ask a 1949 audience to sing at all, it was presumptuous to get them to imitate bird-calls, like children on a night prowl in an Arthur Ransome novel. The song, a sound-impression of the Alde estuary

at night, divides the audience into four groups, like competing teams of
Cubs and Brownies, and requires each to imitate a bird-call: 'Tu-whoo!'
'Keah!' 'Prr-ooo!' 'Pink! Pink! Pink! Imogen Holst recalls that this caused
'consternation' at the audience rehearsal during the first performance, but
Elizabeth Sweeting remembers Scott Goddard of the *News Chronicle*, who
this year had received a press ticket, entering totally into the spirit of the
occasion: 'a tall, lean, bespectacled figure rose from his seat among the
doves . . . "Dear Mr Conductor," he said, "I do not feel that my voice is
compatible with the doves. May I please change my seat to be among the
herons?" In a gale of laughter this was duly effected and everyone relaxed.'

By this stage of the opera, then, the audience has been lured by Britten
into behaving like infants. They must participate too in the final stage of
Sammy's regressive journey. The third scene of the opera opens with the
children's cheerful ''Morning, Sammy! Lovely weather,' an ensemble
which not only evokes a sense of sparkling innocence regained, but carries
a reminder of a similar moment in *The Rape of Lucretia* after innocence
has been violated. Then Sammy is hidden away in the darkness of the
visiting children's trunk, so that he can depart secretly with them. Though
his journey is ostensibly about to begin, it has really ended, for – like
Charles Kingsley's Tom in his watery playground – Sammy is metaphorically back in the womb ('Are you all right, Sammy?' asks one of the
girls, and receives the reply, 'Yes, thank you, Miss! Very comfortable').
Hence the last words of this final song – which is a musical recollection of
Tarquinius's ride to Rome in *Lucretia* – are about arrival rather than
departure: 'Time to stop, our journey's done. / Goodbye to you everyone!'
Happy families are greatly preferable to the adult world, but it is best not
to have been born at all.

*

'Once upon a time lived an unhappy little boy called Sam,' wrote Frank
Howes in *The Times* on 15 June 1949, the day after the first performance
of *The Little Sweep* in the Jubilee Hall. He summarized the plot, and
continued:

> But that is only what happens in the second act of Benjamin Britten's
> delightful new entertainment for young people, *Let's Make an Opera*
> . . . in the first act we are allowed to watch [the cast] rehearsing so that
> we can learn all the things we ought to know about an opera: what an
> aria is, and an ensemble . . . During this rehearsal, too, Mr Norman Del
> Mar, the conductor, with great patience and kindliness and humour,
> teaches us four songs so that we in the audience can also play a part in
> the performance.

Crozier had provided *The Little Sweep* with an introductory play showing how an opera is written and rehearsed. The producer was Basil Coleman, who had helped Guthrie to stage *The Beggar's Opera*. The small orchestra for *The Little Sweep* included Marion Stein as one of the two pianists. Norman Del Mar had been recommended to Britten by her father, who had heard him conduct on the Third Programme. In the interval during the first performance, after he had rehearsed the audience songs, Del Mar hurried round to Crag House to change into white tie and tails for *The Little Sweep* itself. Britten came with him, bursting with praise for Del Mar's handling of the audience, and telling him there was 'no limit' to what they might achieve together. Del Mar was delighted and astonished, especially as he had not found Britten altogether easy to work for: 'On occasion, he would take me for a long walk, and it would emerge that, for example, I had not been quite strict enough in this or that respect. You could go wrong without knowing it.' On the other hand after Del Mar, who was a horn player rather than a pianist, had accompanied the violinist Manoug Parikian (then leading the EOG orchestra) in a Festival recital, Britten told him: 'I wish I could play the piano like that.' Del Mar comments: 'I mean, *that* from *Ben*! This was preposterous. But it was so sweet of him to say it.'

Britten had auditioned the children for *The Little Sweep* himself. 'We went ... to Ipswich & heard 37 children for the opera!' he wrote to Pears. 'Some, happily, *very* promising, & one poppet of a tough small boy!' Basil Coleman writes that 'Britten attended as many rehearsals as his composing allowed ... There was always added excitement when he joined us, as he and the children responded so well to each other.' *Let's Make an Opera* was performed again by the EOG at the Lyric, Hammersmith, at Christmas 1949, and subsequently toured Britain with considerable success, being revived at various times during the fifties. 'I wasn't sure that in the end we didn't go on doing it too long,' says Del Mar.

During this second Aldeburgh Festival, which included revivals of *The Rape of Lucretia* and *Albert Herring*, Arthur Ransome lectured on 'Sailing in East Anglia', and the Cambridge University Madrigal Society gave an open-air performance on Thorpeness Meare. Meanwhile Britten was scoring the *Spring Symphony* under huge pressure of time. It was premièred at the Holland Festival on 14 July, exactly a month after the first performance of *The Little Sweep*. Koussevitzky was not pleased that, yet again, a Britten work commissioned by him did not receive its first hearing at Tanglewood, and Britten wrote to him to apologize, explaining that the 'doubts and miseries' he had experienced while composing it made him want 'to hear the work as soon as possible'. After the première, given by the Concertgebouw Orchestra conducted by Edward van Beinum, with Pears, Kathleen Ferrier and the soprano Jo Vincent as soloists, Britten sent a telegram to Koussevitzky: 'DELIGHTED TO TELL YOU SYMPHONY GREAT SUCCESS IN HOLLAND'.

Both Eric Crozier and Elizabeth Sweeting believe that the *Spring Symphony* owes its existence to a particular Suffolk landscape, 'somewhere between Snape and Ufford', writes Crozier; 'I have forgotten the precise locality, nor does this matter.' According to Elizabeth Sweeting, Britten visited this spot on a picnic with her, his housekeeper and Pears. It was a 'glorious Spring day, one of those that seem to be out of time', and she believes that this experience crystallized his love of the Suffolk countryside. In fact the *Spring Symphony* had been commissioned in 1946, a year before she came to work at Aldeburgh, though at first Britten seems to have imagined it very differently. Writing to Koussevitzky in January 1947, he referred to it merely as 'the Symphony', and went on: 'By-the-way, I am planning it for chorus & soloists, as I think you wanted; but it is a real symphony (the emphasis is on the orchestra) & consequently I am using Latin words.' What these were he does not say. His later decision to use a series of English poems portraying aspects of the spring may well have been the result of the picnic.

Crozier also believes that the Symphony might have turned out as an opera. He describes how, one spring morning in 1948, he and Britten paid a visit to Constable's water-mill at Flatford. 'It was a superb day . . . Then and there we resolved that an opera must be written about a Suffolk homestead, in music that would capture the full radiance of an English spring.' Indeed the *Spring Symphony* seems like excerpts from such an opera: a series of scene settings and choral dances which have somehow become detached from the main plot. It does have a narrative line; Britten described it as 'the progress from winter to spring and the reawakening of the earth and life which that means'. Winter is portrayed in the first section of the opening movement. 'It is such cold music', Britten told Pears while he was sketching this, 'that it is depressing to write, & I yearn for the Spring to begin, & to get on to the 3 trumpets & Tenor Solo!' Thereafter his chief concern seems to have been to impose some sort of symphonic form on what was really a song-cycle. 'The formal problem is a corker,' he wrote to Pears in November 1948. 'But I like the plan of the work, & its atmosphere, anyhow. I've got some sweet poems.'

Sweetness is the words' predominant character – most of the poems are in the pastoral tradition – and it is much to Britten's credit that the music never becomes cloying. This is largely due to the orchestration. Coming to it from the exigencies of the EOG chamber ensemble, Britten treats the full-size symphony orchestra of the *Spring Symphony* (triple woodwind, four percussionists and two harps) as a palette from which he selects only a few colours at a time, with stunning results. Only occasionally – as in the lilting setting of Nashe's 'Spring, the sweet spring' – is the entire orchestra heard. Usually he devises some unconventional instrumental combination to colour the poems: for example, tuba representing the lumbering farm animals and wind ensemble and tambourine for harness bells in the setting of John Clare's 'driving boy, beside his team ... / Cracking his whip in starts of joy', or violins playing close to the bridge to suggest the evening rain in Vaughan's 'Waters Above'. Even when the full orchestra is heard, the sound is usually unconventional, most memorably in the last movement, when, above the tenor soloist's description of May festivities from Beaumont and Fletcher's *The Knight of the Burning Pestle*, blares the primitive, disturbing sound of a 'cow horn', the alpenhorn under an English name.

Crozier recalls that for a long while Britten 'simply could not find a text for his finale, the climax of the whole composition'. This difficulty may have been related to the fact that, as Peter Evans puts it, the *Spring Symphony* 'almost entirely excludes any representation of some of Britten's most intense sentiments'. The subject of spring was laden with overtones of sexuality and childhood, but he chose to exclude these issues. The *Spring Symphony* is a *Serenade* without the Invisible Worm.

*

Desmond Shawe-Taylor, listening to the première of the *Spring Symphony* relayed from Amsterdam on the Third Programme, complimented (in the *New Statesman*) the Dutch chorus and boys' choir for the 'assurance and verve' with which they tackled the English words. Ronald Duncan, who was present at the final rehearsals, testifies that this was largely Britten's achievement: 'I recall Ben's concern with the chorus of boys, and how he repeatedly interrupted the rehearsals ... because he was worried about the articulation ... "You want to bite your consonants as though they were an apple," he said emphatically.' Duncan had not allowed his superannuation as librettist to end his friendship with Britten, who agreed to write incidental music for Duncan's 1949 play *Stratton*; and when Lord Harewood – who also came to Holland to hear the *Spring Symphony* – announced his engagement to Marion Stein, Britten asked Duncan to write words for a wedding anthem.

The wedding took place at St Mark's, North Audley Street, on 29 September 1949, in the presence of King George VI and Queen Elizabeth

(Harewood was a nephew of the King). A manuscript of the Britten–Duncan anthem, *Amo Ergo Sum* – a title which Duncan had taken from (of all places) Ezra Pound's motto on his printed letterhead – was afterwards interred beneath the foundations of the Royal Festival Hall, then being built, along with other artefacts intended to represent British life of the day. The congregation at the wedding included William Walton and his wife. Lady Walton writes that her husband 'claimed that Marion Stein and George Harewood were both admirers of Benjamin Britten's music and were marrying each other because of this bond'. Some weeks before the public announcement of the engagement, Britten wrote to Marion:

> I feel that *absolutely nothing* should weigh in importance beside whether you really love, & feel you'd like to spend your life with him. It isn't of the slightest importance that I personally like him a lot, only you can answer that question. Don't worry about or let people exaggerate to you the difficulties which may arise owing to his position. After all, they might not arise . . .

Basil Coleman gives another glimpse of Britten in the role of sympathetic friend and counsellor: 'I can't tell you how marvellous he was to me when I was experiencing a big emotional crisis at one stage of my life. He and Peter both made me go down to Aldeburgh to talk it out. Ben showed marvellous affection and care and sensitivity toward how one was feeling.'

Soon after the Harewood–Stein wedding Britten and Pears set off for their first-ever recital tour of the USA and Canada. It occupied them until nearly the end of 1949. '*Please,* PLEASE get Eric to do something about Billy Budd script,' Britten wrote to Erwin Stein from New York, which had now become for him 'this terrible night-mare city'. He found it 'maddening' not to be able to think about the new opera 'with all these train journeys'.

Herman Melville spent the last years of his life writing and rewriting the story of the handsome young sailor, Billy Budd, who is hanged from the yard-arm on the orders of Captain Vere, because he has struck and killed the ship's master-at-arms, Claggart, when mendaciously accused by him of mutiny. His novella *Billy Budd*, only a fraction of the various forms of the tale that he had drafted, did not appear in print until 1924, thirty-three years after his death. Three years later, giving the Clark Lectures at Cambridge which were published as *Aspects of the Novel*, E. M. Forster singled out this then still obscure work as containing a wonderful example of 'a real villain', Claggart, and also for the portrayal of Billy, who has 'goodness of the glowing sort which cannot exist unless it has evil to consume'. Fifteen years later, Auden referred to *Billy Budd* in a poem on Melville:

> Evil is unspectacular and always human,
> And shares our bed and eats at our own table,
> And we are introduced to Goodness every day,
> Even in drawing-rooms among a crowd of faults;
> He has a name like Billy and is almost perfect,
> But wears a stammer like a decoration:
> And every time they meet the same thing has to happen;
> It is Evil that is helpless like a lover
> And has to pick a quarrel and succeeds
> And both are openly destroyed before our eyes.

It may have been this poem, published in Auden's *Another Time* (1940), which introduced Britten to the Billy Budd story, which it so shrewdly summarizes; though Britten's own recollection was that he had bought a 'little reprint' of the novella – probably the 1947 edition with an introduction by William Plomer – while 'somewhere on tour in England'. It 'excited me very much'.

While not explicitly homosexual, Melville's novel is full of innuendo about Billy's appeal to the other sailors, Claggart among them. Blond and blue-eyed, he is portrayed as having an 'all but feminine' complexion, and his arrival on the *Bellipotent*, as Melville names the ship, is described as 'something analogous to that of a rustic beauty transplanted from the provinces and brought into competition with the highborn dames of the court'. Claggart 'could even have loved Billy but for fate and ban', and Captain Vere, commander of the ship, who behaves in a 'fatherly' manner towards Billy, is full of 'suppressed emotion' when he conducts the drumhead court-martial which orders Billy's execution.

It was on a day late in 1948 that Crozier, who had moved from Crag House to a rented hut overlooking the beach at Southwold where he was writing *The Little Sweep*, received a summons to come to Aldeburgh as quickly as possible. He took a train the next morning, and arrived to find Forster breakfasting with Britten. They gave him coffee, toast, and a copy of *Billy Budd*, which he had never read, and left him alone with it, asking him to decide whether it would make an opera. He observes: 'Their eagerness for a favourable verdict was all too plain.' (Crozier's letters to Nancy Evans – whom he had not yet married – show that he had been consulted about the project some months earlier. On 24 August 1948 he reported that 'Ben wants the three of us to work together on planning an opera,' and he, Forster and Britten had another discussion in November, though a subject had not yet been found. Crozier gathered that 'Forster felt himself insufficiently experienced in dramatic writing' to undertake the libretto alone.)

That winter's day at Crag House, he finished the novella by mid-morning. 'The moment I emerged, they began to question me. That went on the rest of the morning, through lunch, all afternoon. Clearly they wanted me to like the story as much as they did – but as a practical man of the theatre I felt obliged to stress certain disadvantages and the enormous difficulty of the undertaking.' He wondered 'whether a big opera could be done for a place like Covent Garden with no women at all involved ... and with this inherently homosexual subject'. He did not specify this last point to Britten and Forster. They swept aside his hesitations, Britten produced a notebook, and they spent the evening going methodically through the story, making lists of characters and events. Something unexpected soon became clear to Crozier: 'Most composers, I am certain, would have allocated the tenor role to the innocent young hero Billy: Britten took it for granted that it must go to Melville's wise and thoughtful naval commander, Vere, who would be sung by Peter Pears.'

On that first day of discussions, the idea arose that the action should be framed by a Prologue and Epilogue in which the elderly Vere looks back to the tragedy. A week later, Forster, who had returned to Cambridge, sent Crozier a draft of the Prologue which began 'I am an old man who has experienced much ...' Crozier thought it good – it remains much the same in the finished opera – and sent it on to Britten, who was on his convalescent holiday in Italy with Pears, telling him:

> Morgan & I are planning an expedition to the *Victory* [Nelson's ship] at Portsmouth, but not until after your return in case you would like to join the party. Waterloo Station, with sandwiches for the day, bottles of ginger-pop and whistles on lanyards. And don't forget your pocket-compass or the First Aid set. Morgan will be dressed as Commissioner of the Trumpington Street Wolf-Cubs.

The Prologue, like the rest of the libretto with the exception of the sea shanties and excerpts from Melville's ballad about Billy imprisoned, was in prose. Britten has recalled of this that Forster 'was worried that his writing in prose would inhibit my music; on the contrary, I found his terse, vivid sentences, with their strong rhythms, melodically inspiring'.

The three collaborators met again in Aldeburgh at the beginning of

March, but Crozier reported to Nancy Evans that he and Forster had
found Britten 'tired, depressed and strained' from the worry of exceptionally high tides which were threatening the sea-front and Crag House
– the cellars had been flooded and the street was under water. Crozier
still had to complete *Let's Make an Opera*, but there was no holding
back 'Morgan's great enthusiasm' for *Billy Budd*. Every morning for the
next two weeks, while Britten laboured at the *Spring Symphony* in his
upstairs study, the two librettists settled down on either side of the
fireplace, re-reading and discussing Melville's text passage by passage
and drafting their own versions of each episode. 'Sometimes one of us did
this, sometimes both,' writes Crozier. 'I was mostly responsible for the
technical scenes and the dialogues: Forster undertook what he called "the
big slabs of narrative". Then we would read our drafts aloud, comparing
and criticizing them.' During the mid-morning coffee break Britten
would come in to read what they had done. At lunch the three would talk
about progress and problems, and there was more discussion during an
afternoon walk – since Britten was merely scoring the *Spring Symphony*
and had not yet begun *The Little Sweep* he was willing to give up his
'thinking walk' to *Billy Budd*. He and the librettists parted company for
more work in separate rooms until supper time. At the end of the
fortnight some forty typed pages of the libretto were finished, with a few
blanks for passages requiring nautical research. Crozier and Forster were
now working easily as a team. 'Morgan is the careful, wise mind,'
Crozier wrote to Nancy Evans, 'I am the technician.' However, he began
to sense a barrier between the pair of them and Britten.

'Something is worrying him,' he told Nancy Evans,

> spoiling his temper, jamming his work, and throwing his tummy out of
> gear. I can't make out what is the cause. Domestic changes, perhaps –
> Anni [a Swiss maid who had replaced the neurotic housekeeper]
> leaving, and a new man-servant taking over: perhaps the symphony
> and its great problems: even, I begin to suspect, that he does not really
> want to do *Billy* as an opera but feels that he cannot withdraw now
> that Morgan and I are so earnestly at work ... It is worrying ... and
> the long hours that Morgan and I are spending cloistered together
> seem almost to make him a little jealous ...

A few days later, on 6 March 1949:

> I was right in my guess about Ben's wretchedness. He was going
> through a period of revulsion against *Billy Budd*, from a misunder-
> standing about the purpose of the story, and he wanted to give the

whole thing up. But now he has come through and he sees that his feeling was muddled, and with that change everything has improved – health, temper, outlook, work on the symphony, and spirits.

This letter does not specify what Britten's 'misunderstanding' was, but since Britten himself, in a letter written that month to a Dutch friend, described the subject of the opera as 'provocative' it is likely that he was becoming frightened of the story's sexual implications.

Crozier was now very confident about *Billy Budd*. 'It is going to be a stupendous opera,' he told Nancy Evans. 'Like *Grimes* – with a much better story.' However, he felt he must resign from his staff job with the EOG, giving as his reason the small salary, too small for him to maintain his first wife and their daughters. A letter to Nancy Evans in July 1949 also suggests that he was making moves to leave the Britten 'family' because he felt that otherwise he would soon be ejected:

> ... I have always recognised that any ordinary person must outlive his usefulness to a great creative artist. When that happens, the only thing is to accept it and not to make matters worse by clinging to a relationship that is outworn. I have known since early this year that Ben was done with me and that we could not work together again – not for some years, anyway. But ... perhaps, during the leisure of August, there may be a chance of talking with Ben in greater freedom, and the air may clear a bit.

Britten gave no overt sign of wishing to be rid of Crozier. A letter to him, undated but from this period, expresses sympathy with his 'beastly financial jam', offers kindly advice about difficulties with his first wife, and concludes: 'Now, dear Eric, *please* tell me in future what will be happening to you, & what you're thinking & planning.' He implied that it was Crozier rather than himself who seemed to be ending the friendship: 'We can't afford, personally or professionally, to let these "iron curtains" interfere.'

Crozier accepted a job as artistic director for the 1951 Bournemouth Festival, but he was back in Aldeburgh in August 1949 to continue work on *Billy Budd*. Britten had studied the librettists' first draft very closely and wanted to discuss revisions and simplifications with them both. Crozier had brought his daughters and was renting a small cottage; Forster was staying at Crag House. 'This afternoon,' Crozier wrote to Nancy Evans on 14 August, 'Ben and Peter gave a picnic-party on the beach for a dozen children and various grown-ups. First we swam, then we ate, then some of us went out in a fishing-boat. Aldeburgh looks charming from the sea, and I was astonished to realise that I had never seen it from there before.' The boat belonged to Billy Burrell, an Aldeburgh fisherman whose friendship Britten had begun to cultivate.

They had first met in 1947, when Burrell was twenty-two and Britten had just moved into Crag House. The Burrell family, fishermen for many generations, augmented their income by running a bathing station on the beach. Because of storm damage they had to move their beach huts on to the shingle just outside Britten's windows. Billy Burrell went to Britten and warned him that his view of the sea would be obscured by school bathing parties. Britten raised no objection 'And Ben and I started talking in general,' says Burrell.

> There was definitely at that time class distinction, but not with Ben. He started to talk about what birds I'd seen, and he said, 'Do you mind if I come out with you in your boat?' I said, 'No, not at all.' He came out with me many times, and then George and Marion Harewood came out fishing with me, and then Morgan Forster, and we became firm friends. And Ben loved the herrings for breakfast, and when there was a herring I'd bring it early for him, so he had a fresh herring for breakfast. And I would go into the house, and he would say to the housekeeper, 'Oh, bring a cup in for Billy, will you?' And he'd say, 'Good morning, Bill, what's the fishing like?'

Forster's biographer P. N. Furbank has suggested that in Forster's and Britten's eyes Burrell had 'a "noble savage" quality faintly evocative of Billy Budd's'. In a letter to Forster, Britten refers to Burrell as 'the other Billy B.', while in print twenty years later he described him as 'curiously resembling the Billy we were writing about'. Furbank quotes Forster referring to Burrell as 'adorable', and Burrell admits that he realized he had a romantic appeal to Forster, but says this was 'as far as it went'.

Britten, too, found fishermen attractive. In November 1948, after a visit to the fish market at Lowestoft, he wrote to Pears mentioning 'some remarkably fine looking fishermen & boys, terrifically tanned & strong, in their curiously attractive clothes'. Again, Burrell emphasizes that 'in all the years I've known Ben and his friends, I never saw or heard anything unforeseen' – that is, improper.

When in August 1949 *Picture Post* decided to publish a feature on the writing of *Billy Budd* (with a text by Crozier), it was decided to photograph Britten and Forster in Burrell's boat. Over the caption 'Background for an Opera of the Sea: Author and Composer Go for a Sail' was printed a picture of the three men in the stern of the boat, with an unidentified boy seated in front of Britten, holding the tiller. This was

Robin Long, aged about twelve, known to Burrell as 'Nipper', who frequented the bathing station after school. Burrell describes him:

> He was a sneaky little devil. Nipper used to come on the beach; he loved swimming – he went to Leiston secondary school – and didn't care a damn about nothing. He'd come down, and he'd fling his satchel in my lap; 'Billy, I'm going for a swim, do my sums for me, will you?' And he was that sort of boy that the girls would strip him off, with nothing on at all, and he didn't care a damn! And then he'd run from one hut to another (because we segregated them), and he was a real devil! Ben said to me one morning: 'Bill, they want me to see if I'll put Nipper to school' [pay his fees at a private school]. I said, 'You want to forget that.' He wanted more or less to adopt him. And I said, 'That's the biggest mistake you'll ever make.'

'Nipper' was killed in a road accident in Scotland some years after his friendship with Britten.

*

During the August 1949 session with Forster and Britten, Crozier noted that he had had 'a pleasant talk with Ben', and they were 'more relaxed' together than for some time past. 'He still seems to me tense, though: not specially in relation to me, but as though he were going through a prolonged internal crisis.' Returning from his American tour shortly before Christmas 1949, Britten wrote to wish Crozier well for his impending marriage to Nancy Evans, and asked: 'The ship at the start is hove to – hadn't we better start her? How does one do this?'

Though the new opera had been conceived with Covent Garden in mind, it had not yet been formally commissioned. The idea came up at the Arts Council that Sadler's Wells should present it at the 1951 Edinburgh Festival. Britten was doubtful both about the Wells – 'could they afford it?' – and Edinburgh, which he feared would mean 'an international snob audience'. Meanwhile Pears became very ill with shingles, and the new manservant at Crag House 'went mad – quite literally! It was very weird,' Britten wrote to a friend. Crozier describes how the man 'developed some very peculiar fantasies and habits . . . thinking of himself as a great composer and of Britten as his servant: he would get up in the middle of the night and come downstairs to play crashing discords on the piano'. Finally the man's mother came to remove him. It was at this point that Britten turned his full attention to *Billy Budd*. 'I have to-day written the first notes of the new opera,' he announced on 3 February 1950.

Forster wanted *Billy Budd* to be a tract on the redeeming power of homosexual love, with Billy as a specimen of lower-class goodness, like

Alec Scudder in his then unpublished novel *Maurice* which he showed to Britten and Pears, destroying the 'perverted' aspect of homosexuality (Claggart) and becoming a saviour-figure to the rest of the ship. In a 1960 radio discussion about the opera with Britten and Crozier he said that he was chiefly interested in 'this question of goodness, and of making goodness interesting', and in a letter to Britten soon after the opera was finished he described it as 'my Nunc Dimittis', implying that his eyes had seen the salvation bestowed by Billy. This approach was very different to Britten's. Already in *Peter Grimes* he had uncovered and destroyed the Claggart in himself. He did not share Forster's faith and optimism, and was probably frightened of bringing his own dark side out of the cupboard again, as would be necessary if he were to do justice to Claggart. Faced with this predicament, he took avoiding action. In the 1960 radio discussion he makes it perfectly clear on which character he had focused when composing the opera: 'Billy always attracted me, of course, the radiant young figure; I felt there was going to be quite an opportunity for writing nice dark music for Claggart; but I must admit that Vere, who has what seems to me the main moral problem of the whole work, round [him] the drama was going to centre.' By casting Pears as Vere, and trying to shift attention away from the Claggart–Billy axis on which Melville's story turns, he presumably hoped to defuse its dangerous power and reduce it to a purely ethical debate. In the radio discussion he also said: 'I think it was the quality of conflict in Vere's mind . . . which attracted me to this particular subject. The fact that he realized later that he could have saved Billy, and yet circumstances forced him to sacrifice him.'

Pears has recalled that he found the part of Vere very easy dramatically. 'That was me,' he has said, citing his naval uncles and brothers as making the role 'natural for me'. Britten was probably not very interested in the aspect of Vere that Pears implies here, the upright naval man torn between his own humanitarianism and keeping the rules. For him, Vere seems rather to have been a return to the better nature of Grimes. In an article published in *Opera* in April 1950, and therefore probably written just as he was beginning the composition sketch of *Billy Budd*, he describes a radio broadcast of *Peter Grimes* which he had heard in Canada: 'The Peter Grimes of William Morton was quite remarkable . . . It was not too heavy, which makes the character simply a sadist, nor was it too lyric, which makes it a boring opera about a sentimental poet *manqué*; but it had, as it should, the elements of both.' Besides showing how clearly Britten himself now understood the hero of his earlier opera, this throws considerable light on *Billy Budd*, for Claggart and Vere, both in Melville and the Forster–Crozier libretto, are just such a pair of characters, a sadist and a poet *manqué*. Probably Britten's intention at the outset of composition was to pay little attention to the former, and to present Vere as a reworking of the visionary side of Grimes, who this time was somehow to be saved rather than destroyed by his relationship with the apprentice (Billy). Once again the boy would be annihilated, but only the Claggart part of 'Grimes' would go with him. The rest would remain, somehow transfigured. (It is notable that actual boys play no real part in *Billy Budd*. Four Midshipmen, sung by boy trebles, make brief vocal appearances in the opening scene but, apart from the tuneless chattering of Powder-monkeys in the battle scene and a few lines spoken by Vere's cabin boy, unbroken voices are not heard again after Billy has made his first entry, as if he had taken on all boyish qualities.)

It was one thing to plan a sanitized *Billy Budd* along these lines, another to create it. In the 1960 radio discussion Britten admitted that during composition his operas usually acquired 'a greater depth than perhaps I'm intending'. *Billy Budd* was no exception.

Forster, who was often at Crag House while Britten was composing it – 'Morgan ... doesn't like me taking a moment off Billy Budd!' Britten reported to Crozier in May 1950 – began to worry that the music of Act I, when he heard Britten playing it, conveyed little sense of the sea. He complained that there was 'a tendency to dry-dock feeling'. It is true that, while Britten was taking considerable trouble to portray life aboard *The Indomitable*, as Melville's ship had been renamed, suppressing the sexual implication of *Bellipotent*, he was not repeating his *Peter Grimes* tour de force of picturing the sea itself. 'I have been lost on the infinite sea,' declares Vere in the Prologue, referring to the chaos of human experience, and the sea has this metaphorical role throughout. Similarly the ship in the opera resembles something quite un-nautical.

Melville's *Bellipotent* houses an American-style community of different nationalities and cultures who rub along cheerfully. The opera takes place in a very different sort of society, intensely hierarchical, with each rank, however humble, bellowing commands to those below it, and behaving obsequiously to superiors. This may or may not be a convincing portrait of British naval life in Napoleonic times, but it is certainly an accurate representation of a world in which the composer and both his librettists had lived, and which they had all hated, the English single-sex school. Forster had been bitterly unhappy at Tonbridge, and devoted much of his fiction to attacking public-school values. Crozier had been equally miserable at a boys' day-school in London. When reworking *Billy Budd* for the operatic stage, they and Britten turned Melville's novella into an example of that genre of fiction to which Britten had been devoted in his RCM days, the school story. For Britten, this meant revisiting a painful area of his past.

In Melville, a mere half-dozen lines are devoted to the flogging of a young seaman for dereliction of duty. In the opera this incident is spread out to occupy, on stage and off, much of the first scene. Yet while in the novella Billy witnesses the actual flogging – 'Billy saw the culprit's naked back under the scourge, gridironed with red welts and worse' – in the opera the victim is led away crying in curiously schoolboyish language, 'Sir, no! not me! Don't have me flogged! I can't bear it!', and the punishment is administered out of sight. We are back at South Lodge, with the victim being displayed to the whole school before being led upstairs by Sewell. Whereas in Melville the seaman is punished for a major infringement of discipline which has resulted in a 'rather serious hitch' to the ship's progress, in the opera he is picked on merely for being slightly cheeky. One is reminded of John Pounder's observation that at South Lodge 'you got beaten on the slightest pretext'.

Strikingly, the flogging of the Novice is not ordered by Claggart, who has not yet made an appearance, but by the Bo'sun, a mere cog in the machine. When Claggart does appear, the music – reiterated minor-key figures on tuba and timpani – announces him as a 'heavy' character, but carries no suggestion of corruption. His first action, the mechanical reiteration of 'Your name? Your age?' to each of the newly pressed men, suggests a school prefect conducting a roll-call. Even his observation that Billy is 'A beauty, a jewel' contains no musical indication of a corrupt personality. Britten sets it to a series of major triads, indicating that it is natural for male beauty to be admired.

Certainly when left alone Claggart reveals his malevolence, but it takes a very trivial form. Instructing his lackey Squeak to make life difficult for Billy (to a scurrying woodwind figure which emphasizes the childishness of the plot), he tells him to 'tangle up his hammock, mess his kit, spill his grog, splash his soup'. This is not the subtle Claggart of Melville but a mere school bully, a Flashman to Billy's Tom Brown, as much a product of the system as the flogging and the constant issuing of orders.

Although when he was writing it, Britten could not be certain which company would perform *Billy Budd* or with what resources, he scored the opera for an enormous orchestra, including four flutes, four trumpets and six percussionists. The intention was probably to provide plenty of high wind and brass to make up for the absence of women's or boys' voices. Among the instruments called for is an alto saxophone, and to its half-mournful, oily sounds the flogged Novice is led on stage, unable to walk after his punishment. When a friend consoles him with the words

'The pain'll soon pass', he replies: 'The shame'll never pass, the shame'll never pass, the shame'll never, never, never, never pass.' No great shame was attached to corporal punishment in English preparatory and public schools. Indeed a certain heroism was accorded to boys who endured beatings stoically. On the other hand if, as he had told Crozier, Britten was sexually abused at South Lodge, possibly while undergoing a flogging, he would surely have responded in just this fashion: the shame would never pass. At the same time the ambiguous saxophone seems to suggest that the experience held a horrified fascination for him.

If *Billy Budd* is a school story then Vere stands for the headmaster. Billy is at first only able to contemplate him from a distance. 'What's the Captain like?' he asks a shipmate, just as Britten might have inquired about Captain Sewell, and receives the reply 'Starry Vere we call him', sung to a rising five-note figure which suggests that the Captain is on a higher plane than the rest of the ship. Yet as Erwin Stein noticed when he studied the score of *Billy Budd*, 'Vere's motif . . . is the exact inversion of the motif of the lament . . . of the flogged Novice' (the saxophone motif expressing the emotions aroused by the beating).

When we actually see Vere in his cabin at the opening of the second scene (in the two-act version of the opera which is performed these days; in the original four-act version he appeared briefly in a 'Captain's Muster' at the end of the first act), the orchestra's shifting chromaticism indicates that he is a man very much 'at sea' morally and emotionally. His first decisive action is to lead two officers in a patriotic set piece, 'Don't like the French!', the banal sentiments of which are mirrored in the music; an indication that Vere is very much part of the system and accepts its ideas unquestioningly. The only sin recognized by such a society is a refusal to accept its values, in naval terms mutiny, and this is the subject of Vere's first substantial set piece, 'Revolution, sedition . . . We must be on our guard.' In fact the ordinary seamen are contentedly below decks in their dormitory, singing sexually suggestive sea shanties. Claggart, doing his rounds like a prefect, comes to tell them 'Lights out'.

Britten reached this point in the composition sketch at the end of 1950. The first act (Act I scene 1 in the revised version) had occupied him till August, with various interruptions, among them the third Aldeburgh Festival. This included the first-ever complete performance in Britain of Bach's *St Matthew Passion* in its original German, with Pears as Evangelist and a choir and orchestra from Rotterdam, '*really* well done,' Britten wrote to Lennox Berkeley; also the distinguished viola player William Primrose giving the first performance of Britten's *Lachrymae* for viola and piano, a series of 'Reflections' on a song by Dowland, written 'to reward him for coming to the Festival'. A briefer distraction was a fund-raising fancy dress ball held by the EOG in London in April 1950. Britten came to it dressed in a sailor suit.

*

'I am, on the whole, pleased with Act I,' Britten wrote to Crozier on 29 August 1950. 'It was after all the act that we were least emotionally interested in, & I think it was the most difficult to bring off. But I don't minimise the daunting job ahead!' During October, illness made him cancel a recital with Pears – 'I'm sorry to be a bloody nuisance . . . but I feel absolutely done in, & depressed' – but left him energetic enough to press on with *Billy Budd*. 'Billy is being quite a tyrant', he told Marion Harewood, '– fascinating problems, difficult but rewarding. It is a strange business this, creating a world which finally ends by dominating oneself.'

As he progressed further into the opera, tension developed between him and Forster. Billy Burrell

> felt very sorry for Morgan, because he came down to Ben for one weekend, and he said he'd like to come the next weekend. Well, Ben didn't want him down that week. Morgan was – what shall we say? Oh, he was slow; I wouldn't say he was in the way, but you'd have to fetch him from Cambridge, or Saxmundham, you'd have to take him back – he was that sort of man. So anyhow I said, 'Well, Morgan, if you want, we're only simple humble people, but you're quite welcome to come to us, and stay whenever you want.' Which he did.

Burrell and his wife made Forster welcome on this and subesquent occasions in their bungalow in Linden Close, near the Aldeburgh golf club, though Burrell admits that Forster never gave them any sort of present in gratitude for hospitality, until their first child was born some time later. 'He never bought Barbara a bunch of flowers, a little box of chocolates – never.'

Forster's resentment at Britten's discouragement of his coming to stay whenever he chose soon became apparent. In November 1950, while working on the sea shanty scene, Britten went to Cambridge with Crozier for a performance of *Let's Make an Opera*, and they called on Forster. 'To me,' writes Crozier, 'he was chilly but polite. To Britten, he was outrageous: he spoke to him like some low-class servant who deserved to be whipped. Then he stalked off into the night.' A month later Crozier wrote to Nancy Evans that Britten 'has received from Morgan a very deflating letter, full of sharply-pointed doubts about *Billy*, and he is still not certain, after long discussion with Peter and with Erwin Stein, how much the criticisms are deserved'. Crozier also reported that 'troubles between Sadler's Wells Opera and the Edinburgh Festival and the Arts Council' about the production had come to Forster's ear, and he was very angry that Britten had not kept him informed.

Britten wrote to Forster, explaining that Sadler's Wells and Edinburgh had fallen out over money, so the opera would be performed at Covent Garden after all. He made no reference to Forster's criticisms of the music. These had centred on Claggart's soliloquy, which Britten had recently completed. Claggart contemplates Billy's 'beauty, handsomeness, goodness', and asks himself: 'Having seen you, what choice remains to me?' Forster was deeply dissatisfied with the way Britten had set this passage. 'It is my most important piece of writing,' he told him,

> and I did not, at my first hearing, feel it sufficiently important musically. I want *passion* – love constricted, perverted, poisoned, but never the less *flowing* down its agonized channel; a sexual discharge gone evil. Not soggy depression or growling remorse. I seemed [to be] turning from one musical discomfort to another, and was dissatisfied. I looked for an aria perhaps, for a more recognizable form.

His disappointment was shared privately by Crozier, who says he felt that Claggart had come out as a 'boring, black-masked villain, not a tormented individual who is driven into evil by some kind of inadequacy in his nature. I felt Britten wasn't sufficiently interested in Claggart; he was interested in Vere.'

In the middle of the soliloquy, Claggart seems briefly to become musically identical to Vere. When he sings 'Having seen you, what choice remains to me?' it is to the rising 'Starry Vere' motif. Peter Evans suggests that this is an accidental 'inapposite' echo of Vere, but Britten would surely have recognized his own motifs. Philip Brett points out another overlap between the two characters in a later scene, when Vere repeats both the words and music of Claggart's 'O beauty, handsomeness, goodness'. Donald Mitchell describes this as an extraordinary 'invasion' of Vere's music by Claggart, and finds it 'uncomfortable, disorienting'. Perhaps Britten is suggesting that the two men are the same person beneath the skin, neither a sadist nor a poet *manqué*, but simply a typical product of this 'world which finally ends by dominating oneself'.

For all its obsession with male beauty, it is a world in which sexual fulfilment is constantly frustrated. This is emphasized by the librettists' invention of a scene, which opens the second half of the opera, in which one of the ship's guns fires at the French but the shot falls short, and the men groan with disappointment. It is in this atmosphere of implied sexual frustration that Claggart makes his accusation of mutinous conspiracy

against Billy. This assault on Billy's innocence is the one metaphorically
sexual action which achieves anything as the ship sails on through the
mist – the fog of human emotions and taboos.

Britten reached this point in the composition sketch during January
1951. Though he had been badly thrown by Forster's criticisms he
invited him to stay again at Crag House. '. . . no mishaps', Britten reported
to Pears on 28 January, after the visit. 'He is very well & is in splendid
form, helpful over Billy, agreeing to postpone Claggart problems, &
understanding the working situation' (Britten's inability to devote all his
time to the opera). 'So I didn't need to worry!' A month later David
Webster came to hear some of the music, and was much moved. 'Webster
cried a little, & embraced me – !) & is generally nice about everything,'
Britten told Pears. Piers Dunkerley was due to pay a visit, but Britten
developed laryngitis, put him off, and pressed on with the opera. 'Every
bar is written with depression & insecurity looking over my shoulders',
he wrote to Imogen Holst, '– but somehow I believe it's coming out well.'

During February he wrote the crucial scene in Vere's cabin in which
Billy is accused and strikes Claggart dead. Forster was puzzled by a detail
in Melville. In April 1949 he had written to Lionel Trilling: 'N.B. why is
it Vere's touch on Billy's shoulder that precipitates the blow.' Britten had
an answer. In the opera the scene opens with Vere, alone in the cabin,
declaring that he is not deceived by Claggart's accusation against Billy:
'He is good, you are evil. I've studied men and their ways. The mists are
vanishing, and you shall fail.' Britten set these last words to fanfare-style
music reminiscent of 'The splendour falls on castle walls' in the *Serenade*,
a resemblance heightened a moment later, when Billy enters, by the
sound of solo horn and strings. But Claggart has already made a similar
claim for himself – 'Have I never studied men and man's weaknesses?' –
and in the Prologue we have heard an older and wiser Vere admitting
that there is always an invisible worm: 'Much good has been shown me
and much evil, and the good has never been perfect. There is always some
flaw in it, some defect, some imperfection in the divine image . . . So that
the Devil still has something to do with every human consignment to this
planet of earth.' What follows in the scene in Vere's cabin suggests that
this may be profoundly true of Vere himself.

In the novella Billy, summoned to Vere's cabin, wonders 'if he's going
to make me his coxswain'. The libretto expands this into a passionate
outpouring: 'You wanted to see me. I knew it, I knew I'd be called.
Captain of the mizzen! Oh, the honour! And you telling me! . . . To be
near you . . . I'll look after you . . . I'd die for you . . . Didn't know what
life was before now . . . Let me be your coxswain!' Claggart is admitted

and makes his accusation, whereupon Billy becomes tongue-tied. It is now that Vere lays his hand on the lad's shoulder, and Britten marks this with a soft D major chord in the strings, clashing with Billy's 'stammer' music. D major was the key in which Vere asserted that he could distinguish good from evil, and in which Billy vowed love and loyalty to his captain. Yet sustained quiet major chords of this sort, often in the same key, have already been heard – as Philip Brett points out – whenever Claggart addresses Billy. Britten seems to be suggesting that Vere and Claggart's feelings for the boy are identical. Assured by the D major chord that his love for Vere is reciprocated, Billy strikes down Claggart. With the headmaster's implicit approval the school bully has been destroyed. But the rules must be kept, and the headmaster's favourite (Billy) must become the victim and receive his punishment.

At this point in the novella Vere utters two pithy sentences: 'Struck dead by an angel of God! Yet the angel must hang!' In the opera he reacts quite differently, with elaborate expressions of anguish and guilt:

> The mists have cleared. O terror, what do I see? Scylla and Charybdis, and the straits of Hell. I sight them too late; I see all the mists concealed. Beauty, handsomeness, goodness coming to trial. How can I condemn him? How can I save him? How? My heart's broken, my life's broken. It isn't his trial, it is mine. It is I whom the devil awaits.

In an article on the libretto of *Billy Budd*, Clifford Hindley points out that these words were a late addition to the text, added not long before musical composition began, apparently by Britten himself, since in his working typescript of the libretto they appear in his own handwriting, with deletions and revisions suggesting that he drafted them.

Why should Britten want Vere to admit that he is 'broken' and consigned to Hell by the prospect of Billy's trial and punishment? What sin has Vere committed, or is he about to commit, that justifies his statement 'It is I whom the devil awaits'? The answer probably lies in the most mysterious section of the opera, an instrumental passage of thirty-four bars which comes at the end of this scene, after the drumhead court has sentenced Billy to hang from the yard-arm. Vere tells his officers that he will himself announce the decision to Billy, who has gone to an inner cabin while sentence and verdict are being deliberated. Vere contemplates the news he must bring Billy: 'Beauty, handsomeness, goodness, it is for me to destroy you . . . I am the messenger of death. How can he pardon? How receive me?' He then goes through the door into the inner cabin, and the instrumental passage follows, ending the scene and presumably answering Vere's question.

It consists of thirty-four triads, each held for four beats, beginning loudly and rising to a *fff* climax, then sinking gradually (with two slight returns, to *f* and *mf*) to *ppp*. The chords progress through a wide range of keys, with D major making a few weak appearances and F major, in which the officers had deliberated their sentence, predominating – as if Vere's personal feelings for Billy are being overwhelmed by his sense of duty. So much we might expect. But the *fff* climactic chord is in A flat, a key which (until this scene, when it appears in Vere's soliloquy before he tells Billy he must hang) has not been used before in the opera.

Interpretations of these 'Interview Chords', as they are known, differ widely. Donald Mitchell, writing in 1952, judged that they were 'the true musical realization of the ultimate passions involved, when, in Melville's words, "two of great Nature's nobler order embrace".' Erwin Stein suggested that they 'convey rapid changes of emotion, ranging, one might conjecture, from surprise to fright – from terror to resignation and composure; an even higher state of mind is perhaps suggested by the last chords of the divided strings and the muted brass' (Stein seems to assume that the chords describe Billy's state of mind rather than Vere's). John Culshaw made no attempt at an explanation in his 1968 sleeve note to the Decca recording of *Billy Budd*: 'One can no more define why this passage is so profound than one can reveal, by an analysis of his sentences, why Melville's story of Billy Budd is so much more than an account of misadventure and misjudgement at sea.' As to more recent commentators, Peter Evans writes of 'the mysterious cleansing process of the great succession of chords', while Philip Brett feels that they 'suggest that in Platonic terms, the love of Ideal Beauty can lead to wisdom, knowledge and forgiveness; and that in Christian terms, goodness and love have the power to forgive. This moment of unalloyed optimism is perhaps the crux of the opera.' Clifford Hindley even believes that 'a positive and indeed idealised form of homosexual love' is 'implicit in the relationship between Billy and Vere'.

All these commentators regard the 'Interview Chords' as some sort of process of redemption or salvation. If this is so, why does Vere declare 'It is I whom the devil awaits?' The Chords could be interpreted quite differently. Beneath his cultivated exterior, might not Vere be experiencing sadistic delight in passing sentence of death? At the very least, in casting the most crucial moment of the opera as wordless instrumental music, Britten seems to be responding to his own uncertainty about the real nature of Vere and his feelings for Billy, and is deliberately leaving the crisis in the realms of ambiguity.

However, Forster felt no such uncertainty about the rectitude of Vere and the power of Billy-as-saviour, and the remainder of the opera becomes something of a struggle between him and Britten as he tries to press this message home. Billy declares that he has 'sighted a sail' in the storm, / The far-shining sail that's not fate'. In a note among the libretto drafts Froster specifies that this is 'the sail of love'. For him therefore the opera ended optimistically. The music suggests that Britten felt differently. Billy's hanging takes place simply as an event, without further musical reflection, and in the Epilogue the aged Vere tries to reassert the Forsterian belief in personal salvation through love of another human being, declaring that Billy 'has saved me and blessed me, and the love that passes understanding has come to me'. Yet the accompaniment to this passes through a harmonic sequence much like the Interview Chords, rising with much discord to a brutal *ff* on a chord of B flat. Though this is the key in which Billy has declared his faith in the 'far-shining sail' of love, the manner in which it is arrived at seems once again to suggest, at the very least, ambiguity in Britten's view of Vere.

*

'Budd goes on apace – murder over, & I'm well on – but it's *very* hard going & I get madly depressed,' Britten wrote to Marion Harewood on 4 March 1951. 'I've never been so obsessed by a piece. I long to play it to you & see what you feel.' By the end of March the composition sketch was finished except for the Epilogue, and Britten's life began to be crowded with other commitments: performing with Pears in Vienna at Easter; conducting his realization of Purcell's *Dido and Aeneas* as part of an EOG season at the Lyric, Hammersmith during May; conducting the *Spring Symphony* at the new Royal Festival Hall later the same month; travelling at the end of May with the EOG to Wiesbaden, where Josef Krips was to conduct a revival of *The Rape of Lucretia*; and overseeing the fourth Aldeburgh Festival, which included the première of his own *Six Metamorphoses after Ovid* for solo oboe, played by Joy Boughton on Thorpeness Meare, as well as performances of *Dido*. He and Pears also performed Tippett's new song-cycle *The Heart's Assurance*, which had been commissioned by Pears and which they had premiered at the Wigmore Hall a month earlier.

Despite the commission Tippett says he did not think of Britten and Pears as 'the exact people I was writing for'. Pears 'didn't have a top B natural of the kind I wanted', and Britten found the piano part demanding 'even for his considerable technique'. *The Heart's Assurance* was soon dropped from the Britten–Pears repertoire. Tippett had been invited to stay at Crag House while he was recuperating from hepatitis (he says it was 'very very nice' of Britten and Pears to ask him), and was allowed to see some of the drafts of *Billy Budd*. As with *Peter Grimes*, he felt there was a certain naïvety in the libretto. In particular he recalls a 'marvellous remark – I think it got changed – when they were going to clear the decks in order to let off the gun, and the wonderful order, given by Claggart or somebody, "Clear the decks of *seamen*!" I roared with laughter!'

Although he had still to score *Billy Budd*, which was scheduled for performance at Covent Garden in December 1951, only a few months away, Britten found time to consider writing another children's opera, for pairing with *The Little Sweep*, thereby creating a more satisfactory full-length programme than *Let's Make an Opera*. This idea originated with Crozier (who had left the Bournemouth Festival after three months because of the impossibility of working for a bossy alderman, and was now scraping a living from humdrum writing jobs and reading manuscripts for publishers), and at first Britten seemed inclined to collaborate with him on it. 'He is in a very good mood these days and I am sure that we shall not get any unhappy reactions,' Britten wrote to Basil Coleman in March 1951. However, a little later in the year he was intending to use William Plomer as librettist. He wrote several letters to Plomer discussing Beatrix Potter's *The Tale of Mr Tod* as a possible subject. He said it would be 'a wonderful relief after the Tale of Mr Budd!', but since the Potter story describes a vicious badger shutting up a family of baby rabbits in an oven with the intention of killing and eating them, it is hard to imagine that the opera would have been entirely comic.

By August 1951 he was scoring *Billy Budd* – 'o, o, what an *awful* lot of notes' – and had decided not to see the new Stravinsky opera, *The Rake's Progress*, with libretto by Auden and Chester Kallman, which was to open in Venice the next month. A few weeks later he wrote about it to the Harewoods:

> I feel miserably disappointed (I have done since I first saw the libretto & first few pages of the score) that easily the greatest composer alive should have such an irresponsible & perverse view of opera, (of the voice & of the setting of words & of characterisation in particular). Of course I am sure it will contain a lot of beautiful music, & it will be throughout original & distinguished, but I'm not yet convinced that it helps to keep opera alive one little bit – & I feel Auden to be largely to blame, being the cleverer & more sophisticated of the two. What these two *could* have produced — ! But the subject seems quite wrong for them both.

Auden meanwhile told Stravinsky that Britten admired the opera very much, 'everything but the music'. Stravinsky was not amused.

Britten's attitude to *The Rake's Progress* may have been affected by an unfortunate meeting with Stravinsky in America during the Britten–Pears 1949 recital tour of America, described by Lord Harewood:

Stravinsky talked a bit about the music of Britten's he knew – *Peter Grimes* from the score only, *Lucretia* from local performance. When was Stravinsky himself going to write a full-length opera, asked Britten. 'I have one in progress even now,' said the old master. 'But opera, not music drama, is my interest – and I shall write it in closed forms.' 'Just as I did in *Lucretia*,' said Britten. 'Not at all,' said Stravinsky. 'My opera will have *secco* recitative accompanied only by piano, not by orchestra!' Britten was dumbfounded. Had he not done exactly that in *Lucretia*, which Stravinsky claimed to have heard? Either the master was a liar, or a fool.

Forster had his first opportunity to hear the whole of *Billy Budd* during a visit to Crag House in September 1951, but Britten told Erwin Stein he had been

in a funny abstracted mood, rather selfish, in demanding lots of treatment and extra consideration unnecessarily. He's done some work with me, & demanded to have the work played to him – but cannot remember *at all* what he's previously heard of it! I've played him Acts II, III, & IV – & apart from excitement about Claggart's Monologue (rather ironical that!), no comment *at all*, not even of disapproval! He doesn't seem to be able to grasp it at all – or really interested in the musical side of the opera. Still, I must be grateful for a wonderful libretto.

Basil Coleman was to produce the opera, and he too was given a play-through at Cragg House. He describes how

Britten half sang all the vocal parts, giving a vivid idea of the characterizations he had in mind . . . as the daylight faded in the room round him and the terrible events of the story developed, Britten became more and more immersed in them himself. At the finish he was exhausted, physically and emotionally. It was very apparent how much the work meant to him.

Britten wrote of the opera to the Harewoods, when asking permission to dedicate it to them: 'It is by far the biggest, & I think the best, piece I've written for some time.'

His expectations of Covent Garden were not high – to Forster he mentioned worries about 'the size of the house, state of company, lack of co-operation' – and he persuaded David Webster to bring in additional singers. His own first choice for the part of Billy was Geraint Evans, then twenty-two and beginning to make a name, but Evans found that some of the part lay too high for him – he was cast as the Sailing Master instead – and during a visit to the USA Webster discovered Theodor Uppman, a Californian baritone with film-star looks who appeared much younger than his thirty years. 'At that time', recalls Uppman, 'I was very blond and curly-haired, and I had been working a good deal of the summer out of doors, rolling great big barrels of oil, my shirt off, and I had a pretty good set of muscles and I was nice and tanned.' He says that when Britten first saw him and heard him sing, 'apparently he felt that I *was* Billy Budd'.

The casting of Claggart was not so successful. A bass named Frederick Dalberg was chosen, but though Britten described him as 'acting with phenominal energy' Crozier felt he was 'a dull singer in a dull part'. John Piper was again the designer, and Josef Krips, whose handling of *The Rape of Lucretia* had pleased Britten, was engaged to conduct. However, the orchestral score was not finished until about a month before the first night, and Krips found the photostats impossible to read. A week before the opening performance it was announced that Britten would be conducting the opera himself. 'Ben was the one who should have done it anyway,' says Theodor Uppman, who found him superb to sing for.

> I think we, all of us on stage, felt we were his children, so to speak, and that he was going to guide us. I have never worked with anybody that gave me that same feeling. We all know that Ben went through great turmoils whenever he had to perform, or whenever he had to conduct, but once he was there and doing it, there was nobody who could do it better – just the little looks and the coaxings that you could see from his hand as he was conducting; you knew what he wanted. He was a great conductor.

(Britten's habit of finishing the orchestral score at the last minute caused problems again in 1960, when George Malcolm, sharing the conducting of *A Midsummer Night's Dream* with Britten, was given the original pencil score – the only one that then existed – to use in the pit. 'I really couldn't read it in those conditions, and I replaced it with the printed vocal score, heavily annotated by me with instrumental cues. Ben was a bit shocked.')

The first performance of *Billy Budd* was on Saturday 1 December 1951. 'There were tears running down more than one cheek at Covent Garden last night when the final curtain came down,' reported the *Sunday Times* next morning. 'Then, as a release from pent-up emotions, a torrent of applause greeted the composer ... The enthusiasm recalled

the première of *Peter Grimes* at Sadler's Wells six years ago. Sharing
Britten's honours were his two librettists . . . The performance which ran
late ended shortly before eleven and was followed by a reception in the
Crush Bar.' A few days later Crozier wrote to Britten that the impact of
the opera seemed to be 'really tremendous. Grimes made enough of a stir,
but this new achievement of yours has fired the imagination of an
astonishing number of people. I liked particularly the remark made by K.
[Sir Kenneth Clark] to Morgan that "it is one of the great masterpieces
that change human conduct."' Joan Cross, however, was 'terrified by the
cruelty of it', and Michael Tippett 'wasn't good' at enjoying the opera,
especially the moment 'when the Novice is brought on and he's been
flogged, like a Crucifixion. It wasn't me.'

Britten's own reaction to the opera's reception was characteristically
cautious. Among his letters of thanks to those who had praised it was one
to Lennox Berkeley, two weeks after the opening night. Berkeley had
quoted several comments by reviewers, and Britten replied:

> I haven't seen many of the latters' efforts (I avoid them like the plague
> – since they make me angry for at least 2 hours – much too long!) but
> they have obviously been up to standard! What a race – vermin, living
> off others' leavings! But luckily, they don't really affect the public
> much – only those dreary middlebrows who don't know what to think
> till they read the *New Statesman*!

To another correspondent who had not yet seen the opera he wrote: 'I
hope you'll like the piece. It is a strange one, one which seems to have
written itself in some way.' In February 1953 Imogen Holst wrote in her
diary that Britten had 'talked about *Budd* and said that although it would
never be a popular success he was very glad he'd written it, and to a few
of his intimate friends it would always mean a great deal'.

6: The power of love . . .
the love of power

The *New Statesman*, mentioned by Britten in his acid comments on reviews of *Billy Budd*, was among the few journals whose critic was not entirely enthusiastic about the opera. Desmond Shawe-Taylor wrote about it in advance of the first performance, on the basis of the vocal score, observing: 'Benjamin Britten has more genius in his little finger than most of his contemporaries in their whole bodies.' Yet after seeing *Billy Budd* performed, he wrote (a week later): 'I must confess that the opera as a whole does not quite fulfil the hopes I had built on it . . . Composer and librettists . . . have turned [Vere] from credible naval officer into moralising lay preacher . . .'

Most critics had no such reservations. William McNaught in the *Musical Times* disliked 'the total absence of female characters' but found the music 'unflagging and unfailing' and called Britten 'the most inventive mind and mobile instinct that we have in music today'. In a symposium in *Opera*, Fred Goldbeck described *Billy Budd* as 'fantastically well conceived and carried out', and Winton Dean judged it 'an even finer work than *Peter Grimes*'. Frank Howes in *The Times* felt that this was the opera Britten's admirers had been waiting for: 'To those . . . who have wondered whether and when he would sound the deeper music of humanity, *Billy Budd* provides the answer.' Britten, then, had little to complain about from the critics, yet he chose this moment to make his resentment of them publicly known.

He had hinted at it in July 1951 when he received the Freedom of the Borough of Lowestoft, remarking in his speech of thanks:

Artists are artists because they have an extra sensitivity – a skin less, perhaps, than other people; and the great ones have an uncomfortable habit of being right about many things, long before their time . . . So . . . when you hear of an artist saying or doing something strange and unpopular, think of that extra sensitivity – that skin less . . . before you condemn him.

Three months after the première of *Billy Budd* he contributed to a symposium on criticism in *Opera* (which had recently been founded and was being edited by Lord Harewood), revealing his feelings in an article entitled 'Variations on a Critical Theme'.

He observed that critics had not changed much in the twenty years during which his work had been reviewed: 'practically all have been unobservant if not actually inane'. Without naming them, he alluded to Frank Howes's review of *Albert Herring* nearly causing Peter Diamand to cancel the Dutch performances and Desmond Shawe-Taylor changing his mind about *Billy Budd* – 'confusing for his readers'. He was also scathing about an admission by Scott Goddard that he had been bewildered by both the *Spring Symphony* and *Billy Budd*, 'works which certainly appeared to make no bewildering effect on the first night audiences'. (Goddard's review of the opera was by no means unenthusiastic. He had merely observed that 'it cannot be assessed, let alone understood, quickly'.) Britten concluded by suggesting that reviews should be written by composers, performers and others actively engaged in music rather than by a '*failed* artist who has had to turn to criticism to live'.

Goddard responded with a pained article in the *News Chronicle* saying he thought that Britten had sympathized when, in conversation, they had discussed the difficulty of reviewing substantial works. In the *New Statesman*, Shawe-Taylor was more abrasive, suggesting that Britten had 'persecution mania'. In fact the *Opera* article had merely allowed him to express publicly the acute resentment criticism had always caused him when it came from anyone except himself. John Amis writes of this:

> I soon learned . . . that with Ben it was not a question of 'love me, love my music' but love every single bit of my music even if I run it down myself. I met him one day in Boosey & Hawkes, just after his Prelude and Fugue for eighteen strings . . . had been performed. Ben made some deprecatory remark about his piece and not only did I agree with him but I went on to ask him why he still needed to accept commissions if he wasn't happy with the result? Wrong. He turned on his heel and did not speak to me again for some time.

Amis blundered again when, at a party after the première of *A Child of Our Time*, Joan Cross and Tyrone Guthrie persuaded him to do his Peter Pears imitation (which was much like Dudley Moore's in *Beyond the Fringe* some years later, a kind of strangulated wobble). 'At which Peter laughed graciously but Ben looked furious.' Amis gradually realized that Britten 'simply could not take criticism of any kind about any person or composer that he loved. Even a crack about Dowland or Purcell would not be permitted.' Consequently 'most critics were automatically enemies'.

Though the *Billy Budd* reviews contained little hint of it, a definite antagonism was now building up in certain quarters of the musical world, not so much against Britten himself as against those surrounding him. When late in 1948 Eric Walter White's book on him was published by Boosey & Hawkes, the anonymous reviewer in the *Times Literary Supplement* attacked it ferociously not so much for what White had said about Britten as for what the book allegedly symbolized:

> Every religion at an early stage in its development becomes possessed of a canon of sacred writings . . . It was, therefore, to be foreseen that the latest and most flourishing of our musical sects would furnish itself with . . . a neat and unpretentious gospel discreetly combining the qualities of hagiography with those of a modern publicity agency . . . The rest of the world . . . recognizes in Mr Britten a composer of quite exceptional natural gifts in great danger of being spoiled by too-easy success, and . . . adulation.

The reviewer, who in the correspondence which followed signed himself as Bene Latul, went on to discuss *Peter Grimes* in such a way as to hint at Britten's homosexuality:

> In casting a Byronic aura round this man [Grimes], whose only claim to our interest is that he has been involved in the death of several small boys and is therefore an object of suspicion and dislike among his neighbours, composer and librettist seem to be attaching some mystical value to the mere fact of being in opposition to society . . . The absence of any feminine figure, except the purely maternal schoolmistress and the cardboard caricatures of femininity in its most unpleasing or ludicrous forms, accentuates the extraordinary emotional unbalance of the whole plot.

The review concluded with a final swipe at 'the small but powerful sect which threatens to kill with kindness one of the most naturally gifted of contemporary British composers'.

Accusations of cliqueishness were also directed at the Aldeburgh Festival. An article in the magazine *Public Opinion* in the spring of 1951 had suggested that the 'brilliant' Britten should not use Aldeburgh as his principal platform. The town was not the quaint fishing port it pretended to be but simply a 'block of *rentiers* and retired people', and though the few remaining fishermen and their families welcomed the visitors for economic reasons, they 'do not go to the concerts'. (A cartoon by Horner in the *News Chronicle* around this time showed a group of fishermen among the dinner-jacketed concert-goers, one old salt remarking: 'Ar, in the old days a man could break into a bit of a shanty any time without someone a'bobbin' up to arrange it for'm.')

The *Public Opinion* article did admit that the Festival stage hands in the Jubilee Hall included a member of the sea-going Burrell clan, and remarked that they were 'far more companionable with the opera-singers than they ever are with the residents'. Describing the Festival as it was in the early years, Billy Burrell recalls a great camaraderie with the performers: 'In those days, it was not unusual after a concert to go on to the beach – a real summer's night – get a case or two of wine out, and they would drink away, and one singer would start, and then another would start, and then another, and that sort of atmosphere was better than the opera itself!' On one such occasion, Pears 'was really liquidated! And he started singing. And I said, "Well, whoever needs to go to the opera when you can hear this?"'

In September 1951, just as Britten was finishing *Billy Budd*, he and Pears were passengers on a trip across the North Sea and up the Rhine in a thirteen-ton launch crewed by Billy Burrell and other Aldeburgh men, with Basil Coleman and Arthur Oldham (the young composer who had helped with the score of *Peter Grimes*) also on board. The role of cabin boy was filled by Robin Long, 'my little fisherboy friend ("the Nipper")' as Britten described him in a letter to Eric Walter White. Oldham says that it was on the whole a sober and serious journey. A diary kept by the Nipper and published in his school magazine is chiefly a record of conscientious sightseeing in Germany: 'up the Drachenfels, to a large fortress on the mountain. Ben, Basil, Arthur, Peter, Bill and I went by horse and trap to the top, where a wonderful view was improved by ham and bread and ice-cream. Bill took photos and Ben bought me a hat.' Britten took Billy Burrell to see *Billy Budd* – 'He kitted me up to go to Covent Garden' – but Burrell found the opera too 'long drawn-out' to enjoy it.

The 1952 Aldeburgh Festival included Arthur Oldham's realization of the eighteenth-century ballad opera *Love in a Village*, performed by the EOG, and Britten's new *Canticle II: Abraham and Isaac*, for alto, tenor and piano, performed by Kathleen Ferrier, Pears and Britten. Once again Britten had used a short work to form an epilogue to his most recent opera. In the *Billy Budd* novella Melville writes that, in the interview when he tells Billy he must hang, Vere 'may in the end have caught Billy to his heart, even as Abraham many have caught young Isaac on the brink of resolutely offering him up in obedience to the exacting behest'. In A. W. Pollard's edition of the English Miracle Plays, which Crozier had given him a few years earlier, Britten found a section of the Chester Play which vividly presents the Abraham and Isaac story, and he made this into what he called a 'naïve little piece'.

Canticle II is most effective when, as in Britten and Pears's 1961 Decca recording, the part of Isaac is taken by a boy with a voice just about to break. The lilting style of the music as man and boy set off up the hill, the boy still suspecting nothing, gives way to almost self-parodying melo-drama (*tremolando* chords in the piano) as the tenor reveals his true intention, and Britten seems to be amused by Isaac's attempts to wriggle out of what is coming: 'If I have trespassed in any degree / With a yard you may beat me'. In a letter, Britten called this 'Isaac using every wile to try & escape . . . I don't think there'll be a dry eye in the place – – –!' Sir Michael Tippett mentions the opening of *Canticle II* as one of the 'wonderful things' in Britten's music, and recalls 'Ben saying to me, "Yes, that's worth a million dollars", and I knew he was correct.'

*

By the time that *Canticle II* was performed at Aldeburgh, Britten was already working on his next opera. Over the winter of 1951–2 discus-sions had continued with William Plomer about *The Tale of Mr Tod*, but copyright problems soon diverted them into planning an original story for a children's opera, a science fiction piece with the working title 'Tyco the Vegan'. In March 1952 Britten wrote to Plomer from Austria, where he and Pears were on a skiing holiday with the Harewoods, suggesting an audience song: 'the children are doubtful about whether to return to Earth or not . . . the audience is directly appealed to (Tinkerbell like!), & sings a song about missing them'. A later letter to Plomer mentions 'the Marcus-Rose duet, & the Plato aria'. However, during the skiing holiday Lord Harewood came up with an entirely different suggestion.

They had been talking about quintessentially 'national' operas: *The Bartered Bride* for the Czechs, *Boris Godunov* for Russia, *Meistersinger* for the Germans, and for the Italians, *Aida*. Britten asked where was the English equivalent, and received the reply: 'Well, you'd better write one.' Harewood continues:

> The next three or four hours were spent discussing a period – the Merrie England of the Tudors or Elizabethans? – and a subject –

Henry VIII? too obvious, and an unattractive hero. Queen Elizabeth? highly appropriate! What about a national opera in time for next year's Coronation [George VI had just died]? We talked into the night, agreed that Lytton Strachey's *Elizabeth and Essex*, which I had recently read, would make a good starting point, and then started to face the difficulties.

The most obvious of these, that the Coronation was only a year away, did not worry Britten. Indeed, he wanted a firm deadline for the project. Harewood writes that he 'insisted that his Coronation opera was made in some way official, not quite commanded but at least accepted as part of the celebrations'.

On his return from the holiday Britten was still thinking about 'Tyco the Vegan', but he encouraged Harewood to pursue the Coronation opera idea. Harewood 'bought a paperback of *Elizabeth and Essex* and started to divide it into operatic scenes ... and got in touch with my cousin Tommy Lascelles, the Queen's private secretary, to tell him the great idea and to ask his advice'. Harewood saw Lascelles at Buckingham Palace on 23 April 1952 (his second meeting with him about the opera), and four days later Britten wrote to William Plomer: 'it is imperative that I see you; about what I can only explain, when I see you'. They met in London at the beginning of May, and Plomer responded rather warily to Britten's proposal. A few days later the royal approval of the project was granted, and assurance was given by David Webster that if Covent Garden could not put up the commission money the Treasury would. The opera was to be called *Gloriana*. Plomer then agreed to write the libretto. Britten told him on 11 May: 'I long to start planning with you ... A tall order, but I think we can do it!'

Britten's new librettist was ten years older than him, South African by birth, and discreetly homosexual – so discreet that there was scarcely a hint of it in his novels and poetry, to their detriment. In the twenties Virginia Woolf described him as 'a compressed inarticulate young man ... trying to be like other people ... very self-contained ... determined not to be rushed in any way ... tells a nice dry prim story; but has the wild eyes which I once noted in Tom [Eliot], & take to be the true index of what goes on within'. Despite Plomer's determination to hide his true self, she judged him much more 'solid' than many of her Bloomsbury friends.

A description of Plomer as he had become when Britten first knew him is provided by the writer James Stern: 'With his clipped moustache, dark hair brushed straight back, the thick-lensed horn-rimmed spectacles, the considerate, enquiring, courteous manner, he struck me as a cross between a doctor and an army chaplain with a sense, a surprising sense, of humour.' Plomer knew little about music but had greatly enjoyed those Aldeburgh Festivals at which, in consequence of his friendship with Forster, he had been invited to lecture. After the rough ride Forster had given him as librettist, Britten was probably attracted to the collaboration by Plomer's muted personality.

As soon as word got out about the royal approval, Plomer found himself pestered for interviews, which he refused to give. He sent Britten a copy of J. E. Neale's straightforward biography of Elizabeth I 'as a sort of corrective to Lytton Strachey', but in the same letter suggested using a scene from Strachey, in which Essex, returned from his failure to defeat the Irish rebel Tyrone, bursts in on the Queen before she has dressed and finds her (in Strachey's words) 'without her wig, her grey hair hanging in wisps about her face'. Britten's reply on 11 May made no reference to this, and indicated that he had only had time to give superficial thought to the project: 'My feelings at the moment are that I want the opera to be crystal-clear, with lovely pageantry (however you spell it) but linked by a strong story about the Queen & Essex.' He and Plomer met in early June and again a month later. By mid-July Plomer was able to send Britten, now on tour with Pears in Europe, a version of the first act which had already undergone revision. 'Terribly good,' Britten wrote from Aix-en-Provence on 24 July.

> I am delighted with it & ideas come fast & furious. I'd like to start the tournament [in Act I scene 1] *earlier*, so, in fact, that practically the whole of it could be described by Cuffe [a courtier]. Could Essex have some more asides – such as "Hearuss" – "I can't bear it" kind of thing? Which leads to one *general* worry – – – I think that metre & rhyme (especially the latter) may make the recitatives *very* square, & unconversational. Can we take out a word here & there to break them up?

Britten generally discussed such matters face to face with his librettists or on the telephone, but Plomer did not often come to Aldeburgh and had an aversion to telephone calls.

Britten described the libretto for the second scene, in which Essex sings lute songs to the Queen, as 'a lovely, a really lovely scene', though he suggested that Elizabeth might address Essex as 'Robin', as she is recorded to have done: 'it would be nice & tender, I think'. He concluded his letter with a big idea about the end of the opera, which I'll hint at, only, now. After the great discussion, & the deputations about Essex' execution, & signing of the Warrant – could we make a quite unrealistic slow fade out of the Queen? Like this. Signing of warrant. Take lights down except for a spot on Elizabeth. Then, so as to suggest her mind is on Essex, play an orchestral version of the 'Bramblebury' song, while people come & hand her documents to sign, consult her on matters – to which she replies automatically or not at all. Then finally, perhaps one might suggest she's dying; some doctor tells her to go to bed – she won't, but continues to stand there gauntly, like some majestic fowl, & slow fade of all lights to show the end. Could you think about this?

The Harewoods were with Britten and Pears in France, and noticed that Pears was 'glum' about the new opera. He resented being deprived of his accompanist while it was being written – Noel Mewton-Wood was to deputize for Britten at recitals in the coming months – and was wary of the 'official' nature of the project. He also felt he was unsuited to playing Essex, which Britten had assigned to him. Harewood suspected that he was not keen on acting the 'young, ardent lover' of Joan Cross who was to sing Elizabeth. Pears suggested he could be cast in the minor role of Cecil instead. Harewood felt that Essex could perfectly well be a bass. But 'Ben . . . wanted Peter for Essex, and he was accustomed to getting his own way.'

*

Composition of *Gloriana* began when Britten returned to Aldeburgh at the end of the summer of 1952 – '(hush!) I have already penned – no pencilled – the first notes!' he told Eric Walter White on 8 September. He was confident that he could complete the opera on time, provided that his health did not let him down. 'Marion and I used to say that some of his illnesses were psychosomatic,' writes Harewood. Britten 'agreed, but maintained that knowing it didn't make him feel any better'.

On 14 September he told Plomer that the first part of Act I scene 1 was written, though he had made 'drastic changes' in the libretto. 'I have been searching for ages for the correct form for the music for it, & *think* I've got it at last.' Meanwhile the EOG had raised objections to Britten diverting his energies yet again from them to Covent Garden, when they needed new chamber operas. Basil Coleman, who was to produce *Gloriana*, encouraged Britten to be 'selfish' towards them, and Britten replied on 25 September:

> I *am* that naturally, I fear – for now the problem of writing a *good* opera is more in my mind than anything else – other problems seem

remoter every day! It is going well, especially from the libretto problem. William's been here again, & we have sketched out fully all the
work except the last two scenes – & very satisfactorily sketched too.
He is a great sweet, & fine to work with; reasonable & skillful. John
P[iper] (with Myfanwy) is coming here next week-end to talk about it,
& also, I expect The Turn of the Screw.

A new chamber opera had been commissioned from Britten for performance in Venice, and had had to be postponed for a year because of
Gloriana. Britten was already discussing it with the Pipers.

The same letter mentioned that 'Festival matters are a bit upside down
here', but 'dear Imo Holst is taking up residence next week to help
straighten things out'. The previous year Pears had undertaken some
teaching at Dartington, where Imogen Holst was still on the staff, and he
wrote to Britten: 'This morning I attended a harmony class of Imo's
where we studied a Bach chorale – She is quite *brilliant* – revealing,
exciting.' At the end of the course: 'I am quite sure that somehow we
have got to use Imo in the biggest way – as editor, as trainer, as teacher,
etc – she is *most* impressive.' Shortly afterwards, she left Dartington and
became freelance. One of her first jobs was to orchestrate Britten's
Rejoice in the Lamb for performance at the 1952 Aldeburgh Festival.
The month after it, Britten wrote to her: 'always supposing you would
like to come in & help us, & in future on a really professional [i.e. paid]
basis, will you count yourself as definitely engaged – in the preparations,
& running of Aldeburgh Festivals nos 6, 7, 8, 9 – – –? Please say yes!' She
said yes, and soon after arrival found herself involved in the writing of
Gloriana.

Covent Garden had asked that vocal scores be available for the singers
by February 1953, so it was necessary for work to begin on this at once.
In the past Erwin Stein had adapted Britten's composition sketches into
the form of vocal score (piano part with vocal lines), but the urgency of
Gloriana made it preferable to use somebody whom Britten could overlook and advise. Imogen Holst began at once. 'His pencil sketches were
remarkably clear to read,' she recalls. 'He gave me helpful advice about
my piano reductions, telling me to add a *tremolando* in brackets for a
gradual *crescendo* on slow sustained brass chords, and . . . he never
allowed a convenient pianistic division between the two hands on the
keyboard to disguise the clear outlines of the music.' She was also struck
by the ease with which he could move from one task to another, could

have a detailed meeting discussing plans for the Festival immediately
after finishing the scene for the new opera he was writing upstairs. I've

never known anything like it, that power of going from one thing to another without any fuss at all, and in every committee meeting I've ever been to, Ben has always been the clearest-headed of them.

Imogen Holst was then aged forty-five, unmarried, the only child of Gustav Holst. Eric Crozier says she was characterized by 'indefatigable enthusiasm'. As a child, she had been briefly to the Jinner-Mawer School, where she learnt 'Greek dancing' – 'which accounted for some of Imo's more extravagant gestures', says Rosamund Strode. A bout of typhoid at the age of eight put paid to hopes of her becoming a professional dancer. She went to St Paul's Girls' School, where her father was teaching, and then to the Royal College of Music, studying piano, composition and conducting (she remained sporadically active as a composer to the end of her life). At the RCM she also attended ballet classes, and performed as a dancer in several student productions. From the age of sixteen she was also a keen member of the English Folk Dance Society, occasionally dancing in their international team. To the end of her life she used ballet exercises to warm herself on a cold day. When conducting she would move about the rostrum like a dancer.

John Francis says of her conducting: 'She was a bit of a comic turn, but her extremely fine musicianship did come over.' William Servaes, who worked with her in the seventies, remarks that 'in a way she was a caricature of herself, and she deliberately played up to it. But she was ruthlessly professional, very clear and astute. She was hooked on the memory of her father, and on Ben – not on Peter.' Colin Matthews, who like Servaes came to know her in the seventies, remarks that 'she didn't trust Peter on a musical level. She once said to me, "Peter is a philistine." She herself had an extraordinarily open mind. Once I looked at her copy of the prospectus of the next Prom season, and the only thing she'd ringed as an absolute must was an all-John Cage concert!'

During the thirties she was on the staff of the English Folk Dance & Song Society (as it had then been named) and during the war was CEMA organizer for the South West, coping with the vast amount of travelling that this entailed although she did not drive a car. Rosamund Strode, who studied under her at Dartington, talks of her ability to encourage amateurs – 'to make music enjoyable for everyone – even a bad cornet player with only B flat and D at his disposal'. When in 1952 she took over the auditioning of Suffolk amateurs for the Aldeburgh Festival choir, she made it clear that accepting some singers and rejecting others was against her principles: her father had always believed in letting everyone make music who wanted to. In the autumn of 1952 she moved to Aldeburgh. Eric Crozier describes her 'on London trains, enthusiastically conducting from a score in total unawareness of her fellow passengers, or dancing down Aldeburgh High Street like a six-year-old because Ben had just said "Good morning" to her'. Billy Burrell remarks of her devotion to Britten: 'She kissed the ground that he walked on.' Colin Matthews puts this more strongly: 'She could be so wonderfully perspicacious about everybody except Ben, whom she absolutely worshipped.'

At times he found her difficult to work with. 'Imo good, but pretty wild – I'm doing my best to keep my temper!' he wrote to Pears seven years after she had come to Aldeburgh. In another letter he describes 'Imo's panics' as '*ff* staccato'. Anne Wood calls her 'a very, very strange character, and very unstable, I thought. I was walking up Baker Street with a friend, and towards us came Imogen, who'd been to a recital of mine, and as she reached us she went down on her knees, and said, "Anne, you sang *wonderfully*." I said, "Imogen, *get up*."' Myfanwy Piper remarks: 'Imo was a joke, but she had got a spark of genius, real quality.'

Rosamund Strode, who eventually succeeded her as Britten's amanuensis, says that after settling in Aldeburgh she lived in 'extremely spartan conditions. One of the rather sad things was that Ben had absolutely no idea that she was entirely without money – she had made over her share of Gustav's estate to her mother. It didn't cross Ben's mind that she might be poorly off.' (She was paid piecemeal by him, and was never on a salary.) As to his occasional irritation with her, Rosamund Strode admits that 'she had very much a disciple-at-his-feet attitude, which must have been very difficult. And she had a tendency to carry dutifulness to extremes. She'd say, "I can't come out in case Ben rings up," which irritated him slightly. But that didn't mean that he hadn't got boundless affection for her, and didn't constantly ask her advice.'

*

Soon after arriving in Aldeburgh and beginning work on *Gloriana*, in the autumn of 1952, she began to keep a diary. It gives a vivid portrait of many aspects of Britten; for example in these few excerpts:

> *8 October 1952* ... When I said he'd got the right Elizabethan flavour with contemporary materials [in *Gloriana*] he said I was to swear to tell him directly it began to turn into a pastiche.

> *10 October* He said he always knew what Michael [Tippett] was *feeling* in his music, and it moved him, but he didn't think Michael always managed to convey what he was thinking.

20 October   He was in the depths of depression owing to weariness: he told me of the row he'd had about the Festival and said that he'd been so angry that his heart had beat so violently that he could hardly speak or move.

24 October   Ben walked in just before 4 and said come for a walk: he'd only got till 4.30, so we drove to Slaughden and walked along the ridge beyond the boat. He talked about the flight of birds, how they all kept perfectly together, never touched each other, and all without a conductor! 'And we talk about orchestral technique and ensemble but we haven't *begun* to get near it!'

   He talked about rehearsals and he said what he *could* do was to do a *very* little rehearsing and then just mesmerize them into doing it properly. 'That's probably what I'm meant for, – I'm no good at rehearsing, I just get bored and irritated. I can rehearse with Peter till the cows come home: and I can rehearse with Joan. But not other people.'

She found that he was 'mystified' by descriptions of Elizabethan dances in a standard work on the subject, so she volunteered to go to Oxford and 'have lessons on the Pavane, Galliard, Coranto and La Volta' from a friend who was expert in them. On her return she 'made Peter do the La Volta straight away', and demonstrated all the steps to Britten.

19 November   Ben rang to say would I go to supper. We talked about *Gloriana* – he's decided to have a Coranto at the end of the scene. I was so delighted that I leapt up from the meal to kiss him and just at that moment Miss Hudson came in to say why hadn't he found the shepherd's pie in the oven: it was a *very* comic meal! He talked about *Norma* and said 'If *only* I could write a real tune: – one day I will.' I thought of several answers but none were adequate.

On 27 November he told her that David Webster had offered him the post of musical director at Covent Garden (to succeed Karl Rankl).

Ben said that the only thing that would make him do it would be if Covent Garden would take on all of them, i.e. the Group. Webster said he couldn't do that because people would say it was turning into a clique. Ben was furious, and said that everything that ever got done in music was done by a clique – that was the word that was used when people disapproved, and that when they approved they called it something else ... Then he went on to say that he couldn't be a 'public figure' ... And that he couldn't manage dealing with people, except when he loved them or was interested in them ...

Over tea in front of a blazing fire he suddenly said 'Did your father get terribly depressed?' ... Then he began talking about his compositions that he wrote when he was a child, and tried to find the full score of his first symphony ... He said the only value in the stuff he kept from those early years was the chance it gave of seeing how a child's mind worked.

In his autobiography, Tippett describes Walton's comment on Britten being offered the Covent Garden job: 'There are enough buggers in the place already, it's time it was stopped.' Tippett records that

Walton associated himself at that time with a cabal of composers who were trying to debunk Ben or undermine his reputation: figures like Elisabeth Lutyens, Constant Lambert, Alan Rawsthorne, all of whom used to indulge in heavy drinking bouts with the critic Cecil Gray, the writers Dylan Thomas, Louis MacNeice and the painter Michael Ayrton. They all had great chips on the shoulder and entertained absurd fantasies about a homosexual conspiracy in music, led by Britten and Pears ...

Willie never lost his sense of rivalry with Ben. Once ... he let out a great cry, saying, 'Everyone is queer and I'm just normal, so my music will never succeed.' ... Ben told me that when they met, on another occasion, Willie took out his chequebook and showed him the cheque-stubs. 'There,' he said, 'you can't pay out that kind of money.'

On 2 December 1952 Britten told Imogen Holst that

he'd been reading Sibelius symphonies as a bedside book every night from 11 onwards. He said he couldn't help having a conscience, and every now and then he had to get out the things he disliked and take another look at them to be quite sure he hadn't been mistaken. 'Anyway I've done Brahms now and needn't get him out again for another three years or so.' He'd been through the Arch-Duke that afternoon. Sibelius, he decided, probably wrote when he was drunk. He realised why people liked him: – because he went on and on and it was sufficiently like the nineteenth century not to be upsetting, but with a suggestion of something 'new', and a certain amount of 'atmosphere'.

(Later, after hearing a performance of the Fourth Symphony, Britten became more impressed.)

One diary entry gives a hint of the strength of Imogen's feelings for Britten:

Back that afternoon at 5.30 for the committee meeting ... The committee members began putting on their coats to go, and I went into the hall to fetch mine and Ben followed me and said 'pretend to go and then have a meal with us and go to the films with us' ... So I ran up the hill and changed into my Cresta frock and ran back and was there just before 7.30 and was looking at the pictures over the fireplace when he came in looking *so* beautiful that my heart turned over so that it was thumping when he embraced me, but I explained that I'd run down the hill too fast. Peter came in in his old blue sweater and Ben made him go and change which I thought *very* odd of him ... The film was frightful beyond belief ...

*

As *Gloriana* progressed during the autumn of 1952, the Covent Garden Ballet complained to David Webster that they had not been invited to give the Coronation gala. 'They forget', Britten observed to Basil Coleman, 'that if we'd not had the idea of the new Opera & George H. hadn't bullied the Queen there wouldn't have been a gala at all ... But ... I've said that if they want there are two little ballets in the opera where they can hop around & make their little bows – further than that I can't go.' He asked Webster if John Cranko could undertake the choreography for the opera. Aged twenty-five, Cranko had just achieved an enormous success with his Gilbert and Sullivan ballet *Pineapple Poll*. John and Myfanwy Piper had introduced him to Britten, who told Webster: 'I know he is sympathetic to my music.'

During November 1952 Plomer went into hospital, and Britten had to write music for words that did not yet exist. On 23 November he thanked Plomer for 'the lovely Essex speech which fits what I'd planned (& even sketched in!) like a glove. A lovely case of thought transference!' When Plomer came out of hospital Britten had him to stay at Crag House. 'You would be *really* no trouble,' Britten assured him. '[You] could be coddled (both Miss Hudson & I are expert at that)'. Britten had finally found the ideal housekeeper, Nellie Hudson, whose uncle had been the miller at Snape. She was in her fifties when she came to work at Crag House. Believing that Britten and Pears were 'just concert people', she was surprised to find 'actors and actresses' – opera singers – frequenting the house as well. 'I don't know that I would have gone to live with him if I'd known that, because in my young days we'd never looked at actors and actresses as respectable class.' If she was aware that Britten, Pears and many of their friends were homosexual, in an interview in 1979 she gave no sign of it. 'I never saw anything out of place, you know, in the house.'

In this interview she describes Britten's fondness for plain cooking: 'nursery food ... milk pudding ... spotted dog', whereas 'Mr Pears was more fancy ... he liked spices and things [and] would come back from abroad and bring a continental receipt for me to do.' She regarded her job as 'mothering Mr Britten', but kept her distance. 'I never really knew him well, you know.'

By mid-January 1953 the composition sketch of *Gloriana* had reached the middle of the last act. On the night of 31 January a huge storm hit the East Anglian coast, bursting over Aldeburgh and causing about a hundred houses to be evacuated. Britten was away – Elizabeth Sweeting rescued his manuscripts from the ground floor sitting room – but he hurried back and wrote to his sister Barbara a few days later: 'We are slowly getting the water out of the house, but there's plenty of mud left!' Clearing up took two weeks, and Britten admitted that the floods had 'increased the pressure of work on Gloriana to almost breaking point', but the opera was ready for him to give a complete play-through – 'three hours nervous playing', he called it to Plomer – at Covent Garden on 14 February.

Just as *Gloriana* was being finished, something like open warfare over Britten broke out in the musical press. Donald Mitchell, then twenty-seven, who had been a prep schoolmaster and was now making his name as a freelance music critic, had since 1949 edited, with Hans Keller, the journal *Music Survey*. The 1950 spring number was a 'Britten issue', and from this came a symposium on Britten in book form. Forty years later, Mitchell describes this as

> a necessary corrective to critical attitudes to Britten at that time. These were often prejudiced or ignorant; and even when they weren't, it seemed to us that the positive comment was almost as ill-informed as the negative. Now, of course, the tone of the whole thing makes me cringe a bit. But I certainly don't disown it; nor would Hans have done. On the contrary, our symposium, for all its faults, successfully insisted that Britten's gifts were not to be taken for granted but – above all – *seriously*. It opened up the possibility of a radical change in critical approach to Britten and his music, and I'm not at all apologetic about claiming for the book a certain historical importance. Its critics of course tried to rubbish it. But who remembers them now? As for the music, it's won its (and our) case, hasn't it?

Mitchell and Keller's contributors included Pears, Harewood, Erwin Stein, Lennox Berkeley, Arthur Oldham, Norman Del Mar and Imogen Holst. The book appeared late in 1952 as *Benjamin Britten: a commentary on his works by a group of specialists*. Ernest Newman in the *Sunday*

Times complained that it was 'frankly of the adoring order'. Robin Mayhead in *Scrutiny*, under the heading 'The Cult of Benjamin Britten', suggested that the editors had only invited contributions from those whom they knew would 'preserve intact and unclouded the picture of their idol's near-perfection', Peter Tranchell in *Music and Letters* dismissed much of the book as 'incoherent verbiage' and 'hero-worship', and observed that 'Britten is too potent a figure to require a bodyguard', and Dyneley Hussey in the *Listener* deplored 'the thurifers who regard any balanced criticism of their idol as "detraction", and who are in reality doing great harm to the object of their uncritical attention'.

At times the book was indeed dangerously close to hero-worship. Keller's essay on 'The Musical Character' of Britten's works included this paragraph:

> This is not the time, and I am not the man, to decide about the relative greatness of Mozart and Britten; to assess how far with Britten, too, 'the world-spirit wishes to show that here is pure sound, conforming to the weightless cosmos, triumphant over all chaotic earthliness, spirit of the world-spirit' [a quotation from Einstein]; but as one who is soaked in the music of both Mozart and Britten I may be allowed to claim that for the first time Mozart, the universal musician who masters everything with a somnambulistic surefootedness and grace, has found a companion. And personally, I regard Britten as the greatest of all living composers whose music I understand.

There was a general assumption among the contributors that all Britten's music was equally admirable and faultless. However, as several reviewers rather grudgingly allowed, the book was full of innovative musical analysis, and it was wrong to suppose that the editors had been motivated by their own friendship with Britten. Keller has said that he was 'not particularly fond of Britten as a person', while Mitchell had not yet met him. Pears was introduced to Mitchell just after the book came out and described him to Britten as 'very sweet, young, dotty & enthusiastic', and Britten himself wrote to Mitchell and Keller that he was 'pleased & flattered' by the book, and suggested that they might now meet '& have a good talk'. He told Imogen Holst that 'On the whole he was pleased with the book:– said he liked George Malcolm's chapters [on Britten's Purcell realizations and his *Dido and Aeneas*] v. much. But the analysis diagram . . . made him think of one of Bill [Burrell]'s nets. He said he'd no idea he was as clever as that:– "I've come to the conclusion I must have a very clever subconscious."' Two weeks later 'We talked about the book about him:– he said it made him feel like a small and harmless rabbit being cut up by a lot of grubby schoolboys when he'd *much* rather be frisking about in the fields.'

In his letter to Mitchell and Keller he particularly commended their own articles on him. Keller's essay included this passage:

> Britten is a pacifist. It is an established fact that strong and heavily repressed sadism underlies pacifistic attitudes. About the vital aggressive element in Britten's music (as distinct from his extra-musical character) there cannot indeed be the faintest doubt, and those whose ears are not sensitive enough to recognize the sadistic component at least in his treatment of the percussion, will still be able to confirm our observation upon an inspection of his libretti, children's opera included ... What distinguishes Britten's musical personality is the violent repressive counter-force against his sadism.

Imogen Holst wrote of this in her diary that Britten 'read out a terrible sentence about "sado-masochism":– he said they must have noticed in my chapter that his favourite instrument was the whip!' Ten years later Britten was asked by an interviewer what he thought of Keller's remarks. He answered: 'It is difficult, if not impossible, to comment objectively on what is written about oneself. But I admire Keller's intelligence and courage enormously, and certainly about *others* he is very perceptive!'

*

Britten began work on the orchestral score of *Gloriana* early in February 1953, with Imogen Holst at his elbow. Her diary records their labours:

> *15 February* ... I realised that I shall *never* be able to keep up with him. He writes it quicker than one could ever believe would be possible. He's leaving doublings [of instruments and voices] for me to fill in, and he *thinks* he can get through by the time they go away in mid-March ...

> *16 February* The hardest day's work I've ever done ... Ben had written 28 pages of full score in one day. I suppose I shall learn to be quicker as it goes on, but I hope to heaven I don't keep him waiting. He was v. kind and never got peevish.

> *18 February* ... In spite of being rushed and weary he kept up a priceless intermittent conversation throughout the hours of work, saying how glad he was that he'd refused that Dr. of music the day before.

> *2nd March* ... He reckoned to get the dance scene finished by 4, but he finished it at *12.20*!! Absolutely incredible. As usual, he turned round from putting in the last note and said 'Now in the *next* scene' ...

He completed the enormous score in one month, and then took two weeks' holiday in Ireland with Pears and the Harewoods. They had intended to go to Greece, but Imogen noted that 'they were refusing him a permit because he'd signed a petition about the [Greek] prisoners who'd not had a fair trial'. On his return he ran through the role of Elizabeth with Joan Cross – 'It suits her down to the ground,' he wrote to Plomer on 8th April – then attended rehearsals in the Crush Bar at Covent Garden. John Pritchard was conducting. Both Joan Cross and Basil Coleman say he contributed nothing to the opera. Cross calls him 'hopeless – he didn't give you any help at all; he didn't know the score well enough'. Imogen's diary alludes to this:

> At the second orch. rehearsal Ben said he was going to conduct the 1st ½hr and as we were alone in the passage I said 'Oh, now it will be *right*!' and he blew up in an absolute fury, the first time he's ever lost his temper with me:– absolutely terrifying – hard, set face and no love in his eyes and a feeling of utter removal to an immense distance. I was so shattered that I could hardly listen . . . In the pub, over a meal . . . I realised that he'd been angry because I'd said what was in his own mind, which he didn't want to think. He said 'Everyone will have to help me to think that Pritchard is going to be all right.' He also said 'I wish I didn't get so angry', so I said that he was the calmest and most patient person in the world.

As to Pears's interpretation of Essex, Joan Cross began to find that while he was delivering 'a very good performance' it was as usual difficult to act with him – 'We never got together over it.' (She mentions that in *Peter Grimes*, when Grimes was supposed to strike Ellen, 'Peter would never hit me – he could *not* hit me!') Long afterwards Pears admitted that he had been uncomfortable about playing Essex: 'I'm not sure, but I think somebody else should have done it rather than me.'

On 18 May the Harewoods held a private dinner party at their London house in Orme Square for the Queen and the Duke of Edinburgh. Britten, Pears and Cross were among the guests, and they performed extracts from the opera. Plomer, who was also there, amused the Queen by describing the Lord Chamberlain's insistence that the object emptied over Essex's rebels in Act III should not be a chamber pot, and Harewood judged the royal couple 'an appreciative audience' for the extracts, though Joan Cross says it was 'not my favourite evening', and doubts whether the Queen and the Duke enjoyed it 'any more than we did'. Two weeks later, on 1 June, Britten was created a Companion of Honour in the Coronation honours list.

The gala première of *Gloriana* had been arranged for Monday 8 June, six days after the Coronation. Harewood hoped that the audience would consist largely of 'artistic Britain', but seats had been found for such people at the public dress rehearsal, and the gala night audience, as Plomer put it, was 'so largely official that it was afraid the stuffing might run out of its stuffed shirts'. However, talking to the Duke of Edinburgh, Plomer was pleased to discover that he had been reading the libretto carefully since the private preview, '& I think he now knows it better than I do'.

Philip Hope-Wallace in the *Manchester Guardian* described the appearance of the Opera House that night:

> gorgeously dressed with flags and flowers; full evening dress, medals, and jewels glittered at the back as the Queen and the royal party entered the royal box after a fanfare of trumpets. As the audience turned towards the royal box and the National Anthem crashed out from the orchestra, it seemed as if one of those legendary nights of the Edwardian golden age of opera had come again. But in those days a royal gala would have meant titbits from *Aida* and *Bohème*. Tonight there was the great difference that on the stage we were to see and hear a completely new opera . . .

It was an opera which, despite its subject matter, Britten had managed to make into a part of his continuing private debate about himself. *Gloriana* is an examination of the choices an artist has to make, and the perils he faces, when he reaches Britten's level of achievement.

*

By 1953, the year of *Gloriana*, many of those who worked for him felt that a significant change had taken place since the earliest Aldeburgh Festivals. Norman Del Mar says that, at the beginning, the Festival had been such a happy affair that it was in danger of becoming 'just one big private party'. It had been the same in the early EOG tours. Norman Lumsden, the original Sergeant Budd in *Albert Herring* and Black Bob in *The Little Sweep*, remarks that 'when we went abroad, Ben and Peter were with us all the time, second class, on the boats, no differentiation, one of the boys you might say. But then it gradually changed, just like the Festival changed, until it was very difficult to approach them. We called them the Royal Family.' John Francis uses the same phrase: 'They grew into a kind of Royal Family. People were very much *in*, then they got dropped. Ben would be all over some singer or other. Then after a while they'd be left out in the cold.'

Conductors and tenors in particular felt that they had a hard time of it.

Anne Wood, the first EOG manager, says that conductors 'never felt really that they were doing what Ben wanted, but he couldn't tell them what to do, and that's why they all came to grief'. Norman Del Mar describes how 'somebody would whisper to you, "Move it on – Ben's getting stomach cramps." You had to discern when he was getting fidgety, to *know* that he was gnawing his fingernails in the background.' Del Mar also recalls how on an EOG tour

> I blotted my copybook inadvertently because I started reading one of the crits in the interval to Ben and Peter and Joan. And I hadn't read the crit ahead, and it said that I'd conducted it as well as Ben, and that didn't go down at all well. And I suddenly realized that I had put my foot in it without meaning to. The silence was rather awful. I mean, all right, I was Ben's conductor, but that I should actually be able to challenge him on his own territory – no, that didn't do.

As to tenors, when Richard Lewis sang the Male Chorus in *The Rape of Lucretia*, Anne Wood says that Britten 'would *not* rehearse with him, he would *not*'. She believes it was because Lewis's top register was stronger than Pears's, 'and I think Ben, on Peter's behalf, was jealous of it. Richard would come to me and say, "I've still not had any rehearsals with Ben. I can't understand – can't he find time?"' Basil Douglas, who took over as EOG manager in 1951, remarks that Britten 'couldn't bear other tenors', while Norman Lumsden observes that 'there was always this business that Peter had to be Number One. Anybody who was too good was a threat to Peter. And Peter was, I think, the power behind the throne all the time.'

Lumsden says that he and his fellow singers soon learnt that 'you'd only got to make one little slip, and you were out of the door'. George Malcolm, who conducted the EOG on various occasions from 1951, remembers that 'after a while there was an organization called the Club. It consisted of people who *used* to sing or play for Ben. They used to say, "You'd better be careful, or you'll be joining the Club."'

The organist Ralph Downes, the only musician to perform at every Aldeburgh Festival in Britten's lifetime, says that 'many people got themselves a first-class exit ticket simply by giving a bad performance'. Some were not re-engaged because Britten had found a better player or singer. Herbert Wilson, percussionist in the EOG orchestra, was replaced by James Blades, and George Malcolm says that the moment Britten heard Osian Ellis play the harp, 'Osian was *the* harpist and Enid Simon was out on her ear'.

Victims would usually complain that Britten had given them no warning, nor any explanation why he was discarding them. Anne Wood recalls the crisis over Lesley Bedford, who sang Lucia in the first production of *The Rape of Lucretia* and Emmie in the original *Albert Herring*, both juvenile roles, though she was approaching middle age. 'It was grotesque. And it suddenly came to the point when Ben saw that it was grotesque. And he could not, he *could not* make up his mind to say anything to her. I had to do it. And she was distraught.' Lesley Bedford's son, the conductor Steuart Bedford, says his mother had fallen entirely under Britten's spell, and agrees that she was utterly crushed by the rejection.

Elizabeth Sweeting says that people often fell from favour because they made their adoration of Britten too obvious, and behaved too possessively towards him, 'something which Ben abhorred; as soon as people began to make demands, he ran a mile'. Anne Wood says it was wisest to keep one's distance. 'You really needed just a little bit to be apart, or you really did risk annihilation.'

Fidelity Cranbrook's nephew Jonathan Gathorne-Hardy recalls that the atmosphere surrounding Britten by the early fifties was 'like a girls' school, or a court – crushes, favourites, who's in, who's out'. George Malcolm says that invitations to lunch at Crag House during the Festival were considered 'very much a sign of one's personal status. If one went through an entire Festival without being invited to lunch, that was a bad sign.'

Malcolm says that dismissals were common in other musical circles where the highest standards were observed – for example Walter Legge, running the Philharmonia Orchestra, would replace a musician if he found another who was 'only five per cent better'. Lord Harewood suggests that the regret which performers felt at finding themselves not re-engaged by Britten arose 'because of Ben's charisma. They *minded*, more than people usually minded, because of what Ben was like. If Malcolm Sargent didn't engage you for his *Messiah*, you said, "Stupid old Malcolm, he never knew anything about singing anyway." But if Ben didn't, you *minded* not being asked back.'

Myfanwy Piper wonders whether Britten's treatment of people might have been influenced by Auden's 1942 injunction to 'suffer, and make others suffer' – she suggests that it could have been a 'childish, unsubtle interpretation of this'. Joan Cross says bluntly: 'He just used people, and he finished with them, and that was that.' Elizabeth, the part written for Joan Cross in *Gloriana*, seems to do precisely that with Essex. The opera can be interpreted as partly a self-portrait of this aspect of Britten, and an examination of the stresses experienced by a public figure such as he had now become.

*

The orchestral prelude to the opening scene of *Gloriana* is a set of busy variations on a theme stated in a brass fanfare. For the first time since *Albert Herring* we are in the public world. 'The opera has two selves,' writes Donald Mitchell, 'the public and the private, which reflect the very constitution of the Queen herself and of her relation to Essex, which is in itself a symbol of her dilemma.'

The action opens with Essex enviously hearing of his rival Mountjoy's success in a tournament. So might a struggling young composer receive reports of another's achievements. Essex here seems to represent the vulnerable aspect of the artist – the envyer, the man of action, easily deflated by others' success as well as his own failures. As to the Queen herself, her entrance is heralded by lengthy fanfares from trumpets on the stage. Throughout *Gloriana* her presence creates music, not just the narrative music of the opera but specific performances of songs, dances, fanfares and other occasional pieces, and it is these which give the opera its particular flavour. Britten seems to be asserting that the public facet of the artist can be immensely productive, creating occasional music of the highest order. (Eleven years after *Gloriana*, in his 1964 Aspen Award speech, he remarked that 'almost every piece I have ever written has been composed with a certain occasion in mind'.)

In Act I of *Gloriana* the pieces which Elizabeth engenders are the chorus's 'Crownèd Rose' hymn of loyalty, after she has reconciled Essex and Mountjoy, and in the second scene, two lute songs performed at her request by Essex in her private chamber. Their theme is the manic-depressive artistic personality. The first song recommends creative energy as a remedy for depression – 'Quick music is best / When the heart is oppressed' – and the second describes the self-doubting artist's desire to live 'obscure / From all society'. The Queen taunts Essex with being a creature of mood swings: 'You man of moods! . . . Now up, now down.' His vulnerability is contrasted with her own apparently impregnable self-control. Act II brings these two sides of the artistic personality, the vulnerable self-absorbed creative genius and the public-minded figure of power, into open conflict. In the first scene Elizabeth watches a masque on the theme of Time and Concord, a highly relevant subject for a power-figure: in Act I she has established concord between rival factions, as any politician must do, and Act III will deal with the one thing that makes her vulnerable, the passing of time. The masque is made up of 'Choral Dances'. It irritates Essex, who is impatient to advance towards power. The Queen, however, knows that her people's love and trust, which the masque is intended to express to her, *is* her source of power – an artist must be in touch with his or her audience. The music of the

Choral Dances exactly catches the nature of the debate. To a self-centred artist, such as Essex appears to represent, it might seem mock-Elizabethan pastiche, but in fact Britten has, with great harmonic and rhythmic ingenuity, trodden the fine line between evoking a sixteenth-century court entertainment and sounding like himself.

The second scene of Act II, like that in Act I, seems about to deal with 'private' issues, but again ends up by being concerned with public ones. It opens with a romantic assignation between Mountjoy and his mistress, Lady Rich, Essex's sister, but Mountjoy anticipates her arrival with a song so exactly like a drawing-room ballad – 'A garden by a river at a trysting / Is perfect in the evening for a pair' – that Britten seems to be asserting that there is no such thing as 'private' music. Sure enough the tryst quickly turns into a four-handed debate (between the lovers and Essex and his wife) in which admiration for 'the power of love' quickly gives way to an admission of 'the love of power' (Lady Rich's words). Essex declares that he wants to see power slip from the grasp of the ageing Elizabeth into his own: 'The Queen is old, and time will steal / Sceptre and orb from out her hand'. So it will, but Essex's impetuosity leads him into a fatal error. At a court ball he has his wife arrayed in a dress so splendid that the Queen is jealous. By a trick she steals it from Lady Essex and puts it on herself. Commentators on the opera have generally seen this as a revelation of personal weakness in the Queen, but the grotesque music which accompanies Elizabeth as she enters in the gorgeous gown – the tuba mimics the La Volta which the court has been dancing – gives no hint that Britten regards her as unwise, let alone deranged. The joke is on her, and it is a sharp and effective response to *lèse-majesté*. That she proceeds directly from this to appointing Essex her Lord Deputy in Ireland, the job he has been seeking, shows not that she wishes to make amends for her behaviour but that she is going to let Essex hang on his own rope, for nothing we have heard from him suggests that he will be able to cope with public responsibility. Sure enough the first scene of Act III brings him hastening back impetuously from Ireland, where he has not subdued the rebels but merely made a truce. He crashes into the Queen's dressing-room before she is ready to receive him, and thereby shows us at last the 'real' Elizabeth – an old woman in a dressing-gown. 'You see me as I am,' she admits candidly to him in simple unadorned music. Only Time can undo the lovers of power.

Essex blurts out that 'The gale of the world has caught me . . . / the world is full of lying tongues . . . / foes beset me now / Here, in England, at home'. The Queen is puzzled – 'What foes are they?' – as might be a reader of *Elizabeth and Essex*, the opera's source. Though the scene in the

Queen's dressing-room is in Strachey's book, Essex is given no such words – according to Strachey, all his troubles lie in Ireland. Britten and Plomer's Essex, the vulnerable self-destructive side of the artist, seems to be experiencing the kind of attack from 'the world' that Britten always felt the critics were making on him. It is too much for Essex, and this is the last we see of him in the opera, whereas the Queen immediately gets a grip on herself by means of another piece of occasional music, the Dressing Table Song, sung by the maids as they adorn her for the populace to behold. In the next scene another kind of public music is ingeniously introduced, for Essex's attempt at rebellion is narrated by a ballad singer in the street, accompanied on a gittern. Perhaps Britten is suggesting that a headstrong artist like Essex will eventually engender nothing more than this musical doggerel, inspired by his fall. Or perhaps he is saying the opposite, that even at our lowest and most foolish moments we can create some form of art.

One might expect her destruction of Essex to arouse in the Queen the sort of passion which Billy's destruction possibly arouses in Vere, but Elizabeth is not really annihilating another human being. The 'public' aspect of the artist is suppressing another part of his or her own artistic personality, the vulnerable, human and impetuous side. Elizabeth has already made it clear earlier in the scene that it is one side of herself that she is destroying when she sends Essex to the scaffold: 'I am, and am not; freeze, and yet I burn; / Since from myself my other self I turn.' Once the deed is done she is left in the Epilogue to the opera 'standing alone in a strong light against an indeterminate background. Time and place are becoming less and less important to her' (so reads the stage direction). Having destroyed all that is human and fallible in himself or herself, the artist can only survive by being utterly detached from time, place and other people. It is not a happy prospect, and it is notable that in the Epilogue, Elizabeth speaks rather than sings – and other voices are heard speaking to her as the final years of her reign are sketched impressionistically. Like Grimes she has gone beyond music, though she does sing two phrases from Essex's second lute song – a sad admission, now that it is too late, that she has destroyed the real artist and left only a husk, the public figure. *Gloriana* may have been intended by Britten as a celebration of impregnability, a powerful argument in support of ruthlessness in the artist, but in the end he concedes the impossibility of artistic achievement without human warmth.

*

Lord Harewood describes the gala first night of *Gloriana* as

> one of the great disasters of operatic history. The audience ...
> applauded if at all with their kid gloves on and the press, critics as well
> as journalists, gathered next day to castigate composer, performance,
> and choice ... it was clear that some sort of simple-minded glorifica-
> tion was what had been expected, not the passionate, tender drama ...
> that Ben had contrived.

Certainly the audience was difficult. Joan Cross, on stage, noticed two
grandes dames asleep against each other in the front stalls, and Pears said
it was like performing to an empty auditorium. One report describes a
'faint drizzle' of applause at the end, and at a party afterwards the opera
was jokingly referred to as 'Boriana' or 'Yawniana'. The journal *Musical
Opinion* quipped 'Sic transit *Gloriana*'. However, when the curtain had
risen for Act III scene 2 spontaneous clapping broke out for John Piper's
set – Philip Hope-Wallace described Piper's designs as 'witty, dry, ellip-
tical sketches of Tudor ostentation' – and there was enough applause at
the final curtain for Britten and Plomer to take a bow alongside John
Pritchard and John Cranko. Nor were the critics as uniformly harsh as
Harewood suggests.

Certainly there were unfavourable reviews. Ernest Newman in the
Sunday Times wrote: 'The bulk of the music is hardly more than pastiche, sometimes very clever pastiche, sometimes not so clever ... In
general the music seems to me to fall far below the level we have come to
expect from a composer of Mr Britten's gifts.' Martin Cooper in the
Spectator on 12 June, judging the opera on the vocal score and the radio
broadcast of the first night, wrote: 'My impression is that Britten has ...
fulfilled his commission with brilliant success.' But Richard Capell in the
Daily Telegraph on 13 June asserted that Britten had written 'uneasily
nervous, ungenerous music', and Martin Cooper repeated this very
phrase in his second review of *Gloriana*, in the *Spectator* on 19 June,
written after he had seen the opera (and had obviously read Capell's
piece too): 'the emotional drama ... finds expression in thin-blooded,
nervous, ungenerous music that teases and irritates, instead of satisfying
ear and heart'.

Frank Howes in *The Times* thought the opposite: 'In the music Britten
has dealt with a wider range of emotion than hitherto ... The librettist
has provided him with opportunity for gay, capricious, and ceremonious
music, upon which he has brought to bear his astonishingly fertile
resource and invention. What he has not quite commanded is the full-
blooded vigour of the age he set out to depict.' Desmond Shawe-Taylor

in the *New Statesman* hinted at the relevance of the opera's subject matter to Britten himself:

> For this royally commissioned opera the composer has had recourse to yet another librettist, William Plomer – his sixth, if we count the collaboration of Auden in the forgotten *Paul Bunyan*. This Tudor fickleness provides welcome evidence of discontent; nevertheless, if solid masterpieces are to be achieved, it is time to settle down. Can we look for a Catherine Parr in Plomer . . .?

Far from feeling – as Harewood says the critics felt – that the evening would have been better served by an innocuous pageant, Shawe-Taylor complained that the opera was 'more pageant than drama . . . Only now and again . . . are we emotionally affected'. Similarly Philip Hope-Wallace in the *Manchester Guardian* observed that as late as the ending of Act II 'one is still . . . wondering if the opera will ever "get off the ground"'. However, Andrew Porter in *Music and Letters* judged it 'a work of great imagination and power . . . an opera remarkable for its truth to history, for its effect in the theatre and for the unfailing interest of its music'. Most critics in the musical journals came to the same opinion.

The sort of rebuke which Harewood describes came not from reviewers but in the correspondence columns of *The Times*, where Dr Marie Stopes (an unlikely commentator on opera) alleged that there was 'public resentment, intense and widespread' at the 'inharmonious and wearisome' *Gloriana*, in which there were 'at least two scenes profoundly affronting the glorious memory of Queen Elizabeth I, hence unsuitable for public performance before Queen Elizabeth II'. A resident of Aldeburgh wrote to complain about the waste of public money, but while Woodrow Wyatt said he had gone to Covent Garden 'prepared to be bored or worse', he had decided that 'money has been well spent'. Anthony Lewis, then Professor of Music at Birmingham University, praised the 'superb richness and invention' of the score. There was also a letter from Vaughan Williams, who said he refused to judge *Gloriana* 'after a single hearing', but observed that 'for the first time in history' an English sovereign had commissioned an opera by a British composer, and that must be entirely to the good.

Auden was in England on a visit, and went to see a performance of *Gloriana*. Afterwards he wrote to Elizabeth Mayer that it had 'some of the best operatic music in it, I think, that Ben has done yet . . . Didn't care for the libretto and neither Joan Cross nor Peter should sing any more on the stage.' Auden went to Aldeburgh in the same month as the *Gloriana* première to lecture at the Festival, but suspected that he would not 'be able to have a real talk' with Britten. Sure enough he told Elizabeth Mayer after the visit: 'Everyone was charming, but I was never allowed to see Ben alone – I feared as much, still, I was a bit sad.' Stephen Spender believes that after seeing one of Britten's operas – most likely *Gloriana*, though it may have been *Billy Budd*, which William Walton alleged that Auden had seen in Paris in 1952 and had described as 'absolutely the end' – Auden sent Britten a letter including praise but also criticisms. Spender says that Britten sent it back, torn to pieces. Certainly after their 1953 meeting at Aldeburgh, Britten would have nothing further to do with Auden. 'We'd invite Ben to dinner from time to time when Auden was staying with us,' says Spender, 'but Ben *never* appeared – he always got ill.' Spender adds that Auden was 'very deeply hurt' by this, and others of Auden's friends recall him saying in later years that in the course of his life he had only lost one friend, obviously meaning Britten, though he was too loyal to name him.

Auden's friend, patron of the dance, Lincoln Kirstein, asked in a 1991 interview about the break between Auden and Britten, said: 'it was what seemed Ben's lack of daring, his desire to be The Establishment that irritated Wystan most; the playing it safe, settling for amiability as a guard against his queerity, but insisting on the innocence of adolescence as if this was a courageous attitude.'

*

Britten's letters following the *Gloriana* première did not give the impression that he was too downcast. He wrote to Plomer: 'I expect that you, like me, have felt a bit kicked around over it – perhaps *more* than me, because I'm a bit more used to the jungle! But the savageness of the wild beasts is always a shock.' He said that the opera had been 'an enormous success' at the box office, and would be repeated at Covent Garden the following year (in fact it had to wait thirteen years before it was next seen on stage). Despite this apparent resilience, Harewood realized that Britten was 'mortified' by the public reaction to *Gloriana*. He confided to Harewood 'that he had received a broadside from Peter – did not the reception confirm his worst fears? Should they not in future stick to the public that wanted them, the loyal Aldeburgh friends, and not get mixed up with something that was none of their concern? Ben was in the mood to take his advice.'

Walter Hussey, who went down to Aldeburgh to preach at the 1953 Festival service, saw him in black mood. After church they went to Crag House for lunch.

Peter came in before lunch and said, 'Ben won't be in to lunch, if you wouldn't mind carrying on on your own. He's just a bit worried. But if he *does* come, take no notice at all – but I'm sure he won't.' So we all sat down to lunch . . . And we were having a discussion on the parable of the talents [which Harewood had read as a lesson during the service]. Suddenly the door opened and in came Ben, looking like death . . . And he never said a word . . . And we went on busily discussing the talents and almost forgot him. Then suddenly we were interrupted by a hysterical voice from the other end of the table. 'It's those who have no talents at all – they're the real problem!' And of course we were absolutely silenced . . . I said, 'meaning yourself, Ben?' And he said in the same hysterical tone: 'There are times when I feel I have no talents – no talents at all!' And so again, a great silence. Then I leant forward and said, 'You know, Ben, when you're in this mood we love you best of all.' And he simply gave a great shout. 'I hate you, Walter!' From that moment, he was entirely all right! It was very strange: a tremendous tension built up, and then it was like lancing a boil. After that he chatted and was friendly and went off and gave a marvellous concert.

7: A sort of spiritual corruption

Britten's behaviour at lunch that day may have been caused by the public response to *Gloriana*, but since he had to give a concert after the meal it is just as likely to have been a manifestation of performance nerves, which were getting worse as he grew older. As a young man he had seemed to have complete self-confidence as a performer, playing his Piano Concerto at the Proms almost before he had had time to learn it. After his return from America that confidence had seemed to evaporate. Lord Harewood recalls that during the 1949 Britten–Pears tour of the USA

> Schoenberg came to his dressing room at the interval of a concert that Ben was conducting, something which away from Aldeburgh always crippled him with nerves, and was turned away from the door by an attendant who assured him – correctly, I am certain – that the maestro was in the bathroom being sick. Schoenberg put it down to drink rather than nerves and, the least charitable of letter-writers, conveyed as much to Erwin [Stein].

The performance nerves were not only experienced away from Aldeburgh. Isador Caplan (Britten's solicitor) was astonished by 'the bouts of nerves he had in the Jubilee Hall before a recital, accompanying Peter, though half the people in the audience he knew by sight, if not by name!'

George Malcolm was not particularly surprised by Britten's anxiety before keyboard-playing – 'most of us get that way' – and believes it was partly because 'Ben was an instinctive rather than a scientific pianist'. Britten told Imogen Holst

> how he'd once been playing Mozart with Clifford [Curzon], (presumably the D major [Sonata for Two Pianos]) and when it was over Clifford had been thrilled and had insisted on taking his chair and

sitting by Ben's piano and asking him how he'd done certain phrases, and when he asked him how he'd fingered something Ben not only didn't know but was physically incapable of playing the passage in order to find out!

Britten's next composition after *Gloriana* – his only work between it and *The Turn of the Screw*, which he was already planning – was his first song-cycle for Pears since *The Holy Sonnets of John Donne*. They gave its first performance together at Harewood House on 8 October 1953, as part of the Leeds Festival. *Winter Words*, a setting of eight poems by Thomas Hardy (whose verse Britten had known and admired for some while) is a transitional work between the 'public' territory of *Gloriana* and the landscape of his next opera.

The first song, 'At Day-Close in November', was probably intended by Hardy as a sketch of the transitory nature of existence, with the tall pines, tossing their dark heads against the autumn sky, reminding us that there was 'A time when no tall trees grew here', and that 'none will in time be seen'. However, for Britten the crucial lines in this poem may have been 'I set every tree in my June time, / And now they obscure the sky', a suggestion of an increasing obsession, once apparently innocent, which has now mastered the personality. The second song, 'Midnight on the Great Western', set to childish train-whistle and clanking-wheels music, has obviously been selected because Hardy's 'journeying boy', travelling alone to some unknown destination, is a wonderfully clear symbol of innocence in a corrupt world, 'This region of sin that you find you in, / But are not of'. Similarly the perky 'Wagtail and Baby' is a bitter little parable showing that sin comes only from human beings, not from the remainder of the living world – the baby watches the wagtail drinking placidly despite the passing by of all manner of terrifying beasts (bull, stallion, mongrel), but it flees when 'A perfect gentleman' approaches. As to the fourth song, 'The Little Old Table', Britten may have selected it because it is a hinge between the childlike and the adult. The piano depicts the creaking table as if this were a nursery song, but the table was a gift with an ulterior motive: 'she looked at me with a thought / that I did not understand'.

Winter Words is like the *Serenade* in reverse, for its first half sketches corruption and its second innocence. The fifth song, 'The Choirmaster's Burial', reminds us that the simple (the village choir) are frequently wiser than the sophisticated (the vicar). 'Proud Songsters' is a vigorous imper-sonation of the exuberance of the very young ('brand-new birds of twelve-months' growing'), and 'At the Railway Station, Upway' has the piano mimicking the open strings of 'the boy with a violin' as he plays to a convict who symbolizes experience and the extent to which adults are imprisoned by their own natures – 'The man in the handcuffs'. If we are still in any doubt as to the meaning of *Winter Words*, Britten spells it out in his final choice from Hardy, 'Before Life and After': 'A time there was . . . / Before the birth of consciousness, / When all went well . . . / But the disease of feeling germed, / And primal rightness took the tinct of wrong . . . – lines that would serve almost as well as Yeats's 'The Second Coming' as epigraph for *The Turn of the Screw*.

*

The new opera arose out of the idea that the EOG might make a film. 'There were two film possibilities,' recalls Eric Crozier.

> After *Peter Grimes*, Gabriel Pascal got in touch with Britten, and wanted to make a film of it . . . Later on, when we started the English Opera Group, Ben and John Piper and I thought of making a film as a way of raising money to finance our future projects. We hadn't got any particular subject at that time. It was simply that we felt we could get support from Michael Balcon [the film producer], who was interested in us.

While this idea was in the air, the EOG organized a gala fund-raising performance of a film of *The Tales of Hoffman*. Piper's wife, Myfanwy, was among those in the audience. She says she 'really rather hated' the style of the Offenbach film,

> and I remember meeting Peter in the foyer and saying 'If Ben's got to do a film, why doesn't he look at *The Turn of the Screw*?' And because we were all busy, no more was said. And then some time later Ben was casting about for something to do, and Peter said he'd just re-read *The Turn of the Screw*, and he remembered that I'd suggested it.

Britten had heard Henry James's novella dramatized on the radio in 1932 – 'a wonderful impressive but terribly eerie & scarey play', he wrote in his diary. He read it the following January: 'glorious & eerie . . . An incredible masterpiece'. This opinion was not shared by William Plomer, who said he had 'never been a James fan', and, coming from South Africa where a vigorous belief in the supernatural was widespread, found James's northern European hauntings rather namby-pamby. Plomer only said this after Myfanwy Piper had completed the libretto of the new opera, so it may have been motivated by jealousy. Britten had once again changed librettists.

Myfanwy Evans, born in 1911 of an English mother and a Welsh father (a London pharmacist), was educated at the North London Collegiate

School and at St Hugh's College, Oxford, where she read English. John Betjeman, whom she came to know through his work with John Piper on the *Architectural Review* and the *Shell Guides*, fantasized about her schoolgirl and undergraduate days in a pair of poems, 'Myfanwy' and 'Myfanwy at Oxford', published in 1940:

> ... a
> Willowy figure with lips apart,
> Strong and willowy, strong to pillow me,
> Gold Myfanwy, kisses and art.

(She says that the poems are 'all wrong' factually.) After Oxford she worked for the Times Book Club and held an evening class in writing at Morley College. In 1935 she and John Piper went to live in the farmhouse near Henley which remained their home thereafter, and she married him when he became divorced from his first wife. She edited a journal of abstract art, and wrote on modern painting, but had to devote most of her time to her husband and their four children, born between 1938 and 1950. Britten had known her for many years and had often discussed libretto problems with her:

> I think he turned to me because, with the *Lucretias* and *Herrings* and the various things which John and I had been through with Ben, he often talked to us about the words. He'd say 'What am I to do here? I don't like this', and I was very much aware of the kind of things he didn't like. So although I hadn't got any qualifications for writing a libretto, it didn't disturb me.

The actual collaboration began informally: 'Ben said to me, "Would you try and think of a way it [*The Turn of the Screw*] might be done and then we might get someone in to write it." ... So I worked out a possible way, and then we began to work on it together, and there seemed no reason to ask anyone else.' She found him 'very easy to work with, because he knew what he wanted – he was quite definite'.

The EOG was now being managed by Basil Douglas, Pears's flatmate from Charlotte Street days, who had given up a BBC career to run it – 'I was so delighted to be of any service to Ben.' He had been sent out to Venice to obtain a commission for *The Turn of the Screw* from the festival committee which wanted a new Britten opera, and on his return to London was dismayed to be told by Britten, 'looking at me out of the corner of his eye', that it would have to be postponed for a year because of *Gloriana*. (Imogen Holst's diary records that he had hoped to be able to write it 'during the spring and summer of rehearsals and performances of *Gloriana*', but she realized that this was 'madness'.) The Venetian committee reluctantly agreed to the postponement, but as soon as *Gloriana* was out of the way there was a further threat.

At the end of October 1953, just as he should have been starting work on the James opera, Britten was ordered by his doctors to stop using his right arm. 'Yousee,' he wrote to E. M. Forster, typing with his left hand, 'i have had a horrid complaint boyling up for some time called BURSITIS [inflammation of a sac in his right shoulder]. All through the summer i have been fighting it, & trying this autumn to go on doing concerts as usual, but the doctors have at last put thier feet down – so herei am – at least 3 months without my moving the right arm.' The cause of the inflammation may have been his tenseness when conducting, but he may also have been frightened of beginning work on the opera. James's story of Miles and Flora, two children in a remote country house who may have been sexually corrupted by Peter Quint, a manservant, now dead, was bound to cause further murmurs among Britten's detractors. Anne Wood remarks that 'you never knew when these things would arise. There was always tension.' For example she recalls that William Parsons, who sang the vicar in the first production of *Albert Herring*, was highly critical of Britten and Pears behind their backs – 'the pacifism he couldn't stand, and the homosexuality'.

Britten's letters while he was suffering from bursitis give no indications of regret that he could not begin *The Turn of the Screw*. He found that he could write music with his left hand, but made no effort to start the opera. 'My arm, in spite of taking great care and following the doctors' instructions precisely, is not improving,' he reported on 2 December 1953, 'and it now looks as if I must go abroad for some weeks and give up all ideas of work until the trouble is cleared up.' He spent Christmas and the New Year in Germany as the guest of Prince Ludwig of Hesse and the Rhine, a cousin of Lord Harewood, and his British-born wife Margaret, née Geddes, always known as 'Peg'. Britten had been introduced to them by the Harewoods. Prince Ludwig ('Lu') had become engaged to his wife in the thirties before succeeding to the title. Their wedding was to be held in London, and five of his relatives, including the then Prince and his heir, were killed on their way to it, when their plane crashed at Ostend. 'We were married in black at St Peter's, Eaton Square,' says Peg Hesse, 'and then travelled to Germany with five coffins. I think Ben was gripped by the story of that. Lu was a poet, and the two of them understood each other as artists.'

'The German Xmas was very romantic,' Britten wrote to Myfanwy Piper from Schloss Wolfsgarten near Frankfurt, the Hesses' principal home,

very holy & serious, but inclined to be abit sloppy & 'heilige Nacht'
... I've been thinking & thinking about Act I & having lots of ideas.
I've got one idea about the school-room scene, which you may not like
but which we must discuss soon, as it affects the structure of the music.
I wonder if you have had a shot at the Ghosts dialogue, or have left it? I
know it's a corker, but I'm certain we are on the right track so far.

The Turn of the Screw was to be another chamber opera, with a mere six
singers and thirteen instrumentalists, yet with the première only nine
months away and the libretto not yet finished, Britten was setting himself
an even tighter schedule than for *Gloriana*.

By the end of January 1954 his right arm was 'definitely improving',
but he still seemed in no haste. A letter to Myfanwy Piper suggested
words that Miles might sing at the conclusion of Act I – 'You see, I *am*
bad, aren't I? – explaining: 'I like Miles last remark because it is clear,
bright, and in short phrases, which I think is right for the boy's character
and his manner of singing.' He was now contemplating the start of
composition. 'May be with luck I shall be penning the first notes of the
Henry James opera now provisionally called "The Tower and the Lake",'
he wrote to Anthony Gishford, who looked after his business affairs at
Boosey & Hawkes, on the same day (31 January) as the letter to
Myfanwy Piper. The new title referred to the particular places where the
ghosts of Peter Quint and Miss Jessel (a former governess) appear at Bly
(the country house in James's story). The libretto was finalized early in
February – the première was now only seven months away – and Britten
began to talk to George Malcolm, who conducted Westminster Cathedral choir, about how the right children might be discovered to play
Miles and his sister Flora. 'I am longing to get down to finding the right
notes,' he wrote to Myfanwy Piper on 16 February, but added that his
arm was still 'playing me up'.

A police witch-hunt against homosexuals was now taking place in
Britain. In October 1953 there had been rumours in the press that the
Home Secretary, Sir David Maxwell-Fyfe, wanted 'a new drive against
male vice' in the wake of the defection to Moscow in 1952 of Guy
Burgess and Donald Maclean, 'who were known to have pervert associates'. Maclean had been at Gresham's in Britten's time. In January
1954 Lord Montagu of Beaulieu, Michael Pitt-Rivers and Peter Wildeblood were arrested on charges arising from their association with two
working-class young men in the summer of 1952. (Montagu had already
been on trial for an alleged indecent attack on two Boy Scouts, but had
been acquitted.) The hearing began on 15 March 1954, and nine days

later Montagu was sent to prison for a year and Pitt-Rivers and Wilde-blood for eighteen months, even though there was no suggestion that the 'offences' had not been committed between consenting adults. (At this period, buggery still carried a maximum sentence of life imprisonment and 'gross indecency' two years. During 1953–6, 480 adult men in England and Wales were convicted of sexual offences with consenting adults in private.) Meanwhile on 15 January 1954 the editor of the *Evening Standard*, Percy Elland, had written to his proprietor Lord Beaverbrook: 'Scotland Yard are definitely stepping up their activities against the homosexuals. Some weeks ago they interviewed Benjamin Britten. This week I am told they have interviewed Cecil Beaton. No action is to be taken against either.'

*

Not until 30 March did Britten tell Myfanwy Piper: 'I started the opera this morning.' The première in Venice was to be in a little over five months' time.

His arm was still not right. A small operation on the bursal sac had been performed, and the after-effects were 'very painful', so that he was still writing with his left hand. But on this first day of work he reported 'quite good progress' with the first scene – there was as yet no Prologue. He and Myfanwy Piper were still uncertain about the opera's title. She had sent a list of suggestions, and he commented: 'I do not quite feel that we have arrived yet, although something to do with "Bly" is hopeful I think ... I must confess that I have a sneaking, horrid feeling that the original H[enry] J[ames] title describes the musical plan of the work *exactly*!!' James's title is taken from an observation in the conversation about ghost stories which precedes the tale proper: 'If the child [i.e. the involvement of a child in a ghost story] gives the effect another turn of the screw, what do you say to *two* children – ?' The 'musical plan' referred to is the cycle of keys through which the opera progresses, like a screw being gradually tightened. 'The new piece progresses in a *circular* direction,' Britten told Eric Walter White.

Basil Douglas, waiting anxiously to see if Britten could meet the almost impossible deadline, was 'brimming with admiration' for the speed at which he now worked, assisted by 'the great Imogen Holst machine'. As each scene was completed in composition sketch – the first took a mere two days – it was handed to Imogen, who made a fair-copy vocal score and posted it to London for reproduction in batches of six pages at a time. Soon Britten was handing her sections before he had completed scenes. 'It seemed incredible', she writes, 'that a composer could be so sure of what he wanted that he would risk parting with the beginning of a scene before he had written the end of it.'

By 12 April he had 'finished Scene 3' and was 'very pleased with it'. As usual, he was changing the libretto as he went along. 'The tune I have used is "Lavender's Blue" which fits very nicely,' he told Myfanwy Piper of the first nursery rhyme scene. Similarly the final text of the fifth scene, in which the children play teasingly at 'Tom, Tom the Piper's Son' – squealing 'Now chase me!' 'I'll catch you!' 'Let's do it again' – was his own work. The words were sent by him in a letter to Myfanwy Piper on 23 April.

Basil Coleman was again to be the producer. He came down to Aldeburgh, and he and Britten worried that the opera 'is going to be much too short' – the first three scenes occupied only ten minutes. Britten wrote to Myfanwy Piper suggesting 'a prologue?', perhaps based on the conversation about the story's provenance which opens James's novella – 'possibly spoken?' She replied that she was 'afraid a prologue would be repetitive' unless she rewrote the opening scene (which had already been set to music). Over the following weeks she 'tried various things'. Basil Douglas recalls that the Prologue underwent many alterations and 'was never right until the first performance'.

In another letter to his librettist (26 April) Britten reported Pears's suggestion that Mrs Grose, the housekeeper, should not state that Peter Quint had 'made free with everyone' – words used in the draft libretto.

> He feels that '*made free*' is too particular and suggestive, and that we should save this particular phrase until the beginning of the next page. James merely says 'Quint *was* too free with the boy'. I think the sexy suggestion should only refer to his relationship with Miss Jessel, don't you? Incidentally it may help to avert a scandal in Venice!

But he evidently relented when he set the scene, for Mrs Grose's words are: 'Quint, Peter Quint! The Master's valet. Left here in charge . . . I saw things . . . I did not like, when Quint was free with everyone, with little Master Miles! . . . Hours they spent together . . . He made free with her, too, with lovely Miss Jessel . . . He liked them pretty, I can tell you, Miss, and he had his will morning and night.' Pears was wrong to suggest that James's narrative does not imply a sexual relationship between Quint and the boy. 'Quint was much too free,' says Mrs Grose in the novella. 'Too free with *my* boy?' asks the Governess with 'a sudden sickness of disgust'. The housekeeper answers: 'Too free with every one!' A few paragraphs later James describes Quint as suffering from 'secret disorders, vices more than suspected', and when the matter is raised again in the next chapter Mrs Grose states: 'He did what he wished . . . with them all.'

Britten visited the Pipers in Oxfordshire in mid-May – John Piper was again to design the opera – and played through what he had written. 'I'm afraid it was a bad performance,' he wrote to Myfanwy afterwards, adding that he had been distracted by a thunderstorm. (She vividly remembers 'amazing crashes' accompanying Quint's calls to Miles.) On 28 May he hinted to her for the first time that he was nervous about his schedule: 'I hope to goodness there will be an opera ready in time for the Group to perform in Venice.' And to Basil Coleman the next day:

> I am so glad – much encouraged – that you like the way the Screw is Turning. I have never felt so insecure about a work . . . I wonder if you talked to Myfanwy about the churchyard scene? . . . we *must* have something light & gay here, something for the children to be young & charming in (for the last time, almost, in the work) – & I think the idea of the hymn (a kind of 'choir procession') to be the best yet thought of. Goodness – how *difficult* it is to write an opera with the librettist so far away! She is so good, but is so occupied with being a wife & mother.

The Aldeburgh Festival came round again, increasing the pressure on him: 'this is always a bad time,' he told Myfanwy Piper on 5 June, '& this year particularly bad (*two* major items were cancelled yesterday because of illness or so – & must be replaced!)' He and Pears performed *Winter Words*, and the EOG presented Lennox Berkeley's *A Dinner Engagement*. 'There are most lovely things in the piece, my dear, which give one enormous pleasure,' Britten wrote to Berkeley on 6 July. As to the *Screw*, 'wish me luck,' he told Berkeley; 'rehearsals start in a month & I have 5 scenes still to write – O Law!'

*

Why did Myfanwy Piper, who first suggested James's story as the basis of a Britten opera, believe it might be the right subject for him? 'I just thought it was. I knew he was interested in the effect of adult, or bad, ideas on the innocence of children. I also thought it was densely musical prose, which would suit his work.'

James himself had been inclined to make light of the story – 'the thing is essentially a pot-boiler and a *jeu d'esprit*', he wrote to H. G. Wells. But Siegfried Sassoon told William Plomer, who told Britten (in 1964), that 'when Henry James was asked what construction should be put upon *The T of the S*, he said, "The worst possible construction"'. The 'pot-boiler' remark was probably an attempt to distract attention from the story's sexuality – James himself was homosexually inclined. Perhaps the hope of disguising this lies also behind the novella's frequent hints that the ghosts who have supposedly corrupted the children do not exist but are only hallucinations in the mind of the Governess who is narrating.

Lord Harewood discussed this point with Britten when he was planning the opera: 'Ben and I argued about the haunting; had it to be explicit, or could it be the product of the Governess's paranoia – *she* was convinced that something was wrong, but was it really? I insisted on ambivalence, he on the need for the composer to make a decision – and he *had* taken one: that the haunting was real.' However, Myfanwy Piper does not accept that this was necessarily Britten's interpretation of James; 'I don't think Ben really took sides.' The important point to him was 'that evil exists whether in life or in the mind . . . and is capable . . . of causing the loss of innocence'.

Besides being structured on a 'circular' pattern of keys, *The Turn of the Screw* is built on a theme which uses all twelve notes of the chromatic scale (generally referred to as the Screw theme). This does not mean that the opera was written according to the twelve-note serialist system invented by Schoenberg. A decade after composing the new opera, Britten remarked that serialism

> has simply never attracted me as a method, although I respect many composers who have worked in it, and love some of their works. It is beyond me to say why, except that I cannot feel that tonality is outworn, and find many serial 'rules' arbitrary. 'Socially' I am seriously disturbed by its limitations. I can see it taking no part in the music-lover's music-making. Its methods make writing *gratefully* for voices or instruments an impossibility, which inhibits amateurs and young children.

In *The Story of Music*, a lavishly illustrated book for children published in 1958 under the nominal authorship of Britten and Imogen Holst, but in fact written chiefly by the latter, who submitted her drafts to Britten for approval and correction, it is remarked of twelve-note music: 'It is impossible for anyone to say whether this is to be the recognised music of the second half of the twentieth century . . . Some think that it does not matter what style a composer chooses to write in, as long as he has something definite to say and says it clearly.'

The fact that children were to play a vital part in *The Turn of the Screw*, and must be able to sing their music with confidence and understanding, probably helped to dictate its ostensibly simple and accessible musical style. However, Britten wrote to Erwin Stein while planning it: 'I think it was [Donald] Mitchell who made the observation that the easier my music gets the more difficult it is to understand it.' Mitchell says of this: 'In fact, it was Ben who made this remark to me, at a rehearsal of *Gloriana*. Nor did he recollect what he did say quite accurately, which

Top Pears as Peter Grimes and Joan Cross as Ellen Orford. She and her fellow directors of Sadler's Wells knew *Peter Grimes* was 'a major work', but she 'really didn't know' what the opera was about.
(*Angus MacBean*)

Left Pears as Peter Grimes with the original Apprentice, Leonard Thompson, at the première in June 1945. 'Ben . . . had this wonderful gift of communication,' says Thompson, recalling his friendship with Britten.
(*Angus MacBean*)

Britten at the Old Mill in 1946 with the
pre-war Rolls Royce bought after the
success of *Peter Grimes*.
(*George Rodger*)

Britten at Glyndebourne in the summer
of 1946 with two members of the cast of
The Rape of Lucretia, (left to right)
Margaret ('Mab') Ritchie and Anna
Pollak. Pollak worked for Britten for
another eighteen years and was then, as
she puts it, 'sacked'. In 1947 Ritchie
became anxious about Britten's
friendship with the boy actor
David Spenser.

Top   Pears and Britten perform in the drawing-room at Crag House, Aldeburgh, Britten's home from 1947. Listening are (left to right) Ronald Duncan, librettist of *The Rape of Lucretia*, and the young composer Arthur Oldham, for a while Britten's amanuensis and composition pupil. He calls Britten 'an immensely good man'.

Above   A similar scene at 3 Oxford Square, the London house bought by Pears in 1946. The picture was probably taken to publicize the founding of the English Opera Group, in which (left to right) John Piper, Eric Crozier and Joan Cross were principal figures along with Britten and Pears.

Top English Opera Group production team for *Albert Herring* at Glyndebourne in the summer of 1947. (Left to right) Pears, who was singing Albert; Nancy Evans, singing Nancy; Eric Crozier, librettist; John Piper, designer; Frederick Ashton, producer; Britten, composer. Ashton is said to have 'really felt quite vexed by their cliqueishness'.

Above The three children in *Albert Herring* (1947). (Left to right) Anne Sharp (Cis), David Spenser (Harry), and Lesley Duff (Emmie). Duff, the mother of David and Steuart Bedford, was 'distraught' when she later lost the part because she looked too old. Spenser was the first child performer in a Britten opera to be closely befriended by the composer. (*Angus MacBean*)

Top Britten wrote in 1940: 'I always make a resolution never to attend any more first performances . . . I make everyone all round me uncomfortable, by feeling sick.' This photograph shows that he would not go into Aldeburgh parish church for the first performance of *Saint Nicolas*, at the opening concert of the first Aldeburgh Festival, on 5 June 1948, but stayed outside in the churchyard with his librettist Eric Crozier, listening from a distance.

Above A photograph to publicize the second Aldeburgh Festival in 1949. H. W. ('Tommy') Cullum, the local bank manager who was Festival treasurer, rings the bell, while Elizabeth Sweeting, first Festival manager, and conductor Norman Del Mar look on. Early Festivals are remembered as being 'like a family affair'.

Right Britten conducts an English Opera Group rehearsal in Holland in the late forties, with assistant conductor Ivan Clayton at his elbow. Eric Crozier is at the desk behind. (*Maria Austria, Particam*)

Below E. M. Forster, Britten and Ronald Duncan on the marshes near Aldeburgh. In 1948 Britten wrote that it was 'possible that E. M. Forster . . . will collaborate with Eric [Crozier] & me on the next opera . . . which is a dazzling prospect'. (*Kurt Hutton*)

Left Britten and Eric Crozier during the writing of *Billy Budd*. Crozier had enjoyed Britten's 'close and genuine affection' for several years, but now began to feel that 'Ben was done with me and that we could not work together again.' (*Kurt Hutton*)

Below Crozier and Forster at work on the libretto of *Billy Budd*. Crozier wondered 'whether a big opera could be done . . . with no women involved', but Forster's 'great enthusiasm' carried them along. (*Kurt Hutton*)

Top Forster, Britten and Crozier on a hot day at Crag House. The beach huts run by the Burrell family are just beyond the garden wall. (*Kurt Hutton*)

Above Forster and Britten watch as young Robin Long, Britten's 'little fisherboy friend ("the Nipper")', is held spellbound by Billy Burrell, in whose boat they are being photographed for *Picture Post* in the summer of 1949. (*Kurt Hutton*)

Top   Another shot from the *Picture Post* boat trip. Billy Burrell recalls that Britten 'wanted more or less to adopt' the Nipper. (*Kurt Hutton*)

Above   Theodor Uppman as Billy Budd and Pears as Captain Vere at Covent Garden, December 1951. (*Roger Wood*)

Top   George and Marion, Earl and Countess of Harewood, with Britten at the opera at Wiesbaden, 1952. (*Hans Scheffer*)

Above   Lord Harewood, organizer of the 'Coronation opera' scheme, talks to William Plomer, librettist of *Gloriana*. On either side of Plomer sit Harewood's father-in-law and Britten's publisher, Erwin Stein, and Imogen Holst. (*Roger Wood*)

Top   Imogen Holst, Britten's devoted music assistant for a decade, beginning with
Gloriana. 'She kissed the ground that he walked on,' says Billy Burrell.
(*Kurt Hutton*)

Above   Norman Del Mar flanked on the left by Britten, and on the right by
Joan Cross and Pears. 'I was Ben's conductor', says Del Mar, 'but that I should
actually be able to challenge him on his own territory – no, that didn't do.'

Right Pears as Essex and Joan Cross as Elizabeth in the dressing-room scene in *Gloriana*.

Below Britten and Pears at Crag House with the librettist of *The Turn of the Screw*, Myfanwy Piper, and two of her children. 'I hadn't got any qualifications for writing a libretto,' she says, but 'there seemed no reason to ask anyone else'.

Left In Venice for *The Turn of the Screw*. (Left to right) Erwin Stein, Britten, Sofie Stein, Basil Coleman (producer), and Pears.

Below Some of the *Screw* team at 'grumble corner' in Venice. (Left to right) John Piper, Britten, Pears, Myfanwy Piper, Clarissa and Edward Piper, and Basil Douglas (English Opera Group manager). (*Erich Auerbach; Hulton-Deutsch Picture Company*)

Top David Hemmings, the original Miles in *The Turn of the Screw*. 'Of all the people I have worked with', says Hemmings, 'I count my relationship with Ben to have been one of the finest . . . And it was never, under any circumstances, threatening. (*Maria Austria, Particam*)

Above 'Peter Quint, you devil!' Pears, David Hemmings and Jennifer Vyvyan in the original production of *The Turn of the Screw*. (*Denis De Marney*)

Top   Stephen Reiss, manager of the Aldeburgh Festival from 1955 (with Imogen Holst in the background). Anne Wood warned him not to commit himself totally to Britten, but for many years he 'loved every minute' of the job.

Above   Roger Duncan and his sister Briony. Britten asked Ronald Duncan if he could 'share' his son with him.

Top Britten and Pears performing in a television studio in Tokyo during their 1955–6 Far Eastern tour.

Above Pears, the Prince and Princess of Hesse ('Lu' and 'Peg'), and Britten, in traditional costume during their 1956 visit to Bali.

was this: "The simpler I make my music, the more difficult it becomes to perform." His revised version is far more interesting and revealing!'

*

The opera opens with the Prologue that was added as an afterthought, which describes the Governess's commission from the children's guardian in London. The duration of this is less than three minutes, so Britten's claim that it was needed to lengthen the opera may be questioned. Its real function seems to be to provide a frame for the action, like the Prologue to *Peter Grimes*, the use of the Male and Female Chorus in *The Rape of Lucretia*, and the Prologue and Epilogue to *Billy Budd*. The effect is that of a distancing device, which provides a preparation and a warning before we enter the enclosed worlds of these operas.

In the first scene proper, the Governess, journeying to Bly in a coach, imagines her new charges as fairy-tale innocents: 'Poor babies, no father, no mother. But I shall love them as I love my own . . .' However, the excited timpani figure which accompanies her – faintly recalling Tarquinius's journey to Lucretia's bedroom – suggests that something menacing is in store for her. Sure enough, when Miles and Flora appear, Britten makes the two nursery rhymes they sing seem distinctly sinister. 'Lavender's Blue' has a rather disconcerting artificial prettiness, achieved (as Peter Evans points out) by setting its diatonic tune in the middle of a scene which is otherwise chromatic, while, in a later scene, 'Tom, Tom the Piper's Son', with its bass line in another key from the melody and the ecstatic harp glissandi which follow each verse, suggests more than mere nursery games. (Jonathan Miller's 1979 production of the opera hinted, in this scene, at incest between the children.) Nevertheless the Governess ignores these signs, and when a letter comes dismissing Miles from school on account of some mysterious and unspecified wickedness, she persuades Mrs Grose that 'The child is an angel.' Britten may be mocking his own inclination to regard childhood as an unsullied Eden.

Each scene in *The Turn of the Screw* is preceded by a short orchestral interlude, a variation on the Screw theme, which establishes the scene's musical colour. Following the arrival of the letter, the orchestra takes us into the woods around Bly, with woodwind bird-calls based, as Christopher Palmer has observed, on the pentatonic scale. We can assume from Britten's use of it here to depict the woodland birds that he intends it, in the musical language of this opera, to stand for the natural world, the right and proper order of things (like the natural harmonics on the horn in the *Serenade*). The bird-song interlude leads into a scene by the tower, which opens with the Governess, still backed by pentatonic bird-song, admiring the beauty of the setting: 'How beautiful it is . . . The birds fly home to these great trees.' It is now that the ghost of Quint first appears, standing on the tower (James's use of tower and lake as male and female symbols are retained in the opera).

Quint's presence is indicated by the sound of the celesta, an instrument only once before heard in Britten's music – in Grimes's hut, when the boy has fallen down the cliff and Grimes has descended after him. From that context we might assume that despite its 'celestial' associations the instrument means for Britten a *fall*, perhaps a specifically sexual fall. This would explain its use for Quint, whose relationship with Miles begins, so to speak, where Grimes's with the apprentice left off. Yet the instrument is playing sets of notes which belong to the pentatonic scale. Indeed, as Christopher Palmer writes, '*all* its music' in the opera – and it only plays when Quint is present – belongs to this scale. Why are we apparently being told that Quint belongs to the natural order?

Palmer's answer is that Britten is being ironic, and has given Quint 'good' music because the opera deliberately inverts the 'natural' musical order in order to heighten the sense of evil (and to avoid cliché in portraying wickedness). Another critic, Clifford Hindley, believes that there is no irony, and that Britten simply means us to regard Quint's seduction of Miles as natural – that 'the situation with which they are associated is essentially one of beauty and goodness'. Both Palmer's and Hindley's interpretations ignore the fact that, while Quint's music is pentatonic, it is also full of harmonic clashes. *Two* pentatonic scales are played simultaneously by the celesta when he first appears, in G flat and G major, a collision of a semitone, which in Britten's harmonic language always suggests some sort of tension or contradiction. Later in the opera, the clashes in Quint's celesta music are less violent (G flat and C, and in the night scene when the ghosts call to the children G flat and A flat), but it is never unequivocally 'natural'.

There can be little doubt, however, that Britten wishes us to consider with open minds the moral balance between Quint and his rival for Miles's love, the Governess. The melisma (a group of notes sung to a single syllable) with which Quint seductively calls Miles's name in the night scene may seem like an oriental charm, but it has its origin in a piece of medieval church music, a setting of *Beata Viscera* by Perotin, sung by Pears in Aldeburgh Church a few months before Britten composed *The Turn of the Screw* – Lord Harewood has pointed out the resemblance. There is no reason to doubt the Governess's assertion that 'things have been done here that are not good' (her words are accompanied by semitonal clashes). But Britten evidently does not regard Quint as a black villain like Claggart, rather as a set of natural impulses which have led to disaster because they are incompatible with each other, like the two clashing pentatonic scales. One would guess that he is thinking of the love of children and the sexual impulse.

The Governess's own musical identity is surprisingly tied up with Quint's. When in her first scene she sings 'Oh why, why did I come?' it is to a series of notes we will eventually recognize as a weaker version of Quint's 'Miles' melisma night call. Evidently Britten believes that she and Quint have the same intentions at heart – the possession of Miles – and are maybe ultimately the same person, or the same set of desires, ostensibly divided, like Claggart and Vere, Elizabeth and Essex, into two personalities.

The ambiguity in these two central characters is found equally in Britten's portrayal of Miles himself. (Flora seems little more than a reflection of the boy, just as Miss Jessel lacks independent identity and is simply an aspect of Quint.) Myfanwy Piper writes that it was Britten himself who found Miles's Latin mnemonic-rhyme in 'an old-fashioned Latin grammar that an aunt of mine produced':

> *Malo*, I would rather be,
> *Malo*, in an apple tree,
> *Malo*, than a naughty boy,
> *Malo*, in adversity.

(Tippett remarks that what fascinated him in *The Turn of the Screw* was Britten's device of 'using one thing for each scene – the piano-playing, or Latin verbs, and so on'.) The accompaniment to this rhyme is a series of major triads, suggesting that Miles is still pure and 'natural', yet his vocal line is based on Quint's celesta music. Myfanwy Piper describes Miles as 'inexperienced and innocent', but Jonathan Gathorne-Hardy, who knew Britten well in the forties and fifties, observes that 'Miles seems a male Lolita'. Certainly the boy's hypnotic responses as Quint calls to him in the night scene – 'I'm here, O I'm here' – suggest compliance. Act I concludes with him stating – 'simply', says the instruction in the vocal score – 'You see – I am bad, I am bad, aren't I?'

If Britten had indeed experienced sexual abuse at school, then his portrayal of Miles might be another stage in his coming to terms with it. Yet any self-portraiture in the opera is rather to be found in the Governess and Quint. During the period between *Peter Grimes* and *The Turn of the Screw*, Britten had displayed characteristics of both of them in his own relationships with children.

*

In the original production of *Albert Herring* at Glyndebourne in 1947 the part of the boy Harry was played by thirteen-year-old David Spenser. He and his mother and brother had come to England in 1940 from Ceylon, where David had been born and where his father remained. David began to work as a child actor in radio and the West End, and was noticed by Nancy Evans during a broadcast of Honegger's *Joan of Arc*. He auditioned for Britten, and though untrained as a singer was judged an adequate Harry. He was dark and good-looking in a slightly oriental way.

David Spenser describes the Glyndebourne rehearsals as 'a golden summer, and everyone without fail was terribly nice to me'. He stayed with the EOG during the trip to Holland and Lucerne, and it was now that 'Peter and Ben became terribly sweet, and used to go out swimming with me in the afternoon. Peter taught me how to dive between their legs – it was totally harmless, just a game; the old arch thing, and you went under.' His mother came on the European tour, and he had a chaperon on the English tour which followed, but Anne Wood, managing the EOG, began to be concerned about Britten's growing friendship with the boy. 'I made it my business to interfere, going in and out of rooms. I was very worried. I just prayed we would get through with it but I often wondered whether we would. And David Spenser's mother was a most extraordinary woman!' David himself confirms this: 'I must be fair to somebody who was struggling financially, but she was certainly very aware that her sons were not unattractive. I mean, she'd have sold either my brother or me to the nearest bidder!'

Joan Cross, singing Lady Billows in *Albert Herring*, noticed that Margaret ('Mab') Ritchie, playing the schoolmistress Miss Wordsworth, made it her job off-stage as well as on to look after her boy pupil. 'And she was horrified really – he got a lot of attention from Ben.' David himself remembers Mab Ritchie's concern for him, though he thought nothing of it at the time, and also recalls Britten taking him out to tea in Lucerne and telling him 'that certain women had said I was taking advantage of my position' – again he did not understand what was meant.

After the tour, Mab Ritchie called on Eric Crozier in the EOG London office. 'She was a remarkable character,' he says, 'an ardent Christian Scientist' – she had sung for Mrs Britten and the Musical Society in Lowestoft – 'and she came to ask me, could I use my influence with Ben to stop him using small boys in his operas? She felt it was a moral duty to try and protect these small creatures from a danger that she foresaw.' Meanwhile, between the European and English tours of *Albert Herring*, in the late summer of 1947, Britten invited David Spenser to stay for a few nights at Aldeburgh, where he had just moved into Crag House.

'Peter wasn't there,' recalls David. 'Ben was alone, and that was the reason we had to share the same bedroom, because the house wasn't ready. He said that Peter might come back during the night, and might need his own room, so we shared the double bed in Ben's room.'

Nothing happened between them, and next morning David was 'conscious enough' that it was unusual 'to write to my mother' to say that they had shared the bed, 'so it must have stuck out in my mind that it wasn't what I was expecting. But also the very fact that I wrote that to my mother would mean that I had no personal guilt.'

David Spenser describes himself as sexually a very knowing child by that age. 'Not having a father around, my brother and I had the facts of life explained to us by every well-meaning male that my mother came across.' Moreover 'the odd naughty parish priest' had sometimes gone 'a little too far' with him. 'I mean, nobody ever did anything disastrous: I never lost my virginity or anything. But certain people's hands were exploratory, and then you had to say, "Please sir, I don't like that." But I can't truly remember ever having to say that to Ben.' There were, however, hugs, cuddles and kisses.

I mean, if he were sitting, he would put his arm round me if he was looking at the same book, or looking to see what I was reading. The cuddle was like a protective 'I'm here, and everything's all right', nothing beyond that. The cuddle last thing at night said slightly more. And I would have thought that had he done that when we were in bed, I would have remembered it. He didn't do that when we were actually in the same bed. He used to kiss me goodnight – he kissed me on the mouth, but not a lingering, long kiss (I didn't have real kisses until I was nearly twenty). It seemed natural, and it wasn't to the point where you said, 'Please don't do that.' There was something very chaste about him; he was like a school prefect.

Anne Wood had been worried about Britten's interest in David Spenser partly 'from Peter's point of view. One could just see cracks in the relationship, and that seemed so important it was a pity.' After David's first visit to Crag House, Britten wrote to Pears, on 4 September 1947:

Little David went off yesterday morning – rather sadly, poor thing. His home life is hell, but I think his existance [*sic*] has been made a little brighter by being treated properly for a few days. Barbara was very sweet to him, & he poured out his heart to me – rather self consciously, but the old feelings were genuine, I'm sure.

David Spenser does not know what Britten meant by 'the old feelings', but guesses that it was the warmth and trust he demonstrated by talking to Britten about 'my not quite ecstatic home life ... I very very rarely talked about my mother. I had an over-developed sense of loyalty.'

He remembers that he showed Britten a bruise made by his mother, and when on a later visit to Crag House he mentioned that a man had made sexual advances to him on a bus, Britten

> was very protective, and very concerned that this should have happened to me. I remember that particular night was one when he came and sat on my bed and kissed me. It was as though he didn't want to have 'Little David' – if that's what he called me – to have to experience that kind of thing. So I think that innocence was very important to him.

On these later visits, Pears was sometimes there, and 'was always terribly nice – he went out of his way to be really sweet. Peter was much jollier with me than Ben was, a very boisterous companion – it was more altogether party time.' David noticed that Britten became a different person when no other adult was present – even Pears's absence made a difference to his behaviour. 'On our walks, when we were absolutely alone, he seemed to have a kind of sweetness – it's an awful word, so sugary – but a sweetness and warmth that he never had when a third person was there.'

Others noticed the change that came over Britten in the presence of children. 'It was almost a return to his own youth,' says Eric Crozier,

> but a kind of idealized image of himself at the age of ten or twelve, the gay, attractive, charming young Lowestoft boy, unerringly skilful in his use of a cricket bat or a tennis racket, and being able to do things with a ball that no other child of his age could do. It was like a flirtation that he carried on with any child that he met, particularly of course young boys, trying to dazzle them and astonish them by his virtuosity and his charm, making them his undying friends.

Sometimes it was achieved with party tricks. He was adept at winding up an invisible handle by his ear and then sticking out his tongue to imitate the opening of a cash register, and turning his head round while opening and shutting his eyes, as if he were a lighthouse. Steuart Bedford recalls him creating loud twangs with a knife on the edge of a restaurant table. Rose Marie Duncan describes him walking along a Suffolk cliff with her children, Roger and Briony, 'and he suddenly disappeared – he leapt over the edge of the cliff! And *we* didn't know (but of course he did) that there was a ledge only about ten feet below.' Briony observes that 'he was just so like a little boy' when in the company of children. 'He had this way of entering into one's world,' says David Spenser.

He seems to have preferred it to the adult world. John Drummond of the BBC noticed that at a party after a Britten–Pears recital televised during the sixties

> there were two children, a boy and a girl, about fourteen and twelve, and Ben obviously didn't want to speak to anyone else, and he sat down in a corner and talked to them – absolutely at his ease, absolutely relaxed, having a really serious conversation with these two kids. And then he turned and looked at the room, and a kind of frown came over his face as the world had to be confronted again.

Nancy Evans feels that this ability to empathize with children is evident in his music: 'He never wrote down – he sensed ways in which they could do things which other composers would think were too difficult for them, because he could fit into their mentality and their spirit. It was a sort of Peter Pan thing.'

During one of his visits to Crag House, David Spenser sat in Britten's study while he was writing music.

> He brought out a book of Hieronymus Bosch's paintings, and said, 'Have a look at these while I go on working.' And I looked at the paintings, and was also watching his pencil – it seemed to be moving far too fast, and I said to him, 'You're writing that awfully quickly.' And he said, 'Well, yes, I find it easier than writing letters.' He said that watching the sea always gave him ideas for music – he loved it from that window.

David Spenser realizes that Bosch was an odd choice of painter to amuse him. 'I was amazed at the close-ups. I was aware that they were very sensual and physical. I found them quite exciting in a funny kind of way, but I was also, you see, a good Catholic, and very frightened of Hell, and determined to be a very good saint.' If there was a hint of sexual suggestion in showing David the Bosch paintings, Britten gave no such signals in any other way.

> I never felt he was leading up to something. There was an oldish actor, about seventy, at about the same time, and when he kissed me he used to get a look on his face which I didn't like – lust, I suppose. I can't remember Ben ever having that look. There was a slight soppiness, but not lustful. I mean, if I'd suddenly thrown my arms round him or

whipped down my trousers, God knows what would have happened. But he didn't seem to expect it. I was aware that he felt a great affection for me, but not necessarily an unnatural one.

Britten's friendship with David Spenser lasted until 1949, when David was fifteen and beginning to shave. 'I was aware', David says, 'that whatever there had been was no longer there.' By this time his part in *Albert Herring* had been taken over by Alan Thompson, younger brother of Leonard who had played the Apprentice in *Peter Grimes*. Unlike the Spenser brothers, the Thompson boys grew up entirely unaware of homosexuality or paedophilia, and Alan (like Leonard) did not perceive anything unusual in Britten's friendly interest in him. 'He was always very nice. And I just didn't know anything at all about homosexuality. I always wondered why someone like Nancy Evans wasn't in love with Peter Pears.'

Britten took a close interest in the casting for the original *Let's Make an Opera* in 1949 and its subsequent revivals. In March 1951, after auditioning children for a new production, he wrote to Basil Douglas: 'We've got a fine Sammy – dark with longish uncontrollable hair & hypnotic dark eyes – also a tiny impediment which stops him saying his r's properly – most engaging!' It may be that some of the boys who appeared in the show had close attention paid to them, or even came to stay at Crag House, but there is no mention of this in Britten's letters to Pears, which usually alluded to such things.

It seems, in fact, that after David Spenser he looked for his friendships with boys not among children performing in his operas – perhaps because of the gossip that the Spenser friendship had caused in the EOG – but among the schoolboy sons of friends. These included David and Steuart Bedford (children of Lesley Bedford), to whom, in the late forties and early fifties, when they were approaching their early teens, he wrote friendly letters. For example, on 2 January 1949:

> My dear Stewy,
>   I think it is very clever of you to choose me such a beautiful tie . . . I am glad that you had a lovely Christmas . . . We have had some very rough seas, and alot of the beach has got washed away. Unless they put breakwaters or a big wall in front of us, it looks as if we might be washed away too. Perhaps I ought to sleep in a rubber boat in future? . . .

Steuart Bedford says that the friendship never became close; Britten remained simply a family friend.

In March 1949 Britten spent what he called a 'charming afternoon' at Eton, visiting Humphrey Maud, dedicatee of *The Young Person's Guide to the Orchestra*, and Fidelity Cranbrook's son Gathorne, who were aged fourteen and fifteen respectively. (Lady Cranbrook recalls her son's housemaster asking rather suspiciously about Britten's character.) 'By-the-way,' Britten wrote from Aldeburgh to the Mauds after this visit, 'I suggested that Humphrey might like to come here for a few days next holidays to get on with his boat-making.' Humphrey did stay at Crag House on several occasions, both with his parents and by himself. He played tennis with Britten – 'I did not come within miles of beating him!' – and was taken fishing by Billy Burrell. At no point did he detect anything other than a normal friendly interest in him.

> Ben was just a very good friend, a person with whom I felt absolutely at ease talking. I think there was something very boyish in his own nature. I remember actually saying to him, one time, 'I do enjoy talking to you, because I find my mother' – I wouldn't have used the term, but I was talking about inhibitions – 'and I feel able to talk to you very freely, and feel like shaking the wings out of the nest', that kind of feeling. And he was a very good talker; he was very instructive without setting himself up as a teacher.

In the company of Humphrey, an excellent musician (he played the cello in the National Youth Orchestra), Britten was willing to talk about music in a way he rarely would with adults.

> He made lots of remarks about Mozart and Verdi as *the* prime influences for his operas. He had no time for Brahms, although he played through his works every year in order to see if he came to a different conclusion. He had been a fanatic for Beethoven as a boy, with a house full of statues, but he now found that Beethoven shouted his message. I remember saying, 'Oh, come on, you can't say that about Beethoven's slow movements.' And he said, 'Yes, that's precisely what I do mean. It's all so *obvious*.' I remember debating with him his tremendous admiration for Mozart, and asking if Haydn didn't display greater inventiveness, and Ben saying that Mozart's greatness often lay in when he actually *didn't* change key, he didn't modulate. And the observation that it was particularly for his operas that Mozart had to be remembered.

In 1963 Britten mentioned in a letter to Ronald Duncan 'the Beethoven coolness which is now on me – which I don't shout about, since it is my own personal, practical & technical, affair ... my switch to Mozart and

Schubert . . .' Myfanwy Piper says he described Beethoven's music as 'just like sacks of potatoes'.

Even David Spenser, though not a musician, was allowed to glimpse some of this side of Britten:

> I did adore music, and my favourite composers at the time were Brahms and Chopin. And I asked him, would he play the Chopin Preludes? I lay back on the sofa, and he played, and never did he show any signs that he wasn't enjoying it. And that was the first time I heard the Brahms Variations on the St Anthony Chorale, though actually what I liked were the romantic things. And it was long after, a later visit, when he suddenly said to me could he try a different kind of music, and played this very charming piece, and I said that I didn't like it all that much, that I preferred Brahms. And he said to me, '*One* day, David, you will realize that Mozart is the greatest composer that has ever lived and that Brahms is easily the worst.'

The conductor Sir Charles Mackerras recalls that Britten would whistle parodies of the Brahms symphonies, and 'used to joke that it was a pity that, because of the alphabet, he was always put next to Brahms on library shelves!'

David Spenser remembers that on another occasion Britten

> went behind the piano – there were some chintz curtains, and he drew them back, and there were *masses* and masses of manuscripts. I think he might have been talking about being talented when young, and it was that evening that he played something I think he said he'd composed when he was four. And I heard two or three of those early pieces.

Humphrey Maud would bring his cello to Crag House

> and always played with him. I remember particularly playing the first two of the Bach gamba and keyboard sonatas. And his remarks about the importance of being able to play *slowly*. He gave one a real sense of partnership. He was genuinely interested in one's musical evolution, and I tested all sorts of ideas on him, and he was always prepared to sit and listen.

Humphrey's parents had not imagined that there could be anything improper in the friendship, but they happened to mention it to a friend who was himself homosexual, and who warned them that, while it 'might be all right', the risk should not be taken. 'Humphrey was a very fetching boy,' recalls his mother, 'and in the end we thought he'd better not go there, though it was terribly insulting to Ben.' John Maud spoke to

Britten about it, and Myfanwy Piper remembers that 'Ben was *deeply* hurt, he was *terribly* upset.' In 1954 Dermot Bowesman, nephew of Britten's old school friend Francis Barton, received an invitation to spend a weekend at Crag House. His mother Joy Bowesman writes that 'one of our relatives expressed great concern at allowing him to go "to people like that". We ignored it: I *knew* Ben.'

Another of Britten's friendships from this period was with Jonathan Gathorne-Hardy, nephew of Lord Cranbrook, then in his teens (he was born in 1933). He was at a school at Bryanston, where he had become acutely aware of homosexuality. His family lived in Aldeburgh. He gradually noticed Britten's interest in him. 'The thing about Ben and teenage boys, if I'm any guide,' he says, 'is that he was extraordinarily circumspect, very, very delicate and sensitive and nervous.'

In this case the friendship began with tennis. 'I was very good at tennis when I was young, and we used to play.' This revealed a side of Britten which initially surprised Jonny.

> Ben was intensely, remorselessly competitive in an almost sadistic way playing games. When you were beaten by him at squash or tennis, as I invariably was (though I was good at both), you did literally feel that he'd been *beating* you. If you were three down, and he could get you six down, he would. It was a very noticeable element. In *Grimes*, I sometimes wonder whether the beating is more than a symbol.

Following their game, Jonny would sometimes be invited to supper at Crag House. If Pears was present, Jonny found him 'a great deal easier to get on with than Ben – very charming and easy. Ben was rather difficult; he was tense quite often. He had great charm, but could turn rapidly waspish about other people.' Britten would give Jonny plenty to drink, including Martinis before the meal – he was now about sixteen – and 'sometimes I would find I'd drunk too much'.

Jonny was now 'aware that he was keen on me', and began to play up to it.

> I remember once sending Ben a postcard from Italy saying 'Brown all over, even my bottom', and as soon as I'd posted it being appalled with embarrassment. The thought still makes me go slightly hot. But my intense, completely unspoken awareness that he desired me made it irresistible to flirt, or perhaps that is too strong – the awareness itself was a sort of flirting, and I think Ben was aware of this, or wondered if I was in fact aware, and it was the whole edgy tension of it that stimulated him.

Britten's own letters, meanwhile, were playfully affectionate. 'My dear Jonny,' he wrote on 8 August 1950,

> I was awfully pleased to get your letter. It was a very nice one ... I hope you'll be coming here soon. I look forward to challenging you on the tennis-courts (either on the select hard one at the club, or the more friendly bumpy one over at Glemham). I hear you're frightfully good, so I think I'd better buy a new racquet ... send me a p.c. when you're coming & you must come over in a big way.
>
> Love to your parents, & to Sammy if he's there – only I believe he's in France.
>
> > and to yourself
> > Ben.

And on 10 January 1952, by which time Jonny was eighteen: 'I'm taking 24 kids – the midshipmen, powder monkeys, & cabin boys from B. Budd to 'Let's Make' next Saturday. Luckily there is a very charming Jonny in the cast, so they won't get a false idea of you.' (Like other members of his family, Jonny had given his name to a character in *The Little Sweep*.)

Jonny now began to notice 'each step' that Britten was taking with him, 'gradually, gradually. He would say things like, "Well, Jonny, don't go back home to change after tennis today – you're staying to dinner, so why don't you have your bath here this time?" And so we had baths.' The bath was in a room adjoining Britten's bedroom,

> and I would have my bath, and Ben would sit on the edge, or Ben would have the bath and I would sit on the edge. And we'd both be in towels, wandering about, and Ben saying 'Oh, I see, you think you might take up play-acting and give up writing?' or 'What I always found about chemistry was –' and that sort of talk. And I, of course, was aware of all this, down to the last blink of Ben's eyelids. And was prepared for it. Again, I feel rather bashful!
>
> But finally, one day as I got out of the bath and came in in my towel, Ben came up with an extremely soppy, sentimental look on his face, and put his arms round me, and kissed me on the top of the head. And I made the speech which I'd long prepared. I said, 'No, Ben, it is not to be!' Ben didn't break out into guffaws – he must have felt slightly surprised; it might have been an opera, really. In fact I should have sung it! And we sort of manoeuvred.
>
> Ben sort of went into the bathroom, gulped, came back and again approached me – he wasn't put off by this – and again put his arms round me, and again – I don't know if I actually repeated my aria, but I

said, 'No, no, Ben, I can't', or something. And he was perfectly nice. We went down and had our Martini and wine.

And then, just as it had very, very slowly built up to this climax, so, very, very slowly it went down, from there on. I mean, instead of playing tennis five times each holidays, it would be four, and then three, and then there'd be one holiday when I didn't get asked to dinner, but did get asked to tea. It was done with *such* care – noticeable only to a public schoolboy. But I felt that there was no question that, had I relaxed, we would have been in that double bed.

Jonny's younger brother Sammy, who had given his name to the hero of *The Little Sweep*, had a similar experience with Britten when he was about thirteen (this would make it 1949 or 1950) and had just gone to public school:

Ben was obviously very fond of me, I would say perhaps physically attracted. There was a quite definite feeling that one was somebody special. You were told quite clearly that you had the free run of the house whenever you liked. But they were very against homosexual acts at school, and when the pressure was on with him I said, 'People who want to behave like that can do, but it doesn't interest me.' And that was rather the end of it.

Asked if there was any specific pass made at him, Sammy Gathorne-Hardy says: 'It's terribly hard to remember, because one mistakes a hand on the shoulder for genuine friendship. I think the nearest was having a game of squash, and then back to his house, having a bath, and him coming in in the nude.'

Asked if he thinks it possible that Britten chose himself and Jonny for these attentions because, having used them as characters in an opera, he may have felt them to be in some way his property, Sammy answers: 'Yes, I think he might have. But one was just coming to the age of being one's own man, and looking for girls oneself, and the thought of walking down Aldeburgh High Street, and somebody saying, "There's Ben's latest" – !' Such remarks were beginning to be made by the mid-fifties. Bill Servaes who worked for Britten some years later, was astonished at the way that local mothers 'used to throw their sons at Ben'.

Unlike his brother, when he made it clear that he did not want this sort of relationship, Sammy experienced 'quite a severe rejection' by Britten, and was made to feel 'slightly guilty, as though he'd wasted a lot of time on me!'

Jonathan Gathorne-Hardy emphasizes Britten's generosity to him and his brother: 'Our relative poverty, the minuteness of our house, my mother's continual anxiety about money all made it possible for him to feel sorry for me and Sammy. When he got me into Covent Garden or seats at some Aldeburgh concert or a lift up to London, he knew I wouldn't be able to have any of them without his help.' Michael Berkeley, son of Lennox and a godson of Britten, who was invited to stay with Britten in the later fifties together with some school friends from Westminster Cathedral Choir School, recalls an occasion which demonstrated Britten's 'sympathetic intuition into the feelings of children'. He had given each of the boys ten shillings to spend on a fair in Aldeburgh, but Michael lost his, and lacked the courage to say so, merely telling Britten: 'I'm not well, I won't go.' Britten said nothing, but as he took the other boys to the car he slipped another banknote into Michael's top pocket; he had guessed. 'Ben knew that I would be embarrassed to admit I had lost the money in front of the other boys, and indeed they never found out. He saved me from losing face.' Michael Berkeley says that this sort of intuition 'contributed to my great affection for him'.

Asked how he relates Britten's interest in him (and other boys) to the relationship with Pears, Jonathan Gathorne-Hardy (nowadays an author who has written much about sexual complexities) answers: 'It's a common homosexual situation, actually, when their passions are in one place, and their hearts and affections in another.' He emphasizes that he did not sense any jealousy on Pears's part: 'Not a bit, not remotely. If anything, encouraging it, I think. And Ben showed no anxiety in front of him, or about him in any way.' Britten's casual mentions in his letters to Pears of the names of various boy visitors to Crag House confirms this. And when he was ill and depressed in the winter of 1948–9, Pears had written to him: '*don't* worry and remember there are lovely things in the world still – children, boys, sunshine, the sea, Mozart, you and me . . .'

Each partner seems to have become tolerant of the other's interests. In January 1950 Britten reported to Pears that, on a train-journey through Berkshire, he was distracted by 'young Pangbournians' (boys returning to Pangbourne College), and was particularly struck by 'a heavenly meeting between two flowers on Reading Station – such pleasure at re-uniting after the holidays was heart-warming – the Greek Anthology level'. The same letter, addressed to Pears at a Swiss clinic, imagined his 'quick eye roving round for the blonds'. Another letter to Pears mentions the difficulty of working in his study at Crag House 'with all the little naked figures disporting on the beach to distract me!' Nevertheless it is possible that the severe depressions from which Britten suffered during the forties, and the 'prolonged internal crisis' which Crozier felt he had detected in

Britten while they were working on *Billy Budd*, may have been related to his feelings about boys.

Basil Coleman, who often stayed at Crag House, says that, though Pears was away much of the time, 'Ben always looked forward so much to his coming back, and it was always very touching when he did – the affection, the hand going out at table to touch him . . . They were in love.' Colin Graham, who stage-managed *The Turn of the Screw* (and eventually succeeded Coleman as EOG producer), says much the same: 'I do know there was an abiding *love* there.' Graham suspects that by now, 'as with many long marriages', sex no longer played much part in the relationship, and that Britten had become 'really more or less celibate'. He believes that by this time 'Ben was quite at ease with his sexuality.' Donald Mitchell suggests that 'Ben's own highly charged feelings about very young males was something that could not find fulfilment, and that, paradoxically, in a way that may have helped to keep the other (and more important) relationship stable. It wasn't as if he was sexually interested in other men.'

In his 1966 'Notes' on Britten (the document which contains the allegation of Britten having been raped at school), Eric Crozier wrote: 'Having been corrupted as a boy, he seemed to be under a compulsion to corrupt other small boys.' Jonathan Gathorne-Hardy, too, uses the word 'corruption', but in a different fashion: 'It struck me that it was a sort of – if it isn't a contradiction in terms – spiritual corruption. He did want to corrupt me, and would eventually have got me into bed, but the whole thing was done with such delicacy, compared with what obviously went on in his head.'

We cannot be certain what did go on in Britten's head. There is some evidence that he had no conscious sexual designs, that, as with Piers Dunkerley in the thirties, he believed, or tried to believe, that his intentions were merely fatherly. On 7 October 1952 Imogen Holst wrote in her diary that Britten had

> told me that he was thinking of adopting two children from the Hessen's displaced persons camp in Germany:– he wanted a girl and a boy but it would probably have to be two boys because of regulations about a predominantly male household. He said he'd been thinking about it for ages because he realised that it was unlikely that he'd ever marry and have children of his own, and he'd got such an immense instinct of love for them that it spilled over and was wasted. Also that he felt that otherwise he might get more selfish. That he'd try & find the right school for them and then would arrange all his concert tours

in the term time so as to be free for them in the holidays. He said he'd probably spoil them, but I said no, he wouldn't.

Donald Mitchell believes that some of the boys who were befriended by Britten, such as Jonathan Gathorne-Hardy, may have misinterpreted Britten's behaviour towards them, or – as Gathorne-Hardy admits – to some extent have made the advances themselves:

> Once, when Ben and I were talking about one of his young friends who was being especially demanding, he said: 'It's often a problem that these youngsters seem to think I want to go to bed with them.' One may well conclude, with some impatience, that this was a problem he brought on himself. But it's a remark that has stayed with me vividly, and perhaps one worth bearing in mind when assessing some of the more highly-coloured reminiscences clamouring for our attention. In any event, Ben didn't seem to have much success in his role of seducer, did he?

After Britten's death, John Evans was told by Pears that Britten had 'needed the active figure (Peter) to his passive, but he also needed to be active to a boy's passive. And I've always had the impression that Peter meant that both types of relationship had been consummated – which left me absolutely thunderstruck.'

Myfanwy Piper says that Britten 'did talk to me a bit' about his friendships with boys. 'He would go for long walks – I remember one occasion when he did, perhaps two – and he would say that it was very upsetting for him, worrying. He found it a temptation, and he was very worried about it.' She did not know that 'he'd gone so far' as to kiss boys, or offer kisses, and is sure that nothing further went on: 'I think he kept the rules.'

*

It is not clear in the Britten–Piper *The Turn of the Screw* whether Quint has seduced Miles, or even tried to. His invitations to the boy are couched partly in seductive terms – 'I am the smooth world's double face ... the hidden life that stirs / When the candle is out ... The unknown gesture, the soft persistent word' – but also appeal to a boyish spirit of adventure: 'I'm all things strange and bold, / The riderless horse, / Snorting, stamping on the hard sea sand, / The hero highwayman...' Myfanwy Piper remarks of these lines:

> People have often said to me how absurd it was that the language I gave to Quint was so extremely un-evil. That's not the point. The point is how he maintained his attraction. And the only way he could attract

a comparatively innocent child was through the imagination, which is, if you like, why people were attracted to Ben.

Although Miles, with his ecstatic sighs, seems to respond sexually to Quint's words, the scene does not build to a climax, and the ghosts' wooing of the children is interrupted by the Governess and Mrs Grose. A peak is not reached until the beginning of the second act, when the ghosts sing, to swoops of harp and percussion, Yeats's line 'The ceremony of innocence is drowned'.

After they have sung this line excitedly as if they are especially roused by the contemplation of corrupted innocence, the Governess declares: 'Innocence, you have corrupted me.' The line is Myfanwy Piper's own, not Yeats's or James's, so what did she mean by it? 'I think that's about her own innocence, that she was a person who was innocent in all her approaches to everything, but she realized that you can't *be* innocent, you can't afford to be innocent, so that her innocence has let her down.' It might be felt that Britten himself, by this stage of his life, was caught up, perhaps sexually, with the idea of innocence – that it was in this sense a corrupting influence. Myfanwy Piper says that she 'did think of that, to some extent'.

The only sin which Miles definitely commits in the opera is his theft of a letter from the Governess reporting her suspicions to the children's guardian. We do not know whether these suspicions are justified, whether Miles and his sister have really been corrupted. So why, at the end of the opera, and to a passacaglia in the orchestra, does Miles die?

It seems to be once again a victory of bourgeois convention over bohemianism. The Governess, like the Borough, stands for socially acceptable yet in some respects deplorable attitudes (her selfish possessiveness towards Miles). She has banished Quint, who in the end may be no more than a voice for her own unspoken desires. The consequence of this banishment is disastrous: the child, who surely stands for the visionary, the artist (Miles, a precocious pianist, could be Britten himself as a child), is destroyed by the struggle to subdue the personality's own dark side.

Does Myfanwy Piper accept that, on one level, the opera is about the struggle between the two facets of Britten's own nature? 'I never thought of that. It seems to me that it may be the two sides of anybody's sexuality. But that was in the story, and was why he chose to do it.'

*

Britten finished the composition sketch of *The Turn of the Screw* on 23 July 1954. It had taken three and a half months. The orchestral score seems to have been written at lightning speed, in the middle of singers' rehearsals, which were held in the working men's club at Thorpeness, just to the north of Aldeburgh. The orchestral parts were written out by Imogen Holst, working around the clock.

The part of Mrs Grose had been designed for Joan Cross, although she says she 'didn't want it' – she was fifty-four and contemplating retirement from singing. She also felt 'rather indifferent' about the opera at first hearing. Jennifer Vyvyan, who had sung Penelope Rich in *Gloriana*, was cast as the Governess. The casting of Miles proved difficult. 'One of the few boys brought back for a second hearing,' writes Basil Coleman. 'was a very shy but quite personable little twelve-year-old, with a true but very small treble voice. Despite this it was decided to risk casting him, in the hope that the voice would develop and grow during rehearsals – the boy was David Hemmings.' A magazine feature on the child star of the new Britten opera reported:

> David began having his voice trained only two and a half years ago. One wet afternoon, while on holiday at Margate, his father persuaded him to enter a singing contest 'for fun'. To everyone's surprise, he won it. As a result, he entered other competitions and festivals. Now he has one singing lesson a week, but the fact that he is considered to have a musical career ahead of him has not made him less ambitious to win a scholarship, go to Cambridge and eventually become a science master.

John Amis, whose wife Olive Zorian was leading the EOG orchestra for *The Turn of the Screw*, writes that Hemmings

> sang well and he acted well – too well sometimes, overdoing the evil side of Miles so that Jennifer [Vyvyan] used to get frightened and slap him down. But he sang accurately and in Ben's eyes he could do no wrong. The composer seemed besotted with the boy. Cast and players noticed that Peter and Ben were at odds.

Basil Douglas confirms that Britten '*loved* David. He was in love with him, but as far as I know there was nothing more.' He adds: 'Ben was very self-restrained. I took my hat off to him for that. Because he was really smitten, and didn't David know it! He was very advanced for his age.' Colin Graham writes of this:

> We rehearsed for many weeks in Thorpeness. Ben always wanted that, so that people would be separated from the usual humdrum cares of London. He was quite right, but life did become very incestuous, and, inevitably, people would 'talk' about whatever their eyes could grab

hold of. The Ben–David Hemmings relationship was therefore very vulnerable. David was an extraordinary actor and really seemed made for the part. Clearly he was everything Ben had ever hoped for, even though his voice was not great. Ben needed a lot of time with him to get the voice to approximate to what he needed, and so of course people had plenty of food for discussion. He also made sure David got a proper rest in the afternoon (we always worked 10 am–1 pm and 4–7 pm) so that he would always be at his optimum – and of course the rest had to be away from the parents. Who resented it. So there was plenty of ammunition for 'talk', though, judging from everything Ben said to me subsequently, there were no other grounds for it but that.

Yes, he was very fond of him – as he was of adult singers who carried out his work to the optimum, and of course David, being a little devil himself, traded on this very much and quite overtly flattered Ben.

Throughout, whatever people may say, Peter behaved angelically and with enormous understanding. He knew Ben too well and was too sure of him to be jealous – it was neither necessary nor realistic.

Many years later, after Britten's death, Pears talked to Raymond Leppard about Britten's feelings for boys. 'Peter spoke with great understanding of it,' he writes,

> and, I felt, compassion, for it must have been hard to bear for both of them. Only one episode did he specially mention as nearly catastrophic ... David Hemmings ... at the time of *The Turn of the Screw* in Venice. Ben, it seems, became quite distracted. Peter told me that he had to take Ben away by train or it would have escalated into a major scandal. For how long I don't know, at any rate a cooling off time.

Colin Graham doubts this, remarking that there would not have been time for such a journey.

Asked for his own memories of Britten and *The Turn of the Screw*, David Hemmings says:

> He was incredibly warm to me, yes. Was he infatuated with me? Yes, he was. He was a gentleman; there was no sort of overt sexuality about it whatsoever. It was a very kind and very loving and very gentle relationship.
>
> Did he kiss me? Yes, he did. But that was more my need as a young boy alone in his house than it was any threat. I slept in his bed, when I was frightened, and I still felt no sexual threat whatsoever. And I think it would have embarrassed him a damn sight more than it would have embarrassed me at the time.

When told of Leppard's story of Britten being taken away from Venice by Pears for a 'cooling off', Hemmings says he was not aware of this happening. He goes on:

> Of all the people I have worked with, I count my relationship with Ben to have been one of the finest. And also my relationship with Peter too. And it was never, under any circumstances, threatening.
>
> Was I aware of his homosexuality? Yes, I was. Was I aware that he had a proclivity for young boys? Yes, I was. Did I find that threatening? No, because I learnt an awful lot through it. Did I feel that he was desperately fond of me? I suppose I did, but I must say I thought far more in a sort of fatherly fashion; and I had a very bad father–son relationship.
>
> He wanted me to go on to Gresham's School, and he wanted me to be trained as a tenor. I don't really have the frame for a tenor, nor the temperament either. But there is no man in my entire life that has been more influential on my attitudes than Ben.

*

Early in September 1954 the *Screw* company left Aldeburgh for Venice, arriving a week before the opening night. 'It was written in my contract,' says Basil Douglas,

> that we were to have the stage of the Fenice for one week before the first performance. When I arrived in Venice, I discovered that there were two other companies who both had it written in theirs! And so the beginning of the day was always frantic, because we all wanted the stage, and the manager of the festival had a wonderful way of not being there. John Piper was such a great help to me. But the rehearsals were very fraught.

Basil Coleman remembers Britten as 'more than usually upset' when things went wrong during rehearsals, and says he was 'very nervous' about the opening night.

Much more than usual was at stake. The *Spectator* music critic, Martin Cooper, had written in June 1953 of the reception of *Gloriana* 'by the musical world in general' that he perceived 'an almost sadistic relish or glee' at the opera's apparent failure.

> The fact is that the fashion has changed and it is now smart to underrate Britten's music ... Britten and his music have been 'news' for something like ten years, a long run for any fashion ... He has been ill-served, with the best of intentions, by a fanatical clique of admirers ... Finally, it has been felt that Britten has had the advantage of special

patronage . . . This offends the sense of 'fair play' still very strong in the British public and has probably lent the note of bitterness to what might otherwise have been merely a change of musical fashion.

Cooper felt that 'nothing short of a spectacular success' could prevent Britten's reputation for remaining in the doldrums. Six months after *Gloriana*, Britten had talked to Imogen Holst about the resemblance to her father's career: 'He said . . . that the reception of *Grimes* was like the reception of *The Planets*, and that people were disappointed with what came afterwards.'

There was also the delicate subject matter of the new opera. Colin Graham writes that

> Ben was very vulnerable about this opera, about which he cared so much. As a result, the 'family', the Pipers, Basils C. and D., Ben and Peter, and others, went about Venice as a little clique doing nothing but worry. (There's a wonderful picture of all of them having a picnic on a bridge over a canal which became known as 'grumble corner'.) The rest of us had a glorious if difficult time!

The difficulties included the Fenice stage hands threatening to go on strike because they had to dismantle and reassemble the *Screw* set to allow for concerts between rehearsals. Graham, who had taught himself Italian for the occasion, 'had to mediate with the unions, while my superiors hid'.

Lord Harewood, who had come out to Venice for the première, says it was to be 'a lower-keyed event' than the *Gloriana* gala first night. Nevertheless on the evening of 14 September 1954 the Fenice Theatre was *en fête*, the air heavy with the scent of roses which had been set out in each box in the auditorium. The performance was to be broadcast live on the BBC Third Programme and several European stations, and Basil Douglas 'got more and more anxious, because we couldn't start on time because another broadcast was over-running. And there was slow hand-clapping going on.' At last the opera began. All went smoothly, though the numerous scene-changes were noisier than had been hoped. During the interval the Italians in the audience could be seen in little groups, explaining the significance of James's tale volubly to each other. Harewood says that when the curtain came down it was obvious from the reception that the opera was a 'genuine success'.

Despite this, next morning *Il Popolo* printed an unenthusiastic review by Ricardo Malipiero, complaining that the chamber orchestra did not give the opera sufficient orchestral weight – a criticism repeated later by some other reviewers – and regretting that it was not another *Peter Grimes*. However, the only British review to appear that day, by Colin Mason in the *Manchester Guardian* (who had evidently seen the vocal score before the performance), judged that Britten had 'tackled yet another problem, brought off yet another tour de force, and, it seems likely, created another masterpiece'.

The Times carried its review a day later. Frank Howes wondered why Britten had chosen 'this subject', adding: 'It is an improper question for criticism to ask, but it recurs so invariably that it must have some relevance to his art.' Howes affected to be unsurprised by the opera: 'We all know by now that Mr Britten's sheer musical ability is equal to any demands made on it . . .' Antoine Golea in the Paris newspaper *L'Express* was more specific in his comment on the subject matter, writing of 'the composer's customary intense preoccupation with homosexual love and the futility of struggling against it'. This seems to have been the first time that homosexuality was mentioned in print in connection with Britten.

Many critics were impressed by David Hemmings. Virgil Thomson in the *New York Herald Tribune*, who was genuinely enthusiastic if a little condescending ('an opera that seems to me to have beauty and power in it . . . I predict it will travel'), called Hemmings 'adorable all round'. Felix Aprahamian in the *Sunday Times* judged him 'remarkable', and was the first critic to suggest that *The Turn of the Screw* was the peak of Britten's achievement so far – 'not only Britten's most gripping score . . . his finest'. The cast had mostly come to the same opinion. Joan Cross still preferred *Peter Grimes*, but recognized that the new opera was 'a great work'. Basil Douglas says that 'I think we all realized that this was the best ever. I still think so.'

After one more performance in Venice the *Screw* company returned to England, where the opera was staged at Sadler's Wells during October, before being taken to the Holland Festival and Sweden. It was recorded in January 1955 – the first Britten opera to be put on the new long-playing gramophone records – and in September that year was staged again in London as part of an EOG season at the Scala Theatre. The part of Miles was taken over at one performance by the understudy, Robin Fairhearst, 'quite different from David,' wrote Britten, 'but singing beautifully, & with a touching tragic personality'. David Hemmings appeared during the Scala season as Sammy in *The Little Sweep*; 'simple & touching', wrote Britten, though by now his feelings about Hemmings were mixed: 'a good boy – I've seen quite alot of him & am fond of him but puzzled by his two completely opposite sides'. Hemmings sang in the recordings of *Saint Nicolas* and *The Little Sweep*, also put on long-playing records by Decca during

1955, and then his association with Britten ended. He went on to achieve fame in films.

During the autumn of 1954 John Ireland wrote to a friend:

> I have listened twice to Britten's new opera *The Turn of the Screw*. I am no judge of opera as such, but this contains the most remarkable and original music I have ever heard from the pen of a British composer – and it is on a firmly *diatonic* and *tonal* basis. Also, what he has accomplished in sound by the use of only 13 instruments was, to me, inexplicable; almost miraculous. This is not to say I *liked* the music, but it is gripping, vital and often terrifying. I am now (perhaps *reluctantly*) compelled to regard Britten as possessing ten times the musical talent, intuition and ability of all other living British composers put together.

Britten himself wrote to Eric Walter White two months after the première of *The Turn of the Screw*: 'I am delighted in your reaction to my latest baby – one is always so delighted that one's sympathetic friends find the last work the best. It was certainly a difficult work to bring off technically and spiritually.' And to Desmond Shawe-Taylor during the same month: 'I think in many ways you are right about the subject being, as it were, nearest to me of any I have yet chosen, (although what that indicates of my own character I shouldn't like to say!).'

PART FOUR
1954–76

Happy family

1: The middle of life

As usual, there was an epilogue to the opera. *Canticle III: Still falls the rain* was written in November 1954, three months after the première of *The Turn of the Screw*. Writing to Anthony Gishford at Boosey & Hawkes, Britten said he had been 'deeply moved' by the Edith Sitwell poem, '& felt at last that one could get away from the immediate impacts of the war & write about it'. Certainly Sitwell's subject matter is the Second World War ('Still falls the Rain ... / Blind as the nineteen hundred and forty nails / Upon the Cross'). But the Britten setting, for tenor, horn and piano seems to have an additional meaning. John Amis had asked Britten to write something for a memorial concert for Noel Mewton-Wood, who had died two years earlier, aged thirty-one. Besides accompanying Pears and playing at the Aldeburgh Festival, Mewton-Wood had given the first performance of the revised version of Britten's Piano Concerto – with a new third movement – in 1946. Amis describes him as a discreet homosexual who suddenly 'came out': 'He met Bill Fedricks and set up house with him ... We [were] made to feel that heterosexuality was abnormal and just a little bit dirty.' Fedricks eventually died, and Mewton-Wood took prussic acid and killed himself. Britten explained to Edith Sitwell that in her poem's 'courage & light seen through horror & darkness' he found 'something very right for the poor boy'. Imogen Holst's diary records Britten receiving the news of Mewton-Wood's death: 'He was looking grey and worried, and talked of the terrifyingly small gap between madness and non-madness, and said why was it that the people one really liked found life so difficult.'

Dennis Brain took part in the first performance of *Canticle III*. He was killed in a car crash two years later and, at a memorial concert held by the Chelsea Music Club, Britten conducted a performance of the Sonnet 'O soft embalmer of the still midnight' from the *Serenade*, the one movement in that work in which the horn is silent.

On 18 April 1955 Britten told Edith Sitwell that *The Turn of the Screw* and *Canticle III* made him feel 'on the threshold of a new musical world', and that he was 'taking off next winter to do some deep thinking'. At present he was as busy as ever. With Plomer, he was again discussing a children's opera, this time looking in classical legend for a suitable story featuring a boy, such as that of Phaeton, or of Icarus, or of Medea's murdered brother Absyrtus. More immediately he had to write a ballet for Covent Garden.

John Cranko had been asked by David Webster to create the ballet, and had devised a fairy-tale scenario. Asking Britten's advice about possible composers, he was astonished and delighted to find that he was keen to undertake it himself. They worked on a detailed plan which included timings of each section. However, by the time he was free to begin the music, Britten was in a state of exhaustion. Looking back at 1954 and *The Turn of the Screw* he promised himself that there would be 'no more years like this in a hurry'. Indeed there had scarcely been a let-up in his speed and intensity of work since *Peter Grimes* ten years earlier. He told Cranko that 'I have been at it for months, even years, without a break.'

In February 1955 he went off on a Swiss skiing holiday with Pears and Ronald and Rose Marie Duncan. The librettist of *The Rape of Lucretia* had continued to hope for further collaborations, but was constantly disappointed. 'However,' writes Duncan, 'during this bleak period I continued to hear what he was writing and where he was going from my son Roger who was in constant touch with him.' Britten had known Roger Duncan, born in 1943, since he was a baby, and began a friendship with him in 1954, when the boy was eleven and *The Turn of the Screw* was being written. A letter from Britten to Basil Coleman in February 1955 describes David Hemmings as 'no Roger, I'm afraid!' In the summer of 1955 Britten stayed with the Duncans in Devon, and Ronnie Duncan describes Britten asking to go for a walk with him so that he could beg a favour. According to Duncan, the conversation ran as follows:

> 'Ronnie, I've got a problem. I love children and as you know, I can't marry.'
> 'Yes, I know. Why don't you adopt one?'
> 'That's what I want to do.'
> 'Then there's no problem.'
> 'You don't understand. It's Roger I like. I want to be as a father to him. But I don't want to put your nose out of joint. Will you allow me

to give him presents, visit him at school, and let him spend part of his school holidays with me – in other words share him?'

'Of course. He's fond of you too. And as you see, we've always got Briony.'

They then returned to the Duncans' farm, Britten looking 'as if I had given him three opera houses'. Duncan continues:

For the next ten years Ben was a second father to my son, giving him affection and advice as he grew up. He wrote to him once or even twice a week ... I felt some shame at my own inadequacy, at my own lack that I had failed to give my son the support he had received from Ben. The only thing I can say in my defence is that I knew Ben was writing these letters, visiting him at school, giving him a room in his house where he invariably spent part of his holidays.

Roger Duncan says that at the time he knew nothing of the agreement made about him between Britten and his father. 'My father told me that a lot later.' He agrees that his father was an inadequate parent. 'He had a series of girl-friends and affairs, and was not very attentive to me and my sister, or my mother.' Roger says he has 'psychological scars' from this lack of fathering. However, 'Ben largely filled the father gap.'

Britten would call on him at All Hallows, his prep school in Somerset, arriving in the Rolls Royce – 'FLX 8, it's amazing how one can remember the registration'. Roger began to spend at least a week of every school holidays staying at Crag House. 'Ben bought me a new bicycle, a Raleigh, and I used to spend time cycling around Aldeburgh, which was nice. And in the afternoon we would go out looking at parish churches.' The boy was developing an interest in architecture, and Britten had decided to foster this, taking him, *Shell Guide* in hand, to what Roger calls 'literally hundreds of East Anglian churches – he knew his way to all of them, virtually'. On these drives and in other talks together, 'the main thing that Ben had was the ability to talk at my level without talking down to me, and I felt an adult'.

Roger had no ability at music, but 'spending a quarter of my holidays with Ben I naturally went to hundreds of concerts, and it did instil itself into me, and I enjoyed it.' He says he preferred Britten's more joyful music, such as the *Spring Symphony* and *A Ceremony of Carols*. He found the operas 'too taut and fraught'. When Imogen Holst was writing *The Story of Music* – the book nominally co-authored with Britten – Roger was shown the text and asked for his opinion. 'Ben deliberately had me as a philistine, musically, review it and give some comments.'

Roger's mother, Rose Marie Duncan, when asked if she was not worried by the friendship, says:

> I wouldn't have denied Roger the benefit of what Ben could give him, which was amazing. I mean, to be taken around, and given lovely presents! I was so fascinated by Ben himself – he was such a very fascinating creature – that I don't think it occurred to me that anything would go wrong, because I remember Ronnie saying that he'd made Ben absolutely promise that he'd behave. And I suppose because we wanted to believe it, we believed it. But I'll never know.

Roger's sister Briony observes of her parents' attitude: 'They were slightly oblivious, really.'

Fidelity Cranbrook says that on some days when Roger was staying at Crag House, he would be sent over to her at Great Glemham to be looked after. 'And as the time drew near for him to be collected, he'd keep saying "When's Ben coming? When's Ben coming?" And when Ben arrived, Roger would run and take his hand.' Roger himself says that Britten was 'extremely warm, and extremely loving, and generated those genuine feelings. But they weren't physical.'

He admits that in the early days of the friendship he was 'naïve and innocent', and 'it didn't occur to me' that Britten was homosexual. However, when he went from All Hallows to Harrow he encountered homosexuality, became aware that Britten was attracted to him, and decided that 'I wasn't homosexually inclined, so it became just a platonic friendship'. Britten 'respected the fact that I was heterosexual, interested in girls, and had girl-friends. So, you know, he used to kiss me, and that's about it. And I understood that he was homosexual, obviously, and it didn't worry me.'

Colin Graham, who came to know Britten closely during the period of his friendship with Roger Duncan, writes: 'I am sure that those compulsorily platonic relationships did put a lot of strain upon him. But I also believe it was always *in loco parentis* that he saw himself, and the father–son relationship is a very strong one.'

*

In 1952 and 1953 the Aldeburgh Festival had made substantial losses, and the 1955 programme book stated that because of a 'financial bottleneck' it had been decided to 'dispense with the services of a professional general manager. All Festival visitors will be very sorry to know that this present Festival is Elizabeth Sweeting's last.' The job of manager was not being dispensed with. It was immediately taken over by Stephen Reiss, though the next year's programme book disguised this by calling him 'Hon. Secretary'.

Elizabeth Sweeting says of her departure that 'it was not my actual going, being pushed if you like, but the manner of it which angered me', though she adds that 'as dismissal came to so many, I knew my turn would come eventually'. It came one day when she returned from London and found a letter awaiting her. She observes wryly: 'Not everyone was lucky enough to have a letter – usually it was a woundingly silent cold shoulder!'

The Festival gave her what she calls 'a marvellous send-off' – a benefit concert in which Britten and Pears took part – and she remains 'grateful for so many happy & successful years' at Aldeburgh. (She soon became manager of the Oxford Playhouse.) Nevertheless the treasurer of the Festival, Tommy Cullum, who was the Aldeburgh bank manager and had been involved since the beginning, resigned in protest at her removal from office, and she herself writes of the manner of her departure that it was 'typical Ben. I recognized the mixture of guilt and consequent cowardice at dealing a blow, because I had seen it before, and indeed connived at it.'

Her successor, Stephen Reiss, had entered Gresham's School a little while after Britten, and had heard him perform in school concerts. After the war he settled in Aldeburgh with his wife and children in the hope of making a success as a painter, meanwhile supporting his family by teaching and working part-time for an art dealer. He was brought on to the Festival council after proving to be an excellent exhibition organizer. He was disconcerted by Britten's pretence that Elizabeth Sweeting's job was being abolished, which he calls 'a little devious; but that was typical of Ben, and I later came to suffer from the same thing myself'. Anne Wood warned him what might be in store if he committed himself to Britten:

> Many years before, she and I had been neighbours. She came partly to congratulate but also to commiserate and warn. In effect, she was saying he devoured people and spewed out what was left and no use to him. Or she may have used the metaphor of moths getting too close to a flame. But she thought I might survive because I had my own independent interests outside the music world. He could not so easily possess me, or I might be wise to see he didn't.

Word was spreading in the musical world about the risks inherent in working for the EOG and at Aldeburgh. Heather Harper, who made her first Festival appearance in 1956 in Imogen Holst's realization of Blow's *Venus and Adonis*, 'was warned, by I can't remember who, "When you go down there, you do your work, and then get away. Don't try to get involved too closely. Otherwise you'll get your fingers burnt."' The difficulty was that, as Lord Harewood puts it, Britten's personality was 'mesmeric', and it was all too easy to get drawn into something closer than a merely professional relationship. 'What I'm avoiding saying,' continues Harewood,

> because it suggests homosexual overtones – and my regard and feeling for Ben wasn't that way – is that it really was like being with someone you were in love with. You wanted him to be there, and you minded that he was going, and it was good that you were going to see him again. It was a very good feeling.

*

Roger Duncan's first holiday visit to Crag House was in September 1955. 'I had little Roger here for a fortnight,' Britten wrote to Basil Coleman on 25 September,

> which was enchanting. He is a dear child, & a most sweet & gay companion. He stayed a few days with us in Chester Gate [Pears's current London home, 5 Chester Gate, NW1] last week seeing the operas before he went back to school. His is not an easy home life, you know, & I think it's a relief to him to have an avuncular refuge! It was a pretty tearful parting, with the prospect of not seeing each other till Easter.

Britten and Pears were about to set out on a lengthy journey across Europe, giving concerts, to the Far East. Before leaving, Britten told Covent Garden that he could not complete the ballet – of which the first act had been sketched – in the promised time. There was a 'ghastly deadline' for him to finish the full score of all three acts by October 1956, but he was not prepared to work at it without stopping. He had anaemia and badly needed a holiday.

He sent Roger Duncan a series of long letters from the various stages of the foreign trip during the winter of 1955–6. Beginning 'My darling old Roger', and ending 'lots of love, old boy', they described seeing Mozart manuscripts in Salzburg, glimpsing Tito at a reception in Belgrade, and lunching with Nehru and his daughter Mrs Gandhi in Delhi. India astonished him – 'how *extraordinary* it all is', he wrote to Plomer. It was followed by a disappointing encounter with Singapore and 'a week of hectic concerts & dotty travelling in Java'. Then in mid-January 1956, accompanied now by Lu and Peg Hesse, he and Pears reached Bali.

'I am writing this early in the morning,' Britten began his letter to Roger on 18 January 1956.

The sun is already up, and it is as warm as a lovely English mid-day. I am sitting outside Peter's and my room in the courtyard of a palace in this little Balinese village [Ubud]. The palace is owned by a prince who takes guests, specially selected (but paying too!); it isn't a palace in the Buckingham ditto sense, since it's really a collection of innumerable thatched tents, nestling around a complicated and exotic-looking Hindu temple. Even at this hour there is the sound of a musical gong; in fact the air is always filled by the sound of native music – flutes, xylophones, metalphones and extraordinary booming gongs – just as it is filled by the oddest spicey smells, of flowers, of trees, and of cooking, as one's eye is filled by similar sights plus that of the really most beautiful people, of a lovely dark brown colour, sweet pathetic expressive faces, wearing strange clothes, sarongs of vivid colours, and sometimes wearing nothing at all. Sorry, old boy, to write in this 'high-falutin' way, but one is really knocked sideways . . .

And to Imogen Holst:

The music is *fantastically* rich – melodically, rhythmically, texture (such orchestration!!) & above all *formally*. It is a remarkable culture. We are lucky in being taken around everywhere by an intelligent Dutch musicologist – so we go to rehearsals, find out about & visit cremations, trance dances, shadow plays – a bewildering richness. At last I'm beginning to catch on to the technique, but it's about as complicated as Schönberg.

Britten had encountered the music of Bali sixteen years before he came to the island. During the winter of 1939–40 Elizabeth Mayer had introduced him to a patient of her husband's, a composer named Colin McPhee, who had just returned from spending several years on Bali studying and transcribing its music. At first, Britten does not seem to have been very excited by it. The copy of the transcriptions which McPhee gave him is inscribed 'To Ben – hoping he will find something in this music after all.' However, several commentators have shown that it influenced his work before the journey to Bali in 1956; for example, in the 'Moon Turns Blue' episode in the Prologue to *Paul Bunyan*, which Donald Mitchell has described as Britten putting Balinese principles 'to bold, if brief, use'.

During his two weeks on the island in January 1956 Britten noted fragments of pieces he heard played by the Balinese gamelan orchestras, one of which consisted entirely of 'little boys less than 14 years old', and the various five-note scales on which these were based. He turned to this material when he resumed work on the ballet later in the year, though its effect on his music went far beyond that particular score. Lu Hesse, too, was overwhelmed by the music, and disturbed by it. In his travel diary he describes an evening performance by a gamelan orchestra and two child dancers:

> The whole thing is stimulating and soporific at the same time. Hanging over the bamboo barrier and lying beside it are many sleeping children as young as the dancers. But two priests in white robes with white headbands seem intensely and almost dangerously adult . . . There is an odd atmosphere in this place. The dancing and the sleeping children and the drugged audience give one the impression that something sinister is going on. Here, the charming and musical tinkling and singing of the gamelan seems to produce these odd and long-drawn-out sounds one hears before one is overwhelmed by an anaesthetic.

Hesse summed up the experience as 'exciting, burningly interesting; but one is not quite certain if it is good that such things should be'.

'And so we go on to Japan,' Britten wrote to Roger Duncan on 8 February 1956, after a visit to Hong Kong. 'I must say I don't want to, awfully, I don't like what I know about the country or the people . . . But I mustn't be silly.' Japan proved as great an excitement as Bali. 'It is far the strangest country we have yet been to.' Britten told Roger, comparing the inhabitants to 'a very intelligent kind of insect', and describing the oddity of Japanese hotels. Then:

> One thing I unreservedly loved in Japan was the theatre. They have two principal kinds – the Noh, and the Kabuki. The Noh is very severe and classical – very traditional without any scenery to speak of, or lighting, and there are very few characters – one main one, who wears a mask, and two or three supporting ones and usually a very small boy too. There is a chorus that sits at the side, chanting, a kind of orchestra of two drums (who also moan in the oddest way) and a flute, that squat in the centre of the stage, almost in the middle of the action. At first it all seemed too silly, and we giggled a lot. But soon we began to catch on a bit.

The British Council representative in Japan in 1956, Reg Close, writes that he and his wife had

> asked Ben and Peter whether they would care to see a Noh play, warning them that it might turn out to be as boring as a game of cricket. They said they would just go along to see what it was like and

we agreed that we would all slip away at the first interval if they found it unbearable.

Peg Hesse recalls that the four of them had been to an official lunch, the seats were hard and uncomfortable, and for the first half-hour or so they all thought the play 'hilarious', with its absurd groaning voices and other strange sounds – 'We were rolling with laughter.' Then the principal character came on. 'The play was *Sumidagawa*, the Sumida River,' explains Reg Close, 'and the principal character was a woman mourning for a lost child. Ben and Peter sat silently ... When ... we asked if they wished to slip away, Ben started as if from a trance, and said, "What? Leave this? I couldn't possibly."'

After the performance, Close managed to obtain a tape recording of *Sumidagawa* for Britten, who also bought transcriptions of Japanese music. He wrote to Plomer of 'my incredibly strong reactions to Japan', and said he was 'longing to talk about these Noh plays'.

*

After two weeks the party went on via Bangkok to Ceylon, where they stayed for a further fortnight. Britten and Pears were back in England in mid-March 1956, and at the end of that month Britten reported that he had 'cancelled every concert for some time now in order to get on with the Ballet'. On 1 May he told David Webster that it was 'progressing well', but 'there is a colossal amount to write, and the date-line' (still the autumn) 'is beginning to keep me awake of nights'. By mid-May the ballet was still 'only ½ written', and when Britten heard that Ernest Ansermet, his and Covent Garden's choice of conductor, would not be available he told Webster that 'any postponement of the first night would be a god-send to me'. Two months later he wrote to Ronald Duncan that the ballet had been

postponed till at least Christmas – I can't get the 600 pages of score written in time – I'm too old & tired to keep up the 14 hours a day schedule which it intails [*sic*]. It's all disappointing, but since the music's now all written, & I like it, I suppose it isn't the end of the world ... Just off to Switzerland to try & recover.

He remarked to Rosamund Strode, who was helping Imogen Holst with the full score of the ballet: 'I've never written so many notes in my life – all those bits of thistledown dancing on the stage actually need a tremendous amount of music.'

Oliver Knussen suggests that the pace Britten had maintained in the years immediately following *Peter Grimes*, and the sheer quantity of music written, is even more remarkable than Mozart's:

Nobody can cover that much paper! I don't see how it's possible to conceive those large pieces, write them down at that speed and get it right. People, Britten included, have marvelled at the fecundity of a Mozart or a Schubert. Well, most of their pieces aren't quite as big as *Grimes* or the *Spring Symphony* or the others, which are enormous undertakings, and the operas are through-composed, too.

Britten's perceptible slowing of pace after *The Turn of the Screw* may not have been due solely to exhaustion. With that opera, the personal debate which began with *Peter Grimes* had come, at the very least, to a punctuation mark. Some sort of change of direction was now needed. The ballet was not the obvious work to provide it.

In Switzerland, Britten and Pears stayed in a medieval castle belonging to Lu Hesse. Roger Duncan came too; so did Imogen Holst, who worked with Britten on the full score of the ballet. Rehearsals began towards the end of the year, with Britten himself on the rostrum, though he told Plomer: 'I never wished to conduct, was already seedy when the rehearsals started, & the performances were really agonising.' Imogen Holst was struck by Pears's total lack of interest in the ballet and its music. Colin Matthews remembers 'an Imo story of Peter at rehearsals, and Ben in terrible straits saying, "Oh, what *am* I going to do?" and Peter saying, "Well, I don't know about you, but *I'm* going to get my hair cut."'

The Prince of the Pagodas opened at Covent Garden on New Year's Day 1957, with Svetlana Beriosova as Belle Rose and David Blair as the Prince. The sets were by John Piper – 'gorgeous', reported Britten. Cranko had constructed a *King Lear*-like story about an ageing Emperor who disdains his younger daughter and allows the cruel elder sister to inherit. The younger, Belle Rose, is carried off magically to Pagoda Land, where she dances with a Salamander which sloughs off its skin and reveals itself as a Prince. The two return to Belle Rose's kingdom where her villainous sister is routed. The ballet concludes in Pagoda Land with a *divertissement* on the theme of Love and Freedom. Critics were not much taken with the plot. The *Manchester Guardian* complained that it was 'wild and woolly' and *The Times* remarked on its 'sags in tension'. Felix Aprahamian in the *Sunday Times* judged that Britten had 'matched John Cranko's scenario with music more significant than it deserves'.

There was enough in the story – Belle Rose's treatment by her father and sister, and the monstrous Salamander's metamorphosis into the Prince – for Britten to have made the score into yet another work about innocence, corruption and sexuality. But he chose to take Cranko's

scenario at face-value, and provided it with charming and highly accom-
plished fairy-tale music. The score's most immediately striking feature is
its deft imitation of Balinese gamelan music, in the passages for tuned
percussion which portray Pagoda Land. There are nods too in the direction of Stravinsky, Prokofiev and Tchaikovsky. Britten told Ronald
Duncan that he had the score of *The Sleeping Beauty* by his bed while he
was writing *The Prince of the Pagodas* – 'who else can I take as model?'
Colin Matthews remarks that 'for me *The Prince of the Pagodas* is the
best Britten opera. It's such uninhibited music – something which of
course isn't possible when you have to worry about voices.'

He conducted only the first three performances, after which 'my doctor
put his foot down'. He was ordered to rest for a month. 'I *must* give up
conducting,' he had written to Basil Coleman some months earlier.
However, he conducted the Decca recording of the ballet score (in a
slightly abbreviated form) a few weeks later, and a month after the first
night he wrote enthusiastically about the ballet to Coleman:

> Johnny's part is full of wonderful invention, although there are some
> moments of inexperience, & not altogether absorbed classical idioms
> ... Beriosova, & Blair (a splendid chap) are lovely, & there are others
> – but the general level of small parts & corps de ballet is pretty poor,
> even to my novice's eyes ... But all of this we can alter & improve ...
> it is a terrific success, playing to packed houses, & they've just added
> 10 more performances – snooks to the critics! ... I hope you'll like the
> music – alot of it I honestly think is good, altho' a 3 acter is a colossal
> task.

The Prince of the Pagodas received twenty-three performances at Covent
Garden during 1957, and a further ten during an American tour by the
company. It was also produced at La Scala, Milan in the spring of that
year, with Britten, Pears and the Hesses in the audience – they were on a
two-week Italian holiday together. By the end of the year Britten, who
had had to spend much time correcting the orchestral hire parts for Boosey
& Hawkes, was calling it 'that beastly work', and it soon began to fade
from the Covent Garden repertoire. It had a further five performances
there in 1958, but only three in 1959 and three in 1960, after which it
disappeared altogether from the stage – though there were occasional
performances of a concert suite from the ballet, devised by Norman Del
Mar, and the abridged recording of the ballet score, conducted by
Britten, kept interest in it alive. Donald Mitchell writes that for the
remainder of his life Britten 'could rarely be persuaded to return to his
score, either to look at it with a view to publication or to discuss a

possible new production'. This, however, may have been the result of his falling out with Cranko in 1960 over *A Midsummer Night's Dream*. There is nothing to suggest that he came to think poorly of the music. Certainly he was enthusiastic when, around 1970, Covent Garden made efforts to revive the ballet, with new choreography by Kenneth Mac-Millan. However, Britten and MacMillan had widely differing views about possible cuts, and it was not until 1989 that the MacMillan *Prince of the Pagodas*, with Cranko's scenario substantially rewritten by Colin Thubron, was seen at the Royal Opera House.

*

In January 1957, the month of the first performance of *The Prince of the Pagodas*, Britten wrote to Basil Coleman about the financial difficulties of the EOG: 'we've performed less & less & the administrative costs soar'. This letter was critical of the EOG manager Basil Douglas: 'one's affection & admiration (in certain ways) for Basil remain constant. But as you know the poor dear gets out of his depth easily, & the burden falls more & more on all of us.'

Douglas's duties included explaining to various members of the EOG that Britten no longer required their services. These included Olive Zorian, whose place as leader of the orchestra was taken by Emanuel Hurwitz, one of a number of players Britten had decided to import from the Goldsborough Orchestra, later the English Chamber Orchestra. John Amis, still married to her at that time, describes her dismissal as being conducted in 'typical Aldeburgh fashion', in that 'neither Ben nor Peter had the nerve to tell her. A situation arose when she was the only person in the organization who did not know that she was for the chop.' Another who left around this time was Norman Del Mar. His non-re-engagement by the EOG followed a disagreement with Britten about whether the conductor should come on stage when rehearsing the audience in *Let's Make an Opera* – Del Mar wished to remain in the orchestra pit. He suspects that this disagreement was only a pretext on Britten's part. 'It's conceivable that he wanted any stick to beat a dog – that he wanted a change.' Basil Douglas says that 'Ben couldn't face anything unpleasant, and when it came to the time for Norman to be sacked, I had to do the sacking. And this happened to two other conductors, and with designers and producers. And I became awfully unpopular! And it was very sad.' Douglas remarks of these dismissals, 'I never met a more ruthless person than Ben.' Yet he emphasizes that Britten 'produced such cogent reasons for getting rid of these people that I didn't question it. I was absolutely devoted to him, as so many of us were.'

Del Mar observes of this aspect of working for Britten: 'We all knew that our time wasn't going to be for ever. I got the chop in due course, and after I'd got the chop from Basil Douglas, within six months *he'd* got the chop!' Douglas himself recalls how

> when the awkward moment came when Ben decided *I* wasn't any good to him any more, there was nobody to tell me! The only way I learnt what was in the wind was when dear Imogen Holst came into the office, and said, 'Basil, I want you to know that, whatever happens, I shall always be your friend.' So I knew that was it!

Douglas had given up a BBC career to work for Britten, and at first he felt 'very bitter' about his sacking. Later, when he had established himself in artists' management, he resumed his friendship with Britten and Pears, 'I think more particularly with Peter; Ben was rather more guarded.' Del Mar remarks that 'what was nice was that Ben never really forgot one, and one came back, often as not. Many is the one like myself who found themselves suddenly asked back, and how much that gave one pleasure is impossible to say.' John Amis recalls that 'years later, when Ben needed Olive for something, he was charming and she went back. I think she was right to do that. Geniuses are exceptional, aren't they? They can break the rules.' Basil Douglas puts it a little differently: 'One was so devoted to Ben's music that one just had to take the personality with a pinch of salt.'

*

Douglas was not replaced as manager of the EOG. His workload was added to that of the already hard-pressed Stephen Reiss, who was running the Aldeburgh Festival. 'Ben said, "Let's combine the Festival and the Opera Group,"' says Reiss,

> and we would only put the operas on in Aldeburgh. If other people wanted to do them elsewhere, let them organize it themselves. I told Ben that I was willing to run the Opera Group on that basis, as an extension of the Festival. But he didn't really mean what he'd said – and I eventually discovered that this was typical. As soon as we had done *Noye's Fludde* at Aldeburgh in 1958 he said, 'We've got to take it to London.' So we took it to London.

A year later, Reiss had to organize a Holland Festival appearance by the EOG. He managed all this with no permanent staff besides a part-time typist and, questioned about his salary, admits that this was 'nowhere remotely near' what it ought to have been, 'though you might say that was my own fault'. When a Festival club was opened in Aldeburgh he was allowed free meals there – in exchange for managing it as well as his other duties. Nevertheless he says of his early years in the job, or jobs: 'I enjoyed it absolutely hugely. I loved every minute of it.'

A month after the tenth Aldeburgh Festival, in July 1957, Britten reported to William Plomer that he was having 'a frustrating year, as far as writing is concerned'. His commitments included conducting the EOG in *The Turn of the Screw* at Stratford, Ontario, and again at the Berlin Festival. Plomer was keen to work on a libretto based on the Noh play *Sumidagawa*. He had spent two years in Japan when he was young, and Britten's suggestion struck him 'as a gong or bell is struck'. Britten, however, wished to wait a while. 'The "Sumidagawa" doesn't come into any *immediate* plans,' he told Plomer in July 1957: 'I've rather pushed it to the back of my mind; but anytime you feel you'd like to talk about it, it can be brought forward again. It is something I'm deeply interested in, & determined to do sometime.' In another letter this year, to Ronald Duncan, he discussed his habit of delaying the start of work on important projects:

> I get terribly worked up about a thing, then cool off, & then, if the idea was originally a good one, come back with renewed vigour to it. The work has gone on boiling in the back of the old mind, & usually to good effect. Grimes was like this (I delayed over a year on starting the music after Slater had finished the first draft of the libretto) – so was the Spring Symphony, & the Turn of the Screw.

The tenth Festival was his last at Crag House. The windows were easily visible from the sea-front, and passers-by would stare at him as he worked in his study, and even walk into the house uninvited (Fidelity Cranbrook recalls names being scratched on the backs of chairs). During 1957 Britten decided to move out of the centre of Aldeburgh. In 1951 Stephen Potter, author of books about 'Gamesmanship' and similar humorous concepts, had moved from London with his wife and two sons to a large converted farmhouse overlooking the Aldeburgh golf course. It was named the Red House, a common Suffolk term for brick buildings. Potter was a member of the BBC music committee and had known Britten a little before arriving in Aldeburgh, but it was his wife Mary who really made friends with him. She learnt to play the recorder in the Aldeburgh music club, founded with Britten and Pears's encouragement in the early fifties to promote amateur music-making – Britten himself played the viola and treble recorder in it – and when she came on the spring 1955 skiing holiday with Britten, Pears and the Duncans and retired hurt after the first day on skis, Britten wrote on the spot an *Alpine Suite* for recorders to give her something to practise. She was a talented painter whose career had been halted by bringing up a family, and with Britten's encouragement she began to resume it, painting portraits of him, Imogen Holst, Nellie Hudson and Roger Duncan. By the mid-fifties her marriage had broken up and her husband had returned to London. Her boys were now adults, and the Red House was too big for her needs. It was her son Julian who suggested that she and Britten might exchange homes. The legal arrangements took some while, but the double move was finally achieved in mid-November 1957.

'We are very excited about life at the Red House, & have countless plans for it,' Britten wrote to his sister Barbara. 'Peter ... is highly occupied & enjoying himself, moving this & that, & fixing curtains, carpets, etc. etc.' The house dated partly from the sixteenth century, and had numerous outbuildings, including a garage above which Britten made his study, and a substantial garden with tennis court (Britten soon added a swimming-pool). It was reached by a gravel lane on the outskirts of the town, and was only visible to golfers. When Norman Del Mar came back to Aldeburgh some while after the move, he thought it rather a pity that Britten was now out of sight. It had seemed to him that 'Ben and Peter living in that house on the sea-front, and people going past, and knowing they were just there – even that apparently superficial element was important to the Festival. The Red House was a retreat.' Britten himself described it, in a letter to Edith Sitwell, as 'alas, away from the sea, but thankfully away from the gaping faces, & irritating publicity of that sea-front. It is a lovely house, with a big garden all round, & I've made myself a nice remote studio where I can bang away to my heart's content.'

He told Donald Mitchell that his brother Robert, after being shown around the Red House, asked: 'But Ben, do you think you really *deserve* all this?' (The move had in fact cost very little money; it was almost a straight swap.) Michael Tippett thought the departure from Crag House 'strange, in a sense, because there he was going from his beloved sea. But by that time he was living, to some degree, a different kind of life.' Tippett says that by now he found it impossible for him and Britten to 'talk composition together, colleague to colleague. That ceased. I missed it.' Tippett's music was often performed at Aldeburgh, but Britten did not seem to wish to continue the old intimacy. 'If I had to go to Aldeburgh,' Tippett says,

> I used to send him a postcard, and say, 'I shall be staying in a hotel, and I know you'll be extremely busy because of the Festival, and I won't therefore expect to see you.' And I didn't see him at the Red House,

because I didn't want to particularly, and *he* certainly didn't want it – I couldn't tell you the reason why. If I met him in the street, he would be as nice as nice. We never quarrelled. There was no problem. But it was sad for me.

Tippett felt that Britten was now making too much musical use of Pears: 'As the works began to come out involving Peter, I thought it would be very good for Ben as a composer if he had another voice, possibly a woman's voice. *I* couldn't have picked out one tenor voice, whether it was a lover or not. And I didn't really feel that it was a very good way to go.'

Britten's first work written after the move was *Songs from the Chinese*, with words from Arthur Waley's collection of translations, to be sung by Pears, accompanied by the guitarist Julian Bream, who had now begun to give recitals with him. It was another cycle with a personal narrative. Written around the time of Britten's forty-fourth birthday in November 1957, it is concerned with middle age. The first song recommends the avoidance of the race for worldly fame and fortune: 'Don't help on the big chariot; / You will only make yourself dusty.' The second, 'The Old Lute', laments the fickleness of popular taste, which is always changing (is Britten commenting dryly on the critics' constant 'revaluations' of him?). The cycle now turns to love, and in 'The Autumn Wind' past *amours* are recalled amid the consciousness of ageing. Next, as if in further illustration of love recollected, comes a lilting portrait of a boy with an ox, 'The Herd-Boy'. Another reminder of approaching old age, 'Depression' ('Turned to jade are the boy's rosy cheeks'), is built around eerie guitar glissandi. In the concluding 'Dance Song' vigour returns, and we are plunged into an erotic chase, a hunt for a unicorn, the traditional symbol of chastity. The implication seems to be that the only remedy for despair at ageing is love and sexuality, though the singer's reiterated cries of 'Alas!' suggest that, despite the passing of years, guilt about this has not vanished.

The work Britten composed immediately after *Songs from the Chinese* appears at first sight to have no connection with the cycle. 'My dear Owen,' he wrote to Owen Brannigan on 7 December 1957, 'You may have heard that I am writing an operatic version of one of the Chester Mystery Plays, "Noah's Deluge" for the Aldeburgh Festival ... for next year ... Noah, as you can imagine, is a very big part ... Would you consider doing it for us?' To Edith Sitwell, in a letter a week later, he described it as 'a new children's opera – a charming 14th century Mystery Play', and told her that the music was 'punctuated by hammer-blows' because there were workmen at the Red House. To Brannigan, he explained: 'I am writing it for two grown-ups and six professional children, and literally hundreds of

local school children in the choruses. We are doing two or three performances in a very beautiful local church (Orford), very much in the naïve
medieval style.'

Noye's Fludde originated in a commission from Boris Ford, then in
charge of schools' programmes at Associated Rediffusion, the London
commercial television company, for a 'Britten version' of one of the
English medieval mystery plays. Britten responded enthusiastically, telling Ford that 'he had indeed for some months or a year vaguely been
thinking of doing something with the miracle plays'. Ford lost his job and
Associated Rediffusion lost interest, but Britten decided to go ahead
independently. He found his new text in his copy of A. W. Pollard's
selection from the English mystery plays, from which he had already
taken the words for *Canticle II: Abraham and Isaac*. Like that story, the
Noah play deals with a paternal–filial relationship, doubly so, for it
treats of Noah's obedience to God the Father as well as his harmonious
dealings with his own sons.

Noye's Fludde opens with the congregational hymn 'Lord Jesus, think
on me', but from the introductory bars to the very end the bass line is out
of step with the singing. The hymn's prayer to 'purge away my sin . . .
make me pure within' seems to have little hope of success. If the hymn
suggests an adult world where purity is unattainable, the music which
introduces Noye's children conjures up the blissful optimism of childhood which cannot perceive that any unpleasantness is in store. The
children's first song is full of impatient, enthusiastic syncopation and
excited key changes. Into this happiness, Mrs Noye intrudes with jarring
cynicism, and though Noye manages to get her under control she boxes
his ears – a detail invented by Britten, perhaps with another domineering
mother in mind. Meanwhile with the building of the Ark we encounter
the work's musical innovation, the use of children not merely as singers
but in the orchestra: beginner string players, a recorder group, and a
team of young percussionists. This is bold in itself, but the effect they
produce is thoroughly startling. The repetition of two-note figures on the
recorders, aligned with open string pizzicato and the tapping of oriental
temple-blocks, leads us into the musical world of Bali. Wilfrid Mellers
has written of Quint's music in *The Turn of the Screw* that it 'open[s]
magic casements, revealing realms wildly mysterious, remote from the
pieties of the Victorian country house'. If for the last three words one
substitutes 'English parish church' the same is true of the effect produced
by the child instrumentalists in *Noye's Fludde*.

Britten has still more startling effects to come. With the Ark built and
ready to float there begins a march which brings in the animals, the

chorus of schoolchildren mentioned in the letter to Brannigan. They arrive to the sound of bugles. This may seem an unlikely instrument for a pacifist composer, but for Britten the bugle's associations were not with the army but school. David Layton, who was at Gresham's with him, is convinced that the 'bugle theme' in *Noye's Fludde* is a recollection of the school's Officer Training Corps band practising in front of the cricket pavilion, where there was a 'grand echo', while he and Britten were nearby in the nets. Most other English ex-public schoolboys would have similar memories, while others would think of a boys' brigade band marching past on a Sunday morning. The bugle, then, is an instrument evoking boyhood.

To its sound, in march the child-animals, like the Hamelin rats following the Pied Piper. Because of the martial character of the music it is easy to miss the significance of the words they are singing, 'Kyrie eleison', that is, 'Lord have mercy'. It soon becomes apparent that the storm from which they are sheltering is no mere matter of wind and water. It begins not with any crash of thunder but once again with a piece of nursery-like instrumentation. Imogen Holst describes how Britten.

> had the idea of hitting teacups with teaspoons to represent the sound of the first raindrops falling on the ark, but he came round to me one afternoon saying that he'd tried it out at tea-time and it wouldn't work. By great good fortune I had once had to teach Women's Institute percussion groups during a wartime 'social half hour', so I was able to take him into my kitchen and show him how a row of china mugs hanging on a length of string could be hit with a large wooden spoon.

This sound is soon joined by swirling recorders (representing the wind) and beginner strings and young percussionists (thunder and lightning). The storm, then, is made up entirely of childlike materials. It takes the form of a passacaglia.

As this builds excitedly towards its peak, those on board the Ark pray for deliverance, not in the medieval language of the Chester Play, but in the words and melody of a Victorian hymn, 'Eternal Father, strong to save'. Perhaps unlike Britten's own young days, when he may have felt that no strong father had stepped in to protect him, the prayer is answered. Just as the storm is about to reach its climax, the orchestra falls silent and the organ breaks out, accompanying the final verse of the hymn with untroubled Anglican harmonies. Innocence has not been lost.

No wonder that, as they leave the Ark, the child-animals sing a thankful Alleluia. But the danger has not quite vanished. As the voice of God promises that there will never be another such storm, his words are accompanied by a sound faintly suggesting Quint's celesta music, a Balinese-style note-cluster (chord of closely spaced notes) from a team of handbell ringers. Imogen Holst has described how the handbells got into *Noye's Fludde*:

> They [the ringers] were members of the local Aldeburgh Youth Club, whom Ben used to invite in every now and then, and give them his foreign stamps, from all those hundreds of letters he got from abroad. And one day, one of the boys said, 'Well, I've got to go now.' And Ben said, 'What are you doing?' And they were practising hand-bells. And Ben said, 'Oh, I'd love to hear them. Will you come and play them to me tomorrow afternoon?' And so they came, and played in his garden – *Little Brown Jug* I think it was. And he was so thrilled that he gave that marvellous moment in *Noye's Fludde* to those little boys.

The sound produced by the 'little boys' dominates the remainder of *Noye's Fludde*. God may have promised the end of all storms, and cast and congregation join together to assure themselves of the triumph of the rational mind over instinct: 'In reason's ear they all rejoice, / And utter forth a glorious voice . . .' Yet insistently above the 'godly' G major of Tallis's Canon (G is the key used throughout *Noye's Fludde* to suggest man's harmony with God) there rings out the B flat call of the bugles, joined now by the handbells. As God speaks his final, paternally loving words to Noye, 'My vengeance shall noe more appeare / And nowe fare well, my darlinge deare', and the orchestra comes to rest on a 'natural' G major triad, the young ringers still faintly sound their oriental charm in their own key. The magic casements have not yet utterly closed.

There is a curious detail in the music just before the key of G major is reached in the third verse of Tallis's Canon (the preceding verse has been in F). The organ is heard by itself, going through a series of discordant chromatic contortions, full of note-clusters like those sounded on the handbells, before it resolves itself rather unconvincingly into G for the final verse. Peter Evans calls this passage 'the only jarring note in *Noye's Fludde*', and suggests that Britten is recalling 'all those meretricious devices by which officious organists have found it necessary to demonstrate changes of key to presumedly witless congregations'. Britten must have meant this elaborate and overblown modulation to jar. He seems to be portraying people who attain a sense of godliness (G major) by repressing their real natures. On the other hand a few moments earlier G major has arrived effortlessly, without warning, out of the handbells' note-cluster of B flat with an added sixth (the note G). This magical moment, remarked on appreciatively by almost every commentator on

Noye's Fludde, seems intended to show that real godliness, a true sense of oneness with the universe (as opposed to Anglican-style 'churchiness'), arises out of total acceptance of the sensual (the Balinese-style B flat with added sixth) – a view rarely expressed in Britten's music.

*

Britten dedicated *Noye's Fludde* to Beth Welford's children and also to 'my young friend Roger Duncan'. Some months before writing it, he told Basil Coleman: 'I see more & more of little (now quite big!) Roger, as his parents get more & more unhappy. He spends about ½ his holidays from Harrow here, & is an enchanting & deeply affectionate boy.'

Britten asked Charles Mackerras, who had taken over from Norman Del Mar as EOG conductor, to direct the music for the first production of *Noye's Fludde*. Mackerras had a heavy workload at the 1958 Aldeburgh Festival. Besides the new work, he was in the pit for a revival of *The Rape of Lucretia*, and for Poulenc's comic opera *Les Mamelles de Tirésias* ('The Breasts of Tirésias'), in which Peter Pears was to take the part of a husband who has a sex change and gives birth to a multitude of babies. (Poulenc himself, who had first taken part in the Festival in 1956, was due to play, with Britten, one of the two pianos which were to accompany the opera, but had to cancel.) Although the opera was billed decorously in the programme book as *Tirésias*, Mackerras assumed, 'as it turned out mistakenly', that the choice of such a ribald piece and the casting of Pears meant that 'Ben and Peter were starting to be able to laugh at themselves a bit'.

The tendency among musicians of the Walton–Beecham–Constant Lambert circle to crack jokes about Britten and Pears ('Twilight of the Sods', 'Bugger's Opera', 'The Stern of the Crew' and others) had spread to certain members of the EOG, who had devised words for the horn call which opens the *Serenade*: 'I like boys, I like young boys, big boys ...' Mackerras, who participated in some of these jokes, says they were partly a reaction to uneasiness:

> I always felt slightly uncomfortable in Ben and Peter's presence, because you couldn't ever quite say what you thought. You always had to couch everything in slightly false terms not to offend them. But the fact that people laughed at the homosexuality didn't mean that we didn't all worship Britten as a musician, and even as a person.

During preparations for *Noye's Fludde*, Mackerras realized that 'it had more boys than any Britten work to date – masses of boys! – though there were girls too. And I made a remark about this to someone, who mentioned it to John Cranko, who took it straight to Ben.' (The boys included the young Michael Crawford as Jaffet. Under his real name of Michael Ingram he had already appeared as Sammy in *The Little Sweep.*)

Cranko was producing *Les Mamelles de Tirésias*. He and Mackerras had collaborated on the creation of two successful ballets, *Pineapple Poll* and *The Lady and the Fool*. Mackerras accused him of telling tales to Britten. Cranko's response was: 'When suddenly you hear something like that, however long you may have worked together, suddenly you hate that person.' Mackerras comments: 'But he was a homosexual, and I'm not, and there is a sort of Freemasonry among them.'

Mackerras now received

a horrible letter from Peter, saying, 'You've ruined the pleasure of *Noye's Fludde.*' I was told to go to the Red House, and when I got there Ben said to me, 'Because I like to be with boys, and because I appreciate young people, am I therefore a lecher?' He actually said that to me. And I couldn't explain to him that on the one hand we worshipped him, and on the other hand we were amused by this. I must say, though, that he was extraordinarily restrained, extraordinarily calm. It was I who was white with nerves!

Mackerras was allowed to remain as conductor of *Noye's Fludde*, 'and I did a good job I believe'. Britten was playing one of the pianos in *Tirésias*, 'and he was marvellous in that, and said, "I'm sorry if I'm not following the beat." We were very, very polite to each other, and I know he was trying hard to be nice, and I was trying hard to make up, of course. But after that I didn't get employed by Aldeburgh for some time.' Stephen Reiss saw Britten before he had managed to control his anger and confront Mackerras calmly:

We were having a rehearsal of *Noye's Fludde* in the young people's club, and Ben came in at the door, and it was something superhuman. The anger that came out, it was just phenomenal. And I thought, 'My God, what on earth has happened?' He didn't say anything, he was just standing there in the doorway. And I asked him what was the matter, and he told me about it, and he was absolutely furious. He said, 'It's as if I was stealing money out of the till!'

*

'The sleepy village of Orford, near the Suffolk coast,' wrote Felix Apra-hamian in the *Sunday Times* on 22 June 1958, 'was disturbed last Wednesday afternoon by invading crowds who came to its parish church from far and wide to witness the first performance of Benjamin Britten's latest work.' Aprahamian judged *Noye's Fludde* to be a 'curiously moving spiritual and musical experience'. The producer was Colin Graham. He had been promoted from EOG stage-manager to take over from Basil Coleman, who was now working in Canada. Coleman says he decided to leave the EOG 'because I felt I needed to grow up'. Colin Graham writes:

> I had wanted to be involved in opera from a very early age. When I finally accepted that my voice was never going to be good enough to sing it, I turned to the possibilities of directing ... The very first recordings I ever possessed were the old 78s of *Lucretia* with which I was hopelessly in love. I had cut out pictures of *Peter Grimes* from *Picture Post* when at school, and Britten was already a hero for me. I never got to see an opera of his until the 1951 EOG season at the Lyric, Hammersmith (Festival of Britain), when I saw all that was available, and this cemented my passion for his operas. After two years at drama school (RADA) I went into rep as an actor and stage manager. Out of work the following summer, I was overjoyed to receive a call from the EOG, who desperately needed an ASM for *The Beggar's Opera* at the Taw and Torridge Festival. It seemed a call from heaven.

For *Noye's Fludde* he also designed the scenery; the costumes were devised by the painter Ceri Richards. Martin Cooper in the *Daily Telegraph* praised the 'gay colours ... fantastic head-dresses of the animals', and judged that 'the future of the work will lie in village churches such as this and with amateur musicians, for whom Britten has written something both wholly new and outstandingly original'.

'I am so glad you enjoyed Noye; we are all very pleased with the reception it has had,' Britten wrote a few days later to Ernst Roth, one of the directors of Boosey & Hawkes. Since its completion there had been many distractions from his work: 'the builders were in the house, without interval, from mid-November to mid-June', he told William Plomer. Also, 'I've had a series of silly, & unimportant illnesses (culminating in Pleurisy ...)' As to *Sumidagawa*, 'I can't write about the No play idea now, except to say that it's boiling up inside me, but that I have so many things to talk to you about – the style & all – before I start on it.' Meanwhile he was writing a work for the Leeds Festival at the invitation of Lord Harewood, artistic director for 1958, its centenary year. 'I have been in such a really dreary state recently,' Britten told Marion Harewood in August, 'stupid little health things going wrong, never has work been so difficult (it is a real "wrestling with the angel" to get the

Dream piece written).' He was referring to what Lord Harewood calls 'the strangely beautiful *Nocturne*', a setting for tenor, seven 'obligato' (Britten's preferred spelling) instruments, and strings, of eight poems with the common theme of dreaming. It was given its first performance by Pears and the BBC Symphony Orchestra conducted by Rudolf Schwarz in Leeds Town Hall on 16 October 1958.

'It won't be madly popular because it is the strangest & remotest thing – but then dreams are strange & remote,' Britten wrote of the *Nocturne* to Marion Harewood. In an interview with Donald Mitchell a decade later he spoke of dreaming as an important part of the process of composition – 'it gives a chance for your subconscious mind to work when your conscious mind is happily asleep ... if I don't sleep, I find that ... in the morning [I am] unprepared for my next day's work' – but admitted that dreams could also 'release many things which one thinks had better not be released'. The *Nocturne* is an examination of both these aspects of dreams.

It is linked by a recurring passage for strings, a gently rocking rhythm which critics have interpreted as the breathing of the sleeper, though if this is what Britten had in mind the breaths seem unusually fast and shallow. Colin Matthews points out that it is also found in Britten's setting of 'Now sleeps the crimson petal', written for but not included in the *Serenade*.

The cycle begins with a Shelley poem which expounds Britten's belief that dreams are the artist's workshop. Next comes a setting of Tennyson's lines about the Kraken sleeping beneath the waves, obviously a symbol for the dark side of the personality which dreams can reveal. Coleridge's vision of 'A lovely Boy ... plucking fruits', with a melismatic vocal line, is followed by an onomatopoeic setting of a poem which Britten called 'a mad piece about night noises' – Middleton's 'Midnight's bell goes ting, ting, ting, ting'. Wordsworth's lines from *The Prelude* about night fears engendered by the French Revolution, which Britten provides with a dramatic timpani 'obligato', lead to a sombre setting of a Wilfred Owen poem about a woman (symbol of the British nation) who sleeps undisturbed by the knowledge that the innocent have died to keep her in comfort – her 'palace wall' is constructed out of 'boys on boys and doom on dooms'. Gaiety breaks out again briefly in Keats's 'What is more gentle than a wind in summer?', which Britten sets in the manner of 'English pastoral' music, but the conclusion of the cycle, a setting of Shakespeare's sonnet 'When most I wink, then do mine eyes best see', is in Mahlerian mood – the *Nocturne* is dedicated to Mahler's widow Alma – and seems to be an assertion, perhaps in antithesis to the seductive dream world, of the necessity of a stable love relationship. 'Peter is a rock, a very solid rock,' Britten once said to Beata Mayer.

*

'My very dearest George & Marion,' Britten wrote to the Harewoods four days after the first performance of the *Nocturne*, 'Forgive the double letter but we are rushing around madly ... trying to record those little Canticles, Donne Sonnets & Hölderlin too ...' *Sechs Hölderlin-Fragmente* was written, like the *Nocturne*, during the summer of 1958 and recorded by Britten and Pears for a broadcast a month after the Leeds Festival. It owed its inception to Prince Ludwig of Hesse, to whom it was dedicated, and who had introduced Britten to the work of this strange eighteenth-century German poet who died insane. The cycle deals with the same subject matter as *Songs from the Chinese*, and though the musical style is more severe, with a distinct nod at Lieder, Britten's standpoint with regard to middle age and love becomes even clearer. As in the Chinese songs, the cycle opens with a contemptuous glance at worldly fame, 'Menschenbeifall' ('The Applause of Man'), which is fol-lowed in 'Die Heimat' ('Home') by a lyrical plea for a return to the security of childhood. Then comes Hölderlin's short poem about Socrates' love for the young Alcibiades. An inquirer asks the philosopher why he dotes on such a stripling. Socrates' reply, that those of deep mind love liveliness, virtue and beauty, is set to a series of major triads, which are (of course) Britten's language for 'naturalness'. He seems to be answering Mackerras's jibe by asserting that his love for the young has nothing unnatural about it. This assertion is reiterated in 'Die Jugend' ('Youth'), in which Ganymede delightedly describes how the love of the gods made him a man. Britten's Schubertian piano part raises no doubts about the rightness of such a love.

Yet in the next song, 'Hälfte des Lebens' ('The Middle of Life'), the music becomes disturbed and anxious. The immediate cause is merely an awareness of middle age, but in the last song, 'Die Linien des Lebens' ('Lines of Life'), there seems to be a more fundamental self-doubt. The four-line poem declares that what we are in this life will be completed by God in the next world, 'Mitt Harmonien und ew'gem Lohn und Frieden', 'With harmony, reward and peace eternal', but the music here becomes full of discord, which persists until the end. Britten does not seem to share Hölderlin's spiritual optimism.

Sechs Hölderlin-Fragmente were performed by Britten and Pears at Schloss Wolfsgarten on 20 November 1958, Lu Hesse's fiftieth birth-day. Two days later they all celebrated Britten's forty-fifth. He took with him to Germany a draft by William Plomer of a libretto based on

Sumidagawa, and reported that he was 'about to start a new opera'. On his return he conducted a recording for Decca of *Peter Grimes*, in Walthamstow Town Hall, with Pears, Claire Watson as Ellen (Joan Cross had now retired from singing), Owen Brannigan as Swallow and Geraint Evans as Ned Keene. Britten had been nervous beforehand – 'I've never conducted it before & the schedule is terrifying (with no time-safety valve)' – and, though the recording was superb, by the end he had 'managed to put a bone in my back out, which made breathing impossible'. He then spent two months off work with flu, and in early March 1959 told Plomer there was 'a big job (500th Anniversary of Basel to be celebrated by a cantata) which I want to get out of the way before I started [*sic*] on the Noh play'. *Cantata Academica*, commissioned for the quincentenary of the University of Basle, is a setting for soloists, chorus and orchestra of a ponderous Latin text. Britten admitted to Plomer that he 'wasn't frankly awfully interested' in the job, though he was 'amused by the rather school-boyish Latin'. The music gives no indication of a more than superficial commitment to the task. Possibly he accepted the commission in order to put off, yet again, work on the Noh play.

'I've more or less finished my Basel chore, & the decks v slowly clearing for the Noh,' he told Plomer on 3 April 1959. And in another letter: 'I think the Noh Libretto is wonderful.' But on 15 April he wrote that he and Pears had 'A new idea . . . of making it a *Christian* work'. He had been worried about producing 'a *pastiche* of a Noh play'. Admittedly, Christianizing the story would 'lose the magic of the Japanese names, & atmosphere', and there might be 'No good reason for Peter to do a female part', though this could be solved 'if we made it Mediaeval, or possibly earlier', that is, if they set it in a period in which 'it would be accurate that no women should be used'. One such possibility was 'pre-conquest East Anglia'. Plomer replied good-humouredly that he was not surprised that Britten was 'setting fire to your – and indeed my – kimono', and agreed that it would have been 'a pasticcio grosso' in its Japanese form, though it was 'a little electrifying to have to think of transposing the story into Christian terms'. He already had one suggestion: 'that the missing child has come to be regarded locally as a saint (perhaps he could have been martyred) & that his grave has already become a place of pilgrimage'. But he feared that, however formalized the style remained, 'it might seem odd for the mother to be a man'.

Britten and Pears visited Plomer in May 1959 and agreed on a working title of 'The River', though shortly afterwards Plomer suggested 'Curlew River'. 'I am very excited about it now,' Britten wrote to him after their meeting. 'I feel that we are really a long way along the road, & I can scarcely wait until I take over the musical reins!' But still he did not begin work on it.

For some time he had promised George Malcolm a Mass for the boys of the Westminster Cathedral choir, where Malcolm was organist. Malcolm disagreed with the usual approach to boys' voices in cathedrals – trying to smooth out any roughness – and had managed to bring out their natural timbre with its raw edge. When Britten heard Malcolm's boys in January 1959 he wrote to him: 'the whole choir sang with a brilliance & authority which was staggering – owing to you, my dear, I know'. In another letter he referred to Malcolm's 'incredible boys'. Malcolm says that one day a little later that year he met Britten by chance and mentioned that he would be leaving the cathedral in the summer to go freelance. 'He didn't say, as some of my friends kindly had, "What a loss for English church music." He just said, "What about my Mass?" and three weeks later he delivered it, very badly copied and duplicated by Boosey's, just in time for me to conduct it. I was immensely pleased.' Britten's *Missa Brevis in D* for three-part boys' voices and organ is a vivacious piece designed to show off the choristers' paces, and makes little concession to the liturgical words. It was first heard in Westminster Cathedral at a service on 22 July 1959, under Malcolm's direction, with Britten in the congregation.

Three weeks later Britten wrote again to Plomer:

> my mind has been working hard about 'The River' ... I fear I must postpone this piece, still near to my heart, for a year. For many reasons. Partly time; because of my 'change of location', moving it from Japan to Mediaeval England, we are well behind our schedule ... The other reason is that we are going this coming winter to rebuild the Jubilee Hall, make it a proper little Opera House, with dressing rooms, bigger stage, bigger orchestral pit, changing & increasing the seating, etc, etc, and we must have a new big opera to open it with next June. The 'River', being for a church, wouldn't do, also, it is scarcely festive. So I am going to do the Midsummer Night's Dream – which uses a bigger cast, orchestra, & has the essential advantage of having a libretto ready (it is an old idea of mine, & Peter & I have already done much work, cutting up poor old Shakespeare). I hope you won't be too cross ... I am determined on doing ['The River'] for the next year ...

From the earliest days of the Festival it had been hoped that there might eventually be a purpose-built auditorium, larger than the cramped Jubilee Hall. During the fifties this scheme had advanced and ebbed with the Festival's finances. By 1957 a site had been bought on high ground overlooking Aldeburgh High Street, and Britten was asking friends' advice about fund-raising (one scheme was to get Marilyn Monroe to open a garden party). However, Stephen Reiss felt that a more urgent priority was to 'develop what we'd got', and it was eventually decided to enlarge the Jubilee Hall at a cost of £18,000 as opposed to the £40,000 required for the theatre. The land for the theatre was sold again and the Friends of the Aldeburgh Festival raised most of the money for the alterations during the winter of 1959–60, while the work was going on. The costs included the acquisition of the building next door to the hall, which would provide space for the enlargement of the auditorium, and also a directors' box, 'a sort of private gallery for Ben and Peter,' says Fidelity Cranbrook, 'so that they could slip in and out'. Stephen Reiss says that this was essential: 'If they were going to come into events to hear them at all, they had to be free to go in and out.'

Plomer accepted the further postponement without complaint, and set about Christianizing and East Anglianizing the Noh play at his leisure. Meanwhile Britten had already been to see John and Myfanwy Piper in Oxfordshire to discuss the Shakespeare opera. 'They were thrilled with the idea of Midsummer Night's Dream,' Britten told Pears on 24 July 1959, '& we discussed it endlessly. I'm just sending off to Myfanwy our projected scheme for it; she has some good ideas about it.' Myfanwy Piper says that, while she did make a few suggestions, Pears was 'extremely possessive' about his role as co-librettist, or co-editor of Shakespeare, 'and didn't want to forgo his collaboration with Ben at all'. She adds that 'he did consider himself to be the literate one'.

On 18 August, Britten wrote to Alfred Deller, whom Michael Tippett had discovered singing in Canterbury Cathedral Choir during the war. With Tippett's encouragement he had achieved a one-man revival of the Purcellian counter-tenor voice. Britten had often heard him, and hoped he would be available to sing Oberon: 'I see you and hear your voice very clearly in this part ...' Deller replied that he had only minimal stage experience, but when Pears assured him that 'Your height and presence will be absolutely right (– so will your beard!),' Deller committed himself enthusiastically to the opera. Meanwhile Britten and Pears were busily cutting Shakespeare, reducing the play by roughly half, omitting the opening in Athens and transferring certain lines to different characters. Conscious of 'the tremendous challenge of those Shakespearean words', Britten began the composition sketch during October.

His health was bad during the winter. By the beginning of December he was in bed with gastric flu, and his arm was playing up again. However, Act I was sketched by the end of November, and Imogen Holst began work on the vocal score. 'I dragged the dogs out for a good long walk round the river-wall this afternoon, to collect ideas for Act II,' Britten told Pears on 9 December. The Red House ménage now included two dogs, one of them 'the smallest Dachshund ever, called Clytie' – named after Clytie Mundy. Five days later: 'I'm having fun with Thisby now – well into the 2nd Act, & going fairly well, I think.' John Piper had done 'some spiffing new designs', and John Cranko, who was to produce, was coming down to Aldeburgh for discussions. Two months later: 'I am afraid I'm still very much under the weather here – oscillating between bed & drawing-room. The cold's got into the sinuses, & I stream from nose & eyes, & can't breathe or hear ... However I'm pushing on with the score.'

Cranko began to disappoint as producer. His private life was in a mess, and he was showing little interest in the opera. 'We mustn't be foolish & throw him over *too* soon,' Pears wrote to Britten on 8 January 1960, in a letter which gives a rare glimpse of Pears's part in such matters. Later in the same letter: 'Oh dear – no. I suppose he's hopeless – we'd better forget him. Do you think a tactful, affectionate letter to Fred. A[shton] would get *him*? He might do a lovely job of it.' In the event they decided it was too late to change producers. This side of Pears did not escape the notice of Lord Harewood:

> I watched him with people who were friends of theirs, and saw what I think may have been Peter's rather malevolent influence over Ben. You could say that it was a benevolent one, that it was better for Ben to be cut off from them. But Ben was very easily influenced in such things, and had a naïve side to his personality, and I think Peter influenced him against a lot of friends. I've always thought that eventually he did against me, though I have no proof of it.

By 22 February 1960, Britten had finished the orchestral score of Act II of *A Midsummer Night's Dream*, but had not yet sketched much of Act III. Work was eventually completed at Easter – 'not up to the speed of Mozart or Verdi,' wrote Britten, 'but ... the fastest of any big opera I have written'. Owing to delays in copying (Imogen Holst was ill) George Malcolm, who was training the boy fairies, did not receive the vocal score for Act III until about two weeks before the first performance. 'I was horror-struck by the difficulty of the music, and I told him, "Ben, the boys won't be able to sing everything you've written – it's too damn difficult." But somehow they did.'

A Midsummer Night's Dream (dedicated to Stephen Reiss and his wife) is 'big' in that it uses a larger orchestra than the chamber operas –

the improvements to the Jubilee Hall included the enlargement of the orchestral pit – but it has a less intricate construction than *The Turn of the Screw*, which had been written at far greater speed. Britten himself, in an article published in the *Observer* a few days before the first perform-ance, described it as 'more relaxed' than its immediate predecessor. This article fails to give any clear indication of why he was attracted to the Shakespeare play. The most he says is that he has 'always loved' it, feels it to be the work of 'a very young man', and finds it 'especially exciting' as operatic material because 'there are three quite separate groups – the lovers, the rustics, and the fairies'. More of a clue as to why he chose it for his next opera, postponing the Noh play, lies in the opening music, which takes us back into the sound world of the *Nocturne*, of the child instrumentalists in *Noye's Fludde*, and of Peter Quint.

This music consists of a series of glissando chords, establishing the character of the magic wood where, in the Britten–Pears version of Shakespeare, nearly the entire action takes place. These chords, which really do have the rhythm of a sleeper's breathing (though they also recall the ecstatic sighs of Miles), are in discordant relationship to each other and range through all twelve keys, but are themselves triads. Britten is establishing a world that is both 'natural' (triads) and 'unnatural' (dis-cords and chromaticism), a place where normal rules do not apply. That this world is familiar to us is indicated (following these chords) by the tuned percussion and harps which introduce the boy-treble fairies. We have passed through the magic casements and are actually in the amoral landscape of which earlier Britten works have given us a glimpse.

'Amoral' is a word Britten himself uses in his *Observer* article to describe the first individual to appear in the magic wood, Puck: 'He seems to be to be absolutely amoral and yet innocent.' The same might have been said of Miles, and Puck could be Miles growing up. He does not sing; Britten directs that his words be spoken rhythmically by a boy acrobat. In the *Observer* article he explains: 'I got the idea of doing Puck like this in Stockholm, where I saw some Swedish child actors with extraordinary agility and powers of mimicry, and suddenly realised we could do Puck that way.' Though the score does not specify the age of the boy, in the original production and a later revival supervised by Britten the part was given to a teenager with a just-broken voice. This suggests that Britten imagined Puck as having just passed puberty, an age at which many boys are indeed unable to sing properly, as their voices are settling into the lower register.

If Puck is an older Miles, Oberon seems to be an ethereal version of Quint. Throughout the opera he is musically characterized by celesta and harp, and like Quint's his vocal music is melismatic and has a 'home' key of E flat. Whereas in *The Turn of the Screw* the use of a pentatonic scale conferred moral ambiguity on Quint, Oberon's spell theme is made up of major seconds and shifts between incompatible keys (E flat and E minor). His music is always intensely beautiful, but Britten makes no pretence that he belongs, so to speak, to the world of the Governess. As to the use of the counter-tenor voice for Oberon, Michael Tippett has described Deller's singing as conveying 'almost no emotional irrelevancies [to] distract us from the absolutely pure musical quality', and it may be that Britten simply wished Oberon to sound as unhuman as possible – Myfanwy Piper describes Deller's singing of the part as 'unearthly'. It is also worth remembering that Purcell himself sang counter-tenor, so possibly Britten, writing neo-Purcellian music for Deller, was paying a double tribute to his great predecessor. However, many people would disagree with Tippett's assertion that a counter-tenor's voice has nothing emotionally distracting. In 1960 Deller was still regarded as something of a curiosity. Though he was the father of three children and sported a beard he still had to endure insinuations about his virility. (Robert Tear has a story of a German woman inquiring 'You are eunuch, Herr Deller?' and Deller replying, 'I'm sure you mean *unique*, Madam.') It may be that Britten, far from wanting Oberon to seem neutral, intended to suggest that there was something different about him sexually, possibly that he was a kind of Peter Pan who would never 'grow up' into puberty.

'I seek a friend – / Obedient to follow where I lead, / Slick as a juggler's mate to catch my thought, / Proud, curious, agile . . .' So Quint describes his hopes for Miles, and these words exactly catch the nature of Puck's relationship to Oberon. Established from the outset, that relationship is a datum of the opera rather than the area of its musical and dramatic conflict. Britten is obliged – since, for all their cuts, he and Pears have not tampered significantly with their Shakespearean original – to occupy himself largely with the mortal lovers who stray into the magic wood, and their music is based on a suitably tortuous motif which is first heard to Lysander's words 'The course of true love never did run smooth'. The parts of the opera which find him at full stretch are those which depict the interaction of the amoral fairy world with the third group of characters, Shakespeare's 'mechanicals', whom Britten refers to as 'rustics'.

After Bottom has been transformed into an ass in Act II, Britten, with considerable subtlety, depicts both the apparent and the real nature of Tytania's (as the opera, following some Shakespearian texts, spells her name) love for him. She sings him a sugary-sweet little waltz song, which seems to be in the 'innocent' key of C major, but all the time pedal notes are pulling it back towards the 'magic' key of E flat. Similarly the boy fairies chant 'Hail, mortal' to Bottom in 'pure' treble voices but with a sharpened fourth and flattened seventh which pull the phrase out of a 'natural' shape into something hypnotic and disturbing. When they perform innocent-sounding tunes, one of which closely resembles 'Girls and Boys, Come Out to Play', to divert him, their superficially childlike instruments – recorders, woodblocks and small cymbals – produce a 'magic casements' effect similar to that in *Noye's Fludde*.

Like the child-animals in the Ark, Bottom survives the storm of Tytania's sexual passion unscathed. Indeed he scarcely notices it. He is still singing what Peter Evans calls his 'earthy *parlando*' as he falls asleep in her lap. There is no question of his succumbing to the seductiveness of the immortals as Miles perhaps does to Quint's. In this scene, the pivot of *A Midsummer Night's Dream*, Britten is exploring two kinds of innocence: that of the fairy world, which has an ulterior seductive purpose, and the real purity of Bottom.

Having encountered seduction and survived it intact, Bottom and his fellows have a similarly blameless encounter in Act III with courtly life. The parody-opera which Britten makes out of their 'Pyramus and Thisbe' play has sometimes been criticized for the crudeness of its musical jokes, but it too is a celebration of innocence, or at least of naïvety. At the time of the first production of *A Midsummer Night's Dream* this scene was built around a topical joke. In February 1959 Joan Sutherland had scored an immense hit at Covent Garden in Zeffirelli's production of *Lucia di Lammermoor*. Britten's 'Pyramus and Thisbe' is largely a parody of Donizetti, and in the original production Pears took the part of Flute/Thisbe. (Hugues Cuenod, the Swiss tenor specializing in broadly comic roles, was offered the part, but was not available.) Myfanwy Piper says that Pears made Thisbe into 'a really wicked imitation of Joan Sutherland', both in appearance and vocal mannerisms. George Malcolm, who conducted the second performance at Aldeburgh, says Pears was so funny that 'I could hardly keep my place in the score for laughing'.

Alfred Deller loved the music Britten had written for him, but when rehearsals began he found Cranko a perfunctory producer who could not rise above the limitations of the tiny Jubilee Hall stage. Desmond Shawe-Taylor, reviewing the first performance on the opening night of the 1960 Aldeburgh Festival, observed that 'Cranko's production did not wholly avoid the village-hall effect'. He judged Puck to have been 'brilliantly performed by Leonide Massine II' (fifteen-year-old son of the choreographer), but though he commended Deller for 'some exquisite soft singing', he called his performance 'undramatic' and thought it a mistake to have dressed him in 'a capacious black magician's gown, half mandarin and half Prospero'. David Drew, writing in the *New Statesman*, observed the link between the new opera and *The Turn of the Screw*: 'The choice of a counter-tenor ... brilliantly confirms the equivocacy of Oberon's "unnatural" character ... Britten's Oberon is a more grimly effective horror than the Peter Quint who called from the Tower and had no Puck to help him.' Though he felt that *A Midsummer Night's Dream* had 'more than one superior' among Britten's earlier operas, Drew judged it 'an achievement far beyond the capacity of any other living composer'. Shawe-Taylor called the opera 'captivating', and praised the comedy of Owen Brannigan as Bottom and Pears as 'a saffron-clad Thisbe', while Donald Mitchell in the *Daily Telegraph* welcomed the news that the opera would be seen at Covent Garden in a few months: 'The interval of time is welcome for the opportunity it gives one's astounded, spellbound ears to come to grips with the audacious inspiration of a score in which extreme economy of invention and lavish imagination walk hand-in-hand in truly dream-like amity.' However, when Auden saw the opera he described it as 'dreadful! Pure Kensington', and Michael Tippett felt that it defined the real difference between him and Britten: '*Midsummer Marriage* comes out of the magic wood of *A Midsummer Night's Dream* on one side, but it's a different magic wood.'

A Midsummer Night's Dream reached Covent Garden in February 1961, having in the meanwhile been seen at the Holland Festival. There were major changes for the London performances: John Gielgud took over from Cranko as producer, Georg Solti conducted, Pears was replaced by John Lanigan, and Oberon was sung by the young American counter-tenor Russell Oberlin. (Gielgud writes: 'I never knew Ben or Peter at all well, although of course I met them many times – they used always to come round when they came to see me act. I had an ambitious desire to film *The Tempest*, and Ben promised he would compose the music, which was a most thrilling idea.' Donald Mitchell says that the plan was to make the film on Bali, with gamelan music for Ariel and the other spirits. Richard Attenborough was envisaged as director.)

Deller's biographers allege that his removal from *A Midsummer Night's Dream* came as an unpleasant shock to him and brought on a severe depression. However, immediately after the first performance and the appearance of the reviews, he had written to Britten, observing that his presence in the cast was obviously doing the opera no good with the critics, and telling him to 'delete me when you think fit'. He added: 'I shall always be grateful for being given such a wonderful opportunity.'

2: A kind of reparation

'It *was* a joy setting those heavenly words,' Britten wrote to Marjorie Fass in July 1960, the month after the première of *A Midsummer Night's Dream*. This summer he began to plan what he described as 'a big commission from Coventry, a full evening's choral work' to mark the opening of the new cathedral, though he was irritated that the clergy there hoped to avoid paying him a fee. 'My feeling is that ... they must be prepared to pay for it just as they have had to pay the workmen to build the Cathedral.' He was also, in consultation with Forster and Crozier, reorganizing *Billy Budd* from four acts into two for a BBC radio broadcast in the autumn, and in the hope of a new stage production. (This finally took place in January 1964 at Covent Garden, with Georg Solti conducting, Basil Coleman producing, Richard Lewis as Vere, Forbes Robinson as Claggart and Robert Kerns as Billy. Britten was 'not too happy with the cast' but called Solti 'wonderful'. The reviews were excellent; Desmond Shawe-Taylor called it 'an absurdity' that the opera had not previously been acknowledged universally as 'a self-evident and cast-iron masterpiece'.)

Britten gave pressure of work as his reason for declining an invitation to take part in a broadcast discussion with Shostakovich, who was in London in September 1960 for the first British performance of his Cello Concerto, though he said he hoped to meet the Russian composer 'for a moment'. On the evening of the concert, given by the Leningrad Symphony Orchestra on 21 September, he accepted an invitation from Shostakovich to sit in his box at the Royal Festival Hall. The opening item on the programme was *The Young Person's Guide to the Orchestra*. Then came the Concerto, premièred in Moscow the previous year. The soloist was the thirty-three-year-old cellist Mstislav Rostropovich, for whom it had been written.

Before he went on to the platform, Rostropovich was told that Britten was in the audience. 'I knew some of his works. In fact, I was extremely fond of them, but I had never seen the composer himself, not even a photograph of him. I wondered what he looked like. But then . . . it was time to go out on the stage.' Britten had listened to Rostropovich on the radio a few days earlier, 'and thought this was the most extraordinary 'cello playing I'd ever heard'. Now, during the Cello Concerto, Shostakovich saw Britten bobbing up and down like a schoolboy, even nudging him with happiness at the music. At the end of the concert, Shostakovich introduced Britten to Rostropovich, and the cellist, who had been led by Britten's music to expect a large and imposing figure, was momentarily thrown off balance by his slight build. Talking through an interpreter, Rostropovich 'attacked Britten there and then and pleaded most sincerely and passionately with him to write something for the cello. He replied that we'd have to talk it over in greater detail. Honestly,' concludes Rostropovich, 'I did not expect a reply so simple and yet so serious.'

Britten suggested that he come to Rostropovich's hotel the next day. Rostropovich, whose English vocabulary consisted solely of 'Goodbye' and 'Thank you very much', felt some consternation, since the Soviet concert agency, who took most of his earnings from foreign tours, had booked him into a cheap place in Kensington. However, he gave Britten the address, and excitedly told Genadi Rozhdestvensky, who had been conducting, about the caller he would be receiving tomorrow. Rozhdestvensky was present when Britten arrived, and Rostropovich says that both of them were struck by Britten's 'exceptional magnetism'. Britten said he was very keen to write a sonata for cello and piano, on the condition that Rostropovich would give the first performance at next summer's Aldeburgh Festival. Rostropovich was delighted, but warned Britten that he would have to obtain permission from the Soviet authorities. Britten quickly drafted a letter, sending it to Rostropovich for his approval, and on 25 September the cellist, who was still in London, wrote to him through a translator:

Dear and highly respected Mr Benjamin Britten!

I finally received the so much expected letter from you with the programme of the Festival. Your letter to the Minister is written in a perfect way though my personal qualities are considerably exaggerated. Thank you for this from the bottom of my heart. Not for a second do I doubt the success of this venture . . . From now on, all my life is expectation of your new composition . . . I am taking with me from England many recordings of your music (including *Noye's Fludde*) . . .

Truly yours
M. Rostropovich

On 12 October, back in Moscow, Rostropovich wrote again to say that the minister of culture had given permission for his Aldeburgh visit.

> If you have no objections I intend to come ten days before our concert in Aldeburgh and to learn your sonata there putting in it all my love and skill. Please don't worry that I shall not have time to learn the sonata well, for I am rather quick to learn. For instance I learned Shostakovich's concerto in four days.

He added that he was thrilled by listening to the records of *Peter Grimes*, and hoped that Britten might conduct it in Moscow. 'All my musician friends are asking me about my meeting you.'

For the remaining weeks of 1960, Britten was occupied with the recording of *Billy Budd* for the BBC and the *Spring Symphony* for Decca, and a recital tour of Germany and Switzerland with Pears. He was not able to begin the Sonata in C for cello and piano until after Christmas. 'As far as I can I've got the cello piece in order,' he wrote to Pears on 17 January 1961,

> at least I *must* stop fiddling with it & get on with something else. I played it to Imo who was quite impressed, &, as if an omen, as soon as I'd played it over, the telephone rang & there was 'Slava' [Rostropovich] from Paris, & I had a wild & dotty conversation in broken German (*very* broken) with him. But he is a dear, & his warmth & excitement came over inspite of the bad line & crazy language. He is going to come to London on the way to South America early in March to work with us, which is a good thing . . .

Rostropovich has said of their *lingua franca*: 'My German is such that no German understands it. Ben's was classical by comparison. But we understood each other all the time. We called our special language "Aldeburgh Deutsch".'

In Moscow, Rostropovich was waiting for the Sonata to arrive. 'Patiently is not the word,' he writes. 'The wait was actually painful.' Then, one day early in February 1961, he was called to the telephone and told that a parcel had come from England. 'I'm sure I broke all records for the 880 yards hurdles for cellists.' Accompanying the MS was this letter from Britten:

> My dear Slava,
> I hope the Sonata in C will arrive at the same time as this note. I have copied the cello part and had the piano part roughly photographed (so you can see what's going on!). I hope you can make something of it. I

have put some suggestions of bowing, but I haven't had much *first-hand* experience of the cello and may have made some mistakes. The pizzicato movement (II) will amuse you; I hope it's possible! . . .

On his return to his apartment, Rostropovich 'made a dash for my cello, locked myself in and went at that Sonata. It was a case of love at first sight.'

Britten's first important piece of purely instrumental music since his String Quartet No. 2 in 1945 seems to be in part a portrait of the exuberant musician for whom it was written. In her autobiography, Rostropovich's wife, the soprano Galina Vishnevskaya, gives vivid glimpses of her husband's engagingly manic character – 'a man with a kind of frantic motor inside him', she writes; 'once Rostropovich had made up his mind to do something and had decided he was right, no force on earth could stop him.' The Sonata is full of mood swings such as Vishnevskaya describes as typical of her husband: 'now high and expressive, now low and grumbling, now gay and carefree,' Britten writes of the last movement in his sleeve note to the Decca recording. Rostropovich himself calls this movement 'irresponsible and tempestuous'. Having read through the Sonata, he rushed off and sent a telegram to Britten: 'ADMIRING AND IN LOVE WITH YOUR GREAT SONATA . . . LOVE ROSTROPOVICH.'

*

Nearly a month later, on 5 March 1961, Rostropovich stopped off in England for a day, while changing planes on the way to South America, to try the Sonata with Britten. They met at Pears's current London flat, in Anne Wood's house at 59 Marlborough Place, St John's Wood, and Rostropovich was at first very nervous.

Fifteen minutes passed after I entered the tiny room with the piano, then twenty, but still I was afraid to begin playing. I took a long time settling down with my cello. I took still longer in preparing my instrument and music. It appeared to me that Britten was also in not too much of a hurry. Drinks were served. 'Let's have a drink, maybe it'll go easier,' said the composer.

Elsewhere Rostropovich alleges that it took 'four or five large whiskies' before they could find the courage to begin. He was still so nervous that 'I could not even tell how we played. I only noticed that we came to the end of the first movement at the same time. I jumped up, hopped over the cello, and rushed to the composer to embrace him in a burst of spontaneous gratefulness. After that things went easier.' They played through the entire Sonata 'an endless number of times without stopping to thrash out nuances and interpretations. Then at Britten's suggestion we hurried out to a nearby restaurant where we dined in virtual silence.' During the meal, Britten began to hum the theme of the first movement in such a way that Rostropovich realized he wanted it played slightly differently – it was his only comment on the performance. 'After gulping down our meal,' continues Rostropovich, 'we hurried back and played and played and played . . .' Then it was time for the cellist to return to the airport.

Three weeks later Britten wrote to Galina Vishnevskaya 'to tell you how much I enjoyed working with Slava . . . He had understood the work perfectly, and of course played it like no-one else in the world could.' The letter invited her to come to Aldeburgh with her husband, to sing. 'I have recently heard several of your wonderful records, which have made me a great admirer of yours.' She was keen to accept, and though the Soviet concert agency threatened a last-minute ban because the Aldeburgh fees were not high enough, Rostropovich arrived in London a few days before the 1961 Festival to rehearse with Britten, and Vishnevskaya followed shortly afterwards. Among the works to be performed was the Schumann Cello Concerto, with Britten conducting the London Symphony Orchestra, and when they ran through this in London, Rostropovich was greatly impressed by Britten on the rostrum. 'How simple and expressive his gestures were . . . Britten-the-conductor makes any music he is conducting . . . reveal . . . its initial beauty, unspoiled by any "interpretation".' They set off for Aldeburgh in Britten's car – the Rolls had been replaced by an open-topped Alvis – and when they arrived and Rostropovich was shown to his room in the Wentworth Hotel, he was delighted by the place: 'What a wonderfully cosy and enticing town it is!' Vishnevskaya, joining him there a few days later, was equally entranced: 'I had been to London before, but the bustle of the capital . . . had given me no opportunity to get to know the English themselves.' She calls Aldeburgh 'that enchanting nook on the seashore where the spirit of Old England is still preserved'. As for their host, 'I met Ben the day I arrived, and my heart opened to him instantly. From the beginning I felt at ease with him. I'm sure that everyone who was lucky enough to know that charming man must have felt the same sense of simplicity and naturalness in his company.'

Britten's new Russian friends had brought out his warmest qualities. Vishnevskaya was as radiant a personality as her husband. Raised in the direst poverty, she had buried the child of a previous marriage with her own hands because there was no money for a funeral. Now she was a star of the Bolshoi and the darling of Soviet society – Marshal Bulganin,

Soviet premier in the mid-fifties, had courted her ardently – but like Rostropovich she retained the impetuous and demonstrative nature of a child, as did no other of Britten's adult friends. Pears has said of Rostropovich: 'He is a bully, of course, Slava is a strong personality . . . and you really can't resist him!' Britten was equally susceptible to Vishnevskaya. 'No one who knew him would ever say he could not love women,' writes Colin Graham. 'He was *passionately* fond of Galina Vishnevskaya.'

In Aldeburgh, Rostropovich rehearsed the programme for his recital with Britten, which was to include Schubert's Arpeggione Sonata. Rostropovich had never played it before, and had left it 'rather late' to learn it. 'Some of the difficult spots tripped me up at the rehearsal. Britten . . . tried to make it easier . . . putting me in a cradle so to say . . . [so] that I was able to play all the notes that were there without panicking.' He judged that 'Britten-the-pianist closely resembled Britten-the-composer', a remark which Imogen Holst thought the best summing up of Britten as accompanist. 'He used to accompany songs by Schubert,' she writes, 'with such intimate concern that the music sounded as if it were his own.'

This was demonstrated when the 1961 Aldeburgh Festival began, for it included Pears and Britten giving their first complete public performance of Schubert's *Winterreise*. Pears had not felt ready to sing the cycle until he was fifty. William Mann, who had succeeded Frank Howes as chief music critic of *The Times*, wrote that Britten demonstrated 'an astonishingly full and vivid understanding of what Schubert's musical vocabulary says in *Winterreise* – for example, the equestrian rhythm in 'Die Post' refers not only to the pounding along of the mail coach, but also to the even more urgent pounding of the foot-traveller's heart, for which reason the song is taken much more quickly than usual.' Robert Tear remarks: 'I think it must be admitted that when [Britten] played Schubert for Peter the songs (because of his huge personality) did sound remarkably like Britten: but his insight was peerless.' Rosamund Strode strongly disagrees: 'What it sounded like was not Britten but *the real thing* – it didn't sound studied or learned.'

Four days later Rostropovich and Britten gave their joint recital in the Jubilee Hall. Mann called it 'stunning', and felt that in accompanying the Schubert Sonata and Debussy's Cello Sonata, Britten had surpassed himself:

his artistry as a pianist, established fact though it is, seemed to move into a higher gear as he matched Mr Rostropovich's masterly phrasing and articulation with feats of his own. Often he seems to be playing for the delight of musician friends; this time he was met with a cellist who plays with him as though he had to satisfy the rigorous judgement of the composers themselves. Mr Britten is musician enough to play at this pitch, and the challenge roused from him virtuoso qualities of pianism to which he usually does not aspire.

Of Britten's new Sonata, the crowning piece of the recital, Mann wrote:

> There is a suggestion in the nature of the sonata that Britten may have intended it (as Shostakovich did in his cello concerto for Mr Rostropovich) to reflect his own impression of the character of the player to whom it is dedicated: gay, charming, an astonishingly brilliant executant, but behind all these qualities a searching musician with the mind of a philosopher.

The last two movements were repeated as an encore – 'we would gladly have heard the whole sonata again, on the spot', writes Mann – and then Rostropovich brought Pears on to the platform alongside Britten, made a speech of thanks to them for their hospitality, and joined with them in performing an aria, with cello obbligato, from Bach's Cantata No. 41.

Rostropovich had thrown himself utterly into the spirit of the Festival. He was the piano accompanist for Vishnevskaya's recital, which Mann judged 'thrilling ... In the Jubilee Hall her soprano voice sounded enormous, monumentally rich and full from top to bottom'. Vishnevskaya herself writes:

> It was at my solo concert, with Slava accompanying me, that Britten heard me for the first time. He must have thought I was a madwoman. Indeed, thinking back, I can't believe such a programme was possible. In addition to songs by Prokoviev, Tchaikovsky, Richard Strauss and Schumann, plus arias from *Norma, Manon Lescaut, La Forza del Destino,* and *Lady Macbeth of Mtensk*, for dessert I sang Mussorgsky's *Songs and Dances of Death.*

Mann wrote that the Mussorgsky was 'the outstanding experience of the recital ... Mme Vishnevskaya ... wheedled and whispered and ranted, and assumed a dozen vocal disguises, each of them vital and compelling; and in her husband she had a worthy partner – his musicianship is as evident at the piano as on the cello.' Mann reported that 'at the end of the recital Mr Rostropovich, beaming with pleasure like any schoolboy, announced in English that they would sing another song, and that "dear Ben" would play the piano. It was the aria from the fifth of Villa-Lobos's *Bachianas brasileiras ...*'

When he was not performing, Rostropovich attended everything that was going on. He sat 'spellbound' through *The Turn of the Screw* (a revival conducted by Meredith Davies, with George Maran as the Prologue and Quint); Rostropovich adds that when Shostakovich heard it the next year he said it had made a 'tremendous impact' on him. Rostropovich was also in Orford Church for a performance of *Noye's Fludde* (this was the production, conducted by Norman Del Mar, which Decca recorded), and could not restrain himself from joining in the congregational hymns, 'not knowing the words and not even being able to read them. My neighbours looked at me in surprise and even consternation, for my voice is unique in its unreliability . . .'

Leaving the Wentworth with Vishnevskaya on his last morning, waving goodbye to Britten and Pears through a light Suffolk drizzle, Rostropovich was full of emotion. A few days later came this letter:

> Dear, dear Ben and Peter!
>
> It is quite impossible to express in a letter our feelings of sorrow and loneliness which we feel being away from you . . . We never happened to meet people so cordial and warm-hearted, so genuinely gifted, so sincere and frank, so simple and unsophisticated . . .
>
> Yours affectionately
> Slava and Galina

*

Britten had come up to Vishnevskaya after her recital and 'said he was particularly glad he had heard me right at that moment because he had begun to write his *War Requiem* and now wanted to write in a part for me'. He told her that 'his composition, which was a call for peace, would bring together representatives of the three nations that had suffered most during the war: an Englishman, Peter Pears; a German, Fischer-Dieskau; and a Russian, myself.' On 16 February 1961 Britten had written to Dietrich Fischer-Dieskau:

> Please forgive me for writing to such a busy man as yourself . . . Coventry Cathedral, like so many wonderful buildings in Europe, was destroyed in the last war. It has now been rebuilt in a very remarkable fashion, and for the reconsecration of the new building they are holding a big Festival at the end of May and beginning of June next year. I have been asked to write a new work for what is to us all a most significant occasion.
>
> I am writing what I think will be one of my most important works. It is a full-scale Requiem Mass for chorus and orchestra (in memory of those of all nations who died in the last war), and I am interspersing the Latin text with many poems of a great English poet, Wilfred Owen,

who was killed in the First World War. These magnificent poems, full of the hate of destruction, are a kind of commentary on the Mass; they are, of course, in English. These poems will be set for tenor and baritone, with an accompaniment of chamber orchestra, placed in the middle of the other forces. They will need singing with the utmost beauty, intensity and sincerity.

Peter Pears has agreed to sing the tenor part, and with great temerity I am asking you whether you would sing the baritone.

Pears had performed alongside Fischer-Dieskau in Germany in 1956, when he described him as 'very nice, & is very musical, but grand'.

In his book *Working with Britten*, Ronald Duncan says that the dropping of the atomic bomb on Hiroshima in 1945 made him propose to Britten that they write an oratorio, *Mea Culpa*, in reaction to 'this savage atrocity'. Duncan recalls that 'It was to be a full-scale work with chorus, soloists and symphony orchestra, almost like the *Messe des Morts*.' He says it came to nothing because of a stalemate regarding a commission between Boosey & Hawkes and the BBC. 'It was a pity: the *War Requiem* could have been written in 1946 instead of 1961.'

In February 1948 Britten wrote to Ralph Hawkes that 'the death of Gandhi has been a great shock to one of my strong convictions, & I am determined to commemorate this occasion in, possibly, some form of requiem, to his honour. When I shall complete this piece I cannot say.' Hawkes encouraged him, but nothing came of it, probably due to Britten's enormous workload at this period. However, it is evident that when the Coventry arts committee first approached Britten in October 1958, requesting a work for the new cathedral, he was to some extent able to respond with an existing scheme.

His letter to Fischer-Dieskau makes no mention of a soprano soloist. It seems that the addition of this voice was entirely due to his hearing Vishnevskaya in Aldeburgh. She describes him asking her on that occasion: '"Have you ever sung in English?" "No, of course not. Only in Italian." "Then I'll write your part in Latin. Do you know Latin?" "Yes!" I exclaimed, and joyfully threw my arms around his neck.'

Britten's choice of England, Russia and Germany as 'the three nations that had suffered most during the war' is odd in that it omits the Jews. In fact for Britten himself the *War Requiem* may also have been a response to a private tragedy which occurred two years before he began to write it. The published score and recording bear this dedication:

In loving memory of

Roger Burney,	*Sub-Lieutenant*
	Royal Naval Volunteer Reserve
Piers Dunkerley,	*Captain*
	Royal Marines
David Gill,	*Ordinary Seaman*
	Royal Navy
Michael Halliday,	*Lieutenant*
	Royal New Zealand Volunteer Reserve

The programme note which was printed for several London perform-ances of the *War Requiem* in the sixties, by William Mann, states: 'Britten, a Christian pacifist and zealous humanitarian, had pondered for some years a large work of this sort . . . and inscribed it to the memory of four friends who died in the second world war.' In truth, only three of the dedicatees were killed in the war. The fourth, Piers Dunkerley, commit-ted suicide in the summer of 1959.

Roger Burney was a young friend of Pears's (nine years his junior), discreetly homosexual, who died on board the French submarine *Surcouf* in 1942 – 'Alas! alas! he was a sweet dear person,' Pears wrote when news came of his death. David Gill was a cousin of the Reeve family in Lowestoft; during Britten's adolescence he had sometimes stayed there when on holiday from St Paul's Cathedral choir school in London, where he was a chorister. In November 1961, while at work on the *War Requiem*, Britten wrote to Gill's mother:

> Although he was a bit younger than I [about eight years], I was very fond of him, and he helped a great deal by singing over music I had written. I am engaged on a big work now for the re-opening of Coventry Cathedral, a War Requiem, and I wish to inscribe it to several of my friends who were killed in this last terrible war. I was very shocked when I heard later that David had been one of these, and I wonder if you would allow me to write his name with the others, as a tribute, at the head of the Requiem.

Gill was killed in action in the Mediterranean. Michael Halliday had been a schoolboy at South Lodge in Britten's days there, and Britten continued to see him during the thirties when he was in the merchant navy. 'Isn't it tragic about Michael Halliday being missing,' Britten wrote to Pears in the spring of 1944. 'I feel very odd about it now – poor silly old dear that he was.' John Pounder calls Halliday rather an odd sort of character – lonely and sad. He wasn't a Lowestoft boy, but came from some distance. There was some sort of unfortunate family background, and he always seemed rather an outsider until Ben took him in hand, and looked after him. He was short, stocky, medium-sized, rather tough-looking and dour; very much on his own.

Piers Dunkerley was wounded during the 1944 Normandy Landings, and was reported missing. At the end of the war he was discovered in a German prison camp. He remained in the Royal Marines, served on HMS *Vanguard*, then became ADC to the governor of Gibraltar, and returned to civilian life in about 1958, when he was thirty-seven. He had remained unmarried, and visited Britten when he could; for example he was at Crag House for Christmas 1954. After leaving the Marines he found it hard to get a job, but was eventually taken on by Charrington's the coal merchants. His sister-in-law Barbara Dunkerley says that he had 'lots and lots of girl-friends', and early in 1959 he became engaged to a young woman doctor. They planned to marry in August, and Dunkerley wrote to Britten asking him to be best man. Britten declined, saying he was too busy, and Dunkerley wrote again:

we shall both be *very* disappointed if you cannot come at all. I only intend to get married once, and you *must* be there ... Longing to see you sometime. Much love as always, you dear old thing.

Piers

About three months before the wedding Dunkerley lost his job. On the night of 7 June 1959 he was staying with his fiancée and her parents at Poole in Dorset. According to reports at the inquest the couple had 'a heated discussion about the future'. They had dined at a yacht club, where Dunkerley had drunk 'a fair amount of whisky'. They returned to the fiancée's house. The *Daily Sketch* for 11 June 1959 takes up the story:

'I knew he slept badly after such discussions,' [Dunkerley's fiancée] said, 'and I gave him two seconal sodium tablets. There were between 30 and 40 tablets in the box which – as far as I can remember – I put on my dressing-table. I went for a drink of water, leaving Captain Dunkerley in my room for the time being.' The box which had contained the tablets was found in his room when she found him dead in the morning ... The coroner, Mr J. W. Miller, found that death was due to seconal poisoning, 'self-administered while his mind was befogged owing to taking seconal and spirits'.

The fiancée's mother told the inquest that she had seen a light under Piers's door during the night, and had gone in. 'He seemed "dopey" and said: "I can't do without [her]." She told him: "You won't have to. You'll be better in the morning." The *News Chronicle* adds that his fiancée 'had definitely assured Mr Dunkerley that the engagement was still on'.

Barbara Dunkerley, while again emphasizing that Piers 'loved girls', was struck by the amount of time he spent with Britten in the years between the war and his death: 'Always when we said to Piers, "Come for Christmas", or "Come to one of the children's christenings", there was always something that he was doing somewhere else with Ben and Peter Pears. He always seemed to be there.'

There are no references to Dunkerley's suicide in Britten's letters, but the painter Sidney Nolan has a recollection of Britten referring, during a conversation in 1970, to 'a friend of his who tragically hanged himself on the morning of his wedding. I think it was at Oxford – I don't know, he didn't tell me who it was, but it was quite a deep thing in him.' Though the details are inaccurate, this seems to be Dunkerley.

On quite another occasion Nolan brought up the subject of the *War Requiem*. He says that Britten told him: 'Really what the whole thing is, it's a kind of reparation. That's what the *War Requiem* is about; it is reparation.'

*

In the summer of 1961, when Britten was beginning work on the *War Requiem*, Christopher Isherwood, with whom he had remained loosely in touch since the thirties, sent him a book containing a photograph of Wilfred Owen. 'I am delighted to have it,' wrote Britten. 'I am so involved with him at the moment, & I wanted to see what he looked like: I might have guessed, it's just what I expected, really.' This may be the photograph printed in the booklet accompanying the *War Requiem* recording, in which the young Owen, smiling shyly in his officer's uniform, looks not unlike surviving wartime snapshots of Piers Dunkerley. William Plomer wrote to Britten in July 1961 suggesting that he meet Owen's brother Harold, who was still alive. 'I'm not sure about visiting the brother,' Britten replied. 'I am so involved with the work that the chance may not present itself, & also I don't want to be disturbed, maybe, in that direction.' Plomer may already have hinted that Wilfred Owen had homosexual leanings.

At the end of August 1961, Britten told Boosey & Hawkes that he had finished 'the first large chunk of the War Requiem', and two months later he wrote to Basil Coleman: 'I go on working at the Coventry piece. Sometimes it seems the best ever, more often the worst – but it is always with me.' Meredith Davies, who had conducted the EOG for Britten on several occasions, began to rehearse the amateur choirs who were to provide the chorus in Coventry. By Christmas the Soviet authorities were showing reluctance to give permission for Vishnevskaya to take part, though Britten was 'hopeful that this will change'. He intended to conduct the first performance, though he admitted that 'I am not crazy about conducting big works'.

Early in the New Year he went with Pears for a month's holiday in Greece, where he completed the orchestral score. 'I was completely absorbed in this piece, as really never before,' he wrote to a friend at the beginning of March 1962, 'but with considerable agony in finding the adequate notes for such a subject (& such words!), & dread discovering that I've not succeeded.' Rostropovich, who had been ill with heart trouble, wrote that he and Vishnevskaya, who had been sent the vocal score, were both 'mad about Requiem. It is a profound and extraordinarily powerful work! It's majestic!' Britten was delighted by their reaction, but at Easter he told E. M. Forster that 'the Soviets have forbidden me to have my precious Russian Soprano . . . the combination of "Cathedral" & Reconciliation with W. Germany . . . was too much for them.' Vishnevskaya writes that Ekaterina Furtseva, the minister of culture, asked her: 'How can you, a Soviet woman, stand next to a German and an Englishman and perform a political work?' Vishnevskaya was replaced by Heather Harper, who 'had ten days to learn it. And I had three performances of *A Midsummer Night's Dream* and another concert during that period. Ben happened to be in London, so I took it round to his flat and we went through it.'

A few weeks before this, Britten had had a minor operation, apparently for piles. He was also suffering once again from 'a rotten arm'. When he arrived at Coventry for final rehearsals he found conditions in the new cathedral 'appalling'. The acoustics, which he had been assured would be wonderful, were 'lunatic', while the cathedral staff were waging 'really Trollopian clerical battles, but with modern weapons' against the *War Requiem* performance. The builders were making continuous noise, the authorities refused permission for a tiered platform in front of the altar for orchestra and chorus, and the entire chorus threatened to walk out when an attempt was made to reduce their numbers because of lack of space. Britten and Meredith Davies decided that the performance could only be saved if one of them directed the orchestra, chorus and Heather Harper, leaving the other to conduct the chamber orchestra, Pears and Fischer-Dieskau. Britten, whose arm was still playing up, chose the latter.

On the evening of the first performance, 30 May 1962, the cathedral staff were still making difficulties, insisting on admitting the vast audience through one small doorway. 'The queue stretched into the distance,' writes Richard Butt of the BBC's midland region, who was producing the live broadcast, 'and it was quite obvious that many of them would not be in their seats by the time we were due to start at eight o'clock. It took a good deal of persuasion before more doors were eventually opened.' The broadcast began with the announcer reading a lengthy introduction, but when he finished the audience was still coming in. Butt tried to persuade Britten to start. He refused: 'We can't go on yet, it's like a market-place.' The announcer had nothing left to say, and there was a long gap before the first notes were heard. Afterwards Butt was amused to receive letters thanking the BBC for 'that wonderful pause' before the *War Requiem* began.

Five days previously William Mann had written in *The Times*, on the basis of studying the score, that the new piece was 'Britten's masterpiece'. (Michael Tippett says he thought it 'silly' of Mann to make such an extreme judgement before hearing the *War Requiem*, though he praises it as 'the one musical masterwork we possess with overt pacifist meanings'.) After the performance, Mann called it 'the most masterly and nobly imagined work that Britten has ever given us'. Britten himself wrote to Plomer that 'dear Heather Harper did splendidly; and weren't the two chaps marvellous? Poor F-Dieskau was so upset at the end that Peter couldn't get him out of the choir-stalls! It was that wonderful "Strange Meeting"' – the setting, which concludes the *War Requiem*, of Owen's poem in which a dead British soldier meets the German he has killed. Fischer-Dieskau confirms this in his memoirs: 'I was completely undone; I did not know where to hide my face. Dead friends and past suffering arose in my mind.' The playwright Peter Shaffer, reviewing the performance for *Time & Tide*, was equally moved: 'I believe it to be the most impressive and moving piece of sacred music ever to be composed in this country . . . the most profound and moving thing which this most committed of geniuses has so far achieved. It makes criticism impertinent.'

The next performance was in Berlin in November, on the anniversary of the Armistice. Britten was to have conducted, but the shoulder trouble made him stand down, and Colin Davis took his place. The London première took place on 6 December in Westminster Abbey, with Meredith Davies and Britten conducting, and a Yugoslav, Vladimir Ruzdjak, singing the baritone part. The Abbey's acoustics suited the work no better than Coventry's, and Desmond Shawe-Taylor wrote in the *Sunday*

Times that he had 'gathered only a blurred and distant impression of the musical facts'. Conditions were a little better at the Albert Hall performance on 9 January 1963, at which Galina Vishnevskaya at last sang the part that had been written for her – 'singing it at some points with less purity of tone than Heather Harper,' wrote Shawe-Taylor, 'but with an individual colour and intensity of experience'. But the *War Requiem* only made its full impact when Decca released the two-disc set, in a striking black box with white lettering, of the recording that Britten had directed, without an associate conductor, at the Kingsway Hall during the week before the Albert Hall performance, with the three soloists for whom the music was intended. Within five months the recording had sold 200,000 copies, an unprecedented figure for contemporary music.

'The *War Requiem* has caught the public imagination to an almost unheard-of degree,' wrote William Mann after a Festival Hall performance in December 1963, at which Britten (uniquely for a live performance) was the sole conductor. The work was becoming identified with the peace movements and left-wing intellectualism of the sixties, just as *Peter Grimes* had harmonized with the mood of the forties. Critical acclaim remained high throughout the decade. 'If the work has its faults, I cannot yet see them,' observed Shawe-Taylor some months after the first performance, while William Mann alleged that 'practically everyone who has heard it has instantly acknowledged it to be a masterpiece'. Stravinsky, whose envy of Britten was becoming perceptible, observed that to dare to criticize the *War Requiem* in Britain would be 'as if one had failed to stand up for *God Save the Queen*'. Later there was a reaction. The composer Robin Holloway, aged twenty when the *War Requiem* was first performed, wrote in 1977 that he became disenchanted by 'the "public" manner' of the work, which seemed to him a betrayal of the private concerns of Britten's greatest music. It also began to be remarked how much the setting of the Requiem itself evoked Verdi's. In a 1969 interview with Donald Mitchell, Britten said of this:

> I would think . . . it's useful to know how someone else has gone there [i.e. written a requiem]. And I think that I would be a fool if I didn't take notice of how Mozart, Verdi, Dvořák – whoever you like to name – had written their Masses. I mean, many people have pointed out to me the similarities between the Verdi *Requiem* and bits of my own *War Requiem*, and they may be there. If I have not absorbed that, that's too bad. But that's because I'm not a good enough composer, it's not because I'm wrong.

He himself had had enormous hopes for the *War Requiem*, saying that it had been 'a precious idea with me for ages', and he felt that it had succeeded. 'The idea of the W.R. *did* come off I think,' he wrote to his sister Barbara just after the first performance; 'arn't those poems wonderful, & how one thinks of that bloody 1914–18 war especially – I hope it'll make people think abit.'

3: Across the river

The 1962 Aldeburgh Festival was the first at which Keith Grant was administrator of the English Opera Group. After *A Midsummer Night's Dream*, Britten had asked the Arts Council to provide the EOG with greater financial security. Their response was to suggest that it be managed by either Sadler's Wells or Covent Garden. 'Ben was known to be deeply suspicious of David Webster at Covent Garden,' says Keith Grant, 'and was disappointed at the way they had handled his work in the past. But I think he was frightened that Sadler's Wells was too close in character to the EOG not to swallow it up.' So he chose Covent Garden, and Grant, who was in his late twenties and had just been taken on to the staff of the Opera House, found himself responsible for the EOG.

The first Aldeburgh production on which Grant worked was *Dido and Aeneas* with Janet Baker as Dido. Grant brought a stage-manager and chief electrician down from Covent Garden, but the stage crew was made up of workmen from the Aldeburgh building firm Reade's, 'and very good they were too,' says Grant.

> But they tended to be members of the lifeboat crew, and at the sound of a maroon off they went. There had been a lifeboat call-out during one of the rehearsals of *A Midsummer Night's Dream*, so Reade's were asked that in future nobody sent for stage work should be a lifeboatman. Well, on the first night of *Dido* we found, on turning up at the Jubilee Hall, that the crew weren't there, because they were members of the voluntary fire brigade, and they were all fire-fighting in Tunstall Forest! So my memory of that night is of, dressed in a dinner-jacket, hauling ropes backstage, together with the assistant conductor, James Gibson, who was equally attired!

David Webster and his second-in-command John Tooley knew that the relationship between the EOG and Covent Garden would never work if

Britten felt he were taking second place to the Opera House. 'I gave my first priority to Aldeburgh,' says Keith Grant. 'My relationship with Ben was peaceful because I was never unavailable.' Two years after Grant had begun to work for Britten the Opera House closed for rebuilding, and the Covent Garden Opera Company went on tour to Coventry and Manchester. Grant spent as much time as possible at rehearsals for the Aldeburgh Festival, but was obliged to devote three days a week to the Opera Company, disappearing from Aldeburgh while he did so. 'Ben pretended that I wasn't doing this. We did the deal, but he pretended it wasn't happening, and he never referred to it.'

Casting for EOG productions was always a delicate business, since not only Britten's but Pears's agreement was required. 'I always found Peter much more difficult to deal with than Ben,' says Grant.

> Ben would vacillate a bit, but there would come a point where he would stand firm. Peter never reached that point. I'd spend hours at the Red House talking to them, and Peter would constantly undermine things, with his second, third, fourth, fifth and sixth thoughts. They were often very good thoughts, but there was an impracticality about it.

Sue Phipps, who became Pears's and Britten's agent in the sixties (first at Ibbs & Tillett and then independently with her husband Jack), had the same difficulty with her uncle. 'I adored Peter, but I could never anticipate what he was going to think. Whereas I almost always knew with Ben, I always got it wrong with Peter. If you tried to pin him down, he would just divert.'

Keith Grant's duties sometimes included recruiting boys for revivals of *The Turn of the Screw*:

> I found the sexual overtones of that opera rather hard to handle. I used to feel distinctly uneasy at taking eleven- or twelve-year-old boys from their families and contriving that they should take part in this thing, the subtleties of which would not be obvious to them. There was never any impropriety on Ben's part, but he did get involved with them in the sense that he was intensely protective and interested in them. It was folly in one way, because any sort of close interest in a boy from a man like that is obviously going to be noticed and commented on. And so Ben was indiscreet in being warm and interested towards them, because the gossips would immediately respond.

Grant also had to explain to certain performers that Britten did not wish to re-engage them. Asked if there were many such occurrences, Grant says:

Yes, there were, but I won't be thanked by those who are still living if I name them! There were cases which were insignificant, because they were members of the chorus, for example, but I think that in my eleven or twelve years there must have been a good half-dozen famous unloadings. I will name one, purely as an example: Anna Pollak, who was a very distinguished figure with Sadler's Wells, and indeed with the EOG. [She was the original Bianca in *The Rape of Lucretia* in 1946.] She had been cast as Mrs Peachum in the 1963 revival of Britten's version of *The Beggar's Opera*, and Ben became dissatisfied with her voice.

She was a wonderful stage actress, a really commanding figure, and I personally would have forgiven her any vocal defect in a role like that – did it matter if she couldn't quite catch the top notes if she was a powerful performer? But Ben couldn't be doing with that. He had to have every note right, and if she couldn't reach the top without faking it he wasn't prepared to forgive her. So that was the end of that. She did it at Aldeburgh and the Edinburgh Festival, but we were due to take it to Russia in 1964, and I had a very embarrassing telephone conversation in which I told her she wouldn't be required for that.

Dame Janet Baker says that 'Anna Pollak was such a character, such a colleague, such a personality, that to me it infinitely outweighed the sound she was making, and I would have thought Ben would have recognized that. But he had a perfect right to do it. This is a cruel profession, and you have to be up to the mark.' Anna Pollak herself takes the same attitude:

I was cast as Mrs Peachum . . . a bawdy slut in filthy Hogarth costume, wig and cap awry, and with a thick Cockney accent. I was in conflict about her singing voice and so evidently was Ben, for after Aldeburgh and a season in Edinburgh I was sacked. Poor Keith Grant had the executioner's job. I can't recall being very hurt. I didn't like the role or the piece, and I consider rejection part of the hazards of any branch of show-business. Ben had rather a reputation for going off people. A lot of us do! In any case, in all opera companies one has to bear disappointments, jealousies, criticisms, and – oh dear – failure. None of it, however, outweighing the fun and excitement and triumphs.

Asked if he was ever requested to remove a singer from the cast on the spot, in the middle of a run of performances, Grant says: 'I don't think so. We came near to it, but no.' However, Colin Graham recalls that, during one of the *Beggar's Opera* revivals, 'the poor chap singing Filch was fired after a dress rehearsal, having been found wanting by them both' (Britten and Pears). Grant says he would often 'put up a fight to try and save these people, and often I did succeed, by saying to Ben, "You *can't*, it's too public."' But he does not dispute that it was his task rather than Britten's to do the sackings. 'That was my job.'

Though Grant, Baker and Pollak all feel that the Britten dismissals were characteristic of the operatic world, Thomas Hemsley, the original Demetrius in *A Midsummer Night's Dream*, disagrees:

> I have to say that my experience of being in opera companies for a very long time is that there's much less of it than people outside the profession think there is. I've always been surprised about how comradely people are with each other in opera houses. Of course it happens, if the director decides that somebody has to go. But very often it's done as kindly as possible, as uncruelly. At Aldeburgh and in the EOG, when people were dropped – and there were lots of them, especially tenors – there was never any reason given.

Ursula Strebi, managing director of the English Chamber Orchestra when it was working for Britten (and wife of Philip Jones, whose brass ensemble made its first solo appearance at the 1962 Aldeburgh Festival), had much the same task as Keith Grant – to make sure that Britten had only the instrumentalists he wanted: 'He would have his dislikes, and say, "I don't want to see so-and-so any more." I do remember one player who had been there a very long time, and he didn't want him any longer, and it was embarrassing. We agreed about it, but it was difficult.' Emanuel Hurwitz, leader of the English Chamber Orchestra in those days, says: 'If somebody had, say, made faces at a first performance of Ben's when he was conducting them at the age of twenty-five, he'd remember. He wasn't at all a vindictive man, but he felt nervous, off-balance, if he knew someone didn't like his music.' Hurwitz adds that Britten was uncomfortable when conducting unfamiliar orchestras, however good they might be. '"Between ourselves," he would say, "however well it went, I'm still happier working with my own friends."'

Like Keith Grant, Ursula Strebi does not dispute that it was her job to remove people Britten did not want: 'It was right that I had to do it.' Grant emphasizes that, despite the tension of working for him, Britten was an easier master than others might have been:

> Willie Walton, for example, who was an entirely different character, you had to handle *very* carefully. He was very suspicious and thin-skinned, and could be very difficult. And while there were things about

Willie which I think were entirely admirable, I don't think I would ever have hit it off with him as well as I did with Ben.

*

'Dear Ben and Peter,' wrote Rostropovich in March 1962, sending news of his recent illness, 'if you want me to recover completely I ask you to see the doctor whose address is: The Red House, Aldeburgh, Suffolk. Only he can bring me to life by composing a brilliant violoncello concerto.' Britten replied that 'your doctors in Aldeburgh' were longing to see him, while as to a concerto, 'I am determined to write one for you.' According to Rostropovich, Britten eventually signed a pledge to write 'six major works for cello in recompense for which Slava Rostropovich will agree not to perform his pirouette in front of Princess Mary'. Marion Thorpe (then Lady Harewood, the Princess's daughter-in-law) says:

> the 'contract' was signed on the back of a menu at a restaurant in Lincoln, on the way from the Aldeburgh Festival of 1964 to Rosehill in Cumbria, where Britten and Rostropovich were to give a recital. We were breaking the journey at Harewood House in Yorkshire, where Princess Mary was in residence. Rostropovich had threatened to make an elaborate curtsey, which would have highly embarrassed the shy Princess. When Ben and I realized that Slava's threat was serious, this 'blackmail' solution was found! The 'contract' was for six solo cello suites, to equal the number by Bach. The 'contract' is now buried, with other relevant papers, in the foundation stone of the Britten Theatre at the Royal College of Music.

Britten's own health continued to bother him. 'I've had a dreary summer,' he wrote to E. M. Forster in August 1962, three months after the first performance of the *War Requiem*, 'endless doctors, & quite a lot of boring pain in this shoulder.' But he sent the first movement of the new cello work to Rostropovich on 15 November. 'As you see,' he wrote,

> it is going to be rather a big piece; this is only the first of four big movements – very much shaped like a symphony in fact, I wonder whether it would not be better to call it Sinfonia Concertante ... I hope you will like it so far, dear Slava; I must confess I can hear you in every note and every bar, although I fear it may not be worthy of your great art.

Rostropovich wrote back that the movement was 'the very top of everything ever written for cello'.

Britten had hoped to have the Cello Symphony, as the work was eventually named, ready for performance by Rostropovich in March

1963, when Britten himself was due to visit Moscow and Leningrad as part of a festival of British music. But during the autumn he was plagued by bad digestion. 'I am so dreadfully worried I'm being such a broken reed at the moment – it is the bloodiest nuisance from every point of view,' he wrote to Pears.

> I suppose one can't help having weak spots, and being a jumpy neurotic type – but . . . it isn't fun to feel like the wrong end of a broken down bus for most of the time . . . But from now on you'll see a new me, – I hope –, & one that's not a drag on you, a worry for you, & a bit more worthy of my beloved P.

Pears's reply came by return of post from Liverpool, where he was singing:

> My darling Ben,
>   Your letter simply makes me go hot with shame – That *you* should be asking me to forgive you for being ill, when it is I that should be looking after you & loving you, should long ago have thrown my silly career out of the window & come & tried to protect you a bit from worry and tension, instead of adding to them with my own worries and tetchinesses! . .

The Cello Symphony was not finished when Britten set off for Moscow in March. 'This does not distress me very much,' he told Rostropovich, 'because it means there will be an excuse to come back to Russia the following year!' Pears went with him; the festival programme was to include the *Serenade, Winter Words*, and the *Sechs Hölderlin-Fragmente*, as well as the Cello Sonata. Britten found the schedule strenuous, but told Plomer that 'it was really eminently worth it, & we were touched & moved by the warmth we met everywhere'. During the trip he was interviewed for *Pravda*, and told the reporter that the Russian audiences were proving wonderfully responsive to his music, which he had feared they might find strange. He was also quoted as saying that 'the artist's social duty' was 'to form, educate and develop [the] people's artistic taste'. This, square brackets and all, was how the *Daily Telegraph* quoted the *Pravda* article. Its chief music critic, Martin Cooper, queried whether Britten had said 'people' or 'the people', and wondered whether he realized the important ideological difference between the two when speaking to Soviet citizens. Citing Britten's further remark, at the end of the interview, that 'between the arts of our two peoples there are no barriers', Cooper suggested that readers of *Pravda* would assume from this 'that he was in fact subscribing to the full Communist doctrine of art as an instrument of ideological propaganda'. Cooper pointed out that Khruschev had recently made a violent attack on all art that could not be interpreted as actively supporting the Communist cause.

'I was sickened by Pravda getting me all wrong,' Britten wrote to Plomer on 7 April,

> & of course people who don't know me at all have rushed eagerly for the wrong end of the stick! I had to walk *very* gingerly around this difficult problem, but did what I hoped was a sympathetic tactful talk, which of course the blighters got deliberately wrong. However that isn't unique to USSR, is it?

In another letter to Plomer, two months before the Russian trip, Britten had touched on the question of the artist's relationship with society. Asking if Plomer would give a speech at a formal dinner at that year's Aldeburgh Festival, Britten suggested as the topic 'some subject like the Artist and his Patron (or – and Society). To me this is a burning question to-day, when so many artists refuse to have a Patron, or won't try & please him – or some cow-tow completely (thinking of film-writers . . . & some – not all – Russians).'

Despite the experience of *Gloriana*, Britten himself had no qualms about accepting royal patronage. During the 1962 Aldeburgh Festival the Duke of Edinburgh had opened a new Festival club and gallery in the High Street, in a building bought and refurbished with money raised by an auction of works of art donated by artists and collectors. (Billy Burrell remarks that Aldeburgh was now 'being strangled' by the growth of the Festival and its takeover of buildings, but Fidelity Cranbrook says that the new club gave previously hostile factions – the golf club, the sailing fraternity and the Festival supporters – a chance to mingle and 'actually look at each other and *smile*'.) During 1961 Britten had composed a *Jubilate Deo* intended for performance at St George's Chapel, Windsor. He explained that it was merely the first result of 'a proposal from the Duke of Edinburgh that I should write some music for St George's. His proposal was a rather major one, and which I would rather not talk about at the moment . . .' In fact he wrote nothing further for the royal chapel, and a letter to Pears in July 1963 affectionately compares Peg and Lu Hesse to 'all these other dreary HRH's, you know – these hopeless misfits who go around condemning everything new in their snobbish way'.

Replying, Pears observed that it was remarkable that royalty befriended them at all: 'we are after all queer & left & conshies which is enough to put us, or make us put ourselves, outside the pale, apart from being

artists as well'. Yet in the public eye Britten was now an entirely 'establishment' figure, as was shown by the celebrations in 1963 of his fiftieth
birthday.

'What's so special about being 50?' he asked Ronald Duncan before it
all began. He managed to stop Duncan writing a profile of him for the
Sunday Times, but other coverage could not be avoided. There were
lengthy radio and television tributes, though Britten pleaded to the BBC
'could you not wait until my 75th birthday?' and warned them 'I do not
like being interviewed, nor do I do it well.' He always asked to see the
questions in advance. Eric Crozier, who chaired the 1960 radio discussion
with him and Forster about *Billy Budd*, noticed that, whereas Forster was
completely relaxed in the studio, Britten was tense and spoke in a
'schoolmasterly voice which gave a false impression of his normal speech'.

On 12 September 1963 there was a Britten 'birthday' Promenade
concert at the Albert Hall, with Britten himself conducting the *Sinfonia da
Requiem*, the *Spring Symphony*, and the first British performance of his
Cantata Misericordium, commissioned for the centenary of the International Red Cross and first heard at their celebrations in Geneva a few
days earlier. Donald Mitchell wrote in the *Daily Telegraph* that Britten
had 'received a rousing ovation' at the end of the Prom, 'which must have
convinced him that his music forms a living and cherished part of the
experience of a very wide public'. In fact Britten was taking, or affected to
take, a gloomy view of the celebrations. 'I feel that . . . these concerts are
memorial rather than celebratory, & these nice things being written are
really obituaries,' he told William Plomer a few days before his actual
birthday. When William Walton sent a generously worded birthday letter
('In the last years your music has come to mean more and more to me – it
shines out as a beacon . . . in . . . a chaotic and barren musical world and I
am sure it does for thousands of others'), Britten replied: 'I don't think any
composer has ever felt less confident than I – especially somehow when the
public praise seems to have got rather out of hand!'

Lavish newspaper tributes were paid by Michael Tippett ('Of all the
musicians I have met, Britten is the most sheerly musical – music seems to
flow out of his mind, out of his body') and Hans Keller ('by way of
quinquagenery tribute, I personally would not hesitate to call Britten the
greatest composer alive'). In contrast Britten himself, writing in the
Sunday Telegraph under the heading 'Britten Looking Back', devoted the
entire article to praise of Frank Bridge's teaching, and concluded: 'I am
enormously aware that I haven't yet come up to the technical standards
Bridge set me.' Similarly he spoke, around this time, to the young
composer, Nicholas Maw, of the 'howlers' in his earlier work, at the same

time encouraging him to write as much as possible while still young, 'because it gets more difficult as you grow older'. And in a BBC interview: 'It is becoming, as I get older, more and more difficult to satisfy my ear that I have found the right notes to express my ideas with.' Would he write as much in the future? 'No, I shall probably not write as much. I can see that one is slowing down as one gets older.'

Another question raised in this interview was his state of religious belief. 'I'm certainly a dedicated Christian,' he answered, 'but I must confess I am influenced by the Bishop of Woolwich and Bonhoeffer, and these people whom he quotes, and at the moment I do not find myself worshipping as regularly as perhaps I will later.' (John A. T. Robinson, Bishop of Woolwich, had caused a storm with his radical *Honest to God*, published in the spring of 1963.)

The birthday proper, Friday 22 November, was marked by a concert performance of *Gloriana* at the Royal Festival Hall, with Sylvia Fisher and Pears in the main roles. Britten reported that it 'went surprisingly well, & was rather interesting', though the celebrations were considerably dampened by the news, which filtered in during the performance, of President Kennedy's assassination. Anthony Gishford of Boosey & Hawkes had been clandestinely assembling a *Festschrift*, which was now published by Faber and Faber as *Tribute to Benjamin Britten on his Fiftieth Birthday*. Contributions included a previously unpublished fragment of fiction by Forster. Britten, who had been told nothing about it in advance, said: 'I am *very* proud of that book.'

Eric Crozier was among those invited to contribute to the book. For it he wrote a short story, 'Albert in Later Life', a sequel to *Albert Herring*. This describes how, after the death of his mother, Albert leaves Loxford to see the world. He gets a job at a hotel in Lowestoft, where he extracts money from the proprietor after surprising him in a compromising situation; is taken into the employment of a clergyman with a penchant for curly-headed youths, from whom he again extorts cash; turns bookseller, specializing in erotica; meets Cissie Woodger, who is now an operatic prima donna; and is persuaded by his business partner to dispose of her by setting fire to the theatre in which she is appearing. She survives unscathed, marries him, and takes him back to Loxford, where she will obviously bully him just as his mother did. Anthony Gishford told Crozier that the story had 'entertained me vastly', and intended to put it in the book. After discussing it with Fabers' he wrote again: 'I am afraid that the voice of caution warns me against using a story [about] blackmail, pederasty, pornography and arson.'

*

When it was put to Britten in one of the birthday interviews that he was primarily an opera composer, he answered: 'Well, I don't know . . . At the moment, I think the finest thing I've written is my work for cello and orchestra which hasn't yet been performed.' The Cello Symphony had been completed in May 1963, but owing to Rostropovich's continuing heart trouble was having to wait for performance. The other work for large forces which Britten had completed since the *War Requiem*, the *Cantata Misericordium*, was conceived – as Britten explained to Fischer-Dieskau, who with Pears took part in the Geneva performance – as 'a very *direct & simple*' setting of the Good Samaritan story. The Latin words, by Patrick Wilkinson, a Cambridge friend of Forster, were meant to be suitable 'for such an *International non-musical occasion*!' However, Britten told Forster after the performance: 'I did mind very much about the Cantata, & am delighted that it came over [the radio] so strongly.' William Mann in *The Times* praised it for the 'instantaneous vividness' with which it evoked the characters in the biblical story, 'the heedless passers-by . . . the traveller's spurs on his donkey's flanks . . . and the Samaritan's lullaby . . . Like most of Britten's music it may, on first hearing, sound unimpressively bland, if one has not appreciated the diversified unity of the musical ideas.' Mann compared it to the *War Requiem*, and judged that 'on its smaller scale is it also a humanitarian document'.

On 13 November 1963 Britten wrote to Hans Werne Henze: 'I am having a difficult time with all the celebrations of my birthday, which are touching but take a lot of time and energy which one would rather spend on writing new works. Still, I have managed to do a big new piece for Julian.' The *Nocturnal after John Dowland*, for guitar, was first performed by Julian Bream at the 1964 Aldeburgh Festival. (Henze, a friend of the Hesses, knew both Britten and Bream from their visits to Wolfsgarten.) The piece is in vivid contrast to the 'public' works Britten had been producing since *A Midsummer Night's Dream* three years earlier. Subtitled 'reflections', its theme is Dowland's 'Come, heavy sleep', which is not heard in full till the end, suggesting that sleep does not come for a long while. The preceding movements are undoubtedly meant to portray the various stages of insomnia. They have such markings as 'Very agitated', 'Restless', and 'Uneasy'. Uncharacteristically, Britten admitted (in a 1969 interview) that the *Nocturnal* 'has some very, to me, disturbing images in it'. He did not say what they were.

Some years later, Julian Bream recalled of the *Nocturnal*:

When the piece arrived, I found I didn't have to change anything, not one note. It's the *only* piece written for me of which that is true. Oh yes, except for one tiny blemish, where Britten had contrived to place two notes on the same string. When I pointed this out to him he was simply horrified! It was as though you'd pointed out some terrible gaff in his social behaviour.

Donald Mitchell, who published the *Nocturnal*, remembers it differently:

Ben would sometimes consult Julian, and ask, 'Is this possible on the guitar?' And Julian would say, 'No it isn't.' But then he would take it away and try it and find that it *was* possible, that it worked. Julian himself made the point that this was an example of a composer writing ahead of an instrument's established technique, exploring potentialities that the player (however gifted) had not foreseen. It was rather like Mozart and the clarinet – what he composed for it advanced the instrument's technical (and thus expressive) possibilities.

Bream was now regularly accompanying Pears, and he has spoken of the vicissitudes of working at Aldeburgh, remembering in particular

a wonderful time when it was said that my Dowland was slipping! I remember Willie Walton was always amused at that, and whenever I saw Willie, he said, 'Now, Julian, tell me, I want to know one thing – *is your Dowland slipping?*' And so I would be out the following year, not asked. Then I'd hitch it up, and be back!

A 1959 letter from Pears (in Germany with Bream) to Britten observes: 'Julian ... was disturbed when I told him you were worried about his playing, but he played pretty superbly at Nymphenburg.'

The Cello Symphony, still waiting for performance when the *Nocturnal* was written, is an equally 'private' work. Britten told Rostropovich that it had been 'very difficult to write'. Far from being 'unimpressively bland' at first hearing, it is tense and frequently frightening, no mere show-piece for cello but an intricately constructed dialogue in which orchestra and soloist are equal partners – Britten himself described it as 'an argument on equal terms, rather than just a pure background for the orchestra'. Restlessness and a sense of internal struggle predominate among its moods. John Warrack wrote in the *Musical Times* of 'the dark intricacy of the first movement and its nervous, shifty scherzo companion', while Peter Evans remarks on the 'furtive, claustrophobic atmosphere' of the second movement.

*

Roger Duncan was now twenty. He had continued to spend much of his school holidays at Aldeburgh throughout his time at Harrow, but his mother had the sense that he had now been superseded in Britten's affections: 'Ben did a rather nasty thing. He came down to the farm with another little boy, when Roger was there, and I felt very strongly for Roger about that, though when I referred to it, Roger said, "Oh, I couldn't care less."' Writing to Forster when Roger was nineteen, Britten remarked that Harrow had given him a certain 'glossiness', very different from the 'lively, intelligent & tender little boy' of earlier years. Roger himself recalls the incident of the other boy arriving in Britten's company, and allows that it was 'upsetting'. He says it was clear that 'Ben's affection for me had waned'. He married young, and went to Canada. Ronald Duncan writes that Britten sent his son 'a splendid desk as a wedding present'. Roger confirms this, and adds that Britten 'offered to write a piece of music for my wedding, but that didn't come to pass'.

*

When Britten was in residence at Aldeburgh his daily routine was much the same as ever – work in the morning, a walk in the afternoon, and more work before supper. He was still sometimes playing children's games in the evening. (Mary Potter presented him with a homemade set of Happy Families cards, with what Rosamund Strode describes as 'wickedly accurate characters of some Aldeburgh people. Ben and Mary were both utterly terrified that both the fact of these cards and also the details of some of them might get out while the persons depicted very transparently in them were still alive.') But by 1963 it was becoming increasingly difficult to keep to his ideal day's timetable without constant distractions. That winter he decided to try the experiment of going away to write his next work. 'I go off abroad in January for 6 weeks to do the bulk of a new opera which I've been planning for a time,' he told Yehudi Menuhin at Christmas 1963. This was, at last, *Curlew River*. It had now been in his mind for nearly eight years, though he was still uncertain about the title. To Plomer, during the autumn of 1963, he suggested 'The other side of the River', 'Across the River', or 'Over the River'.

He had chosen to work in Venice, where he and Pears arrived in mid-January 1964, staying in an apartment in the Palazzo Mocenigo – 'part of a dotty but rather fine Palazzo – where Byron stayed!' The weather was 'arctic', and at first work on the opera went 'badly'. At the last minute Britten had suggested to Plomer that he might come out to Venice so that they could alter the libretto together when the music required it, but no reply came from Plomer, and Britten had to make the changes himself with the help of Colin Graham, who was to produce, and who had travelled to Venice to discuss the staging. (Imogen Holst also joined them, to work on the vocal score while Britten wrote.) Three weeks after beginning work Britten reported to Donald Mitchell, who, besides being on the music staff of the *Daily Telegraph*, now had a part-time consultancy at Boosey & Hawkes:

> I am getting on quite well with the new opera. It was hellishly hard to start with; I found I was tireder than I thought . . . And I wasn't so well prepared to start with as I'd like to have been . . . Apart from finding the right notes (& because there are so few of them, it seems harder than ever), one of the problems is how to write it down: there being no conductor, & the tempo is kind of 'controlled floating'.

The sparse instrumentation – a mere seven players – and the absence of a conductor were modelled on the method of presenting *Sumidagawa* when Britten had seen it in Tokyo in 1956, but he told Plomer he was still wary of the 'strong influence' of Japan, which might lead him into pastiche.

For this reason he had forbidden Colin Graham to see any Noh theatre. 'He wanted our movement style to be our own,' writes Graham, 'not a pastiche.' Graham describes how during their sessions in the Palazzo Mocenigo

> Ben would discuss what he was about to write in the afternoon, play what he had just written, and discuss the practicalities of how to stage it. I had to demonstrate the kind of movement I envisaged for each episode. He would then build these strengths and softnesses into that day's music and then I had to do them again when the music was written. And so on.

Graham adds that Pears would always listen to these play-throughs, 'but he would never make suggestions or interfere or take part in any way'.

On 15 February 1964, a week before leaving Venice, Britten sent Plomer a progress report:

> When we arrived I was tireder than I thought . . . & honestly I still couldn't quite see the style of it all clearly enough. I was still very drawn towards the Nô, too close for comfort. However, a few days here, although Arctic in temperature, the Gothic beauty & warmth, and above all the occasional Masses one attended, began to make their effect. It was a slow start, but after that it rushed ahead, & after little more than a month I am well towards the end. Apart from the usual bits that need clarifying, I am *very* pleased with it . . . Oddly enough, as the work progressed the *Curlew* grew in significance, & my inclination is to go back to Curlew River as a title!!

The Masses were in the island church of San Giorgio Maggiore, where the monks still sang plainsong. Colin Graham writes that he and Britten 'were impressed and moved by the ritual robing – the robes were unfolded from a linen chest with extreme delicacy and reverence. This led Britten to follow the Abbot's address [in *Curlew River*] with a robing ceremony.'

At the end of February, back in Aldeburgh, Britten wrote to Plomer: 'It will be lovely to see you, & to play you the piece.' Plomer came down to Aldeburgh at once. After his visit Britten thanked him for being 'unbelievably quick to understand what Curlew River was about & what needed to be done'. This letter, written on 7 March, announced that Britten was 'Just off Eastwards in a whirl of music, visas, warm clothes'. Following the success of his 1963 Russian trip he had been invited back by the Soviet authorities to conduct the première of his Cello Symphony in Moscow with a repeat in Leningrad. John Warrack wrote in the *Musical Times* that 'Britten has become ... a part of the Russian musical scene: he was the only contemporary English or American composer whose music I noticed in Soviet editions when in Russia recently.' Warrack was in Moscow for the Cello Symphony performance, and went to the Great Hall of the Moscow Conservatoire to hear the final rehearsal:

> Snow was falling. The orchestra trudged past, shedding coats and fur hats. Inside, the hall was warm, and romanticised pictures of Bach, Mozart and Tchaikovsky simpered down on the platform. I wondered how long it would be before Benjamin Britten found himself among them ... But he was very much alive, clearing up a point with the timpanist, looking at his watch as Rostropovich failed to turn up, in his element among friendly musicians. A noise from the back, and Rostropovich's cello appeared, with the apologetic musician propelling it. The rehearsal was barely more than a run-through.

That evening in the Great Hall,

> the English colony was out in force. So was the musical establishment – Shostakovich's grey, impassive face in the third row, Khachaturian enthroned in a box. Britten appeared, was cordially greeted, and everyone settled down except for the cameramen, whose clicks and probing searchlights went on unremittingly.

Britten himself wrote that the orchestra, the Moscow Philharmonic, was 'excellent', and that 'Rostropovich played incredibly well'. Warrack writes that the musical establishment applauded politely, but 'the students in the gallery were overjoyed, stamping and hand-clapping until they got the finale encored. I later heard from a professor that no work had so excited the younger generation for years.' On his arrival in Leningrad, Britten was surprised and delighted by what Warrack calls 'the "present" of a carefully prepared performance of the first half of the *War Requiem* by the students of Leningrad Conservatory', and throughout the trip 'was surprised to be involved in expert discussions about works he had almost forgotten'. In a 1965 letter Britten mentions that 'the Leningrad Conservatoire . . . paid me the stunning compliment of an improvised performance of the War Requiem (and jolly good it was too) at a time when the work was virtually forbidden in Russia'. Meanwhile he was building up a good relationship with Furtseva, the minister of culture. He proposed to her that Rostropovich should have the exclusive right to perform the Cello Symphony until the end of 1965. She was 'enthusiastic and grateful', and reciprocated by giving permission for Rostropovich to record it for Decca – at a time when few Russian artists were allowed to record abroad.

Britten returned from Russia to face a critical situation with regard to the publication of his music. His relations with Boosey & Hawkes had been poor since the death of Erwin Stein in 1958. (Ralph Hawkes, who had done so much to further Britten's career, had died eight years before Stein.) There was no longer anyone in the firm whose musical abilities he really respected, and he was astonished to discover that Decca had found Boosey's uncooperative and even hostile over recordings of his works. Ernst Roth, who had taken over responsibility for his music after Stein's death, had had his tastes formed in the age of Richard Strauss and showed little understanding of contemporary composers. In June 1962 Britten wrote to Leslie Boosey that the firm was 'not really in touch or in sympathy with serious music today'. He dropped hints that he might go to another publisher, but Roth 'pooh-poohed my idea of leaving B & H (where to?, he said)'. This was indeed the problem. Schott's were publishing a number of contemporary British composers, including Tippett, but their head office was in Germany, and the only other British firm able to cope with a musician of Britten's stature was Oxford University Press, with whom he had parted company years earlier.

Britten hoped that the solution had been found when, at his suggestion, Boosey's recruited Donald Mitchell on a part-time basis, to look after his affairs, and also to acquire, whenever possible, young composers – 'Ben was very anxious about that,' he says, 'as well as about his own music.' However, early in 1964 Roth gave Mitchell three months' notice on the thinnest of pretexts. Mitchell had also been acting as adviser on books about music to Faber & Faber, and on 5 February 1964, from

Venice, Britten wrote to Mitchell: 'Don't worry ... I'm sure there'll be some future. I occasionally dream of Faber & Faber – music publishers!' Fabers' had never published music and were not equipped to do so. However, Mitchell took the letter to the firm's chairman, Richard de la Mare, son of Walter, and was told: 'I have no idea how this can be done, but clearly we have to do it.'

No serious music publishing firm had been set up in Britain since the founding of the Oxford University Press Music Department in 1925, and the project would require heavy financial commitment, but Fabers' pressed ahead enthusiastically, and soon Peter du Sautoy, one of the directors (and the son-in-law of Sir Francis Floud who had chaired Britten's Conscientious Objector appeal tribunal in 1942), was in touch with Britten about it. Britten emphasized that he would not be the only composer to benefit: 'I do feel that a lively new music publishing firm can be of the utmost value to the musical life of this country.' His existing publishing agreement with Boosey's had expired at the end of 1963, so things moved quickly. On 16 May 1964 the *Daily Telegraph* reported:

> Faber and Faber, who today announce their plans to enter the field of music publishing, must be the first firm who have started such a venture by attracting the leading English composer of the day to their side ... Benjamin Britten is now likely to stay firmly in the Faber camp. They are starting with two new works to be introduced at the Aldeburgh Festival in June, *Curlew River*, A Parable for Church Performance, and a Nocturnal for guitar. The head of Fabers' new music department will be Donald Mitchell, the *Daily Telegraph* music critic, who now hopes to add some of the younger English composers to his first formidable capture.

The young gradually arrived, but for a long while Faber Music had to be supported by its parent firm. Britten, who had agreed to serve on the board of directors, helped by allowing payments to him to be deferred. Meanwhile his letters to Mitchell were full of praise for the excellent standard of design and production and for the devotion with which Mitchell looked after his interests. 'I had never dreamed that published music could again become a delight to the eye & a stimulus to performance,' he told Mitchell, '& I am deeply impressed and very very grateful.'

The term 'Parable', mentioned in Fabers' publicity for *Curlew River*, had been carefully devised by Britten, who wrote to Plomer on 2 April 1964: 'I have been looking for a sub-title which will make it clear it is *not* an opera, in the accepted sense, & *must* be done in Church. Do you like Curlew River – *a parable* (I must learn how to spell it) *for church performance?* We all like the parable-idea.' In the same letter he announced that the writing of *Curlew River* was 'all finished, & the machinery is grinding away at producing parts for everyone to learn'. A crucial part of the 'machinery' was Rosamund Strode, who this year took over Imogen Holst's work as Britten's music assistant, at first working under Imogen's supervison. She had first met Britten in 1948 when she was a postgraduate student of Imogen's at Dartington, having previously studied singing and viola at the RCM. She became a professional soprano, was a founder member of the Purcell Singers, a small choir which often performed at the Aldeburgh Festival from 1954, and began to assist Imogen as extra copyist for Britten's full scores, beginning with *The Prince of the Pagodas*. Imogen had intended to retire in 1967, when she would be sixty, and to devote her remaining years to looking after her father's musical estate. In the event she stopped working as Britten's amanuensis three years earlier. Rosamund Strode says this was because there was so much preparation for the Holst centenary, which would fall in 1974, but Fidelity Cranbrook believes that Britten had begun to be exasperated by her, and that, realizing this, she had the wisdom to leave of her own accord. Certainly Britten was dismayed by her frequent, studiedly casual references to a gynaecological operation she had recently undergone, and Rosamund Strode admits that this became 'a slightly naughty Red House joke. She had no idea how it curled Ben up.' She continued to live in Aldeburgh and was as closely involved as ever in the running of the Festival. Rosamund Strode observes that, once you had come to Aldeburgh, it was almost impossible to get away: 'It's a flypaper.'

Rosamund Strode made no claims to most of Imogen's vast talents, and it was agreed that her musical work would be restricted to copying, proof-reading and other sorts of straightforward paperwork, plus some secretarial duties, leaving the making of vocal and rehearsal scores to others. 'I used to wake up in the night for ages,' she says, 'thinking, "I *can't* really be working for Benjamin Britten!"' She found that it took a little time to learn his language:

> He'd ring up and say, 'Would you like to come to lunch?' Actually it was a command. And although he could plan rehearsals in detail six months ahead – when the wind and brass would be required, and so on – he organized each particular day that morning. So he would telephone at very short notice, and say, 'Come and have a meeting.' And you had to.

Like others before her, she found Pears in some respects more opaque than Britten:

He had this rather withdrawn quality, an apartness – I think it was to do with being a performer. On the other hand you could approach Peter at any hour of the day, interrupt him, whereas you couldn't interrupt Ben. So if I was fielding a really tricky telephone call, I could immediately go upstairs to Peter's study and say, 'Sorry, there's bad news,' and Peter would then go and break it to Ben. I couldn't walk into Ben's study when he was working. It would be frightfully agitating.

Though her position as fender-off of nuisances and interruptions made her seem to many people a member of the innermost circle at the Red House, Rosamund Strode emphasizes that this was not so: 'I didn't feel myself that I was on that step of the ladder. And it actually felt much more comfortable not to be. I always referred to myself as a cog, because that's how I saw myself.' On the other hand she was made completely welcome: 'I felt like a junior member of the Britten family.'

While she was copying the instrumental parts of *Curlew River*, Britten and Pears went to Prague and Budapest for concert appearances – 'those brave and exciting peoples', Britten called the Czechs and Hungarians in a letter to Plomer on his return, though their journey back via the Berlin Wall 'lowered our spirits considerably'. Rehearsals for *Curlew River* began at the Thorpeness working men's club in May 1964. Eric Crozier recalls that, when word got around Aldeburgh that Pears would be appearing as a woman, 'there was almost a scandal'. The twenty-five-year-old tenor Robert Tear, who the previous year had sung Quint in a revival of *The Turn of the Screw*, had been engaged to understudy Pears and sing his role in certain performances. Tear watched Pears struggling with the Madwoman's costume in rehearsal, and describes an exchange about this between him and Britten: 'Peter . . . brought the rehearsal to an end, saying, "Really, Ben, I just can't work with this frock." To which Ben replied to Colin Graham (producer), "Oh, for Christ's sake, Colin, give her a crin."' Colin Graham says that the remark was 'a joke, not a snap', and recalls that Tear 'was much more concerned than Peter about not appearing to be effeminate; he infuriated Ben by resolutely detaching himself from the role – whereas the whole ethic of Noh-Playing is Total Identification!'

Twelve-year-old Oliver Knussen, whose father Stuart was the double-bass player in *Curlew River*, came to the final rehearsals: 'Some of the players couldn't work out how in the blazes they would be able to play at different speeds, or together accurately, without a conductor, and were afraid it couldn't really work.' Rosamund Strode was kept up late at night rewriting the elaborately cued instrumental parts so that different players could lead the others at particular moments. Britten had also devised new effects for certain instruments. Philip Ledger, who was playing the chamber organ, recalls that 'there was a bit on the harp, and Osian Ellis said, "Ben, I can't play that – I don't think it's possible." And Ben said, "Well, if you tried that pedal, and played it like this –" And there was Ben giving Osian a lesson on where to find the notes on *his* harp!'

The 1964 Aldeburgh Festival opened three days before the first performance of *Curlew River*. Exhibitions included paintings (inspired by Shakespeare sonnets) by Sidney Nolan, who had been introduced to Britten some years earlier by Kenneth Clark; also bronzes by Georg Ehrlich, described by Pears in the Festival programme book as an artist 'without rival in his bronzes of animals and children'. Britten and Pears had bought a large number of Ehrlich's works, chiefly bronzes and pencil sketches of boys, which were displayed at the Red House. Britten had written to Ehrlich in 1956: 'You know how much your art has meant to me for many years.'

The Festival included the first British performance of the Cello Symphony, given in Blythburgh Church by Rostropovich with the English Chamber Orchestra conducted by Britten. 'Rostropovich played the work as though he had composed it himself,' wrote Desmond Shawe-Taylor, and William Mann judged it 'plainly . . . a masterpiece'. Rostropovich himself wrote to Britten some months later: 'Dearest Ben! Wherever I can I play your great Symphony! Only now the performances are beginning to have a more genuine quality. Only now do I begin to understand what it really is!' He now had his own names for his Aldeburgh friends, 'Benusenka and Peterchik', and could write a few words of English. 'MY DIEREST, DIEREST Benusenka!' reads one note, 'MY HARD with ju! Slava.' He told friends he had 'learnt to phrase' from Pears's singing.

Richard Butt, who was producing the BBC broadcast of the Cello Symphony from Blythburgh, met Pears after the final rehearsal. 'He said, "How did it go?" And I said. "Marvellous. It's a wonderful piece, isn't it?" And Peter said, "I don't know. I've never heard it."' Butt was struck by Pears's apparent indifference towards a Britten work in which he was not performing. Later in the sixties Britten remarked to Donald Mitchell in conversation: 'When I have ideas which may seem very new or bold, I'm nervous sometimes of telling Peter about them. He's such a strong personality that if he says "no" or takes a negative view, I'm discouraged, and can't go on with them.' Mitchell comments:

I remember Imo saying much the same thing. I don't know that it added up to a problem in their relationship, but clearly Peter was intensely interested in the works Ben wrote for him, and altogether less interested in those that weren't. Ben's output might have been different in character – there might conceivably have been greater diversity – if he had set up in life with someone other than a singer. On Peter's part there was self-evidently a high degree of self-interest involved: the production-line should be kept going with as few interruptions as possible. Did Peter in this sense keep Ben creatively on too tight a rein? It may be doing Peter an injustice even to ask the question, but it has to be asked, I think.

There was great excitement over a last-minute addition to the 1964 Festival. 'RICHTER DROPS IN TO PLAY SCHUBERT,' read the *Daily Telegraph* headline. 'Dropping in unannounced, Sviatoslav Richter sat down in Aldeburgh's parish church yesterday to give a truly unforgett-able recital of Schubert's piano music. Where else but in Aldeburgh is one likely to stumble inadvertently on the experience of a lifetime? – and Mr Richter's performance of the E minor Sonata was no less than that.' Rostropovich had introduced Britten to Richter in London in 1961, and they had spent a lively evening at Boulestin's. During Richter's Alde-burgh recital (on 20 June 1964) Britten sat down with him to play Schubert's A flat Variations for Piano Duet. 'The somewhat matter-of-fact and dry exposition of the first few pieces,' wrote Peter Stadlen in the *Daily Telegraph*, 'emphasised the indescribably powerful expressiveness of the ones in the minor and the coda.' Stadlen 'could not see who did the pedalling', but it must have been Richter, for though Britten normally took control of the pedal when playing duets he would undoubtedly have deferred to Richter, whom, writing to Lord Harewood in 1961, he called 'the best pianist ever'.

Pears has said that Britten

greatly admired Richter, was very fond of him, though of course he's not the same outgoing type as Slava [Rostropovich], and though Slava Richter would have loved a piano piece from him, Ben, honestly, was not specially, honestly interested in the piano in the same way. He was never all that sympathetic to the piano. Early on in his career he was happy to write the Piano Concerto and a few other pieces, but the piano was an instrument that he had very mixed feelings about, and I don't think he could really face getting down, sitting down to that again, writing another Piano Concerto as it were.

Michael Berkeley thinks it odd that later in his life Britten wrote no solo piano music, other than the short *Night Piece (Notturno)* (1963), composed at Marion Harewood's request for the first Leeds International Piano Competition, which she had founded with the piano teacher Fanny Waterman. Berkeley suggests that as virtually all Britten's music was intended for particular performers, the one person he would apparently not write for was himself. When questioned in 1962 about why he had not written for solo piano since the war, Britten answered: 'I don't feel inclined. I like the piano very much as a background instrument, but I don't feel inclined to treat it as a melodic instrument. I find that it's limited in colour. I don't really *like* the sound of a modern piano.' Donald Mitchell, however, remarks on the 'exceptional quantity of virtuoso piano music that forms part of the song-cycles – those extraordinarily elaborate and subtly conceived accompaniments that require an interpreter and executant quite the equal of the singer. "Accompaniments" does not adequately describe them.' Rosamund Strode, making the same point, adds: 'He would write things that even he found extremely difficult. There were some pieces in the repertoire with Peter that he had to practise like blazes.'

*

On the evening of Saturday 13 June 1964 the audience assembled in Orford Church for the first performance of *Curlew River*, which being only a little over an hour in length was not starting until 9 p.m.

'Our arrival at Orford Church was greeted by a violent storm,' wrote Leslie Ayre in the *Evening News*, 'during which lightning struck at the electricity system and delayed the start of the performance for half an hour. Yet there was something almost appropriate about it. For Benjamin Britten's latest dramatic work, *Curlew River*, is full of a mystic sense of powers beyond those of men.' Keith Grant says that when the electricity was cut

> it was quite astonishing the way Ben rallied to the occasion. *Curlew River* had been a particularly stressful opera in rehearsal, because Ben was very conscious of the fact that he was pushing the boat out in a new direction, and he was worried about the reception that Peter might get in a drag part, so we were all strung up like fiddle-strings. And then suddenly this bathos, when the lights went out, and you might have expected Ben, being easily upset by nature, to curl up and die. But on the contrary, he had obviously decided that the way to handle it was not to care, but only to care about the artists, to keep their morale up. And he went round, he talked, showed his good-humoured side, and was exemplary.

–433–

At last the performance began. The singers and instrumentalists, robed as monks, processed from the vestry to the acting area at the west end of the church, where a special round stage designed by Colin Graham had been constructed, singing the Gregorian chant *Te lucis ante terminum*, 'Before the ending of the day'. One of the audience that night writes that, from this moment until the end of the performance, everyone listening in the church 'scarcely breathed'.

Writing in the Britten fiftieth birthday *Festschrift*, Prince Ludwig of Hesse gave a vivid description of *Sumidagawa* as he and Britten had seen it in Tokyo in 1956:

> The play which is hard to forget is the play about the Sumida river: the ferryman is waiting in his boat, a traveller turns up and tells him about a woman who will soon be coming to the river. The woman is mad, she is looking for her lost child. Then she appears and the ferryman does not wish to take a mad person, but in the end he lets her into his boat. On the way across the river the two passengers sit behind each other on the floor as if in a narrow boat, while the ferryman stands behind them, symbolically punting with a light stick. The ferryman tells the story of a little boy who came this way a year ago this very day. The child was very tired for he had escaped from robbers who had held him. He crossed the river in this boat, but he died from exhaustion on the other side. The woman starts crying. It was her son. The ferryman is sorry for her and takes her to the child's grave.
>
> The mother is acted by a tall man in woman's clothing with a small woman's mask on his face. Accessories help you to understand what is going on: a bamboo branch in the hand indicates madness, a long stick is the ferryman's punting pole, a very small gong is beaten for the sorrowing at the graveside. As soon as these props are no longer necessary, stagehands who have brought them to the actors take them away again.
>
> The sorrowful declamations of the mother rising and subsiding in that oddly pressed voice, the movement of her hand to the brim of her hat as if to protect her sadness from the outside world, the small 'ping' of the little gong which she beats at the child's grave, become as absorbing as does the sudden foot-stamping which emphasizes important passages. The play ends in the chanting of the chorus. We feel this is more than an interesting experience.

In a *Radio Times* article previewing the broadcast of *Curlew River* from the 1964 Aldeburgh Festival, William Plomer observed that by 'a strangely fortunate chance' Britten had seen the one Noh play out of the whole repertoire that was most likely to appeal to him, 'with its motif of innocence wronged'. This may well have been the particular feature of the play – the boy's tragic death following the kidnapping – which caught Britten's attention in the Tokyo performance. But both the Noh play and the Britten–Plomer reworking concentrate not on the child but on the mother, or as she is named in *Curlew River* – and the change is significant – the Madwoman.

Britten's letter to Plomer from Venice while he was writing *Curlew River* indicates that it was he rather than the librettist who chose *Te lucis ante terminum* for the opening plainchant. Like the hymn which opens *Noye's Fludde* it is a prayer for purity, an appeal for aid in the struggle against moral contamination. 'From all ill dreams defend our eyes,' reads the second verse as translated in the *English Hymnal*, 'From nightly fears and fantasies; / Tread under foot our ghostly foe, / That no pollution we may know.' The plainchant is part of a three-decker 'frame' introducing the work, the other two sections being the Abbot's address to the audience, and an instrumental fantasy on *Te lucis*, played while the actors don their costumes and masks. In his programme note to *Curlew River*, Britten states of *Te lucis* that 'from it the whole piece may be said to have grown', by which he means – as Peter Evans has demonstrated – that the chant is the source of almost all the motifs in the work. Yet the music which Britten draws from it is anything but liturgical in character.

As the chant itself dies away, untuned drums of different pitches begin a nervous tapping, and the chamber organ spreads out a rich chord, a note-cluster reminiscent of the celesta music in *The Turn of the Screw*. (Donald Mitchell points out that the cluster is 'virtually a precise transcription of the chord produced by the Japanese *shō* [a type of mouth organ] which Britten heard in Tokyo'.) The Abbot may assure the audience in his Prologue that the play will demonstrate 'God's grace', but beneath his voice the organ becomes more and more discordant, and the drums tap away obsessively. Two different worlds, the Christian and something else, seem to be in tension with each other.

After the Ferryman has announced himself to the accompaniment of a brash horn call ('I am the ferryman / I row the boat / Over the Curlew . . .') the chorus observes: 'Between two kingdoms the river flows; / On this side the Land of the West, / On the other, the Eastern fens.' It has already become apparent that, musically speaking, the river is the meeting point between the styles of East and West, and the same is true on the dramatic level. As the Ferryman sits down in his boat the Traveller arrives on the western bank, announced by a plodding double-bass suggesting weary feet and a harp whose shifting arpeggios hint at mental restlessness. This is Western Man on his relentless journey through life, pushing 'the big chariot' up the hill to fame and fortune in classic northern European fashion, as if it were the only way to exist. We may assume that on the eastern side of the Curlew they live very differently.

As the Traveller in *Curlew River* climbs into the boat, the cry of the Madwoman is heard as she approaches on the western side, accompanied by a bird-like flutter-tongued flute. She does not sound as if she is tortured by sorrow. The leaping chromatic motif which Britten has given her suggests not bereavement but excitement, while her words indicate that she is trying to find the answer to a riddle:

> You mock me! You ask me!
> Whither I, whither I go.
> You mock me! You ask me!
> How should I, how should I, how should I know?

Then comes the riddle itself:

> Where the nest of the curlew
> Is not filled with snow,
> Where the eyes of the lamb
> Are untorn by the crow,
> There let me, there let me, there let me go!
> Let me in!
> Let me out!
> Tell me the, tell me the way!

Unlike her fellow Westerner, the Traveller, she seems aware that there is another, less bleak way of living than the West practises. Her words suggest that it may be found within one's own psyche ('Let me in!'), but that to achieve it requires escape from the limitations of one's own obsessions ('Let me out!'). She is not mad, but visionary.

The casting of a male singer as the Madwoman was, of course, suggested by the Noh play, but like the use of a counter-tenor as Oberon it carries hints of unorthodox sexuality. (Pears has said of the role: 'I didn't really find it all that difficult, because I found it so sympathetic ... I certainly adored doing it.') The Madwoman's description of life with her boy before his kidnap is musically tense and disturbing. She sings in an eerie monotone, ending each phrase with a glissando. When the Ferryman, who despite the significance of his job seems to represent the blunt-minded common man, refuses her a place in his boat unless she entertains the passengers with her crazy singing, she cites 'a riddle' once made by a 'famous traveller ... In this very place':

> Birds of the Fenland, though you float or fly,
> Wild birds, I cannot understand your cry.
> Tell me, does the one I love
> In this world still live?

This is taken up by the other singers as a big number. Clearly the Curlew, the bird as well as the river, is an important symbol. Yet its actual cry, impersonated by the flute, is simply the Madwoman's own motif. She and the bird seem to be two halves of a divided personality; Britten is once more setting up a pair of balanced opposites. The Madwoman seems to be the mundane, physical aspect of human nature (though with visionary possibilities), the Curlew to be the human spirit purged of the commonplace. It is the age-old tragedy that one side cannot communicate with the other: 'Wild birds, I cannot understand your cry.'

The Ferryman warns the Madwoman that

> To navigate the ferry boat
> Is not easy.
> The river is glassy,
> But the Devil himself
> With strong-flowing currents
> Can drag the boat aside,
> And carry away all who are in her . . .
> God have mercy upon us!

The most frightful moral dangers lie in wait for those who abandon the Western way of life (bourgeois convention) for something more exotic. Sure enough when the boat moves off from the bank the slow glissandi in double-bass and harp, while vividly evoking the swirling of the water as the Ferryman pushes with his punt pole, also recall the music of the amoral and erotic fairy wood in *A Midsummer Night's Dream*. These glissandi continue during the Ferryman's narrative of the death of the boy ('a gentle boy, twelve years old'). While the libretto gives a plain account of the child collapsing from exhaustion and dying by the wayside, the music suggests something quite different.

When the Madwoman learns of his death she blames the river – the journey away from bourgeois convention: 'O Curlew River, cruel Curlew.' She and the others kneel at the boy's grave and pray, but though Britten now introduces another plainchant, *Custodes hominum* (a hymn to the guardian angels), the Christian force of this is in tension with note-clusters from organ and harp and gamelan-like *tremolandi* on handbells (played with beaters). One is reminded of Prince Ludwig's description of the Balinese dancers: 'The whole thing is stimulating and soporific at the same time . . . There is an odd atmosphere in this place.' It is at this moment that the dead boy's spirit is heard, singing within his tomb.

He emerges and circles around the Madwoman. Then he returns to the tomb and is heard singing again. At moments the music is purely Christian – the boy's 'Go your way in peace, mother, / The dead shall rise again' sounds like part of the Mass – but at other times becomes oriental and seductive. The child's final 'God be with you, mother' ends on a sighing glissando like Miles responding to Quint, while the Madwoman's response to this, a melismatic 'Amen', might evoke Quint even if the two roles had not been sung by the same performer. Here the dramatic action of *Curlew River* concludes, and we are back in the three-decker frame: instrumental music for disrobing, the Abbot's Epilogue to the audience, and *Te lucis* sung as a recessional. *Sumidagawa* ends in the same fashion, with the chorus making a final comment. Plomer's libretto retains some features of the Japanese text, but its most striking passages, such as the Madwoman's riddle-asking, are his own invention.

*

Oliver Knussen has studied an earlier version of the boy's spirit's appearance from the tomb, rejected by Britten in rehearsal:

> The music was very fast and nervous. The Madwoman was supposed to reach out and try to grab the ghost as it went past – which is not only musically out of place in a piece that is predominantly slow and contemplative, but also dramatically (if you can imagine it) very strange indeed – a man dressed as a woman grasping for a small boy. The music that replaced it is the most extraordinarily beautiful in the opera, and I'm still staggered that it was written as a patch-up over the weekend before dress rehearsals.

This grasping is in fact what happens in *Sumidagawa*, but Britten may have felt that it was open to misinterpretation. Fidelity Cranbrook says that she and others at Aldeburgh who knew about *Curlew River* in advance 'had our hearts in our boots in case somebody started giggling at Peter dressed up as a woman', but nobody did, and her neighbour in the audience was moved to tears by his performance. William Mann in *The Times* commended Pears for avoiding the manner of a pantomime dame 'to an astonishing degree', and suggested that *Curlew River* might be 'the start of a new, perhaps the most important, stage in Britten's creative life'. Mann had praise too for Colin Graham's 'miraculously tactful production' and the 'formalized oriental gestures' in which the cast had been coached by Claude Chagrin, the French mime artist. Martin Cooper in the

Daily Telegraph was just as enthusiastic, though he felt that the Christian denouement struck a 'questionable note' in the middle of the brilliant 'East–West musical cross-fertilization'.

Pears sang the Madwoman again at the third performance, while at the second and fourth the role was taken by Robert Tear. 'Mr Tear was outstandingly successful,' wrote one of Mann's second-string critics in *The Times*. 'His actual singing of this florid part impressed particularly for its precision and control.' Tear recalls how, after he had sung the part for the first time, he and the other principals waited backstage for Britten's comments – and Pears's:

> Ben came first and was sweet, casting however a weather eye over his shoulder. Peter followed on closely. He said to John Shirley-Quirk . . . [the Ferryman], 'Absolutely stunning, John'; to Bryan Drake [the Traveller], 'Bravo, Bryan, well done'; and to me, 'Lipstick a little too white, I feel.' I was bemused but at that time too green to understand.

Steuart Bedford, who later worked with both singers, says that Tear's top register was far stronger than Pears's, and Pears knew it.

From Orford, *Curlew River* moved to Southwark Cathedral, where Tear again sang the Madwoman. A few moments before he was due to go on, Britten came backstage and 'astonished' Tear by saying: 'I'm very disappointed with your work, you're using my music as a vocal exercise.' In his book *Tear Here* (1990), Tear gives this as an example of Britten's 'cruelty', but in an interview with the musical journalist Alan Blyth ten years earlier he suggested that Britten was being 'devastatingly waspish' in order to challenge him to greater heights of performance.

Talking about Britten in 1991, Tear suggested that the spirit of the boy in *Curlew River* 'could have been the son that Ben and Peter might have wished for'. A few months after the first performance, Britten invited John Newton, who had sung the part of the boy in the second cast, to stay at the Red House. He wrote to Pears: 'He is a sweet affectionate child – makes one feel rather what one has missed in not having a child . . . John is a little bit of a substitute, and I'm really lucky!'

4: We do not lack enemies

'Got a good idea for another opera in the same style – so be prepared!'
Britten wrote to Plomer from Amsterdam, where *Curlew River* was being
performed at the 1964 Holland Festival. At the end of July he had to fly
to Aspen, Colorado, to receive the first-ever Aspen Award, a prize of
$30,000 donated by the chairman of the Institute of Humanistic Studies
in that city for an outstanding contribution 'to the advancement of the
humanities'. Britten invited Elizabeth Mayer to come to Aspen as his
guest, but she felt she was too old for such a journey. He had to make a
speech of acceptance, and Pears helped him write it; Britten referred to it
as '*our* speech ... which I think you've done marvellously for me'. But
the ideas were obviously Britten's own.

The speech is a consideration of the composer's role in society. Britten
begins by emphasizing that he believes 'in *occasional* music', written for
particular performers, places and times. 'A lot of it cannot make much
sense after its first performance,' he asserts. Robert Tear noticed that the
first production of any of his operas 'was the definitive version' for
Britten, 'and any future workings with different people could only result
[he believed] in the deterioration of the piece'.

In the speech, he regrets the present-day domination of music by
recordings, so that 'Anyone, anywhere, at any time, can listen to the B
minor Mass ... No qualification is required of any sort – faith, virtue,
education, experience, age.' Although he is unhappy that twentieth-
century Britain 'has for years treated the musician as a curiosity to be
barely tolerated', he deplores the fact that, by means of the transistor,
'Music is now free for all.' The loudspeaker, he asserts,

> is the principal enemy of music ... I don't mean that I am not grateful
> to it as a means of education or study ... But it is not part of true
> musical *experience* ... Music demands ... from a listener ... some

preparation, some effort, a journey to a special place, saving up for a ticket ... It demands as much effort on the listener's part as the other two corners of the triangle, this holy triangle of composer, performer and listener.

He concluded his speech by expressing his gratitude to America for showing him 'in the unhappy summer of 1941' that he had to go home to East Anglia: 'I belong at home – there in Aldeburgh. I have tried to bring music *to* it in the shape of our local Festival; and all the music I write comes *from* it. I believe in roots, in associations, in backgrounds, in personal relationships.' It was a very Forsterian conclusion, and Forster himself supplied a 'blurb' for the speech when it was published by Faber Music: 'A confession of faith from a great musician which should awake a response in the hearts of the rest of us, whether we are musicians or not, and whether we are great or small.'

Five years later, in an interview with the *New York Times*, Britten took an even stronger line about the composer being in the service of society rather than the other way round:

Until the 19th century, the composer was the servant of society ... [Then] composers began to blow up their egos ... Now the artist is the glorified mouthpiece of God ... I believe in the reverse of that. I believe in the artist serving society. It is better to be a bad composer writing for society than to be a bad composer writing against it. At least your work can be of *some* use.

His hostility in his Aspen speech to the gramophone and radio aroused some comment – was it a conscious echo of his father's dislike for those devices? – and a few years later he admitted that he might have 'slightly overstated the case'. Just before making the speech he had, after all, been recording the Cello Symphony in London with Rostropovich, and a few months later he was conducting the *Sinfonia da Requiem* for Decca. There was also a suggestion of élitism in his implication that people who wanted to hear his music should buy tickets for the Aldeburgh Festival. In fact a number of young people with limited funds were now able to come to the Festival, thanks to a scheme suggested by Peg Hesse in 1959, by which bursaries were provided for students. By the mid-sixties about forty such Hesse Students attended the Festival each year. Britten explained that they were expected to 'help in the Festival in some way ... working on the stage, helping to paint scenery, etc. – and in return they get their board and lodgings, and can attend all performances'. Rosamund Strode says that the majority of them were employed in 'endless chair-moving', though 'Imo used to nab the most musical ones for turning over and other sorts of musical stooging.'

At the conclusion of the Aspen speech, Britten raised the question of what he was going to do with the $30,000 award. He said he hoped 'to give an annual Aspen Prize for a British composition'. This precise scheme did not materialize in his lifetime (though the Trustees of the Britten–Pears Foundation now award composition prizes in his name), but by the spring of 1965 he had established what he called 'a small charitable fund for the commissioning of works of young composers', named the Benjamin Britten Aspen Fund, with Imogen Holst and Stephen Reiss as trustees. Nicholas Maw was the first beneficiary; his *Sinfonia*, premièred in 1966, was commissioned by the Fund.

Britten was now receiving unsolicited work by child composers, encouraged to approach him by their parents, and he usually replied encouragingly. In 1963 the nine-year-old Robert Saxton began corresponding with him – 'I kept asking my mother how I could be a composer, and she said, "Why don't you write to someone? There's Stravinsky, there's Britten"' – and two years later Saxton came to the Red House for a composition lesson: 'I'd set Gray's *Elegy* for violin and voice, and he gave me a very professional lesson on it. He said, "Look, you can't set it as 'The curfew tolls *the* knell' – the accentuation's wrong."' Saxton continued to send his work to Britten until he was in his mid-teens. 'He was always going on at me to write "character" pieces, waltzes, marches, "things that *other* composers have done"; in other words, don't try and write noises or be original, but try and become a craftsman. One of the great sentences in his letters to me is, "Sounding right is all that matters."' After a while Saxton began to study composition regularly with Elisabeth Lutyens. 'When I was about fifteen, Britten told me not to send him any more music until I'd done this and that. I thought perhaps he was cooling off a bit, but I wasn't hurt.'

Another who sent scores was Lennox Berkeley's son Michael, born in 1948, who described Britten as a 'fantastically considerate' godfather, and says the great lesson Britten taught him was to compose away from the piano; he told him: 'You will be amazed how much you can do without it.' One of Britten's letters to Robert Saxton touches on this:

If it worries you too much to work away from the piano, I should go back to it. Only try & think what kind of thing you want to write *before* you sit down at it. And remember that there won't always be 10 fingers playing the music – that violins, oboes & voices work differently from pianos ... Try & think of the melody, the rhythm, the accompaniment, the colour of it all (what instruments) as far as possible *all together*! Certainly not always just the tune first. (I am sure that in Schubert's Trout he thought of the accompaniment first.) Go on writing, play & sing as much of what you write as you can, & find out *why* you don't like the bits that don't work.

*

On his return from receiving the Aspen Award, Britten replied to a letter from the thirty-year-old Peter Maxwell Davies, whom he described in a *Times* interview few months later as 'immensely gifted': 'I was extremely pleased that you liked Curlew River. It was extremely difficult to do – to write and to perform, & I'm not sure we've altogether solved all the problems. But I wanted to do it, & I'm determined to make the *next* one much better.' Three months later, in November 1964, he wrote to Pears: 'I've been madly low & depressed – you being away mostly I expect, but worried about my work which seems so bad always ... I *must* get a better composer somehow – but how –– but how –––?' This was a deliberate echo of Albert Herring's 'But how ...' at the end of Act II as he contemplates the possibility of breaking loose. Oliver Knussen remarks that Britten sometimes 'had big crises of confidence, but a real crisis for a composer is when you stop composing. And I don't think that ever happened to him.'

Interviewed for Tony Palmer's film, *A Time There Was*, Pears remarked that Britten's low opinion of himself did not mean he had a higher one of his contemporaries: 'He thought he knew nothing, but he thought he knew more than anybody else! ... But while he may have thought he could do better than the others, it was still very little.'

*

In October 1964 the EOG toured Russia, with a company which included Janet Baker as Lucretia. They also performed *Albert Herring* and *The Turn of the Screw*. 'I must say,' Britten wrote to Plomer,

> when one is rehearsing the boy in T of the S ... it is difficult to avoid 'the worst possible construction' [James's own comment on the story, which Plomer had just passed to Britten] in answering the polite queries! But it is extraordinary how children don't put 2 and 2 together, & just get on with the job. We have had a staggering Miles for USSR.

The music critic of the Leningrad edition of *Pravda* did not put two and two together either, for he wrote of *The Turn of the Screw* as if it were a simple ghost story, and judged it 'a trifling subject' for Britten's immense talent. Britten commented to a reporter from *The Times*: 'Of course, *The*

Screw is not the kind of work they are used to – its subject would be
considered ideologically unsound ... But once they grasped what it was
all about the reaction was very warm.'

During the autumn of 1964 Britten told Plomer he was thinking a lot
'about Church Parable II', and longed to discuss 'Shadrach etc – – – or
possibly Tobias & the angel. Do you have any feelings?' He was not
going to write it yet. 'Peter & I are having 1965 off ... Doctors ... have
now very seriously advised me to be strict about taking this rest.' It was
to be 'our sabbatical', and was to begin with a lengthy holiday in India
with the Hesses. Just before he left England, in January 1965, Britten
wrote a short letter to Lord Harewood, whose marriage to Marion had
been going through difficulties for some while, and who had recently
fathered an illegitimate son by Patricia Tuckwell:

> My dear George,
>   I hate to write this letter. Although our paths have recently gone in
> different directions, I often think of you with admiration & affection,
> and with gratitude for your very timely support at the very early stages
> of our various enterprises, and of the many occasions on which we
> have both worked together on the things we have both believed in. All
> the same, we must face facts, & that it doesn't seem possible, at any
> rate for the time being, for you to come to our Aldeburgh Festivals. Do
> you think, therefore, that it makes any sense your continuing to be our
> President? People are already beginning to notice your absence, & will
> soon begin to ask questions. If you agree with me, would you please
> just write a line of resignation to Fidelity Cranbrook?
>
>   Yours, with sincere regret,
>   Ben.

Harewood waited to reply until Britten had returned from India. He said
he had hesitated to send his resignation, but had now done so, and ended
by assuring Britten of his affection and admiration.

Britten's letter had not come out of the blue. In his memoirs Harewood
writes:

> I had gone to the Holland Festival in the summer of 1964 at a different
> time from Marion, and was at a concert in Scheveningen which Ben
> was conducting ... At the end I went round with Maria Diamand [wife
> of Peter, director of the Festival] to the dressing room to see Ben and
> Peter, only to watch them push out past the queue and go off into the
> night. I sensed that their precipitate departure had to do with me ... I
> was told by Maria next day ... that Ben had asked her to drive with

him to the port to catch his ship and had had to stop to be sick on the way to relieve his nerves ... When I got back to London there was a curt note from him saying that my behaviour to Marion had alienated him so much that he was putting an end to our association.

Fidelity Cranbrook says that Britten asked her to write to Harewood requesting his resignation as president of the Aldeburgh Festival, but she refused. She thought Britten's attitude 'awfully prissy, pompous and silly', and adds that 'my much more conventional husband' felt the same as her. However, Harewood was also obliged to give up the directorship of the Edinburgh Festival, which he had been running for five years, and Donald Mitchell says that Britten was by no means alone in ostracizing him – Mitchell witnessed two members of British smart society cutting him dead in a picture gallery in Hamburg. Mitchell also says that 'Ben and Peter thought of Marion as if she were a daughter. It was through them that she had met George, and the marriage, so to say, had happened under their roof and with their blessing. The rupture came as a terrific shock.' Marion herself says that Britten was 'very supportive of me'. She emphasizes that 'in those situations, people take sides'.

However, Harewood was puzzled as well as deeply hurt by Britten's behaviour, because six years earlier Britten had been a 'sympathetic listener' when Harewood told him he was in love with Patricia Tuckwell. He says of Britten's rejection of him in 1964–5: 'I thought it mistaken, wrong, misguided, but it didn't cause me to hate Ben in any sense – though I found it gave one a peculiar pang listening to his music.'

Stephen Reiss says Britten spoke to him 'a lot' about the whole business: 'On the one hand he thought Harewood should have merely kept it as an affair without separating from Marion, and on the other he thought he should have been dutiful, like Tatiana in *Onegin*.' Reiss adds:

It was the disloyalty to *himself*, really, rather than the disloyalty to Marion that seemed to matter to Ben, partly because he was so ridiculously and madly – but understandably in one sense – sensitive about any kind of scandal. He wanted everything to be as pure as gold, because he was ashamed of his own position. He felt that if there was a scandal, then *he* would be dragged into it.

By this time Reiss realized that Britten intensely desired to be thought of as normal in every way: 'He would all but say to me that his relationship with Peter was nothing. He would try and submerge that whole aspect of himself. He wanted to be just an absolutely normal person.'

*

Britten wrote a series of long letters describing his 1965 trip to India, just as he had to Roger Duncan nine years earlier. This time the recipient was John Newton, the boy who had sung in *Curlew River* and stayed at the Red House a few months later. Compared to the discovery of Balinese music and *Sumidagawa* in 1956, there was little to report, but the letters give two examples of Britten's mesmeric effect on children. While he and the others were visiting Old Delhi, the party and their guide

> were joined by a serious young boy, about 12 or 13, who seemed to be trying to follow what the guide said (in English). Wherever we went he came too, but seriously not cheekily. I smiled at him once or twice, and when we finally got into the car to go off, I waved to him.
>
> We drove through the crowded streets of Old Delhi, and whenever I looked back there he was following us, running. Once or twice we were stopped by the jumble of cars, bicycles, people and cows ... and he came right up to the car window, looking appealing. Then, after nearly half an hour he could keep it up no longer and faded into the distance, still waving. He was a well dressed child, so it wasn't money he wanted, and he didn't look unhappy. One was only sorry we could not take him into the car and find out about him, as we could not speak his language.

The other occasion was at a bird sanctuary near Mysore, by a lake:

> as we got out of the boat, a small boy, possibly the son of the rower, helped us out on to the muddy bank. We thanked him, no more. Two days later the Prince of Hesse and I went back again ... this boy (about 12) saw me from a neighbouring field where he was working, dashed across and then for a solid hour he followed me around.

Britten's reading on the Indian trip included *Anna Karenina*. On his 1963 Russian journey he had heard Vishnevskaya sing Natasha in Prokoviev's *War and Peace*, and Colin Graham had suggested that he and Britten might convert Tolstoy's other great novel into an operatic vehicle for her. 'Anna was an obvious role for her,' writes Graham, adding that Pears would have played Karenin and Rostropovich would have conducted. Graham believes that Britten 'was *very* challenged by people's short-sighted belief that he couldn't / wouldn't write great love music – or even music of sensuality'. However, Britten seems to have been less interested in Anna's romantic tragedy than in the parallel between 'these two couples' (Anna and Vronsky, Kitty and Levin), 'the one living only for "self" ... the other, for God or Goodness'. He concluded his February 1965 letter about it to Graham: 'I hope we can do it, because I can think of nothing more important in one's life than finding another medium (the operatic) for this wonderful story.'

After writing a first draft of the libretto Graham realized 'how important it was for Ben to have each character speak in a different way, a different style, with different vocabulary ... So lots of re-writing. Meanwhile, a very detailed synopsis, running into ten pages, had been translated into Russian for Slava and Galya [Galina Vishnevskaya] to get their teeth into. They were over the moon.' It was originally intended that Plomer should help to write the finished libretto, but he declined, saying he thought Graham's words were fine as they stood, and that in his experience Britten's music could 'transcend anything!'

The project had not reached this stage until the end of 1967, and the Russian invasion of Czechoslovakia the following summer made it impossible for Britten to accept a commission for *Anna Karenina* from the Bolshoi. 'The Foreign Office even gave him what was more or less a directive,' writes Graham, 'but he had already made up his mind. He then turned to the idea that Heather Harper should do it at the Aldeburgh Festival, and that we should revamp the work on a smaller scale.' Word was now spreading about the project – the Swedish Opera asked to do the first European production, with Elisabeth Söderström – and Graham says that this began to inhibit Britten, who 'couldn't bear the idea of the world hanging on his coat tails for the next work. Just as he couldn't bear being quizzed on what he was "writing now" or "how was it going?" '

Rosamund Strode recalls Britten's discomfort when news of *Anna Karenina* leaked out:

Ben actually said to me, 'Did you talk about it to so-and-so?' It was like a court of law. I said, 'No, and I never do.' He said, 'I know you don't, but I had to ask you.' And I knew that at the formative stage things could be put off, aborted, like this. So I made this private rule not to know, or try to find out, about things which were still in the germinal stage.

Colin Graham feels 'sad at the loss of this opera he might have written – one which I believe would have shown a range of passions and emotional depths different to those he had yet charted'.

Another operatic project came to grief for the same reason in 1963. During the recording of the *War Requiem*, Fischer-Dieskau suggested that Britten should bring to reality 'my old dream of an opera of Shakespeare's *King Lear*. Ben seemed interested at once ... he thought [that] just as I was the only one who could sing Lear, only Peter could be considered for the Fool.' On 17 November 1963 a *Sunday Times* article by Desmond Shawe-Taylor to mark Britten's fiftieth birthday quoted him as saying: 'I have no intention of abandoning large-scale opera altogether. In fact I have been thinking about *King Lear* for a long time, and *Lear* would hardly do in the Jubilee Hall, would it? ... It's really well in my mind; I've even thought about the casting.' Nothing more was heard of the project, and in 1971 Britten said that it was Shawe-Taylor's article which had killed it. However, Donald Mitchell and Rosamund Strode both wonder whether the press report had not merely provided Britten with an excuse for jettisoning a project which was not proving viable.

*

Shortly after his return from the Indian trip in March 1965 it was announced that Britten had been awarded the Order of Merit, a distinction conferred personally by the Sovereign and limited to twenty-four holders at one time. Britten replaced T. S. Eliot, who had died two months earlier. 'I am delighted to join the select band,' Britten wrote to Peter du Sautoy at Fabers', 'but how I wish that Eliot was still with us to keep me company in it.' (Valerie Eliot says that her husband had been delighted by the founding of Faber Music to publish Britten.) To Yehudi Menuhin, Britten wrote: 'Honours, as you know only too well, don't really touch one; but there are moments in one's depressions, when one feels one's work to be hopelessly inadequate (all too often!) that they *do* encourage ...'

Britten had written one piece of music during the Indian holiday. He explained its origin to John Culshaw, who was producing his recordings for Decca:

> when Peter and I were in Budapest last year we were staggered by the virtuosity and versatility of two young Hungarian twins – sons of the fine flautist of the Opera orchestra. I have written them a piece which they are coming over to play at the Festival in June. It is in the form of a tribute to Kodaly, a quartet for two players (they each play the piano, one the violin and the other the flute). It is quite an extended piece, lasting about fifteen minutes, brilliant but with some serious moments, ending with a fugue for all four instruments and quite a bit of stage managing ... It might not turn out 100% since we have only heard them once and cannot guarantee that they have developed as we expected, but judging from their enthusiastic and highly intelligent letters describing their progress with the rehearsals I think there is a good chance ... They are the most engaging little chaps.

Britten wrote to Donald Mitchell that the twins, thirteen-year-old Zoltán and Gábor Jeney, had sent him 'a sweet letter' saying that the *Gemini Variations* 'is "not too easy and not too difficult" & "1000 kisses for your majestic present"! I long to hear them bash at it!'

Another performer who had been invited to the 1965 Aldeburgh Festival was Dietrich Fischer-Dieskau. Britten promised him a new piece as part of his programme, 'big and serious – words by Blake'. *Songs and Proverbs of William Blake*, for baritone and piano, was begun after the return from India. 'I'm getting on quite well with the Blake,' Britten told Pears on 16 March, 'but finding it pretty difficult & doubtful. Frankly I find *other* singers rather non-inspiring to write for – I'm too choosy about the performers I fear!' The published score of the cycle states that the words were 'selected by Peter Pears' from *Proverbs of Hell, Songs of Experience* and *Auguries of Innocence*. Though Pears had certainly made suggestions for poems that might be used in previous cycles, Britten had never before handed over the entire choice to him, and this suggests a certain detachment on Britten's own part. In any case Blake's voice is so strong and distinctive in the cycle, which is full of such bitter observations as 'Prisons are built with stones of Law, / Brothels with bricks of Religion', that Britten is concerned to illustrate the words rather than construct his own narrative. Certainly the cycle, which is sung as a continuous piece rather than separate songs, scarcely rises above black despondency, even in the settings of 'Tyger! Tyger!' and 'The Chimney Sweeper'. But the determining factor was probably the sombre character, even in its higher register, of Fischer-Dieskau's voice, which had given the Wilfred Owen poems such distinctive colouring in the *War Requiem*. (In his memoirs Fischer-Dieskau says that the cycle was written for him after the death of his first wife in childbirth, and this too may have affected its mood.) Britten's own comment on the cycle was: 'when I think of the wonderful words I feel rather inadequate'.

After he had heard it performed by Fischer-Dieskau and Britten at Aldeburgh in June 1965 William Mann guessed that *Songs and Proverbs of William Blake* would be judged 'Britten's deepest and most subtle song-cycle', while in the *Daily Telegraph* John Warrack wrote that Britten 'has, I feel, here come most fully to terms with the darkness and sense of cruelty that has always stalked his art'. In contrast the *Gemini Variations*, performed by the Jeney twins in Aldeburgh parish church, were in Mann's opinion largely intended to 'induce a smile'. The theme of the work was taken from an 'Epigram' by Kodály, and the eighty-two-year-old Hungarian composer was guest of honour at Aldeburgh that summer. The Festival also included Rostropovich giving the first performance of Britten's new unaccompanied Suite for Cello. William Mann suspected that it was 'less harmless than it first sounds'. At even the first hearing he had noticed 'discomforting harmonic implications'. Mann also announced, in *The Times* on 2 July, that Britten's 'next sacred music-drama . . . is to be about Nebucchadnezzar'.

In the spring Britten had written to Plomer that he was 'excited' by the choice of 'the Firy [*sic*] Boys' (as he termed Ananias, Azarias and Misael) as subject matter for the next church parable, and just before the Festival they met and worked out a 'synopsis of the "3 Boys"'. Britten's sabbatical year had now become 'terribly busy', and he had also accepted a commission to write a cantata for the twentieth anniversary of the founding of the United Nations, a setting of 'suitable sentences . . . from the great peace lovers of history'. It proved very hard to find texts – Plomer and Donald Mitchell both gave advice, and Pears made the final arrangement of the words – and Britten could not find time to begin composition until July, only three months before the work was to be given simultaneous performances in New York, London and Paris. Understandably *Voices for Today*, for adult and children's chorus and optional organ accompaniment, is a deliberately low-keyed, gentle work which opens with the setting of a sequence of exhortatory sentences, among them Auden's 'We must love one another or die', and ends with an excerpt from Virgil's Fourth Eclogue, which looks forward to the coming of a golden age of peace. Donald Mitchell recalls that Auden was perfectly agreeable to the use of his text.

While Britten was writing it he went with Fidelity Cranbrook to Cliveden, the Berkshire home of the Astors, which had been in the news two years earlier as the scene of scandalous goings-on during the Profumo affair. Britten was to be made an honorary member of the Worshipful Company of Musicians, in which Lord Astor held high office. Fidelity Cranbrook says that from the outset he was very nervous – he had only accepted on the understanding that it was to be 'a quiet little party', and 'he was very suspicious of Bill Astor'. She went to fetch him from his room to attend the ceremony. Eric Crozier, to whom she told the story, recounts what happened next:

> At this point, an unpleasant and dissolute painter [who knew Britten slightly, and was himself homosexual] made his way upstairs, seemingly having drunk too much, and began to taunt Britten about his 'hypocrisy' in writing church operas like *Curlew River* which centred upon little boys being saved or redeemed by a miracle. Ben controlled himself admirably in the face of this offensive provocation, painful though it must have been to listen to such things in the presence of a third person – but from Fidelity's account of the scene I formed the impression (which may or may not have been true) that the assailant on this occasion was acting almost like a blackmailer.

Fidelity Cranbrook confirms this account, and calls the incident 'torture, agony'. She adds: 'We somehow got through the visit, then fled to the safety of Aldeburgh.'

*

Shortly after this episode, at the beginning of August 1965, Britten and Pears flew to Russia to continue their sabbatical by holidaying with Rostropovich and Vishnevskaya. Most of their time was spent at a composers' colony in Armenia, where the hospitality was overwhelming and Britten was treated almost as a god by the local musicians. 'The three Armenian composers of whom we have seen most are ... all good friends,' Pears wrote in his diary of the trip. Trying to imagine a British parallel, he asked himself: 'Can one imagine Arthur Bliss, William Walton and Ben and lots more taking their holidays together on Windermere and entertaining Fischer-Dieskau and Henze for a month? Not quite.' Britten envied the Russian composers' salaried employment by the state. 'The dangers of too much security are so small compared to those of worrying artists as we do,' he wrote in the *Sunday Telegraph* on his return. 'I can't believe an artist is often ruined by too much security, and without it one may frighten off potentially useful creators.' However, he was unimpressed by the contemporary works he heard, judging that the symphonic pieces (mostly in the style of Tchaikovsky) were 'written to satisfy a demand only, and not from aesthetic conviction'.

His stomach played up during the trip. Several events had to be cancelled because of this, and Pears described in his diary how

> every imaginable remedy was proffered and taken, Alka-Seltzer, Enterobioform, manganese in solution and stewed pomegranate leaves. All of which, in ensemble, proved effective and Ben was O.K. in 48 hours ... Ben's two days *hors de combat*, one in bed and one on sofa, produced, as it so often does, intense creative energy. He has now just written his 5th Pushkin song ...

Britten had bought a bilingual edition of Pushkin's poems when leaving Heathrow, deciding that,

> setting some Pushkin might help my obstinately bad Russian. I got Slava and Galya to read the poems I chose from the English crib in my Penguin, and painstakingly they set about teaching me to pronounce them properly. I worked out a transliteration of six of them, and began setting them to music.
>
> I would write a song, then play it over and get Slava to correct the prosody. It is not perhaps a method I would recommend to composers

setting foreign words: it is best to learn the language first. But it was nice to find that I seemed to have got the emphasis right, and have caught something of the mood of these vivid, haunting poems; if I haven't, Pushkin still remains intact!

The result we have called, in Russian, *Echo Poeta*, literally *Poet's Echo*. It is really a dialogue between the poet and the unresponsiveness of the natural world he describes.

The Poet's Echo, written for Vishnevskaya, is designed to demonstrate her wide dramatic range, so that the songs, as the pianist Graham Johnson writes, switch 'with volatile energy from inconsolable loneliness to expansive glee'. Vishnevskaya writes that she was delighted by Britten's understanding of Pushkin – 'he had succeeded in penetrating the very heart of the verse' – and describes a memorable evening when Britten and Pears tried out the songs in the Pushkin House Museum:

> The room was cloaked in semi-darkness – only two candles burned. They reached the last song, 'Insomnia': 'I can't sleep, and there's no fire / Dull dreams and darkness all around / All I hear is, next to me, / The ticking clock's monotonous sound.' The moment Ben started to play the prelude, which he had written to suggest the ticking of a clock, Pushkin's clock began to strike midnight, and the twelve strokes chimed in exact synchrony with Ben's music. We all froze. I stopped breathing, and felt my scalp prickle. Pushkin's portrait was looking straight at Ben. He was shaken and pale, but didn't stop playing – *The Poet's Echo* – Not daring to speak, we silently dispersed to our rooms.

Pears describes this scene, in his diary, in only slightly less melodramatic fashion – 'Pushkin's clock joining in his song. It seemed to strike more than midnight, to go on all through the song, and afterwards we sat spell-bound.'

On the last night of the holiday they all went to Shostakovich's dacha, where he welcomed them with a feast and insisted on listening to the new song-cycle. Pears noted: 'he is clearly fond of Ben and was glad to see him ... he was, as always, physically strung-up'. Vishnevskaya remarks 'how different' were Britten and Shostakovich in this respect:

> With Ben I could be open ... How often I ran my hand through his wiry hair! He would purr with pleasure, and say that in a past incarnation he must have been a horse. I would stroke his face, and could kiss him. But did I ever hug Dmitri Dmitriyevich when we met or parted? ... For him, an outward demonstration of feelings – even toward the people closest to him – was unnatural.

Donald Mitchell's wife Kathleen comments in the same fashion on Britten's physical warmth: 'He was very overtly warm and affectionate. He would hug you, and would hold your hand for a long time in the car – anything like that, and it was very companionable. You didn't have to speak to him, but you felt this extraordinary pressure of the hand.'

*

Britten began work on the new church parable soon after his return from the Russian holiday, in October 1965. Its title was not yet decided. Writing to Plomer, he referred to it as '*Strangers in Babylon* or *The Fourth Man* or *The Fiery Furnace*', but the second of these bore too much resemblance to *The Third Man*, and soon he and Plomer settled on *The Burning Fiery Furnace*. 'Anyhow I have now got down to the BFF & although I am enjoying it, it can't be really said to have caught fire yet,' he told Plomer on 27 October. 'Still, it is progressing &, as you know from previous experience, as I progress little changes here & there creep in . . .' In mid-November he reported difficulties: 'the truth is that I have been having a very worrying time, & I rather wanted to wait until it was over before I wrote to you. I have been tired & not awfully well, & I have had a family problem which has distressed me & absorbed my time to an alarming degree.' This was the plight of his sister Beth, who was now suffering from a broken marriage and drinking heavily. Even without external worries, Britten could not maintain his former pace. 'I loathe date-lines now,' he told Walter Hussey, '& write everso slowly.' Pears, too, observed the change of pace. 'Ben is very tired (or rather, easily tired) these days,' he wrote to Donald Mitchell.

By early December 1965 Britten could report that 'about half the music is sketched out'. Rostropovich and Vishnevskaya were guests at the Red House during Christmas. Vishnevskaya turned out to be 'a virtuoso at Happy Families', and there was a children's party in the 'library' – largely a room for rehearsals and small-scale performances – which had now been made from an outbuilding. After a conjuror had performed, Rostropovich and Vishnevskaya 'did the Pushkin songs to about 30 of us; a very touching occasion'.

John Newton, the boy from *Curlew River*, paid a visit after Christmas. 'He is a dear boy, & was very sweet to me here,' Britten wrote to Pears. The same letter reported: 'I work pretty hard in the mornings – the tum feels really much better.' In an interview three years earlier, Britten had acknowledged: 'My state of mind is reflected in my body.' However, a physical cause (or possibly effect) of his digestive troubles had now been diagnosed, and a 'major op.' for diverticulitis, the development of pockets in the wall of the colon, had to be arranged. Before he went into

the Royal London Homeopathic Hospital in February 1966 he managed
to finish the composition sketch of *The Burning Fiery Furnace*, and
half completed the full score. He told Rosamund Strode that he had lain
awake one night counting the number of people whose employment
depended on his finishing the parable in time: a double cast, the orchestra
and second orchestra (two sets of instrumentalists rehearsed the parables
to give a safety-margin), and so on. 'And when I got to seventy, I stopped,
because I got frightened.' On the other hand Pears observed: 'The only
real dread is the anaesthetic which he loathes!'

He was in hospital for three weeks, and a nurse was sent to the Red
House with him when he was discharged. 'I totter around the garden,' he
wrote to William Walton, who had just had an operation for cancer, 'go
for gentle drives, play "scrabble", & return to bed quite exhausted.' On 3
April he wrote to Pears:

> My darling Peter,
>   . . . I am sorry I have been such a drag on you these last years; with
> so much to think about, it has been wretched for you to have the extra
> worry of my tum . . . It may not seem like it to you, but what you think
> or feel is really the most important thing in my life. It is an unbelievable
> thing to be spending my life with you: I can't think what the Gods were
> doing to allow it to happen!

Marion Thorpe remarks that 'Ben always got very worried and unhappy
when Peter was ill, but Peter got cross when Ben was ill.'

Rehearsals of *The Burning Fiery Furnace* began in mid-May. Around
that time, Britten wrote to Prince Philip:

> Sir,
> Dear Prince Philip,
>   I do not know if you remember, but when you came to the Alde-
> burgh Festival a few years ago, you suggested that the Queen might
> enjoy a similar visit sometime, and, well, we are taking you at your
> word & writing to Her Majesty & suggesting such a visit next year.
> The occasion would be the opening of a new concert hall, a disused
> Maltings, on a river a few miles up from Aldeburgh, which we are now
> converting . . .

*

Stephen Reiss describes the beginning of the Maltings project:

> Ben felt that there were certain works that couldn't be done in our
> existing buildings, in particular large-scale secular works, which
> simply did not seem to be right in a church (Blythburgh or Orford).

Although we'd had the changes in the Jubilee Hall, he wasn't happy with the acoustic. He kept saying to me, 'Forget about large-scale opera, but we can't perform these big secular works, and the repertoire of the Festival is getting too emaciated without the capability of doing works with larger forces.'

I racked my brains about it. There was a big place just south of Ipswich – we looked at all sorts of places. Then there was a question of storage of scenery for the EOG (things like the staging for *Noye's Fludde*), and I had heard that the Maltings at Snape had changed hands, and that there might be a place there where we could store it. And I went over and had a look.

I had no idea quite what the buildings behind the road frontage were like. I saw this great barn-like place, one of the buildings that was up for rent, and thought, 'I wonder whether there's something we could do there.'

The making of brewer's malt was begun at Snape in 1854 by the Garrett family, who constructed a fine group of agricultural buildings in mellow red brick, some of them very sizeable. Malting went on there until 1965, and when the business was shut down the buildings were bought by the firm of Gooderham & Hayward, who ear-marked some of them for the manufacture of animal feeds and advertised the rest for renting. It was at this stage that Reiss made his visit.

Fidelity Cranbrook recalls how, one day during 1965, 'an amazing suggestion was put forward' about a new concert-hall for the Festival. 'What about the semi-derelict Maltings at Snape? Charles Gifford, the treasurer, and I went to see it and were aghast. We decided it was a madness.' But Britten was determined.

In October 1965 Reiss wrote to the civil engineer Ove Arup, who had worked on Coventry Cathedral and was currently involved with the building of Sydney Opera House and the Queen Elizabeth Hall in London. His letter was passed to a member of Arup Associates, Derek Sugden, who (like Arup himself) had been attending the Aldeburgh Festival for some years, though he was unknown to Britten and Reiss. Sugden had often admired the Maltings road-frontage when driving from Aldeburgh to Orford with his wife: 'We used to pass this fabulous range of agricultural buildings. And it was a time when people had begun to draw architects' attention to how amazing these structures of the nineteenth century were.'

Sugden came down to Snape to examine the malt-house that Reiss had picked as a possible concert-hall:

I had a good nose round, and climbed up into the roof. Ben and Peter and Stephen had seen this big shed and felt you didn't really have to do a lot to it. But it was a space-divided structure, with cross-walls that formed the kilns, and the roof had turned into charcoal from the heat of the malting. So I knew it would all have to come off, and the big cross-walls and the charging-floors would have to come out.

I remember Ben said to me, 'How much will it cost?' I hadn't got the faintest idea! And I stalled by saying, 'How many seats do you want?' 'Oh, eight hundred or a thousand.' The Queen Elizabeth Hall was to be that size, and I knew the final cost of that was going to be about three million. And Ben said, 'We can't spend a penny more than fifty thousand.' So I did some quick calculations of the number of square feet, and said, 'It's going to be a hundred thousand at least.' 'Oh,' he said, 'we'll never raise anything like that.' But we left that on one side for the present.

John Culshaw of Decca was invited to Snape to give his opinion:

We walked round the Maltings and then clambered inside. It was all but impossible to imagine what it would be like when gutted, because it consisted of floor upon floor with no through sight-line. We kept on descending until we reached the ovens in the basement. And yet – there was a feeling about the place, about its setting by the river with the view of Iken church through the reeds and across the marshes that made it right. If Ben was to have a concert hall on his doorstep, this was it.

Culshaw's views were particularly important to Britten, who intended that the new hall should become his personal recording studio, eliminating the need to go to London to make records. It was much like the founding of the EOG and the Festival two decades earlier: another move away from the outside world and into the closed circle of his 'family'.

Derek Sugden asked Britten what sort of acoustic he and Decca wanted.

He said, 'To give you an idea of the sound I like, I prefer the *War Requiem* in Ely Cathedral, when I can't hear all the words, to the Festival Hall, when I can. I'd like it as *full* as possible, a full sound. And it's got to be as good as Kingsway Hall [in London, used for many Decca recordings].' I said, 'Steady – it's nothing like the size of Kingsway Hall, and the acoustic Decca love there is when it's *empty*.' But it gave us a guide.

Sugden was 'terribly impressed' with Stephen Reiss: 'He was one of the best clients I've ever had. He gave us a marvellously clear brief, in a single letter, and when we'd done a thorough survey and produced a report, Stephen rang me up and just said, "Start!" I loved that.'

This was in December 1965. Sugden warned Reiss that, since Arup Associates were overwhelmed with work, and detailed drawings and specifications would take a considerable time to produce, it would be difficult to get tenders from contractors before the 1966 Aldeburgh Festival. 'Stephen said, "But Ben expects the hall to be ready by then!" I said, "Don't you realize, it will be difficult enough to finish it in time for the 1967 Festival?" At which there was a great pause! But I agreed to try and do it for the '67 Festival.'

In a letter to the Queen, Britten admitted that fund-raising for the new hall would be 'by far the greatest undertaking we have attempted', but said he was convinced that the Maltings would be 'a turning point in the life of the Festival'. An appeal was launched, and money began to come in from Decca, the Arts Council, and the Gulbenkian Trust, who gave a grant of £25,000 for an orchestra pit and stage lighting. The Arup Associates' brief was to create 'a concert hall with certain facilities for opera', and Derek Sugden says that Britten told him: ' "I want a concert hall, with a concert hall acoustic. We'll put in pit and a lighting system and we'll try opera there, and if it works that's a bonus. But we won't compromise the acoustic or turn it into half an opera house." He'd seen all those multi-purpose halls which are neither fish, flesh nor fowl.' Sugden says there was 'pressure' from Colin Graham and others involved with the EOG to 'push it more towards the opera house mode', and that in particular Graham wanted a lavish lighting board. Sugden recalls Graham's long face when Britten vetoed this, and Britten telling him: 'Come on, Colin, they did it at Esterháza [Haydn's opera house] with *candles*!'

The 1966 Festival programme book included photographs of 'Snape Malt House' before the conversion, and a picture of the architect's model of the new hall. Looking back at that summer, Wilfrid Wren, who sang in the Festival chorus each year, describes it as 'the last year of the "old" type of Festival, with concerts, operas and recitals having perforce to be scattered around the countryside, with cramped conditions for the choir and inadequate seating and facilities for the audiences.' Wren observes that those who never knew the Festival before the opening of the Maltings could not imagine the 'miracles of hard work and improvisation' it had required, nor guess 'how much fun' it had been.

Dame Janet Baker describes the 'sense of camaraderie' which still characterized the Festival in the early sixties:

The English Chamber Orchestra were very much in evidence, and I'd
started to work quite a lot with them, so there were a lot of familiar
faces, and a sense of being not exactly part of a family, but music-
making in a joyous sense, like the summer festivals in America –
relaxed, with people wandering about the streets and shopping with
the kids. You saw your colleagues in a different dimension, and there
was an air of tremendous friendliness, and normal life going on. It was
different from anything else I'd come across at that time.

She used to share a flat with Heather Harper on the top floor of the home
of Britten's doctor, Ian Tait, and his family. 'That again was lovely, being
part of the town.'

The atmosphere of that last pre-Maltings Festival, in 1966, was caught
by Geoffrey Moorhouse in an article in the *Guardian* a few days after it
opened. He observed that in view of what Britten had done for Aldeburgh it was

> no wonder that picture postcards of the Red House outside Baggott
> and Son's shop have a pencilled notice on top which says very firmly
> 'View of Mr Britten's House'. To the more knowing and less respectful
> ones who circulate around the Fesival, though, he is 'Ben'. Even young
> ladies who refer to 'Papa' over breakfast in the Wentworth Hotel can
> be heard calling Mr Britten 'Ben' ... Wiry women in dirndl skirts and
> young men in gay pants are to be seen dabbing ochre on stage scenery
> in somebody's back yard. Extracts from *The Creation* issue, *con brio*,
> from solo voices practising behind half-a-dozen wide open bedroom
> windows ... And miraculously this annual visitation and the reputa-
> tion that trails throughout the year has not spoiled Aldeburgh.

The Creation, in Orford Church, with Britten conducting Heather
Harper, Pears, John Shirley-Quirk and the English Chamber Orchestra
was a highlight that year – Wilfrid Wren calls it a 'cataclysmic' performance – but, as Desmond Shawe-Taylor wrote in the *Sunday Times*, 'The
great event ... is the presentation of Benjamin Britten's second parable
for church performance.'

*

Before he began to write *The Burning Fiery Furnace*, Britten had described it in *Faber Music News* as a 'much less sombre, altogether gayer
affair' than *Curlew River*. Colin Graham's production notes in the score
explain that this time the visual style was inspired not by Noh theatre –
though the stylized gestures were retained, and many characters wore
masks – but by 'the colours and action in the stained-glass windows at

Chartres Cathedral', which Graham and Britten had visited together. Graham also wrote that 'The political aspect of the story, the schism between the Babylonians and the three young Jews, should be continually stressed.'

In Plomer's libretto the Astrologer observes that 'This rash innovation, / Invasion of immigrants, / Puts Babylon in danger.' Immigration was becoming a sensitive political issue in Britain in 1966 (Enoch Powell's infamous speech calling for repatriation came two years later), and the topicality of this aspect of *The Burning Fiery Furnace* does not seem altogether accidental (*Curlew River*, though conceived long before the sixties, nevertheless fitted well with the growing popularity in that decade of oriental religions and music). Similarly the austere musical style of the church parables allowed Britten to use certain techniques which were fashionable among younger composers – such as 'non-alignment', in which the coincidence of notes is left to chance in the performance, and the repetition of patterns in different superimpositions – without committing himself fully to the avant-garde. Shortly before writing *Curlew River* he had told an interviewer: 'I am prepared to experiment with organizing my music on different lines.' But he added: 'I think there is a snobbery of enormous pretentions connected with the most recent trends in music. People in this country who thought Schoenberg was mad until recently have suddenly swung the other way and they think it's all wonderful. Neither estimation is honest.' In a 1968 letter to the composer Jonathan Harvey (born in 1939) he wrote: 'Another difficulty I find with many composers of your generation is, that inspite of the considerable interest & ingenuity of the colour of the music, I often find a lack of interesting shapes in the phrases. Lack of basic *ideas* can become boring after a time.' In a 1962 interview, in which Peter Pears (who was also taking part) remarked that even the avant-garde composers themselves were often unable to distinguish between right and wrong notes when their music was performed, Britten observed: 'There's no doubt that the best composers are writing in the avant-garde manner, which is sad.' The avant-garde reciprocated his dislike. John Amis describes the left-wing Italian composer Luigi Nono, who was teaching at Dartington in 1959, making 'vitriolically scornful' remarks about Britten to his classes, and refusing even to meet him – Britten was there to perform with Pears.

However, 'the three Boys', as the Israelites are called in Britten's letters to Plomer about *The Burning Fiery Furnace*, are not simply representations of a sixties political debate. When they remark to each other that

> We do not lack enemies
> We might have known jealousy
> Would work against us

the words are reminiscent of one of Britten's letters to Elizabeth Mayer in 1943: 'I have my great friends for my work, and at the moment they seem easily to outweigh my enemies – but for how long, one can't say.' He had encountered a frightening example of enmity in the taunts of the painter at Cliveden, shortly before writing the second church parable, and this may have made him identify the more closely with the Israelites in Babylon, misunderstood individuals in a hostile society.

Like its predecessor, *The Burning Fiery Furnace* opens with a plainsong prayer for purity, *Salus aeterna, indeficiens mundi vita*; in the English Hymnal translation this reads: 'Saviour eternal ... / Grieving that the ages of men must perish / Through the tempter's subtlety, / ... O Christ, our souls and bodies cleanse ...' Again the melody of this provides the source of most of the music in the parable, but Babylon is given a very different musical personality from the 'East' in *Curlew River*. Nebuchadnezzar's entrance takes place to a chorus of almost Verdian grandeur ('Great King, whom all you rule'), and the beat is marked by the clang of an anvil which sounds remarkably like an Anglican parish bell summoning Church and State to Matins. There are even shades of Lady Billows. (James Blades produced the anvil sound that Britten wanted with a piece of a spring from an old Rolls Royce, one of several examples of his inventing percussion instruments to suit Britten's precise needs.)

The king's music (the role of Nebuchadnezzar was written for Pears) remains thoroughly formal and imperial as he grants the three Israelites jobs in his government. But with the entry of the boy Entertainers who are to provide a cabaret while the Babylonians dine, a new mood is evoked, introduced by the childish tapping of wood-blocks and sweeping chords on the harp. The words for this cabaret sequence appear trivial, but an important statement is being made:

Entertainer 1	The waters of Babylon,
	The flowing waters,
	All ran dry.
	Do you know why?
Entertainer 2	Of course I do!
Entertainer 1	And so do I!
Entertainer 2	The gardens of Babylon,
	The hanging gardens,

> Grew like mad.
> Do you know why?

Entertainer 1   Of course I do!
Entertainer 2   And so do I!
Entertainer 1   The people of Babylon,
> The thievish people,
> Ate the figs,
> They ate the melons and ate the grapes,
> The thievish people of Babylon ate the grapes –
> Do you know why?

The last verse supplies the answers, all of them obvious. The waters ran dry because 'somebody had monkeyed with the water supply', the gardens grew 'because of all the water they'd had', and the people ate the fruit because 'Babylonians are greedy pigs!' Beneath the 'prep school language', as several reviewers dismissively called it, we are being shown a society with a degenerate secret life. Nature is being diverted out of its course, illicit passions grow 'like mad', and the people indulge themselves shamelessly. Babylon, it seems, is another Sodom. The 'Empire' respectability of the Babylonians' music is just a façade.

Merodak, the heathen image raised up by the Babylonians, is musically characterized by glissandi, which sound especially gross because Britten has added, to the instruments used in *Curlew River*, an alto trombone, representing the 'sackbut' mentioned in the biblical text. It slides about the notes grotesquely in the Merodak music, and also emphasizes the pomposity of the 'Empire' passages. The connection between the public and private life of Babylon is ingeniously indicated during the instrumentalists' procession around the church while the idol is raised up. In this, a series of formal-sounding fanfares on each instrument gradually accumulates into what Robin Holloway calls an 'orgy of abasement before "Merodak" . . . ice-cold, horrible, and completely stunning'.

If the Babylonians are a society whose real nature, like that of the Borough, is masked by hypocrisy, who are 'the three Boys'? There may have been some divergence here between Plomer and Britten. The libretto has them declaim:

> They have given us new names
> To disguise our true natures
> But our names cannot change us.
> What we are, we remain,
> And so must continue . . .
> Lord, help us in our loneliness.

Plomer was surely thinking of the plight of the homosexual in British society, still widely persecuted in 1966. Though the Sexual Offences Act which legalized homosexual acts between consenting adults in private was only a year away, the police were prosecuting offenders against the old law as energetically as ever. (In 1943 Plomer himself had nearly been caught by it; he got into trouble for propositioning a sailor on Paddington Station, and the military police were only persuaded with difficulty to drop the matter. In 1959 John Cranko was arrested for importuning in a public lavatory.) Britten, on the other hand, seems to be responding to the taunts of people like the painter at Cliveden, who assumed that because he was attracted to boys he was a practising paedophile. *The Burning Fiery Furnace* seems musically speaking to be a passionate assertion of his innocence.

Rejecting the seductiveness implied by the boy Entertainers – whose cabaret is one of Britten's most lyrical and alluring creations – the three allow themselves to be cast into a furnace which for Britten surely represents the test of moral will-power. What they find inside it is another boy, this time in the role of the Angel, who 'purifies' their music into fourths (whereas before it contained some semitonal clashes, and shifted almost as uneasily as that of the Babylonians). The fourths are taken up by Nebuchadnezzar and his courtiers, and the parable comes to its conclusion with a Benedicite built entirely around this interval. Britten seems to believe not only in his own innocence but in the power of his music to heal society of its corruption.

Desmond Shawe-Taylor in the *Sunday Times* felt that *The Burning Fiery Furnace* lacked 'the intense pathos and single-minded purity of *Curlew River*', but observed that it had a 'modern relevance' not easily discernible in its predecessor. He did not say what this relevance might be, but Jeremy Noble in the *New Statesman* suggested that Britten and Plomer were attacking 'nationalism ... with its concomitant evils of conformism, intolerance and racial hatred'. All the critics were greatly impressed by the orgiastic effect of the instrumentalists' procession, but there was some disagreement about the portrayal of the furnace and the Angel. Andrew Porter in the *Financial Times* wrote admiringly that the boy sang 'shining unelaborated notes ... casting a steady celestial radiance on ... the song of human praise rising below', but Noble said that 'the treble angel ... reminded me only of Miles's ecstatic "I'm here" in *The Turn of the Screw*'.

*

The Burning Fiery Furnace was dedicated to Donald and Kathleen Mitchell. Britten, as Mitchell recalls, asked their permission in the most diffident way imaginable:

He said ... something like ... 'I want to dedicate the *Furnace* to you both, but I want to be *absolutely* sure you like the idea.' And before I had a chance even to respond, he was continuing: 'Please, if you *don't* like the idea, say so – I shall *perfectly* understand', and he looked at me anxiously and repeated this assurance at least two times more, as if there were indeed a serious possibility that the offer might not be accepted. It was an altogether characteristic exchange.

Mitchell was encouraging Britten to revise and publish some of his juvenilia. 'I enjoyed your week-end here so much,' Britten wrote to him after they had looked through early manuscripts together. 'I hope I didn't talk & play too awfully much, but I've had great fun as a result – I re-did 5 early songs yesterday alone! It felt funny re-writing something I wrote 45 years ago!' During the late sixties Faber Music published *A Wealden Trio*, his Walter de la Mare settings, and other pieces written in his teens.

'We are just off to Kings Lynn for Fiery Furnace etc. and one night at Sandringham with H.M. Mum, which should be cosy,' Britten wrote to Anthony Gishford towards the end of July 1966, six weeks after the first performance of *The Burning Fiery Furnace*. He, Pears and the EOG had become regular participants in the King's Lynn Festival, organized annually by Lady Fermoy, a member of the royal household, and in consequence there had been invitations to stay with the Queen Mother at Sandringham, not far from Lynn. The first such visit had been in July 1964, when Britten – who went alone – reported to Pears: 'very nice Queen Mum, but the whole set up rather juvenile & irritating (one has to behave so stupidly with Royalty).' Basil Coleman comments:

> Ben did like grand company, the titles and the royals – there was no doubt about that. I can remember us talking about it once. He'd come back from seeing the Queen Mother at Sandringham, and was very pleased, and I think I must have been a bit cool, and I remember saying that I didn't want him to be thought of as a snob, so fond of the royals. And Ben did say, 'Well, yes, I suppose I am a snob.'

Donald Mitchell does not believe, however, that Britten lionized the Royal Family:

> If anything it was rather the other way round. I think Ben and Peter were very fond of the Queen Mother, because they found her to be what she is – genuinely a most musical person. I recall how openly moved she was by the first performance of *A Time There Was* at Snape. The Queen was another story – music is clearly not one of her principal interests. On the other hand she was exceptionally supportive

of Snape – visiting the hall twice, don't forget, once before and once after the fire – and Ben and Peter were very grateful for that truly gracious gesture. As for the occasional visits to Sandringham or elsewhere, I remember them saying how dire these could be, with everybody keeping their mouths shut for fear of saying something that might give offence, or prove controversial or indeed just interesting! I thought they were pretty level-headed about it all.

Dame Janet Baker observes, as had others before now, that Britten himself had certain 'royal' traits:

I remember he made a great effort to put me at my ease. I don't think he quite succeeded because to be with him was a bit like being with the Queen: in those circumstances you're never quite natural. I suppose it's almost like the sensation of being in love. Something happens to time, and one seems to be living in a highly volatile present. Nothing matters except the other person and the moments you spend with them. Just because you're in that state, all other experiences seem heightened.

Robert Tear, for whom the part of Misael in *The Burning Fiery Furnace* had been written – 'the youngest, nervous and impulsive,' says the character note in the rehearsal score – writes of Britten in much the same terms: 'I remember those times when Ben was so wonderfully charming that when he spoke to me the world seemed to stop.'

Stephen Reiss observes that Britten 'had the gift of making people feel they were special to him, that everything about them mattered to him'. This gift was not only exercised to other musicians, people working for him, or the young. Kathleen Mitchell experienced it: 'He had that incredible quality of making you feel that you were the most important person in the world – that you really were everything to him.' Robert Tear echoes this: 'He could make you believe you were the only person in the world.' Keith Grant says: 'He had a gift of relating to you in conversation which made you feel as if you were in a warm bath.' Pears, on the other hand, seemed as opaque and unknowable as ever. 'I certainly feel,' says Donald Mitchell,

that I never knew him as I feel I knew Ben or as one knew other close friends. And I've really never met anybody who claims to have known him well, except people who *didn't* know him well, who had simply found him charming, agreeable, courteous. But that's knowing only those few outward signs that he was willing to release in his social relationships.

5: The finest hall of its kind

'We are tremendously thrilled that the Queen will come with the Duke of Edinburgh to open our new Concert Hall in Snape on June 2nd,' Britten wrote to Buckingham Palace in December 1966. *Gloriana* had been revived at Sadler's Wells two months earlier, with Sylvia Fisher in the title role, and Britten told Plomer that 'The nice Queen Mum was asking about dates of it – but I do hope all *that* isn't going to start again.' Another revival in the autumn of 1966 was *Billy Budd*, shown on BBC TV in a studio production by Basil Coleman. Britten was present during the recording, and judged television 'a cumbersome medium' (the orchestra was in one studio, the singers in another), but began to 'think furiously' about writing an opera especially for it. This *Billy Budd* was conducted by Charles Mackerras, who says that Britten now seemed to have forgiven him completely – he later (1973) conducted a *Messiah* at Aldeburgh, and Britten wrote to him praising his performances of his works. 'Although we had never been bosom pals,' says Mackerras, 'we became perfectly good friends again.' (Britten had similarly made his peace with Norman Del Mar, who in 1963 shared with him the conducting of a Britten fiftieth birthday concert in Basle – though on the night Britten went down with 'nervous tummy' and Del Mar conducted the entire programme.)

The role of the Novice in the television *Billy Budd* was played by Robert Tear. Britten wrote to him, calling his performance 'splendid and touching', and told him: 'I am highly interested in the development of your career, which has started so brilliantly.' Tear sang Snout when *A Midsummer Night's Dream* was recorded for Decca during the autumn of 1966, with Deller as Oberon once again ('*very* impressive', wrote Britten to Pears). Puck's lines were spoken on the recording by a fifteen-year-old London schoolboy, Stephen Terry, who came to stay at the Red House in August to practise them, and to pose for a Mary Potter painting. In 1963 she had moved from Crag House into a house-cum-studio which Britten and Pears had built for her in the Red House grounds. It was around now that she began to paint the big semi-abstract oils, mostly studies of light, which are her most distinguished work – Kenneth Clark claimed that she had become one of the finest painters in the country. She would see Britten for a meal or a drink two or three times a week, and was buoyed up by his encouragement and interest in her work. Her son Julian calls it 'the most productive time of her life'.

'Stephen Terry is being a good, if voluble, little visitor, but helpful for errands etc.,' Britten told Pears during his visit. 'We work hard at Puck (coming along well). Mary gets him to pose at the pool' – this was a painting showing several boy bathers – 'while I get a certain amount of work done'. Stephen had come to Britten's notice as a member of the London Boy Singers, a choir founded with his encouragement to continue the vocal training methods of George Malcolm. At the age of twelve Stephen was picked out from the Singers to play Harry in the Decca recording of *Albert Herring*, made in the Jubilee Hall in 1964. It was after this that he began to receive invitations to the Red House. He would bring his bicycle on the train from London and be met by Britten:

> He'd collect me from the station in his Alvis, a wonderful, beautiful car, extraordinarily luxurious – walnut and leather, and the hood down in the summer. We'd go out for a drive, and there was a yellowhammer singing, and I remember sensing Ben's response to nature – which, coming from a North London suburb, was something alien to me – and his different priorities: stopping to listen to a bird singing was not a waste of time.

Stephen knew that Britten and Pears were homosexual – at school he was teased about his friendship with Britten – and he was surprised to find that at the Red House the two men had separate bedrooms (as they always had since moving from Crag House), though it also struck him that 'Ben's bedroom had an enormously big bed'. Ludmilla Cooper, who in 1972 succeeded Nellie Hudson as Britten's housekeeper, says: 'Ben, when he took me round the house the first time, said, "Look at this great big bed in my room. But I *like* a big bed." And I never saw any sign of Peter anywhere near that bed. Nor anybody else.'

Stephen Terry detected nothing sexual in Britten's behaviour towards him:

> He was the kind father / uncle figure. I can remember thinking, 'I wish he was my father, I wish I could be his son', because of the whole

richness of his intellectual, aesthetic and emotional life. There was an incredible tenderness as well, no sexuality, but a great sense of gentle, almost fragile being. And in comparison Peter always seemed strong and severe and slightly judgmental. I think I felt there was a resentment of me there. I felt Peter as a slightly hostile presence.

Asked if Britten's 'tenderness' was expressed in any physical way, Stephen Terry says: 'I can remember a paternal kiss on the forehead before going to sleep one night. That's about all. I think there was also the occasional arm round the shoulder, that sort of thing. But it all came across to me as paternal rather than amorous. And he was a tired man, incredibly busy.'

Stephen appeared as Puck in the 1967 production of *A Midsummer Night's Dream*, but not long afterwards, at about the age of seventeen, experienced 'a feeling of rejection' by Britten. 'I wrote asking to come and stay, and he said, "No, you can't because we're too busy, but I'll arrange for you to stay with Jeremy Cullum [Britten's chauffeur / secretary and son of Tommy Cullum, the original Festival treasurer, who lived with his wife in Aldeburgh]." And I went to stay there, and felt that I wasn't in the inner circle any more. I was out.' Writing to Britten, he had signed letters 'Lots of love' and 'All my love', as other boys befriended by Britten had done before him. He says of this, 'I think there was an unrealized relationship being expressed there which maybe was easier on paper than in real life.'

Besides acting as patron of the London Boy Singers, Britten gave much encouragement to the choir of Wandsworth Boys' School, who under the directorship of Russell Burgess became notable interpreters of his music during the later sixties. The tenor Adrian Thompson was a member of the choir at this time. He says that when they visited Aldeburgh to perform, Britten treated them with great kindness, giving them the run of the Red House swimming-pool and tennis court. Thompson says that he and the other boys never felt that Britten was interested in them sexually. 'I'm not saying that he didn't feel any attraction – it could well have been – but he was far too intelligent to let it get in the way.'

The 'work' mentioned by Britten in his August 1966 letter describing Stephen Terry's visit was the writing of *The Golden Vanity*, a tragi-comic 'vaudeville' for boys' voices and piano, to be sung by the Vienna Boys' Choir at the first concert in the Maltings following its official opening. Colin Graham had adapted the words from an old English ballad about a sea-captain's treachery and the death of a cabin-boy. Graham describes the story as 'a mini-*Billy Budd*'. Britten called the libretto 'very stimulating', but, perhaps on account of the celebratory occasion of the first performance, he chose to make it chiefly an entertainment rather than to explore the story's darker implications. Graham writes that though the Vienna Boys gave a 'riotous' rendering of it, when they returned to England to repeat it at the Festival Hall some months later they were 'absolutely shattered and exhausted' after 'one of their interminable world tours'. Britten 'was furious and lodged a formal complaint with the director of the choir for exploiting and exhausting the boys'. Consequently *The Golden Vanity* was dropped from their repertoire.

*

Building work had begun at the Maltings in May 1966. To speed things up, and in order to employ local craftsmen, Arup Associates had not put the job out to tender but had negotiated a price – totalling about £110,000 – with Reade's of Aldeburgh, who were to be the main contractors. 'The most important man, right from the start,' says Derek Sugden of Arup Associates, 'was Reade's foreman, Bill Muttit. He didn't have to have any project managers telling him what to do next. It was all in his head.' Despite excellent and speedy workmanship by Reade's and their various Suffolk sub-contractors, during the autumn the project slipped about a month behind schedule, chiefly due to problems in getting the sheer volume of timber to the specification needed to give the roof its special structural and acoustic properties. Sugden went to the Red House with a warning:

> I saw Ben and Peter and Stephen, and said, 'We've done our best, but we've been hunting all over Europe for the wood, and the roof's not going to be erected before Christmas. I think it would be prudent to ask you to find other venues for the 1967 Festival.' There was frost all round the room. That's when I first saw Ben's toughness. He said, 'It's virtually certain that the Queen is coming to open it.' And he gave me a whole list of performers who'd made special arrangements to be present, and concluded: 'I don't think we can take this discussion any further, Derek. You've just got to finish it on time.' And I was going skiing with my family next day, and I thought I could forget Aldeburgh for a little, but it was my birthday, and my wife gave me as a present Imogen Holst's new book on Ben!

This was *Britten*, published in March 1966 by Faber and Faber, the book in which Imogen Holst completely omitted to mention Eric Crozier's work for Britten. The names of Montagu Slater and Ronald Duncan were similarly left out in reference to *Peter Grimes* and *The Rape of Lucretia*. The following year John Drummond, wanting Britten to take part in a

BBC TV documentary he was producing about Kathleen Ferrier, used John Culshaw as go-between to conduct negotiations. 'Ben agreed, and I only discovered subsequently what his terms were: that neither Nancy Evans nor Eric Crozier would be allowed to take part in the film. I found that, at the time, troubling. Twenty-five years later I find it absolutely shocking. But I'm afraid it was rather typical of what happened when people were out of favour.'

Returning from his skiing holiday, Derek Sugden managed to speed up the delivery of timber for the Maltings roof. Meanwhile there had been much difficulty in finding suitable chairs for the auditorium. 'Derek, they mustn't be too comfortable!' Imogen Holst told him. 'They should make people sit properly. And when there's something special in the music, they should be able to *sit up straight*!' It was Richard Butt of the BBC who suggested copying the cane-seated chairs from Wagner's festival theatre at Bayreuth. Sugden wrote to Wolfgang Wagner, the composer's grandson,

> and he was fantastically helpful. He sent me a lovely letter with photographs of the chairs and a drawing done by him, with dimensions. He said the only ones of the original 1876 chairs they'd had to replace after the Second World War were 'those damaged by the American occupation forces'! We had only allowed something like four pounds a chair in the budget, and the lowest Wrinch & Sons of Ipswich could make them for was £6 4s 3d, so we accepted that. It was a fabulously good price.

Another problem was the screens which had been built to reduce the stage area during performances by small groups or soloists. By this time Sugden

> was absolutely exhausted, doing several other big jobs as well as Snape, and I hadn't seen my family for weeks, and I was in the concert-hall one Friday night, and we were trying at the last minute to decide on the layout of the screens we had designed and modelled for the platform. Ben and Peter kept rearranging the layout, and I said, 'Well, I must leave it to you, because I'm going to spend the weekend with my family.' Ben turned to me and said, 'Pulling out, Sugden?' I thought he was joking. But he wasn't.

Sugden was similarly astonished when Britten complained to him of one of the EOG staff who had become pregnant by another member of the Group, and would be unable to work for the next few months. 'He said, "I don't mind them getting into bed together, but you would think that my opera was far more important." And it was really serious – he was furious!'

By the beginning of December 1966, with the opening of the Maltings six months away, Britten was becoming 'paralized [*sic*] with worry about commissions & commitments. But I am going to have a long holiday after Xmas, the best part of 2 months, & after that I am sure I will feel better & able to tackle things again.' The first part of the holiday was in Russia, 'because Slava and Galya spent last Christmas at Aldeburgh and they insisted on returning the hospitality,' writes Pears in his diary of the trip. Christmas Day was spent with Shostakovich and his wife:

> S. in good form, talkative, nervous, Irina gentle, quiet, a marvellous foil for him. After dinner, we produced a specially bought pack of 'Happy Families' ... Slava had been champion at Aldeburgh Christmas '65, but this time in Moscow it was Dmitri who triumphed ... Ben tells his recent dream of Stravinsky as a monumental hunchback pointing with quivering finger at a passage in the Cello Symphony: 'How dare you write that?'

Pears noted that a recital he and Britten gave in Moscow 'Went well on the whole, and my memory wasn't too bad at all'. Robert Tear remembers 'Britten telling me that Pears had a terrible memory', and himself describes Pears struggling to recall Nebuchadnezzar's opening lines in *The Burning Fiery Furnace*, and disguising a memory lapse in *Curlew River* with a series of nonsense syllables. (Steuart Bedford writes that Pears's own term for this method of covering up was 'verbal chewing-gum'.) Wilfred Wren, witnessing a similar incident in a Purcell performance some years later, was struck by Pears's astonishing skill in coping with the near-disaster:

> He had forgotten his spectacles, and ... could neither remember nor see the printed words ... With inimitable flair he sang nonsense words for a whole page until the counter-tenor came in: he leaned over to catch the words from the other singer, joining in so incredibly smoothly that nobody in the audience knew that anything untoward had happened.

Pears was fifty-six by the time of the Moscow visit, an age by which many singers have retired, but Julian Bream observes that 'one of the staggering things about Peter's achievement was that, as he got older, he was improving all the time ... singing more and more beautifully. And his voice was getting better.' Lord Harewood agrees: 'I think it acquired a kind of burnished sound that it didn't have before.' This was partly due to the teaching of Lucie Manén, to whom Pears first went for lessons in 1965. Thomas Hemsley introduced her to Pears:

> Peter and Ben had taken a sabbatical, and had been away, and Peter hadn't sung for some months, and found it very difficult to get his voice going again. And we sang together in Geneva, in the *War Requiem*. I was vocalizing a bit before the concert, and Peter knocked on my dressing-room door and said, 'Tom, I've always thought you had a particularly secure vocal technique – I believe you have a little woman round the corner who looks after it?' I said, 'Peter, I wouldn't describe her as a little woman!' But I put him in touch with Lucie, and she did help him.

Lucie Manén writes that Pears 'studied with me like any youngster', accepting that he had to go back to basics of voice production. Sue Phipps says that Pears's new teacher 'spent a lot of time bringing out his baritone qualities, really working on the lower part of the voice'. Britten wrote to Lucie Manén in 1965: 'It is a great thing for Peter that he has met you and worked with you, Lucie.' She told Hemsley that Pears 'had a much more heroic voice than he ever allowed himself to use, but it was a psychological thing – he didn't want to sing like that. He could have sung much heavier roles, but he didn't want to.' John Evans, who knew Pears towards the end of his life, recalls his admiration for the classic Italian tenor voice, radically different as it was from his own. 'I remember Peter coming back from a performance of *Otello* at Covent Garden with Placido Domingo and Margaret Price, and saying, "I've been for a singing lesson to London" – to hear Domingo singing Otello.'

During the Christmas 1966 Russian trip, which also took them to Leningrad, Pears and Britten went to the Hermitage and looked at 'some of the greatest Rembrandts in the world . . . surely greatest of all, the Prodigal Son (with his broken back, shaven head, worn sole to his one foot out of its shoe, the father all loving-understanding, the three diverse characters looking on, judging, grudging and surprised). Of course, this is the subject for the next Church Parable.' It seems that the Rembrandt gave Britten the idea. Certainly Plomer knew nothing about it as yet. On his return from Russia, and before going for a fortnight's further holiday in the Caribbean, Britten wrote to him that there was no time to 'say all the things I want to say (such as the subject of the 3rd Church Parable)'. He seems to have proposed the Prodigal Son to Plomer on his return from the Caribbean trip. On 17 March he wrote: 'I was so glad that you liked the idea of the Prodigal Son so much. Alas, I couldn't get a postcard of the Rembrandt, but it is in most of the R. books . . . I want to do it for next year – it would be wonderful to complete the trilogy when one's mind is working in this direction . . .'

The Caribbean holiday, on the small island of Nevis, was a success, but immediately on his return Britten 'caught a chill in a nerve in my back and have been virtually paralised [*sic*] ever since!' By 6 February 1967 he was 'feeling as near death as only 'flu can make me'. However, the conversion of the Maltings was 'going frightfully well, and we are all most excited by it'. (The Queen Elizabeth Hall in London was opened at the beginning of March; Britten conducted the two inaugural concerts.) On 1 April the *Guardian* carried an article about the Maltings by Edward Greenfield, who had been shown round it by Stephen Reiss:

> Thanks to his energy, The Maltings will have changed its face in little over a year . . . at the moment the last few slates are being laid on the roof . . . The side walls of the main building had to be raised 3 ft . . . and a complete new roof has been built with a steeper rake than before . . . in making the changes, Benjamin Britten was concerned above all in getting a sufficiently spacious acoustic, and judging by the healthy reverberation of pneumatic drills he has succeeded.

Derek Sugden says that, largely thanks to Bill Muttit, the project was now nearly a month ahead of schedule. Detailed acoustic tests (including a concert with an invited audience) were held during May, and the reverberation time proved to be 'bang on two seconds, with the place full', which was exactly on target.

Greenfield stated that the conversion had cost 'paltry sums by the standards of cultural budgeting today . . . although Reiss puts in a reminder that the appeal is still £25,000 short'. The article speculated how the new hall, located several miles from Aldeburgh, would affect the character of the Festival – there was a danger that the Maltings might become 'a sort of Glyndebourne', and Greenfield thought it fortunate that the ground landlords were still carrying on their own business elsewhere on the premises. (However, Fidelity Cranbrook now feels that the building should have been bought outright rather than leased, so that the Festival would not have had 'the worry of rising rent' in subsequent years.)

William Mann came down to Snape a few days before the official opening, and thought the 800 seater hall 'most striking', with its 'wide and deep apron stage without proscenium or flies'. He called the view from the restaurant windows across the Alde estuary and Iken Marshes 'breathtaking', and was impressed by the trouble taken to make such features as the glass-fronted lighting box blend with the character of the building. There was also 'a small, low-ceilinged box for the artistic director and his guests'. (John Evans says that, when the Maltings came into use, 'artists would often bow to the directors' box almost as though it contained Royalty – especially if it was a Britten work', and Robert Tear describes the box as 'a kind of enormous bread oven', observing that when Britten and his fellow directors were in it they tended to look like 'Beelzebub and his cronies'.)

At midday on Friday 2 June 1967 the Queen and Prince Philip landed at RAF Bentwaters, a few miles from Snape, and were driven to Alde-burgh, where they visited the Moot Hall and went to the Red House for lunch. Britten had invited the Hesses, the Cranbrooks and Marion Harewood to join the party. His sister Barbara was looking after the domestic arrangements. 'My dearest, dear, Barbara,' he wrote to her afterwards, 'You were on splendid form this year, & handled us all with great, but kind, firmness!' A new front entrance had been added to the Red House in time for the the royal visit, though Rosamund Strode says that Britten and Pears had been 'thinking about it for ages – it just spurred them into doing it'.

After lunch the Queen was driven to the Maltings, where she opened the main door with a gold-plated key, briefly inspected the empty audi-torium (the audience was waiting outside), then went to the restaurant where some of those most closely concerned with the Festival and the conversion were presented to her. A BBC crew was filming the event under the direction of Tony Palmer, then a young trainee, and Prince Philip came up to him and 'asked me very conspiratorially, "What's the old man written for us this time?"' Palmer said that Britten had com-posed an overture called *The Building of the House*. A few weeks later, in an article in the *London Magazine*, he reported this conversation – and received a letter of complaint not from Buckingham Palace but the Red House, written by Pears. 'Three or four months later,' says Palmer, 'I saw Peter across the other side of the BBC canteen, and he waved at me and grinned, so I went over and apologized. And he waved a hand dismiss-ively, and said, "I thought you knew us well enough to guess why I had to write. What upset Ben was the word *old*."'

As the Queen came into the hall to take her seat for the concert, military trumpeters struck up a fanfare from *Gloriana*. There followed Britten's own arrangement of the National Anthem, written for the 1962 Leeds Festival. Wilfred Wren, who was singing in the choir, writes:

> Never, the Queen afterwards declared, had she been so affected by the National Anthem as when Britten had led the chorus in its singing on that occasion ('and I have heard it once or twice before', she added).

After the whispering *pianissimo* of the first verse, the triumphant brass and chorus in the second stanza lifted the tension almost to unbearable heights.

Next came *The Building of the House*, for orchestra and optional chorus. 'This begins with a merry bustle,' wrote Andrew Porter in the *Financial Times*: 'it might be the prelude to some operatic scene of surging industry; then from the activity there rises, soaring and strong, a chorale'. The words were taken from a metrical version of Psalm 127, 'Except the Lord the house doth make', and Porter judged the piece to have 'a richness and subtlety' that would give it 'lasting value'. Britten then conducted the English Chamber Orchestra in Delius's *Summer Night on the River*, which the programme note observed 'could easily be a tone-painting of the River Alde', after which Imogen Holst took over the rostrum for her father's *St Paul's Suite*. Wilfrid Wren quotes a critic writing of her conducting that afternoon: 'It was as if the composer's spirit descended upon her. She lived the music so vividly that it would have been no surprise if she had suddenly risen in a state of levitation.' It had been agreed that there would be no 'curtain calls', but the applause for this item was so tremendous that Britten had to go backstage and fetch her out for another bow. He himself then conducted the final item, a shortened version of Handel's *Ode for St Cecilia's Day* with Heather Harper, Pears, and Philip Jones as trumpet soloist.

Praise for the building was unanimous. 'A first visit suggests that the Maltings is the best concert hall we have,' wrote Andrew Porter. 'Diapason' of the *East Anglian Daily Times*, a veteran of the Festival, stated that 'by general consent it is the finest hall of its kind anywhere in the country'. On the Wednesday after the official opening the building's suitability as an opera house was put to the test with *A Midsummer Night's Dream*, newly produced by Colin Graham. Robert Tear was Lysander and the newly discovered counter-tenor James Bowman appeared as Oberon. Felix Aprahamian judged the Maltings 'as apt for opera as it is for concerts', though he regretted the absence of a proscenium arch. Bowman's performance attracted universal praise. Aprahamian called him 'Deller's worthiest successor'.

Some were already regretting the Festival's shift of focus away from Aldeburgh itself. Elizabeth Sweeting, who attended the opening of the Maltings, noticed that the town seemed deserted when there was an event going on at Snape, and a correspondent to the *Leiston Observer* suggested that Aldeburgh railway station, recently closed, would have made a better site for the new auditorium. In fact plenty was still going on in the town. At the Jubilee Hall the EOG were staging two one-act operas, Lennox Berkeley's *Castaway* and Walton's *The Bear*. Sean Day-Lewis in the *Daily Telegraph* reported that suggestions that in future the entire Festival might take place in the Maltings were being 'firmly resisted'.

As intended, the Maltings made it possible to present big-scale secular works. The *Spring Symphony* and Richter playing Britten's Piano Concerto were both on the 1967 programme. Britten wrote of Richter's performance as 'magnificent', and felt that it 'clearly resurrected the old work'. In a letter to Yehudi Menuhin a few weeks after the end of the Festival, he described the Maltings as 'quite a success'. And to another corrrespondent: 'It has been a most magnificent success, as marvellous to listen in as it is to look at. Recording & television companies are queuing up to use it.' During the autumn *Opera* magazine printed an interview with Britten in which he suggested that 'a new open-stage technique of opera production might well be evolved' at the Maltings, and added: 'We'd like to have the building next door to the new concert hall at Snape', though he did not say for what purpose. In an interview with an American magazine in July he mentioned the possibility of an opera written specially for television – 'It could be a Henry James again' – but he told *Opera* that his immediate task was 'completing my trilogy of church operas for next summer'.

*

'Dare I ask if you have had time to put pen to paper over "Prodigal Son"?' he asked Plomer a month after the 1967 Festival. Plomer and Colin Graham both spent time at the Red House in August, and Britten was excited by the libretto which Plomer quickly produced: 'I look forward passionately to getting down to work on it – if only I can find the right notes to match your strong, simple, yet touching words.' Before he could begin, he had to undertake a two-month trip to Canada, New York, and 'almost to the bottom of South America' – Mexico, Peru and Chile. Donald Mitchell was with them in Montreal and New York, and was astonished by the degree to which Britten now suffered from performance nerves. He describes it as 'totally incapacitating. Ben was fine the night before, but immediately after breakfast the agonizing wait for the concert began. He had to rely on Complan to keep him going. Everything else he brought up.' Rosamund Strode describes how 'Ben would go out of the dressing-room and he'd come back, and Peter would say, "All right?" And he'd say, "Mm." After a bit I discovered that this probably meant he'd been to the loo and thrown up.' Sue Phipps says that

Peter frequently was sent nearly crazy by Ben's nerves ... Often Peter would say: 'Ben, if you're going to go on behaving like this, I simply cannot go on.' It took a terrific amount of will-power for Peter to go through with some of those performances, because he had to carry Ben's nerves as well. And that, for a singer, was quite awful.

When the pianist Graham Johnson remarked to Britten 'how wonderful it must be to be famous and not have to be nervous', Britten replied: 'You're quite wrong; it gets much worse the more famous you become – you have to prove yourself from the first note.'

Mitchell says that Britten would 'have a drink to steady his nerves before going to the hall'. George Malcolm remarks of this:

Ben used to drink heavily to sedate his performance nerves. I remember him saying after a recital with Peter, 'Well, that went pretty smoothly.' 'So it should have', said Peter, 'after that bottle of brandy you downed.' 'It wasn't a bottle,' Ben said indignantly, 'it was only half a bottle.' Yet I never knew Ben drunk or even impaired by the drink. H seemed to absorb it.

Mitchell reiterates this – 'I can't remember a single instance when Ben was adversely affected by alcohol' – and wonders why Britten suffered from these terrors 'when in fact he had a consummate technique seemingly permanently in place, which meant he never had to practise. All he had to do was to release it, set it in motion.' Possibly the nerves were not only about his ability to play or conduct. Making a speech terrified him even more than giving a musical performance, and according to his driver Jeremy Cullum he was equally nervous when faced with having to go to London: 'We always used to have to drive there sideways through Suffolk, and pretend we weren't going there. He used to be physically sick before setting off for London.'

Donald Mitchell believes that, despite the nerves, Britten had a vital need to go on performing:

Perhaps as he grew older, Ben did find submitting himself to public scrutiny – summoning up the necessary smiles and bows, receiving applause, all the obligatory stage business which is part of the perform-ance – an increasing trial, and he had to screw himself up to get on the platform. In later years, undoubtedly, recitals exacted a heavy toll. But one shouldn't overlook the rewards, not just for audiences but for him. I sometimes think of his role as a performer in the same perspective that I think of Mahler as a conductor. A love / hate relationship with performance in both cases; but also an indication of a fundamental *need*. Britten would not have been the *composer* he was if he had not also been a *performer*.

Heather Harper says that, when he was conducting, he was tense until the very end of performances: 'He would take my hand for the bow, and he would be trembling like anything.' Janet Baker noticed this too, and found it wonderfully encouraging: 'I used to think, "My God, he's just as frightened as me", and I used to find that so touching.' Pears says that, in recitals, 'quite often the first song or two was very awkward for him, very difficult', but 'after a song or two he warmed up and that was it'. Bill Servaes witnessed the nerves towards the end of Britten's performing career:

> One used to go into their dressing-room, and there was Ben in a sort of knot, all arms and legs – he was the most extraordinarily gangly kind of person – and somewhere there was always a glass of brandy. And he'd say, 'Oh God, I feel terrible, I've been sick six times.' And I said to him once, 'Why do you do it? You don't have to.' And he said, 'It's only the first five minutes. After that it's *wonderful*.'

*

From New York in September 1967, Britten wrote to Rosamund Strode that he and Pears had had 'the most grievous disappointment that we've not seen Elizabeth Mayer, who had a stroke 2 days ago'. Beata Sauerlander says:

> My mother had already had her first stroke, a slight stroke, and she was in hospital. And Ben and Peter gave a concert, in the Town Hall, I think. And she looked forward to being there. I went to the concert, and later on we went on to some place, and I said, 'Are you going to see her?' They were in New York for a few days and had the use of a limousine from some record company. And Ben said, 'Well, it probably makes no sense to see Elizabeth, you know, she's in hospital.' And I was very angry, and I told Ben, and I said, 'You go and see her.' And they did go.

Donald Mitchell says of this:

> Beata ... had to keep on reminding them not to leave New York without seeing Elizabeth; and finally they did, by having the limousine stop by on the way to the airport en route for South America ... it took time to get themselves organized. But those few days in New York, as I recall them, were made complicated by all kinds of unforeseen events, principal among them Peter arriving from Montreal

without a voice. This meant the postponing of his first recital with Ben, a flurry of visits to a doctor, a crescendo of nerves and tension – and an avalanche of telephone calls. Not so many people are aware of the fraught circumstances of a tour of this kind. On top of Peter's incapacity, when the recital finally got itself reinstated, there was Ben's own incapacitating pre-concert nausea which could knock out a whole morning. And then the welcome but unscheduled visits *from* friends (Copland and Victor Kraft [Copland's pupil and friend] among them) and commitments made long in advance, like the meeting with U Thant, the then Secretary General of the United Nations. The demands made on them – by themselves and others – were often ferocious; and a reminder of a personal obligation could sometimes seem to be the last straw. But this particular story had a happy outcome: there was a joyful reunion. And I had a hand in arranging, at Ben's request, a modest but regular contribution to the costs of Elizabeth's hospitalization.

*

'I am launched on the Prodigal,' Britten told Plomer on 22 November 1967, soon after his return to Aldeburgh from South America, 'i.e. I have found a splendid Plain-song to start me off, & useful ideas are popping up.' This time he chose *Jam lucis orto sidere*, another evening prayer for deliverance from temptation. 'My chief worries are still the nature & presentation of the temptations, & the character of the Tempter which I still haven't found the exact prototype for.' A month later he was still stuck on this point: 'The vexed question of the Temptations we haven't solved yet I fear – mostly my fault because I cannot get them clear in my mind. I am spending sometime in January discussing them together with Colin.'

Much of December was taken up with conducting *Billy Budd* for Decca, which left him exhausted and under a doctor's warning that he must 'do less next year'. He had decided to go to Venice to write *The Prodigal Son*, and by mid-January 1968 had arrived at the Palazzo Mocenigo. '. . . it's *bitterly* cold,' he reported to Rosamund Strode. 'Now I'm down to it, & the Prodigal Son is started.' To Plomer on 20 January: 'I have started my routine of working all the morning, & in the afternoons wandering, looking into churches (*when* they are open, not very often, I fear), & generally [being] fascinated by this beautiful, but very much lived in, museum of a city.' Pears, who was with him at first, soon had to leave to go on tour. Rosamund Strode and Mary Potter arrived, and also Colin Graham, '& we started discussing the Temptations immediately,' Britten told Plomer. 'I had the idea of seductive, acolyte, voices "off" to add to the night-mare atmosphere.'

Pears was to play the Tempter, the diabolical figure who leads the Younger Son astray. He was to be 'Lucifer, rather than Mephistopheles' (a fallen angel rather than pure devilry) '& also the other side of the Younger Son's nature'. (This alter ego idea could be easily conveyed in performance thanks to the close vocal resemblance between Pears and Robert Tear, who would sing the Younger Son.) There is no Tempter in the biblical story (Luke xv, 11–32) in which it is merely stated that the Younger Son squanders his inheritance in reckless living, nor in the Rembrandt painting, which depicts the father embracing him on his return. Though Britten had been deeply irritated by *The Rake's Progress*, it may have been the Auden–Kallman libretto for Stravinsky's opera, which borrows from the Faust story the detail of a devilish tempter, that gave him and Plomer the idea of remodelling the New Testament parable in this fashion.

Auden seems to be involved with *The Prodigal Son* in another respect, for the Tempter, whose music portrays him as an especially agile Quint, plays much the same role in the Younger Son's growing- up as Auden had played in Britten's. When he sings to him 'Act out your desires', there is an echo of Auden's 'Act from thought should quickly follow ... / Strike and you shall conquer' in the first of his two 1936 poems exhorting Britten. The Younger Son is portrayed instrumentally by the viola, which, as Michael Kennedy suggests, may be a hint of autobiography.

As to the home which the Tempter persuades the Younger Son to leave, Britten characterizes it as right-minded but repressive. When considering the character of the Father, he wrote to Plomer: 'I see them all sitting round him, while he describes in rather heavy slow words the kind of life they lead ... while the orchestra makes pretty pastoral noises!' These noises emanate from the alto flute, and the Father's vocal lines, while certainly 'heavy' and 'slow', nevertheless do not clash with the bird-song depicted by this instrument. Evidently there is nothing about him which goes against nature. On the other hand his statement of paternal authority, 'I am father to you all', is accompanied by a series of loud B flat major triads in the orchestra which seem to be at odds with the bird-song. Britten may be suggesting that while the Father's values are the right ones there is something repressive and constraining about such a well-ordered home. Moreover his words are dangerously close to the clichés of bourgeois moralizing: 'Evil lurks everywhere / Watching for idleness, / When evil is lurking / Repel it by work.'

Escaping from this oppressively correct household, the Younger Son is led by the Tempter to the wicked city, which is depicted by a garish trumpet and the 'seductive' boys' voices mentioned by Britten in his letter to Plomer. While *Curlew River* could justify its all-male cast because of its Noh play source, and no female characters were required for *The Burning Fiery Furnace*, women are a striking omission from *The Prodigal Son*, in which sexual temptation plays a central part. No wonder Britten found difficulty in presenting this section of the story.

The off-stage boys' voices do no more than introduce each Temptation. 'Nights of ecstasy, / joys of fierce completeness,' they sing before the brothel scene, 'Beauty offers / Pangs of piercing sweetness.' The scene itself, in which growling male voices hint at 'dark delights', is considerably less orgiastic than the Merodak music in *The Burning Fiery Furnace*. (Colin Graham says that the barcarolle-like music in this scene was inspired by Britten's memory of the Barcarolle from *The Tales of Hoffman* playing on the gramophone in the Paris brothel he visited with Ronald Duncan just before his mother's death.) Much more striking is the Tempter's incitement to the Younger Son, in which, accompanied by glissandi on string harmonics, we hear him in *Sprechgesang* (half-speaking, half-singing): 'My boy, indulge yourself! Show yourself to be a man!' The words 'my boy' occur so frequently in Pears's own early letters to Britten that this scene – made more personal by Pears's very distinctive speaking voice – may have private overtones.

After the Temptations, the Tempter declares to the audience that he has kept his promise that he would break up the Younger Son's family. But he has not. The Father is waiting for the repentant Younger Son with his B flat triad, though it is now only heard twice, and softly, as if the Younger Son no longer feels that home is a restraint. He has come back to what Auden, in his 1942 letter to Britten, called 'a warm nest of love'.

*

'I worked as almost never before, with the result that I'm about ¾ done,' Britten told Plomer on 20 February 1968, on his return from Venice,

> & have a pretty clear idea of what's to follow ... that glorious city ... has really done me & the Prodigal Son proud. To be in a place where man can still dominate (even over the pigeons!) somehow gives one confidence again in one's own capacity – machinery just *has* to take a back seat ... here [at the Red House] of course one has aeroplanes, telephones, every sort of business & artistic complication ...

American fighter planes from Bentwaters flew regularly over the house, which they used as a landmark, and were an increasing irritation. This and the other distractions mentioned in the letter to Plomer had made Britten and Pears begin the search for a retreat. In the autumn of 1967 they were looking for a cottage 'on the sea between Cork and Wexford'.

Britten was just about to write the remainder of *The Prodigal Son* when he was struck down by what seemed to be flu. 'I went down with a high temperature & had a horrid day with deliriums,' he told Pears on 24 February, and five days later: 'It's *awfully* frustrating just to lie here & feel wuzzy & sweaty, hot & cold, & *not to be able to work at all . . .*' At the beginning of March he was taken to hospital in Ipswich, still with a high temperature and 'a certain amount of discomfort & pain'. Here the specialists diagnosed sub-acute (also known as infective) endocarditis, an infection of the innermost layers of the chambers and valves of the heart.

He had had no trouble with his heart since infancy, but it is possible that his illness soon after birth, which had allegedly left him with some sort of heart defect, lay behind the present trouble; endocarditis often strikes those who have had rheumatic fever in childhood. Britten was treated with penicillin, administered intravenously – 'I've just had my 100th injection,' he told Plomer – and by 18 March, though still in hospital, he was able to do 'a couple of hours work this morning without absolutely collapsing!' When he finally left hospital 'after 4 fairly grim weeks', a nurse began to come daily to the Red House to continue the injections.

By now, *The Prodigal Son* was due to go into rehearsal in a month. 'By breaking all doctors' orders, & really thrashing my poor old self, I have finished Prodigal Son – score & all,' Britten told Plomer on 29 April. 'It is sickening that it had to be the most difficult & important bit of the whole work which remained to be done.' In the biblical story the most important passage is indeed the conclusion, in which the Elder Son objects to the lavishness of the Father's welcome of the repentant prodigal. The Father's reponse points the moral of the whole parable: 'Your brother here was dead and has come back to life, was lost and is found.' Yet when *The Prodigal Son* received its first performance in Orford Church on 10 June 1968, reviewers detected skimpiness not in the conclusion but in the presentation of the Temptations. Martin Cooper in the *Daily Telegraph* felt that 'the city's allurements' were 'palely described . . . mild and unreal . . . hardly more than perfunctory', while the *Observer* critic, Peter Heyworth, remarked that 'the prodigal's sinful living never looks remotely like rocking the piece's moral edifice'. With the trilogy of church parables complete, William Mann judged *The Prodigal Son* 'sufficiently distinctive', but 'for me the predicament of the Madwoman in *Curlew River* is unsurpassable and her music outstrips anything in the other two church operas'. Peter Heyworth was even doubtful about the whole genre of the church parables: 'somehow the props ... the village church at twilight, the hooded monks, the plainsong ... finally seem more theatrical than conventional theatre, and the other-worldliness they evoke less a confrontation with the world than a germ-free refuge from it.'

*

Britten dedicated *The Prodigal Son* to Shostakovich, who was to have attended the 1968 Aldeburgh Festival but had to cancel because of illness. That year the Festival was extended to three weeks. It included the Sadler's Wells production of *Gloriana* at the Maltings, Harrison Birtwistle's new opera *Punch and Judy* at the Jubilee Hall, and Rostropovich playing Britten's Second Suite for Cello, written the previous August. John Higgins in the *Financial Times* described the happy 'end of term atmosphere' at a recital given by Vishnevskaya and Rostropovich, and Vishnevskaya herself recalls their departure at the end of their Aldeburgh visit as hilarious. Rostropovich had bought a Land Rover and had equipped it with a horn that gave out a cow-moo:

> All the people who had come to see us off were gathered on the lawn at the Red House. We were faced with the problem of what to christen our ship ... Ben thought up the name 'Buttercup', the cow's favourite flower, and then mysteriously vanished ... Soon Ben returned and solemnly handed Peter, Slava and me our parts in his just-completed cantata for soprano, tenor and cow, entitled *Buttercup*, as a blessing for the trip ahead of us. Everyone assembled in the car, Ben waved his baton, Peter and I started to sing, and Slava climbed into the car and started 'mooing' ... We were on our way.

On the other hand, at the same Festival, Richard Butt witnessed a joke which did not go down with Britten. Birtwistle's *Punch and Judy* had proved an endurance test for many of its audience – 'my goodness, how I would have liked to slope off halfway through', wrote Desmond Shawe-Taylor in the *Sunday Times* – and Butt says that 'Ben and Peter had crawled from the directors' box after five minutes – they couldn't bear it'. Birtwistle's opera had been commissioned for the EOG, with Britten's approval, by David Webster's deputy at Covent Garden, John Tooley. He says that 'Ben was quite appalled by what he heard. He hated the subject matter, he disliked the writing – I have to say in defence of Harry [Birtwistle] that it was performed in the Jubilee Hall, and the noise in there was indescribable.' Rosamund Strode questions whether Britten and Pears actually walked out, but Tooley is definite that they 'started to withdraw' from the directors' box into the ante-room behind. 'I wasn't quite sure whether it was with the intent of actually going, or just trying to see if it sounded a little better from the back!' Stephen Reiss confirms that 'Ben and Peter were there for most of it but didn't like it. Behind the box there was an anteroom and they retired to have a drink.'

Richard Butt's reminiscence of the 1968 Festival continues:

> It was also the year that the old Sadler's Wells came and did *Gloriana*. And the lady who was the stage director had been incarcerated with *Punch and Judy*, and came over to Snape for a dress rehearsal of *Gloriana*. And she ran across Ben in the corridor at the back of the Maltings and said 'Oh, Ben, how marvellous to hear *Gloriana*. After *Punch and Judy* it's as tuneful as *The Desert Song!*' Not a flicker of amusement from Ben. And next day she said to me, 'I quite expected him to send a note dismissing me.'

Julian Bream recalls that at the 1966 Aldeburgh Festival he had 'got together a little jazz group' – himself and Ken Sykora (guitars), Emanuel Hurwitz (violin), George Malcolm (piano) and Adrian Beers (double-bass) – to play for a Festival party in the Jubilee Hall,

> and Peter wanted to sing a couple of songs, 'Miss Otis Regrets' and 'Night and Day'. Come the evening, Ben was near the front, and I think he was faintly amused by our first few numbers. And then Peter got up and sang 'Miss Otis regrets', which I think went down quite well. And when we got to the other song, Ben's face changed to a note of sourness. He disapproved of the way Peter was singing. And Peter was giving it his all, and we were driving Peter on, and the rhythm section was getting faster, and Peter was getting carried away, and he was really singing fantastically. And the more Peter was giving – the more fantastic Peter was – the more saddened Ben's expression. I think Peter probably got a rocket when he got back.

Myfanwy Piper remarks that Britten had played 'Night and Day' as a piano duet with Auden at her house in 1937. Emanuel Hurwitz confirms Bream's story, and adds:

> Ray Leppard [the conductor] committed an unforgivable sin. He found a lot of very dubious songs by people like Purcell, and Ben wasn't pleased to find Peter singing these sort of Doll Tearsheet lyrics, you know. On the other hand he had been very happy [in 1958] to have him singing the *Mamelles de Tirésias*, complete with balloon tit-busting with pins! I think you could do naughty things if Ben decided personally.

Raymond Leppard himself writes of this cabaret which he organized:

> Ben hated it. There were several reasons. Firstly I was by then tied up
> with Glyndebourne and he felt a resentment about that, some illogical
> sense of betrayal; the cabaret had a few of the ruder rounds and some
> delectable Dryden numbers of dubious implication; possibly worst of
> all, I improvised the accompaniments and did not use Ben's realiz-
> ations of Purcell which I didn't like. A froideur persisted for some years
> and then gradually faded, and they often came for dinner to Trinity
> [College, Cambridge] while I was a Fellow, and occasionally to stay on
> the way from Aldeburgh to London.

Jeremy Cullum gives an example of what Britten did consider funny.
'Once he received a letter from a lady written all in capitals. I said, "I
wonder what's wrong with her," and Ben said, "I expect she's deaf!"
That was my sort of sense of humour too, a schoolboy type. And driving
through Yorkshire he would suddenly come out with, "Oh, I do feel
Thirsky. How about having one?"'

*

At the end of July 1968, Britten and Pears were again 'staying with Q.
Mum' at Sandringham, for the King's Lynn Festival. They also had a
Welsh holiday with Stephen Reiss and his wife Beth. ('We had four
holidays with Ben and Peter,' writes Reiss, 'in 1966 to the Dordogne, in
1967 to Holland, in 1968 to Wales, and in 1969 to the Border country
mostly. At their expense.') In August 1968 Britten and Pears went to the
Edinburgh Festival, which this year was featuring the music of Britten
and Schubert, with a performance of the *War Requiem* as a highlight.
Donald and Kathleen Mitchell shared a house with them, and Kathleen
kept a diary of their lives together. Once again Britten's performance
nerves were much in evidence. 'Ben on Complan but Peter in good
spirits,' she noted before their performance of *Winterreise*, while before
the *War Requiem*, in which Britten was to conduct the chamber orchestra, 'I held his hand in the car & could feel him trembling all over.' The
prospect of giving a short speech at a public reception made him 'pale
with anticipation', though in the event his performance was 'brief and
witty', quite the best of the evening. He was also 'very nervous' before
hearing Menuhin play his Violin Concerto, even though he was not
conducting. In fact Kathleen had the impression that listening to a
performance of his own music 'is as much agony as performing or
conducting – perhaps more'.

The Rostropovichs were in Edinburgh, and the cellist tucked into a
malt whisky which Donald Mitchell had bought:

Slava drank a glassful straight down, as if it was water, & poured out another glass & downed that, all the while roaring with laughter, removing his jacket, stripping a banana & eating it, detaching a bunch of grapes & dropping them down his throat & finally biting juicily into a peach. Another glass of Laphroaig & he went gaily upstairs with Ben to rehearse the Cello Sonata!

In contrast was Britten's evident fear of departing from his nursery diet, in which mince and rice pudding played a large part:

> Peter had bought glorious *lobster* but out of deference to Ben's quite violent dislike of shellfish (the night before we had supped off crayfish *in* their shells before his fascinated & horrified eyes) the lobster had all been taken from the shell & harmlessly served on reassuring plates with obscuring salad!

(Myfanwy Piper adds that, besides shellfish, 'Ben also couldn't stand tomatoes, pears or mushrooms. I think it was the texture.') Yet as a whole Kathleen Mitchell felt the household was remarkably harmonious: 'We have become a family, with our jokes, our special words & phrases, our exaggerations & our drawbridges up protecting us.'

Kathleen was impressed by Britten's *lingua franca* with Rostropovich: 'Ben's Aldeburgh Deutsch is tremendously fluent & marvellously grammatical. He amuses me as his spoken *cadences* remain exactly the same whether he is speaking English or German.' Britten expressed his irritation with one of the Melos Ensemble, the chamber orchestra in the *War Requiem*, who was 'reading a newspaper throughout yesterday's rehearsal' – this was mentioned 'at least 4 times. So he's going to be slow to forgive this insult. His immersion in his music is total & he can't conceive how a musician *could* read a newspaper while waiting for his entries.'

On 21 August news came of the Russian invasion of Czechoslovakia. This 'left us all stunned & bewildered, Ben thinking particularly of Slava & Galya'. During the next week it was 'the main topic of conversation at breakfast', with 'Ben & Peter inclined to equate Russian occupation of Czechoslovakia with the American "occupation" of Bentwaters' (the USAF airbase near Aldeburgh whose planes roared over the Red House). Britten was contacted by the Czech conductor Rafael Kubelik and asked to sign a telegram of protest, but decided against it, according to Kathleen,

> as he wasn't in favour of severing the life lines between artists in Britain & the invading countries . . . I think Ben may write to Kubelik to explain his attitude which is wholesale condemnation of the invasion & all Russian tactics but belief in keeping cultural & intellectual links

strongly forged between individuals, who might between them be able to make some impression on a country's policy.

No such letter seems to have been sent. In 1971 Britten told the *Guardian*: 'I haven't made open declarations about Czechoslovakia because I was involved with a lot of Russian friends at that moment, and anyhow I prefer to do it privately, which I did do. I can't say exactly how I did, but I did.'

After Britten's death, Pears was asked whether his and Britten's political views in the post-war years had differed from those in the thirties. 'They were a little more fluid, I suppose,' he answered. 'Ben ... always said he could never see himself voting Conservative. He voted either Liberal or Labour all his life, and varied as to which he thought looked like the best policy at the time ... He was never a member of any political party, other than the Peace Pledge Union ... That was roughly my stand too.' Donald Mitchell observes:

As Ben and Peter got older, yes, they seemed reluctant overtly to express support for causes one presumed they had at heart. I remember [the composer] Gordon Crosse once saying to me at general election time, 'Ben told me, and I don't doubt it, that he'd never voted Conservative and has always voted Labour. Well, I wish he'd say so publicly, or put a poster up.' There was undeniably a sense of disengagement from immediate politics, the consequence perhaps of regarding politicians in general as 'ghastly', as Ben remarked in the early 1960s – a somewhat undiscriminating conclusion, it seemed and seems to me: don't we then get the politicians we deserve? The truth, I think, lies elsewhere. Ben may not have shown much enthusiasm for putting up posters or signing petitions or letters to *The Times* (though he did sign some of those). For him, political deeds were his works; and if we want to locate the 'social feelings' that were *his* politics, then we must turn to *War Requiem*, to *Voices for Today*, *Children's Crusade* and *Owen Wingrave*, each of which represents commitment to a specific social belief – 'I profoundly disbelieve in power and violence' – and a form of protest. These were the true successors of the more overtly 'political' works of the thirties. It was a tradition to which Britten was to remain faithful throughout his life.

Rosamund Strode believes that though Britten 'went through semi-socialist periods, he wasn't really very socialist. I think he was a non-political animal, like a lot of artists.' Basil Coleman adds: 'I do remember Ben saying, "As one gets older, one gets more conservative."'

*

By the spring of 1968 Britten had decided to make Henry James's *Owen Wingrave* into an opera for television. He had begun to discuss it with Myfanwy Piper – making no mention of it in his frequent letters to Plomer. She writes that he had 'thought of it as a subject for years and had spoken of it before he wrote the *War Requiem*'. He also talked of it to Basil Coleman, who it was assumed would direct it, but detailed planning was impossible on his return from Edinburgh in the autumn of 1968 because of many 'chores'. These included a heavy schedule of Decca recordings at the Maltings – Schubert songs with Pears, all the Brandenburg Concertos with the English Chamber Orchestra (Marion Thorpe calls his Brandenburg performances 'incredible, full of energy and bounce; every note had a nerve-end to it'), an LP of string music by Purcell, Elgar, Delius and Bridge, and a selection of pieces by Percy Grainger, whom Britten had met on one of his visits to England not long before his death in 1961. By Christmas, Britten was feeling 'tired and ill', and thought he had not really recovered from 'the various medical crises of the last years', but there was little time to rest, for February 1969 was to be taken up by the videotaping of *Peter Grimes* by the BBC, at the Maltings. John Culshaw, who had moved from Decca to be head of music programmes at BBC TV, was determined to achieve this before Pears became too old for the role.

Britten and Culshaw both wanted Basil Coleman to direct, but Coleman felt from his experience of televising *Billy Budd* that the job could only be done properly in the London studios, as it had with that opera, whereas Britten was determined to use the Maltings. In *Billy Budd* the orchestra had had to be placed in a different studio from the singers, and Britten, who was to conduct the televised *Peter Grimes*, believed this would severely limit communication between himself and the cast. He was also convinced that the acoustics of the Maltings would greatly enhance the sound. Neither party would budge. Culshaw and his team had no objection to working at Snape, and eventually Coleman left the project. Writing to him, Britten said his decision had been 'a great disappointment', and concluded: 'Well – there we are! I hope & expect we shall work together on other occasions; it is only sad that it won't be in Peter Grimes. Much love & good luck to you, my dear.'

It was decided that Joan Cross should rehearse the performers – 'no one knows it better than she', observed Britten – with the BBC's Brian Large directing the cameras. Rehearsals took two weeks, and the cast of sixty-five and huge technical crew and equipment so filled the Maltings that, as Britten told Plomer, 'They achieved the miracle of making the place look about one foot square.' It was 'a really wonderful cast', with

Heather Harper as a 'simply superb' Ellen, but much time was wasted putting corrections into the orchestral parts which had been made during the 1958 Decca recording but then erased by over-zealous hands at Boosey & Hawkes. Press photographs taken during recording show Britten, in a cramped position among television equipment, with a huge jar of peppermints at his side to keep him going, looking utterly exhausted.

When the programme was transmitted in November 1969 the television critics were unenthusiastic. James Thomas in the *Daily Express* thought it a mistake to record 'in the confines of the stage at The Maltings when the whole idea cried out for the wide open spaces and facilities of the studios', and Peter Black in the *Daily Mail* judged it 'considerably less satisfying' than Coleman's *Billy Budd*. 'Director Brian Large had to throw away the pictorial mobility that TV opera has been steadily working towards ... What we had was the limited mobility and groupings of a theatre, but without the heightened excitement that a theatre audience gets.' Black added that in the title role, 'Peter Pears looked no more misanthropic than the kindly chairman of a juvenile court.'

Another 'chore' for Britten during the winter of 1968–9 was the writing of a piece to mark the fiftieth anniversary of the Save the Children Fund. Following the success of *The Golden Vanity*, which had had excellent reviews at its 1967 Aldeburgh première, he decided to set another ballad for boys' voices, this time Bertolt Brecht's *Kinderkreuz-zug*, which describes the wanderings of a group of refugee children at the outbreak of the Second World War. Hans Keller made an English translation to fit Britten's music (which had been composed to the German words), and when Britten had finished *Children's Crusade* he described it as 'a very grisly piece'. It was performed on 19 May 1969 in St Paul's Cathedral, London, during what Britten called a 'curious service', by the Wandsworth boys (with percussionists from the school) under Russell Burgess. In a letter to Plomer, Britten wrote that 'the boys (singing & hitting) made a tremendous impression of passion & sincerity along side the assinine pomposity of the established church! I'd love you to hear it properly one day. I react strongly to the roughness of the Brecht.' William Mann remarked on this in *The Times*: 'The music ... has a tough, realistic quality of sound to match the diction of Brecht's poem.' Edward Greenfield in the *Guardian* noticed how 'Britten uses every possible image for musical illustration. The one that will unfailingly catch first attention is the use of a scraper to represent the gruff bark of a dog whom the children befriend.' Greenfield judged the depiction of the children's death to be 'as compelling as anything in the *War Requiem*'. Britten told Osian Ellis that the Suite for Harp, written this spring at Ellis's request, was 'rather in reaction' to the grimness of *Children's Crusade*. 'I feel it is rather 18th century harp writing, but somehow it came out that way.'

'BRITTEN STARTS WORK ON TV OPERA', announced the *Daily Telegraph* on 17 March, and he was indeed working with Myfanwy Piper on the details of the libretto of *Owen Wingrave* this spring. 'If you could think of a bit more for Kate & Lechmere, perhaps on p. 7,' he wrote to her on 14 April; 'more flattery from Kate, & L. becoming more maudlin? It could be in regular rhythm (without G. & S. rhymes!) if you'd like.' A month later: 'I have been working a bit on the opera from a more musical point of view, & one thing does strike me: I think we need a sort of musical flowering for Coyle & Mrs C. in the first scenes, & what has occurred to me could be two little numbers about *Youth*.' But there was no time to do much before the 1969 Aldeburgh Festival, the third since the completion of the Maltings.

'The Maltings Concert Hall, Snape, opened exactly two years ago, has now virtually been paid for, we are glad to say,' announced Stephen Reiss in the programme book. Besides the Festival and the Decca and BBC recordings the hall had been used for a Bach weekend, an antiques fair, some summer orchestral and band concerts and a *Jazz at the Maltings* series for BBC TV. Extensions and extra facilities were now being planned, and Britten and Pears were to give a week of concerts in America to raise funds for these. The 1969 Festival began at 3 p.m. on Saturday 7 June with a chamber concert in the Maltings given by the Amadeus Quartet with Adrian Beers (double-bass), and Britten as pianist in Schubert's *Trout*. Then at 8.30 p.m. in the Jubilee Hall the EOG presented a double bill by Gordon Crosse, *In Purgatory* and *The Grace of Todd*. It was as the curtain came down on these, shortly before 11 p.m., that passers-by in Snape observed that the Maltings was on fire.

6: I am so tired

The first person to realize that something was wrong was a farmer's son, Henry Gibson, who was leaving the Crown pub in Snape village when he saw a red glow over the Maltings. Shortly afterwards another local man drew up at the Crown in his car to telephone for the fire brigade, having noticed a gleam in one of the roof ventilators when driving past. The call was passed to Saxmundham Fire Station, about five miles away, which was manned by part-timers. The fire had now taken hold of the roof, and residents of Snape who had gone to bed were woken by sounds like rifle shots as the tiles burst in the heat. As the Saxmundham brigade arrived – the first of many contingents of firemen from various stations in East Suffolk – the roof came crashing down.

In Aldeburgh, Stephen Reiss had just come out of the Gordon Crosse operas in the Jubilee Hall with the rest of the audience when

> somebody rushed up to me and said, 'The Maltings is on fire!' So I dashed into my car and rushed over, thinking that it was probably a false alarm, because there had been a fire there before, and it had turned out to be of no significance – it wasn't in the hall but in one of Gooderham's buildings. But as soon as I came round the Snape corner, up by the church, I could see the flames. And of course when I got there it was just devastation.

The caretaker, Oscar Rumsey, and a team of helpers from the Snape pubs had managed to rescue some BBC equipment, and Keith Grant and members of the EOG, arriving at about the same time as Reiss, were allowed to fetch costumes out of the dressing-room block, which had not been reached by the fire. Reiss decided not to stay. 'I immediately saw my obligation was to go back to the Red House and tell Britten.'

Reiss himself was 'absolutely destroyed by seeing this whole thing that we'd just built, all this money, absolutely going up in flames'. But when he found Britten – who was on the point of going to bed – and told him, 'Ben was instantly practical, no shedding tears or anything'. Keith Grant, who arrived at the Red House shortly afterwards, confirms this: 'We only briefly talked about the disaster – that there was no roof, there were no seats, the walls might fall down in the morning. Ben said, "Let's not worry about that. Let's just think what we're going to do about *Idomeneo* and the other performances, and how soon we can reopen the place."' Afterwards, Britten admitted that his first reaction 'was one of shock and desperation, and a feeling that we had better go away and forget all about the Festival for a week or two. But this was followed almost immediately by a determination that the Festival must go on.'

Britten, Pears and Reiss spent several hours discussing what could be done. 'Ben was just amazing,' says Reiss. Nineteen events were due to be staged at the Maltings during the Festival, and it seemed possible to move most of them to Blythburgh Church. But could Mozart's *Idomeneo*, which had been due to open at the Maltings in three days' time (with Pears in the title role and Britten conducting) possibly be fitted into Blythburgh?

At breakfast time on the Sunday morning the diocesan bishop rang up, giving the Festival *carte blanche* to use Blythburgh or any other church. The Queen also telephoned personally to express sympathy. 'Everybody has been so kind,' said Britten later that day, 'and that has kept us going.' He himself had stayed at the Red House all night and had not seen the devastation. Reiss returned to Snape at dawn – 'it was a beautiful morning, and the birds were singing' – and realized that things were not quite so bad as he had feared. 'The walls were intact, and I could see that we were going to rebuild.' The walls had survived largely because Derek Sugden had designed one end of the new roof to slide freely over them in storm-force winds; without this, the expansion of the roof in the heat would probably have brought them down.

The foyer, restaurant and dressing-rooms were only slightly damaged. On the other hand nothing remained of Britten's own Steinway concert grand piano, brought down to the Maltings for the Amadeus concert, except the twisted metal of the frame. Also, Adrian Beers had lost the fine eighteenth-century double-bass which he used for chamber music.

The destruction of the hall itself was felt by many as a personal bereavement. As Britten told reporters later that day, 'people have grown to love it in the past two years with a curious tenderness and affection'. When Derek Sugden, at home in Hertfordshire, was told the news by his wife, who had taken the telephone call from Stephen Reiss, 'it was like losing a child'.

Charles Gifford, the festival treasurer, went anxiously into the Festival offices early in the morning to check the insurance policy. Although it was Sunday he managed to contact the insurers, who confirmed that they would pay the cost of rebuilding. Meanwhile Stephen Reiss located a set of stacking chairs and worked out how to fit them into Blythburgh Church facing the west end, so that *Idomeneo* could be staged there. Keith Grant arranged with Covent Garden and Sadler's Wells to borrow costumes to replace those damaged in the fire.

At the Maltings, reporters were now being allowed to examine the ruins. 'Floodlights hung limply from twisted pieces of molten metal,' wrote one. 'Steel floor joists formed a crazy patchwork over death-black cinders.' However, Edward Greenfield of the *Guardian* noted that much of the woodwork in the foyer was 'practically untouched', and when Derek Sugden arrived, having driven from his home as soon as he heard the news, he told Britten that the walls seemed to be 'still sound'. Sugden was still shaken by the catastrophe,

> but by then Ben and Peter had got over it. Ben said, 'It's all right, we're going to build it again. We'll start tomorrow!' And my heart sank because Arup Associates were terribly busy. And I said, 'Exactly as it was?' he said, 'Oh yes, exactly.' And Peter said, 'Well, Ben, just one or two little things . . .'

Meanwhile the next item in the Festival was already taking place, a recital by the violinist Norbert Brainin and George Malcolm at Blythburgh. One event had had to be cancelled, a big choral concert by the Cambridge University Musical Society, due to be held in the Maltings on the Sunday evening (Britten was to have conducted them in *The Building of the House*). Otherwise nothing was being scratched from the programme.

On the Sunday evening Britten held a press conference in the library at the Red House. He indicated the empty space in the room where his Steinway had stood. 'It was the nicest piano I have ever played on,' he told the reporters. 'But it was only one of many valuable objects lost.' He emphasized that the hall had been fully insured and that, if the walls were as sound as Sugden believed, 'there is nothing that we cannot replace speedily. Our aim is to have the concert hall in operation again in time for next year's Festival.' The opportunity would be taken to improve on some features of the original design. A lift would be added to lower and raise the orchestra pit, and there would, of course, be better fire precautions. He concluded by assuring everyone that the Maltings 'is going to rise again, like the phoenix, from the ashes . . . We shall soon see the same glorious roof and the same glorious brick.'

By Monday morning, workmen from Reade's were constructing a stage in Blythburgh Church, and a marquee was being erected on a nearby lawn for dressing-rooms. Not all ticket-holders could be accommodated in the church, and local people were responding to an appeal to give up their seats so that those from further afield could see the opera (Britten had promised that *Idomeneo* would be staged again in the Maltings in a year's time). That day, *The Times* carried a letter from Fidelity Cranbrook and Charles Gifford announcing the establishment of the Snape Maltings Rebuilding Fund to pay for improvements. Britten had already received a cheque for £2,000 from one Festival-goer. Another early contributor was William Plomer. 'It was sweet of you to write so promptly after the disaster,' Britten wrote to him, '& to send that generous cheque. We have been incredibly moved by the reaction & encouraged to rebuild as soon as we possibly can!'

The Tuesday morning after the fire was taken up with a dress rehearsal of a somewhat slimmed-down *Idomeneo*. The orchestra had been reduced because of lack of space, and Britten conducted from a corner of the tiny stage. 'The singers came so close to him at times,' writes Rosamund Strode, 'that he feared he'd poke somebody's eye out with his baton, even though he kept snapping pieces off it to make it shorter.' The performance that evening was unforgettable. 'Because everybody was improvising in many respects,' says Robert Tear, who sang Arbace, 'it had the feel of an improvisation, as if it were literally a first performance. I can't begin to tell you how wonderfully Ben conducted. I've done it since with many great conductors, but it's ruined that piece for me now, simply because Ben — well, what a musician he was.' William Mann wrote that the evening had been 'beautiful, exciting, unforgettable. If a devastated opera production could be restored so quickly, nobody could doubt that the Maltings will rise upon its own ruins, as gloriously as before, within the year.'

Tear was one of many Festival artists that year who donated fees to the Rebuilding Fund. Meanwhile the local papers reported that the cause of the fire was 'unknown', though *The Times* quoted the county's chief fire officer as saying that 'Heating had dehydrated woodwork in the heavily timbered building' and 'There were miles of electric cable and hundreds of people, many of them smokers.' Derek Sugden says that no electrical fault was discovered, and believes that the fire started among costumes stored beneath the stage; a trap-door had been left open, which would have allowed the blaze to spread quickly. Various Festival helpers had been in the building not long before the fire was detected, and Fidelity

Cranbrook recalls 'the usual rumours that somebody was smoking a cigarette, that someone was drunk and did this and that'.

*

'I am up to my eyes in work ... a position made doubly difficult by the complications following the Maltings disaster,' Britten told Yehudi Menuhin on 19 August 1969. The financial problems triggered by the fire were 'hideous', and he had to spend much time writing begging letters to millionaires and charitable foundations, though during September the insurance company paid out £50,000 'on account' for the rebuilding which by then was well in hand, with Bill Muttit again as foreman – 'of course he knew the whole job inside out', says Derek Sugden, 'and we had it done in forty-two weeks, which was quite extraordinary'. Even before the fire, Britten and Pears had been booked to spend a week in New York during October, giving recitals and raising money for the next stage of the Maltings project. The *New York Times* reported that thanks to the fire they 'need $200,000'. Meanwhile Britten somehow found time to begin work on *Owen Wingrave*. (His commission fee of £10,000 from the BBC went straight into the Rebuilding Fund.)

Basil Coleman was still led to believe that, despite his disagreement with Britten over the TV *Peter Grimes*, he would be in charge of the production. 'I was going to write to you about O. Wingrave,' Britten told him in a letter during the summer, 'but now is not the moment – but we won't & mustn't let an artistic difference of opinion break an old & valuable friendship, will we? must we?' However, when discussions about the production began during the autumn, Coleman was not invited to take part. Colin Graham was to direct in tandem with Brian Large, with John Culshaw producing. As to designs, 'I long to hear your ideas,' Britten wrote to John Piper in November. Piper – who did not in fact design *Owen Wingrave* until it reached the stage, though he was design adviser to the BBC production – writes that Britten always wanted to know what an opera would look like before he began to write it. 'What are we going to get next?' he would ask Piper, explaining that 'I can't compose the music until I know exactly what's going to happen [on stage].'

As with *Peter Grimes*, the intention with *Owen Wingrave* was to use the (rebuilt) Maltings as the television studio, and Britten may have felt that Coleman would oppose this. However, he never discussed it with him, and when Coleman realized that he was not being asked to direct, he was deeply hurt.

I wrote Ben a letter, saying I was very sad and sorry that this was so, and I would have felt differently about doing a small-cast opera like this in the Maltings. But I never had an answer back. And various people tried to make approaches to Ben for me, and failed, and I was very hurt when I heard this. It was the last thing I wanted.

Myfanwy Piper came to stay several times at the Red House while she and Britten worked on the new opera (there was still no mention of it in Britten's letters to Plomer). 'I loved staying there,' she says, 'but I always had indigestion. I *never* get indigestion, but when I went there I was absolutely terrified – I'd got all this work to do with Ben, and I didn't know what was going to happen.' She found him involved with the problems of a fifteen-year-old pianist, Ronan Magill, who had been one of the first pupils at the Menuhin School of Music and was now at Ampleforth, the Catholic public school. Britten described him as 'a passionate impulsive boy ... intensely, obsessively musical', who 'desperately needs help' because 'his playing has got into a muddle both technically & stylistically'.

Ronan Magill's mother, the wife of a Dublin doctor, had written to Britten, asking for his advice, and in September 1969 the boy visited him and Pears at their current London home, 99 Offord Road, N1, which they were sharing with Sue and Jack Phipps. 'We were all enchanted by him,' Britten wrote to Mrs Magill, 'and I was amazed at his general musicality and intelligence, and his is a remarkable gift.' Ronan spent a further two days with Britten in London in October, and stayed for several nights at the Red House during November. 'It was useful in that I could really spend some time working on his piano playing with him and coming to one or two conclusions,' Britten told Ronan's headmaster. Besides giving him lessons himself (Ronan recalls that Britten was perfectly willing to work with him on Brahms and Beethoven, despite his feelings about them), he sent the boy to Fanny Waterman for work on his technique. After a few months Mrs Magill, whose husband had now left her, gave up her Dublin home and brought the family to live in Saxmundham (later in Aldeburgh itself) so that Ronan could be near Britten. The boy was strikingly good-looking and had tousled black hair. Britten nicknamed him 'Tyger'.

*

Donald Mitchell accompanied Britten and Pears on their New York trip in October 1969. They also visited Boston, and on the shuttle flight Mitchell witnessed an impromptu rehearsal of a Percy Grainger folksong setting which had been giving Pears trouble:

Up comes B.B's brief-case on to his knees, to form an improvised dumb keyboard, and his long, delicately shaped but strong fingers tap out

P.G.'s rhythmic patterns on the bulging leather surface. At his side, *sotto-sotto voce*, Peter sings the song over. Now and again they stop and patiently go over a tricky entry, then continue . . .

Mitchell noticed how, after a recital was over, Britten would praise Pears's performance but would deflect compliments on his own playing with 'Well, it's a glorious *piece*, isn't it?'

During November, Britten told John Piper that *Owen Wingrave* was 'very difficult, & taking a blasted long time to write. But I am, oddly enough, enormously enjoying working on it.' He and Pears went to Venice at Christmas, but the holiday proved 'a washout' as Britten was unwell all the time. He resumed work on the opera in January 1970. 'I slog away at O.W. Going fairly well, except for one bad bit.' The same letter, to Pears, reported: 'Just sending off Horham cheque to Isador [Caplan] – completion on Feb. 6th.' After a long search for a retreat from aircraft noise, he and Pears had settled on a cottage in mid-Suffolk, tucked down a lane beside the Baptist chapel in the out-of-the-way village of Horham. They enlarged it and named it Chapel House.

In mid-January he went for several weeks to stay with the now widowed Peg Hesse at Wolfsgarten, where he continued work on *Owen Wingrave*. She then accompanied him and Pears on a two-month trip to Australia, where the EOG was to perform the church parables at the Adelaide Festival. Sidney Nolan, who had now painted many pictures inspired by Britten's music, was with them for much of the journey around his native country. After the Adelaide performances he took Britten to see the central desert, which Britten called 'a tremendous experience'. At Alice Springs airport they glimpsed a group of Aboriginal boys walking across an almost bare landscape. 'And the light was crystal clear and the landscape was pink,' recalls Nolan, 'and these boys just walking across it and [Britten] said, "That's marvellous."' Later in the trip they visited the grave of Nolan's younger brother, killed in the war. It was here that Britten alluded to Piers Dunkerley's suicide, in the course of a conversation in which, as Nolan recalls it, he declared that

> he would do a ballet and it would be on Australia, and he wanted me to work out something to do with the Aboriginals, and he had a story of a friend of his who [killed] himself . . . and he was going to combine these [in] two ways – because he had the feeling that Western civiliza-tion wasn't bringing up its children properly, and he felt that the Aboriginals in the past had. That . . . they reared their children to deal with life and be at one with it, and we hadn't done that. We'd got it more kind of complicated and more difficult. And he was going to try

and show on the stage the two things simultaneously – the life of the boy
growing up in the Australian Aboriginal tribe and the life of a boy
growing up . . . English . . . and the tragic ending, on the one hand, of the
English boy . . . and a kind of *Magic Flute* ending for the Aboriginal boy.

On his return to England, Britten mentioned this project to John Tooley,
who had now succeeded David Webster at Covent Garden. Nolan was to
have been the designer for the ballet.

Nolan says that this conversation with Britten revealed

a side of him that I had never actually seen. And it lasted for about an
hour and a half, and we had about three brandies. I was kind of
overwhelmed by this revelation of his identity, of his character. And
then we were due to land at Cairns for the Barrier Reef in about twenty
minutes and he suddenly said, 'Well, that's the end of that. When I get
back to England I won't be like that any more. My destiny is to be in
harness and to die in harness.'

*

Britten had in fact recently written a work not unlike his Aboriginal–
English scheme. The song-cycle *Who Are These Children?*, composed in
the summer of 1969 but not performed in its entirety until two years
later, contrasts a 'natural' childhood with the conditions inflicted on
children by modern society, especially in time of war. The words were
taken from poems by William Soutar, a Scottish poet who died in middle
age in 1943, having spent his last years crippled with arthritis of the
spine. Eight of the twelve poems Britten set are in Scots dialect, and
portray the colourful, innocent world of nursery, schoolroom and family
supper. These are interleaved with four stark English poems describing
the inroads of war on this world. Two are unforgettable; the events in
both take place immediately after wartime air raids.

'The Children' describes the ground stained with the blood of child
casualties. Graham Johnson, who was present when Britten and Pears
rehearsed the cycle, says that the music here replicates the notes of the
Second World War air-raid sirens. The title song, 'Who are These Children?', describes a fox-hunting party in its blood-red uniform riding
through a bomb-damaged village while a group of children look on at
this demonstration of ceaseless inhumanity – Soutar saw a newspaper
photograph of this scene.

The final song, 'The Auld Aik', brings the strands of the cycle together
in its simple description of the felling of an ancient oak, symbol of man's
relentless destruction of the innocent natural world. The last line, as set
by Britten, reiterates: 'But noo it's doun, doun, but noo it's doun, doun,

doun.' Graham Johnson recalls that Britten 'asked me, with disarming simplicity ... was "doun" repeated too many times? Before I could reply, he defended the repetitions: "It really *is* down, you see; it's the end of everything."'

During his New York visit in the autumn of 1969 he was asked by an interviewer about his 'involvement or identification with the young'. He gave what seemed to be the answer to a different question:

> I try to avoid giving that kind of thing any thought. Do you know the book Sartre wrote on Genet? Genet said that after he read it he found it impossible to work. I do know that violence worries me. I become frightfully angry when children are treated badly. Maybe ... there is something in my subconscious that gives rise to this and I am suppressing it.

The reporter noted that 'the composer smiled' during this last remark.

*

On 28 May 1970, a week before the opening of the Aldeburgh Festival, Britten wrote to Marion Harewood: 'Snape looks fine & it's lovely to work there again!' There were fresh acoustic tests, and Derek Sugden recalls that 'there were some people who said it sounded even better – though in fact it was exactly the same'. The opening concert, on 5 June, was described by William Mann in *The Times*:

> It seemed barely imaginable that the intricate structure of the Maltings would really be reassembled in all its splendour only a year after its destruction by fire. But there it was, the familiar outline, as we rounded the corner, and there, too, was all the world and his wife waiting in the glorious sunshine, Union Jacks at the ready, to cheer the royal party.

The concert was attended by the Queen and Prince Philip, but there was no formal reopening. 'Fate was not tempted,' writes Wilfrid Wren, 'for *The Building of the House* was not repeated.' Three days later *Idomeneo* was staged as had been intended the previous year. Mann was hugely impressed by the richness of sound emerging from the new orchestra pit – 'as rich and exact in detail and instrumental personality as the concert platform of the same hall – as glorious, indeed, as at any opera house I know'. The other highlight of the 1970 Festival was Shostakovich's Fourteenth Symphony, which was given its first performance outside the USSR, conducted by Britten, to whom it had been dedicated. 'Everybody in the Maltings,' wrote Mann,

–498–

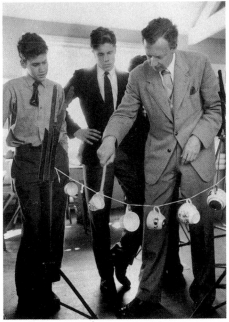

Above Mary Potter and Britten playing tennis at the Red House, Aldeburgh, into which Britten moved in November 1957. Michael Tippett thought it 'strange' that he chose to leave 'his beloved sea'.

Left Britten giving instructions to Suffolk schoolboy percussionists in the use of 'slung mugs' to represent raindrops, during the original production of *Noye's Fludde* in 1958. (*Kurt Hutton*)

Top   Pears, John Cranko and Britten at the Jubilee Hall, Aldeburgh, during its 1959–60 enlargements. Cranko was producing Britten's *A Midsummer Night's Dream*, written for the enlarged hall. (*Keystone Press*)

Above   Pears as Thisbe in *A Midsummer Night's Dream*. George Malcolm 'could hardly keep my place in the score for laughing'. (*Maria Austria, Particam*)

Top   Mstislav Rostropovich leaning against Britten's open-topped Alvis.
Britten thought his was 'the most extraordinary 'cello playing I'd ever heard'.

Above   Rostropovich and Britten communicate in 'Aldeburgh Deutsch'.

Galina Vishnevskaya and Britten. She writes: 'I met Ben . . . and my heart opened to him instantly.' (*Erich Auerbach; Hulton-Deutsch Picture Company*)

Pears as the Madwoman in *Curlew River*, during a performance at the 1964 Holland Festival. (*Maria Austria, Particam*)

Six shots by Jack Phipps of Britten
conducting Bach's *Christmas Oratorio*
for BBC Television at Long Melford
church, Suffolk, in September 1967.
Emanuel Hurwitz describes him as
'a quite wonderful conductor in
the greatest sense of the word . . . who
made the orchestra feel they wanted
to play for him'.

Top Britten leads the Queen into the Maltings during the opening ceremony on 2 June 1967. (*East Anglian Daily Times*)

Above Britten and Pears in front of the Maltings in the spring of 1969. (*Peter Warren*)

Top   On Sunday 8 June 1969, Britten stands in the shell of the burnt-out Maltings. (*East Anglian Daily Times*)

Above   Imogen Holst and Colin Graham in the rebuilt Maltings. (*Nigel Luckhurst*)

Above A group taken during recording for Decca at Orford Church in 1967. (Left to right) John Mandler (Decca), John Culshaw, Britten, Robert Tear and John Shirley-Quirk.

Right Michael Tippett with Britten and Pears. (*Erich Auerbach; Hulton-Deutsch Picture Company*)

Above A grim-faced
Britten conducting *Owen
Wingrave* for BBC
Television at the Maltings
at the end of 1970. 'Ben
didn't really care whether it
went out on TV or not,'
says Colin Graham; 'he was
so fed up with the duplicity
and self-seeking attitudes.'

Left Fidelity, Lady
Cranbrook, in the seventies.
Stephen Reiss's rift with
Britten led her to consider
resigning her Aldeburgh
Festival chairmanship.

Pears with Nellie Hudson, for many years housekeeper at the Red House.

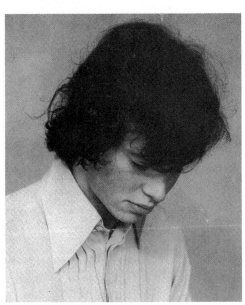

Ronan Magill, whom Britten called 'Tyger'.

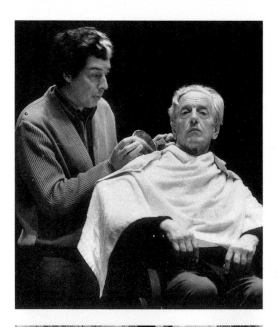

John Shirley-Quirk and
Pears rehearsing for the first
production of *Death in
Venice* in 1973.
(*John Garner*)

Britten at Chapel House,
Horham, photographed by
Rita Thomson, who nursed
him following his 1973
heart operation.

Top   Bill Servaes with Britten in Venice in November 1975.

Above   Janet Baker and Steuart Bedford with Britten in the Maltings during the 1976 Aldeburgh Festival, Britten's last, at which his *Phaedra*, written for Baker, was given its first performance. George Malcolm 'just couldn't believe that the man who had written it was in that condition'. (*The Times*)

Top   Britten talks to Donald Mitchell during the garden party at the Red House on
12 June 1976 to celebrate his peerage. (*Nigel Luckhurst*)

Above   Pears, Britten and Rita Thomson on holiday in Norway during July 1976.
(*Hans H. Rowe*)

Top   Mourners at Britten's funeral, Aldeburgh, 7 December 1976.
(Left to right) Sally Lange (daughter of Britten's sister Beth), Rostropovich,
Hansjürg Lange (Sally's husband), Peg Hesse, Pears, Rita Thomson, Barbara Britten.
(*East Anglian Daily Times*)

Above   Britten and Pears in 1974, photographed by Victor Parker.

could see and hear that Britten was conducting a work which had touched his heart profoundly and which he had prepared as a strenuous labour of love. The vocal music must also have been written for today's soloists, Galina Vishnevskaya and Mark Rezhetin, singers of truly Slavonic intensity ... The words tell us that the symphony is about death.

Two days after the opening of the 1970 Festival, the *Observer* colour magazine carried an article by John Lucas entitled 'At the Court of Benjamin Britten'. Though in the main highly complimentary to Britten, it included this passage:

Like all the best courts, this one has feuds and intrigues of Byzantine complexity, details of which sometimes filter out to the goggle-eyed plebs. Occasionally a courtier drops out of favour, and there is a wailing and a gnashing of teeth. Quite balanced men who have expected, but have not been granted, the call to refreshments at Britten's home after a concert have thrown tantrums.

Stephen Reiss says of this that the official entertaining of artists was generally done at the Festival club or at the Maltings, and while Britten and Pears certainly entertained at the Red House this was generally confined to people with whom they themselves had been performing. 'Ben and Peter had to rehearse, and work, and they'd get tired. I don't know who made these complaints about not being invited. Ben was certainly very concerned that performers received the proper hospitality.' Robert Tear says that to receive an invitation to drinks at the Red House was definitely a mark of special favour. He himself was invited 'quite a lot at the beginning', but not later. Emanuel Hurwitz, on the other hand, particularly remembers that

when Rostropovich was first playing all the new cello pieces, and rehearsing up at the Red House, Ben would invite anybody from the orchestra who fancied it to come and listen. And my son, who's now on the front desk of the Philharmonia, came with me and heard these things at the age of nine or ten.

Lucas's article also dealt with the matter of local working-class attitudes to the Festival and its growth:

The only opposition is to be found in the hinterland of the Snape marshes. Occasionally, in remoter pubs, you meet men in cloth caps, their hands grimy from years of shifting sugarbeet, who resent the middle class cultural invasion of Snape, seeing it as some undefined threat to their lives and livelihood. One hinted that he knew who burnt the Maltings down. It is unlikely that he did: a cigarette-end, carelessly thrown away, may have started the fire.

Stephen Reiss emphasizes that 'there was no evidence of arson'. However, Billy Burrell, speaking about local people's attitudes to the Festival, confirms that there was a degree of resentment:

> Aldeburgh wanted a Festival. And when they first had their operas, the rehearsal night was free. But then it got to the point where Lady this or Lady that wanted twenty tickets – class distinction – and slowly, money was able to buy. Now, in the centre of town, they were able to buy the Festival club; they were able to get the RNLI out of their place; they were able to buy or part-own the Jubilee Hall, which was donated to the town when it was built, which meant that for six weeks the Aldeburgh people couldn't use it; and they were able to buy the house next door to it. Money talks.

The *Observer* article also dealt with what Lucas called the 'constant unconsidered hero-worship' of Britten:

> If you go on the social rounds in Suffolk, you often hear him being called the greatest this and the greatest that by people who don't listen to a note of music outside festival hours. A huge number of people love Britten's music very much indeed, finding it expressive, exciting, clear and easy to grasp; and a lot of people don't, finding it self-conscious, lacking in true intensity, too often extrovert or too unadventurous. If you belong to the second group, it is as well to keep your trap shut around Aldeburgh, unless you are aware of the company.

Britten himself did not comment publicly on the article, but Pears received a letter about it from a lady in Wales, to whom he replied: 'I cannot believe that anyone who loves his music could trust half – no, a quarter – of that "Observer" article – smart, edgy, jealous, full of false emphasis, sensational . . . *either* believe his music or believe the Observer article. They don't make sense together.'

Lucas's assertions are mild compared with passages in two books published after Britten's death. In *Working with Britten* (1981) Ronald Duncan writes:

> The atmosphere at Aldeburgh was reminiscent of Berchtesgarten. It was fraught with sycophancy: 'there was whispering behind shuttering', nobody knew precisely who was 'in' or who was 'out'. It was a tiny ducal court where Ben was Weimar and Goethe combined; the

greatest toady became the latest chancellor. Those who had just been elevated turned to disparage colleagues who had just been abandoned.

In *Tear Here* (1990), Robert Tear calls the Aldeburgh atmosphere 'weird, personal, unhealthy, obsessive, perhaps incestuous, but above all these, seductive', and writes in another passage about the Festival: 'I remember ... the terrible atmosphere of Aldeburgh – an atmosphere laden with waspishness, bitterness, cold, hard eyes, with cabalistic meetings ... with the inscrutability of the élite. It was an atmosphere of secrecy.'

Specifically both Duncan and Tear are critical of Britten for surrounding himself with an entourage. Tear caricatures Britten and Pears with their followers as 'Pope, King, a couple of sycophantic academics and perhaps a handmaiden or two strewing palms', and Duncan writes: 'I always used to blame his entourage for ousting anybody who approached the sacred flame too closely.' He goes on to say that he was 'unjust and incorrect' in this, and asserts that the dismissals were really a manifestation of a split in Britten's own personality: 'No man had more charm, could be more generous or kind – as I should know; but behind that mask was another person, a sadist, psychologically crippled and bent. Perhaps that's that we all are, but with less power, and with less charm to attract others to us, we do less harm and cause less pain than he.' Myfanwy Piper comments of this passage in Duncan's book: 'Ronnie *would* say that. And Ronnie was not a nice character.' She is less severe on Tear's picture of Britten: 'Bob, I think, probably did go a bit far. But it's got to be said.'

In *Tear Here*, Tear is particularly critical of the way dismissals took place: 'I remember the weekends people were kept waiting before they were told if they were sacked or not.' Questioned about this, he produces only one example, a singer who knew that his place in the second cast of *Curlew River* was under threat, 'and they kept him in sheer agony for a week or two'. But he emphasizes that 'there was always something up, never a day which one felt was without machinations of some sort. Ben and Peter obviously needed it; they needed to be on that tightrope.' Keith Grant, from his experience managing the EOG, agrees with this: 'Oh yes, the buzz between them never stopped. They were constantly dissecting the artistic achievement of something or somebody. That's how it worked.' Tear describes Britten and Pears as 'a diumvirate of secrecy', but Grant feels that there were good aspects to their dual control: 'I think Ben without Peter would have felt tremendously isolated and insecure. Peter sharing so much of his feelings about a voice or some matter of musical taste would fortify Ben.' Grant agrees, however, with Tear's assertion that there was an entourage surrounding Britten, which made access difficult:

> There were kitchen cabinets, and entourages, and groups of people who had his ear, and good luck to them! That particular scene was constantly changing. There were certain people who were real friends, in spite of everything – Marion Harewood being one, and Lu and Peg Hesse. But for the rest, they had their ups and downs and their ins and outs. Some quite old friends might find themselves in the wilderness for a long time before being welcomed back.

Donald Mitchell accepts that there was an inner group of people forming a wall between Britten and the world, but believes it was necessary: 'Given the kind of people that Ben and Peter were, and the activities and events that depended on them, there had to be a kind of inside and outside. How could they have survived otherwise? Ben needed people to keep unnecessary, distracting and trivial parts of the world at bay.' Bill Servaes, who worked for Britten from 1971, says of the entourage forming a wall around him: 'We all did it, because the people who used to try and move in on him were frightful. We were constantly criticized for it, and we were perfectly right to do it!'

Complaints about the entourage have been voiced by some of those who might have been supposed to belong to it. Colin Graham speaks scathingly of 'lords and ladies of the bedchamber' whose job was to 'keep others at bay', and Ursula Strebi (of the English Chamber Orchestra) says:

> We were all in awe of Ben, and everybody made you feel that you mustn't go anywhere near. He had his entourage, and you couldn't talk to Ben directly. They made sure that you didn't get anywhere near. It was a bit like a wall around him. And perhaps in one way he wanted it, but on the other hand he was always tremendously spontaneous when you were with him alone. I wish I had not taken too much notice of them all!

John Drummond, who sometimes approached the Red House on behalf of the BBC, says that 'when one wanted Ben to do something, or to go somewhere, one was treated really as if one were an obscene caller'. Drummond adds: 'You had this feeling, as I've often had with incontestably great people, that they somehow choose the wrong intermediaries.'

Rosamund Strode says of Colin Graham's phrase 'lords and ladies of the bedchamber':

I suppose I might have been considered one of them. But you simply had to protect him from certain people. There were the totally crazy people who sometimes turned up uninvited. And yes, there were people on his Christmas card list who nevertheless caused a groan when they were mentioned – though they (and this was definitely Ben and Peter, not just Ben) wouldn't have dreamt of cutting them out altogether. You might call it grit in the machinery. And a highly-tuned machine cannot stand grit.

One incident bears out the truth of this. Fidelity Cranbrook says she was irritated by the 'tremendous amount of protection' around Britten, which on one occasion kept from him the news that the burghers of Aldeburgh did not want the Moot Hall used for a Festival exhibition. She was told that if this came to Britten's ears if would 'stop him writing for a week'. In fact Stephen Reiss recalls that while *Noye's Fludde* was being written, Britten heard that a faction in Orford was opposed to its being performed in the church there, 'and for about three months he absolutely dried up as a composer because he was so distressed. It was from that point on that I realized that he had to be protected from things like that.'

Emanuel Hurwitz says of Britten's use of Rosamund Strode as a fender-off: 'Rosamund, bless her, encouraged it, because she just worshipped him. And you can imagine how many people wanted to speak to Ben, and how many of them were just a bloody nuisance. And I think she did a noble job.' Tony Palmer agrees: 'I think Rosamund was extremely good news, because she had a clear job and she did it, and she was very good at it.' Britten himself described her, in a 1973 letter, as 'a wizard'.

Asked about Britten's need to surround himself with his own 'family', Michael Tippett draws a parallel in musical history:

Ben needed this group around him; there's no question that he did. So did Schoenberg. Bartok didn't. Bartok was nearer my temperament. I didn't want it. Bartok faced exactly the same problems that Schoenberg did, but alone. Schoenberg simply had to have this group of people with him, who believed in him. You either do or you don't; it's as old as the hills.

While he totally dismisses Ronald Duncan's assertion that Britten was a sadist, Donald Mitchell allows that he sometimes caused unnecessary suffering, albeit unintentionally:

I can say with my hand on my heart that, in all the years I worked closely alongside Britten, I never witnessed an occasion of his *deliberately* causing a person hurt. But I'm sure there were cases where he could have spared colleagues unnecessary pain if he could have wound himself up to say, on perfectly justifiable artistic (or whatever) grounds, 'Look, this can't be continued, we've got to have a change.' But there was a distinct distaste for confrontation of any kind. It was a feature of Ben's personality – perhaps of Peter's too – which sometimes gave rise to the very hurt it was supposed to avoid.

Keith Grant, too, dismisses the charge against Britten of sadism, though with qualifications:

He was very apt, when I was relying on him to make a decision, to brush me aside, not in an unpleasant way, but very firmly – to say, 'I can't do this, and it's up to you,' sometimes on occasions when it was very much for *him* to decide. Heads would roll if we got it wrong. So to that extent, maybe, I will go along with the accusation of cruelty. Not sadism, because sadism means you take pleasure out of it, but there was a sort of cruelty in it. He would know perfectly well that some of us lesser mortals would be made to suffer afterwards if we got it wrong. And often we would be in risk of getting it wrong for the lack of a few more minutes of his care and attention.

Lord Harewood, though he was ejected dramatically from the Britten 'family', says of the sadism suggestion: 'It wouldn't ever have occurred to me; it never crossed my mind at all.'

Donald Mitchell says that serious problems were often caused by Britten's excessive enthusiasm for people when he first discovered them, and his habit when disillusion set in – as it almost inevitably did after the first excitement had worn off – of leaving others to remove the now unwanted person. Stephen Reiss agrees that Britten 'did tend to go overboard' about people he believed would be useful to him. Rosamund Strode calls this 'straw-clutching, the trait of someone who's desperate for help'. Mitchell says that real harm could be done if Britten's latest enthusiasm displaced a valuable colleague. He cites the case of John Culshaw and Basil Coleman:

Ben fell for what Culshaw was selling him, and I was sorry to see him taken in by it. John treated him like a version of Wagner – 'Yes, Master, No, Master' – and I didn't care for it. The manipulative side of it was all too transparent. John certainly made an innovative and influential contribution to the record industry, and we must all be indebted to him for his historic series of Britten recordings. But at the BBC he seemed to me to be out of his depth. A result of his appointment there was the displacement of Basil Coleman, to my mind someone with a hundred times more musical insight and taste, and certainly with more experience of the practicalities and potentialities of taking opera into the television studio. That Ben allowed this to happen represented a failure of good sense and good judgement on his part, caused by an excess of incense being burnt at the altar. He came to recognize that he had acted unwisely and much regretted it, but by then the damage had been done. The long-term sufferers were Ben, *Owen Wingrave*, Basil, and of course John himself.

Does Mitchell think that Britten was susceptible to flattery?

I'm absolutely sure of it. We all are, and Ben wasn't a saint, for God's sake. He could sometimes be influenced by people who were yes-men because they saw it as a way of furthering their own interests and ambitions. But sooner or later – and one certainly often wished it could have been sooner – these toadies came unstuck, especially when they didn't deliver the promised goods. Then no amount of yea-saying would save them from the dustbin.

Mitchell says that these situations were all the harder to rectify because

when Ben got an idea in his head, he was like a powerful railway engine. It was useless to contest his will with one's own; one had to find a way of getting round the problem, so that it didn't develop into a confrontation. Then he could be the most reasonable person in the world, and one might well end up with what one had had in mind at the beginning, because he would see the good sense of it. But one certainly had to deploy a terrific amount of tact and diplomacy.

Rosamund Strode agrees: 'You had to go along with him.'

Mitchell says that Britten did not favour homosexuals in his choice of performers or collaborators: 'I'm quite sure that this was never an influential factor.' Richard Butt noticed that, despite the increasingly liberal public attitude to homosexuality (no longer illegal in Britain by 1970), Britten never alluded to it. 'Peter occasionally talked about it – about how marvellous it was that two men could actually love one another – did I agree that it was a good thing? I said it seemed to be perfectly all right. But otherwise nothing.' Fidelity Cranbrook recalls Britten remarking to her of some outrageous behaviour by the homosexual painter who had taunted him at Cliveden, 'Extraordinary the way those sort of people behave.' Robert Tear blundered one day in 1970 when he put on a camp performance in Britten's presence. He was dressed for the Male Chorus in a revival of *The Rape of Lucretia* at that year's Aldeburgh Festival, and had donned some chic easy-rider dark glasses . . . and walked out into the corridor at the Maltings – when I say walk, I think I mean mince – singing that hideous line, 'With you two arm-in-arm again, Rome can sleep secure', in a very queeny way and bumped straight into Ben. He appeared very angry and said, 'This is hardly the way to treat my grand opera.'

Those who lasted the course with Britten and did not fall from favour generally managed it by keeping a certain distance. Janet Baker made a 'decision not to allow myself to approach too close too often', and Thomas Hemsley says: 'I never became dependent on the EOG and the Aldeburgh set-up. I think people who became too dependent made them feel uncomfortable.' Keith Grant was conscious of not wanting to become a close friend of Britten's. 'It would have been quite easy to contrive a deeper social relationship, if I had wanted to', but he felt it was safer to keep a little apart. Steuart Bedford, who in 1970 became Britten's latest conductor-protegé – that year he conducted *The Rape of Lucretia* at the Maltings – remembered the experience of his mother Lesley Duff, who had been ousted from the EOG: 'It meant sometimes saying "no" when you were asked to the Red House for lunch.'

No such care was taken by Jennifer Vyvyan, who had sung Penelope Rich in *Gloriana*, the Governess in *The Turn of the Screw*, and Tytania in *A Midsummer Night's Dream*. 'She was the only one out of the cast who had always been invited to the Red House,' says Thomas Hemsley. 'She was the Queen of Aldeburgh, the prima donna, and they adored her. And then suddenly it stopped. Whether she sang one performance not very well, I don't know, but suddenly they went off her.' John Amis says that Britten and Pears cut her in the street, not once but twice, so that she knew she had fallen from favour. Hemsley says she was 'deeply, *deeply* hurt. It was so easy for that to happen. They would just suddenly withdraw.'

Even Britten's loyal sister Beth refers, in her book *My Brother Benjamin*, to the frequent dismissals from his circle. 'I think he needed us,' she writes, 'certainly his two sisters, for as the people fell round him (and I fear they often did – he had to be ruthless), we were always there.' She adds: 'Barbara . . . was his whipping boy and he would fly out at her when he felt he needed to be nasty to someone.' Her choice of words suggests that she suspected her brother of deliberate cruelty. However, Beth herself was now drinking heavily, and her relationship with Britten was going through such a stormy period that she cannot be regarded as a detached witness. Her nephew Alan (son of Robert Britten) says she would send Robert 'letters of a vitriol you cannot conceive to the effect that my father was worthless and Ben was so wonderful; they were obscenely unkind.' She behaved equally aggressively at times to Britten himself.

Robert Tear says that his own 'final break' with Britten occurred after the 1970 Festival, 'when both he and Michael [Tippett] offered me a part in their new operas'. Britten's offer was of the headstrong Lechmere in *Owen Wingrave*. The Tippett role was Dov in *The Knot Garden*, though Tippett himself says the offer was made 'by Covent Garden, not by me; I never ask for anybody – I'm not that way inclined'. Tear says he 'accepted the role of Dov and . . . was dismissed from celestial Suffolk, with few fond farewells'. In fact he was soon working again for Britten, and Keith Grant thinks he is 'overreacting' in suggesting that he experienced a full-scale dismissal. Tony Palmer guesses that for a while Britten may have thought of Tear as a possible replacement for Pears, 'since it must have occurred to Ben that Peter wouldn't go on for ever', but then decided against it. Tippett suggests that Tear 'had to get out' from the Britten circle, since 'he was really becoming like that voice' (Pears's). Thomas Hemsley says much the same, that Tear, 'an absolute beginner when he came to Aldeburgh', had so far 'made his career by sounding like Peter', which caused tension between him and Pears. Hemsley adds: 'I think Bob has absolutely no cause to feel that he was badly treated. Ben and Peter made him. Of course a lot of people find it difficult to feel gratitude to people who helped them in their early stages.'

*

'Please excuse scribble,' Britten wrote to Yehudi Menuhin on 30 November 1970, 'but I am in the middle of a month-long BBCTV thing – a curious mixture of excitement, boredom & complete frustration – just like life?' Henry James wrote the short story on which *Owen Wingrave*, Britten's opera for television, is based in 1892, six years before *The Turn of the Screw*. Although it was intended simply as a piece of hack work for the Christmas number of a magazine, the account of a young man studying for Sandhurst who appals his family by declaring that war is 'crass barbarism' expressed James's own pacifist feelings, which had been fermenting since the American Civil War.

There is another element in the story. Owen meets his death by spending the night in a room in his family's mansion, Paramore (the name has erotic rather than military overtones), which is haunted by an ancestor who 'struck in a fit of passion one of his children, a lad just growing up, a blow in the head of which the unhappy child died'. Though James may have meant this to exemplify the Wingraves' tradition of violence against which Owen is rebelling, something more seems to be implied. In the story – not the opera – Owen has already passed one night in the haunted room before the fatal one, and the household comments on his shocked manner: '"I'm sure he *did* see something or hear something." . . . "Why then shouldn't he name it?" Young Lechmere wondered and found. "Perhaps it's too bad to mention."' This is the territory of Quint. Writing to Eric Walter White in 1954, Britten described *Owen Wingrave* as having 'much the same quality as the *Screw*'.

George Bernard Shaw complained to James that he should not have allowed a ghost to kill a man; the man should kill the ghost. Certainly the story is no plain pacifist tract. James concludes it with the words: 'Owen . . . lay dead on the spot on which his ancestor had been found. He was all the young soldier on the gained field.' But in what struggle has Owen been victorious? Modern readers and critics seem to find the tale unsatisfactory; it does not appear in popular selections of James's short stories, and Leon Edel, the leading James scholar, simply remarks that it 'reflects to the full the novelist's subterranean anxieties'. Britten, however, seems to have been attracted to it as soon as he read it, around the time that he was writing *The Turn of the Screw*. In June 1970 he told Alan Blyth that he had been 'thinking for some time' of turning it into an opera, and 'felt that it would be suitable for TV because it's a very intimate, reasonable story'. Myfanwy Piper describes Owen's struggle with his family as representing 'the battle of all Conscientious Objectors against the pressures of righteous aggression', but nowhere in his remarks to Blyth does Britten mention pacifism or link his interest in the story with his own wartime conscientious objection. Colin Graham states that 'the offer from the BBC to commission a television opera' came 'when Britten was feeling strongly about the Vietnam War and the shooting of students at Kent University', but the Kent State (Ohio) shootings were in May 1970, by which time the opera was virtually written.

His score for *Owen Wingrave* begins with a motif for percussion, harp and piano – which form a kind of Balinese-style band-within-an-orchestra throughout the opera – marked 'Martial'. This and its fanfare-like rhythm have led commentators to suppose that it represents the militarism of the Wingraves, but the sound quality of this band suggests 'magic casements' rather than the parade ground. Britten seems to be indicating that, though war and peace are the ostensible subjects of the opera, he is also making the journey back into the magic wood.

The score specifies that during the Prelude to the opera we are to be shown, one by one, the family portraits of the Wingraves, with Owen himself as the last of them. The opera is going to be a study of how the individual is hemmed in by the past – by heredity and tradition, but also by decisions made long ago which now act as stifling limitations to freedom of choice.

When questioned by Alan Blyth about note-rows and his views on serialism, just as he was finishing *Owen Wingrave*, Britten observed: 'You could say people are my note rows.' This remark, subsequently much quoted, was printed in the interview (in *Gramophone*) to make it appear that Britten was talking about performers. Certainly *Owen Wingrave*, like all his other operas, was tailored to its original cast, and is to some extent a set of portraits of their own personalities. But it also seems to be about certain other people in Britten's life, in particular two 'families', one past, the other present.

The first scene establishes the relationship between Owen (Benjamin Luxon in the original production) and Mr Coyle (John Shirley-Quirk), the 'crammer' with whom he is studying military history for entrance to Sandhurst. Peter Evans describes Coyle's music as 'fatherly in tone . . . a reminder of Britten's early style'. In particular the figure for strings which introduces Coyle could have come from *Variations on a Theme of Frank Bridge*. It seems likely that in the liberal-minded (but not pacifist) Coyle and his gently wise wife (Heather Harper), with their kindly but not oppressive concern for Owen, Britten was affectionately portraying Frank and Ethel Bridge. (Myfanwy Piper agrees that this is 'very likely – though *I* didn't know them, of course'.)

The part of Lechmere, Owen's fellow pupil at Mr Coyle's, was the role offered to Robert Tear, and it may be that Lechmere's impetuous, tactless, puppyishly enthusiastic musical personality owes something to Britten's perception of Tear (Nigel Douglas took the role). As to Owen himself, after he has announced his hatred of war to Coyle, we find him reading on a bench in Hyde Park, while the music seems to delineate his inner peacefulness. Yet we have heard exactly this combination of gently rocking strings in 6/8 rhythm, punctuated by high figures on the harp, before, in the music which opens the first scene of *The Rape of Lucretia*, where it establishes the tense and stuffy mood of a summer's night that is about to burst into storm. Owen declares that he is 'strong, not mad or weak', but against this bottled-up musical background his words do not carry complete assurance.

Making use of the possibilities of television, the opera cross-cuts in this scene between Owen in the Park and Miss Wingrave, his aunt, reacting to the news of his pacifism. Britten gives her Lady Billows-style music – the part was written for Sylvia Fisher, who had sung Lady Billows and who in *Owen Wingrave* gave what Pears described as a 'splendid dreadnought performance'. Up to this point it looks as if Britten is presenting us with another of his contests between bohemianism (Owen) and the accepted mores of society (the Wingraves). Yet when Lechmere asks of Owen's family, 'Are they so very terrible?', he is answered by the percussion band, which plays the 'magic casements' motif that opened the opera. Britten is endowing Paramore, the Wingraves' home, with the emotional overtones which James's choice of name for it implies.

Before the head of the Paramore household, Owen's grandfather, makes his appearance we are introduced to the three women who form his entourage. Miss Wingrave we have met already, but now her rigid militarism – 'Wingraves are soldiers, they go when they are called' – no longer seems comical in the Lady Billows style. On the superficial level she clearly represents the type of woman who handed out white feathers in the First World War. More subtly, she seems to stand for the species of utterly single-minded Englishwoman who brushes aside all human feeling, her own and others', in her determination to further a supposedly good cause. Britten had encountered many such people; there were some in his 'family'. In the other two female members of the Wingrave household, the fussy, nervy Mrs Julian (Jennifer Vyvyan), a lame-duck dependent relative who is both bossy and unsure of her own position, and her haughty and socially ambitious daughter Kate (Janet Baker), one may again detect portraits of women who had attached themselves to Britten.

When Owen's grandfather, General Sir Philip Wingrave, makes his entrance in the television production it is in the person of Peter Pears. His vocal lines throughout *Owen Wingrave* are characterized by melisma, which Britten here uses to suggest the shaking voice of an old man. Colin Matthews has a suspicion that this might be 'a caricature of Peter's singing style and the fact that his voice was ageing'.

Sir Philip's arrival triggers off the household's attack on Owen, which starts calmly but ominously with glissandi in both voices and instruments, and soon whips itself up into an out-of-control frenzy. No wonder that Owen now declares: 'I'm in a state of siege ... blockaded by the past, starved by lack of love.' In Britten's personal story 'the past' could mean his decision in the forties to establish a 'family ' for himself in Aldeburgh, which had now in many ways become a prison – the buying of the Horham bolt-hole was as much an escape from this as from aircraft noise – while 'lack of love' could be his refusal to allow his relationships with boys to go beyond sentimental friendship. In the dinner scene which ends Act I, Mrs Coyle observes: 'Owen has scruples' – which touches off another nightmare ensemble from the Paramoreans, who this time repeatedly chant the word 'Scruples!'

Act II begins with an entirely new musical and dramatic element, a ballad which narrates how Owen's ancestor killed his son. (The opera adds to Henry James by providing a motive for the striking of the blow. We are told that the father was furious because the boy had refused a playmate's challenge to fight.) The ballad, which is more sinuously chromatic than one might expect in such a folk-genre, is sung in the television production by Pears, with the boys of Wandsworth providing a distant refrain – the same 'seductive' effect that Britten had devised for *The Prodigal Son*. He is sketching another aspect of his past, for the story of the boy's death is a recollection of Grimes and the Apprentice, Claggart and Billy, Quint and Miles. No wonder Owen reacts to the ballad with: 'I can't forget them, the bully and the boy.'

Their tragedy is still a live issue for him (and Britten): 'He [the murderer] was my ancestor in every sense,' sings Owen. 'For me it is not the past, but now, renewed with every thought and breath.' And when Pears as Sir Philip confronts Owen in a room off-stage, we relive the interview between Vere and Billy. (Like Billy, Owen is sung by a baritone.) Here, Britten gives Pears his biggest melisma ever, on the words 'Never return!' as Sir Philip disinherits the boy. There is no appearance of rectitude as there was with Vere; this is unashamed delight in destruction. 'I half thought the old man would knock me down, or worse,' observes Owen when at last he emerges.

Now Kate comes to the fore. Janet Baker says she found it 'very painful' getting into Kate's character in rehearsal, 'because everybody else was playing themselves', and Myfanwy Piper writes that she had tried to make Britten feel some sympathy for the girl, but was hardly successful: 'I felt that in spite of her insufferable behaviour she was as much a victim of her background as Owen, but lacked his opportunities to think again ... Britten took Mrs Coyle's view of her that she was an impossible and arrogant girl, not worthy of the thoughtful Owen.' In James's story she is an impetuous girl of eighteen. In writing the part for Janet Baker, who had sung Dido and Lucretia for him, Britten totally changed Kate's significance as well as her age. In the opera she seems to represent the threat to Owen of a permanent involvement with a mature person – the suffocating side of Britten's commitment to Pears. Owen complains that Kate and the other women have loved his 'image' rather than his real self, an accusation which Britten could have levelled at many who had attached themselves to him:

> I was surrounded with love,
> nursed in hope,
> spoiled with admiration,
> but all for the image they made of me.

Britten had told Sidney Nolan, 'My destiny is ... to die in harness.' Owen decides not to. He rejects everything Paramore has to offer. So what other choice is available? In the calm after the storms of being disinherited by his grandfather and rejected by Kate, he tells Coyle: 'Now I feel I have escaped, / Only I am so tired.' (It is the weariness which by 1970 was so often perceptible in Britten.) Coyle bids him goodnight and, left alone, Owen is at last able to be himself. The main orchestra states a series of great major triads, while above it floats the Balinese sound of the percussion band, whose glittering arpeggios suggest how all the passionate impulses in a human being may be allowed to co-exist harmoniously with a natural way of life (the triads). Britten has never made a musical statement like this before, but then no character in his operas has ever before won through, by personal courage, to this sort of sanity.

As to what Owen means by 'peace' in his words during this great passage in *Owen Wingrave* –

> In peace I have found my image,
> I have found myself.
> In peace I rejoice amongst men
> and yet walk alone

– one might turn to another of Sidney Nolan's recollections of his and Britten's time together in Australia. Britten told Nolan that 'Schubert always said he liked to go for a walk with somebody as long as they didn't speak', and Nolan says of this that he and Britten 'had an instinctive understanding of silence'. Janet Baker has written: 'I often used to wish I could communicate with Ben on his own level, the level of his creative work; an utterly futile wish.' Perhaps Nolan had the answer. 'Peace' in *Owen Wingrave* means not pacifism in the anti-war sense – though it does not negate that – but the possibility of being at peace with oneself, rather than 'in harness' to one's duties and obsessions.

If this inner calm is achieved, the obsessions fade like apparitions. As Owen makes his great 'peace' statement, the ghosts of his ancestors – the bully and the murdered boy – step out of their picture and begin to walk through the house. Owen tells them, in speech (it is one of those moments in Britten's operas that are too intense for singing): 'You two will never walk for me again.' And to the boy: 'Your fate and his no longer frighten me. Tell him his power has gone and I have won, and at last I shall have peace.' But suddenly Kate comes downstairs, accuses Owen of cowardice, and challenges him to spend the night in the haunted room. It is as if Auden had suddenly returned and had again thrown down his 1942 gauntlet: 'If you are really to develop to your full stature, you will have, I think, to suffer, and make others suffer . . . against every conscious value that you have.' Owen responds, as Britten might have done: 'Ah! I thought I'd done with that . . . Would you drag me back?' But he accepts the challenge and goes to his fate, as if Grimes were once more striding off to his and the Apprentice's 'fall' in the hut.

Neither James's story nor the opera explores what happens next. There is no Passacaglia, no musical hint of what Owen experiences when he unwillingly deserts his newly won calm for what awaits him in that room, just his off-stage death and an abrupt ending to *Owen Wingrave*. Myfanwy Piper recalls that Sir Philip's words when he sees Owen lying dead in the haunted room, 'My boy!', were imposed on her by Pears – 'I didn't think it was very successful – it's not really dramatic.' She was unaware that Pears had addressed Britten in these words in his early letters to him.

Britten had not yet really dared to confront in his operas what lay in his own haunted room. Even in *The Turn of the Screw* there had been no more than hints of it. But *Owen Wingrave* seems finally to have given him courage to attempt it. Myfanwy Piper had just begun to relax after the tensions of writing the television opera when, shortly before videotaping began at Snape, Britten suddenly asked her to collaborate with him on a new project. 'My first thought when I heard its subject,' she writes, 'was that it was impossible.' This was *Death in Venice*.

7: Under the lash

Colin Graham describes the videotaping of *Owen Wingrave* by the BBC as a 'horrid' experience for everyone:

> Ben Luxon, Janet Baker and Nigel Douglas all felt themselves too old for the roles, and . . . were all three nervous about how they would turn out in the merciless close-up of TV! That was only a start! The TV guys, John Culshaw, Brian Large, and David Myerscough-Jones (the designer) were all held in deepest suspicion by Ben – in spite of a very satisfactory relationship with John over the years of recording with Decca.

Graham says that Britten now felt guilty at not having chosen Basil Coleman to direct the opera. Realizing that Large 'never actually directed the singers, or the drama, only the cameras' he had insisted on Graham (who had worked in television) being joint director. The BBC team 'hated the idea, and therefore me!' says Graham. By the time recording began, Britten was recovering from a hernia operation. He asked Steuart Bedford to supervise the music during the daytime camera rehearsals, and himself only took charge for the actual taping, in the evening, so that he was often presented with decisions not to his liking. Stephen Reiss says Britten had also found 'his beloved acoustic' in the Maltings 'totally negated by all the scenery and equipment which had to be introduced', and there were 'many technical difficulties which could have been avoided in a proper studio'.

At the very end of the recording there was a showdown between Britten and the BBC, he demanding retakes, they refusing. Graham says that Brian Large 'might have known what he was up against. For the first time in BBC history Ben achieved the impossible: whole scenes and interludes were to be re-shot. He had final approval in his contract.' Graham realized that

Ben didn't really care whether it went out on TV or not; he was so fed up with the duplicity and self-seeking attitudes he had had to put up with ... On more than one occasion he said to me, always with a naughty grin, that he felt the opera would work better in the theatre anyway: he already had the stage première lined up with Covent Garden.

William Walton, meanwhile, was referring to the new opera as 'Godfrey Winngrave'.

'We have had rather a bad time,' Britten wrote to Walter Hussey on 6 January 1971:

the new Television Opera had to be written in order to help build the new Maltings; then came the preparation & recording of it. Now I have had to clear all the decks in order to write a big new piece for Peter, which cannot be delayed. Peter ... is (like most of us) not growing any younger, may not have many more years of singing, & this new piece (about which I will tell you one day) needs him to launch it.

The same day, Britten wrote to John Piper: 'I do hope to write very soon & suggest a plan for Venetian discussions (I feel so nervous about even mentioning the name of the new opera!). I had a very interesting time with Golo Mann in Germany who was just as nice & helpful as I remember him from N. York in early 40s.' Britten had met Thomas Mann's son during a Christmas visit to Wolfsgarten. Golo Mann was very keen on an opera based on his father's *Death in Venice*, and told Britten that Mann, who had died in 1955, used to say that Britten would be the ideal person to write music for his *Doctor Faustus* (in which the hero is a composer) were it ever to be dramatized. However, Luchino Visconti was currently filming *Death in Venice* for Warner Brothers, which presented copyright difficulties. 'The stories about the rights (one might even call them *wrongs*) to do with the film are scarifying, & we aren't quite out of the wood yet,' Britten told Piper; 'but nothing bad enough to stop us all discussing it.' He and the Pipers arranged to go on holiday to France at the end of January.

In the letter to Piper on 6 January, Britten also wrote: 'Thank you very much for getting hold of the advance copy of Susan Hill's stories for me. I have read enough to show me how good they are.' Susan Hill, who was in her late twenties, had been 'overwhelmingly affected by Britten' since she first heard the Sea Interludes from *Peter Grimes* as a schoolgirl in Coventry. She became 'completely obsessed' by the opera itself, and then 'gradually, by the rest of Britten's life and work'. It was not until 1970, by which time she had published several novels, that she made her 'first pilgrimage' to Aldeburgh. That brief visit produced *The Albatross*, a novella set in 'Heype' (Aldeburgh), about a dim-witted young man torn between loyalty to his domineering crippled mother and his fascination with the tough masculine world of the fishermen. Myfanwy Piper, who knew Susan Hill, felt the story was 'up Ben's street', and passed on an advance copy of *The Albatross and Other Stories* (1971) to him.

Susan Hill was now working on a novel about the First World War, *Strange Meeting*, a project first contemplated after she had been 'dazed' by the *War Requiem* nine years earlier. She decided to rent a cottage in Aldeburgh and work on it there. She arrived at the beginning of 1971, and received a letter from Britten inviting her to telephone and arrange to meet him:

> When a voice answered – and I didn't know this rather beautiful very cultured voice he had, with a cello timbre – I thought it was a secretary or someone, and said, 'May I either speak to Mr Britten or leave a message for him, please?' And there was silence, and the voice said, 'Who is this?' in a very tight way. So I said rather clearly, 'Susan Hill.' 'Oh, I'm *so* sorry, this is Ben Britten. Can you come to lunch next Wednesday – if you're not too busy?' As if I could be too busy for that! And he gave me very precise directions for finding the Red House, warning me to watch my car springs when I turned off the main road on to the track. 'And when you get out of the car, mind you're not hit by a golf ball!'

Robert Tear suggests that Britten's highly emphatic 'Oxford' manner of speaking may owe something to Auden's influence in the thirties. Colin Matthews writes that his voice 'had such an extraordinary quality, which especially when relaxed was very seductive, that I've often wondered whether he had consciously chosen a manner of speaking'.

When the day came, Susan Hill arrived at the Red House, parked, and was ushered into the house by a local girl in a white overall.

> And in the drawing room there was Peter, sitting in a corner reading the *East Anglian Daily Times*, and he leapt up and was terribly nice straight away, making me feel completely at home. There was a little dachshund they had called Gilda, running about the place, and I sat down on the sofa and the dog jumped up and put its paw in my lap, and Peter said, 'My goodness, you are honoured, she doesn't do that normally.' We talked about John and Myfanwy, and suddenly there

were footsteps, and the door opened, and in bounded Britten.

It was like somebody on the run. He came leaping in. I think he'd just run down the stairs and bounded into the room. And he was immediately so charming that I didn't feel in the least overawed. He offered me a drink, and he and Peter had an argument about whether the sherry was really dry, and Peter said it was, and Ben said he wasn't at all sure; if I were him I wouldn't take Peter's word for it, and if it wasn't very nice I was to give it back.

Mary Potter joined them for lunch – 'She was rather like Mrs Tiggywinkle, small and dumpy, shy and diffident in manner, and it came out sometimes as being rather brusque and abrupt, though it wasn't' – and they had soup, roast pheasant with braised celery, and treacle tart. 'What struck me', says Susan Hill,

> was the obvious, natural domestic affection between Ben and Peter, just like a husband and wife. I remember thinking that this was a perfectly ordinary relationship which just happened to be between two men. And I would never have detected any note of the camp in Ben, either his voice or his manner, though Peter did have a very slight nuance.

She accepted a second slice of treacle tart. Britten asked if she liked sweet things, and went on: '"Do you know what I like best of all? If I can't sleep at night, I go down to the kitchen and open a tin of condensed milk, and eat it with a spoon." And Peter gave a shudder, saying, "I don't know how he can!"'

During lunch,

> Peter was much easier to talk to, much more relaxed. You got the feeling that if you said the wrong thing to him, it wouldn't have mattered. He might have come back at you, but you wouldn't be beyond the pale for ever. If you said the wrong thing to Ben, you'd get a look from those cold blue eyes, and that would have been that. I did say one thing – I can't remember what, and it was only a remark in passing, but I remember that look. And Peter jumped straight in, putting me at my ease, as if this happened often.

It did. The accompanist Graham Johnson, who in the early seventies was a music student recently arrived from Rhodesia, recalls

> a really sticky patch when I was staying at the Red House – I'm almost sure it was New Year's Eve 1971, and Marion was at dinner too. The subject of *Der Rosenkavalier* came up:

B.B.: It is utterly loathsome. I almost get sick hearing it – even the overture makes me physically sick.

G.J.: But it's got so many beautiful things in it, hasn't it?

B.B.: What do you like about it?

G.J.: Well, that Trio (*singing, unwisely*) 'Marie Thérèse . . .'

B.B. (*utterly icily*): I know how it goes, thank you very much, and I don't need you to sing it to me.

(*Horrible silence. Close examination of plate-ware by other guests. Peter activates the foot-bell for Heather to bring the next course.*)

Of course I was utterly crushed, and said nothing more all evening – which may have been the aim of the exercise! Peter tried to be consoling at bedtime for I was almost in tears. I felt Ben had, after all, asked my opinion. The next morning I suppose Peter had told him I was upset. Ben said, consolingly calling me 'old thing', that what he loathed about this piece was its lesbianism – something he felt unable to talk about in front of Marion. I felt very disappointed about this because it seemed wrong for him to be 'against' lesbianism for its own sake. Now I am much older, I understand very well what he meant. It was not the lesbianism, but Strauss's voyeuristic enjoyment of it . . . There is a salaciousness in this music that sits in the sidelines and *watches* the Marschallin and Oktavian . . . whereas everything Ben wrote from the deeper well-springs of his sexuality was absolutely self-revealing. I think it is this covert quality that Ben found revolting.

Even Marion Thorpe herself says:

I think one was a bit careful sometimes not to touch on certain subjects, or say certain things. One knew what he wouldn't like, so one avoided it. There was a kind of – wariness is too strong a word, but one was aware that he was very, very sensitive, and one didn't want to upset him.

Susan Hill left her lunch at the same time as Mary Potter. Britten and Pears came to see them both off, 'and I remember when they'd gone Mary stopped and said, "And now I can have a cigarette!" She was a chain-smoker, but she wouldn't have dreamt of smoking in their company, though it was a serious deprivation for her.'

*

During the French holiday with the Pipers in late January and early February 1971, Britten sat in the back of the car with Myfanwy, talking over *Death in Venice* and working out a preliminary scenario (John Piper drove and Pears map-read). Britten had now been shown 'a few deplorable photographs' of the Visconti film, which made him 'determine to miss' seeing it. In any case the lawyers had told him not to, so that there could be no accusation of plagiarism. 'I warn you,' he told Anthony Gishford on 3 April, '*nothing* can now put me off writing it!'

The same letter mentioned that he was 'deep in the recording of the St John Passion at Maltings – an absorbing matter!' Robert Tear was engaged to sing the tenor arias. After the run-through of 'Ach mein Sinn' – 'that fearful aria', Tear calls it – Britten's only comment was: 'Well, if that's all you can do, you'd better go on doing it.' Nevertheless Tear was back at the 1972 Aldeburgh Festival, singing Vaughan Williams and Tchaikovsky in a chamber concert.

Owen Wingrave was transmitted on BBC2 on the evening of Sunday 16 May 1971. 'It was such a new world for me,' Britten wrote to Eric Walter White, 'that I am still not quite sure that it works "on the box". What a difficult medium!' Writing in *The Times* the day before the programme, William Mann had no such doubts: 'This is certainly the most impressive piece of ambitious T.V. drama I have yet seen.' He judged that Britten was 'at the masterly height of his career as a composer'. In the *Sunday Times*, Desmond Shawe-Taylor called *Owen Wingrave* 'highly successful, even if not as masterly an achievement as . . . *The Turn of the Screw*', while Martin Cooper in the *Daily Telegraph* thought it 'unmistakably one of the composer's most powerful utterances'. However, in the same newspaper Sean Day-Lewis judged that the production was 'very much opera first and television second', and was 'not calculated to convert' those who had no taste for Britten or opera. Britten himself wrote even more harshly about it to William Plomer: 'Owen Wingrave seems to have made an impact – let's hope the story has sunk in a bit too! But o, what a terrible medium – between ourselves it looked pretty awful, & John P[iper] could do virtually nothing to help.' And to Anne Macnaghten: 'I hope you'll see it on the *stage* before too long.'

Despite his hatred of rumours about his plans for new works, word of *Death in Venice* was already getting round. In *The Times* on 2 June, Alan Blyth reported that Britten was writing 'a new opera to be given at The Maltings, Snape, in September 1972', though 'For contractual reasons the subject cannot yet be announced'. Blyth added that Britten was 'also planning a large-scale solo piano piece for Sviatoslav Richter' (this was never written). Richter was due to perform at the 1971 Aldeburgh Festival, but neither he nor the Borodin Quartet (also billed) managed to get there, and William Mann reported that 'Russian absenteeism has left Britten . . . as this year's principal star. He will conduct, among other works, Mozart's *Requiem* and Elgar's *Dream of Gerontius*, and will take part in the first performance of his new fourth canticle *The Journey of the Magi*.' After the performance, Mann described Britten's interpretation of Elgar as 'urgent, unsentimental and totally lacking in bombast', and when the Britten recording of the work, with Pears again singing Gerontius, was issued the following year Alan Blyth in the *Gramophone* called it 'a searing re-creation of the drama that I find at all times involving and convincing ... Britten removes the veneer of sentimentality, even sanctimoniousness, that has for long come between us and Elgar's compulsive vision.'

As to the new Canticle, performed in the Maltings on the penultimate day of the 1971 Festival, Mann was a little puzzled by the apparent simplicity of Britten's setting of Eliot: 'It is not a hard-hitting piece; for once Britten is not voicing deep discontent, or below the surface is he?' Mann wondered if it had been written chiefly to provide a piece for the 'three trusty colleagues' who sang it, James Bowman, Pears and John Shirley-Quirk (Rosamund Strode says this was indeed the case.) Since these were eventually to be the three principals in *Death in Venice*, it is tempting to regard *Canticle IV* as some sort of prologue to that opera. However, the month before the new Canticle was performed Donald Mitchell made a note that Britten had told him there would be only two principals in *Death in Venice*, Pears as Aschenbach and Shirley-Quirk in a variety of roles as a 'symbolic figure of death'.

A few days after the 1971 Festival, Britten wrote to Rosamund Strode to thank her for her hard work, adding: 'We have had some nice days in Horham, but unfortunately the affaire ——, with all its quick-sand feeling of ungraspable tensions, has rather coloured it ... it makes me sick even to write about it.' The name left blank is that of the then caretaker at the Maltings, appointed during the rebuilding, whose job had now been dignified with the title Snape Warden. Disagreement over the man's competence and suitability was now catastrophically widening the rift that had been appearing for some time between Britten and Stephen Reiss.

Rosamund Strode describes Reiss as 'the most wonderful planner, planning everything in advance, so that he was free to deal with the emergencies while the Festival was actually happening'. During the Festival itself, Reiss, a mild-mannered man who went around whenever possible in a loose cardigan rather than a suit, could frequently be seen setting out the chairs for concerts, a hands-on approach to his job which won approval from most but earned him the reputation of someone who disliked delegating even the humblest duty. This and his hatred of elaborate paper-work made Isador Caplan feel that 'Reiss was still trying to administer the Festival as the quite delightful family affair it used to be, by continuing (as I put it) making his notes on the back of a cigarette pack.' However Ursula Strebi emphatically refutes any suggestion that Reiss was amateurish: 'He gave you the impression that he was vague, but behind it he held the strings very well. Stephen was as much Aldeburgh for us as Ben was.' Dame Janet Baker puts it similarly: 'He was very much part of the fabric, both he and Beth [Reiss's wife]; for a long time he *was* the Festival.'

Besides running the Festival and the Festival club in Aldeburgh High Street, where he presided as an affable *patron* until late at night (somewhat to the disapproval of Britten, who used the club to entertain guests but was not an *habitué*), Reiss had undertaken most of the fund-raising for the Jubilee Hall improvements in 1959–60, the purchase of the club premises in 1962, and the building and rebuilding of the Maltings in 1965–7 and 1969–70. During the early autumn of 1969 he went to New York to set up meetings for Britten and Pears's own fund-raising trip a few weeks later. He found American interest hard to stir up because the Maltings had been fully insured, so that fund-raising for the rebuilding seemed unnecessary – it was hard to get across the need for improvements to the building. Also, he says, 'I found out that you couldn't really succeed in raising money in America unless you had a professional fund-raiser. I had to recommend that we did this, but it was going to be extremely expensive. Ben and Peter turned the suggestion down.'

Reiss says it was around the time of his return from America that 'the cracks began to appear' in his relationship with Britten and Pears.

> They were absolutely bowled over by the success of the Maltings, and by the fact that we were managing to rebuild it in a year, and they thought, 'Everything's going to come our way.' And I'd say, 'I expect it will, Ben, but perhaps not tomorrow.' But he would say to me: 'I'm not going to live for ever; we must get on with it.'

Reiss explains that Britten's plan for the Maltings was now far grander than mere rebuilding of the concert-hall with improvements: 'He wanted a full-scale arts centre, a total thing – we were talking about having a little opera house (not a big one) as well. And we were talking about performances all the year round, about a major art gallery – a total arts centre.' A music school for young performers, later to become a feature of the Maltings, was 'hardly mentioned.' at this stage, says Reiss. 'We would have hostels, where people could come and stay, and yes, there would be a school, but only as one aspect.' (Yet in 1953 Britten told

Imogen Holst she must be 'Principal of our new school of music when we get it', and said that it '*must* be residential and *needn't* be in London – in fact, it would be an advantage for it *not* to be'.)

In the spring of 1970, shortly before the rebuilding of the concert-hall was completed, Arup Associates issued a document entitled 'Snape: The Next Twenty-Five Years', being 'a synopsis' of a full-scale report on the further development of the Maltings then being written for the Aldeburgh Festival committee. This stated:

> As the use of the Snape Maltings has grown, the Artistic Directors believe that Snape provides an ideal location for a more comprehensive arts centre. In addition to music and opera, they would like to extend facilities for other performing arts, such as dance and drama. Snape should also become a place for the study of music and a workshop for the visual arts.
>
> The needs are for rehearsal rooms, a music library, an art gallery, artists' studios, permanent exhibition space and scenery workshops.

Derek Sugden of Arup Associates says that the library was to house Imogen Holst's father's books, and that the art gallery would be 'a home for Sidney Nolan's paintings'. No opera house was included in the plans printed with the synopsis, but Sugden says that 'Britten did go on talking about it – I think there was a lot of pressure to have one from Colin Graham and others. I thought you could fit a small auditorium in, a three-to-four hundred seater.' He comments of the plan as a whole: 'Ben was wanting to leave something like Bayreuth.' Stephen Reiss agrees: 'That's right – totally and completely.'

Reiss's previous successes made Britten believe he could do anything. 'Everything had gone my way, and he thought I was a bit of a wizard, I suppose. He compared me to Diaghilev, which was totally inappropriate, because I'm nothing like that.' Reiss told Britten he could not see how the grand Maltings plan would be possible 'unless it was a national decision, totally at Government level, that they would allocate money. It wasn't a thing we could do by fund-raising.' Consequently in October 1969, while rebuilding was going on at the Maltings, Britten and Reiss went to see Lord Goodman, then chairman of the Arts Council. Reiss recalls that 'Goodman spread before us the most wonderful scenario: Ben would give all his assets to the nation and, in return, the nation would see that he got everything he wanted.' By 'assets', Reiss means copyrights and royalties. He adds that 'Goodman made the parallel that this had happened in some way over Henry Moore – he'd bequeathed his works and everything. And Ben said, "Yes, I'll do it."' Asked in 1991 what he remembered of the discussions, Lord Goodman replied: 'I have only the most sketchy recollection, although I believe that the intention was that – on receiving an assignment of the royalties on his music – the Arts Council would have been willing to give full support.'

As they left Goodman's office, Reiss saw that Britten was 'absolutely bowled over' by the idea, but 'I'm afraid I was cautious.' Reiss suspected that the Arts Council would not be in a position to meet the commitment. 'What Goodman meant was, "This is what *ought* to happen," but Ben thought it *would* happen. And he felt that I was dragging my feet.' Setting out for London that day, Reiss had left his wallet behind, and had had to borrow five pounds from Britten for his rail ticket. 'The next day – back in Aldeburgh – Ben sent round his secretary to collect that £5. Considering all we had done together for sixteen years, he would never have dreamt of doing such a thing had he not been exceedingly angry at my reaction to the Goodman proposal.'

Simultaneously, there came what Reiss calls a 'débâcle' over a woman working in the Festival office. Believing that Reiss needed more help, Britten had persuaded him to take on this person, who had written to the Red House offering her services. 'Ben introduced her', says Reiss, 'although he'd never met her – he'd only had this long letter.' Keith Cable, a member of an old Aldeburgh sea-going family who had worked part-time for the festival since his teens, calls her 'the kind of lady that put on gloves to turn on the television', and Reiss describes her as

> quite frankly a disaster. She was with us for the year the Maltings burnt down. Unknown to me, because she knew her days were numbered, she went and complained about me to Ben, and that was pretty unpleasant, because Ben didn't see that she was hopeless – she presented herself quite well. But nobody liked her.

Just as Britten was in disagreement with Reiss over the Goodman plan, she handed in her resignation. Britten wrote to Reiss, calling her departure 'a bomb-shell', and adding: 'I think to have lost a really first-class professional at the time when we are planning great developments at the Maltings is a real tragedy.'

By January 1971 Arup Associates had issued detailed plans for the new development. In May the *Daily Telegraph* reported that activities at the new arts centre 'would be spread round the year'. Reiss still felt that 'Ben was trying to rush fences,' and he remarked on this to one of Britten's advisers, adding

'On no account must you say anything of what I'm telling you to Ben and Peter', because I knew that the one thing Ben could not tolerate above all else was tittle-tattle behind his back. Then things became very frigid with the Red House, and I really didn't know why. And then I discovered that this person had gone straight to tell Ben and Peter.

Reiss adds that Fidelity Cranbrook, who agreed with him about the Goodman proposal,

slightly fell into the same trap. She meant well, but she said to them, 'You're giving Stephen a bit of a tough time,' and that was a terrible mistake, because again it meant I had been talking behind their backs. And also Ben was so sharp, so cunning, that he would cross-question quick as lightning, and would get out of people things they had never meant to say, even things they didn't honestly mean. The net result was that I just got more and more unpopular with them. I just couldn't do right.

By now it was becoming apparent to others that Britten had lost confidence in Reiss. 'Stephen was a terrific friend of mine,' says Keith Grant, 'and it was very, very painful to see him falling from favour the way he did, and to feel unable to help. But it's like when you see a marriage falling apart, and you know both people very well, and you can't actually do anything.' Charles Gifford suggested to Britten that he was treating Reiss unfairly, and had this reply:

we really are not 'gunning' for Stephen, but are worried that his curious methods and general over-work are causing some matters to be mismanaged or overlooked . . . I am sure a tactful word from you will readily find out what the situation is & put our minds at rest. And I am sure you can do it without lessening Sephen's confidence, particularly in relation to us.

For a while things quietened down, but then came the affair of the Maltings caretaker. 'Arising from the fire,' says Reiss,

we decided that we had to have a full-time caretaker at the Maltings, and Ben and Peter were very keen that I shouldn't engage the person myself, but it ought to be a collaborative effort, a collective decision. Anyway we engaged this chap before reopening in 1970. He was an absolute disaster, but he had this very, very beautiful son, who was athletic to boot – he was practically an England international. I think he was more or less the prototype for the boy in *Death in Venice*. Ben and Peter were crazy about him.

Reiss adds that the caretaker and his wife were 'obviously thrilled' by Britten and Pears's interest in their son, who acted as driver for them. Rosamund Strode says that the boy had 'film-star looks' but was 'dumb'. Fidelity Cranbrook describes him as 'this pretty boy of seventeen' and calls Britten and Pears's interest in him 'so blatant'.

Reiss has the impression that Britten was under some tension sexually:

> I remember one day Ben said to me (we were walking together), à propos of nothing in particular, that he envied the chickens – or some animal or other – because if they felt like it, they could do it. I don't remember exactly how he put it, but that was what he meant. And he was a person who was, I would say, very highly sexed. Probably like most outstandingly positive and creative people, he had a very, very strong urge that way. But he was also, I think, highly controlled, and held himself in check, and didn't do it.

Richard Butt wonders whether Britten's habit of dismissing people from his favour had something to do with the sexual tension which Reiss detected: 'Maybe the kind of frustration which might well have been there because of that has a great deal to do with everything else – a lack of total personal fulfilment which seeped into other things.'

By April 1971, Reiss was telling Britten and Pears that the caretaker would have to go.

> And it was particularly serious because we were building a beautiful caretaker's flat at the Maltings. But they would not talk about it. And I could not talk to them like I used to; it was quite impossible, Anyway, when the 1971 Festival finished they pushed off to Horham. I checked with every single person apart from them whether people agreed with me that we'd got to give the man the sack. And they all agreed.

Reiss saw the caretaker and persuaded him to resign. On 6 July he wrote to Britten:

> I did not dismiss him; I simply said that I was bound to tell him of the report that I was going to make. Not unnaturally he felt that it was going to be impossible to continue under these conditions . . . I do hope you will forgive me, if what I have done has upset you.
>
> Yours,
> Stephen.

By the time he received this letter, Britten had already heard the news from the caretaker himself, who was living not far from Horham. 'Ben and Peter came back to Aldeburgh in a complete storm,' says Reiss,

and said to Fidelity, more or less, 'We're going to pull out of the
Festival – we're not going to go on. We're not totally resigning, but all
but resigning' – I think it was that they wouldn't be artistic directors
any more. And it was quite obvious that they were saying it was either
them or me. And I said, well, in that case it obviously means that I've
got to resign.

In fact Britten only threatened to resign from the Festival management
committee. A letter from him to Fidelity Cranbrook on 8 July 1971,
which makes no mention of Pears, says he no longer has 'the time and
energy' to participate in it, but indicates that he will continue as an
artistic director. It may be that Reiss's recollection is wrong, and that his
resignation was not brought about by this comparatively small matter
but by a confrontation between him and Britten which Fidelity Cranbrook vividly recalls.

Reiss says of Britten's habit of getting others to do the dismissals:

> Though he did mind about causing pain to the person concerned, he
> didn't want the unpleasantness of a calm confrontation – actually to
> go calmly to someone and say, 'Please understand.' But he could do it
> on the spur of the moment if something happened which made him
> lose control of himself.

This is what now occurred. Fidelity Cranbrook describes Britten, 'quite
white in the face', attacking Reiss verbally in the drawing-room at the
Red House: 'It was like watching a cowering animal being whipped.'
Asked what Pears was doing meanwhile, she replies: 'Oh, he just sat
there, silent.'

Reiss himself only has a 'misty' memory of the occasion, though he
says: 'I know this, that if it had been in Elizabethan times, he would quite
happily have had me murdered. I'm not joking. When he was angry, it
really was anger.' Yet he denies that Britten was sadistic: 'Yes, he could
be dreadfully cruel, and he knew exactly how to make it hurt. But I still
don't think he was a sadist, which I take to mean getting pleasure from
seeing someone suffer.' Fidelity Cranbrook simply says: 'Cruel? Of
course he was.'

She describes the end of Britten's tirade: 'Stephen wasn't told, "Get
out" – he was told how *hopeless* he had been. Finally he retreated, and I
had this ghastly feeling, "What do I do now? Do I walk out after him?"
But I stayed.' Reiss sent in his resignation by letter to Fidelity Cranbrook
on 18 July, giving as his reason: 'I believe that I have lost the confidence
of Ben and Peter.' As soon as they received news that he had resigned,

Britten and Pears hurried, early in the morning, to see Charles Gifford, telling him that a terrible mistake had been made and Reiss should be asked to withdraw the resignation. Gifford said it was too late for that. Meanwhile Fidelity Cranbrook, outraged by the treatment of Reiss, was still pondering what she should do. Joyce Grenfell and her husband Reggie happened to be visiting her, and Joyce was 'dumbfounded' by what had happened. But, says Fidelity Cranbrook, 'she was a very level-headed and sophisticated person', and advised: 'I think the Festival is bigger than these personal crises.' Reggie, on the other hand, thought that Fidelity should definitely resign.

At one point she decided to go. Keith Cable recalls that she called the Festival staff to the Aldeburgh cinema (which the Festival now owned) and told them, virtually in tears, that she was resigning on account of the treatment of Reiss. It was at this juncture that a report appeared in the *Guardian*:

> The Countess of Cranbrook, who heads the Aldeburgh Festival com-
> mittee, is on the point of resigning, following the resignation last
> month of the Festival's general manager, Stephen Reiss. Reiss, whose
> job is now being advertised at 'not less than £3,000 a year', left after
> what were called 'differences of approach' ... with Benjamin Britten
> ... Others in the Aldeburgh inner circle have become involved – not
> out of any desire for a factional squabble, which everyone wants to
> avoid, but in anger at the apparent inability of those involved to patch
> things up.

Keith Grant says: 'The Stephen thing was a tremendous test of loyalties.'

According to Reiss, Britten made considerable efforts to win round the Festival staff:

> He went to Bill Ewer, who was our carpenter – an absolutely fabulous
> man – and who had a particular affection for the Jubilee Hall. And Ben
> said he was going to do a new piece specially for the hall, a new little
> opera, and he hoped that Bill would come in and help. It was all
> absolutely fictitious, but Bill lapped it up. Ben was adept at this game
> of playing people to get what he wanted.

Meanwhile Fidelity Cranbrook had been persuaded to stay on. She did so with grave doubts. 'They gave me an OBE, I suppose because I said I was resigning.'

On the day after Reiss's resignation, Britten had written to him:

My dear Stephen,

I do understand so well why you feel you must resign. This deplorable tension and lack of communication between us is really unbearable, and something had to break. The only thing I can say is that when I think back on your years in working with us here, I shall remember your warm and lovable personality and your marvellous devotion to the whole idea of the Festival and the vision of the Maltings. I shall remember your selfless work & real goodness as a man, & I shall quickly forget the unhappy incidents of the last two years. I send you & Beth, & your two dear children, warmest love & gratitude, & hope it won't be long before you feel you can meet us.

> love
> Ben

He did not send this letter until 30 July, when he enclosed with it another one:

My dear Stephen,

As you see from its date, the enclosed note is rather old! I didn't feel somehow that you would want to hear from me then. But now, when I hear from all sides how generous & marvellously helpful you are being, I feel I was stupid – so I send it, for what it's worth.

> With love & gratitude,
> Ben

'Peter wrote too,' says Reiss, 'and there was a benefit fund organized for me. Only recently I discovered that by far the largest sum was given by Peter.' Pears wrote to Peg Hesse: 'I shall definitely feel less guilty if I give a great deal more than I can afford!!'

It was now that Reiss remembered Anne Wood's warning sixteen years earlier that Britten 'devoured people and spewed out what was left and no use to him'. He was luckier than some; Lord Goodman gave him a temporary job running an arts event called Fanfare for Europe – 'I suspect he half realized he had put me in the cart,' says Reiss. He then spent several years as manager of the London Symphony Orchestra. Today he runs his own art gallery in Norwich. Looking back on his Festival years he writes that he has 'never seen a lot wrong' with Britten's treatment of himself and others. 'To give as much as he gave, there had to be a lot of taking, and if one was lucky enough to be able to contribute, this was more than reward enough. My only regrets are that he was sometimes misled. In many ways he was extraordinarily naïve and gullible.' Reiss continued to live in Aldeburgh, but 'I never saw Ben again. That is, I may have seen him in the distance, but we never met.'

*

'That was the Stephen Reiss year,' says Susan Hill of 1971. As a visitor to Aldeburgh she noticed how the town regarded Britten as 'very much "ours"', and was quick to smooth over the cracks made by the Reiss affair. 'But the one area where I felt there was genuine unhappiness, an area that was very difficult, was Viola Tunnard.'

Three years younger than Britten, Viola Tunnard had been a busy accompanist and *répétiteur*, a devoted member of Britten's team during the sixties. She played duets with him in Festival concerts and gave him enormous help with the church parables. Keith Grant describes her work with the EOG:

> The best title she ever got out of us was Chief of Music Staff, but that does her less than credit, because she was really in effect musical director, reporting directly to Ben, for a lot of time – Meredith Davies didn't last that long as musical director, and we had Jimmy Loughran for a *very* short time. Steuart Bedford eventually haled up over the horizon around 1970, but Viola really was the custodian of the standard for a long time. She was a particular friend of mine.

Robert Tear calls her 'a great musician – she wasn't a very great player as such, but she had wonderful musical insight. I learnt rather a lot from her, when I come to think of it.'

Susan Hill got to know her in 1971, not long after her lunch at the Red House:

> I met Viola at the Red Studio [Mary Potter's house in the Red House garden], where Mary had asked me to a drink to meet her and the Cowans, with whom she was living. Mary explained that she had this terrible illness. At that stage, she still had the use of her hands, but she was no longer able to walk. My overwhelming impression was of this incredibly sweet person, this extraordinary luminous quality which sometimes comes over people with terrible illnesses – concentrating on things that she could still enjoy.

Rosamund Strode says that, during her illness, she was 'like a wise woman; you came away revitalized from seeing her'. Susan Hill agrees:

> She was the first person I'd ever met who was like that. You went in feeling sorry for Viola, and came out forgetting that you had any reason to. I didn't know what was going on, except Mary saying to me

warningly, 'Don't talk about Ben.' I then got bits of the story, mostly from Gordon Crosse, who went to see Viola rather a lot. And this was the first inkling I had – apart from the Stephen Reiss business, which was still happening and which for all I knew was just a disagreement on professional grounds – that there was this side to Ben.

Jean Cowan, who with her husband Christopher gave Viola Tunnard a home during her illness, in a tiny fisherman's cottage in the garden of their home on the Aldeburgh sea-front, says that Viola had been working on the television recording of *Peter Grimes* during February 1969 when she fell on the ice. She felt worried that it had happened because something was wrong with her legs, and she was soon limping badly, but she put it down to the fall and seems not to have consulted a doctor. In that year's Festival she played piano duets with Britten and was *répétiteur* for *Idomeneo*, but (says Susan Hill) 'it was a bit like Jacqueline du Pré – she didn't know what was happening, and she began to get numb in the fingers, and couldn't play properly'. Keith Grant witnessed Britten's behaviour to her:

> She was a very stoical person, not given to confiding in people at all about aches and pains, so Ben is entirely to be forgiven for the fact that he had no idea that she was in any difficulty whatsoever. But what he did have an idea of was that she was not delivering musically. And, because she wasn't prepared to make the excuse of failing health or feeling weak, he judged her – as he tended to judge everybody – by the most exacting standard, and got fiercer and fiercer with her.

Robert Tear recalls Britten snapping at her, during rehearsals of *Idomeneo* (a few days before the Maltings fire), 'For God's sake, Viola, what's the matter? What *is* the matter with you?' Tear says he 'saw her in tears when he snapped at her'.

According to Tear, she offered to step down from playing the harpsichord in performances of *Idomeneo*, and Britten's reply was: 'You'd better stay, we've tried everybody else and no one is free.' Tear cites this as an example of Britten's brutality, and remarks: 'She could see nothing but glory in Ben, and it was all the more galling when one saw somebody so doglike in their obedience and love getting smashed in such an absolutely brutal way.' However, Keith Grant emphasizes that 'Viola was a very difficult person herself. She was quite capable of making remarks, in the days of her best health, to the effect that "I don't want to do this . . ." Viola was constantly going on about how she didn't want to do this and that – read Joyce Grenfell's biography.' Viola Tunnard had been Joyce Grenfell's accompanist on service tours during the war, and

Joyce had found 'Darling Vole' lovable but unpredictable and difficult. Heather Harper says that if you invited Viola to dinner she might fail to arrive and then be found wandering in the street, too shy to ring the bell. Keith Grant believes that Britten's rejoinder to her offer to step down was 'that of someone who knew her only too well, and was not going to stand any of that nonsense'. He allows, though, that it was 'a very difficult test of loyalty when Viola appeared to be coming under the lash in the *Idomeneo* rehearsals'.

During the autumn of 1969 she went on trying to work, living with a friend in London and struggling to play at the BBC and Covent Garden. After a few months it appeared that something was going seriously wrong with her body. The eventual diagnosis was the rare, incurable and fatal Motor Neurone Disease. In March 1970 Britten wrote to Rosamund Strode on the subject of a planned concert in that year's Festival: 'We'd like to ask Viola to do the other piano . . . I think she'll be honest & say if she can't, but we know it would help her to be asked.' Unfortunately it was now too late for such gestures. Jean Cowan guesses that this was Britten 'feeling remorseful', and Keith Grant knows that he felt guilty: 'He told me himself that it was agony when he realized that he'd been tough with her, in rehearsals, in front of people, and she was struggling in this way. It sort of wasn't his fault, it really wasn't. But a lot of people would have thought it was culpable of him to be so demanding.'

During 1971 Viola Tunnard was brought down from London by Janet Baker and her husband, and moved into the Cowans' cottage, where she remained until her death. Jean Cowan says that Britten 'didn't visit her for a long time, and all her chums were very bitter about this'. Indeed the story got around that he never visited her. 'But one day,' continues Jean Cowan,

> Rosamund rang and said, 'Ben and Peter would like to come and see Viola this afternoon.' And I called through the door. 'Ben and Peter want to come to tea.' And she said, 'No!' But I came back and said to Rosamund, 'Yes, she'd love it.' And after that they came about four or five times. And when they were doing *Noye's Fludde* I took her in her wheelchair, and Ben came up and talked to her, and then said to someone who was with him, 'This is Viola, and she's living in one of the most adorable cottages in Aldeburgh.' She didn't introduce me, so when I got her home I said, 'You *are* a pig – I really felt so foolish sitting there.' And she burst into tears and said, 'How do you think *I* felt, talking to Ben?'

8: Rather a long business

'Aldeburgh has been ... fairly traumatic,' Britten wrote to Donald and Kathleen Mitchell on 18 July 1971, the day Reiss sent his resignation letter.

> Meetings, difficult ones, followed by a resignation, which has been, naturally, accepted. So we are now in the fire, which although a bit of a shock, seems less confusing and frustrating than the frying-pan was. We are surrounded, we feel, by good keen people, & it is wonderful to have Sue Phipps down here with us. I am writing this scribble in the garden at Horham, whence we have fled for a few hours' peace. But I am sure in the end it will have been the right thing to do.

And to Keith Grant on 26 July: 'It has been a most worrying and frustrating couple of weeks, but I think we are coming out into the clear now – except of course that there must be big meetings to decide about the Festival's administrative future.'

The man who shortly afterwards was chosen to be Reiss's successor was William Servaes, a former naval officer who had worked as a shipping executive and as administrator in a prominent London architectural firm. He and his wife Pat, a member of the wealthy Vestey family, lived in the Old Rectory at Orford, where Britten and Pears frequently parked their car during performances in Orford Church. Colin Graham suggested him as a replacement for Reiss. Servaes says that when he arrived in the job 'nobody was talking to Ben and Peter, and they weren't talking to anybody, over the Stephen thing – it was frightful'. Keith Grant says that 'Bill Servaes was the epitome of what they had latterly wanted from Stephen, which Stephen couldn't deliver: the urbane man-about-town with lots of good connections, who would never allow himself to get bogged down in the details of running a Festival club.'

Servaes recommended that the ambitious Maltings development plans be modified: 'I said, "For God's sake, let's stick to what we know about, which is music, and keep it all within the part of the Maltings we're already leasing." And Ben thought that was a good idea.' Servaes says he 'enjoyed working for Ben more than I can tell you, and it really changed me. The marvellous thing about it was that almost anything was possible. Everybody would say, "Oh, you can't do this," and somehow we'd do it.' In a letter to Plomer, Britten described Servaes as 'fantastically good & charming'.

Servaes says he found Britten much easier to deal with when on his own than when Pears was around:

> It was an absolute routine: Peter used to come down from London, and they used to go to Horham for the weekend, and down came the Iron Curtain – you didn't know what was going on there. And on Monday, when Ben was back in Aldeburgh, I'd get a summons to the Red House, and over the weekend they'd got themselves into such a twist about who had said this and who had said that, and what so and so might think about it, and so on. It used to take me twenty minutes to sort it out with Ben, but then he'd say, 'Fine, that's okay', and we'd get on with other things. But once he and Peter got together it was awful.

Servaes believes that Pears was, if not the architect, then certainly the stirrer-up of many of the troubles: 'The only way I can explain why it was that all these heads were broken, blood flowed, was that Peter inflamed Ben. Because Ben was much too busy writing his music. And Peter had a terrific power over Ben, he really did.' Stephen Reiss disagrees:

> I'm very certain that it was Ben who made the running as far as I was concerned. I think in the early days Peter was a bit suspicious of me, but I don't think he was in any sense plotting. Ben once said to me something to the effect: 'Don't worry about Peter. It's me who actually runs the outfit.' It was Ben's anger that dominated. But I agree that Peter didn't help.

Despite the Reiss upheaval, Britten managed during July 1971 to turn his attention back to *Death in Venice*. A second draft of the scenario was worked out with Myfanwy Piper and sent to Frederick Ashton, who had agreed to choreograph the dance sequences. The plan had been to stage the opera in the Maltings in September 1972, but on 20 September 1971 Britten wrote to Ashton: 'I have sadly realised that I cannot guarantee to have the opera ready for next September. Time is too short, & I am desperately keen to make it the best thing I have ever done. We are planning therefore to do it in the Festival in June 1973.' In October, Britten, Pears and the Pipers spent eight days in Venice. Britten reported to the Mitchells that the trip had been 'fruitful (operatically) and he told the Giffords that the party had spent '3 chilly hours in a Gondola, being rowed hither & thither noting all the Gondoliers' cries (a specially selected G. who remembered all the old ones)'. Also while in Venice, Britten bought a music manuscript notebook and began to make musical sketches for the opera, a major departure from his usual method of planning everything in his head before writing a note. (He had jotted a few sketches for *Owen Wingrave*, but they covered a mere seven pages; those for *Death in Venice* eventually spread to thirty.) He may have felt that he no longer had the energy to retain all the ideas without this. He was in hospital in November, this time to have several teeth removed, because it was believed that dental infection had caused his 1968 attack of endocarditis. It is also possible that the use of the notebook reflects a loss of confidence in his usual method, conceivably as a result of his painful awareness around this time that he was going out of fashion with the younger generation.

In 1970 Donald Mitchell had begun to teach at Sussex University, first as visiting fellow and then from 1971–6 as the University's first professor of music. At Sussex, Mitchell found that, among music students,

> any mention of Britten would provoke a dismissive response: 'Old hat; we really don't want to listen to it' – or think about it, I might add. He was absolutely 'out'. In the student generation I taught, fashion had gone totally against him. The only work that seemed to retain something of a reputation was the *War Requiem*, but that had been a popular success – even among students – just before the shift in critical opinion began; perhaps, ironically, its very success helped generate the shift. And the views of my students, of course, reflected those of a whole generation of young composers, not only in England but elsewhere.

In terms of English music, Britten's reputation had been overtaken by that of Tippett. Robert Saxton, who as a child had adored Britten's music and had had a composition lesson from him, was taking music A level around 1970, and one of the set works was Tippett's Second String Quartet. Saxton says that this

> really set me alight. The rhythmic subtlety and radiant energy, combined with springing diatonic counterpoint, impressed me, as had *The*

Midsummer Marriage slightly earlier. For a time I felt a tremendous sense of liberation and joy, and this certainly caused me to puzzle over the vast gap between these two very strong personalities. At that age, I felt Britten's later pieces to be much more icy and closed in, in comparison with Tippett's warm, generous musical embrace.

Britten had always made generous acknowledgement of Tippett's status. In a 1963 interview he had listed 'Stravinsky, Shostakovich, Copland, Tippett', as the living composers he most admired, and Tippett was the dedicatee of *Curlew River*. (Tippett had dedicated his *Concerto for Orchestra* to Britten on the occasion of the latter's fiftieth birthday.) However, Donald Mitchell believes that in Britten's mind

> there lurked a real scepticism about Michael's technique. I'm sure that Ben thought that, technically speaking, means and ends in Michael's music rarely achieved the precise relationship that was his (Britten's) ideal. Everyone was much amused when Ben remarked, in a birthday tribute to Michael, 'I wish your piano parts weren't so difficult!', because it was made by a pianist for whom technical difficulties seemed not to exist. But in fact I think there was an implied and significant criticism buried in the middle of that *plaisanterie*. However, none of this should be taken to diminish the affection, respect and admiration Ben had for Michael, and especially for the works from the forties and early fifties.

Robert Tear puts it more bluntly: 'Ben being a fluent composer, without any technical problems, couldn't take Michael that seriously. And also Michael was fundamentally a mystical composer, while Ben had no idea what mysticism was. I think they had literally nothing in common.' Mitchell also imagines that the subject matter of Tippett's operas, the later ones especially, would have irritated Britten: 'a self-indulgent mix (as Ben would have seen it) of the trendy, the pretentious, and the downright woolly'. Consequently it would have been 'a painful thing' to realize that 'Michael seemed to be ascending in public esteem while he, at best, was stationary.'

Philip Ledger, who played and conducted for Britten from the mid-sixties, believes that

> Ben was concerned a little bit that perhaps his music was not seen as avant-garde enough. He once said to me, 'Perhaps I'd be a better composer if I were more avant-garde.' It was in his mind that maybe he should have been more in the mainstream of where music was at that

time. But I think he was wrong, and I think he knew in his heart he was wrong.

Asked if he was aware of his rise in popularity and Britten's decline, Tippett himself answers: 'To some degree.' He remarks of the slow increase of his reputation from the forties to the seventies:

I used to say, 'Now, why is it taking an awful long time?' The problem first was that I was regarded as a gifted amateur, not a professional. Also, if you write in one form – opera – like Ben did, it's easier to assess it. An œuvre or corpus which is very wide is really in a way more difficult. And of course there weren't performances of my work. Now, *why* there weren't I don't know. I used to get upset about it, but I never worried, because I was arrogant; I knew quite well what was going to happen in the end.

I don't mean I knew they would become critical about Ben, but they said that Rubbra was the great symphonist and would take over the Vaughan Williams mantle, and there were a whole lot of others who were supposed to be marvellous, and I knew they weren't. (I'm sorry – take that gently – perhaps I shouldn't say that, because I've never wanted to go down that kind of road.)

Irritation with Tippett may lie behind a remark in a July 1971 letter from Britten to a young composer, Ian McQueen, who had shown him his work: 'I suspect some bravura in the writing of the notes on paper, which may not always be dictated by the sound imagination. That is what I personally always demand (and where I quarrel with some of my contemporaries).' A year earlier Britten had told a *Guardian* interviewer that he 'likes to get his music "pruned and pruned and pruned" so that it says what he wants it to and no more'.

The same interviewer asked about his continuing preoccupation with 'innocence outraged', and wrote that Britten 'says that, yes, it must be so because so many people have mentioned it. He is never aware of himself thinking, "Here's a nice story about innocence destroyed again," but he supposes he does have an instinctive tug towards it.' Colin Matthews remembers

around *Death in Venice* time, Ben read out to me an article in *Opera* magazine which said, 'All Britten's operas are concerned with the loss of innocence.' And he said, 'This is absolute *rubbish*!' and picked the thing up and threw it to the other side of the room. And I've regretted ever since that I didn't have the courage to say, 'Well, what *are* they about, then?'

*

On 6 December 1971 Bill Servaes issued a press release that the new Britten opera would be based on Thomas Mann's *Death in Venice*. Word of this had already rippled around Aldeburgh, causing (according to Fidelity Cranbrook) a frisson of anxiety. In fact Britten had not yet begun in earnest on the composition sketch. Sustained work was only possible when, after Christmas, he went to stay with Peg Hesse at Wolfsgarten. 'Work progresses – (don't know how well, though),' he wrote to Pears from Germany on 20 January 1972. 'I've just got you on to the Lido!' On 24 January:

> I love you, & think about & with you all the time . . . it inspires me to work for you, & keeps me going in the moments – which I admit I do get – of rather flat homesickness, & Petersickness. Actually it *is* nice here, & at the moment I am working happily with Myfanwy – getting a lot done, & rewriting earlier bits [of the libretto] which have worried me, & over which she has been very helpful indeed . . . Tyger [Ronan Magill] has written a very mad letter . . . Charles, on the other hand, has written a sweet note saying his prep's going better, so I expect I'll take up psychiatry soon.

'Charles' was Charles Tait, son of Britten's doctor in Aldeburgh and, for several years, a pupil at Old Buckenham Hall, successor to South Lodge. (The Sewell family had established the school there after no less than three moves since Lowestoft, on account of their buildings twice being burnt down.) When he was at home in the holidays, Charles played badminton with Britten, was painted by Mary Potter, and was given the freedom of the Red House swimming-pool, where the custom of nude bathing made him a little uneasy. Britten wrote him letters mentioning progress on the opera without referring to its subject matter. From Wolfsgarten in January 1972:

> My dear Charles,
>
> I was very pleased to get your letter . . . I certainly miss you too – and our badminton . . . I am having a very quiet time here, working hard, with lots of people to look after me – cooks, maids & valets, I feel rather grand! Also I have a large bath in my bedroom . . . I upset almost half a bottle of bubble-bath stuff into the bath the other evening, & the room smelt like a chemist shop all night – & I looked rather like *you* did in your bubble-bath at the Red House: almost invisible . . .
>
> Now I've got to go back to that old opera – so lots of love old boy: write again one day
>
> Ben XXX

Charles played the trumpet. Britten bought him an instrument and wrote a short piece for him. He took him to stay at Horham, but Charles was very shy, and recalls that his silences sometimes exasperated Britten, who once burst out: 'Why don't you *say* something?' Looking back, he guesses that Britten was 'very tempted' sexually by the friendship.

Ronan Magill, 'Tyger', now aged nearly eighteen, was fully aware of the subject matter of *Death in Venice* and its implications. This young pianist, whom Britten had begun to help in 1970, had now left Ampleforth and entered the RCM, where he was winning prizes for piano and composition. From his mother's house at Saxmundham he had been writing frequently to Britten. Several of Britten's friends thought Ronan might seem tiresome to Britten, yet he replied regularly and affectionately to Ronan's letters, addressing him as 'My dear old Tyger'. On 28 January 1972, at Wolfsgarten, he drafted this answer to a letter from the boy about money worries:

> This money business has all been a bit bewildering. First you write to say in detail how you want some money, but that I mustn't tell your mother. I then say that I'm happy to give you the odd present (I do understand how expensive life is in London), but without telling your mother I can't give you anything regularly. And then you return the little present I give you, because it isn't money you want, but that you want to feel dependent on me! It is all a bit dotty, isn't it? . . .
>
> Of course there are some things for which you have come to rely on me – I try to help you as much as I can in musical things, because I want to see your gifts grow in what I think is the right way – and I try and help you a bit in life itself, & there arn't many things we don't talk about! I do this because I think you have a real gift, & you know how much you have come to mean to me . . .
>
> from
Ben XX X XX
>
> Actually I think I'm writing some rather good music???

Talking in 1991 about his friendship with Britten, Ronan Magill indicated that he felt some personal involvement with Tadzio, the boy in *Death in Venice* – and that Britten had wanted it to be more than friendship:

> I don't know quite how to say this. Britten was a homosexual; I wasn't. There was a time, when I was in Horham with him, when he wanted to, and I said, 'No.' I have to be quite honest. But that didn't mean to say there weren't moments of deep affection, on a very high level.

He took me to Horham several times. And I saw some wonderful things there. But I wouldn't call it sexual. It wasn't, it wasn't at all. I did not want that. And I knew that I was probably being very cruel. He felt very fragile, and he had an awful lot of things on his mind, and I didn't know the half of it at the time.

He probably thought I was some sort of escape, a sort of Tadzio-like youth, and I think there's certainly a relationship [to the opera] there, though it's not generally known. The theme in the opera when Tadzio is winning all the games, wanting to succeed, wanting to show how good he is, there's certainly a link there. But Tadzio – the fragility of the man, being devastated by it – that's why, whenever I hear that motif, it's with very deep emotion.

I remember holding him, and hearing his heart beat – this was in Horham. I think I was learning a piece by Brahms at the time! And I could hear his heart beat. It had a sort of hollow bang to it.

*

When Pears joined Britten at Wolfsgarten in February 1972, he made a suggestion for *Death in Venice* which Britten passed to Myfanwy Piper, who had returned to England. Britten had been intending to give the role of Apollo to a boy treble. 'I still like the idea of a boy's voice there,' he wrote, 'but Peter has had a stranger idea, but possibly a better one – why not a counter-tenor, colder, not manly or womanly, & a sound there hasn't been used before. What do you think?' Meanwhile Myfanwy Piper had suggested that the boys' beach games should be danced naked. Britten said this idea was 'excellent, & could be wonderfully beautiful, Hellenically evocative', but he added: 'There may be some objections – Fred Ashton might raise some – & I am worried lest the work might cause a certain interest that none of us really wants!' On 19 February, back in Aldeburgh, he wrote to Pears: 'I've written something this morning which I *hope* you'll like singing: I can hear you doing it most beautifully. I'm getting rather attached to Aschenbach, not surprisingly!'

He had to stop work on the opera at Easter, when he conducted the St John Passion in the Maltings. He was beginning to be worried by 'all that music to learn & prepare for the Festival' – he was to give recitals with Fischer-Dieskau and Rostropovich and to conduct a shortened version of Schumann's *Scenes from Goethe's Faust*. Rostropovich was billed to play the première of Britten's Third Cello Suite, written the previous year, but on 22 May he wrote to Britten, on a torn-out sheet from an exercise book, with no address:

To our great chagrin we learned that once again they would not allow us to come to England ... The reasons for all this are never told us. Perhaps you could manage somehow to come to our dacha this summer, if only for a week. We could go to Pushkin once again.

Ben, your suite is sheer genius. If they forbid me going abroad for a long time please give me permission to play it for the first time in Moscow ... Where genuine human love and devotion is concerned we can do without these idiotic 'permissions' and 'restrictions'.

Rostropovich knew very well why permission had been refused. In October 1970 he had written an open letter to the newspapers in defence of Alexander Solzhenitsyn, who had been attacked in the Moscow press after being awarded the Nobel Prize for Literature. Rostropovich's letter called for free speech, referred to the 'claptrap' which had been written about Prokofiev and Shostakovich when they were out of official favour, and objected to the 'absolutely incompetent' government officials who were always meddling in the arts. Soon after the letter was sent – it was never published – the authorities began to harass him, cancelling his foreign trips and Moscow engagements and restricting him to touring the provinces. He was told that he would be restored to favour if he signed a letter against Andrei Sakharov, but he refused – 'Just what kind of a person do you think Rostropovich is?'

News that he would not be coming to Aldeburgh in June 1972 only reached Britten a matter of days before the cellist's first concert was due to take place. At the chamber recital by English Chamber Orchestra and EOG principals which replaced it, Pears made an announcement expressing 'great regret' at the non-appearance of Rostropovich and begged leave of the audience to send on their behalf a telegram to him 'expressing our love and admiration for him'.

The abbreviated *Faust* was performed in the Maltings the day before Rostropovich had been scheduled to appear. Joan Chissell in *The Times* wrote that Britten had conducted an 'unflagging' performance of which the 'climaxes were roof-raising', but Fischer-Dieskau who was singing the title role noticed how exhausted he looked. He writes that Britten was 'tottering slightly during and after the performance ... His "wonderful" at the end was almost inaudible.'

Two months after the Festival, Britten conducted *Faust* again at the Maltings, this time in a complete version for a Decca recording, spread over a week. Rosamund Strode describes this as 'a total nightmare in a lot of ways – the idea had been that the Festival performance should be a run-up for the recording, but not all the same singers were available, and everything had to happen back to front and inside out'. Wilfred Wren, who sang in the chorus, calls it

> a mammoth undertaking, with the double-chorus, semi-chorus and boys' choir scattered at various points in the sloping auditorium seats, and soloists being likewise dotted about to give an enhanced stereo effect. Down at the bottom by the orchestra, Britten was a tiny figure exerting all his incredible drive and personality to reach out over the vast spaces to the furthest performers. Many sections of the music had to be repeated: a terrible weariness showed in Britten's face and stance when the disembodied voice called out flatly 'Take one hundred and thirty-four.' We felt that Britten had made a superhuman effort unbelievable in its intensity. We did not see him again in front of our Aldeburgh choir, and this recording was in fact the last time he conducted anything.

*

Colin Matthews recalls two remarks made by Britten during the rehearsals of *Faust*: 'I so envy Schumann the devotion of a woman like Clara'; and, of Fischer-Dieskau, 'I'm scared of Dieter – he's the school bully.'

He was working at top speed. The 1972 Festival was followed by a two-week holiday in the Orkneys and Shetlands with Pears, Peg Hesse and her brother, but then he was back for 'a whirl of meetings, sessions on the new op. with Myfanwy ... 3 days of Shostakovich & his sweet wife down here.' Rosamund Strode remembers Shostakovich studying the half-completed composition sketch of *Death in Venice*: 'Ben never, *never* showed an incomplete work to anyone, especially another composer, and I remember him looking very tense while Shostakovich sat alone in the Library with it. But when he eventually emerged, he was beaming!' Next in Britten's calendar came 'another week-end of meetings (great developments in the Maltings set-up) & then, thank God at last, Horham – to work – work – work!!!' But a month later, on 16 August 1972, he told Frederick Ashton: 'I have just spoken to my doctor in Aldeburgh & he wants me to go back there [from Horham] & have a check up, as it is a recurrence of an earlier trouble.'

Ian Tait had been Britten's doctor since he joined an Aldeburgh medical practice in 1960. 'When I first started to look after Ben', he writes,

> he told me that he had been diagnosed as suffering from a heart problem in his childhood, and that for some years his activities were restricted on that account. However, it seems that by the time he was at school he played sports more or less normally, and seems to have been a keen physical competitor. Certainly he enjoyed tennis when I

knew him and seemed active and fit. Nevertheless when I first examined him back in 1960 I found evidence of aortic valve disease.

The aortic valve lies between the left ventricle of the heart and the ascending aorta. The left ventricle is the main pump which ejects blood out into the aorta and round the body. The valve can be diseased in two ways. It may narrow by fusion of its cusps, or it may become incompetent because of distortion in the cusps which then allows a backflow of blood into the left ventricle after its contraction. This latter problem was the dominant situation in Ben's case. The cause is most commonly either a malformation present at birth, or the result of rheumatic heart disease. I could not gain any clear history of acute rheumatic fever in Ben's childhood so we must presume the lesion to have been congenital, I think.

Told that in 1938 a doctor had found nothing wrong with Britten's heart, Dr Tait calls this 'an incorrect diagnosis', and adds that in the Second World War 'Ben would *not* have been considered fit for military service.' Britten himself had evidently not been fooled by the 1938 diagnosis; he told Rosamund Strode: 'I've always had a wonky heart.' Mary Potter has recalled that 'when he played tennis he was always aware that a valve in his heart was troubling him. When he said he did not want to take part in the final set, he meant it.' (It has sometimes been suggested that Britten's experience of shoulder or arm pain when conducting was symptomatic of cardiac trouble, but Ian Tait writes that this was 'capsulitis, inflammation of the capsule of the shoulder – a rheumatic condition of unknown cause, thought by some to have psycho-somatic factors in the background; sometimes known as "frozen shoulder". I am sure the pain in conducting was *not* due to his heart.')

Although Britten had been dangerously ill with endocarditis in 1968, Ian Tait writes that 'from a cardiac point of view he seemed to have made an excellent recovery and there was no evidence of any further cardiac damage'. However, when he gave Britten a check-up in August 1972 Dr Tait detected signs of cardiac deterioration. 'Aortic incompetence', he explains,

> throws an increased strain on the heart's muscular work. It may cope with this quite well for many years but at some stage heart failure is likely to complicate the picture. This generally presents with a shortness of breath on exercise and a general fatigue. Pain is not generally a feature as it is with a 'heart attack' (coronary thrombosis).

Tait felt that Britten

> would need cardiac surgery at some stage, and probably quite soon. This is generally the case when the heart starts to fail as it begins to dilate and the muscle works at increasing disadvantage. The situation can be helped with drug treatment – particularly diuretics, which decrease the total body fluids and hence the volume of fluid the heart has to cope with – but this is very much a temporary solution.

He discussed the problem with Britten, who said he was 'very keen not to interrupt his work on *Death in Venice*, which he expressed as being his priority above all else. He seemed to sense that this might be his last major work.'

Donald and Kathleen Mitchell remember Britten mentioning the possibility that, if surgery was delayed, his heart might give out before the opera had been completed. The Mitchells were both

> impressed by his fortitude and the wholly rational way in which he discussed the options open to him. He talked quite calmly and dispassionately to us about the possibility of *not* having the operation, even though it had been made perfectly clear to him that following *that* path could have had only one outcome – the expectation of a very short future life.

Ian Tait writes that after further discussion

> the course of action we agreed on was that he would cut down all 'unnecessary' effort on commitments and save it all for his work on the opera. I felt that it should be possible to control his heart failure [in the meanwhile, with drugs], but we agreed that as soon as the opera was completed he should see a cardiologist with a view to assessment for surgery. Ben was unwilling to see anyone until then because he feared that he would be pressed to accept hospitalisation and perhaps surgery which would prevent his completion of the opera. In the event I think the decision to postpone second opinions was wise.

Later, Britten said he had been 'rather difficult to cope with' when the heart trouble was diagnosed.

> I remember that I wanted passionately to finish this piece [*Death in Venice*] before anything happened. For one thing, it is probably Peter's last major operatic part; for another, it was an opera I had been thinking about for a very long time, and it had already been postponed once. I had to keep going, and then, when I had finished, put myself into the doctors' hands.

In the autumn of 1971 he had written to a friend: 'Peter Pears goes on singing wonderfully, but the strain grows greater (as I find with all performing).' Some years earlier Rostropovich had made Pears promise he would found a school for singers. 'I signed a contract,' Pears recalls, 'in English, Armenian and Russian. Rostropovich simply demanded that I should start a school! Just like that! I think he expected buildings to spring up like mushrooms overnight for me to found my school in.' In contrast to the ambitious plans for the development of the Maltings, the first step towards a school was very modest, 'a little Master Class', as Pears described it in a letter. He was still studying with Lucie Manén, and it was announced that they would jointly hold a class for young professional singers at the Maltings over a weekend in September 1972.

Lay 'observers' were invited to buy tickets and attend, and among these were two schoolteachers who had become devotees of the work of Britten and Pears, Pam Wheeler and Anne Surfling. 'It was very informal,' they recall,

> like the early days of the Festival must have been – just enough people to fill the rehearsal room at the Maltings. We all had to watch a film about whales, because Lucie was convinced that everyone had got an *imposta* that must open when they sang, or otherwise the voice wouldn't carry to the back row. And a physics professor gave a lecture about the inner parts of the human head and their resonances. Among the singers were Neil Mackie and Anthony Rolfe Johnson, and Mary Clarkson, who did the Purcell *Blessed Virgin's Expostulation*. Everyone just sat together. We sat opposite to Britten, in fact. On the last evening, Peter gave a gramophone recital, and among the records was one by Grace Moore. He said, 'I don't know when she recorded this, but she died in 1947 so I think it must have been before that.' And Ben looked across the gangway at us, laughing.

Among the accompanists for the master class was the twenty-two-year-old Graham Johnson:

> I went up with Anthony Rolfe Johnson to play *Winter Words*. And I was as nervous as hell. Everybody was there, and blow me down if I didn't see Britten at the back. And Peter said, 'Now we're going to do *Winter Words*', and I looked again, and Britten had gone. I thought, 'Thank God for that,' and I played very well, because I didn't care about the rest of the audience. And we went right through it, all seven songs, working on them. And at the end I stood up, and Britten materialized from somewhere, and he said, 'Very good, my dear. You

have a marvellous link between hand and pedal. But I think you could use more left hand in the last piece' – and he suddenly became absolutely wonderful about giving me some pointers. I said, 'But you weren't there!' He said, 'I was standing behind that screen all the time, because I thought you wouldn't want me to be there.'

The weekend began with a Britten-Pears recital in the Maltings, on Friday 22 September. The programme included *Winter Words*. This was to be their last full-length recital together in Britain. The next day, sitting across the aisle from Britten, Pam Wheeler noticed how flushed he looked. A pulse was visible in his leg – 'there was a hell of a pounding going on'.

*

A month later, on 21 October, Britten wrote to Frederick Ashton that *Death in Venice*, of which the composition sketch was now nearing completion, was 'either the best or the worst music I've ever written', and said he had a 'terrible dread of playing the piece to anyone'. In November he had to record *Who Are These Children?* and *Canticle IV: Journey of the Magi* for Decca, with Pears, Shirley-Quirk, and James Bowman, who had now been enlisted to sing Apollo in the new opera. However, he handed over the conducting of a second 'Salute to Percy Grainger' LP to Steuart Bedford, whom he had also asked to conduct *Death in Venice* the following summer. Later, Britten said that he had felt 'very bad' physically around this time. 'But work is a funny thing, and while I was still busy on the opera I had good days, and forgot about my condition. But I did feel rotten, and unable to go upstairs without stopping on the way. And there is no doubt that working on such a huge score as *Death in Venice* was extremely exhausting.' Ian Tait writes: 'He was often tired but got through a great deal of work, and he responded well to medical [i.e. drug] treatment.'

The last notes of the composition sketch of the opera were written just before Christmas, and on New Year's Eve, Britten played it through to the Pipers and Colin Graham. On 7 January 1973 he and Pears began a recital tour in Germany – 'a 'flu-ridden 10 days in Bavaria – about the nastiest visit ever,' Britten told Anthony Gishford. 'Doing concerts with high temps. is not my idea of fun!' While he was away Rosamund Strode prepared manuscript paper for the writing of the full score of *Death in Venice*, 'putting in all voice parts, stage directions, clefs, instrument names, bar-lines, etc.' Britten began work on it as soon as he returned. 'I've got 500 pages of the score to write by Easter!' he told his sister Barbara. The young composer Colin Matthews, who had already been making the vocal score from Britten's sketches, was enlisted to help with the orchestral writing, 'filling in some of the more routine instrumentation, or anything else Britten asked him to do', writes Rosamund Strode. 'We were all conscious of the fact that at all costs Britten's strength must be spared; it was known that he was to undergo thorough medical examination once the score was done, and the need for it was all too apparent.'

Colin Matthews says that working for Britten – even a far from well Britten – was 'like being on a production line: the speed at which he turned it out was almost faster than I could copy the vocal score and get it back to him – it was unbelievable.' Matthews says that, while he was working on it, he felt there was an autobiographical element in the opera: that it

> must have some relationship to Britten's infatuation with David Hemmings at the time of the première of *The Turn of the Screw* in Venice. I think that I was probably wrong, but at the time I couldn't comprehend what had led Ben to choose the subject, and I clearly remember that the impression I had was of Aschenbach as almost a caricature of Peter, as if the role wasn't written so much out of love for him as out of some strange desire to wound. That's a simplistic and one-sided way of looking at it, but there is a very dark side to the work that I still can't claim to understand.

One evening around this time, at a restaurant meal in London with Sidney Nolan, Pears suddenly burst out with: 'Ben is writing an evil opera, and it's killing him.'

There was a possibility that the opera might kill Pears. He looked robust, but in 1970 had been warned to take things easy because of high blood pressure. 'I *am* taking it easy,' he wrote to Peg Hesse in April that year. 'My blood-pressure *is* up a bit ... I am doing what the doctor tells me to.' Thomas Hemsley was told by Lucie Manén that 'when Ben described this big project, this big part for Peter, Lucie said, "You realize that you'll probably kill him, don't you?" And Ben said, "I can't imagine a better way for him to go."'

Hemsley also recalls an occasion in Long Melford Church – a television broadcast of the *Christmas Oratorio* – when Britten was conducting with one of his broken-off batons (Rosamund Strode says he was always shortening them, as he had during *Idomeneo*),

> and he suddenly jabbed himself with it, gouging a piece of flesh out of his hand, and it began to pour with blood. I was sitting in a pew with

Peter, waiting to sing, and Peter turned to me and whispered, 'He's a funny fellow, is Ben. He can't resist any opportunity of hurting himself!' I thought, 'You cold-blooded bastard.'

Rosamund Strode recalls that when Pears began to learn the part of Aschenbach he sometimes 'made suggestions for verbal changes which he preferred to the original words'. Myfanwy Piper says that this was 'very, very tiresome, absolutely maddening'. She remembers Pears objecting, for example, to Aschenbach having to sing 'all my art is bent' because it suggested a 'bent policeman' (or more probably, homosexual). John Evans thinks that Pears saved the libretto from several gaffes of this sort.

*

In mid-March 1973, with the orchestral score of *Death in Venice* finished, Britten and Pears went to Wolfsgarten to celebrate Peg Hesse's sixtieth birthday. They played Schubert piano duets but did not give a recital. The same month they also attended Marion Harewood's wedding to Jeremy Thorpe, leader of the Liberal Party. Then, on 30 March, Britten went to London to see a cardiologist.

Ian Tait had referred him to Dr Graham Hayward, a heart specialist who had been at St Bartholomew's Hospital where Tait himself had trained. Tait describes the appointment with Hayward as

quite an outing. Ben, Peter and I were driven up to Harley Street. Ben had to walk quite a way from where the car was parked, and I remember his being quite exhausted by the effort.

Dr Hayward had an excellent reputation as a sound cardiac physician, not given to chasing the latest position but an excellent opinion. In the event I think he may have been the wrong person for Ben from the personal point of view. He was rather strong meat for Ben – a rugger-playing New Zealander – and had a somewhat unbending, uncommunicative and (towards Ben) judgmental attitude, I fear. I remember feeling sad that Ben was not getting the emotional support he needed.

Hayward decided that Britten should go into hospital, 'to try the effect of "energetic" medical [i.e. drug] treatment', writes Ian Tait. On 6 April he was admitted to the London Clinic, but Tait writes that 'no significant improvement in cardiac function' resulted from this intensive medication, and after ten days he was transferred to the National Heart Hospital, where he underwent cardiac catheterization to determine the exact form of surgery he would have to undergo. The catheterization was performed by Dr Hayward's senior registrar at the hospital, Dr Michael Petch, who writes that he 'knew from then onwards that the heart would not make a good functional recovery, even with a successful valve replacement'; on the other hand without the operation 'he would have died quite quickly from heart failure'. It was decided to go ahead with a valve replacement, using a homograft (human tissue) valve rather than a mechanical one. Dr Petch writes that Donald Ross, the leading heart surgeon who was to perform the operation, 'was obtaining outstanding results in certain cases with aortic homografts so it did seem to be the right decision at the time. The operation [to fit a homograft] may take longer [than one to fit a mechanical valve] but in Donald Ross's hands this was not regarded as a significant increase in risk by any of Britten's medical attendants.'

Britten was allowed to return to Aldeburgh for the final week of April. On 2 May he was re-admitted to the London Clinic to await the operation. Although he was bitterly disappointed to miss the rehearsals and Aldeburgh Festival performances of *Death in Venice* his letters were strikingly cheerful. He told the staff at Decca that he was about to have

> a severe operation (replacing a valve in my heart), out of action all the summer, and then I should be as good as new – even conducting! It is of course a huge bore about this summer – missing the production of *Owen Wingrave* [at Covent Garden] and *Death in Venice* and a whole Festival. But as I said the medical chaps are optimistic about the future.

To William Plomer he observed that 'it *is* cheering to realise that 10 years ago they couldn't do these fabulous things', and to Bettina Ehrlich, widow of Georg: 'It is going to be rather a long business, I fear, but it's got to be done. I rather fear for those operas standing on their own rather wobbley legs!'

*

Rita Thomson, who had trained in nursing in her native Scotland and was in her late thirties, was the senior sister on intensive care (surgical) at the National Heart Hospital in Westmoreland Street, near Harley Street. A few days before Britten was due to be admitted for his operation she 'kept getting calls from people saying, "Now, you know Benjamin Britten's coming", and this and that, and I got absolutely fed up with it, because I wasn't that aware of who he was. I knew he was a composer, but I'd never been interested in his music.' For some while in her spare time she had been attending Royal Festival Hall concerts and going to Covent Garden. 'I can remember thinking that I was getting rather old for all those hospital parties. But if I was going to book for something, I'd look down the lists and think, "Oh, Britten, that's modern, I won't enjoy it." I went to things I thought I'd like, such as Mozart.'

When Britten arrived on the ward Rita Thomson thought him 'so nice, and he was obviously nervous and reserved'. Pears and Sue Phipps were with him when he was admitted, but he was soon left by himself, in a bed at the end of the open ward – there were no private rooms in the hospital, so that patients could be constantly under observation. Sister Thomson always made a point of welcoming new arrivals, and she went and chatted with him. 'He always remembered that I said to him, "Don't worry about this, we'll see it through together." He always used to say that, when I was with him towards the end – "We said we'd see it through together."'

The operation took place on Monday 7 May, lasting about six hours. Rita Thomson explains that everything did not go smoothly:

One of the problems was – which sometimes used to happen – that when they disconnected all the bypass machines and everything, the heart took a long time to restart. But that wasn't the real trouble.

Sometimes when they're cutting out the old valve, the very, very minutest particle of calcium gets through the filters and into the bloodstream, and lodges in the brain. And that may have been what happened to him. Because after he came round from his anaesthetic, he hadn't had a stroke – he wasn't paralysed down one side or anything – but he had a weakness there, a sort of spatial thing, that with his right hand he couldn't find where his mouth was. A tiny speck of calcium may have lodged there, and done some damage.

Dr Michael Petch writes of this:

The operation was complicated by a small stroke, not in the traditional sense that he might have been paralysed on one side of his body, but in a more subtle form which led him to have in-coordination of his right hand. This must have been devastating; it was a consequence of the surgery but the exact mechanism will always be speculative. A possible explanation would be that certain bits of debris from the valve entered the circulation and one lodged in his brain.

Donald Mitchell came to see Britten the day after the operation:

Peter prepared me for the visit by telling me that he'd had a slight stroke. And I observed when he was sitting up out of bed, and having his tea – dutifully eating the brown bread and butter – the difficulty he had in raising his right hand. But no one at that stage seemed to be too worried about it. It was something that could happen in major surgery of this kind, and would correct itself.

*

Pears could not spend much time at Britten's bedside because he was appearing in *Owen Wingrave*. The opera opened at Covent Garden three days after the operation, produced by Colin Graham and conducted by Steuart Bedford, with Janice Chapham taking over from Jennifer Vyvyan as Mrs Julian, but the cast otherwise unchanged. The production was only a modest success with critics and public, but Colin Graham writes: 'The same year, I did the USA premiere at Santa Fé. How I wish Ben had been there: the public reaction – so much closer to Vietnam than we Brits were – was *tremendous*. People stood up and cheered in the middle of scenes when the anti-glory-of-war sentiments were expressed!'

After a week in the National Heart Hospital, Britten was moved back to the London Clinic. 'He was still ill, really,' says Rita Thomson,

> and he needed more tender loving care than they would be giving him at the London Clinic, where he'd be in a room by himself, and it would be very lonely for someone who was a bit nervous and frightened. So when he was going – he was leaving the ward on a trolley, and going in an ambulance – and he said to me, 'Please come and see me', I said, 'Oh yes, I will, I'll come soon.' 'Come tonight,' he said.

She went, and found him 'very frightened and very unhappy'. Although friends were constantly visiting, he was essentially on his own in the private room, and Sue Phipps observes that he had never been able to cope with illness alone: 'He was a very peculiar kind of patient. He really didn't take part in his own recovery; he was totally passive about it, very happy to do everything he was told, just leaving himself in the hands of the doctors. But he was at one remove from it; there didn't seem to be any fight in him.'

Rita Thomson says that at the London Clinic he was being given food quite unsuited to a patient having difficulties with his right hand. 'One evening when I was there, they brought in his dinner, and it was in silver dishes on a big tray. He wasn't really able to manoeuvre that, and I opened it up, and it was a big thick steak. Now, he wouldn't have eaten that if he was on top form.' She confirms Sue Phipps's observation: 'He was completely dependent. Some people, when they're in hospital, are very much in charge of themselves. But he was so ready to do just what he was told. And he was the sort of person that you'd want to be extra comforting towards, because he was terribly vulnerable.'

He was now becoming anxious about his lack of control of his right arm. He asked that a clavichord which Pears had given him some years earlier should be brought to the London Clinic from the Red House. It arrived, and Rita Thomson listened while he played it with his right hand. 'To me, it sounded as if he were doing wonderfully, but to him it wasn't right.'

She gathered that

> he was having a private nurse when he came home – Rosamund had managed to arrange one for the Monday. But then they said he could go home on the Friday, but they hadn't got a nurse, and he had nobody to take him home. So I said I would try and get an agency nurse who would travel with him and stay the weekend, until this other nurse came on the Monday. I tried to get one, and couldn't, and as it happened I had that weekend off, and I just said, 'Well, I'll come home with you for the weekend.'

Pears reported to Anthony Gishford: 'Ben is off to Suffolk tomorrow (Friday), with a Sister from the Heart Hospital, with whom he has fallen in love, and she with him. I can easily understand these Nursing Romances – Gratitude to these angelic beings knows no bounds.' He added that he was 'deep in the Venetian lagoon just now, desperately memorizing' (for *Death in Venice*), and reported of Britten's health: 'His right arm and leg are still far from perfect functioning but they are better – and we are told everything will be alright.'

Rita Thomson says the drive back to Suffolk took 'a tremendous lot' out of Britten,

> and he was very exhausted when we arrived (a chap called Leo who worked for a garage in Saxmundham drove us). He was really quite ill. And our ward was being closed for some repair work the following week, and when it came near the Monday he didn't want me to go, because he was frightened of the new nurse coming, who wouldn't know him. So I stayed on for a few more days. And during that week, Peter was rehearsing *Death in Venice* at the Maltings, and I went to the dress rehearsal.

*

Apart from the death of Aschenbach, *Death in Venice* is essentially a true story. In May 1911 Thomas Mann went to stay at the Hôtel des Bains on the Lido with his wife and brother, and his attention was gripped by a beautiful Polish boy who was there with his family. In a 1965 Munich newspaper article, one Wladyslaw Moes, known in childhood as Wladzio or Adzio, identified himself as that boy.

Mann's widow told Donald Mitchell that everything had happened as in the story, except that her husband had only pursued the boy around Venice in his imagination, not in reality. Mann did not regard himself as homosexual, though *Tonio Kröger* (1903) is partly based on his memories of falling in love with another boy in school-days. In a letter, he emphasized that *Death in Venice* is not a narrative about pederasty:

> what I originally wanted to deal with was not anything homoerotic at all. It was the story – seen grotesquely – of the aged Goethe and that little girl in Marienbad whom he was absolutely determined to marry ... Passion as confusion and as a stripping of dignity was really the subject of my tale.

It is also the subject of Britten's opera.

Given that the opera is about a man's response to falling in love with a boy, *Death in Venice* might appear to be a re-run of Britten's corruption-of-innocence theme from the point of view of the corrupter. But the music makes it absolutely clear that this is not so. It is not Aschenbach but Tadzio whom Britten endows with the Balinese sounds which identify him as a citizen of that seductive magic world from which Quint and Oberon also come. In contrast, Aschenbach's wide-ranging musical vocabulary shows that he belongs to the 'real' world, like Miles and Bottom, and is not the seducer but the seduced. It is he whose purity is ravished and corrupted, and who is ultimately destroyed.

Joan Cross, asked for her opinion of the opera, comments sardonically: 'Preaching to the converted.' Similarly Robert Tear, who has himself sung Aschenbach, regards it as a treatise about Britten's sexuality, and believes that it fails to tackle its subject adequately: 'Musically, it's a masterpiece. But there's a cop-out. It mustn't be called sexual lust. It's Beauty, or it's Greek. And that's a cop-out.'

If the opera's theme were simply the nature of Aschenbach's feelings for Tadzio, Tear would be right, for *Death in Venice* conveys less sense of sexuality than *The Turn of the Screw*, *Billy Budd* or even *Peter Grimes*. But if Britten had believed this to be its subject, he would hardly have remarked, as he did, to Donald Mitchell: '*Death in Venice* is everything that Peter and I have stood for.' Mitchell comments: 'I have often wondered since whether in saying that he was not just referring to the opera's frank avowal of his own Tadzio-oriented homosexuality but also to the obligatory consequential constraints, the absence of which ... was ultimately Aschenbach's undoing.' This suggests that *Death in Venice* is not, as Joan Cross asserts, a celebration of paedophilia intended for the

delight of fellow initiates, but the very opposite: an anguished autobiography by Britten, an account of the tension and guilt he had experienced because of his feelings for boys; also an *apologia pro vita sua*
which answers those who, like the malevolent painter at Cliveden, had
assumed the worst of him.

*

In adapting Mann's novella, Britten and Myfanwy Piper wisely decided
to combine as roles for a single performer – in the first production, John
Shirley-Quirk – the various sinister persons who lead Aschenbach along
his downward path: the mysterious traveller in the Munich cemetery, the
rouged old fop who teases him on the boat, the sinister gondolier, the
hotel barber who gives him an artificially youthful appearance, and the
leader of the strolling players whom Aschenbach questions about the
cholera which is infecting Venice. (To these they added the hotel manager, who in Mann's story is a character of no special significance.) From
his description of these persons, Mann indicates that they are meant to
stand for Death, and also for the ferryman who conducts the dead across
the Styx. While retaining this symbolism in the opera – 'Who comes and
goes is my affair,' sings the Hotel Manager, acknowledging that he is
Death – these characters also have another function, clearly indicated by
the music Britten gives to two of them, the Fop and the Leader of the
Players, both of whom break into a sexually ambiguous falsetto. They
are manifestations of temptation to sexual abandon – the same singer
also takes, in the dream scene, the role of Dionysus, the god of unrestrained sexuality – and in particular the Fop is presented as an outrageous queen, all that Britten hated about flamboyant homosexuals, 'those
sort of people', as he had said to Fidelity Cranbrook.

Aschenbach's innocence, then, is doubly under attack, both from the
allure of the amoral creature that Britten has made musically out of
Tadzio (the amorality of Oberon and Puck), and from the malevolent
determination of the fallen (the Fop) to drag others down to their level of
degradation. This, one may guess, is how Britten felt in real life, under
attack both from the seductiveness of children and from the assumptions
of other homosexuals. And the opera seems to invite us to identify
Aschenbach with its composer.

Though Aschenbach is a novelist, his fiction sounds remarkably like
Britten's operas. When he declares wryly, 'I am become like one of my
early heroes, passive in the face of fate', one thinks of Grimes, Lucretia
and Billy. (These words seem to be founded on the passage in Mann's
story which describes 'The new type of hero favoured by Aschenbach',
who displays 'virginal manliness, which clenches its teeth and stands in

modest defiance of the swords and spears that pierce its side'.) In another passage, not based on anything in Mann's text, Aschenbach recalls how he 'turned away from the paradox and daring of my youth, renounced bohemianism and sympathy with the outcast soul, to concentrate on simplicity, beauty, form' – a summary of Britten's later career.

Indeed, the whole opera seems to be Britten's musical autobiography. When Aschenbach walks on the Lido beach in Act I scene 5, we seem to be hearing another Sea Interlude – albeit the warm, lazy Adriatic rather than the bitter North Sea of *Peter Grimes*. The youths on the vessel which carries Aschenbach to Venice sing a shanty that could come from *Billy Budd*: 'We'll meet in the Piazza, / The flags will be flying, / And outside San Marco / The girls we'll be eyeing.' The children's beach games are played to an echo of the whistling music in *Albert Herring*; Tadzio's music, of course, recalls Quint, Pagoda Land and *Curlew River*; there are echoes of all three church parables in the scene where Aschenbach finds Tadzio and his family at prayer in St Mark's – the overlapping plainsong of the Kyrie, interrupted by tolling bells; *Gloriana* is evoked in the choral dances towards the end of Act I; and there are even memories of *Our Hunting Fathers* in the use of the tuba to represent the plague (it has that role in 'Rats Away!' in the earlier work), and of improvised GPO Film Unit sound effects in the use of scrubbing brushes on drums to portray the ship's steam-engines on Aschenbach's voyage to Venice.

This highly coloured musical tapestry, and the cinematic speed at which the story 'dissolves' from one location to another (a technique carried over from *Owen Wingrave*), means that, despite the obsessive nature of its subject matter, *Death in Venice* is the least claustrophobic of Britten's operas. Although analysis reveals it to contain an intricate web of motivic relationships, with a major-third-versus-minor-third conflict (a favourite Britten device) at its heart, it seems to be bursting with spontaneous ideas, as if Britten, in writing more honestly about his own predicament than ever before, is at last at ease with himself.

In one instance, a musical idea was indeed spontaneous. Britten told Donald Mitchell that the theme portraying the view from Aschenbach's hotel room came to him suddenly while travelling through France with the Pipers in January 1971, and he wrote it down 'on the back of an envelope'. On the other hand Tadzio's theme, one of the most beautiful he had ever devised, was worked out mathematically. Britten explained that it 'used up the notes that had been left unused the night before' – that is, the notes not used in the chord that precedes Tadzio's first appearance (which he had written the evening before composing Tadzio's theme).

*

Although he is in a state of innocence at the opening of the opera, Aschenbach is portrayed by the music as vulnerable through having grown – as he admits in Act I scene 5 – 'dependent not upon human relationships but upon work, and again work', which Britten may have felt to be his own predicament. Mann's Aschenbach makes no such admission, though he is described as having a personality like a closed fist rather than an open hand, which would apply equally to Britten.

Peter Evans has suggested that the twelve-note music which characterizes Aschenbach at the beginning of the opera is meant to suggest that he is 'unduly intellectual' in his attitude to life, and that the formal trumpet theme which accompanies his words 'I, Aschenbach, famous as a master writer' indicates that he is 'self-consciously stiff'. This rigidity is softened when, arriving in Venice, he declares to a lilting barcarolle accompaniment, that the 'Serenissima' will 'soothe and revive' him, as he lives 'that magical life / Between the sea and the city' – symbols of the natural world and an ordered social existence. Yet he is also aware that this is 'Ambiguous Venice', an adjective taken by Piper and Britten from one of Mann's letters about Venice, 'Where water is married to stone / . . . And passion confuses the senses' – the overwhelming presence of both Sea and City can disturb the equilibrium. There is, however, no musical warning of the arrival of Tadzio, whose gamelan-style theme is suddenly heard in the midst of the hotel guests' inane multi-lingual chatter.

Aschenbach's first reaction to the boy is to indulge in what he calls 'novelist's speculations', *recitativo secco* meditations about beauty and its relationship to the artist: 'As one who strives to create beauty . . . I might have created him. Perhaps that is why I feel a father's pleasure, a father's warmth, in the contemplation of him.' ('I want to be as a father to him,' Britten had said of Roger Duncan.) Next, Aschenbach tries to sublimate his feelings for Tadzio into his art. Donald Mitchell has described this aspect of *Death in Venice* as 'the unequivocal acknowledgement [by Britten] of a principal and sometimes overriding . . . source of inspiration'. This gives rise to Act I scene 7, 'The Games of Apollo', a masque-like set of choral dances during which the chorus and countertenor voice of Apollo evoke the Platonic and Greek worship of male beauty, while Tadzio and other boys perform a Pentathlon. Colin Graham, looking back at directing the first production of the opera, says he felt that the five events of the Pentathlon were 'too many', and writes that even Frederick Ashton, choreographing this scene, 'was somewhat stumped when confronted by long-jumps and sprinting races'. Graham believes that had he been present at rehearsals Britten would have altered the scene 'drastically'. Yet its considerable length does demonstrate how important he felt this aspect of his life had been – the sublimation of erotic feeling into art.

At the conclusion of the Pentathlon, Aschenbach declares: 'The boy Tadzio shall inspire me. / His pure lines shall form my style . . .' He also tries to persuade himself that 'nothing is more natural' than wanting to 'become friends' with the boy. Here, a massively dissonant orchestral texture indicates that he does not really believe it is natural. Yet when he finally admits, 'I love you', these words are sung to a triad of E major, Aschenbach's 'own' key throughout the opera. Britten is declaring that, despite Aschenbach's sense of horror at falling in love with a boy, this *is* natural.

At the beginning of Act II, Aschenbach tries to intellectualize what has just happened to him: 'This "I love you" must be accepted; ridiculous but sacred too and no, not dishonourable even in these circumstances.' But when he hears of the cholera infection he loses grip on himself, rushing wildly about the city in pursuit of the boy, and hearing only Tadzio's music in the strains of the Piazza café band. As he watches the strolling players, the burlesque romance they perform cruelly mirrors his predica-ment – 'Dearest, my life is guided by your beauty . . . how shall I save my soul?' – while their Leader with his camp falsetto sings a nonsense song mocking the love of the old for the young, with the refrain 'How ridiculous you are!' Yet Aschenbach only realizes how far he has fallen when, in a dream, he experiences the orgasmic rites of Dionysus and, waking, has to come to terms with the lust which lies behind his passion for Tadzio: 'It is all true, it is all true. I can fall no further.'

Dramatically, he can fall further. The Hotel Barber transforms him into a painted queen like the Fop. But intellectually and musically he has, through admission of the real nature of his feelings, come to true under-standing of himself, so that – like no other character in a Britten opera – he has regained his innocence.

In the key of C major, which in Britten's music often stands for calm and purity, and to an accompaniment dominated by piano and harp (probably representing, respectively, the artist-intellectual and the emo-tional life), Aschenbach recalls Plato's dialogue between Socrates and Phaedrus on the subject of beauty, already alluded to in the Games of Apollo. Beauty, declares Socrates, leads to wisdom, but also to passion and therefore the abyss. 'Should we then reject it, Phaedrus, / . . . Seeking only form and pure detachment / Simplicity and discipline . . .?' It is the same challenge as Auden had laid before Britten: experience versus order. Socrates chooses experience, declaring that, deplorable as passion is, the abyss into which it leads is a price worth paying for knowledge and the experience of beauty; and Britten, for the first time, seems to agree. Having reached this wisdom, Aschenbach can go calmly to his death. When it comes, on the beach, it is in response to Tadzio beckoning from the margin of the sea. Aschenbach, the last of Britten's operatic victim-heroes, seems to return at the end to the natural world from which the first of them, Peter Grimes, originally emerged.

*

Colin Graham writes that during rehearsals of *Death in Venice*, Pears was 'simply amazing' to work with, 'always involved, never temperamental, punctual to the dot, a great colleague to all around him'. Graham guesses that with Britten's illness 'it was a great relief for him to have something else to concentrate on'. He calls Pears's performance 'amazing and stupendous'.

A teenager from the Royal Ballet, Robert Huguenin, was cast as Tadzio. 'People thought he was too muscular,' writes Graham, 'but he had to have *some* muscles to dance Ashton's choreography! The great thing about him, apart from his looks, was that he was totally innocent, and therefore ideal – unlike the knowing young man in Visconti's film.' Graham says that Pears quickly developed an 'infatuation' for Huguenin, and in a letter to Britten some time later when he was performing with another Tadzio, Pears observed: 'I miss Bob Huguenin *very* much. This boy ... has *not got IT* at all!! Oh dear! I wouldn't dream of looking at him for more than 5 seconds.'

Britten had planned to perform twice in the 1973 Aldeburgh Festival, playing in Schumann's Piano Quartet with the Amadeus and accompanying Pears in *Die schöne Müllerin*. In the event he was at Horham, with Nellie Hudson (who was still working part time for him) and an agency nurse, when the Festival opened on 15 June. *Death in Venice* was to receive its first performance the following evening, and he sent a note to the Maltings:

> My love and undying gratitude to the cast, orchestra and staff – not forgetting Steuart, Colin, Fred, John, Myfanwy, Charles [Knode, the costume designer],
>
> > O that I were with you all!
> >
> > Ben

Steuart Bedford explained to Alan Blyth in *The Times* that he and Britten had 'been right through the score and talked a great deal about it', but he emphasized that Britten 'usually changes many things when he sees it all unfolding before him. This time Colin Graham, who is producing, and I have had to make the decisions ourselves. It may be something of a strange experience for Britten when he does see it.' Colin Matthews had been present throughout rehearsals at Snape, and was in the audience on the first night. He says that in performance the opera

> knocked me out, because while I was slaving away on the vocal score I thought the thing was going to be something of a disaster. The vocal score looked so spare – I hadn't grasped the extraordinary quality of the sound world – and I couldn't, and still can't, take some aspects of the libretto (it just seems such a naïve way to treat Mann); and yet when it all came together it was absolutely overwhelming.

Matthews thought it remarkable that Pears could sing Aschenbach so magisterially. 'You wouldn't have believed that the voice of a few years before – Sir Philip Wingrave was almost a picture of how it had aged – could cope with such demands.'

The second performance took place on Pears's sixty-third birthday, 22 June. It was broadcast live from the Maltings, and Rosamund Strode writes that Britten found the temptation to listen too strong to resist, 'but turning on the radio at a quiet orchestral moment, he heard an inexplicable bass note which worried him very much – so he quickly switched off again'. It was the hum of electric motors turning the towers which carried John Piper's impressionistic views of Venice, but Britten was so shaken by this experience that he decided not to listen to a recording of the opera until he was stronger.

On 18 June Edward Greenfield wrote in the *Guardian*:

> Benjamin Britten, consistently perverse in his choice of opera subjects, has once again proved the impossible. Thomas Mann's *Death in Venice*, a compressed and intense story, an artist's inner monologue, lacking conversation, lacking plot, has against all the odds become a great opera. Britten has turned it into one of the richest and deepest of operatic character-studies.

In the *Observer*, Peter Heyworth asserted that Britten 'does not penetrate far into the dark side of the subject matter ... Unlike Mann, he seems to flinch before the abyss he evokes, and in the latter stages ... the music lacks ... just those dionysian qualities the story is concerned with.' But Desmond Shawe-Taylor in the *Sunday Times* perceived that the climax of Act II was not 'the Dionysiac nightmare' but the scene 'in which Aschenbach, although by now grotesquely transformed into the semblance of the painted old dandy of the earlier boat scene, sings the words of Socrates' tender dismissal of Phaedrus.' Shawe-Taylor called this 'the most moving episode of all'.

Most critics felt that the Games of Apollo were too long, but there was unanimous praise for the cast (Deanne Bergsma in the silent-but-dancing part of Tadzio's mother received particular commendation), Graham's production, Ashton's choreography, Piper's sets, Bedford's conducting, and most of all Pears's performance, which several reviewers suggested was the apotheosis of his career. Noel Goodwin wrote in *Music and Musicians*: '*Death in Venice* ... adds much to Britten's musico-dramatic achievement, and may well prove to be the gateway to an even more fruitful phase of the career.'

9: The best brought-up little boy
you could imagine

Anthony Gishford had sent congratulations on the opera, and Britten replied, apologizing for his shaky handwriting: 'I must say how glad I am that 'D in V' gave you pleasure. One always *hopes* that the last is the best, but there are always terrible doubts – especially in this case when illness played such a role.' A month later he admitted to William Plomer that he was having 'rather a dreary time with (it seems) more "downs" than "ups", although I *know* I am getting on well and able to do more & more ... writing is still (as you can see!) difficult for me.' During August 1973 he listened to a tape recording of *Death in Venice*, and on 12 September, just before the opera reopened at the Maltings for a short season, a special performance was staged for him. Rosamund Strode recalls that when it was all over

> Ben said, 'I have to meet the orchestra – I haven't seen any of them, and I must talk to them.' He saw people one by one, sitting on a conductor's stool, and they all had the notion that they'd see someone in full working order, and they all came away looking totally shattered, because it hadn't crossed their minds what an ill man this was.

On 28 September, Britten wrote to Fanny Waterman:

> It is a terribly slow business this recuperation and will be a matter, I fear, of years rather than months now, but one must be very patient ... I find writing very difficult and I am terribly inclined just to put it off! ... By the way, you would be very amused to hear me practising the piano. My exercises are still very simple but I have had to start right at the beginning again, although I can manage to play one Chopin Study very slowly!

Rita Thomson explains that, quite apart from the effect of the calcium fragment in the brain, the actual heart operation 'hadn't been a great success'. Before the operation the heart had become very enlarged because of the incompetent valve, and now it was failing to return to normal size. 'If the heart size had gone down to normal, the pumping would have been stronger and the circulation better. Instead, the whole cardiac output really wasn't very good, which meant that he was getting very swollen with fluid.' Confirming this, Ian Tait writes that

> it was evident immediately after his operation that Ben's chances of regaining his capacity for full work and musical creation were very doubtful. There was of course a very strong wish to think otherwise, and also a great wish to encourage him. And though the result of the operation was a great disappointment, I never felt able to discuss this with him openly.

Rosamund Strode remembers Pears at some point suddenly blurting out to her: 'It's no good pretending that this operation has been anything but a failure.'

In September, William Plomer died of a heart attack. 'It is an awful blow & I am still feeling rather stunned,' Britten wrote to Myfanwy Piper. At the end of month came news that Auden had died in Vienna, also of heart failure. Donald Mitchell was with Britten when he heard, 'and it was the only time I'd ever seen Ben weep'.

*

In October, Pears took him on holiday to Wales. 'Peter looks after me like a saint,' he wrote to Myfanwy Piper. However, Donald Mitchell points out that Pears, like many of Britten's friends, had always felt over the years that his illnesses tended to be psychosomatic, and this suspicion seemed to persist even after the heart operation. 'Peter, inexhaustibly encouraging and sympathetic as he was, undoubtedly believed for a time – and on occasions his impatience showed – that the painful slowness of Ben's recovery was partly at least attributable to hypochondria, best dealt with by behaving as if Ben were *not* a chronic invalid.' When Pears's car broke down during the Welsh holiday and they had to return by train, he allowed Britten to carry some of the luggage.

In the hope that it might help Britten regain his right-hand piano technique, Pat Nicholson, wife of his South Lodge school friend John Nicholson and a stalwart of the Aldeburgh Festival chorus, began to come to the Red House to play piano duets with him:

> I was somebody who, not being professional, he felt he could play with. It was mostly Mozart duets, and I remember having the gall to argue with him about how to play something. He couldn't use the

pedal, because his right side had been affected. He played the bass parts, and I played the top. He was struggling to make the right arm work. He found it very frustrating, but he didn't get cross. It was lack of power and energy – you didn't feel that his brain was affected in any way. We went on for about three months, and then it fizzled out, because he found it wasn't making any difference.

Susie Walton, a retired hospital matron who was living in Aldeburgh and sometimes helped look after Britten, 'heard him playing one day, and I said, "Oh, that was lovely." And he said, "Did you listen?" And I said, "Yes, I was just outside the door." And he said, "Dear, never listen to me again." And it was dreadful.' Rosamund Strode has 'never forgotten the awful look of despair on his face when he'd had a session trying to play with Pat, and she'd gone – this abject look of total misery'.

Yet, a few months after he had given up the duets with Pat Nicholson, Britten offered to work with Murray Perahia, who was to accompany Pears in the *Sechs Hölderlin-Fragmente*. Perahia told Alan Blyth that 'although Britten was partially paralysed in his right hand, he was able to show how he wanted the triplet figure in the second song to sound'. More remarkably, when Perahia was unable to achieve the precise effect that Britten wanted, Britten 'played right through the piece' with Pears singing. Perahia calls his playing 'amazingly beautiful'.

Death in Venice opened at Covent Garden on 18 October 1973. Britten was in the audience. Just over a month later his sixtieth birthday was marked by an Albert Hall concert conducted by André Previn, which included the *Spring Symphony* and the *Sinfonia da Requiem*. The BBC Third Programme broadcast a day-long Britten celebration, including a recording of *Death in Venice* and a production of Louis MacNeice's *The Dark Tower*, with the incidental music Britten had composed for it in 1946. His birthday presents included a colour television set from Decca, so that he could watch a lengthy tribute to him on BBC2 that night. He told them he had never before owned a television: 'I have always feared becoming enslaved, but now I think I am old enough to know better.'

Around the time of his birthday, Bill and Pat Servaes found him depressed and virtually alone one evening at the Red House. 'So Pat and I took him to the Festival club. He wouldn't be seen in public, so we went to a little room they had, and we tried to cheer him up. He was in the depths of depression, saying, "When's it all going to get better?"'

He had kept in touch with Rita Thomson – 'he used to ring me up quite a lot,' she says, 'and send little postcards' – and she came down to the Red House several times for the weekend over the winter of 1973–4.

At Easter 1974 she made another visit. 'That was when they did the *Death in Venice* recording, when he was really still quite ill. We used to go to every session at the Maltings, and listen in a dressing-room, where they'd rigged up loudspeakers.' Rosamund Strode says that Britten 'wasn't anything like fit enough' to attend the recording, 'but you couldn't keep him away. After each take, Steuart would come in, and the singers, and discuss it with him. John Shirley-Quirk said that one of his passages wasn't going right, and asked what should be done. And Ben said a half-sentence – something I didn't hear – which made the whole thing work.' Rosamund wrote to Donald Mitchell: 'I've been thankful to have Rita Thomson there . . . it's obvious that it wouldn't have been a workable affair at all without her presence.'

Rita had now 'decided I should move on from the Heart Hospital, because I'd been there for ten years'. In fact she had already left, and was doing freelance work. 'When I got to the Red House that Easter, Ben was obviously quite ill, and I think they all thought he was dying. Ian Tait asked if I could come and look after him for a while. So I said yes, and I went back to London and closed up my flat, and came back, and stayed.'

*

Rita's up-to-date experience of cardiac treatment at the Heart Hospital made her realize that Britten's medication could be improved. 'We tried to get Graham Hayward to come and see him,' she says,

> but he didn't make home visits. So Mike Petch, who was Hayward's senior registrar, came down and suggested some changes in his medication, which helped Ben get rid of the fluid. He lost about two stone, which was nearly all fluid – everybody thought he had been looking rather fat. And of course once you get rid of all that fluid it allows the heart to beat more freely. That helped him quite a lot.

His condition improved enough for him to begin work again. Rita describes his new routine:

> In the mornings he had his breakfast upstairs in bed, and then I would bath and shave him, and dress him. If he had to do it himself, he could have, but then he would have had no energy left over for anything else – he tired very easily. He'd come downstairs at about eleven, and have a beer or something, and then perhaps he'd see Rosamund and work with her, or he would work by himself until lunchtime, usually in the drawing room with a little board on his knee.

Because it tired him to raise his right hand very far, Rosamund cut his usual manuscript paper down to half size, so that only a small upward reach was necessary. She says that 'Britten felt that his writing was now unclear and difficult to read; true, it did not look quite so precise and even as before, but there was very rarely any doubt as to what a particular note might be.' In this fashion, he revised the String Quartet in D major which he had written in 1931, and which Donald Mitchell wanted to publish.

The 1974 Aldeburgh Festival was attended by Bernard Levin, who wrote in his column in *The Times*:

> The *genius loci*, Mr Benjamin Britten, has, as we know, been very ill, and has consequently written nothing lately. We nevertheless had a new work by him, in a manner of speaking; over 30 years ago he wrote a little operetta with an American setting which received a single performance at Columbia University, after which he never got around to the rewriting that he felt was necessary. But, as a kind of homage combined with a get-well card, some of the songs – slight but charming – were performed, and there was the composer to acknowledge the homage and I hope to get well.

Excerpts from *Paul Bunyan* were performed on two occasions during the Festival. The Wandsworth boys sang three of the narrator's ballad numbers, and as part of a recital in the Maltings a further eight pieces were sung by Heather Harper, Janet Baker, Pears and Shirley-Quirk, with Steuart Bedford at the piano. Pears's programme note stated that

> Recently, when pressure was put to bear on Britten to take the score out again in hopes of revising and using it, he came to the same conclusion as he had 33 years ago . . . that major re-writing was needed before publication or further production. But when I saw and heard again some of the songs which I had copied out in those old days, I persuaded the composer to let us sing them . . .

Rosamund Strode suspects that Britten could not have resurrected *Paul Bunyan* while Auden was still alive, because it would have meant working with him again. After Auden's death, 'Ben could take his own decisions'.

Following the Festival, Pears wrote to the Mitchells: 'I am now going to spend some rainy days pondering "Paul Bunyan" & going through its weaknesses (& strengths) with Ben & shaping it! For it certainly *is* worth salvaging, & it was lovely to hear & see people enjoying it.' Britten made some revisions to it while staying with the Mitchells in Sussex that summer. Donald Mitchell writes that they were 'for the most part minor adjustments and modifications of a few numbers; the omission of two numbers; and the composition of a small quantity of "new" music . . . He was always emphatic that these did not amount to a thorough-going "revised version".'

Rita Thomson says that though much of Britten's work was done in the mornings, and he would spend the afternoon resting in bed, he would try to resume after tea. 'He was always working; he worked all the time. The will to work was there. It was the physical part that wasn't so easy.' They spent a lot of time at Horham.

> When Peter wasn't at the Red House, during the week, Ben and I would go over to Horham and stay there three or four days – I would do the cooking – and then come back again. He loved Horham. He could walk round the garden and about the house without help. At the Red House he went upstairs by himself. But at Horham, after the operation, he never worked in the little studio [a small brick building in the garden where Britten had written much of *Death in Venice*] because sitting at a desk was difficult for him.

In August 1974 the *Sunday Telegraph* carried a report that 'Benjamin Britten has begun to write music again . . . he has just completed a new work . . . a long piece for voice and harp, a setting of T. S. Eliot's very early poem, "The Death of Saint Narcissus".' This was Britten's *Canticle V*, and had been finished in July. Donald Mitchell, who gave Britten the newly published collection of Eliot's juvenilia which contained this text, says that after the heart operation Britten found that Eliot was one of the few poets he could bear to read (and Haydn one of the few composers whose scores he could bear to study).

As Arnold Whittall has pointed out (in his *The Music of Britten and Tippett* (1982)), Narcissus in Eliot's poem could be Tadzio: 'He could not live men's ways, / but became a dancer before God . . . / He walked once between the sea / and the highcliffs / When the wind made him aware / of his limbs smoothly passing each other . . .' Britten remarked of the poem to Rosamund Strode: 'I haven't the remotest idea what it's about.' Nevertheless the Canticle, written for Pears and Osian Ellis, vividly follows Eliot's shifts from triumph to loss of innocence ('Then he had been a young girl / Caught in the woods / by a drunken old man') and St Sebastian-like destruction ('his flesh was in love / with the burning arrows'). Though Whittall suggests that Britten saw a correspondence between this and his own physically broken state when he wrote the Canticle, the piece contains no suggestion of self-pity.

Hearing from Eliot's widow Valerie that Britten was at work again, Ronald Duncan was 'tempted to drive straight to Aldeburgh' in the hope of renewing his friendship. Shortly afterwards he heard from Britten's accountant Leslie Periton that 'Ben had said that he wished his relations with George [Harewood] could return to normal.' A 1972 letter from Britten to Plomer mentions 'George Harewood (with whom I am now on writing terms at least)'. Rosamund Strode says: 'I do know Ben felt bad about some of the estrangements which had occurred,' and Stephen Reiss believes that Britten had always had considerable feelings of guilt about the discarded friends: 'He really did mind about that. He did have a conscience over it. He did nothing about it, but he did not enjoy the people who'd been pushed out, at all. He would dearly have liked them to come back, and to have been told, "It's all right, Ben, I don't mind at all." He really didn't like it.'

Harewood writes that he and Patricia, his second wife,

> heard from Joan Cross and Bill Servaes ... that there would be no umbrage taken if Patricia and I came to performances at Aldeburgh or the Snape Maltings, and we ventured down to see *Death in Venice* and later *Paul Bunyan* and talked to Ben for a few moments; he was already very ill and could not get about except on the arm of his nurse ... of course it was too late to renew friendship even if he had wanted to – which he never said he did – as he tired quickly, and saw only a few friends.

A few people were made welcome at the Red House. During 1974 Rostropovich and Vishnevskaya, who had now left the USSR for good, came and were 'shocked by the change in him'. But most were discouraged from coming.

Stephen Reiss, who had written to Britten, had a letter telling him 'I would love to see you some time ... but I am a hopeless invalid at the moment', and when Ronald Duncan suggested a date for a visit he received a telegram from Britten saying it would not be convenient, followed by a brief note apologizing but not offering any other date: 'I am in rather a sorry state for seeing people now-a-days. I get very tired & when I am a bit brighter I want to get on with my work.' Roger Duncan, on a visit from Canada, did come, and was made welcome:

> I was very honoured, because my father was not allowed to go and see him. And Peter picked me up and took me to the cottage that they'd bought. Ben was very poorly. And I was shocked by how old and frail he was. But he was very sweet. He was just the same person he had always been with me.

*

Throughout the summer of 1974, more than a year after the operation, he still seemed to believe he would eventually get back to normal. 'I am getting rather bored with convalescence,' he admitted in a letter, 'but I have got to be patient.' Rita Thomson says it was in the autumn that he reached a 'point of acceptance' that his condition would not improve. 'It was in November, when we were at Wolfsgarten, and Peter was in America doing *Death in Venice*.'

The Metropolitan Opera production, for which Shirley-Quirk, Bedford, Graham, Ashton and Piper were imported to New York as well as Pears, was an enormous success, though Pears wrote in his diary that, when he spoke to Britten on the telephone after the first night, Britten 'was only concerned to know how they had liked *me* – dear Ben!' There was no question of Britten crossing the Atlantic, but he and Rita Thomson were invited to Wolfsgarten by Peg Hesse as a compensation. A private hired plane direct from Suffolk was provided for the journey. Peter du Sautoy, on his way to the Frankfurt Book Fair, and his wife Mollie accompanied Britten and Rita, and Mollie recalls the plane journey as 'agonizing, because the cabin was unpressurized. We were very worried about Ben.' As to the Wolfsgarten visit, 'Peg thought we'd enjoy it,' says Rita,

> which we would have done, except for the weather. Every single day was grey and dreary, with low cloud and fog, and Ben got very, very low. He talked to me a lot about his situation and his health, and whether he was ever going to be able to conduct again, and whether I thought he'd ever be able to go to America again, and be with Peter, performing.

In a letter to his sister Beth from Wolfsgarten, Britten wrote: 'It is lovely here – but I've had a 'fluey cold & have felt lousy, & very jealous of all of them in New York for D in V. It is one of the hardest things to take. Still, I try to do a bit of work. Sorry the writing is so bad, but very difficult still.' His letters to Pears from Wolfsgarten scarcely alluded to his low spirits, and emphasized the work he was doing. 'I am making myself work like a devil (I've finished the Xmas opera schedule already).' Rosamund Strode describes this project as 'a *Noye's Fludde*, but a Christmas one, similarly based on Chester plays (bits out of them). We knew it as "a *Noye's Fludde* for Faber's". What Ben wanted to do was to provide a money-spinner for Faber Music in the way that *Noye's Fludde* had been for Boosey's.' The work was to have its first performance at Pimlico School, the London comprehensive where Kathleen Mitchell was headmistress. She came to Wolfsgarten on her way back from the New York *Death in Venice*, 'to tell him how it had gone, and we sat seriously and he got out the miracle plays text and I told him about the actual performers, and what they could play'. A letter to the Mitchells mentions '"*our*" Xmas piece: what fun that will be!'

The music for this project got no further than a few fragmentary sketches in a notebook, but Britten was able to write to Pears, while still at Wolfsgarten, that he had begun 'the Folk Song suite . . . the first pages of sketches are quite promising'. Donald Mitchell explains that Britten's *Suite on English Folk Tunes: 'A Time There Was'*, begun at Wolfsgarten that autumn and completed in composition sketch in less than a month, was partly

> a way of making a home for 'Hankin Booby', a sombre, even acrid, little piece [for wind and percussion] he wrote for the opening of the Queen Elizabeth Hall in 1967. In its solitary state there was not much of a future for it; and we often talked about the possibility of creating a context for it. The Suite solved the problem.

The *Suite*'s subtitle '*A Time There Was*' is taken from the Hardy poem which concludes *Winter Words*. The first movement, 'Cakes and Ale', seems to evoke the jollity of unfallen childhood; the bitterness of experience is suggested in 'The Bitter Withy' and 'Hankin Booby'; and then comes 'Hunt the Squirrel', one of Britten's representations of frenzied pursuit. Yet, after considerable anguish, the final movement, 'Lord Melbourne', achieves – like the end of *Death in Venice* – a calm not found in Britten's earlier music. *A Time There Was* undoubtedly reflects what Rita Thomson calls his 'point of acceptance' that autumn that his active life was over, and suggests that he had come to terms with more than the imminence of death.

*

'The Folk Song Suite . . . is just finished – good I hope,' Britten wrote to Pears on 17 November 1974. The same letter described his feelings after listening to a BBC broadcast of their last British recital, at the Maltings in September 1972. The letter began:

> My darling heart (perhaps an unfortunate phrase – but I can't use any other) I feel I must write a squiggle which I couldn't say on the telephone [to New York] without bursting into those silly tears – I do love you so terribly, not only glorious *you*, but your singing. I've just listened to a re-broadcast of Winter Words (something like Sept. '72) and honestly you are the greatest artist that ever was – every nuance, subtle & never over-done – those great words, so sad & wise, painted [?] for one, that heavenly sound you make, full but always coloured for words & music. What *have* I done to deserve such an artist and *man* to

write for? I had to switch off before the folk songs because I couldn't anything [*sic*] after – 'how long, how long' [the end of *Winter Words*]. How long? – only till Dec. 20th – I think I can *just* bear it.

> But I love you,
> I love you,
> I love you – – –
> B.

Pears's reply was sent from New York on 21 November:

My dearest darling

No one has ever ever had a lovelier letter than the one which came from you today – You say things which turn my heart over with love and pride, and I love you for every single word you write. But you know, Love is blind – and what your dear eyes do not see is that it is *you* who have given *me* everything, right from the beginning, from yourself in Grand Rapids! through Grimes & Serenade & Michelangelo & Canticles – one thing after another, right up to this great Aschenbach – I am here as your mouthpiece and I live in your music – And I can never be thankful enough to you and to Fate for all the heavenly joy we have had together for 35 years.

> My darling, I love you –
> P.

Whatever they might write to each other, their relationship had been radically altered by Britten's disability. After *Death in Venice* in New York, Pears began to be much in demand as a performer and teacher in America and Canada, and was away from Britten for very long stretches. Judging by a passage in a letter to Peg Hesse in November 1975 he seems to have been reluctant to go to the Red House: 'I find it terribly hard to judge how important Ben's ups and downs are . . . He hasn't mentioned lately my coming back for a visit and he seems to have accepted my being away until Christmas. I must say that the thought of such a visit appals me.' He did not say why, but he told the young tenor Neil Mackie, whom he was teaching: 'I've lost Ben. Rita's taken over.'

Mackie, himself Scottish, says there was a 'Scots couthiness' (cheerful informality) 'about Rita which Ben loved. Her Scottishness took him over.' Some people felt there was an element of role-playing in the relationship, with Rita as Matron, Britten the eternal schoolboy. Colin Matthews thought there was certainly 'something playful about it, as if Britten had reverted to his schoolboy days – though I don't want this to sound like a devaluation of something special.' Rita herself describes

Britten as 'the best brought-up little boy you could imagine'.

Meanwhile Pears seems to have found his own emotional consolations. Donald Mitchell recalls that

> on one of Peter's trips to New York he had got to know a handsome, *farouche* young man who in turn was clearly much attracted by Peter. How far it went, I don't know. But I remember that Kathleen and I were a bit taken aback when he turned up later, presumably at Peter's invitation, at an Aldeburgh Festival. He struck us (and perhaps not only us) as emphatically representative of that younger generation of New York gay men – jeans, leather jacket, open shirt, hairy chest: an advertisement for himself, so to say. He had lots of charm and was a talent. In other circumstances and another location, he would not have been so highly visible. But with Ben beginning to fail, and Peter much taken up with this somewhat exotic young man, I wondered what on earth was going on in Ben's mind, not to speak of the collective Aldeburgh mind, if there was such a thing. Ben, however, made no comment whatsoever to us.

Rita Thomson says that Pears had several sexual relationships around this time, and that Britten told her: 'I don't care what Peter gets up to providing I don't know about it.'

*

On 30 December 1974 *The Times* carried a lengthy report by Alan Blyth of Britten's state of health, which 'has been the subject of all kinds of rumours, most of them totally unfounded on fact'. Blyth stated, after a visit to the Red House, that

> he is neither, in his own words, 'gaga', nor, as some have suggested, fully restored to active service. His heart operation . . . and the slight stroke . . . have left him semi-invalided but . . . able to resume work over short periods . . . The stroke . . . has left him with some trouble in his right arm and leg – he describes it as having 'continuous pins and needles' – although the condition has considerably improved. 'I have now accepted the situation. It has become a *modus vivendi*. I can't look after myself. Getting about has become extremely difficult. But I can write.
>
> 'For a time after the operation I couldn't compose because I had no confidence in my powers of selection. I was worried too about my ideas. Then I suddenly got my confidence back about five months ago, and now composing has become, apart from anything else, a marvellous therapy. Now that I can write again, I have the feeling of being of some use once more . . .

-570-

'I have not had quite my old certainty. For instance I made some small cuts in *Death in Venice* . . . and then I had them restored for the New York performance . . . Writing even a bar or two is quite a sweat. Physically I find it hard to get to the top of a large score so the flutes and piccolos tend to get left out!'

Rita told Blyth: 'When he goes to the Maltings, people think that he looks great, but actually that takes an awful lot out of him. Speaking to you now, he seems well enough, but afterwards he will be very tired.' Britten himself emphasized to Blyth that

when I refuse to do this or that . . . it's simply because I am not capable of fulfilling all the things I would like to . . . So when I do say 'No' to people, I'm not trying to get out of something. If people get upset, that in turn hurts me. Then I'm depressed. As Ian [Tait] says, psychologically that seems important. Whether it is musically [and here some of the old Britten humour came back] only time will tell.

Among the requests he refused was to be interviewed for a radio programme celebrating Tippett's seventieth birthday. 'I am very sorry,' he told the producer. 'Michael is a very old friend of mine and I am second to none in admiration of his works and striking personality. All the same, my main job at the moment is to try and restore my health, and when the doctors and my nurse say no to anything, then I am afraid it is final.'

Tippett came to hear about it, and Britten wrote to him on 10 January 1975:

My dear Michael,
   It was angelic of you to write at such a busy time particularly, but I am furious that you were told about the little trouble we had over an interview for the BBC. They got me so muddled up that my doctor insisted on stopping it all. You know though how much I treasure your friendship and your wonderful music.

Much love
Ben.

Britten had initially agreed to give the interview, and had asked to be told the questions in advance – this seems to be the 'muddle' referred to.

During 1975 Sir Arthur Bliss died, and Britten was consulted by Buckingham Palace about the choice of a new Master of the Queen's Music. Donald Mitchell had a telephone call from him 'to ask me what my ideas were about it! And it was clear that Tippett was not on Ben's shortlist.' The eventual choice, Malcolm Williamson, was apparently made on Britten's recommendation – Britten thought it would break new ground to install a composer from the Commonwealth (Williamson was born in Australia). Tippett comments: 'I wouldn't have done it; I can't write occasional pieces. I haven't got the facility. What seems to have happened is that Ben and Peter felt it shouldn't be a person of my age.'

*

In May 1975, John Shirley-Quirk lent his narrow boat for Rita Thomson and Polly Phipps, stepdaughter of Sue, to take Britten and Pears for a canal holiday in the Midlands. Britten sat in the prow, well wrapped up, in one of the padded swivel-armchairs which had been bought for him to sit and work in at the Red House and Horham. The following month the Aldeburgh Festival included the first performances of *Canticle V* and the *Suite on English Folk Tunes: 'A Time There Was'*. 'With two new works by Britten in the programme,' wrote Jeremy Noble in the *Daily Telegraph*, 'Aldeburgh has seemed like itself again.' He had now completed two more, and was planning a third.

Pears had formed a madrigal group, the Wilbye Consort, named after the sixteenth-century Suffolk madrigal composer, and for them Britten had written, in January 1975, *Sacred and Profane*, a cycle of settings of English medieval lyrics which alternates devotional sentiments with worldly reflections. The musical mood recalls the *Hymn to St Cecilia*, and, in the manner in which the *Hymn* had contemplated the loss of innocence, the last song. 'A death', comes to terms with the proximity of the grave. It begins with a remorseless description of the body's symptoms when death is near, and in the penultimate line comes gruesomely face to face with the reality of being buried – 'Then rests my house upon my nose' (words taken from the modern English translation provided in the score); but Peter Evans rightly describes Britten's setting of the final words, 'For the whole world I don't care one jot', as displaying 'macabre nonchalance'.

Two months after finishing *Sacred and Profane*, Britten completed *A Birthday Hansel*, a cycle for Pears and Osian Ellis with words by Burns, commissioned by the Queen for the seventy-fifth birthday of the Queen Mother, who was now patron of the Aldeburgh Festival. The choice of Scottish words and the generally carefree atmosphere were appropriate to its dedicatee's Scottish childhood, though there may also be some reflection of what Rita Thomson had brought into Britten's life. Then, on 29 June, Britten told the Mitchells: 'I have to-day written page one of *Phaedra*!'

A highlight of the 1975 Aldeburgh Festival had been Janet Baker's singing of Berlioz's cycle *Nuits d'été*. She recalls that Britten said: '"I want to write you a piece like that." I thought, "Oh, good." And I got it well beforehand, had a lovely lot of time to study it on my own.' She describes *Phaedra* as 'passionate, passionate', and says it was 'terrific, the fact that he was in such a physical state, but there was this *feeling* going on as well'.

The libretto of *Phaedra: Dramatic cantata for mezzo-soprano and small orchestra* was drawn by Britten from Robert Lowell's *Phaedra – A Verse Translation of Racine's Phèdre* (1961), which is in heroic couplets, and which, according to George Steiner, is 'a variation on the theme of Phaedra' rather than a translation. (Britten had met Lowell in New York in 1969.) While it was probably Phaedra's insanity which appealed to the mentally unstable Lowell, Britten found in the text the terrible self-reproaches of another Aschenbach, as Phaedra faces her guilty lust for her husband's young son, her 'thick adulterous passion for this youth, / who has rejected me, and knows the truth'. The Britten libretto uses an explicitly sexual image from Lowell: 'Look, this monster, ravenous / for her execution, will not flinch. / I want your sword's spasmodic final inch.' But the music is never frenzied, and Phaedra's obsession is portrayed in a luminous, chilly passage for high strings and untuned drums with a quaver-crotchet rhythm (ti-tum) that suggests a heartbeat.

The drums reiterate this rhythm at many moments in *Phaedra*, and it may be an allusion to Britten's own heart condition. Galina Vishnevskaya describes the 'heavy, hollow beating of his heart' she heard when sitting next to him at dinner in the summer of 1976, and says she saw 'the pronounced throbbing of his shirt on the left side of his chest'. Certainly he must have felt the personal relevance of Phaedra's calm acceptance of imminent death after she has taken poison: 'chills already dart / along my boiling veins and seize my heart, / A cold composure I have never known / gives me a moment's poise.' Beneath these words the orchestra strains for resolution into C major, and finally reaches what Christopher Palmer calls this 'chord [of] consummation and transfiguration' at the very moment of her death. (Strictly speaking the chord is C with added sixth and ninth. Palmer points out that the sixth is used in similar fashion by Mahler in *Das Lied von der Erde* and suggests that the ninth makes Britten's chord 'an even more orientally pentatonic-sounding chord than Mahler's'.) While this is happening Phaedra sings 'My eyes at last give up their light, and see / the day they've soiled resume its purity', and the music indicates that her death is as final and complete an achievement of purity and naturalness as is found anywhere in Britten's music. As Phaedra has already declared, 'Death will give me freedom; oh it's nothing not to live.'

*

Because he could not play through *Phaedra* satisfactorily at the piano, Britten asked Colin Matthews to do this for him as he composed it. 'He himself sat beside me at the right-hand end of the keyboard,' writes Matthews, 'and generally played the vocal line with his left hand.' He made a few changes after he had heard what he had written, most of them very slight.

Phaedra was completed on 12 August 1975, and Matthews was back at the Red House on 22 October to help Britten with his String Quartet No. 3, which he had begun to write earlier that month. The first movement was already complete, the second almost so, and after hearing Matthews play them Britten again only made slight alterations. 'Britten completed the first four movements of the quartet by the end of October,' writes Matthews, 'and in November went for a holiday to Venice, where he composed the Finale.'

Rita Thomson explains the origin of the Venice trip:

> Bill and Pat Servaes were such sweet people, and Bill was always trying to think up nice little things for Ben – they were terribly generous and kind. And it was really Bill's idea to go to Venice. Ben was writing the Third Quartet at the time, and you know the last part's called 'Serenissma', and I don't know whether he discussed that with Bill, but the idea came about of going there to hear the bells again.

Servaes says that 'we were going to Venice anyway, on holiday, and we asked Ben to come along too, and he said straight off that he'd love to'.

Afterwards Britten admitted that he had been frightened of the journey, and at the last minute had wished not to go, but with Bill and Pat Servaes and their Chilean friend Esteban Cerda, as well as Rita, to handle Britten's wheelchair and look after his needs, there were no difficulties. They stayed in the Hotel Danieli, where Britten and Rita were given a two-bedroom suite with a balcony overlooking the Grand Canal, opposite the church of the Salute. Rita recalls that

> the whole place got flooded all the time that November, and you could see from the window everyone walking about on duckboards, But we went out every morning, and when we came to a bridge, would carry him up the steps in his wheelchair. And we went on vaporettos everywhere, to see pictures, and it was wonderful, because there was nobody around. And we used to go to a family restaurant where we'd have a lovely lunch, and then we'd come back and Ben would have a rest while Bill and Pat and Esteban would go out to see something else, and I would get Ben up at about four o'clock, and go out for a walk,

leaving him by the window, listening to the bells. I used to open the window, and you know how in Venice you hear one bell, and then another, and then a few more – he adored that. And he was writing; he finished the Quartet.

David Matthews, who with his brother Colin played through the Quartet to Britten on its completion as a piano duet the following month, writes: 'We cannot but feel that the redemption of Aschenbach which had begun in *Death in Venice* is completed here.' Yet Colin Matthews recalls Britten emphasizing the unresolved character of the Quartet's last two bars, when viola and cello resist the violins' attempt to achieve E major, producing a semitonal clash, after which the cello holds its low D natural by itself. Britten said: 'I want the work to end with a question.'

Arguably the whole Quartet is made up of questions or uncertainties. Peter Evans has shown that the first movement contains reminders of the fretful music to which Aschenbach pursued Tadzio through Venice, while the second, 'Ostinato', strides off confidently but ends with disconcerting abruptness in the middle of a phrase. The third, 'Solo', is marked 'very calm', but Arnold Whittall suggests that this calm is only achieved through self-denial: the first violin, playing above triadic arpeggios, seems determined to avoid both the certainties of the triads and any sort of lyricism of its own. The fourth movement is called 'Burlesque', but Evans allows that it has an 'obsessive . . . frenetic' character – it could be another of Britten's dances of death, and is made the more eerie by a strange whistling tone produced by the viola playing behind the bridge. As to the Finale, if those critics are right who believe that, in striving for Aschenbach's 'own' key of E major, it is aiming to redeem him, it is surely significant that it fails to maintain that key at the end. The most recognizable motif from the opera in this movement is Aschenbach's 'I love you', which is heard, in various distorted forms, again and again.

*

'Just back from 2 weeks in Venice – in a wheel-chair! But what a place – even in floods,' Britten wrote to Bettina Ehrlich in late November 1975. Colin Matthews says that, after he and his brother had played the quartet to Britten, 'Ben was in a relaxed and benevolent mood.' At Christmas the Red House was, as usual, full of family and friends. 'We used to have Christmas dinner at night,' says Rita, 'and we would have Beth and Mary Potter for it. And in the morning we used to have a lot of people – Bill and Pat would come, and Sue and Jack Phipps and their family.' This year Basil Coleman, with whom Britten had been fully reconciled, was among the guests. Around New Year, Britten wrote to Bill Servaes: 'I am in bed, but only recovering from Xmas!' Rita told the Mitchells: 'Ben has stood up to all the visitors & visits very well but is looking forward to some nice quiet days to get down to some more work.' To Oliver Knussen, on 21 January 1976, Britten admitted that he was now only able to manage 'an occasional tiny bit of writing'.

Ian Tait says that, though his cardiac function had improved for a while, he was suffering from 'a slowly progressive inability of the heart muscle to cope with its pumping activity', a condition which often left him 'totally exhausted'. Dr Michael Petch writes that Britten was experiencing 'progressive heart failure which was a consequence of the weakened heart muscle prior to the surgery [weakened by the leaky valve following endocarditis in 1968] and the failure of the aortic homograft valve. You will probably appreciate that despite the best care in the world, some valves taken from humans let you down when transplanted into others'. Dr Petch and others concerned with Britten's case considered 'the question of a repeat operation', but (Dr Petch writes) 'we did not discuss it with Britten or Pears because we all agreed that it would be too much'.

Ian Tait believes that the disability in his right hand had 'very much undermined' Britten's will to go on, and says he also sensed that Britten 'felt drained of creative drive after *Death in Venice* was completed, and was half ready to give up'. Tait believes that such composing as he did manage after the opera was 'more in response to the expectations of others – more not to let them down, than because of any overwhelming passion in himself'.

He fulfilled a promise to Cecil Aronowitz (who had played in the English Opera Group orchestra) to arrange for string orchestra the accompaniment of his 1950 viola piece *Lachrymae: Reflections on a song of John Dowland*, provided Pears and Osian Ellis with eight new folksong arrangements, wrote the theme for a Theme and Variations for solo cello for Rostropovich to perform at a Swiss concert in honour of the conductor Paul Sacher's seventieth birthday – eleven other composers including Berio, Boulez, Henze, Holliger and Lutoslawski supplied the variations – and began work on a *Welcome Ode* for Suffolk schoolchildren to perform in 1977 on a visit by the Queen during her Silver Jubilee. Meanwhile on 1 February, *Paul Bunyan* had its first complete performance for thirty-three years, on BBC Radio Three, with Steuart Bedford conducting, Norma Burrowes as Tiny, George Hamilton IV as the ballad-singing Narrator, and Pears as Johnny Inkslinger. After the broadcast Peter Porter wrote in the *Times Literary Supplement*: '*Paul Bunyan*'s tone is unique. It is a gentle-tempered and uplifting work; it accepts

America with grace and admiration.' Porter also judged Auden – while allowing that he swamped his composers – to have been the greatest librettist of this century, and remarked that many people had regretted that Auden and Britten 'were never to produce an extended masterpiece together'.

The broadcast had been recorded some months earlier in the Manchester studios of the BBC, and Pears was with Britten when he listened to a tape of the performance, in the library at the Red House. So was Donald Mitchell:

> Ben was profoundly moved by re-encountering this forgotten work from a forgotten – virtually suppressed – past. He hadn't remembered that it was such a 'strong piece' – his words; and the impact of the music, combined with all the memories it aroused – of Auden, of the American years, of his own youth, energy and vitality – overwhelmed him. His own physical condition by now was pretty awful, and when we got to the end of the work, to the great Litany that precedes the Epilogue – 'The campfire embers are black and cold, / The banjos are broken, the stories are told, / The woods are cut down and the young are grown old' – Ben was shattered, and he broke down. Ironic, wasn't it?, to find himself confronting a litany for himself that he'd written in 1940! For the rest of us, too. I remember still, very vividly, how tender and loving Peter was, congratulating him on finding so many different ways of harmonizing F (the last few bars of *Bunyan*), which made Ben smile again.

In March, Britten made a new will. There were substantial funds to be disposed of. Isador Caplan writes that he had never been 'sanguine about the prospect of living out his life with an adequate income', and so had been 'very thrifty, at times bordering on the mean'. Donald Mitchell observes that though Britten and Pears had become wealthy men they 'continued to judge expenditure by pre-war norms and by the tradition in which they had been brought up: one of determined middle-class thrift!' In the will, fifty thousand pounds was left outright to Pears, and there were elaborate provisions for charitable donations at the discretion of his executors and Trustees. Britten emphasized to Caplan that the most important responsibility was for Pears: 'Try and keep him comfortable and as happy as you can. This is far more important to me than anything that is going on in Aldeburgh, or anything to do with my music.'

The executors and Trustees were to be Pears, Caplan, Britten's accountant Leslie Periton, and Donald Mitchell, replacing Anthony Gishford, named as an executor in an earlier will, who had now died. Mitchell explains that Gishford, who had worked at Boosey & Hawkes for many years, was to have 'represented the publishing interest', and Britten 'realized that he ought to have another executor with knowledge of musical and publishing matters'. It was also understood between them that Mitchell would eventually write a critical study of Britten. Britten lent him the diaries he had kept as a schoolboy and young man, and when Mitchell told him how fascinating they had been to read, Britten wrote to him: 'Glad you find the old diaries interesting but I fear I wasnt (& am not!) a writer.'

Mitchell recalls that, à propos his writing a biography, Britten said to him: 'I want you to tell the truth about Peter and me.' Several years later, Pears remarked that, at the end of his life, Britten had been glad to see the increasing public tolerance of homosexuality. But he added: 'The word "gay" was not in his vocabulary . . . He resented that [word], I think.'

*

The summer weather at Aldeburgh in 1976 was exceptionally hot – England was suffering from a severe drought – and Rita Thomson says that the heat 'took a lot out' of Britten. He was on what Ian Tait calls 'a fairly complex regime of drugs' to combat the progressive heart-muscle failure, and frequent adjustment had to be made to his medication to combat breathlessness and exhaustion. Around this time he remarked to Pat Nicholson that her husband John was 'lucky' in having dropped dead the previous year.

George Malcolm, who was at the first performance of *Phaedra* at the Aldeburgh Festival on 16 June, thought it 'a young man's music, full of vigour', and was shocked when he went to see Britten in the 'Royal Box' (the artistic directors' box) and found him ill and feeble. 'I just couldn't believe that the man who had written it was in that condition.' Britten rose to his feet to acknowledge the applause. John Culshaw, who was in the audience, writes that this was 'an emotional moment', though 'finally it was the music that was being applauded'; Culshaw calls *Phaedra* a 'triumph'. The *Evening Standard* reported of Britten: 'The way he has triumphed over his heart condition is amazing. It is not so long since people were glumly prophesying that he would write no more. Yet *Phaedra*, along with his *Sacred and Profane* medieval lyrics and his *Birthday Hansel* (also performed in the current Festival) all date from last year.'

The biggest attraction of the 1976 Festival was *Paul Bunyan*, staged in the Maltings with Neil Jenkins as Johnny Inkslinger and a young cast directed by Colin Graham, under the auspices of English Music Theatre, successor to the now disbanded English Opera Group, founded in the hope of establishing a full-time ensemble of young singers. At first Britten had resisted the decision to wind up the EOG, but he admitted to Colin Graham in November 1974: 'It is certainly over to someone else now as I feel that I have done my stuff operatically.' He allowed his name to be given as 'president' of the new company.

Neil Jenkins told the *Guardian* that the *Paul Bunyan* dress rehearsal had been moved to the morning so that Britten could attend. 'He was really excited by it, and passed a message to us that he was thrilled.' The same *Guardian* piece quoted Pears as saying of Britten's current projects: 'He has ideas for a full-scale work, but is not really getting down to it yet.' This was *Praise We Great Men*, a cantata for chorus with soloists and orchestra, with words by Edith Sitwell, written by her in 1959 at Britten's request for recitation at a celebration of the tercentenary of Purcell's birth. Britten intended that the cantata should be performed at Rostropovich's first concert as conductor of the National Symphony Orchestra of Washington DC in 1977. On the other hand even the prospect of orchestrating the simple *Welcome Ode* for the Queen's Jubilee – not yet begun in composition sketch – exhausted Britten, and he asked Colin Matthews to do it for him when the sketch was ready.

'BENJAMIN BRITTEN MADE A PEER,' announced *The Times* on the morning of 12 June, the second Saturday of the 1976 Aldeburgh Festival. 'Mr Benjamin Britten, the composer, is made a life Peer ... in the Queen's Birthday Honours, published today.' Rita Thomson had opened the letter which offered the peerage. 'He'd been offered a knighthood earlier on, and didn't take it. And I said, "Well, if you don't take this, I'll never speak to you again!" "Well," he said, "I'll have to take it then, won't I?"' Although the news was kept secret until the official announcement, an informal garden party was organized at the Red House for 12 June, without explanation. 'And that day,' says Rita, 'they saw in the paper that he was made a lord, and everybody came to the party, and it was wonderful.' Among the guests were Eric Crozier and Nancy Evans, who were once again living in the Aldeburgh district; she had become involved in Pears's singers' master classes at the Maltings, and this had effected a reconciliation with Britten. Indeed the Croziers were among a number of friends and former employees whom Britten, in his March 1976 will, enjoined his Trustees to take care of.

Fidelity Cranbrook, who was at the garden party, says of the life peerage: 'He got there in the end.' Lord Harewood calls Britten's acceptance of it 'curiously unnecessary', and Donald Mitchell observes: 'Somehow it didn't seem sensible to me – "Lord Britten" – I couldn't make much sense of it.' After receiving the peerage, Britten signed several letters 'Britten' rather than 'Benjamin Britten'. He joked to Colin Matthews that this was a good thing because it 'saved energy'.

Donald Mitchell says Britten would have been aware of his likely scepticism. Even before Mitchell had the opportunity to offer congratulations on the day the peerage was announced,

> Ben said to me, with a rather mournful expression, 'Will you ever speak to me again?' I think we have to remember that he was ill, felt isolated – and forgotten. During those last months of his life, he often said, 'No one remembers me, I'm forgotten, I'm not seen out of Aldeburgh.' On top of these largely illusory fears, he also knew that he was no longer *the* fashionable composer, at the top of the musical agenda, as it were. I think the offer of the peerage did something to restore his ailing self-confidence. He felt he was back on the musical map, back in the public eye (though in fact he had never been out of the public ear). That's why he accepted it, I believe.

Rosamund Strode has another explanation: 'Ben didn't mind about himself in the least. He just felt it was marvellous for music.' No British composer had ever been so ennobled.

During July, Britten was taken by Pears and Rita on holiday to Norway, where Pears had performed in the spring, in the hope that it would be cooler and more comfortable for him than Aldeburgh. They stayed at the Solstrand Fjord Hotel near Bergen, but it was almost as hot as in England, and Britten wrote to Donald Mitchell that the journey each way had been 'traumatic in the heat'. In the same letter: 'I am getting on with the Jubilee piece for Ipswich, which I've asked Colin M. to help me with – hope you approve. He is coming down to discuss it next week.' Colin Matthews and Britten talked at Horham on 29 July, after which Matthews 'began the score, working from Ben's sketch (which had very few indications of instrumentation)'. The *Welcome Ode*, a setting for young people's choir and orchestra of various festive Elizabethan lyrics, is in five short movements, very much in the manner of the *Spring Symphony*. Britten completed the sketch in mid-August, and when Matthews had finished the orchestration Britten asked him to start work in the same way on the cantata *Praise We Great Men*. 'We arranged our next meeting for 9 November,' writes Matthews. He says that Britten's physical condition 'changed his personality a good deal. You felt that you could talk to him without the possibility of sparks flying.' On the other hand he also describes the 'terrible tiredness' that 'working just for an hour' would now cause him.

At the end of September the Amadeus Quartet came to the Red House

to work on String Quartet No. 3 with him. On 23 October a performance was held in the Jubilee Hall entitled 'Cabaret: 30 Years On'. Pam
Wheeler and Anne Surfling, who had been observers at the first of Pears's
master classes, were among those who attended:

> It was supposed to celebrate thirty years of the Aldeburgh Festival, but
> the twenty-ninth Festival had only just been held. The real reason was
> unspoken: there was a feeling that Ben wouldn't live to see the thirtieth
> anniversary, so they were holding it now.
>
> Ben was there, up in the directors' box, with Rita, Imo and
> Rosamund, and we all sat at little tables and ate kedgeree, because it
> was a favourite dish of Ben's. And there was singing by a group from
> Cambridge, calling itself the Kings' Swingers, one of whom was Sue
> Phipps' stepson Simon. And Peter was the compère, and he mentioned
> Michael Crawford, and couldn't remember which part he'd played in
> *Noye's Fludde*, and Ben in the box called out 'Jaffet!' loud and clear.
>
> Peter sang three of Ben's *Cabaret Songs*, with Graham Johnson at
> the piano, and they included 'Tell me the truth about love'. And
> towards the end he sang Noel Coward's 'I'll see you again', and there
> was a feeling in it that he really meant the farewell in it to be Ben's.
> And Rita was wiping the sweat off Ben's face. But at the end, when
> there was a toast to 'The next thirty years', Ben got to his feet and
> drained his glass right to the bottom, and stepped out of sight. And
> that was the last time we ever saw him.

On the Red House copy of the programme, Rosamund Strode has
written: 'Ben came to this and sat in the Box: it was his last public
appearance.'

*

A few days later the Mitchells arrived at the Red House. Britten stayed in
bed all the time they were there, but had plenty to say. 'We sat on the bed
and talked a lot,' says Donald Mitchell.

> He showed me how far he'd got with his pencil composition sketch of
> *Praise We Great Men*, and he was lively in mind, and chatty. I think we
> all realized that this was the beginning of the end but the atmosphere,
> yes, was celebratory and relaxed. Ben ordered up a bottle of cham-
> pagne and we all raised our glasses, sitting on the bed, drinking to the
> successful conclusion of the piece. It was the last time that Kathleen
> and I were to see him.

He was still intending to work on the cantata with Colin Matthews, but
their planned meeting on 9 November was cancelled at the last moment

because he was not well enough. He had written about two-fifths of the composition sketch.

Towards the end of October, Pears had crossed the Atlantic to perform and teach in Los Angeles. He then went to Canada to give recitals with Osian Ellis and sing *Saint Nicolas* in Montreal. On 12 November the *Toronto Globe & Mail* carried an interview with him. While he was talking to the reporter he received

> a long-distance phone call from Aldeburgh with a disturbing report of a further deterioration in Britten's health. Pears was clearly distressed [wrote the reporter] but conscientiously continued. 'The festival is secure, thank God. The big push now is to get the study centre at Aldeburgh properly established. It's Ben's greatest wish to see this done, although lately he's not been able to do much about it and so Imogen and myself are scuttling about here and there to do the job.'

From the first master class at the Maltings in September 1972 had emerged a project for a school for young professional musicians with its own building adjacent to the Maltings concert-hall. Meanwhile the classes had continued. During the summer and autumn of 1976, for example, there were courses of string as well as vocal tuition, and a Snape Maltings Training Orchestra rehearsed and performed over a weekend in October.

A few days after Pears had received this telephone call in Toronto, Rita Thomson sent another urgent message. 'I felt Ben was getting worse, and I was very frightened that something might happen with Peter not here.' After discussing the situation with Ian Tait and Mike Petch, who had continued to see Britten at regular intervals, Rita contacted Pears's hosts in Canada, and it was agreed that he should return home at once, from Montreal. He cancelled his appearance in *Saint Nicolas*, but the flight was delayed by a few hours, so the programme was rearranged to begin with *Saint Nicolas*, and he sang in it after all, arriving at the Red House next day still in his evening clothes. Rita says that 'until Peter came back, Ben had found it very difficult to sleep. People who are dying sometimes do that, because they feel that if they go to sleep they won't wake up. And he hadn't slept, hardly, for a couple of nights. And Peter came back in the afternoon, and Ben slept for about twelve hours.' Pears said he had found Britten 'very ill but clear & conscious'. He felt guilty at having been away at this time: 'I broke the tour I was doing, and came back early, but I really shouldn't ever have gone on that. Then I could have spent all those weeks with him.'

On 22 November, Britten's sixty-third birthday, 'he'd really been very ill all night,' says Rita, and he had had oxygen, and I was feeding him with a cup of tea in the morning, and we discussed the fact that it was his birthday, and he said to me, 'Have you arranged a party?' And I said, 'No, I thought you were too ill.' 'Oh,' he said, 'I want a champagne party.' So he told us all the people he wanted to come – Mary Potter, and Bill and Pat Servaes, and Imo, and his sister Barbara who happened to be here, and Beth came, and Peg Hesse was here too. And they all drank champagne downstairs, and Ben asked for people he wanted to see, and they came up to his room one by one, and he had something to say to everybody.

Pears described him as 'so direct and unafraid' as he said goodbye to each of them. His sister Beth told him: 'You know, we can't do without you.' He answered: 'You've got to – I can't go on.'

Rita says that during these days

he asked what dying would be like – would it be painful, would it be uncomfortable, and what did I think happened at death? I told him I felt dying was like going to sleep, and that there was no problem. I said, 'And after all, there's going to be lots of friends waiting there for you. Wystan will be at the top of the stairs, waiting for you!' And he just laughed.

She gathered that he had been 'a very religious boy when he was young', and she says that several times during his final months the Bishop of St Edmundsbury and Ipswich, the Rt Revd Leslie Brown, came to talk, and eventually to read prayers for the dying. 'I think Ben wanted to have religion when he was dying, but he could never really quite come to it, though I remember he and I both had Communion.' This was brought to the house by the bishop. Pears was thinking of this occasion when, in a filmed interview after Britten's death, he said that 'on one occasion he took Communion because he wanted to make someone [i.e. the bishop] happy'. Ian Tait writes that Britten had asked the bishop to visit 'largely because he felt he wanted a spiritual sanctuary', but 'he told me he didn't feel it was quite honourable to join the church so late and in a poor condition when he had rejected it, very largely, when well and active. It seemed to me a very prep-school kind of code. I hope I helped him to a different view of things.' Pears said in the filmed interview: 'I don't think he really had any particular conviction as to what was going to happen after death, but he was certainly not afraid of dying.'

On 25 November, Pears wrote to an old friend, Oliver Holt:

Ben, having had a quick relapse when I was in Canada, hurrying me home, seems to have decided to take his time over the rest of his journey and keep us waiting. He is weak, angelically good and considerate, calm and clear, asking surprising & practical questions from time to time, still very much 'with us'. Not in real pain but of course uncomfortable. Heigh-ho.

The 'practical questions' included the purchase of the former East Suffolk Hotel in Aldeburgh High Street to provide a larger Festival club and administrative offices. On 17 November, Britten had signed, in a clear, firm hand, a codicil to his will authorizing his executors to buy it for the Festival.

On 28 November, Rostropovich, in England to conduct a recording of all the Tchaikovsky symphonies, came down to Aldeburgh. 'Ben was very sick,' he writes,

> his hand trembling. He told me he wanted to be buried at Snape, where there's a small church with a little churchyard. Then he said, 'Slava, I've got a present for you,' and from the piano Peter brought the beginning of a cantata Ben was writing for me to conduct in Washington. You see, Shostakovich had started to write a piece for my first season in Washington, but then he died [in 1975]; so Ben had said, 'Now I must write it twice – once for myself, and once for our Dimity.' Alas, Britten had composed only 14 pages.

On 30 November, Pears made a hasty trip to London to perform in a gala fund-raising concert for the Snape Maltings Foundation at St James's Palace, in the presence of the Queen Mother. He hurried back to Aldeburgh to report its success to Britten. It was around this time that he wrote a short undated note to Philip Ledger: 'Ben is slowly fading – decrescendo e morendo. But he is calm and clear and ready to go – each day a little weaker. So considerate & a wonderful patient, and our Rita has looked after him like an angel. A wonderful end.'

On the evening of Friday 3 December, Mike Petch was staying at the Red House. 'In fact he was the last person Ben spoke to,' says Rita.

> Peter and I were with him too, when I was settling him down for the night, but with me and Peter he didn't need to speak. But because he was so well-mannered, Ben – he was the best brought-up little boy you could imagine – when Mike said to him, 'Well, I'm going to turn in now, goodnight, Ben', he answered, 'Goodnight, Mike.' When you're ill like that, any speaking is an effort.

Petch, Pears and Rita went to bed, leaving Susie Walton, who was helping at night, to sit with Britten. Some time after midnight she woke

Rita and told her that his breathing was deteriorating. 'I got Peter up,' says Rita, 'and Peter said to me, "I'll stay with him, you go and sleep." I felt it was right for Peter to be with him on his own. So I went back to my room, and Susie went and sat in Peter's study across the landing. And then the bell rang and I went back and he was just dying.' Pears said: 'He died in my arms, in fact, peacefully, as far as anybody could be said to be peaceful when he was in fact very ill. But there was no struggle to keep alive, except the purely physical one, which one can't help, to breathe.' In a letter, Pears wrote: 'His hand was in mine.'

The very first entry in Imogen Holst's diary of working for Britten, dated 29 September 1952, reads:

> Ben asked me in after a choir practice of *Timon of Athens*. We were talking about old age and he said that he had a very strong feeling that people died at the right moment, and that the greatness of a person included the time when he was born and the time he endured, but that this was difficult to understand.

*

The Sunday papers on 5 December, carrying the news of Britten's death, reported that the Queen had sent 'a private message of sympathy to tenor Peter Pears, as a representative of all who had worked with Lord Britten'. Pears told Bill Servaes of the royal telegram: 'It's a recognition of the way we lived.' Among the many others who sent condolences were Tippett, Walton, Lennox Berkeley and Wulff Scherchen. As well as a lengthy obituary, *The Times* on Monday 6 December devoted a leader to praise of Britten. The London music critics were somewhat guarded in their assessment of his career, but the *Daily Telegraph* headed its obituary: 'Benjamin Britten, the truly towering talent of his age'.

The funeral was held the following Tuesday; the cortège, with police escort, made a ceremonial drive through Aldeburgh to the parish church while flags flew at half mast and the High Street shops closed out of respect. Bishop Leslie Brown gave the address, which ended: 'Ben will like the sound of the trumpets, though he will find it difficult to believe that they are sounding for him.' The choir, which sang the *Hymn to the Virgin*, was made up of members of the Aldeburgh Festival Singers, among them Stephen Terry, the Puck whom Britten had befriended in the sixties. He says he felt a 'weird sense of disconnection', because the formalities of burial seemed to have nothing to do with Britten: 'It was something that had happened a long time before; a whole child's world, a paradise, a magical world to enter, that had all fallen away.'

The congregation sang the hymns from *Saint Nicolas*, and the coffin was buried not at Snape but in the annexe of the Aldeburgh churchyard, in a grave which had been specially lined with reeds from the marshes of Snape by Bob and Doris Ling, a local couple who were now the Maltings caretakers. Rostropovich had dashed over from Germany to be among the mourners. After the tea and drinks at the Red House which followed the funeral, Pears departed with him for London, on his way to sing *Saint Nicolas* in Cardiff the next day – 'a fearful task,' wrote Pears afterwards, 'and I did *just* make it . . .'

Britten's obituaries had referred in rather coy terms to his relationship with Pears – *The Times* described them as 'socially . . . ideally attuned' – and it was not until nearly three years after Britten's death that Pears began publicly to identify himself as homosexual. The first occasion was in an interview with the American gay magazine *Advocate*. In the issue dated 12 July 1979 he was quoted as saying: 'I've always rather resisted gay demonstrations because I feel that we have to fit into a society and we don't particularly want to make ourselves an extra nuisance. [But] I'm all for plugging away and making it clear to those who have eyes to see what the situation is.' Donald Mitchell says that in his private life Pears became more open about his sexuality: 'I think he'd had to suppress a certain natural flamboyance during his many years with Ben. But now, with young admirers of his own – and I don't say this in any spiteful sense – he could play the role of the queenly elder statesman.' Rita Thomson says of Pears's emotional life after Britten's death: 'I think he dabbled in certain relationships, and was looking for a replacement for Ben, in a way, but really felt in the end that he hadn't found anything he was really needing.'

The year after the *Advocate* interview, Pears told Gillian Widdicombe of the *Observer* that he and Britten had been 'passionately devoted and close'. This interview was a trailer for Tony Palmer's *A Time There Was*, first shown on Easter Day 1980, in which Pears, interviewed by Donald Mitchell, spoke at length – though in guarded terms – of his relationship with Britten:

> I'm particularly aware of his devotion to me. I have had some quite wonderful letters from Ben, and I propose one day to publish them, because he was absolutely devoted to me, and unbelievably good and kind – I mean, it was a quite marvellous relationship, and I'm incredibly grateful for it . . . It was established very early that we were devoted, passionately devoted and close, and that was it. Of course there were one or two little moments when things didn't go – it wasn't a superhuman sort of relationship. But there was very, very little that

disturbed our relationship, and I was terribly conscious of his devotion, his faith in me. I like to think that I returned that as warmly as he gave it, but I can't ever feel that I could reach his particular extraordinary quality of – well, of trust, and faith, and love.

The film and the *Observer* article brought Pears requests from several homosexual organizations to accept their chairmanship or presidency. 'But I wouldn't let him do it,' says Rita.

It soon became noticeable after Britten's death that Pears was not going to stop performing. Sue Phipps remarks that

> There was this strange feeling that all the stuffing went out of him. And yet he had to go on performing. And he went on at a ridiculous pace for a man of his age, as if he really simply wanted to move as fast as he could towards joining Ben. I wanted him to give up so badly – I did everything I could without actually saying directly to him, 'Please stop' ... He was also trying to prove that he could sing to a greater age than any other tenor had ever done! It was a strange thing; he would never have done that while Ben was alive, that I'm quite sure of – Ben would have stopped him.

He continued to give recitals with Osian Ellis and Murray Perahia, and to travel the world singing Britten's music. He was knighted in the New Year's Honours list in 1978, and, that year, aged sixty-eight, appeared as Vere in *Billy Budd* as the Metropolitan Opera, New York. In February 1980 he was heard to remark, 'I must retire next year – can't go on after seventy,' but it was said without conviction.

Even after a stroke in December 1980 ended his singing career (and once again gave Rita Thomson a nursing role at the Red House), he lectured, adjudicated musical competitions, and took the narrator's part in such works as *Peter and the Wolf*. Sue Phipps feels that 'he couldn't let go of adulation and applause'. John Evans, who came to know him very well during this period, while working for the Britten Estate, suggests that he had several motives: 'He couldn't stop performing – there's no doubt about that – because he needed it. He couldn't stop performing Ben's music because he needed the contact with Ben. But I think part of the reason why he couldn't stop was that he didn't really enjoy being back at the Red House.' He was still making public appearances and teaching five years after his stroke, at the age of seventy-five. On the day before his death, 2 April 1986, he gave a class on the Evangelist's recitatives in the *St Matthew Passion*.

Isador Caplan says that Britten had been almost as concerned about

Rita's future as he had about Pears's. Many of Britten's friends were surprised when she stayed on at the Red House after his death. She trained as a health visitor and then worked in that capacity in the Aldeburgh district. She says that when a friend of Pears's, Hugh Bishop, asked him, 'When Ben died, whom did you turn to?', Pears 'was taken aback, but he said, "The only person I really turned to was Rita." And Ben and I had been so close that he felt it was a continuing bit of that, that there was still some contact there.' She adds that she had intended to return to London, but Pears kept asking her to stay a little longer – 'I would never have thought of it but for that.'

Pears even raised the possibility with several of his friends – among them Peg Hesse and Osian Ellis – that he might marry Rita. On the other hand, some while after Britten's death John Evans gathered from Pears that relations between him and Rita had become very difficult. Christopher Headington has written of this: 'Peter did not share Britten's need for a nanny figure, while Rita herself was strong-minded, with an element of Scottish thrawness, and would sometimes snap at him. Sometimes he found her tiresome, and noted that she distrusted his sexuality, or at least his easy attitude to it, and placed obstacles in the way of one young male friend's staying at the house. In her turn, she sensibly did not wish to become his companion-housekeeper and nothing more ...' Pears mentioned his unhappiness to Donald Mitchell, who assured him that the Trustees would provide another home for Rita if this was what he wanted. But he never raised the matter again.

Rita herself says she was unaware that Pears felt any unease, and dismisses the idea that she restrained his sexuality. 'Peter wasn't an argumentative sort of person, but I can imagine that to have a woman around him all the time wasn't as easy as it had been for Ben. On the other hand we never fought, and we used to go on holiday together.'

Rosamund Strode continued to work at the Red House, initially as Secretary to the Britten Estate, then as Keeper of Manuscripts to the Britten–Pears Library – the title which had been given to the Red House library and its contents in 1973, when a Trust was established to maintain it for the benefit of scholars and research students. After Britten's death a 'pre-eminent collection' of manuscripts from his estate became the property of the nation in lieu of estate duty, and was placed on permanent loan at the Britten–Pears Library by the British Library, to whom it belongs.

In 1979 permanent buildings for the Britten–Pears School of Advanced Musical Studies – as the young musicians' training courses were now entitled – were opened alongside the Maltings concert-hall. Pears was in

charge of the singers' master classes, held at various times during the
year, with Nancy Evans as his co-director of singing studies, and many
other instrumentalists and singers – among them, Galina Vishnevskaya
– who had worked with Britten came to teach.

The Aldeburgh Festival continued, with Philip Ledger, Steuart Bedford
and Colin Graham as directors alongside Pears and Imogen Holst, and
the year after Britten's death Rostropovich joined them; but Wilfrid
Wren writes that something now seemed to be missing from the Festival:
'Though outwardly the drive, the enthusiasm, the energy grew greater,
and standards remained high, the Festival seemed to falter as if someone
had thrown a switch in its power-house ... It is not fanciful to believe
that [Britten's] influence was far more all-pervading than anyone had
realised when he was alive.' One thing had not changed. Bill Servaes
resigned as general manager in 1980, partly because he found it impossible to continue working with Pears. Asked if he thinks it striking that
such ruptures should have continued after Britten's death, Servaes says:
'Everything went on the same, all the intrigues, the favouritism, the way
that people who flattered could get Peter's ear – it was all just the same.'

After Pears's death, his and Britten's estates were constituted into the
Britten–Pears Foundation. Donald Mitchell, one of its Trustees, describes
its charitable and other activities:

> We support the Aldeburgh Foundation, including the Festival, with
> substantial grants which in 1991 reached almost £200,000. Another
> major part of the income goes to the upkeep of the Britten–Pears
> Library, the Archive, which holds virtually all Britten's juvenilia and
> the majority of his manuscripts (including those on permanent loan
> from the British Library), and the Red House complex. Thirdly, we
> support the posthumous release and recording of those works of
> Britten we consider worthy of publication and, in the same area,
> sponsor the recording and performance of works that have been neg-
> lected or hitherto unrecorded. And finally, money goes to support
> causes close to Ben's and Peter's hearts – helping young composers,
> indeed creating whenever and wherever possible a high profile for the
> *living* composer, which is the objective of our major Britten Award
> (triennial) and our more modest Benjamin Britten International Com-
> petition for Composers (alternate years). We make a special point of
> assistance to musicians and music education, especially in East Anglia.
>
> Outside the field of music we keep in mind the guidelines Ben and
> Peter left us; for example, that one of our concerns should be to
> encourage civilized attitudes to homosexuality, alas still much needed

in 1992. And we speak out for peace and non-violence – the Falklands and the Gulf Wars were examples – as we believe Ben and Peter would have wanted us to.

The Red House, mentioned by Mitchell, remains much as it was in Britten and Pears's time. It is frequently used by the Trustees, and Rita Thomson continues to live there.

Britten's sisters and brother outlived him by several years; the last survivor, Beth, died in 1989. Imogen Holst, who lived in Aldeburgh until the end of her life, died in 1984. Eric Crozier and Nancy Evans still live in the district, at Great Glemham, not far from Fidelity Cranbrook. Stephen and Beth Reiss now live in Thorpeness.

All the Trustees' charitable work is possible because the income from Britten's music, far from dwindling as he had feared, grew substantially in the years following his death. Today there are more performances of his work than ever. 'It's such a strange turn of the wheel now,' says Mitchell, 'because he's really come back as an example and a model which so many of the succeeding generation of composers want to follow.' Oliver Knussen says that Britten has become 'a phenomenal father-figure' to present-day younger British composers, and Robert Saxton, who today is head of composition at the Guildhall School of Music as well as being an established composer, emphasizes that he has now 'swung back' from his passionate enthusiasm for Tippett to a rediscovery of Britten:

> I actually think some of Britten's late works are masterpieces. I heard the String Quartet No. 3 played at Tanglewood when I was teaching there in 1986, and it was a moving experience to witness a tough American modern music audience, nine hundred or a thousand of them, stunned into silence at the end, before they felt able to applaud. I think when you've got somebody delivering the goods like that ten years after his death, to a hardened American new music audience, you've got to be very careful criticizing him.

Tony Palmer suspects that Tippett's ascendancy over Britten in the seventies may have been partly a matter of personalities: 'I've heard very distinguished musicians arguing forcefully that in the long run it's Tippett who'll be thought of as the great British composer of our time. And then you realize that what they're telling you is that they hate Britten because of something he did to them.'

It is certainly difficult to keep Britten's personality out of any assessment of his music, and vice versa. 'He was a *good* man,' wrote Pears not long after Britten's death. 'How could he not be having written all that beautiful music?' A very different judgement is delivered by Robert Tear: 'There was a great, huge abyss in his soul. That's my explanation of why the music becomes thinner and thinner as time passed. He got into the valley of the shadow of death and couldn't get out.' Leonard Bernstein said in the film *A Time There Was*:

> Ben Britten was a man at odds with the world. It's strange, because on the surface Britten's music would seem to be decorative, positive, charming, but it's so much more than that. When you hear Britten's music, if you really *hear* it, not just listen to it superficially, you become aware of something very dark. There are gears that are grinding and not quite meshing, and they make a great pain.

This, surely, is the source of Britten's greatness – this combined with sheer musicianship on a level that has rarely been reached in the history of music. In an obituary in the *Listener*, Tippett wrote: 'I want to say, here and now, that Britten has been for me the most purely musical person I have ever met and I have ever known.' The use of this vast talent to express his private struggle produced remarkable results. In 1946 Britten was quoted in the *Observer* as saying: 'If I had been born in 1813 rather than 1913 I should have been a romantic, primarily concerned to express my personality in music.' Arguably this was exactly what he was, and what he did.

Robert Tear believes that, without the emotional tensions, Britten 'could have been another Verdi. But he wouldn't give himself. He always stopped. He wouldn't quite go over the top.' Tippett comments: 'That's a silly statement. You can't be Verdi – that belongs to the nineteenth century. But I would have liked to change certain things for Ben, because of his immense possibilities. And there could have been some changes if he had not had Peter. But then Peter did something else for him.'

Chronological list of Britten's compositions

This is an abbreviated list, giving only (a) compositions to which Britten allocated opus numbers; (b) other works mentioned in the text of the biography. For a comprehensive list, see John Evans, Philip Reed and Paul Wilson, *A Britten Source Book*, The Britten Estate Limited, revised edition 1988.

1919–20   Earliest attempts at composition include a fragment of music in the play 'The Royal Falily'; and 'DO YOU NO THAT MY DADDY HAS GONE TO LONDON TODAY'.

1921–5   Numerous juvenila include the songs 'Oh, where are you going to, all you big steamers' (Kipling); and 'Beware!' (Longfellow).

1926   Works include 'Ouverture' for orchestra, submitted to the BBC.

1927   Works include 'Chaos and Cosmos: Symphonic Poem in E' for orchestra.

1928   (12 January: first composition lesson with Frank Bridge.) Works include 'Humoreske in C' for orchestra (February–March); and *Quatre Chansons Françaises* (June–August).

1929   Works include *The Birds* (Belloc) for medium voice and piano; and Bagatelle for violin, viola and piano.

1930   Works include *A Hymn to the Virgin* for mixed voices.

1931   Works include 'Variations on a French Carol' for women's voices, violin, viola and piano; String Quartet in D major; 'Three Small Songs' (Samuel Daniel, John Fletcher) for soprano and small orchestra; and 'Plymouth Town' (scenario by Violet Alford), ballet for small orchestra.

1932   Works include *Phantasy* in F minor for string quintet; *Three Two-part Songs* (de la Mare) for high voices and piano; *Two Part-songs* (Wither and Graves) for mixed voices and piano; *Sinfonietta*, Op. 1, for chamber orchestra; and *Phantasy*, Op. 2, for oboe, violin, viola and cello.

1933   *Alla Marcia* for string quartet.
      Alla Quartetto Serioso: 'Go play, boy, play' for string quartet.

	A Boy was Born, Op. 3, for mixed voices.
1934	*Simple Symphony*, Op. 4, for string orchestra.

Te Deum in C major, for choir and organ.

Holiday Tales (later renamed *Holiday Diary*), Op. 5, for piano.

1935   *Friday Afternoons*, Op. 7, for children's voices and piano.

Incidental music for *The King's Stamp*, *Coal Face*, and other documentary films.

Suite, Op. 6, for violin and piano.

Incidental music for Group Theatre production of *Timon of Athens*.

Incidental music for Left Theatre production of *Easter 1916* (Slater).

1936   Scores for documentary films including *Night Mail* and *Peace of Britain*.

Russian Funeral for brass and percussion.

Incidental music for Left Theatre production of *Stay Down Miner* (Slater).

Our Hunting Fathers, Op. 8 (Auden and others) for high voice and orchestra.

Soirées Musicales, Op. 9 (Rossini arr. Britten) for orchestra.

Score for feature film *Love from a Stranger*.

1937   *Pacifist March* (Duncan) for unison voices and accompaniment.

Incidental music for Group Theatre production of *The Ascent of F6* (Auden and Isherwood).

Cabaret Songs (Auden) for high voice and piano (published posthumously in 1980).

Variations on a Theme of Frank Bridge, Op. 10, for string orchestra.

Incidental music for *The Company of Heaven* (BBC radio).

On This Island, Op. 11 (Auden) for high voice and piano.

Incidental music for *Hadrian's Wall* (BBC radio).

Mont Juic, Op. 12 (with Lennox Berkeley) for orchestra.

1938   Incidental music for *The World of the Spirit* (BBC radio).

Piano Concerto No. 1 [*sic*], Op. 13.

Incidental music for Group Theatre production of *On the Frontier* (Auden and Isherwood).

1939   Incidental music for *Johnson over Jordan* (Priestley).

Advance Democracy (Swingler) for chorus.

Ballad of Heroes, Op. 14 (Auden and Swingler) for tenor or soprano solo, chorus and orchestra.

Incidental music for *The Sword in the Stone* (White) (BBC radio).

Young Apollo, Op. 16, for piano and strings (withdrawn; published posthumously in 1982).

Violin Concerto, Op. 15.

Les Illuminations, Op. 18 (Rimbaud) for high voice and strings.

Canadian Carnival, Op. 19, for orchestra.

1940   *Sinfonia da Requiem*, Op. 20.

Diversions, Op. 21, for piano (left hand) and orchestra.
Seven Sonnets of Michelangelo, Op. 22, for tenor and piano.
Introduction and Rondo alla Burlesca, Op. 23 No. 1, for two pianos.

1941   *Paul Bunyan* (Auden), operetta.
Matinées Musicales, Op. 24 (Rossini arr. Britten) for orchestra.
String Quartet No. 1 in D, Op. 25.
Mazurka Elegiaca, Op. 23 No. 2, for two pianos.
'Occasional Overture' for orchestra (published posthumously in 1985 as *An American Overture*).
Scottish Ballad, Op. 26, for two pianos and orchestra.

1942   *Hymn to St Cecilia*, Op. 27 (Auden) for chorus.
A Ceremony of Carols, Op. 28, for treble voices and harp.
Incidental music for *An American in England* (radio series).

1943   *Serenade*, Op. 31, for tenor, horn and strings.
Prelude and Fugue, Op. 29, for string orchestra.
Folk Songs Volume 1, British Isles (arr. Britten), for high voice and piano.
Rejoice in the Lamb, Op. 30, for soloists, chorus and organ.
The Ballad of Little Musgrave and Lady Barnard, for male voices and piano.

1944   *Festival Te Deum*, Op. 32, for chorus and organ.
A Shepherd's Carol (Auden) for mixed voices.

1945   *Peter Grimes*, Op. 33 (Slater), opera in three acts.
The Holy Sonnets of John Donne, Op. 35, for high voice and piano.
Incidental music for *This Way to the Tomb* (Duncan).
String Quartet No. 2, Op. 36.

1946   *The Young Person's Guide to the Orchestra*, Op. 34, for orchestra.
Incidental music for *The Dark Tower* (MacNeice) (BBC radio).
The Rape of Lucretia, Op. 37 (Duncan), opera in two acts.
Occasional Overture (withdrawn; published posthumously in 1984).
Prelude and Fugue on a Theme of Vittoria, for organ.
Folk Songs Volume 2, France (arr. Britten), for high voice and piano.

1947   *Albert Herring*, Op. 39 (Crozier), comic opera in three acts.
Canticle I: My beloved is mine, Op. 40 (Quarles), for high voice and piano.
A Charm of Lullabies, Op. 41, for mezzo-soprano and piano.
Folk Songs Volume 3, British Isles (arr. Britten), for high voice and piano.

1948   *The Beggar's Opera*, Op. 43 (Gay and Pepusch, real. Britten).
Saint Nicolas, Op. 42 (Crozier), for tenor, chorus and orchestra.

1949   *The Little Sweep*, Op. 45 (Crozier), children's opera in one act.
Spring Symphony, Op. 44, for soloists, chorus and orchestra.
A Wedding Anthem (Amo Ergo Sum), Op. 46 (Duncan), for soprano, tenor, chorus and organ.

1950   *Five Flower Songs*, Op. 47, for chorus.

	Lachrymae, Op. 48, for viola and piano.
1951	*Six Metamorphoses after Ovid*, Op. 49, for oboe.
	Billy Budd, Op. 50 (Forster and Crozier), opera in four acts.
1952	*Canticle II: Abraham and Isaac*, Op. 51 (Chester Miracle Play), for alto, tenor and piano.
1953	*Gloriana*, Op. 53 (Plomer), opera in three acts.
	Winter Words, Op. 52 (Hardy), for high voice and piano.
1954	*The Turn of the Screw*, Op. 54 (Piper), opera in two acts.
	Canticle III: Still falls the rain, Op. 55 (Sitwell) for tenor, horn and piano.
1955	*Alpine Suite* and *Scherzo* for recorders.
	Hymn to St Peter, Op. 56a, for choir and organ.
1956	*Antiphon*, Op. 56b, for choir and organ.
	The Prince of the Pagodas, Op. 57 (Cranko), ballet in three acts.
1957	*Songs from the Chinese*, Op. 58, for high voice and guitar.
	Noye's Fludde, Op. 59, the Chester Miracle Play set to music.
1958	*Nocturne*, Op. 60, for tenor, seven obligato [*sic*] instruments and string orchestra.
	Sechs Hölderlin-Fragmente, Op. 61, for high voice and piano.
1959	*Cantata Academica*, Op. 62, for soloists, chorus and orchestra.
	Missa Brevis in D, Op. 63, for boys' voices and organ.
1960	*A Midsummer Night's Dream*, Op. 64, opera in three acts.
	Folk Songs Volume 4, Moore's Irish Melodies (arr. Britten) for voice and piano.
1961	*Sonata in C*, Op. 65, for cello and piano.
	Jubilate Deo for chorus and organ.
	Folk Songs Volume 5, British Isles (arr. Britten) for voice and piano.
	The National Anthem (arr. Britten) for chorus and orchestra.
	Folk Songs Volume 6, England (arr. Britten) for high voice and guitar.
	War Requiem, Op. 66 (*Missa Pro Defunctis* and the poems of Wilfred Owen), for soprano, tenor and baritone solos, mixed chorus, boy's choir, chamber orchestra, organ and full orchestra.
1962	*Psalm 150*, Op. 67, for children's voices and instruments.
1963	*Cello Symphony*, Op. 68.
	Night Piece (Notturno) for piano.
	Cantata Misericordium, Op. 69, for tenor, baritone, chorus and orchestra.
	Nocturnal after John Dowland, Op. 70, for guitar.
1964	*Curlew River*, Op. 71 (Plomer), parable for church performance.
1965	*Cello Suite*, Op. 72.
	Gemini Variations, Op. 73, quartet for two players.
	Songs and Proverbs of William Blake, Op. 74, for baritone and piano.
	Voices for Today, Op. 75, for chorus of men, women and children, and organ (ad lib.).

The Poet's Echo, Op. 76 (Pushkin), for high voice and piano.

1966　*The Burning Fiery Furnace*, Op. 77 (Plomer), parable for church performance.

The Golden Vanity, Op. 78 (Graham), vaudeville for boys and piano.

Hankin Booby for wind and drums.

1967　*The Building of the House,* Op. 79, for orchestra and optional chorus.

Second Cello Suite, Op. 80.

1968　*The Prodigal Son*, Op. 81 (Plomer), parable for church performance.

Children's Crusade (Kinderkreuzzug), Op. 82 (Brecht), for children's voices and orchestra.

1969　Harp Suite, Op. 83.

Who are these children? Op. 84 (Soutar), for tenor and piano.

1970　*Owen Wingrave*, Op. 85 (Piper), opera for television.

1971　*Canticle IV: Journey of the Magi,* Op. 86 (Eliot), for counter-tenor, tenor, baritone and piano.

Third Cello Suite, Op. 87.

1973　*Death in Venice*, Op. 88 (Piper), opera in two acts.

1974　*Canticle V: The death of St Narcissus*, Op. 89 (Eliot) for tenor and harp.

Suite on English Folk Tunes: 'A Time There Was', Op. 90, for orchestra.

1975　*Sacred and Profane*, Op. 91, for unaccompanied voices.

A Birthday Hansel, Op. 92 (Burns), for high voice and harp.

Phaedra, Op. 93 (Lowell), dramatic cantata for mezzo-soprano and small orchestra.

String Quartet No. 3, Op. 94.

1976　*Eight Folk Song Arrangements* (arr. Britten) for voice and harp.

Welcome Ode, Op. 95, for young people's chorus and orchestra.

Bibliography

Works (and other sources) are arranged in alphabetical order of the initials by which they are referred to in Appendix C.

Alexander	Peter F. Alexander, *William Plomer, a biography*, Oxford University Press, 1989
ALP	Eric Crozier and Nancy Evans, 'After Long Pursuit', unpublished autobiographical typescript
Amis	John Amis, *Amiscellany: My life, my music*, Faber and Faber, 1985
Aspen Award	Benjamin Britten, *On Receiving the First Aspen Award*, Faber and Faber, 1964
ATTW	*A Time There Was: a profile of Benjamin Britten*, film directed by Tony Palmer, with interviews by Donald Mitchell, London Weekend Television, 1980. (Transcripts and tapes at the Britten–Pears Library also include material filmed and recorded but not used in the finished programme, some of which is quoted in the book.)
Auden, *Shorter Poems*	W. H. Auden, *Collected Shorter Poems*, Faber and Faber, 1969
BC	Christopher Palmer (ed.), *The Britten Companion*, Faber and Faber, 1984
Berkeley	*The Instrument of his Soul*, BBC radio documentary on Peter Pears, presented by Michael Berkeley and produced by John Evans, 1988
Betjeman	John Betjeman, *Collected Poems*, John Murray, 1970
Blades	James Blades, *Drum Roll*, Faber and Faber, 1977
BLB	Benjamin Britten, 'Britten Looking Back', *Sunday Telegraph*, 17 November 1963
Blunt	Wilfred Blunt, *John Christie of Glyndebourne*, Geoffrey Bles, 1968

Blythe	Ronald Blythe (ed.) *Aldeburgh Anthology*, Snape Maltings Foundation / Faber Music 1972
Bowen	Meirion Bowen (ed.), *Music of the Angels: Essays and Sketchbooks of Michael Tippett*, Eulenburg Books, 1980
B-PL	The Britten–Pears Library, The Red House, Aldeburgh
Britten/Holst	Benjamin Britten and Imogen Holst, *The Story of Music*, Rathbone, 1958
Carpenter, *Auden*	Humphrey Carpenter, *W. H. Auden: a biography*, Allen & Unwin, 1981
CL	Benjamin Britten, 'How to Become a Composer', *Listener*, 7 November 1946 (extracts from a BBC Schools radio broadcast entitled *The Composer and the Listener*, of which the full text (available to Eric Walter White when he wrote his book on Britten) is now lost).
Crozier, 'Notes'	Eric Crozier, 'Notes on Benjamin Britten', unpublished typescript (1966)
D	The diaries of Benjamin Britten (1928–1939); MSS, at B–PL; many extracts published in L (see below)
Dickinson	Peter Dickinson, *The Music of Lennox Berkeley*, Thames Publishing, 1989
DIV	Donald Mitchell (ed.), *Benjamin Britten: Death in Venice*, Cambridge Opera Handbooks, Cambridge University Press, 1987
DMI	Interviews conducted by Donald Mitchell (see list below)
Duncan	Ronald Duncan, *Working with Britten: a Personal Memoir*, Rebel Press, 1981
EA	W. H. Auden (ed. Edward Mendelson), *The English Auden*, Faber and Faber, 1977
ESI	Interviews by Elizabeth Sweeting (see list below).
Evans	Peter Evans, *The Music of Benjamin Britten*, J. M. Dent, revised edition 1989
Fischer-Dieskau	Dietrich Fischer-Dieskau, *Echoes of a Lifetime*, Macmillan, 1989
Foreman	Lewis Foreman (ed.), *From Parry to Britten: British Music in Letters 1900–1945*, B. T. Batsford, 1987
Fuller	John Fuller, *A Reader's Guide to W. H. Auden*, Thames and Hudson, 1970
Furbank	P. N. Furbank, *E. M. Forster: A Life*, Vol.2, Secker & Warburg, 1978
Gishford	Anthony Gishford (ed.), *Tribute to Benjamin Britten on his Fiftieth Birthday*, Faber and Faber, 1963

Bibliography

Hamilton	Ian Hamilton, *Robert Lowell: a Biography*, Faber and Faber, 1984
Handford	Basil Handford, *Lancing College: History and Memoirs*, Phillimore, 1986
Hardwick	Michael and Mollie Hardwick, *Alfred Deller: A Singularity of Voice*, Proteus, 1980
Harewood	George, Earl of Harewood, *The Tongs and the Bones: The Memoirs of Lord Harewood*, Weidenfeld & Nicolson, 1981
HCI	Interviews conducted by Humphrey Carpenter (see list below)
Headington	Christopher Headington, *Britten*, Eyre Methuen, 1981
Headington, *Pears*	Christopher Headington, *Peter Pears: a Biography*, Faber and Faber, 1992
Holst	Imogen Holst, *Britten* (The Great Composers series), Faber and Faber, third edition 1980
Hussey	Walter Hussey, *Patron of Art*, Weidenfeld & Nicolson, 1985
IHD	Diary of Imogen Holst (unpublished), the Holst Foundation, Aldeburgh
James, *Aspern Papers*	Henry James, *The Aspern Papers and The Turn of the Screw*, ed. Anthony Curtis, Penguin, 1984
James, *Complete Tales*	Leon Edel (ed.), *The Complete Tales of Henry James*, Vol. 9, Hart-Davis, 1964
Kemp	Ian Kemp, *Tippett: the Composer and His Music*, Eulenburg Books, 1984
Kennedy	Michael Kennedy, *Britten* (The Master Musicians series), J. M. Dent, paperback edition 1983
Kennedy, *Walton*	Michael Kennedy, *Portrait of Walton*, Oxford University Press, 1989
L	Donald Mitchell and Philip Reed (eds.), *Letters from a Life: Selected Letters and Diaries of Benjamin Britten 1913–1976*, Vols 1 and 2, Faber and Faber, 1991
Lago / Furbank	Mary Lago and P. N. Furbank (eds.), *Selected Letters of E. M. Forster,* Vol. 2, Collins, 1985
MBB	Beth Britten, *My Brother Benjamin*, The Kensal Press, 1986 (actually published in 1987)
Medley	Robert Medley, *Drawn from the Life*, Faber and Faber, 1983
Miller	Charles H. Miller, *An American Friendship*, Scribner, 1983
M / E	Donald Mitchell and John Evans, *Benjamin Britten: Pictures from a Life 1913–1976*, Faber and Faber, 1978

M / K	Donald Mitchell and Hans Keller (eds.), *Benjamin Britten: A Commentary on his Works from a Group of Specialists*, Rockliff Publishing Corporation, 1952
OBB	David Herbert (ed.), *The Operas of Benjamin Britten*, Hamish Hamilton, 1979
Palmer	Tony Palmer, *Julian Bream: a Life on the Road*, Macdonald, 1982
PB	W. H. Auden, *Paul Bunyan: The Libretto of the Operetta by Benjamin Britten*, with an essay by Donald Mitchell, Faber and Faber, 1988
PG	Philip Brett (ed.) *Benjamin Britten: Peter Grimes*, Cambridge Opera Handbooks, Cambridge University Press, 1983
PGSW	Eric Crozier (ed.), *Benjamin Britten: Peter Grimes*, Sadler's Wells Opera Book No. 3, The Bodley Head, 1945
PPT	Marion Thorpe (ed.), *Peter Pears: A Tribute on his 75th Birthday*, Britten–Pears Library, 1985
Pudney	John Pudney, *Home and Away*, Michael Joseph, 1960
RB	Alan Blyth, *Remembering Britten*, Hutchinson, 1981
Schafer	Murray Schafer, *British Composers in Interview*, Faber and Faber, 1963
Searle	Muriel V. Searle, *John Ireland: The Man and His Music*, Midas Books, 1979
Stallybrass	Oliver Stallybrass (ed.) *Aspects of E. M. Forster*, Edward Arnold, 1969
Symons	Julian Symons, *The Thirties*, Faber and Faber, second edn., 1975
Tear	Robert Tear, *Tear Here*, André Deutsch, 1990
Tippett	Michael Tippett, *Those Twentieth Century Blues: an autobiography*, Hutchinson, 1991
TMS	Transcript of interview recorded with Sir Peter Pears (by Donald Mitchell) for *The Tenor Man's Story*, Central Television, 1985, produced by Jim Berrow
TS	Patricia Howard (ed.), *Benjamin Britten: The Turn of the Screw*, Cambridge Opera Handbooks, Cambridge University Press, 1985
Vishnevskaya	Galina Vishnevskaya, *Galina: a Russian story*, Hodder & Stoughton, 1984
Voice is a Person	*A Voice is a Person*, BBC radio documentary about Kathleen Ferrier, presented by Peter Pears, 1967
Walton	Susana Walton, *William Walton: Behind the Façade*, Oxford University Press, 1988
White	Eric Walter White, *Benjamin Britten: His Life and*

	Operas, second edition (edited by John Evans), Faber and Faber, 1983
Wildeblood	Peter Wildeblood, *Against the Law*, Weidenfeld & Nicolson, 1955
Wood	Sir Henry Wood, *My Life of Music*, Gollancz, 1938
Wren	Wilfred J. Wren, *Voices by the Sea: the story of the Aldeburgh Festival Choir*, Terence Dalton Ltd, 1981
Wright	Paul Wright, *A Brittle Glory*, Weidenfeld & Nicolson, 1968
Wright, *Faber*	David Wright, *Faber Music: the First 25 Years, 1965–1990*, Faber Music, 1990

Interviews by Humphrey Carpenter

These were conducted on the following dates:

Baker, Dame Janet   London, 20 March 1991
Berkeley, Michael   London, 5 December 1990
Britten, Marjorie (née Goldson)   London, 23 March 1991
Burrell, Bill   Aldeburgh, 8 June 1990
Butt, Richard   Oxford, 6 December 1990
Caplan, Isador   Aldeburgh, 8 June 1990
Coleman, Basil   London, 13 November 1990
Cowan, Jean   Aldeburgh, 9 June 1991
Cranbrook, Fidelity, Dowager Countess of   Great Glemham, 25 June 1990, and by telephone on many subsequent occasions
Cross, Joan   Aldeburgh, 8 June 1990
Crozier, Eric, and Evans, Nancy   Great Glemham, 8 June 1990 and 26 June 1990, and by telephone on many subsequent occasions
Del Mar, Norman   London, 29 January 1991
Douglas, Basil   London, 28 September 1990
Downes, Ralph   By telephone, 30 May 1990
Drummond, John   London, 11 June 1991
Duncan, Roger   Reading, 18 June 1991
Duncan, Rose-Marie, and Lawson, Briony (née Duncan)   Charlbury, 10 September 1990
Dunkerley, Barbara   Kirtlington, 16 July 1990
Ellis, Osian   London, 26 September 1991
Evans, John   Oxford, 26 June 1991
Evans, Nancy, see Crozier
Ferguson, Howard   By telephone, 11 June 1990
Francis, John   London, 9 April 1991
Gathorne-Hardy, Jonathan   Binham, 19 July 1990
Gathorne-Hardy, Sammy   By telephone, 23 April 1991

Grant, Keith   London, 12 March 1991
Harewood, George, Earl of   London, 13 March 1991
Harper, Heather   London, 12 March 1991
Hemmings, David   By telephone, 6 October 1991
Hemsley, Thomas   London, 14 May 1991
Hewitt, Jack   London, 22 April 1991
Hill, Susan   Oxford, 27 February 1991
Hurwitz, Emanuel   London, 15 March 1991
Knussen, Oliver   London, 8 May 1991
Ledger, Philip   Aldeburgh, 9 June 1991
Lumsden, Norman   London, 13 March 1991
Mackerras, Sir Charles   London, 21 January 1991
Mackie, Neil   Ruislip, 5 June 1991
Magill, Ronan   London, 27 June 1991
Malcolm, George   London, 3 January 1991
Matthews, Colin   London, 14 May and 4 September 1991
Maud, Hon. Humphrey   By telephone, 4 July 1990
Mitchell, Donald and Kathleen   London, 10 February 1991 and 9 April 1991;
    Horham, 11–13 October 1991
Nicholson, Patricia   Lowestoft, 27 June 1990
Nolan, Sir Sidney   Aldeburgh, 8 June 1991
Oldham, Arthur   By telephone, 28 June 1990
Palmer, Tony   London, 22 March 1991
Phipps, Susan   London, 15 March 1991
Piper, Myfanwy   Oxford, 31 October 1990, Fawley, 15 November 1991
Pounder, John   King's Lynn, 27 June 1990
Reeve, Alan   By telephone, 7 October 1990
Reeve, Eric   By telephone, 9 October 1990
Reiss, Stephen   Thorpeness, 17 and 19 February 1991
Sauerlander, Beata   By telephone, 17 June 1990
Saxton, Robert   London, 8 March 1991
Servaes, William   London, 8 and 14 May 1991
Sewell, Donald   Old Buckenham Hall School, 19 July 1990
Spenser, David   Stambourne, 30 July 1990
Strebi, Ursula   London, 13 March 1991
Strode, Rosamund   Aldeburgh, 17 and 20 February 1991, and by telephone and
    at Aldeburgh on many other occasions
Sugden, Derek   Oxford, 6 July 1991
Sweeting, Elizabeth   Oxford, 2 June 1990
Tear, Robert   London, 9 March 1991
Terry, Stephen   Hedenham, 16 February 1991
Thompson, Alan   By telephone, 10 September 1990
Thompson, Leonard   Oxford, 14 May 1990
Thomson, Rita   Aldeburgh, 19 February and 11 October 1991

Bibliography

Thorpe, Marion   London, 8 March 1991
Tippett, Sir Michael   Calne, 19 March 1991
Tooley, Sir John   London, 1 October 1991
Walker, Marian   Lowestoft, 20 July 1990
Wheeler, Pam and Surfling, Anne   Aldeburgh, 20 February 1991
Wood, Anne   London, 10 October 1990

Interviews by Donald Mitchell

These were conducted on the following dates:

Alston, John   Aldeburgh, 20 June 1988
Douglas, Basil   London, 16 November 1987
Harvey, Trevor   London, 15 December 1980
Isherwood, Christopher   Santa Monica, 22 April 1978
Mayer, Michael   Aldeburgh, 22 June 1988
Reeve, Basil   London, 3 October 1986
Scherchen, Wulff   London, 15 September 1989

Interviews by Elizabeth Sweeting
(transcribed from tapes in the Britten–Pears Library)

These were conducted on the following dates:

Del Mar, Norman   19 November 1985
Piper, John and Myfanwy   September 1986

Notes on sources of quotations

These are identified by the first words quoted. When two or more quotations from the same source follow each other with little intervening narrative, I have generally only used the first quotation for identification. Abbreviations refer to the Bibliography (Appendix B).

In the case of quotations from unpublished letters by Britten, only the name of the recipient and the date are given. Unless otherwise stated, these, and quotations from letters by Pears, are taken from transcripts, photocopies or carbons in the Britten–Pears Library.

PART ONE

1: Once upon a time there was a prep-school boy

page
3 '*determined* that he', L. 12. 'The county wouldn't, HCI. 'nice friendly dentist', HCI. 'he used to come', HCI.
4 'I come from', interview by Henry Comer, CBC, 11 April 1968. 'yeoman farmers', interview by Charles Ford *c.* 1976/7 (B–PL). 'I think my', ibid.
5 'a drunk', ibid. 'very religious', HCI. 'an interesting amateur', HCI. 'My mother was', to Eric Walter White, 2 Dec. 1953. 'probably due', MBB 30.
6 'He looked so', ATTW. 'After the war', MBB 31. 'the sound of', TMS. 'Very few', MBB 23.
7 'had a thought', *Lowestoft Journal*, 10 Dec. 1976. 'We used to', ATTW. 'I believe', to Eric Walter White, 2 Dec. 1953. 'Oh, he was', ATTW. 'I think he', ATTW. 'in skin-coloured', *Tempo*, autumn 1951. 'I remember', White 19.
8 'it was really', L 100. 'beautiful . . . very detailed', MBB 43–4. 'Miss E. K. M. Astle', *Lowestoft Journal*, 17 Sep. 1921. 'soon able', Holst 12. 'at Sotterly', MBB 46. 'we had a secure', MBB 37. 'always rather like', ATTW. 'Bobby, they're', HCI.
9 'about 20', L 76. 'Lift your leg', MBB 44. 'Once upon a', L 77.

10 'As we go', *South Lodge School Magazine (Lowestoft)*, Christmas 1923. 'If you were', HCI. 'I can remember', *Guardian*, 7 June 1971. 'There was some', ATTW. 'It's rather', HCI. 'very pleasant', HCI.

11 'We have to congratulate', *South Lodge School Magazine (Lowestoft)*, Christmas 1924. 'a tremendous debt', *Eastern Daily Press*, 26 April 1952. 'Where did your', HCI. 'much more conscious', White 19.

12 'afraid that if', MBB 51. 'ploughing through', to Alan Frank, 1 September 1970 (Oxford University Press). 'reams and reams', L 78. 'His friends', L 77. 'passionately keen', CL. 'He was just', ATTW. 'We all knew', *Eastern Daily Press*, 30 July 1951. 'A distinctly useful', *South Lodge School Magazine (Lowestoft)*, Summer 1927. 'He could stand', ATTW.

13 'they are still', L 78. 'odd moments', , L 778. 'I can never', D 31 Aug. 1930. 'My Mummie', L 81. 'each mother', MBB 48. 'I was never', John Alston to the author, 9 June 1989.

14 'heard Frank Bridge', BLB. 'an extraordinary', HCI. 'Frank did give', HCI. 'Oh, that', 274. 'Little Benjamin', *Lowestoft Journal*, 31 Jan. 1948. 'spends far too much', ibid. 'developed into', L 83. 'We think that', *South Lodge School Magazine (Lowestoft)*, Summer 1927.

15 'complaining that', MBB 49. 'The outlook', L 90. 'had not talked', MBB 49. 'I spent', BLB. 'By the time', BLB.

16 'When I said', IHD 2 Nov. 1953. 'had no other', BLB. 'was the popular', MBB 54. 'It was a red', Schafer 119. 'Saw Frank', D 12 Jan. 1928. 'Even though', BLB.

17 'I used to get', BLB. 'used to perform', L 101. 'two cardinal', BLB. 'At one point', BLB. 'blinking and twitching', MBB 53. 'often I used', BLB. 'I, who thought', CL.

18 'Work hard', D 23–8 Jan. 1928. 'Finish orchestral', D 6 March 1928. 'very strange', *Rattle on Britten*, BBC TV, 2 Nov. 1985.

19 'the fourteen-year-old', BC 309. 'suppressed all mention', Crozier, 'Notes'.

20 'I wasn't given', HCI. 'I think Ben', HCI. 'Peter and Mother', HCI.

21 'I think if', HCI. 'I don't know', HCI. 'Sewell said', South Lodge old boy who wishes not to be named, to the author, 20 Sept. 1990. 'Set off', D 13 June 1928. 'he could be', HCI. 'We all liked', HCI. 'quite possible', HCI.

22 'The more I', Donald Sewell to the author, 31 Aug 1990. 'Talking to him', HCI. 'You won't send', HCI (Patricia Nicholson). 'he wasn't', HCI. 'born homosexual', HCI.

23 'Was Ben', HCI. 'I can't remember', HCI.

24 'sure something', HCI. 'never heard', HCI. 'a couple of', HCI. 'a feeling of', HCI. 'The point is', ATTW. 'Beth had', HCI. 'I took an', HCI.

2: Utter loneliness

26 'I like this', L 93. 'I am in.' D 21 Sept. 1928. 'In my study', D 23 Sept. 1928. 'His mother', MBB 56.

27 'they don't seem', L 93. 'horrible', L 96. 'My duty', D 1928 (flyleaf). 'very flimsy', L 96, 'So *you*', Holst 20. 'hopeless for', L 96. 'first . . . in my', D 13 Nov. 1928. 'Oh! Beethoven', D 24 June 1929. 'it would be', L 96. 'domed, bald', L 223. 'with no two', L 96.

28 'I am longing', L 94. 'Mummy darling', L 97. 'Wonderful lesson', D 9 Nov. 1928. 'a great', D 18 Jan. 1937. 'wonderful', D 9 Nov. 1928. 'very nice', D 10 Nov. 1928. 'utter loneliness', D 17 Jan. 1929. 'Stravinsky's', D 21 Jan. 1929. 'All the time', D 4 Feb. 1929. 'It is ripping', D 23 Feb. 1929. 'yearning for', D 13 Feb. 1929. 'I still think', L 103. 'Go and see', D 31 July 1929. 'FRANCIS comes', D 5 May 1929. 'It's been', D 13 Sept. 1929. 'He meant', L 105.

29 'Originality', D 19 Nov. 1929. 'The only', D 29 and 30 July 1929. 'The day ends', D 17 July 1929. 'I think that', D 6 Dec. 1929. 'a very reliable', *Gresham*, 14 Dec. 1929.

30 'positively miraculous', L 115. 'I am thinking', D 20 Nov. 1929. 'a marvellous', D 7 April 1930. 'Read quite', D 9 Dec. 1929. 'I find that', D 25 Feb. 1930. 'E. B. Britten's', *Gresham*, 15 Feb. 1930. 'neither the piano', D 10 Dec. 1929. 'Sat. night', D 16 Dec. 1929. 'effort against', D 17 Dec. 1929. 'marvellous lesson', D 10 Jan. 1930. 'How I loathe', D 16 Jan. 1930. 'We knew that', *Gresham*, 29 March 1930.

31 'It goes', D 1 March 1930. 'what Benjamin', *Lowestoft Journal*, 30 May 1986. 'Quite a successful', D 21 June 1930. 'She arranged', L 11. 'the centre', L 14. '. . . the apex', *Gresham*, 7 June 1930.

32 'my pieces', D 29 March 1930. 'Letter from Pop', D 12 May 1930. 'he should go', MBB 55. 'If I have', D 7 May 1930. 'try for a', L 132. 'I have given', D 12 June 1930.

33 'Pt. song', D 19 June 1930. 'took his paper', MBB 59. 'After that', D 19 June 1930. 'That's a splendid', L 132. 'We are *delighted*', L 131. 'Write . . . "Hymn to the Virgin"', D 9 July 1930. 'I spend all', D 27 July 1930.

34 'sketch for strings', D 19 Aug. 1930. 'It is marvellous', D 31 July 1930.

3: What an institution

35 'stressed the amateur', *Modern Music*, Jan/Feb. 1941. 'The attitude', *High Fidelity Magazine*, Dec. 1959. 'This is a topping', L 40. 'It is rather', D 20 Sept. 1930. 'Oh, God', D 23 Sept. 1930. 'rather a cold', HCI.

36 'all Elgar', L 140. 'Much too long', D 23 Sept. 1930. 'I . . . saw', Kennedy 10–11. 'Mr Benjamin', L 140. 'a marvellous', D 8 Oct. 1930. 'Yes, but', Schafer 124. 'says that I', D 3 Dec. 1930. 'Lor', I'm bad', D 13 Jan. 1931.

37 'music class', D 24 Sept. 1930. 'so easy', D 14 Jan. 1931. 'a live composer', L 133. 'positively ripping', D 1 March 1929. 'terribly strict', L 144. 'very beautiful', D 2 Oct. 1930. 'marvellous', D 27 Oct. 1930. 'He is *terribly*', D 16 Oct. 1930. 'still in bed', MBB 59. 'The other two', Schafer 30. 'This is the finest', Searle 80–1. '*not* Vaughan Williams', L 191.

38 'Everything one knows', Kennedy 10. 'not given him', L 46. 'With me', L 146. 'I am plodding', L 144. 'the Palestrina things', D 23 Oct. 1930. 'a choral piece', D 31 Jan. 1931. 'quite pleased', D 8 May 1931. 'grasp of form', L 195. 'That's what makes', RB 171. 'fit only', L 143. 'innumerable Beethoven', D 26 July 1931.

39 'quite liked', D 9 Jan. 1931. 'Remarkable', D 28 Jan. 1931. 'I min of', D 18 Feb. 1931. 'sonorous orchestration', D 6 May 1931. '*terrible execrable*', D 4 Nov. 1931. 'Didn't like Bax', D 4 Feb. 1931. 'thrilling to', D 4 Dec. 1930. 'v. beautiful', D 6 May 1931. 'England's premier', L 143. 'The country', D 20 June 1931. 'rather good', BLB. 'opened my eyes', BLB.

40 'the latest poems', BLB. 'quite drunk', D 22 Oct. 1931. 'He peed', HCI. 'He was most', David Green to the author, 20 Sept. 1990. 'the most highly', L 191. 'Ireland's star', D 26 Feb. 1931. 'V. competant', D 26 Feb. 1931. 'a moaning', L 147. 'very kind', L 147. 'At about', BLB. 'very clever', L 191. 'absolute Farce', D 27 July 1931.

41 'He had written', BLB. 'It's jolly', D 31 Oct. 1930. '*Musical Evening*', D 9 Jan. 1932. 'We made', interviewed by Rosamund Strode, 23 November 1985 (B–PL).

42 'the World's', D 2 Sept. 1932. 'It contains', D 9 Nov. 1932. 'a fine work', D 9 Sept. 1931. 'stood out', D 10 Sept. 1931. 'Elgar was', HCI. 'I feel', D 24 Sept. 1931. 'showed me', L 202. 'high class', Foreman 134. 'delightful and', D 7 June 1932. 'apparently bad', D 11 Aug. 1932. 'very moving', D 25 Nov. 1931.

43 'bad – but', D 22 July 1932. 'complete fiasco', D 11 July 1932. 'I have never heard', D 22 Sept. 1932. 'What an institution', D 13 Oct. 1932. 'so as not', D 4 Nov. 1932.

44 'In many ways', Crozier, 'Notes'. 'the lesbian', HCI. (Donald Mitchell). 'beastly', D 10 Jan. 1932. 'v. good', D 11 April 1932. 'Barrie's little', D 31 Dec. 1933. 'It's good', D 5 April 1931. 'much against', D 26 Dec. 1929. 'a hopeless', HCI. 'positively unhealthy', D 8 April 1930.

45 'slop', D 19 Aug. 1932. 'the most perfect', D 28 March 1933. 'a Suite', D 3 April 1933. 'impressed', D 7 Dec. 1933. 'a sketch', D 13 March 1934. 'a marvellous', D 24 Sept. 1932. 'Why not', D 2 June 1932. 'New Bass', D 24 Nov. 1932. 'I would hunch', Wright 15. 'if one put', L 288.

46 'Elisabeth Lutyens', Iris Lemare to the author, 10 March 1990. 'v. pleased', D 16 March 1932. 'I think it', L 259. 'ought to use', BLB.

47 'incredible', Holst 24. 'You ought', R. Vaughan Williams to Anne Macnaghten, n.d. [1932] (Anne Macnaghten). 'very young', HCI. 'v. well', D 12 Dec. 1932. 'attractive', *The Times*, 16 Dec. 1932. 'good for one', *Music Lover*, 17 Dec. 1932. 'I saw', L 295. 'I can well', *Opera*, Feb. 1952.

48 'quite well', D 31 Jan. 1933. 'Mr Benjamin', *Daily Telegraph*, 1 Feb. 1933. 'Mr Benjamin Britten, after', *The Times*, 3 Feb. 1933. 'very flattering', L 344. 'A Sinfonietta', *Music Lover*, 4 Feb. 1933. 'I do whole-heartedly', L 297.

4: Depressed for English music

49 'protestations', Frank Bridge to Britten, 4 Jan. 1933 (B–PL). 'Lesson with', D 13 Jan. 1933. 'The broadcast', L 304. 'original', *The Times*, 25 Nov. 1933.

50 'a large choral work', L 303. 'My dear', L 310. 'Isn't old', R. V. Britten to Beth Britten, 19 Dec. 1933 (B–PL). 'no doctor', MBB 70. 'slur', D 31 Dec. 1933. 'David's mov.', D 12 March 1935. 'rather rude', Iris Lemare to the author, 3 April 1990.

51 'a different', Schafer 114. 'Listen to', D 13 Feb. 1933. 'thoroughly sincere', D 8 March 1933. 'extraordinarily', D 14 March 1934. 'What I could', D 8 Feb.. 1933. 'unapproachable', D 29 Sept. 1933. 'what music!', D 11 May 1933. 'common-place', D 9 Nov. 1932. 'a mix up', D 23 April 1933. '1st, (& I hope, last)', D 25 April 1933. 'I *am* afraid', D 1 Feb. 1933. 'technically inefficient', D 18 April 1933. 'My struggle', *High Fidelity Magazine*, Dec. 1959.

52 'suggested to the', Schafer 114. 'I said at home', BLB. 'discovered that', Schafer 114. 'There was at', BLB. 'I *am* going', L 328. 'I cannot', L 319. 'F.B. looks', D 11 Jan. 1934.

53 'my "Simple Symphony"'', D 6 March 1934. 'They sing', D 16 Feb. 1934. 'Here in this', *Radio Times*, 16 Feb. 1934.

54 'great extrovert', L 333. 'There was', L 337. 'by Italian', D 2 April 1934. 'After dinner', D 31 July 1934. 'I can't stand', D 7 March 1935. 'Goossens &', D 5 April 1934. 'Lunch given', D 6 April 1934. 'we were the', DMI. 'a marvellous', DMI.

55 'It was', DMI. 'Meet Wulff', D 7 April 1934. 'You know all', MBB 73. 'impossibly ghastly', D 12 Oct. 1933. 'half expecting', MBB 75. 'Pop brightens', D 27 March 1934. 'Goodbye my', R. V. Britten to his children, n.d. [1934] (B–PL). 'a pretty filthy', L 337.

56 'Arr. Newhaven', D 9 April 1934. 'Don't do', D 10 April 1934. 'Mum is', D 10 April 1934. 'Pop dies', D 6 April 1934. 'written by', *Lowestoft Journal*, 14 April 1934. 'A pupil', *Eastern Daily Press*, 20 Feb. 1934.

57 'left us', L 334–5. 'Mum had had', L 337. 'My darling', L 340–1. 'Sketch a school', D 4 May 1934. 'Robert . . . was', Crozier, 'Notes'.

58 'I shall be', D 22 May 1934. 'a man', D 23 May 1934. 'I see Ralph', D 30 May 1934. 'it is an effort', D 30 May 1934. 'Miss Astle', D 13 June 1934. 'long thinking', D 19 June 1934. 'heavenly sunset', D 1 May 1934. 'thinking walk', D 1 April 1935. 'most disconcertingly', D 24 March 1935. 'certainly his', HCI. (Barbara Dunkerley). 'quite well', D 29 June 1934. 'quite well', D 29 June 1934. 'decided to', *Opera*, Feb. 1952.

59 'Benjamin Britten's', *Musical Times*, Aug. 1934. 'unobservant', *Opera*, Feb. 1952. 'to catch', L 344. 'impressions of', L 348. 'a very long', L 353. 'very busy', MBB 80. 'a simply', L 353. 'the Mozart', L 353.

60 'quiet rooms', MBB 82. 'Never such', L 354. 'Meistersinger', L 357–8.

'Benjamin looks', MBB 85. 'go round', MBB 79. 'very nice', D 5 Nov. 1934. 'gets very', MBB 81. 'a bit wobbly', D 7 Nov. 1934. 'Personally I', D 6 Nov. 1934. 'come here', L 354. 'enough to keep', *High Fidelity Magazine*, Dec. 1959. 'I have a', MBB 83.

61 'The five', D 13 Nov. 1934. 'sick', L 357. 'A great', D 24 Nov. 1934. 'thrilling', D 29 Nov. 1934. 'To-day I', D 17 Sept. 1934. 'Try in vain', D 25 Sept. 1934. 'they avoid', *The Times*, 4 Dec. 1934. 'his music', *Observer*, 23 Dec. 1934.

62 'one of the', Hubert Foss to Humphrey Milford, 2 June 1933 (Oxford University Press). 'Now I am', L 364. 'F[oss] has', D 28 Jan. 1935. 'It was *hopeless*', L 363. 'It is no', D 16 Jan. 1935.

63 'There is a', D 8 Feb. 1935. 'A most', D 27 April 1935.

5: The most amazing man

64 'Literal hell', D 1 May 1935. 'I'm having', D 24 Jan. 1935. 'Usual day', D 6 March 1935. 'I had to work', CL.

65 'I don't', L 897. 'At 10.30', D 2 May 1935. 'too nationalistic', D 4 May 1935. 'It was also', CL. 'masterpieces', D 8 April 1935. 'a little', D 12 Feb and 1 March 1935. 'glorious', D 1 July 1935. 'Long talks', D 8 May 1935. 'What a job!', D 16 May 1935. 'It goes quite', D 17 May 1935.

66 'a damn', HCl. 'Spend morning', D 4 June 1935. 'entirely experimental', D 17 June 1935. 'I well remember', CL. 'absolutely dead', D 19 June 1935. 'Everyone's', D 18 June 1935. 'Have a quick', D 5 July 1935.

67 'a very brilliant', D 5 July 1935. 'Walk about', D 6 July 1935. 'extraordinary musical', Carpenter, *Auden*, 178. 'fourteen small', D 11 July 1935.

68 'Go straight', D 2 Sept. 1935. 'not princely', Carpenter, *Auden*, 181. 'seems rather', D 6 Aug. 1935. 'Work with Auden', D 9 Sept. 1935. 'delivering Peace', D 19 Feb. 1935. 'very serious', D 3 Feb. 1935. 'to talk', D 1 Aug. 1935. 'I swear', D 5 Sept. 1935.

69 'Spend day', D 17 Sept. 1935. 'it is partly', D 8 Nov. 1935. 'I am hopelessly', D 3 Sept. 1935. 'Go to Soho', D 10 Oct. 1935. 'I know you', L 378. 'a Kensington', D 23 Oct. 1935.

70 'There was Wystan', Medley 162–3. 'Both very', D 5 Oct. 1935. 'Over dinner', Medley 163. 'A great tragedy', D 6 Nov. 1935.

71 'absolutely no', D 4 Nov. 1935. 'guarantee of', D opening entry, Jan. 1936. 'railway sound', D 12 Nov. 1935. 'pretty violent', D 6 Dec. 1935. 'compressed steam', D 18 Dec. 1935. 'Not very good', D 9 Jan. 1936. 'lovely verse', D 3 Jan. 1936. 'A large orchestra', D 15 Jan. 1936. 'somewhat blasé', Blades 152. 'There is too', D 15 Jan. 1936.

72 'not at all', D 16 Jan. 1936. 'having alot', D opening entry, Jan. 1936. 'riotously funny', D 12 Sept. 1935. 'quite competent', D 27 Jan. 1936. 'It is absolutely', D 10 March 1936. 'it made some', D 28 Feb. 1936. 'They are

72 lovely', D 30 Dec. 1935. 'delightful', D 14 April 1936.

73 'makes one think', D 2 Feb. 1936. 'feel it is', D 9 Feb. 1936. 'revel', D 6 June 1936. 'I suppose', D 27 June 1936. 'surrenders completely', D 21 June 1936. 'a nice', D 22 June 1936. 'playing Beethoven', D 11 June 1936. 'Wagner fever', D 2 June 1936. 'Now I more', D 29 May 1936. 'I feel it', L 391. 'Very amusing', D 26 Jan. 1934. 'Of course', D 18 March 1936.

74 'sole upholder', D 19 March 1936. 'All nervousness', D 13 March 1936. 'It isn't', D 2 March 1936. 'typical respectable', D 10 Jan. 1936. 'a consolation', Symons 39. 'Piers makes', D 10 Jan. 1936. 'Giles Romilly', D 16 Jan. 1936. 'playing the step-father', D 13 July 1936. 'My foster', L 419.

75 'watch some', D 19 Jan. 1936. 'late teens', Duncan 14. 'He is a very', D 23 Feb. 1936. 'Received with', D 25 Feb. 1936. 'Mr Britten', *Daily Telegraph*, 26 Feb. 1936. 'I feel like', D 26 Feb. 1936. 'He is quite', D 24 Jan. 1936. 'Arrive in', D 3 Feb. 1936.

76 'lunch . . . with Auden', D 14 Feb. 1936. 'I am reading', D 31 Jan. 1936.

6: The deluge and the earthquake

77 'Underneath the', EA 160.

78 'very light', D 17 Nov. 1936. 'it goes', D 7 March 1936. 'at great length', D 22 Jan. 1936. 'We talk', D 2 Jan. 1936. 'quibbling about', D 29 Feb. 1936. 'Auden has', L 418–19. 'impressed', D 23 March 1936.

79 'getting ideas', D 11 April 1936 '*very* good', L 429. 'to do music', D 30 March 1936. 'the censor', *Manchester Guardian*, 8 April 1936. 'the now "*famous*"', D 9 April 1936. 'mostly Communists', D 23 Feb. 1936. 'just shattering', D 19 April 1936. 'It is difficult', D 24 April 1936.

80 'the sensuous', D 25 April 1936. 'where the food', D 12 May 1936. 'my 1st', D 22 April 1936. 'Long walk', D 7 April 1936. 'meet Piers', D 15 April 1936. 'Jennifer (aged 6)', D 22 Aug. 1936. 'very nice', D 5 June 1936. 'wonderful fantasy', D 12 Jan. 1936. 'long thinking', D 5 June 1936.

81 'Wystan . . . sent', D 22 May 1936. 'Night covers up', EA 162. 'not poems', Pears to the author, 24 April 1980.

82 'I go to', D 11 May 1936. 'An era', D 19 Feb. 1936. 'lots of bother', D 7 June 1936. 'the periodical', D 11 April 1936. 'She disapproves', D 11 June 1936. 'Now, ma cherie', L 396. 'Much love, my sweet', L 450. 'My darling', L 456–7.

83 'Beethoven's op.', D 8 June 1936. 'Hard going', D 22 July 1936. 'really great', D 15 Aug. 1936. 'I find', D 13 July 1936. 'undress and', D 19 July 1936. 'luxury, but', D 1 Nov. 1936. 'pleasant – if', D 16 July 1936. 'One thing', D 24 July 1936. 'a funeral', D 24 July 1936. 'But what', L 436. 'A boy', MBB 91. 'The small', D 24 May 1936. 'He is a dear', D 26 July 1936.

84 'To its advantage', D 19 June 1936. 'we have', D 28 July 1936. 'Long talks', D 29 July 1936. 'work a lot', D 30 July 1936. 'a very sorrowing', D 30 July 1936. 'we think', D 9 Aug. 1936. 'long intimate', D 19 Aug. 1936.

'Kit & Piers', D 6 Sept. 1936. 'slept only', D 7 Sept. 1936.

85 'rosy' D 3 Sept. 1936. 'a work of', D 3 Sept. 1936. 'very satirical', L 429. 'no discipline', D 19 Sept. 1936. 'the members', MBB 92. 'but he won't', D 20 Sept. 1936. 'Most of the', D 21 Sept. 1936.

86 'looming ahead', D 24 Sept. 1936. 'Mum & Beth', D 25 Sept. 1936. 'I always make', L 799. 'Disgusting!', Kennedy 22. 'difficult to believe', note to EMI CDM 7 69522 2. 'dangerous', HCI.

87 'The soprano', L 444–5. 'account of present-day', D 24 March 1936. 'The orchestra', D 25 Sept. 1936. 'the quintessence', L 433. 'not a very', MBB 92. 'he was very', BLB.

88 'Oh, I do', interviewed by Rosamund Strode, 23 Nov. 1985 (B–PL). 'Notices of', D 26 Sept. 1936. 'only now 23', *The Times*, 26 Sept. 1936. 'It is extremely', L 433. 'a very early', to Carlos Pemberton, 17 Sept. 1957. 'Ben was still', Colin Matthews to the author, 21 July 1991. 'a clear', L 442.

89 'any of Arthur', MBB 88. 'a bit ironicle', D 16 Oct. 1936. 'feed a poor', D 6 Nov. 1936. 'Wystan Auden', D 7 Oct. 1936. 'Mum furnished', MBB 98. 'Piers comes', D 19 Dec. 1936. 'appalling inferiority', D 1 Dec 1936. 'he tells', D 1 Dec 1936. 'charming and', MBB 98. 'being slightly', D 15 Dec 1936. 'Mum takes', D 6 Dec 1936.

90 'To my friend', W. H. Auden and Louis MacNeice, *Letters from Iceland*, Faber & Faber, 1937, 238. 'A happy', D 1 Jan. 1937. 'It is terribly', D 8 Jan. 1937. 'two grand', D 8 Jan. 1937. 'Mum never', L 465. 'even now', L 465.

91 'a commissionaire', D 12 Jan. 1937. 'we are taken', D 12 Jan. 1937. 'not examining', D 14 Jan. 1937. 'He is indeed', D 15 Jan. 1937. 'an attendant', D 16 Jan. 1937.

92 'It is a glorious', D 17 Jan. 1937. 'brilliantly amusing', D 19 Jan. 1937. 'Mum's not feeling', D 19 Jan. 1937. 'Beth is much', D 20 Jan. 1937. 'the coldest, *High Fidelity Magazine*, Dec. 1959. 'holding her', D 21 Jan. 1937. 'seems to be', D 23 Jan. 1937. 'Mum definitely', D 25 Jan. 1937. 'reassuring comments', D 26 Jan. 1937. 'mostly incoherent', D 27 Jan. 1937. 'a fine chance', D 28 Jan. 1937.

93 'Beth still', D 30 Jan. 1937. 'We get a', D 31 Jan. 1937.

PART TWO

1: One's resistance . . . gradually weakening

97 'The undertakers', D 1 Feb. 1937. 'meet us', D 3 Feb. 1937. '. . . it helps', D 10 Feb. 1937. 'a little Mother's', D 11 Feb. 1937. 'O God', D 12 Feb. 1937. 'responsible for', IHD 27 Nov. 1952. 'Certainly when', DMI. 'defeatist', D 18 Feb. 1937. 'it is nice', D 18 Feb. 1937.

98 'a good &', D 26 Feb. 1937. 'I feel that', D 1 March 1937. 'hotly', D 3

98 March 1937. 'emphasises the', D 5 March 1937. 'Lunch with', D 6 March 1937. 'One really', DMI. 'You never', HCI. 'there was', HCI. 'a far more', DMI. 'One always', HCI. 'rather stiff-necked', Crozier, 'Notes'.

99 'very dearly', TMS. 'I never had', Headington, *Pears* 6. '*I had a*', HCI. 'a well behaved', TMS. 'If Peter', DMI. 'took my place', TMS. 'amorous pursuits', Headington, *Pears* 16. 'the wonderful', HCI.

100 'I shall never', TMS. 'My dear', Headington, *Pears* 31–2. 'a rather drab', Headington, *Pears* 39. 'a marvellous', Headington, *Pears* 39.

101 'I wanted', TMS. 'He didn't trust', Headington, *Pears* 43. 'a very small', DMI. 'It wasn't', Headington, *Pears* 54. 'I'm wiser', IHD 13 Jan. 1953. 'Two g-1', Peter Pears, Travel Diary, 1936, unpublished (B–PL).

102 'Peter's romantic', Headington, *Pears* 49. 'Peter was', HCI. 'When I first', Crozier, 'Notes'. 'They had', DMI. 'I catch', D 13 March 1937. 'very pathetic', D 14 March 1937. 'plays with', D 15 March 1937. 'I am very', D 24 March 1937. 'I have such', D 28 March 1937. 'queerness', D 4 April 1937.

103 'He is a dear', D 11 April 1937. 'has suddenly', D 23 April 1937. 'a special pet', D 25 April 1937. 'sentimental memories', D 1 April 1937. 'killed in', D 27 April 1937. 'I was on', TMS. 'dinner with', D 30 April 1937.

104 'Peter Pears', D 7 May 1937. 'the nightingales', TMS. 'He is a', D 11 May 1937. 'exhilarating duel', D 25 May 1937. 'Peter is', D 26 May 1937. 'irritates me', D 23 April 1937. 'Lennox ... has', D 6 April 1937. 'set a serious', D 5 May 1937.

105 'a light one', D 5 May 1937. 'caberet songs', D 10 May 1937. 'it isn't there', D 4 June 1937. 'It is cruel', L 493.

106 'delighting their', D 6 June 1937. 'very clever', D 5 and 6 June 1937. '& a great', D 17 June 1937. 'suitable spots', D 20 June 1937. 'well-nigh hopeless', M/K 239. 'is putting', D 8 June 1937.

107 'The Variations', D 24 June 1937. 'a Mill', D 29 June 1937. 'slightly drunk', D 3 June 1937. 'a grand', D 15 March 1937. 'sex between', Carpenter, *Auden*, 188. 'I know nothing', Sir Stephen Spender to the author, 22 May 1990. 'No doubt', Carpenter, *Auden*, 187–8. 'Well, have we', Headington 35.

108 'a little work', D 4 July 1937. 'I start', D 5 July 1937. 'the end', D 10 July 1937. 'straight in', D 12 July 1937.

109 'I ... cannot', L 576. 'I don't know', Frank Bridge to Britten, 16 March 1938 (B–PL). 'I have never', L 495. 'our cottage', D 20 June 1937.

110 'I lunch', D 3 July 1937. 'Much time', D 15 July 1937. 'I saw', M/K 239. 'He is charming', D 28 July 1937. 'Peter Pears', D 28 July 1937. 'I was rather', Dickinson 46. 'If you want', ibid. 26

111 'Lunch with', D 20 Sept. 1937. 'Ben ... always', DMI. 'I decide', D 30 July 1937. 'Much love', Piers Dunkerley to Britten, n.d. (B–PL). 'all the best', Piers Dunkerley to Britten, n.d. (B–PL). 'a splendid', D 26 June 1937.

'slight over-dose', D 11 Oct. 1937. 'adopt', D 30 April 1937. 'lunch with', D 8 Sept. 1937.

112 'Peter stays', D 8 Sept. 1937. 'much talk', D 9 Sept. 1937. 'he runs thro''', D 10 Sept. 1937. 'an extraordinary', TMS. 'could make', RB 18. 'Ben manages', HCI (Rosamund Strode). 'Ben could', HCI. 'letting it up', HCI. 'It was amazing', TMS. 'Ben wanted', HCI. 'Ben didn't', ATTW.

113 'without slackening', D 21 Sept. 1937. 'nice words', D 29 Sept. 1937. 'In those', DMI. '. . . if he studies', D 15 Oct. 1937. 'and that, the Almighty', L 508. 'Next year', L 518. 'I'll have', L 518. 'The loss', D 20 Oct. 1937. 'flying Dutchman', L 527.

114 'Christopher's one', D 2 Nov. 1937. 'I like', D 17 Nov. 1937. 'fearfully badly', D 25 Nov. 1937. 'they are far', D 19 Nov. 1937. 'I'm having', Marjorie Fass to Daphne Oliver, n.d. [Dec. 1937] (B–PL).

115 'the *pièce*', Medley 141. 'very professionally', L 545. 'Beastly crowd', D 18 and 19 Jan. 1938. 'Sleeping with', D 9 Feb. 1938. 'going marvellously', D 14 Feb. 1938. 'Lunch Peter', D 19 Feb. 1938. 'laid up', L 526. 'so worried', Marjorie Fass to Daphne Oliver, n.d. [Dec. 1937] (B–PL).

116 'it dashes', D 7 Feb. 1938. 'Probably a', D 25 Feb. 1938. 'end to all', D 12 March 1938. 'unfurnished abit', D 16 March 1938. 'He was no', ATTW. 'Stuck in', D 21 March 1938. 'elated', L 553. 'the great move', D 9 April 1938. 'The country', D 15 April 1938. 'for tootling', D 14 April 1938. 'ton', D 15 April 1938. 'Lennox's furniture', D 13 April 1938. 'As I go', D 16 May 1938.

117 'It's been', L 554. 'Ben did not', MBB 106. 'about twelve', MBB 107. 'Andoni is', L 554. 'lovely day', D 6 May 1938. 'José', D 21 May 1938. 'Francis Barton', D 22 May 1938.

118 'Francis sounds', L 559. 'He is a', D 24 May 1938. 'Francis goes', D 27 May 1938. 'The correct line', L 575. 'get down', D 13 June 1938.

2: I daren't mutter the name

119 'I do not', L 562–3. 'We two', L 563–4. 'windmill in', L 563. 'Mind you', L 573. 'always a bit', L 533. 'The piano', L 574.

120 'VIVE LA', L 575. 'If music', L 575. 'dislikes this', *Radio Times*, 12 Aug. 1938. 'simple and', M/E 111. 'brilliant', *Listener*, 25 Aug. 1938. 'he was quite', MBB 107. 'admirable throughout', *Listener*, 25 Aug. 1938.

121 'or is the composer's', *The Times*, 19 Aug. 1938. 'And what', L 575. 'I'm glad', L 580. 'I expect', Marjorie Fass to Daphne Oliver, 19 Aug. 1938 (B–PL). 'Shall I get', L 575. 'On when', L 581. 'Wystan was', DMI. 'I adored', DMI.

122 'strange thing', L 14. 'Benjamin . . . is', L 593. 'a bit', L 589. 'a grand little', D 17 Sept. 1937. 'best so far', D 22 Sept. 1937. 'Rows', D 1 Aug. 1937. 'first since', D 2 Aug. 1937. 'very much', HCI.

123 'music which', *Observer*, 19 Feb. 1939. 'In my mind's', L 591. 'The strain',

123   L 596. 'much more', L 586. 'jitters . . . over', L 611.

124   'Isn't everything', L 615. 'I envy', L 518. 'No composer', *Listener*, 25 Aug.
      1938. 'v. much want', L 587. 'that means', L 610. 'really beautiful', D 18
      Feb. 1935.

125   'now definitely', L 603. 'to do some', L 618. 'time that Britten', *Musical
      Times*, July 1938. 'never be a big', *Observer*, 9 April 1939. 'increasing
      brilliancy', *Listener*, 25 Aug. 1938. 'were travelling', L 604.

126   'two good', L 617. 'beautiful exercises', *Birmingham Post*, 22 April 1939.
      'I did not', MBB 109. 'We thought', interview with Anthony Friese-Greene
      c. 1977 (B–PL). 'Peter'll be', L 618. 'I realized', DMI. 'a singer', L 1337.

127   'I liked him', *High Fidelity Magazine*, Dec. 1959. 'Well, the car', L 615–16.
      'which Ben', HCI. 'Peter always', HCI. 'Benjie my', L 558–9. 'Much love',
      L 616. 'Somehow things', ATTW.

128   'I didn't fit', DMI. 'One relationship', PG 33. 'I say', L 631.

129   'A thousand', L 634. 'What a fool', L 632. 'bloody boring', L 631–2. 'but
      the band', L 641. 'the Rimbaud', L 639. '& I stay', L 645. 'We are getting',
      MBB 111–12. 'I am so', L 195. 'The next time', L 657.

130   'Calypso is', L 657. 'Most shout', L 657–8. 'a letter from', MBB 111. 'as
      often as', L 663–4. 'I wonder', Pears to Britten, n.d. [28 Feb. 1959]. 'I shall
      never', L 759. 'it is *you*', L 60. 'He said that', HCI.

131   'Peter sends', L 702.

3: Stuck here

132   'interviews with', L 665. 'I'm thinking', L 668. 'I might as', L 671. 'I can't
      do', L 672.

133   'It was an', L 674. 'New York is', L 684. 'immense', L 675. 'had to come',
      L 684. 'operetta for', L 675. 'rather inspired', L 691. 'founded on last', L
      742. 'worried constantly', L 678. 'I think you', Aaron Copland to Britten, 6
      Sept. 1939 (B–PL).

134   'You can't tell', L 696. 'I went', Auden to Mrs A.E. Dodds, n.d. [1940]
      (Bodleian Library, Oxford). 'what the Spanish', D 1 Dec. 1936.

135   'my position', Carpenter, *Auden*, 270–1. 'I've seen', L 696. 'It looks', L
      697. 'Thank you', L 698. 'my mother', DMI. 'Ben and Peter', Carpenter,
      Auden, 276. 'Mrs Mayer', L 769. 'She was', TMS.

136   'Peter & I', L 725. 'tho' we eat', L 728. 're other', L 724–5.

137   'oh Hedli', L 720.

138   'a reproof', L 715. 'Peter seemed', HCI. 'My darling', L 758–9.

139   'Do you know', L 761. 'I am worth', Pears to Britten, n.d. [Jan. 1940]. 'I
      was aware', *Guardian*, 18 June 1983. 'Peter wasn't', HCI. 'he could never',
      HCI. 'My darling', L 754–5.

140   'Your very', L 756. 'get you made', L 705. 'simple marketable', L 700. 'a
      short Symphony', L 703. 'to the memory', L 705. 'the Jap:', L 705. 'bigger,
      easier', L 730. 'vile cold', L 769. 'His temperature', L 776.

141 'I remember', ATTW. 'Outwardly the', *High Fidelity Magazine*, Dec. 1959. 'The bug', L 792. 'There is modern', New York Times, 19 March 1940. '. . . Just completed', L 702.

142 '. . . in so many', L 793. 'Personally I'm', L 797. 'the improvement', L 780. 'I've seen', L 752

143 'for the first', Carpenter, *Auden*, 290. 'I suppose', L 798. 'for the moment', L 803. 'a terrible', L 818. 'paid up', L 831. 'I hope', L 843. 'Ben caught', L 836. 'about 103°', L 849. 'one gets', L 849–50.

144 'Actually Peter', L 851. 'Peter & I', L 862–3. 'The house', L 899. 'sordid beyond', 'Conscripts to an Age', unpublished typescript by Caroline Seebohm on 7 Middagh Street (copy in B–PL). 'Peter and George', L 899.

145 'I am *not*', to Elizabeth Mayer, 22 Nov. 1940. 'I find', L 899. 'unfortunate effect', quoted in Humphrey Milford to Hubert Foss, 22 Oct. 1940 (Oxford University Press). 'I feel', L 868. 'express felicitations', L 881. 'after all', L 888. 'just staggering', L 892. 'feel this is', L 868.

146 'So far', L 893. 'believe it', L 893. 'Mr Britten's', L 895. 'I'm making', *New York Sun*, 27 April 1940.

147 'Personally I think', L 909. 'mood of', Evans 58. 'but I have', L 908. 'tremendous', PB, 128. 'Wystan . . . is', L 735–6.

148 'sweet melodies', L 913. 'The opera', L 920. 'something genuine', *New York Times*, 6 May 1941. 'flaccid and', *New York Herald Tribune*, 5 May 1941. 'anemic operetta', *Time*, 19 May 1941.

149 'not only', *New York Times*, 4 May 1941. 'This country', L 800. 'I do hope', Auden to Elizabeth Mayer and others, 22 Feb. 1940 (Berg Collection, New York Public Library). 'a self-portrait', HCI.

150 'That was Peter', PB, 148. 'as long as', L 758. 'The performance', L 920. 'in spite of', L 947. 'I feel', L 947. 'on several', Crozier, 'Notes'. 'I've found it', to Eric Walter White, 6 April 1951. '. . . the reaction', L 919–20.

151 'Benjamin Britten's', *New York Herald Tribune*, 6 May 1941. 'he and I', L 865. 'splendid', L 933. 'The only thing', Voice is a Person. 'the battle', *Sunday Times*, 8 June 1941. 'thoroughbred', *Sunday Times*, 4 May 1941. 'He is in', L 959.

152 'The favour', L 870. 'alive and', L 871. 'the consciousness', L 871. 'I feel', L 957. '. . . we want', L 920–1. 'if possible', L 921.

153 'write the extra', L 936. 'Short notice', L 938. 'The people', L 941–2. '& then God', L 942. 'The attempt', *Modern Music*, Jan.–Feb. 1941.

154 'I think', L 943–4. 'We've just', L 961.

4: O weep away the stain

155 'To talk', *Listener*, 29 May 1941. 'the reading', TMS. 'A famous', *Listener*, 29 May 1941.

156 'I did not know', PG 148. 'it was in', *Aspen Award* 21. 'in a flash', L 962.

157 'nothing more', PG 150. 'began trying', PG 148. 'scraps', L 955.

157 'unnecessary emotional', L 961. 'the little Owls', L 1152.

158 'We haven't', L 960–1. 'One only', L 944. 'after Rimbaud', L 800. 'a garland', BC 290.

159 'Ben complaining', L 801. 'I've had quite', L 966. 'extremely vague', L 977. 'really horrible', L 968. 'released prisoners', L 991. 'our trip', L 983–4. 'I have made', L 987.

160 'content and', L 1002. 'more manner', L 996. 'seeing my agent', L 993. 'maybe I'll', L 994. 'You are such', L 998. 'played at salesman', L 886. 'He wanted', L 999.

161 'He had the', ATTW. 'absolutely no', L 985. 'Bobby was so', ATTW. 'you, especially', L 998.

162 'the weakness', *Modern Music*, Jan–Feb. 1941. 'handsome and', Miller 56–7; also unpublished memoir of his meeting with Britten and Pears written by Miller for this book.

163 'I think', L 1008. 'and when we', L 1008. 'not deep', L 861. 'in about', L 1013. 'any day', L 1014. 'I need scarcely', L 1015–16.

164 'A carefully', L 1021. 'Dearest Ben', L 1016–17.

165 'started ... pushing', L 1017. 'think & think', L 1021. 'There seem', L 1017. 'The Ides', L 887. 'we shall be', L 1024. 'The end', M/E, 160.

166 'God how', L 1027. 'callow, foul', L 1032. 'it was difficult', L 1032. 'one had', L 1037–8. 'the U boat', MBB 177. 'having difficulty', D 19 Jan. 1935.

167 'a product', Fuller 178.

169 'the opera', L 1037.

PART THREE

1: The invisible worm

173 'dazzlingly green', L 1032.' 'drab shabbiness', L 1037. 'there is a', L 1038. 'backwards &', L 1038. 'much older', MBB 177. 'very thin', Marjorie Fass to Daphne Oliver, n.d. [1942] (B-PL). 'My whole', L 653.

174 'So far', L 1037. 'Since I believe', L 1046. 'I was brought', L 1046. 'I have passed', L 1059. 'Snape is', L 1049. 'get atmosphere', L 1050. 'full of respect', L 1059.

175 'He has splendid', L 1037. 'rather altered', L 1061. 'impossible', L 1080. 'the right girl', L 1061. 'until I', L 1050. 'the greater part', L 1049. 'Peter ... was', L 1050. 'a lovely one', L 1053. 'Boohoo', L 1055–6.

176 'I still really' L 1064. 'My dear', L 1067–9. 'I do think', L 1149. 'a dear', L 1089. 'not conscientiously', L 1058.

177 'he would', L 1049. 'good to me', L 1059. 'completely free', L 1087–8. 'guilty about', L 1088. 'cruel', L 1086. 'a *grand*', L 1076. 'I shall', DMI. 'indescribably', *New Statesman*, 3 Oct. 1942. 'There are', L 1078. 'sold

enormously', L 1078. 'screaming', L 1080.

178 'hopelessly inefficient', L 1089. 'particular (hm)', L 1080. 'absolute pain', DMI. 'He remained', Duncan 27–8. 'As to', Pears to Michael Kennedy, n.d. [late 1970s]. 'Of course', HCI. 'Peter was', HCI. 'Ben really', HCI. 'I think Peter', HCI.

179 'I think it', Stephen Reiss to the author, 12 Feb. 1991. 'Britten once', Crozier, 'Notes'. 'became more', IHD 6 April 1953. 'practically no', L 1102. 'as much time', L 1088. 'I just', L 1103. 'Never never', L 269. 'It was very', L 1113. 'a very bad', L 1116. 'boring jobs', L 1117.

180 'towards the solution', L 1122. 'the worst', L 1131. 'pick the', L 1121. 'Immer dein', L 1125. 'would have held', L 1121. 'there are the', L 1124. 'be able to', L 1125. 'the character', L 1130. 'I mean to', L 1128. 'Admits his', PG 50.

181 'wondered whether', TMS. 'Sooner or', PGSW 16. 'It is getting', L 1037.

182 'rather . . . devastating', PG 56. 'A week', ALP. 'a wonderful', HCI. 'not operatic', PPT 22–3. 'I make', HCI. 'Peter . . . is', L 1148. 'He took', HCI. 'the one who', ALP. 'the slight', Berkeley.

183 'For once', *Opera*, May 1951. 'It didn't', Berkeley. 'Ben and I', ALP. 'think of', L 1133. 'Worrying as', L 1103. 'You are so', L 1103. 'O my precious', L 1108.

184 'It was on', HCI. 'always changing', HCI. 'some new improvements', L 1128. 'Peter is', L 1145. 'to write', L 1133. 'I've practically', L 1144.

185 'I took every', *Tempo*, Winter 1958. 'lapping [it] up', L 1118. 'My dear White', L 1126.

186 'The subject', White 46. 'the sin', Duncan 28.

187 'I'm much', L 1146–7. 'impertinent', L 1139.

188 'Something lively', L 283. 'Wystan introduced', L 1172. 'Smart captures', BC 276.

189 'I did croak', *The Muse of St Matthew's*, BBC Radio 4, 1989. 'E. B. Britten', L 1160.

2: The clue whose meaning we avoid

190 'great new friend', L 1151. 'wore surplice', Hussey 11. 'I had no', Bowen 77. 'which I called', Tippett 5. 'Most alarming', Tippett 8–9.

191 'a certain', Kemp 10. 'I never played', Tippett 21. 'Eliot told him', Kemp 24.

192 'Meeting Wilf', Tippett 58. 'I suppose', HCI. 'the music simply', HCI. 'I had been', Foreman 255.

193 'advised me', Bowen 78. 'This I entirely', Bowen 78. 'Schotts are going', Bowen 78. 'We were close', HCI. 'Once, Peter', Tippett 117. 'I'd gone', HCI.

194 'Britten – if', HCI. 'my first', Bowen 77–8. 'I had been', HCI. 'we're all fighting', L 1151–2. 'The question', HCI. 'ring Peter', Foreman 261.

196 'And what the', HCI. 'Ben corresponded', Amis 177–8. 'We weren't', HCI.

197 'I do envy', Kennedy, *Walton* 131. 'England was', HCI. 'I feel', L 1162. 'Ben knew', HCI.

198 'I used to', *Observer*, 24 Oct. 1943. 'I am quickly', L 1173. 'enormous commitment', L 1180. 'at Snape', L 1178. 'Well, at last', L 1181.

199 'gets more charming', L 1181. 'Ben my', L 1189. 'I do hope', L 1140–1. 'The more I', L 1189.

200 'was that it', HCI. '*excellent* for Grimes', L 1173. 'I am making', L 1185–6. 'Grimes is', L 1191. 'My bloody', L 1203. 'the aeroplanes', L 1196. 'I like working', ATTW. 'Always an', MBB 183.

201 'Usually I', Schafer 123. 'I can only', interviewed by Peter Garvie, CBC, 4 Sept. 1962 (B–PL). 'All I knew', ALP. 'Peter Pears has', Headington 92.

202 'Writing music', ALP. 'I do the', BBC radio interview, November 1963. 'My great aim', to Otto Klemperer, 4 Dec. 1961. 'as the most', ALP. 'You get the', interviewed by Peter Garvie, CBC, 4 Sept. 1962 (B–PL). 'I think one', BBC radio interview, November 1963. 'One is', *Guardian*, 7 June 1971. 'In Ben's', Duncan 66.

203 'It wasn't', HCI. 'Well, your', L 1210. 'I've just', L 1211. 'A central', Schafer 116–17.

204 'held the theory', Colin Graham to the author, 15 April 1991.

205 'I have a', libretto draft (B–PL).

208 'I only come', L 1227. 'murders', L 1037. 'P.G.'s Hut', PG 51. '"Boy's suffering"', libretto draft (B–PL). 'is intended', PGSW 43–4.

209 'If you are', L 1016.

211 'By God', libretto draft (B–PL). 'We're seamen', libretto draft (B–PL).

212 'for me an', to Peter Gammond, 20 Aug. 1959. 'the town and', PGSW 48. 'A thick', PGSW 53. 'I do not', BC 104.

213 'People automatically', HCI.

214 'which sounded', ALP. 'Ben came', HCI. 'Ben had', ALP. 'Britten had', HCI. 'went down', L 1219. 'we realized', HCI.

215 'I suppose', ALP. 'nerves', L 1232. 'the part', L 1216.

216 'make you', L 1235. 'one day', L 1201. 'I have actually', L 1241. 'someone with', Gishford 160. 'an impregnable', HCI.

217 'absent-minded', Amis 77. 'almost second', L 1152. 'We are having', L 1243. 'springboard', Duncan 37. 'automatic and', Duncan 39. 'agreed to', L 1243. 'hard to', RB 73.

218 'bowled over', MBB 186. 'It was one', Leonard Thompson to Pears, 30 July 1979 (B–PL). 'completely unaware', HCI.

219 'like someone', ALP. 'could not be', ALP. 'At 31', unidentified cutting in Joan Cross's scrapbook. 'found him', ibid. 'such a piece', ALP. 'mostly those', ALP.

220 'this marvellous', HCI. 'but for how', L 1172. 'enemies', L 1216. 'spiteful antagonism', L 1264. 'Mind you', L 1249. 'completely nerveless', HCI.

3: Have a nice peach?

221 'A slim', *Daily Express*, 8 June 1945. 'stood at', *News Chronicle*, 8 June 1945. 'Whatever happens', RB 72. 'stunning', Hussey 149. 'Actors and', Holst 39.

222 'unforgettable', PPT 48. 'something much', PPT 42. 'I think', TMS. 'threats of', ATTW. 'When the', HCI. 'a few', unidentified cutting in Joan Cross's scrapbook. 'They stood', Holst 39. 'The stage', L 1263. 'Whatever his', Duncan 51.

223 'Everything Ben', L 1263. 'gloomy, harrowing', L 1256–7. 'astonishing', L 1256. 'As for Benjamin', L 1263. 'sharp turns', L 1253–4. 'It is a', L 1258. '*Peter Grimes* . . .', L 1260. 'I was very', Searle 81. 'We are all', L 1252. 'people are', L 1252. 'That'll be', L 1264.

224 'may well be', *Picture Post*, 30 June 1945. 'detailed and', White 15. 'I must', L 1268. 'those ludicrous', L 1272. 'If more', OBE 27. 'Only a few', programme for, *The Rape of Lucretia*, Dublin Opera Theatre, 1990.

225 'Music for', Schafer 118. 'I am keen', to Ralph Hawkes, 30 June 1946.

226 'It may', L 1128–9. 'Plans are', L 1273. 'Benjamin Britten's', Peter Cox to the Trustees of Dartington Hall, 10 August 1945 (Rosamund Strode). 'We plan', L 1269. 'Well, honey', L 1269. 'He urged', L 1271. 'Yehudi was', L 1272. 'Men and women', L 1271–2. 'Somehow one', L 1274.

227 'for some', M/K 70. 'Auden got us', Schafer 115. 'I . . . can't', L 1277. 'on a bed', M/K 70.

228 'was in many', Schafer 122. 'defies the nightmare', M/K 71. 'never talked', Sir Yehudi Menuhin to the author, 2 Oct. 1991. 'how shocking', HCI.

229 'One of my', PGSW 8. 'I had never', from *Talking About Music* with John Amis, BBC sound archives, undated tape (B–PL). 'sometimes had', RB 88. 'an intricate', *Musical Times*, Feb. 1946. 'at the back', L 1241. 'to my mind', L 1285.

230 'It was almost', RB 89. 'felt in some', RB 88. 'listened and', Amis 181. 'a big thing', Schafer 120. 'terribly nervous', Amis 181.

231 'uncanny', M/K 28. 'eerie', Kennedy 179. 'panic-stricken', ibid. 'an instrumental', White 77–8. 'I have a', L 1241. 'long wait', to Basil Wright, 1 April 1946.

232 'I am glad', ibid. 'I haven't', L 1285. 'I think', L 1277.

233 'Her bedroom', Duncan 71.

234 'The days', L 1275.

235 'If she weren't', HCI.

236 'the rhythm', Duncan 83. 'ploughing away', to Pears, n.d. [May 1946]. 'in a pair', programme for *The Rape of Lucretia*, Dublin Opera Theatre, 1990. 'Glyndebourne can', internal report on arts administration, Dartington Hall (Rosamund Strode). 'method by', *Tempo*, March 1946. 'I wish', to Erwin Stein, 24 May 1946. '*far* too', ibid.

237 'very excited', Voice is a Person. 'I couldn't', ibid. 'this lively', ibid. 'The

237 beginning', ibid. 'to begin with', ibid. 'an excellent', to Desmond Shawe-Taylor, 23 June 1946. 'most exciting', to Ralph Hawkes, 30 June 1946. 'growing tension', Duncan 80. 'He was not', TMS.

238 'no music', Blunt 257. 'During the', HCI. 'was Eric's', to Ralph Hawkes, 30 June 1946. 'I myself', Duncan 81. 'I felt', HCI. 'alarmed', Duncan 83. 'polite but', Duncan 85. '*Lucretia* is', *News Chronicle*, 13 July 1946. 'splendid voice', *Times*, 13 July 1946. 'the most striking', *New York Times*, 13 June 1946.

239 'Can slippers', *Sunday Times*, 21 and 28 July 1946. 'went backstage', HCI. 'He seemed', Duncan 86. 'Many of', L 63.

240 'Well, why', ALP. 'It's really', HCI. 'a new Contemporary', programme for *The Rape of Lucretia*, Glyndebourne, July 1946. 'lively student', Headington 81. 'I loved', Auden to Britten, 30 Jan [1946] (B–PL). 'hurt', Miller 74.

241 'Auden's stuff', to Walter Hussey, 26 Feb. 1946. 'Ben was', Pears to the author, 18 April 1980. '"working together"', OBB 117. 'Ben told', MBB 177. 'Peter Pears', ATTW.

242 '. . . the oratorio', to Victor Hely-Hutchinson, 25 Feb. 1946. 'Ben was', Duncan 92. 'Ben could', Duncan 93. 'I suggested', Foreword to 1964 Decca LP set of *Albert Herring*. 'a close', ALP.

243 'frightfully disappointed', PG 42. 'always had', Crozier, 'Notes'. 'I don't', HCI. 'it would', Foreword to 1964 Decca LP set of *Albert Herring*.

244 'very relieved', to Eric Crozier, n.d. [Oct. 1946]. 'liked to think', MBB 190. 'When asked', ALP.

245 'Ben threatened', MBB 190. 'Ben is', *Glyndebourne Festival Opera Programe Book*, 1985. 'Ben . . . is going', ibid. 'I see now', ibid. 'liked to', ALP.

247 'a less', Evans 162. 'small change', Kennedy 186.

248 'Auden is', HCI.

4: A family affair

249 'We've fallen', to Jean Maud, 8 Jan. 1947. 'The opera', *Glyndebourne Festival Opera Programme Book*, 1985. 'We believe', English Opera Group prospectus,. 1947 (B–PL).

250 'They were', to John Lowe, n.d. [spring 1951]. 'stiff &', Marjorie Fass to Daphne Oliver, 22 Aug. 1938 (B–PL). 'Who was', Pudney 99. 'hated', ESI. 'I wish', to E. J. Dent, 18 Dec. 1953. 'Ben used', HCI. 'a quite', HCI.

251 'Ben *liked*', HCI. 'Unlike so', Fischer-Dieskau 273. 'one was', OBB 2. 'a great', RB 73. 'Ansermet was', HCI. 'disliked what', HCI. 'Fred was', HCI. 'a peacemaker', HCI. 'Ben and', HCI.

252 'This isn't', Kennedy 51. 'there was great', *News Chronicle*, 21 June 1947. 'a charade', *Times*, 21 June 1947. 'all these', *Daily Telegraph*, 21 June 1947. 'Britten's phenomenal', *Manchester Guardian*, 21 June 1947. 'a

first-rate', *Sunday Times*, 29 June 1947. 'a work', *Time & Tide*, 28 June 1947. 'Throughout the', *New Statesman*, 28 June 1947.

253 'entirely engrossed', *Manchester Guardian*, 10 Oct. 1947. '"Herring" went', to Walter Hussey, n.d. [June or July 1947]. 'We said', HCI. 'Albert was', to the Maud family, n.d. [Aug. 1947]. 'The rest', *Aldeburgh Festival Programme Book*, 1948. 'I remember', TMS.

254 'I thought', HCI. 'Snape ... is', to Erwin Stein, 8 Aug. 1947. 'It was agreed', *Aldeburgh Festival Programme Book*, 1948. 'It is a', to Pears, 4 Sept. 1947.

255 'thought that Aldeburgh', HCI. 'It was AGREED', Aldeburgh Festival committee minute book (B–PL). 'Peter & I', to Eric Crozier, n.d. [autumn 1947]. 'I confess', Elizabeth Sweeting, 'Let's Make a Festival', unpublished TS (Elizabeth Sweeting).

256 'lovely, absolute', HCI. 'What does', *Listener*, 24 June 1948.

257 'It's the most', HCI. 'first annual', 1948 Aldeburgh Festival hand-out (Lady Redcliffe-Maud). 'Oh, he was', HCI. 'At Snape', ALP. 'The Blake', to Pears, 30 March 1950. '*the most*', Pears to Britten, n.d. [? 1950].

258 'Ben and Peter's', ALP. 'Ben and Peter shared', Walton 124. 'they shared', HCI. 'A man who', Wildeblood 3–4.

259 'PANSY', Headington, *Pears* 128. 'Eric has', to Nancy Evans, 23 Jan. 1948.

260 'Peter did', notes by Isador Caplan on first draft of Headington, *Pears*. 'It was in a district', ALP.

261 'a middle-aged', Crozier, 'Notes'. 'possessive about', HCI. 'we always', HCI. 'When he moved', ALP. 'with nothing', HCI. 'Always, if', Berkeley. 'it was Ben', ATTW. 'He was never', ALP. 'somebody so', HCI.

262 'Ben could', HCI. 'nothing pleased', Crozier, 'Notes'. 'We'd play', HCI. 'Ben didn't', HCI. 'My Canticle', to unidentified correspondent, n.d. [autumn 1947].

263 'Britten did', HCI. 'but I think', HCI. 'The title', to Nancy Evans, 17 Dec. 1947.

264 'a hymn to', Handford 255. 'Eric has', to Pears, n.d. [Sept. 1947]. 'Really grand', to Ronald Duncan, Sept. 1947. 'commercially viable', L 1269. 'I am beginning', to Pears, 18 Dec. 1947.

265 'Oh, never!' Schafer 118. 'The main', ALP. 'I think', to Pears, 18 Dec. 1947. 'During the', Handford 255.

266 'shake normally', BC 81. 'new section', Eric Crozier to Nancy Evans, 19 Dec. 1947 (Eric Crozier). 'I ... haven't', to Ronald Duncan, n.d. [Jan. 1948]. 'as well as', Colin Graham to the author, 27 March 1991. 'probably more', to Pears, 17 March 1948. 'Some of', *Times*, 25 May 1948.

267 'a polite', *Evening Standard*, 25 May 1948. 'You look', HCI. 'as it was', Colin Graham to the author, 27 March 1991. 'After that', HCI. 'We are just', to Lennox Berkeley, 4 June 1948. 'a good', to Pears, 17 March 1948. 'It amuses', PG 20–1. 'the sweetest', Furbank, Vol. II, 282.

268 'It was one', *Listener*, 24 June 1948. 'As he was', ibid. 'belong', *Aldeburgh*

268 *Festival Programme Book*, 1948.

269 'The harp', *Listener*, 24 June 1948. 'the London press', *Listener*, 1 July 1948. 'Ben kept open', HCI. 'no one seemed', *New English Review*, Aug. 1948. 'more than an', ibid.

270 'The whole Festival', HCI. 'We have just', to E. J. Dent, 16 June 1948. 'a universal', Aldeburgh Festival committee minute book (B–PL). 'My dear Morgan', to E. M. Forster, 11 Aug. 1948. 'Peter & I', to Eric Walter White, 11 Aug. 1948. 'reading possible', to Erwin Stein, 24 Aug. 1948. 'I am keen', to Serge Koussevitzky, 12 Jan. 1947. 'I certainly intend', to David Webster, 27 Oct. 1948. 'possible that', to Erwin Stein, 24 Aug. 1948.

271 'each suggested', Stallybrass 89. 'I'd got it', to Pears, n.d. [Nov. 1948]. 'I hope', to Pears, 28 Oct. 1948. 'I am sorry', to Lesley Bedford, 19 Nov. 1948. 'went *all* wrong', to Lesley Bedford, n.d. [Dec. 1948]. 'three months', to Ronald Duncan, 2 Jan. 1949. 'nervous exhaustion', ibid. 'it is a good', to Kathleen Tuttle, 22 Dec. 1948. 'grumpy & nervy', to Ronald Duncan, 2 Jan. 1949. 'Peter is hard', ibid. 'I *do* adore', to Pears, n.d. [Dec. 1948].

272 'when Ben', HCI. 'Peter's taking', to Ronald Duncan, 19 Jan. 1949. 'perfect sun', to Barbara Britten, n.d. [Jan. 1949]. 'Venice has', to Lord Harewood, n.d. [Jan. 1949]. 'when I got', to John Maud, 7 March 1949. 'I am sorry', to Pears, 19 Feb. 1949. 'Perhaps after', to Pears, n.d. [spring 1949]. 'My memories', to Pears, 2 March 1949. '*don't* worry', Pears to Britten, n.d. [late 1948 or early 1949].

5: It is I whom the devil awaits

273 'I don't know', to John Maud, 7 March 1949. 'I have at last got', to Leslie Boosey, 10 March 1969. 'I have at last completed', to Jean Maud, 15 March 1949. 'I can recall', ALP.

274 'Here was our', OBB 168. 'brought up', to Eric Walter White, n.d. [probably 1949]. 'I am pushing', to Pears, 8 April 1949.

275 'went about with', ALP. 'We take these', Holst 44.

276 'a tall, lean', Elizabeth Sweeting, 'Let's Make a Festival', unpublished typescript (Elizabeth Sweeting). 'Once upon a', *Times*, 15 June 1949.

277 'no limit', RB 100. 'On occasion', RB 99. 'I wish I', ESI. 'We went', to Pears, n.d. [spring 1949]. 'Britten attended', OBB 35. 'I wasn't sure', ESI. 'doubts and miseries', to Serge Koussevitzky, 19 April 1949.

278 'DELIGHTED TO', Serge Koussevitzky, n.d. [July 1949]. 'I have forgotten', ALP. 'glorious Spring', Elizabeth Sweeting to the author, 11 June 1990. 'the Symphony', to Serge Koussevitzky, 12 Jan. 1947. 'It was a', ALP. 'It is such', to Pears, 'October 22nd (?) Friday' [1948]. 'The formal problem', to Pears, 2 Nov. 1948.

279 'simply could not', ALP. 'almost entirely', Evans 429. 'assurance and', *New Statesman*, 23 July 1949. 'I recall Ben's', Duncan 106–7.

280 'claimed that Marion', Walton 36. 'I feel that', to Marion Stein, 7 April 1949. 'I can't tell', HCI. '*Please, PLEASE*', to Erwin Stein, 29 Oct. 1949.

281 'Evil is unspectacular', Auden, *Shorter Poems* 145–6. 'Their eagerness', OBB 32. 'Ben wants', Eric Crozier to Nancy Evans, 24 Aug. 1948 (Eric Crozier).

282 'The moment I', ALP. 'whether a big', HCI. 'Most composers', ALP. 'Morgan & I', Eric Crozier to Britten and Pears, n.d. [Jan. or Feb. 1949] (B–PL). 'was worried that', Oliver Stallybrass (ed.), *Aspects of E. M. Forster*, Edward Arnold, 1969, 86.

283 'tired, depressed', ALP. 'Morgan is the', ALP. 'Something is worrying', ALP. 'I was right', ALP.

284 'provocative', to Henriette Bosmans, 18 March 1949. 'It is going', ALP. '. . . I have always', ALP. 'beastly financial', to Eric Crozier, n.d. [*c.* 1949]. 'This afternoon', ALP.

285 'And Ben and I', HCI. 'a "noble savage"', Furbank 285. 'the other Billy B', to E. M. Forster, 14 Dec. 1950. 'curiously resembling', Stallybrass 85. 'adorable', Furbank 303. 'as far as', HCI. 'some remarkably', to Pears, n.d. [Nov. 1948]. 'in all the', HCI.

286 'He was a sneaky', HCI. 'a pleasant', ALP. 'The ship at', to Eric Crozier, n.d. [Dec. 1949]. 'could they afford', to Eric Walter White, 18 Jan. 1950. 'went mad', to Henriette Bosmans, 3 Feb. 1950. 'developed some', Crozier, 'Notes'. 'I have to-day', to Henriette Bosmans, 3 Feb. 1950.

287 'this question of', BBC radio discussion between Britten, Crozier and Forster about *Billy Budd*, 4 Nov. 1960 (B–PL). 'my Nunc Dimittis', Lago / Furbank 246. 'Billy always', BBC radio discussion between Britten, Crozier and Forster about *Billy Budd*, 1960 (B–PL). 'That was me', TMS. 'The Peter Grimes', RB14–15.

288 'a greater depth', BBC radio discussion between Britten, Crozier and Forster about *Billy Budd*, 1960 (B–PL). 'Morgan ... doesn't', to Eric Crozier, 4 May 1950. 'a tendency to', *Music and Letters*, Aug. 1989.

290 *'really* well', to Lennox Berkeley, 27 June 1950.

291 'to reward him', to Eric Crozier, 4 May 1950. 'I am, on', to Eric Crozier, 29 Aug. 1950. 'I'm sorry to be', to Pears, n.d. [5 Oct. 1950]. 'Billy is being', to Marion, Lady Harewood, 22 Oct. 1950. 'felt very sorry', HCI. 'To me', ALP. 'has received from', ALP. 'troubles between', ALP.

292 'It is my', Furbank 285–6. 'boring, black-masked', HCI. 'inapposite', Evans 167. 'invasion', HCI.

293 '. . . no mishaps', to Pears, 28 Jan. 1951. 'Webster cried', to Pears, n.d. [Feb. 1951]. 'Every bar', to Imogen Holst, 12 Feb. 1951. 'N.B. why is it', Lago/Furbank 237.

295 'the true musical', *Music Survey*, 4, 1952. 'convey rapid', M/K 208–9. 'One can no', booklet issued with Decca SET 397–81. 'the mysterious', Evans 173. 'suggest that in', BC 142. 'a positive', *Music and Letters*, Aug. 1989.

296 'Budd goes on', to Marion, Lady Harewood, 4 March 1951. 'the exact people', Berkeley. 'didn't have', HCI. 'even for his', Berkeley. 'very very nice', HCI.

297   'He is in a', to Basil Coleman, 7 March 1951. 'a wonderful relief', to Eric
        Walter White, 22 Aug. 1951. 'o, o, what', ibid. 'I feel miserably', to Lord and
        Lady Harewood, 2 Oct. 1951. 'everything but', Carpenter, *Auden*, 370.

298   'Stravinsky talked', Harewood 132–3. 'in a funny', to Erwin Stein, 9 Sept.
        1951. 'Britten half sang', OBB 35. 'It is by', to Lord and Lady Harewood, 2
        Oct. 1951. 'the size of', to E. M. Forster, 14 Dec. 1950.

299   'I was very', ATTW. 'acting with', to Lord Harewood, 6 April 1952. 'a dull
        singer', HCI. 'Ben was the', ATTW. 'I really couldn't', HCI. 'There were
        tears', *Sunday Times*, 2 Dec. 1951.

300   'really tremendous', ALP. 'terrified by', HCI. 'wasn't good', HCI. 'I haven't
        seen', to Lennox Berkeley, 14 Dec. 1951. 'I hope you'll', to Alec Robertson,
        n.d. [1951]. 'talked about *Budd*'. IHD, 5 Feb. 1953.

6: The power of love . . . the love of power

301   'Benjamin Britten has', *New Statesman*, 1 Dec. 1951. 'I must confess', *New
        Statesman*, 8 Dec. 1951. 'the total absence', *Musical Times*, Jan. 1952.
        'fantastically well', *Opera*, Jan. 1952. 'an even finer', ibid. 'To those', *Times*,
        3 Dec. 1951. 'Artists are', *Tempo*, Autumn 1951.

302   'practically all', *Opera*, March 1952. 'persecution mania', *New Statesman*,
        8 March 1952. 'I soon learned', Amis 180.

303   'Every religion', *Times Literary Supplement*, 19 Feb. 1949. 'brilliant', *Public
        Opinion*, 2 March 1951.

304   'In those days', HCI. 'my little fisherboy', to Eric Walter White, 22 Aug.
        1951. 'up the Drachenfels', *The Leistonian* (Leiston Grammar School), no.
        17, 1952. 'long drawn-out', HCI.

305   'naive little piece', to Jonathan Gathorne-Hardy, 10 Jan. 1952 (Jonathan
        Gathorne-Hardy). 'Isaac using', ibid. 'wonderful things', HCI. 'the children
        are', to William Plomer, 14 March 1952. 'Well, you'd better', Harewood
        134–5.

306   'insisted that his', Harewood 135. 'bought a paperback', Harewood 136. 'it
        is imperative', to William Plomer, 27 April 1952. 'I long to', to William
        Plomer, 11 May 1952. 'a compressed', Alexander 153. 'With his clipped',
        Alexander 261.

307   'I am delighted', to William Plomer, 24 July 1952. 'a lovely', ibid.

308   'glum', Harewood 136. '(hush!) I have', to Eric Walter White, 8 Sept. 1952.
        'Marion and I', Harewood 136. 'drastic changes', to William Plomer, 14
        Sept. 1952. 'I *am* that', to Basil Coleman, 25 Sept. 1952.

309   'This morning', Pears to Britten, 21 Feb. 1951. 'I am quite sure', Pears to
        Britten, 1 March 1951. 'always supposing', to Imogen Holst, 9 July 1952.
        'His pencil sketches', BC 47. 'have a detailed', ATTW.

310   'indefatigable enthusiasm', Crozier, 'Notes'. 'which accounted', HCI. 'She
        was a bit', HCI. 'in a way', HCI. 'she didn't trust', HCI. 'to make music',
        HCI.

311 'on London trains', Crozier, 'Notes'. 'She kissed', HCI. 'She could be', HCI. 'Imo good', to Pears, 17 Feb. 1959. 'Imo's panics', to Pears, 22 Feb. 1959. 'a very, very', HCI. 'Imo was a', HCI. 'extremely spartan', HCI. 'she had very', HCI.

311–12 Extracts from IHD as dated in the text.

312 'mystified', IHD 30 Oct. 1952. 'have lessons', ibid. 'made Peter', IHD 3 Nov. 1952. 'Ben said', IHD 27 Nov. 1952.

313 'There are enough', Tippett 215. 'Walton associated', Tippett 214. 'he'd been reading', IHD 2 Dec. 1952.

314 'Back that afternoon', IHD 20 Jan. 1953. 'They forget', to Basil Coleman, 6 Oct. 1952. 'I know he', to David Webster, 5 Nov. 1952. 'the lovely Essex', to William Plomer, 23 Nov. 1952. 'You would be', to William Plomer, 30 Nov. 1952. 'just concert people', ATTW.

315 'We are slowly', to Barbara Britten, n.d. [Feb. 1953]. 'increased the pressure', to Anthony Gishford, 10 Feb. 1953. 'three hours', to William Plomer, 15 Feb. 1953. 'a necessary corrective', HCI.

316 'frankly of the', *Sunday Times*, undated cutting [1953]. 'preserve intact', *Scrutiny*, spring 1953. 'incoherent verbiage', *Music and Letters*, April 1953. 'This is not', M/K 334. 'very sweet', Pears to Britten, 6 Jan. 1953. 'pleased & flattered', to Hans Keller and Donald Mitchell, 21 Jan. 1953. 'On the whole', IHD 4 Dec. 1952. 'We talked about', IHD 19 Dec. 1952.

317 'Britten is a', M/K 350. 'read out a', IHD 4 Dec. 1952. 'It is difficult', Schafer 117. Extracts from IHD as dated in the text.

318 'they were refusing', IHD 26 Feb. 1953. 'It suits', to William Plomer, 8 April 1953. 'hopeless – he', HCI. 'At the second', IHD undated entry [late May or early June, 1953]. 'a very good', HCI. 'I'm not sure', Headington, *Pears* 166. 'an appreciative', Harewood 137. 'not my favourite', HCI. 'any more than', Headington, *Pears* 166.

319 'artistic Britain', Harewood 138. 'so largely official', Alexander 278. '& I think', Alexander 279. 'gorgeously dressed', *Manchester Guardian Weekly*, 11 June 1953. 'just one big', RB 100. 'when we went', HCI. 'They grew into', HCI.

320 'never felt', HCI. 'somebody would', ESI. 'would *not* rehearse', HCI. 'couldn't bear', HCI. 'there was always', HCI. 'after a while', HCI. 'many people', HCI. 'Osian was', HCI.

321 'It was grotesque', HCI. 'something which Ben', HCI. 'You really needed', HCI. 'like a girls' school', HCI. 'very much a', HCI. 'because of Ben's', HCI. 'childish, unsubtle', HCI. 'He just used', HCI.

322 'The opera has', BC 171. 'almost every piece', *Aspen Award* 11.

325 'one of the great', Harewood 138. 'faint drizzle', *Opera*, August 1953. 'witty, dry', *Manchester Guardian Weekly*, 11 June 1953. 'The bulk of', *Sunday Times*, 14 June 1953. 'My impression', *Spectator*, 12 June 1953. 'uneasily nervous', *Daily Telegraph*, 13 June 1953. 'the emotional drama', *Spectator*, 19 June 1953. 'In the music', *Times*, 9 June 1953.

326   'For this royally', *New Statesman*, 13 June 1953. 'one is still', *Manchester Guardian Weekly*, 11 June 1953. 'a work of', *Music and Letters*, Oct. 1953. 'public resentment', *Times*, 20 June 1953. 'prepared to be', *Times*, 20 June 1953. 'superb richess', *Times*, 16 June 1953. 'after a single', *Times*, 18 June 1953. 'some of the best', Carpenter, *Auden*, 375.

327   'absolutely the', Kennedy, *Walton* 160. 'We'd invite', interviewed by Donald Mitchell, Aldeburgh, 27 Oct. 1990. 'it was what', *W. H. Auden Society Newsletter*, Oct. 1991. 'I expect that', to William Plomer, n.d. [summer 1953]. 'mortified', Harewood 138.

328   'Peter came', Headington 93–4.

7: A sort of spiritual corruption

329   'Schoenberg came', Harewood 132. 'the bouts', HCI. 'most of us', HCI. 'how he'd once', IHD 2 Dec. 1952.

331   'There were two', HCI. 'really rather hated', ESI. 'a wonderful', D 1 June 1932. 'glorious & eerie', D 6 and 7 Jan. 1933. 'never been a', Alexander 259.

332   '. . . a/Willowy figure', Betjeman 88. 'I think he', ESI. 'I was so', HCI.

333   'Yousee', to E. M. Forster, 'Sunday oct.?' [1953]. 'you never knew', HCI. 'My arm', to T. E. Bean, 2 Dec. 1953. 'We were married', conversation with the author, Aldeburgh, 8 June 1991. 'The German Xmas', to Myfanwy Piper, 3 Jan. 1954.

334   'definitely improving', to William Plomer, 31 Jan. 1954. 'I like Miles', to Myfanwy Piper, 31 Jan. 1954. 'May be with', to Anthony Gishford, 31 Jan. 1954. 'I am longing', to Myfanwy Piper, 16 Feb. 1954. 'a new drive', Wildeblood 45–6.

335   'Scotland Yard are', Percy Elland to Lord Beaverbrook, 15 Jan. 1954 (Kathleen Tynan). 'I started the', to Myfanwy Piper, 30 March 1954. 'very painful', ibid. 'quite good progress', ibid. 'I do not quite', ibid. 'The new piece', to Eric Walter White, 21 May 1954. 'brimming with', HCI. 'It seemed incredible', Holst 55.

336   'finished Scene 3', to Myfanwy Piper, 12 April 1954. 'is going to', ibid. 'a prologue', ibid. 'afraid a prologue', OBB 11. 'was never right', HCI. 'He feels that', to Myfanwy Piper, 26 April 1954.

337   'I'm afraid', to Myfanwy Piper, 16 May 1954. 'amazing crashes', HCI. 'I hope to', to Myfanwy Piper, 28 May 1954. 'I am so', to Basil Coleman, 29 May 1954. 'this is always', to Myfanwy Piper, 5 June 1954. 'There are most', to Lennox Berkeley, 6 July 1954. 'wish me luck', ibid. 'I just thought', HCI. 'the thing is', James, *Aspern Papers* 17. 'when Henry James', William Plomer to Britten, 21 Nov. 1964.

338   'Ben and I', Harewood 139. 'I don't think', TS 23. 'has simply never', Schafer 120. 'It is impossible', Britten/Holst 67. 'I think it', to Erwin Stein, 16 Feb. 1954. 'In fact', HCI.

340 '*all* its music', BC 109. 'the situation with', *Musical Quarterly*, Vol. 74 no. 1, 1990.

341 'an old-fashioned', OBB 10. 'using one thing', HCI. 'inexperienced and', OBB 12. 'Miles seems a', Jonathan Gathorne-Hardy to the author, 29 June 1990.

342 'a golden summer', HCI. 'I made it my', HCI. 'I must be fair', HCI. 'And she was', HCI. 'that certain women', HCI. 'She was a', HCI.

343 'Peter wasn't there', HCI. 'from Peter's point', HCI. 'Little David', to Pears, 4 Sept. 1947.

344 'the old feelings', HCI. 'my not quite', David Spenser to the author, 7 Aug. 1990. 'was very protective', HCI. 'but a kind of', HCI. 'and he suddenly', HCI.

345 'he was just', HCI. 'He had this', HCI. 'there were two', HCI. 'He never wrote', HCI. 'He brought out', HCI.

346 'He was always', HCI. 'We've got a fine', to Basil Douglas, 15 March 1951. 'My dear Stewy', to Steuart Bedford, 2 Jan. 1949.

347 'charming afternoon', to John Maud, 7 March 1949. 'By-the-way', ibid. 'I did not come', HCI. 'the Beethoven', to Ronald Duncan, 14 Nov. 1953 (Briony Lawson).

348 'just like sacks', HCI. 'I did adore', HCI. 'used to joke', HCI. 'went behind the', HCI. 'and always played', HCI. 'Humphrey was a', conversation with the author, Oxford, 30 April 1990.

349 'Ben was *deeply*', HCI. 'one of our', L 105. 'The thing about', HCI.

350 'My dear Jonny', to Jonathan Gathorne-Hardy, 8 Aug. 1950 (Jonathan Gathorne-Hardy). 'I'm taking', to Jonathan Gathorne-Hardy, 10 Jan. 1952 (Jonathan Gathorne-Hardy). 'each step', HCI.

351 'Ben was obviously', HCI. 'used to throw', HCI. 'quite a severe', HCI.

352 'Our relative poverty', HCI. 'sympathetic intuition', HCI. 'It's a common', HCI. '*don't* worry', Pears to Britten, n.d. [*c.* Jan. 1949]. 'young Pangbour-nians', to Pears, 29 Jan. 1950. 'with all the little', to Pears, 26 July 1956. 'prolonged internal', HCI.

353 'Ben always looked', HCI. 'I do know', Colin Graham to the author, 15 April 1991. 'Ben's own highly', HCI. 'Having been corrupted', Crozier, 'Notes'. 'It struck me', HCI. 'told me that he', IHD 7 Oct. 1952.

354 'Once, when Ben', HCI. 'needed the active', HCI. 'did talk to', HCI. 'People have', HCI.

356 'didn't want', HCI. 'One of the', OBB 41. 'David began', article by Davina Hughes; unidentified cutting (B–PL). 'sang well', Amis 181. '*loved* David', DMI. 'Ben was very', HCI. 'We rehearsed', Colin Graham to the author, 27 March 1991.

357 'Peter spoke', Raymond Leppard to the author, 26 Sept. 1991. 'He was incredibly', HCI.

358 'It was written', HCI. 'more than usually', OBB 43. 'by the musical', *Spectator*, 19 June 1953.

359 'He said ... that', IHD 15 Dec. 1953. 'Ben was very', Colin Graham to the author, 27 March 1991. 'a lower-keyed', Harewood 139. 'got more and', HCI. 'genuine success', Harewood 139.

360 'tackled yet another', *Manchester Guardian*, 15 Sept. 1954. 'this subject', *Times* 16 Sept. 1954. 'the composer's customary', *L'Express*, 25 Sept. 1954. 'an opera that', *New York Herald Tribune*, 26 Sept. 1954. 'remark-able', *Sunday Times*, 19 Sept. 1954. 'a great work', HCI. 'I think we', HCI. 'quite different from', to Basil Coleman, 25 Sept. 1955. 'a good boy', to Basil Coleman, 3 Feb. 1955.

361 'I have listened', Searle 141. 'I am delighted', to Eric Walter White, 5 Nov. 1954. 'I think in', to Desmond Shawe-Taylor, 6 Nov. 1954.

PART FOUR

1: The middle of life

365 'deeply moved', to Anthony Gishford, 4 Feb. 1955. 'He met Bill', Amis 212. 'courage & light', to Edith Sitwell, 27 Dec. 1954. 'He was looking', IHD 7 Dec. 1953.

366 'on the threshold', to Edith Sitwell, 18 April 1955. 'no more years', to Barbara Britten, 26 Dec. 1954. 'I have been', to John Cranko, 15 Aug. 1955. 'However', Duncan 131. 'no Roger', to Basil Coleman, 3 Feb. 1955. 'Ronnie, I've got', Duncan 132.

367 'For the next', Duncan 132–3. 'My father told', HCI.

368 'I wouldn't have', HCI. 'They were slightly', HCI. 'And as the', HCI. 'extremely warm', HCI. 'I am sure', Colin Graham to the author, 27 March 1991. 'financial bottleneck', *Aldeburgh Festival Programme Book*, 1955.

369 'It was not my', Elizabeth Sweeting to the author, 1 March 1991. 'typical Ben', Elizabeth Sweeting to the author, 7 March 1991. 'a little devious', HCI. 'Many years before', HCI. 'was warned', HCI. 'mesmeric', HCI. 'I had little', to Basil Coleman, 25 Sept. 1955. 'ghastly deadline', to John Cranko, 15 Aug. 1955. 'how *extraordinary*', to William Plomer, n.d. [Dec. 1955]. 'a week of', to Imogen Holst, 17 Jan. 1956. 'I am writing', to Roger Duncan, 18 Jan. 1956.

371 'The music is', to Imogen Holst, 17 Jan. 1956. 'to bold', BC 41. 'little boys', to Roger Duncan, 8 Feb. 1956.

372 'The whole thing', Gishford 58–9. 'And so we', to Roger Duncan, 8 Feb. 1956. 'It is far', to Roger Duncan, 24 Feb. 1956. 'asked Ben and', Reg Close, 'Memories of Benjamin Britten', unpublished typescript (B–PL).

373 'hilarious', conversation with the author, Aldeburgh, 8 June, 1991. 'The play was', Reg Close, 'Memories of Benjamin Britten', unpublished typescript (B–PL). 'my incredibly strong', to William Plomer, 13 May 1956.

'cancelled every concert', to Ronald Duncan, 27 March 1956. 'progressing well', to David Webster, 1 May 1956. 'only ½ written', to David Webster, 28 May 1956. 'any postponement', ibid. 'postponed till', to Ronald Duncan, 2 Aug. 1956. 'I've never written', HCI.

374 'Nobody can cover', HCI. 'I never wished', to William Plomer, 25 Jan. 1957. 'an Imo story', HCI. 'gorgeous', to Barbara Britten, 29 Dec. 1956. 'wild and', *Manchester Guardian*, 2 Jan. 1975. 'sags in', *Times*, 2 Jan. 1957. 'matched John Cranko's', *Sunday Times*, 6 Jan. 1957.

375 'who else can', Duncan 136. 'for me', HCI. 'my doctor', to William Plomer, 25 Jan. 1957. 'I *must*', to Basil Coleman, 25 Sept. 1955. 'Johnny's part', to Basil Coleman, 31 Jan. 1957. 'that beastly', BC 193n. 'could rarely', BC 193.

376 'we've performed', to Basil Coleman, 31 Jan. 1957. 'typical Aldeburgh', Amis 181. 'It's conceivable', HCI. 'Ben couldn't', HCI.

377 'We all knew', ESI. 'when the awkward', HCI. 'what was nice', ESI. 'years later', Amis 182. 'One was so', HCI. 'Ben said', HCI.

378 'a frustrating year', to William Plomer, 10 July 1957. 'as a gong', Alexander 300. 'The "Sumidagawa"', to William Plomer, 10 July 1957. 'I get terribly', to Ronald Duncan, 3 Feb. 1957.

379 'We are very', to Barbara Britten, 11 Nov. 1957. 'Ben and Peter', ESI. 'alas, away', to Edith Sitwell, 3 March 1959. 'But Ben', HCI. 'strange, in a sense', HCI.

380 'My dear Owen', to Owen Brannigan, 7 Dec. 1957. 'a new children's', to Edith Sitwell, 14 Dec. 1957. 'I am writing', to Owen Brannigan, 7 Dec. 1957.

381 'he had indeed', Boris Ford interviewed by Donald Mitchell, 9 Nov. 1989. 'open[s] magic', BC 149.

382 'bugle theme', David Layton to Pamela Wheeler, 28 Oct. 1982 (B–PL). 'had the idea', BC 48–9.

383 'They were members', ATTW.

384 'I see more', to Basil Coleman, 31 Jan. 1957. 'as it turned', HCI.

385 'When suddenly', HCI (Sir Charles Mackerras). 'We were having', HCI. 'The sleepy village', *Sunday Times*, 22 June 1958.

386 'because I felt', HCI. 'I had wanted', Colin Graham to the author, 27 March 1991. 'gay colours', *Daily Telegraph*, 19 June 1958. 'I am so', to Ernst Roth, 23 June 1958. 'the builders', to William Plomer, 12 July 1958. 'I have been', to Marion, Lady Harewood, 20 Aug. 1958.

387 'the strangely', Harewood 141. 'It won't be', to Marion, Lady Harewood, 20 Aug. 1958. 'it gives a', BC 92.

388 'Peter is a', Berkeley. 'My very dearest', to Lord and Lady Harewood, 20 Oct. 1958.

389 'about to start', to Yehudi Menuhin, 27 Nov. 1958. 'I've never conducted', to Marion, Lady Harewood, 20 Aug. 1958. 'managed to put', to Barbara Britten, 15 Dec. 1958. 'a big job', to William Plomer, 8 March 1959. 'I've

389 more or', to William Plomer, 3 April 1959. 'I think the Noh', to William
Plomer, 8 March 1959. 'A new idea', to William Plomer, 15 April 1959.
'setting fire', Alexander 303. 'I am very', to William Plomer, 24 May 1959.

390 'the whole choir', to George Malcolm, 5 Jan. 1959. 'incredible boys', to
Alan Frank, 22 Aug. 1959. 'He didn't say', HCI. 'my mind has been', to
William Plomer, 12 Aug. 1959.

391 'develop what', HCI. 'a sort of', HCI. 'If they were', HCI. 'They were
thrilled', to Pears, 24 July 1959. 'extremely possessive', HCI. 'I see you',
Hardwick 143–4. 'the tremendous', BC 178.

392 'I dragged', to Pears, 9 Dec. 1959. 'the smallest', to William Plomer, 8 Feb.
1954. 'I'm having fun', to Pears, 14 Dec. 1959. 'I am afraid', to Pears, 18
Feb. 1960. 'We mustn't', Pears to Britten, n.d. [8 Jan. 1960]. 'I watched',
HCI. 'not up to', BC 178. 'I was horror-struck', HCI.

393 'more relaxed', BC 178. 'always loved', BC 177. 'He seems to', BC 179. 'I
got the', BC 179.

394 'almost no emotional', Hardwick 75. 'unearthly', HCI. 'You are eunuch',
Tear 55.

395 'earthy *parlando*', Evans 242. 'a really wicked', HCI. 'I could hardly',
HCI. 'Cranko's production', *Sunday Times*, 12 June 1960.

396 'The choice of', *New Statesman*, 17 June 1960. 'captivating', *Sunday
Times*, 12 June 1960. 'The interval', *Daily Telegraph*, 27 June 1960.
'dreadful', Carpenter, *Auden* 428. '*Midsummer Marriage*', HCI. 'I never
knew', Sir John Gielgud to the author, 29 Nov. 1990. 'delete me', Alfred
Deller to Britten, 11 June 1960.

2: A kind of reparation

397 'It *was* a', to Marjorie Fass, 28 July 1960. 'a big commission', to William
Glock, 30 July 1960. 'My feeling', to Ernest Roth, 11 Aug. 1960. 'not too
happy', to William Plomer, 4 Jan. 1964. 'an absurdity', *Sunday Times*, 12
Jan. 1964. 'for a moment', to Ariadne Nicolaeff, n.d. [summer 1960]. 'I
knew some', Gishford 15.

398 'and thought this', radio interview on return from USSR, March 1964
(B–PL). 'attacked Britten', Gishford 15. 'exceptional magnetism', ibid.
'Dear and', Rostropovich to Britten, 25 Sept. 1960 (B–PL).

399 'If you have', Rostropovich to Britten, 12 Oct. 1960 (B–PL). 'As far as', to
Pears, 17 Jan. 1961. 'My German', *Observer*, 27 Nov. 1977. 'Patiently is',
Gishford 15. 'My dear', to Rostropovich, 30 Jan. 1961.

400 'made a dash', Gishford 15–16. 'a man with', Vishnevskaya 143, 198.
'irresponsible and', Gishford 15. 'ADMIRING AND', Rostropovich to
Britten, 11 Feb. 1961 (B–PL). 'Fifteen minutes', Gishford 16–17. 'four or
five', *Observer*, 27 Nov. 1977. 'I could not', Gishford 17.

401 'to tell you', to Galina Vishnevskaya, 1 April 1961. 'How simple', Gishford
17. 'What a wonderfully', ibid. 'I had been', Vishnevskaya 364–5.

402 'He is a bully', ATTW. 'No one who', Colin Graham to the author, 15
April 1991. 'rather late', Gishford 18. 'He used to', Holst 56. 'an astonishingly', *Times*, 5 July 1961. 'I think it', Tear 105. 'What it sounded', HCI.
'stunning', *Times*, 9 July 1961.

403 'thrilling ... In', *Times*, 8 July 1961. 'It was at', Vishnevskaya 365. 'the
outstanding', *Times*, 8 July 1961.

404 'spellbound', Gishford 18–19. 'Dear, dear', Rostropovich and Vishnevskaya to Britten and Pears, 9 July 1961 (B–PL). 'said he was', Vishnevskaya 365. 'Please forgive', to Dietrich Fischer-Dieskau, 16 Feb. 1961.

405 'very nice', Pears to Britten, 24 July 1956. 'this savage', Duncan 54–6. 'the
death of', to Ralph Hawkes, 27 Feb. 1948. '"Have you ever"', Vishnevskaya 365.

406 'Britten, a Christian', programmes for Bach Choir performance on 15 Feb.
1965 and New Philharmonia performance on 16 Jan. 1966, both at the
Royal Albert Hall. 'Alas! alas!', L 1033. 'Although he', to Mrs Gill, 21
Nov. 1961. (Alan Reeve). 'Isn't it tragic', L 1192.

407 'rather an odd', HCI. 'lots and lots', HCI. 'we shall both', Piers Dunkerley
to Britten, n.d. [1959] (B–PL). 'a heated discussion', *News Chronicle*, 11
June 1959. 'I knew he slept', *Daily Sketch*, 11 June 1959.

408 'had definitely', *News Chronicle*, 11 June 1959. 'loved girls', HCI. 'a friend
of', Sir Sidney Nolan interviewed by Donald Mitchell, 11 June 1990.
'Really what', ibid. 'I am delighted', to Christopher Isherwood, 11 Sept.
1961. 'I'm not sure', to William Plomer, 16 July 1961. 'the first large', to
John Andrewes, 29 Aug. 1961. 'I go on', to Basil Coleman, 29 Oct. 1961.

409 'hopeful that', to William Glock, 28 Dec. 1961. 'I am not', ibid. 'I was
completely', to Alec Robertson, 4 March 1962. 'mad about Requiem',
Rostropovich to Britten, n.d. [March 1962] (B–PL). 'the Soviets', to E. M.
Forster, 'Easter Saturday' [1962]. 'How can you', Vishnevskaya 366. 'had
ten days', HCI. 'a rotten arm', to Marjorie Fass, 4 June 1962. 'appalling',
to William Plomer, 5 June 1962.

410 'The queue', '*War Requiem*: The First Performance', programme for gala
tribute to Sir Peter Pears, Royal Opera House, Covent Garden, 30 Nov.
1986. 'We can't go', ibid. 'Britten's masterpiece', *Times*, 25 May 1962.
'silly', HCI. 'the one musical', *The Pacifist*, Jan. 1977. 'the most masterly',
Times, 1 April 1962. 'dear Heather', to William Plomer, 5 June 1962. 'I
was completely', Fischer-Dieskau 258. 'I believe it', *Time & Tide*, 7 June
1962.

411 'gathered only a', *Sunday Times*, 9 Dec. 1962. 'singing it at', *Sunday
Times*, 13 Jan. 1963. 'The *War Requiem*', *Times*, 13 Dec. 1963. 'If the
work', *Sunday Times*, 13 Jan. 1963. 'practically everyone', Kennedy 80. 'as
if one had', Kennedy 80. 'the "public" manner', *Tempo*, March 1977. 'I
would think', BC 96.

412 'a precious idea', to Alec Robertson, 4 June 1962. 'The idea of', to Barbara
Britten, n.d. [summer 1962].

3: Across the river

413 'Ben was known', HCI.

414 'I adored Peter', HCI. 'I found the', HCI.

415 'Anna Pollak was', HCI. 'I was cast', Anna Pollak to the author, 17 Nov. 1991. 'I don't think', HCI. 'the poor chap', Colin Graham to the author, 27 March 1991.

416 'put up a fight', HCI. 'I have to say', HCI. 'He would have', HCI. 'If somebody', HCI. 'It was right', HCI. 'Willie Walton', HCI.

417 'Dear Ben', Rostropovich to Britten and Pears, n.d. [March 1962] (B–PL). 'your doctors', to Rostropovich, 14 March 1962. 'six major works', RB 148. 'the 'contract' was', HCI. 'I've had a', to E. M. Forster, 26 Aug. 1962. 'As you see', to Rostropovich, 15 Nov. 1962. 'the very top', Rostropovich to Britten, n.d. [late 1963] (B–PL).

418 'I am so dreadfully', to Pears, 29 Oct. 1962. 'My darling', Pears to Britten, 30 Oct. 1962. 'This does not', to Rostropovich, 15 Nov. 1962. 'it was really', to William Plomer, 28 March 1963. 'the artist's social', *Daily Telegraph*, 30 March 1963.

419 'I was sickened', to William Plomer, 7 April; 1963. 'some subject like', to William Plomer, 1 Jan. 1963. 'being strangled', HCI. 'actually look at', HCI. 'a proposal from', to Alan Frank, 15 May 1961. 'all those other', to Pears, 18 July 1963. 'we are after', Pears to Britten, n.d. [20 July 1963].

420 'What's so special', to Ronald Duncan, 5 Nov. 1962. 'could you not', to Humphrey Burton, 22 July 1963. 'I do not like', to Lawrence Gilliam, 20 April 1963. 'schoolmasterly voice', Crozier, 'Notes'. 'received a rousing', *Daily Telegraph*, 13 Sept. 1963. 'I feel that', to William Plomer, 10 Nov. 1963. 'In the last', Kennedy, *Walton* 225. 'I don't think', ibid. 'Of all the', *Observer*, 17 Nov. 1963. 'by way of', unidentified cutting [autumn 1963] (B–PL). 'I am enormously', *Sunday Telegraph*, 17 Nov. 1963. 'howlers', *Tempo*, March 1977.

421 'It is becoming', BBC radio interview, Nov. 1963 (B–PL). 'went surprisingly', to Kenneth Clark, 28 Nov. 1963. 'I am *very*', to George Malcolm, 28 Nov. 1963. 'Albert in Later Life' remains in typescript form (Eric Crozier). 'entertained me', quoted in Introduction to 'Albert in Later Life' (Eric Crozier). 'I am afraid', ibid.

422 'Well, I don't', *London Magazine*, Oct. 1963. 'a very *direct*', to Dietrich Fischer-Dieskau, 12 June 1963. 'for such an', ibid. 'I did mind', to E. M. Forster, 16 Sept. 1963. 'instantaneous vividness', *Times*, 13 Sept. 1963. 'I am having', to Hans Werner Henze, 13 Nov. 1963. 'has some very', BC 93. 'When the piece', Palmer 87.

423 'Ben would sometimes', HCI. 'a wonderful time', Berkeley. 'Julian ... was', Pears to Britten, 24 July 1959. 'very difficult', to Rostropovich, 11 April 1963. 'an argument', radio interview on return from USSR, March 1964 (B–PL). 'the dark intricacy', *Musical Times*, June 1964. 'furtive,

claustrophobic', Evans 319.

424 'Ben did a', HCI. 'glossiness', to E. M. Forster, 'Easter Saturday 1962'.
'upsetting', HCI. 'a splendid desk', Duncan 141. 'offered to write', HCI.
'wickedly accurate', HCI. 'I go off', to Yehudi Menuhin, 22 Dec. 1963.
'The other side', to William Plomer, 23 Oct. and 10 Nov. 1963. 'part of a',
to William Plomer, 15 Feb. 1964. 'arctic', to Rosamund Strode, 27 Jan.
1964. 'I am getting', to Donald Mitchell, 5 Feb. 1964. 'strong influence', to
William Plomer, 4 Jan. 1964. 'He wanted our', Colin Graham to the
author, 27 March 1991. 'When we arrived', to William Plomer, 15 Feb.
1964.

426 'were impressed', OBB 49. 'It will be', to William Plomer, n.d. [Feb. 1964].
'unbelievably quick', to William Plomer, 7 March 1964. 'Britten has
become', *Musical Times*, June 1964. 'Snow was falling', *Listener*, undated
cutting [spring 1964] (B–PL). 'excellent', to Ernst Roth, 20 March 1964.
'the students', *Musical Times*, June 1964.

427 'the Leningrad Conservatoire', to David Adams, 27 Nov. 1965. 'enthusiastic and', to Ernst Roth, 20 March 1964. 'not really in', to Leslie Boosey, 13
June 1962. 'pooh-poohed', to Leslie Periton, 15 March 1962. 'Ben was
very', HCI.

428 '... don't worry', to Donald Mitchell, 5 Feb. 1964. 'I have no', Wright,
Faber 5. 'I do feel', to Peter du Sautoy, 20 March 1964. 'Faber and Faber',
Daily Telegraph, 16 May 1964. 'I had never', to Donald Mitchell, 12 Sept.
1969. 'I have been', to William Plomer, 2 April 1964.

429 'a slightly naughty', HCI.

430 'those brave and', to William Plomer, 2 May 1964. 'there was almost',
Berkeley. 'Peter ... brought', Tear 131. 'a joke', Colin Graham to the
author, 15 April 1991. 'Some of', HCI.

431 'there was a bit', HCI. 'without rival', *Aldeburgh Festival Programme
Book*, 1964. 'You know how', to Georg Ehrlich, 2 Aug. 1956. 'Rostro-
povich played', *Sunday Times*, 21 June 1964. 'plainly ... a', *Times*, 19
June 1964. 'Dearest Ben!', Rostropovich to Britten, n.d. [1965]
(B–PL). 'MY DIEREST', Rostropovich to Britten, n.d. (B–PL). 'learnt to
phrase', HCI (Susan Phipps). 'He said', HCI. 'When I have', HCI.

432 'RICHTER DROPS IN', *Daily Telegraph* 20 June 1964. 'The somewhat',
ibid. 'the best pianist', to Lord Harewood, 15 May 1961. 'greatly admired',
ATTW.

433 'I don't feel', interviewed by Peter Garvie, CBC, 4 Sept. 1962 (B–PL).
'exceptional quantity', HCI. 'He would write', HCI. 'Our arrival',
Evening News, 15 June 1964. 'it was quite', HCI.

434 'scarcely breathed', Wren 72. 'The play which', Gishford 61. 'a strangely
fortunate', *Radio Times* 18 June 1964.

435 'virtually a precise', HCI.

436 'I didn't really', ATTW.

438 'The whole thing', Gishford 58. 'The music was', HCI. 'had our hearts',

438 HCI. 'to an astonishing', *Times*, 15 June 1964.

439 'questionable note', *Daily Telegraph*, 15 June 1964. 'Mr Tear', *Times*, 20 June 1964. 'Ben came first', Tear 131. 'astonished', Tear 103. 'devastatingly waspish', RB 152. 'could have been', HCI. 'He is a sweet', to Pears, 17 Nov. 1964.

4: We do not lack enemies

440 'Got a good', to Plomer, n.d. [summer 1964]. '*our* speech', to Pears, 28 July 1964. 'in *occasional* music', *Aspen Award* 11. 'was the definitive', HCI. 'Anyone, anywhere', *Aspen Award* 20.

441 'has for years', *Aspen Award* 15. 'Music is now', *Aspen Award* 20. 'I belong at', *Aspen Award* 21. 'A confession', *Aspen Award* front cover. 'Until the 19th', *New York Times*, 16 Nov. 1969. 'slightly overstated', Kennedy 88. 'help in the Festival', *Opera*, autumn 1966.

442 'endless chair-moving', HCI. 'to give an annual', *Aspen Award* 22. 'a small charitable', to Anthony Gishford, 22 April 1965. 'I kept asking', HCI. 'fantastically considerate', HCI. 'If it worries', to Robert Saxton, 20 Feb. 1968.

443 'immensely gifted', *Times*, 14 Dec. 1964. 'I was extremely', to Peter Maxwell Davies, 12 Aug. 1964. 'I've been madly', to Pears, 17 Nov. 1964. 'had big crises', HCI. 'He thought he', ATTW. 'I must say', to William Plomer, 3 Dec. 1964. 'a trifling', quoted in *Guardian*, 6 Oct. 1964. 'Of course, The Screw', *Times*, 14 Dec. 1964.

444 'about Church', to William Plomer, 8 Sept. 1964. 'My dear George', to Lord Harewood, 15 Jan. 1965. 'I had gone', Harewood 145–6.

445 'awfully prissy', HCI. 'Ben and Peter thought', HCI. 'very supportive', HCI. 'sympathetic listener', Harewood 145. 'I thought it', HCI. 'a lot', Stephen Reiss to the author, 12 Feb. 1991. 'It was the disloyalty', HCI.

446 'were joined by', to John Newton, 19 Jan. 1965. 'as we got', to John Newton, 1 March 1965. 'Anna was an', Colin Graham to the author, 15 April 1991. 'these two couples', to Colin Graham, 19 Feb. 1965.

447 'how important it', Colin Graham to the author, 15 April 1991. 'transcend anything', ibid. 'The Foreign Office', ibid. 'Ben actually', HCI. 'sad at the', OBB 53. 'my old dream', Fischer-Dieskau 259.

448 'I have no intention', *Sunday Times*, 17 Nov. 1963. 'I am delighted', to Peter du Sautoy, 26 March 1965. 'Honours, as you know', to Yehudi Menuhin, 16 May 1965. 'when Peter and I', to John Culshaw, 1 May 1965. 'a sweet letter', to Donald Mitchell, 17 April 1965.

449 'big and serious', to Dietrich Fischer-Dieskau, 15 Jan. 1965. 'I'm getting on', to Pears, 16 March 1965. 'when I think', to Peter du Sautoy, 10 May 1965. 'Britten's deepest', *Times*, 2 July 1965. 'has, I feel', *Daily Telegraph*, 27 June 1965. 'induce a smile', *Times*, 21 June 1965. 'less harmless', *Times*, 2 July 1965.

450 'next sacred', ibid. 'excited', to William Plomer, n.d. [spring 1965]. 'synopsis of', to William Plomer, 30 May 1965. 'terribly busy', to Martin Hall, 22 April 1965. 'suitable sentences', to Donald Mitchell, 10 May 1965. 'a quiet little', HCI. 'At this point', Crozier, 'Notes'.

451 'torture, agony', HCI. 'The three Armenian', Peter Pears, *Armenian Holiday: August 1965*, privately printed, n.d. (copy in B–PL). 'The dangers of', *Sunday Telegraph*, 24 Oct. 1965. 'every imaginable', Peter Pears, *Armenian Holiday: August 1965*, privately printed, n.d. (copy in B–PL). 'setting some Pushkin', *Sunday Telegraph*, 24 Oct. 1965.

452 'with volatile', BC 302. 'he had succeeded', Vishnevskaya 374. '. . . Pushkin's clock', Peter Pears, *Armenian Holiday: August 1965*, privately printed, n.d. (copy in B–PL). 'he is clearly', ibid. 'how different', Vishnevskaya 377.

453 'He was very', HCI. '*Strangers in Babylon*', to William Plomer, 28 July 1965. 'Anyhow I', to William Plomer, 27 Oct. 1965. 'the truth is', to William Plomer, 15 Nov. 1965. 'I loathe date-lines', to Walter Hussey, 24 Nov. 1965. 'Ben is very', to Donald Mitchell, n.d. [late 1965]. 'about half', to William Plomer, n.d. [Dec. 1965]. 'a virtuoso at', to Donald Mitchell, 31 Dec. 1965. 'He is a dear', to Pears, 19 Jan. 1966. 'My state of', Schafer 122. 'major op.', to William Plomer, n.d. [early 1966].

454 'And when I got', HCI. 'The only real', Pears to Lady Clark, 12 Feb. 1966. 'I totter', to William Walton, 9 March 1966. 'My darling', to Pears, 3 April 1966. 'Ben always got', HCI. 'Sir, Dear Prince Philip', to HRH Prince Philip, n.d. [May 1966]. 'Ben felt that', HCI.

455 'an amazing', programme for Aldeburgh Foundation Gala Concert, Barbican Hall, London, March 1990. 'We used to', HCI.

456 'We walked round', BC 66. 'He said', HCI. 'terribly impressed', HCI. 'Stephen said', HCI. 'by far the greatest', to HM the Queen, n.d. [summer 1966]. 'I want a', HCI. 'the last year', Wren 75.

458 'The English Chamber', HCI. 'no wonder that', *Guardian*, 11 June 1966. 'cataclysmic', Wren 76. 'The great event', *Sunday Times*, 12 June 1966. 'much less sombre', Evans 480.

459 'I am prepared', Schafer 120. 'I think there is', Schafer 124. 'Another difficulty', to Jonathan Harvey, 15 Aug. 1968. 'There's no doubt', interviewed by Peter Garvie, CBC, 1962 (B–PL). 'vitriolically scornful', Amis 199.

460 'I have my great', L 1172.

461 'orgy of abasement', BC 221.

462 'the intense pathos', *Sunday Times*, 12 June 1966. 'nationalism . . . with its', *New Statesman*, 17 June 1966. 'shining unelaborated', *Financial Times*, 11 June 1966. 'the treble', *New Statesman*, 17 June 1966.

463 'He said . . . something', *Aldeburgh Festival Programme Book*, 1989. 'I enjoyed your', to Donald Mitchell, 22 Nov. 1967. 'We are just', to Anthony Gishford, 25 July 1966. 'very nice', to Pears, 28 July 1964. 'Ben did like', HCI. 'If anything', HCI.

464 'I remember he', RB 136. 'I remember those', Tear 104. 'had the gift', Stephen Reiss to the author, 12 Feb. 1991. 'He had that', HCI. 'He could make you', HCI. 'He had a gift', HCI. 'I certainly feel,' HCI.

5: The finest hall of its kind

465 'We are tremendously', to Sir Michael Adeane, 8 Dec. 1966. 'The nice Queen', to William Plomer, 5 Aug. 1966. 'a cumbersome', to William Plomer, 20 Sept. 1966. 'think furiously', to Basil Coleman, 12 Sept. 1966. 'Although we', HCI. 'splendid &', to Robert Tear, 22 Dec. 1966. '*very* impressive', to Pears, 6 Oct. 1966.

466 'the most productive', in conversation with the author, Orford, 9 June 1991. 'Stephen Terry is', to Pears, 17 Aug. 1966. 'He'd collect', HCI. 'Ben, when he took', in conversation with the author, Leiston, 8 June 1991. 'He was the kind', HCI.

467 'I'm not saying', in conversation with the author, Chinnor, 30 April 1991. 'a mini-*Billy*', Colin Graham to the author, 15 April 1991. 'very stimulating', to Colin Graham 14 Aug. 1966.

468 'riotous', Colin Graham to the author, 15 April 1991. 'The most important', HCI. 'I saw Ben', HCI.

469 'Ben agreed', HCI. 'Derek, they', HCI. 'and he was', HCI.

470 'paralized with', to Walter Hussey, 4 Dec. 1966. 'because Slava', Peter Pears, *Moscow Christmas: December 1966*, privately printed, n.d. (copy in B–PL). 'S. in good', ibid. 'Went well', ibid. 'Britten telling', Tear 129. 'verbal chewing-gum', PPT 7. 'He had forgotten', Wren 114. 'one of the staggering', Berkeley. 'I think it', Berkeley.

471 'Peter and Ben', HCI. 'studied with me', PPT 60. 'spent a lot', HCI. 'It is a great', PPT 60. 'had a much', HCI. 'I remember Peter', HCI. 'some of the greatest', Peter Pears, *Moscow Christmas: December 1966*, privately printed, n.d. (copy in B–PL). 'say all the', to William Plomer, 6 Jan. 1967. 'I was so', to William Plomer, 17 March 1967.

472 'caught a chill', to Anthony Gishford, 28 Jan. 1967. 'feeling as near', to Eric Walter White, 6 Feb. 1967. 'going frightfully', to James Burnett, 17 Feb. 1967. 'Thanks to his', *Guardian*, 1 April 1967. 'bang on two', HCI. 'paltry sums', *Guardian*, 1 April 1967. 'the worry of', programme for Aldeburgh Foundation Gala Concert, Barbican Hall, London, March 1990. 'most striking', *Times*, 22 May 1967.

473 'artists would often', HCI. 'a kind of', Tear 138. 'My dearest, dear', to Barbara Britten, 16 July 1967. 'thinking about it', HCI. 'asked me very', HCI. 'Three or four', HCI. 'Never, the Queen', Wren 82.

474 'This begins with', *Financial Times*, 3 June 1967. 'It was as if', Wren 83. 'A first visit', *Financial Times*, 3 June 1967. 'by general consent', *East Anglian Daily Times*, 7 July 1967. 'as apt for opera', *Sunday Times* 11 June 1967.

475 'firmly resisted', *Daily Telegraph*, 5 June 1967. 'magnificent', to David

Adams, 26 June 1967. 'quite a success', to Yehudi Menuhin, 29 Aug. 1967. 'It has been a', draft letter to 'Sir Donald', n.d. [1967]. 'a new open-stage', *Opera*, autumn 1967. 'It could be', *Saturday Review*, 29 July 1967. 'completing my trilogy', *Opera*, autumn 1967. 'Dare I ask', to William Plomer, 20 July 1967. 'I look forward', to William Plomer, 17 Aug. 1967. 'almost to the', to Yehudi Menuhin, 6 Sept. 1967. 'totally incapacitating', HCI. 'Ben would go', HCI.

476 'Peter frequently', Berkeley. 'how wonderful', RB 158. 'have a drink', HCI. 'Ben used to', HCI. 'I can't remember', HCI. 'We always used', in conversation with the author, Aldeburgh, 19 Feb. 1991. 'Perhaps as he', HCI.

477 'He would take', HCI. 'I used to', HCI. 'quite often', TMS. 'One used to', HCI. 'the most grievous', to Rosamund Strode, 24 Sept. 1967. 'My mother had', HCI. 'Beata . . . had', HCI.

478 'I am launched', to William Plomer, 22 Nov. 1967. 'The vexed question', to William Plomer, 23 Dec. 1967. 'do less', to William Glock, 17 Dec. 1967. '. . . it's *bitterly*', to Rosamund Strode, 15 Jan. 1968. 'I have started', to William Plomer, 20 Jan. 1968. '& we started', to William Plomer, 20 Jan. 1968.

479 'Lucifer, rather', to William Plomer, 12 Dec. 1967. 'I see them', to William Plomer, 20 Aug. 1967.

480 'I worked as', to William Plomer, 20 Feb. 1968.

481 'on the sea', to Edmund Doyle, 6 Sept. 1967. 'I went down', to Pears, 24 Feb. 1968. 'It's *awfully*', to Pears, 29 Feb. 1968. 'a certain amount', to William Plomer, 4 March 1968. 'I've just had', to William Plomer, n.d. [March 1968]. 'a couple of', to William Plomer, 18 March 1968. 'after 4 fairly', to Eric Walter White, n.d. [spring 1968]. 'By breaking all', to William Plomer, 29 April 1969. 'the city's', *Daily Telegraph*, 13 June 1968. 'the prodigal's', *Observer*, 16 June 1968. 'sufficiently distinctive', *Times*, 12 June 1968.

482 'somehow the props', *Observer*, 16 June 1968. 'end of term', *Financial Times*, 1 July 1968. 'All the people', Vishnevskaya 379. 'my goodness', *Sunday Times*, 16 June 1968. 'Ben and Peter had', HCI. 'Ben was quite', HCI.

483 'Ben and Peter', HCI. 'It was also', HCI. 'got together a', Berkeley. 'Ray Leppard', HCI.

484 'Ben hated it', Raymond Leppard to the author, 12 Aug. 1991. 'Once he received', in conversation with the author, Aldeburgh, 19 Feb. 1991. 'staying with Q. Mum', to William Plomer, 1 July 1968. 'We had four', to the author, 23 Sept. 1991. 'Ben on Complan', Kathleen Mitchell's diary, Edinburgh, 1968 (B–PL).

485 'Slava drank a', ibid. 'Peter had bought', ibid. 'Ben also couldn't', HCI. 'We have become', Kathleen Mitchell's diary, Edinburgh, 1968 (B–PL). 'reading a newspaper', ibid. 'left us all', ibid. 'as he wasn't', ibid.

486 'I haven't made', *Guardian*, 7 June 1971. 'They were a', ATTW. 'As Ben and', HCI. 'went through', HCI. 'I do remember', HCI.

487 'thought of it', OBB 15. 'chores', to Myfanwy Piper, 18 Nov. 1968. 'incredible, full', HCI. 'tired and ill', to Rostropovich, 1 Jan. 1969. 'the various medical', to Joy Bowesman, 10 Dec. 1968. 'a great disappointment', to Basil Coleman, 11 Aug. 1968. 'no one knows', to William Plomer, 5 Feb. 1969. 'They achieved', to William Plomer, 5 Feb. 1969. 'a really wonderful', ibid.

488 'simply superb', to Heather Harper, 5 March 1969. 'in the confines', *Daily Express*, 3 Nov. 1969. 'considerably less', *Daily Mail*, 3 Nov. 1969. 'a very grisly', to Osian Ellis, 31 March 1969. 'curious service', to Diana Menuhin, 20 May 1969. 'the boys', to William Plomer, 22 May 1969. 'The music . . . has', *Times*, 20 May 1969. 'Britten uses', *Guardian*, 20 May 1969.

489 'rather in reaction', to Osian Ellis, 31 March 1969. 'BRITTEN STARTS WORK', *Daily Telegraph*, 17 March 1969. 'If you could', to Myfanwy Piper, 14 April 1969. 'I have been', to Myfanwy Piper, 14 May 1969. 'The Maltings', *Aldeburgh Festival Programme Book*, 1969.

6: I am so tired

490 'somebody rushed', HCI.

491 'We only briefly', HCI. 'was one of', Wren 93. 'Ben was just', HCI. 'Everybody has', *Daily Telegraph*, 9 June 1969. 'it was a', HCI. 'people have grown', *Times*, 9 June 1969. 'it was like losing', HCI.

492 'Floodlights hung', unidentified cutting (B–PL). 'practically untouched', *Guardian*, 9 June 1969. 'still sound', *Times*, 9 June 1969. 'but by then', HCI. 'it was the nicest', *Times*, 9 June 1969. 'there is nothing', *Leiston Observer*, 12 June 1969. 'is going to', *Guardian*, 9 June 1969.

493 'It was sweet', to William Plomer, n.d. [summer 1969]. 'The singers', *Aldeburgh Soundings* (magazine of the Friends of the Aldeburgh Festival), summer 1989. ' Because everybody', HCI. 'beautiful, exciting', *Times*, 11 June 1969. 'unknown', *Leiston Observer*, 12 June 1969. 'Heating had', *Times*, 12 July 1969.

494 'the usual rumours', HCI. 'I am up to', to Yehudi Menuhin, 19 Aug. 1969. 'hideous', to Osian Ellis, 3 Oct. 1969. 'need $200,000', *New York Times*, 16 Nov. 1969. 'I was going', to Basil Coleman, n.d. [summer 1969]. 'I long to hear', to John Piper, 16 Nov. 1969. 'What are we', OBB 6. 'I wrote Ben', HCI.

495 'I loved staying', HCI. 'a passionate', to Fanny Waterman, 9 Nov. 1969. 'We were all', to Mrs J. Magill, 18 Sept. 1969. 'It was useful', to Father Patrick Barry, 25 Nov. 1969. 'Up comes B.B.'s', Blythe 432.

496 'Well, it's a', ibid 433. 'very difficult', to John Piper, 16 Nov. 1969. 'a washout', to Donald Mitchell, 31 Dec. 1969. 'I slog away', to Pears, n.d. [Jan. 1970]. 'a tremendous', to Anthony Gishford, n.d. [Feb. or March 1970]. 'And the light', Sir Sidney Nolan, interviewed by Donald Mitchell, Aldeburgh, 11 June 1990 (B–PL).

498 'asked me', BC 306. 'I try to', *New York Times*, 16 Nov. 1969. 'Snape looks fine', to Marion, Lady Harewood, 28 May 1970. 'there were some', HCI. 'It seemed barely', *Times*, 6 June 1970. 'Fate was not', Wren 96. 'as rich and', *Times*, 9 June 1970. 'Everybody in', *Times*, 15 June 1970.

499 'Like all the best', *Observer* colour magazine, 7 June 1970. 'Ben and Peter had', HCI. 'quite a lot', HCI. 'when Rostropovich', HCI. 'The only opposition', *Observer* colour magazine, 7 June 1970.

500 'there was no', HCI. 'Aldeburgh wanted', HCI. 'If you go', *Observer* colour magazine, 7 June 1970. 'I cannot believe', Headington, *Pears* 233. 'The atmosphere', Duncan 144.

501 'weird, personal', Tear 102. 'I remember', Tear 104. 'Pope, King', Tear 137–8. 'I always used', Duncan 145. 'Ronnie *would*', HCI. 'I remember', Tear 104. 'and they kept', HCI. 'Oh yes', HCI. 'a diumvirate', HCI. 'I think Ben', HCI.

502 'There were kitchen', HCI. 'Given the kind', HCI. 'We all did', HCI. 'lords and ladies', RB 122. 'We were all', HCI. 'when one wanted', HCI.

503 'I suppose I might', HCI. 'tremendous amount', HCI. 'and for about', HCI. 'Rosamund, bless', HCI. 'I think Rosamund', HCI. 'a wizard', to John Britten, 31 Jan 1973. 'Ben needed', HCI. 'I can say', HCI.

504 'He was very', HCI. 'It wouldn't', HCI. 'did tend', HCI. 'straw-clutching', HCI. 'Ben fell for', HCI.

505 'You had to', HCI. 'I'm quite sure', HCI. 'Peter occasionally', HCI. 'Extraordinary the', HCI.

506 'some chic', Tear 104–5. 'decision not', OBB 2. 'I never became', HCI. 'It would have', HCI. 'It meant sometimes', conversation with the author, London, 26 Sept. 1990. 'She was the only', HCI. 'deeply, *deeply*', HCI. 'I think he', MBB 191–2. 'letters of a', conversation with the author, London, 23 March 1991.

507 'final break', Tear 136. 'by Covent Garden', HCI. 'overreacting', HCI. 'since it must', HCI. 'had to get out', HCI. 'an absolute beginner', HCI. 'Please excuse', to Yehudi Menuhin, 30 Nov. 1970.

508 'much the same', to Eric Walter White, 5 Nov. 1954. 'reflects to the', James, *Complete Tales* 9. 'thinking for some', *Gramophone*, June 1970. 'the battle of', OBB 12. 'the offer from', OBB 53.

509 'You could say', *Gramophone*, June 1970. 'fatherly in tone', Evans 520. 'very likely', HCI. 'splendid dreadnought', Pears to Anthony Gishford, n.d. [Nov. or Dec. 1970].

510 'a caricature', HCI.

511 'because everybody', HCI. 'I felt that', OBB 14.

512 'My destiny', Sir Sidney Nolan interviewed by Donald Mitchell, Aldeburgh, 11 June 1990 (B–PL). 'Schubert always', ibid. 'I often used', OBB 3.

513 'I didn't think', HCI. 'My first thought', OBB 15.

7: Under the lash

514 'horrid', Colin Graham to the author, 15 April 1991. 'never actually', ibid. 'his beloved', Stephen Reiss to the author, 12 Feb. 1991. 'might have known', Colin Graham to the author, 15 April 1991.

515 'Godfrey Winngrave', Kennedy, *Walton* 133. 'We have had', to Walter Hussey, 6 Jan. 1971. 'I do hope', to John Piper, 6 Jan. 1971. 'The stories', ibid. 'overwhelmingly affected', HCI.

516 'up Ben's street', HCI. 'When a voice', HCI. 'had such an', Colin Matthews to the author, 27 Sept. 1991. 'And in the drawing', HCI.

517 'a really sticky', Graham Johnson to Donald Mitchell, 19 June 1991 (Donald Mitchell).

518 'I think one', HCI. 'and I remember', HCI. 'a few deplorable', to Anthony Gishford, 3 April 1971.

519 'that fearful', Tear 104. 'It was such', to Eric Walter White, n.d. [May 1971]. 'This is certainly', *Times*, 15 May 1971. 'highly successful', *Sunday Times*, 16 May 1971. 'unmistakably one', *Daily Telegraph*, 17 May 1971. 'very much opera', *Daily Telegraph*, 10 May 1971. 'Owen Wingrave', to William Plomer, n.d. [May 1971]. 'I hope you'll', to Anne Macnaghten, n.d. [May or June 1971]. 'a new opera', *Times*, 2 June 1971. 'Russian absenteeism', *Times*, 7 June 1971.

520 'urgent, unsentimental', *Times*, 11 June 1971. 'a searing', *Gramophone*, June 1972. 'It is not', *Times*, 28 June 1971. 'symbolic figure', DIV 4. 'We have had', to Rosamund Strode, 8 July 1971. 'the most wonderful', HCI.

521 'Reiss was still', notes by Isador Caplan on first draft of Headington, *Pears*. 'He gave you', HCI. 'He was very much', HCI. 'I found out', HCI.

522 'Principal of our', IHD 11 Aug. 1953. 'As the use', 'Snape: The Next Twenty-Five Years', Arup Associates report (Derek Sugden). 'a home for', HCI. 'That's right', HCI.

523 'I have only', Lord Goodman to the author, 19 March 1991. 'absolutely bowled', HCI. 'the kind of', conversation with the author, Aldeburgh, 18 Feb. 1991. 'a bomb-shell', to Stephen Reiss, 7 Oct. 1969. 'would be spread', *Daily Telegraph*, 15 May 1970. 'Ben was trying', HCI.

524 'Stephen was a', HCI. 'we really are', to Charles Gifford, 19 Oct. 1970. 'Arising from the', HCI.

525 'film-star', HCI. 'this pretty', HCI. 'I remember', HCI. 'Maybe the kind', HCI. 'And it was particularly', HCI. 'I did not', Stephen Reiss to Britten, 6 July 1971 (Stephen Reiss). 'Ben and Peter', HCI.

526 'the time and', to the Countess of Cranbrook, 8 July 1971. 'Though he did', HCI. 'quite white', HCI. 'misty', HCI. 'Cruel?', HCI. 'I believe that', Stephen Reiss to the Countess of Cranbrook, 18 July 1971 (Stephen Reiss).

527 'dumbfounded', HCI (the Countess of Cranbrook). 'The Countess', *Guardian*, 31 Aug. 1971. 'The Stephen thing', HCI. 'He went to Bill Ewer', HCI. 'They gave me', HCI.

528 'My dear Stephen', to Stephen Reiss, 19 June 1971 (Stephen Reiss). 'My dear Stephen', to Stephen Reiss, 30 July 1971 (Stephen Reiss). 'Peter wrote too', HCI. 'I shall definitely', Pears to the Princess of Hesse, 1 Sept. [1971]. 'devoured people', HCI.

529 'That was the', HCI. 'The best title', HCI. 'a great musician', HCI. 'I met Viola', HCI. 'like a wise', HCI. 'She was the', HCI.

530 'it was a bit', HCI. 'She was a very', HCI. 'For God's sake', HCI. 'You'd better stay', Tear 104. 'She could see', HCI. 'Viola was a', HCI. 'that of someone', HCI. 'We'd like to ask', to Rosamund Strode, 22 March 1970. 'He told me', HCI. 'didn't visit her', conversation with the author, Aldeburgh, 9 June 1991.

8: Rather a long business

532 'Aldeburgh has been', to Donald and Kathleen Mitchell, 18 July 1971. 'It has been', to Keith Grant, 26 July 1971. 'nobody was talking', HCI. 'Bill Servaes', HCI.

533 'I said', HCI. 'fantastically good', to William Plomer, 21 Nov. 1971. 'It was an absolute', HCI. 'I'm very certain', HCI. 'I have sadly', to Frederick Ashton, 20 Sept. 1971.

534 'fruitful (operatically)', to Donald and Kathleen Mitchell, n.d. [Oct. 1971]. '3 chilly hours', to Laetitia Gifford, 24 Nov. 1971. 'any mention', HCI. 'really set me', HCI.

535 'Stravinsky, Shostakovich', *London Magazine*, Oct. 1963. 'there lurked', HCI. 'Ben being a', HCI. 'a self-indulgent', HCI. 'Ben was concerned', HCI.

536 'To some', HCI. 'I suspect some', to Ian McQueen, 29 July 1971. 'likes to get', *Guardian*, 7 June 1971. 'around *Death*', HCI.

537 'Work progresses', to Pears, 20 Jan. 1972. 'I love you', to Pears, 24 Jan. 1972. 'My dear Charles', to Charles Tait, 26 Jan. 1972 (Charles Tait).

538 'Why don't you', conversation with the author, Aldeburgh, 8 June 1991. 'This money', draft letter to Ronan Magill, 28 Jan. 1972. 'I don't know', HCI.

539 'I still like', to Myfanwy Piper, 6 Feb. 1972. 'excellent, &', ibid. 'I've written', to Pears, 19 Feb. 1972. 'all that music', to Myfanwy Piper, 12 May 1972.

540 'To our great', Rostropovich to Britten, 22 May 1972 (B–PL). 'claptrap', Vishnevskaya 400–1, 445. 'great regret', *East Anglian Daily Times*, 13 June 1972. 'unflagging', *Times*, 13 June 1972. 'tottering slightly', Fischer-Dieskau 273.

541 'a mammoth', Wren 104–5. 'I so envy', HCI. 'a whirl of', to Barbara Britten, 15 July 1972. 'Ben never', HCI. 'another week-end', to Barbara Britten, 15 July 1972. 'I have just', to Frederick Ashton, 16 Aug. 1972. 'When I first', Ian Tait to the author, 7 April 1991.

542 'I've always had', HCI. 'when he played', RB 107. 'capsulitis', Ian Tait to the author, 7 'April 1991. 'from a cardiac', ibid.

543 'impressed by his', HCI. 'the course of', Ian Tait to the author, 7 April 1991. 'rather difficult', *Times*, 30 Dec. 1974.

544 'Peter Pears goes', to Joy Bowesman, 28 Nov. 1971. 'I signed a', Berkeley. 'a little Master', Pears to Fanny Waterman, n.d. (autumn 1971]. 'It was very', HCI. 'I went up', conversation with the author, London, 16 July 1991.

545 'there was a', HCI. 'either the best', to Frederick Ashton, 21 Oct. 1972. 'very bad', *Times*, 30 Dec. 1974. 'He was often', Ian Tait to the author, 7 April 1991. 'a 'flu-ridden', to Anthony Gishford, 18 Jan. 1973. 'putting in', DIV 38. 'I've got 500', to Barbara Britten, 9 Feb. 1973.

546 'filling in some', DIV 38. 'like being on', HCI. 'Ben is writing', conversation with the author, 'Aldeburgh, 8 June 1991. 'I *am* taking', Pears to the Princess of Hesse, n.d. [April 1970]. 'when Ben described', HCI. 'and he suddenly', HCI.

547 'made suggestions', DIV 40. 'very, very', HCI. 'quite an outing', Ian Tait to the author, 7 April 1991.

548 'knew from then', Michael Petch to the author, 6 Nov. 1991. 'a severe operation', to Ray Minshull, 3 April 1973. 'it *is* cheering', to William Plomer, n.d. [April 1973]. 'It is going', to Bettina Ehrlich, 6 April 1973. 'kept getting calls', HCI.

549 'The operation', Michael Petch to the author, 6 Nov. 1991. 'Peter prepared', HCI.

550 'The same year', Colin Graham to the author, 15 April 1991. 'He was still', HCI. 'He was a very', HCI. 'One evening when', HCI.

551 'Ben is off', Pears to Anthony Gishford, n.d. [May 1973]. 'a tremendous', HCI.

552 'what I originally', *Music and Letters*, Nov. 1990. 'Preaching to', HCI. 'Musically, it's', HCI. '*Death in Venice* is', DIV 207. 'I have often', ibid.

554 'on the back', DIV 3. 'used up the', ibid.

555 'unduly intellectual', Evans 527. 'self-consciously stiff', Evans 529. 'I want to', Duncan 132. 'the unequivocal', DIV 207. 'too many', DIV 71.

557 'simply amazing', Colin Graham to the author, 15 April 1991. 'People thought', ibid. 'I miss', Pears to Britten, 12 Oct. 1974. 'My love', undated note [June 1973] (B–PL). 'been right through', *Times*, 12 June 1973.

558 'knocked me out', HCI. 'You wouldn't', HCI. 'but turning on', DIV 41. 'Benjamin Britten', *Guardian*, 18 June 1973. 'does not penetrate', *Observer*, 24 June 1973. 'the Dionysiac', *Sunday Times*, 24 June 1973.

559 '*Death in Venice*', *Music and Musicians*, Aug. 1973.

9: The best brought-up little boy you could imagine

560 'I must say', To Anthony Gishford, n.d. [June 1973]. 'rather a dreary', to

William Plomer, 29 July 1973. 'Ben said', HCI. 'It is a', to Fanny Waterman, 28 Sept. 1973. 'hadn't been', HCI.

561 'it was evident', Ian Tait to the author, 7 and 24 April 1991. 'It's no good',
HCI. 'It is an awful', to Myfanwy Piper, n.d. [Sept. 1973]. 'and it was',
HCI. 'Peter looks', to Myfanwy Piper, 10 Oct. 1973. 'Peter, inexhaustibly',
HCI. 'I was somebody', HCI.

562 'heard him playing', conversation with the author, Aldeburgh 10 Oct.
1991. 'never forgotten', HCI. 'although Britten', RB 168–9. 'I have
always', to Sir Edward Lewis, 16 Nov. 1973. 'So Pat and', HCI. 'he used
to', HCI.

563 'wasn't anything like', HCI. 'I've been thankful', Rosamund Strode to
Donald Mitchell, 25 April 1974 (B–PL). 'decided I should', HCI. 'We tried
to', HCI. 'In the mornings', HCI.

564 'Britten felt that', BC 61. 'The *genius loci*', *Times*, 28 June 1974. 'Recently,
when', *Aldeburgh Festival Programme Book*, 1974. 'Ben could take', HCI.
'I am now', Pears to Donald and Kathleen Mitchell, n.d. [summer 1974].
'for the most', publisher's note in vocal score of *Paul Bunyan*, Faber Music,
1978.

565 'He was always', HCI. 'Benjamin Britten has', *Sunday Telegraph*, 18 Aug.
1974. 'I haven't the', HCI. 'tempted to drive', Duncan 154.

566 'George Harewood', to William Plomer, n.d. [1972]. 'I do know', HCI.
'He really did', HCI. 'heard from Joan', Harewood 147. 'shocked by the',
Vishnevskaya 377. 'I would love', to Stephen Reiss, 14 Sept. 1974. 'I am
in', to Ronald Duncan, n.d. [Jan. 1975]. 'I was very', HCI. 'I am getting',
to Adrian Thompson, n.d. [summer 1974]

567 'point of acceptance', HCI. 'was only concerned', Headington, *Pears* 256.
'agonizing, because', telephone conversation with the author, 25 Nov.
1991. 'Peg thought we'd', HCI. 'It is lovely', to Beth Welford, 17 Oct.
1974. 'I am making', to Pears, 4 Oct. 1974. 'a *Noye's Fludde*', HCI. 'to tell
him', HCI.

568 '"*our*" Xmas', to Donald and Kathleen Mitchell, n.d. [1974]. 'the Folk
Song suite', to Pears, 12 and 26 Oct. 1974. 'a way of', HCI. 'The Folk Song
Suite . . . is', to Pears, 17 Nov. 1974.

569 'My dearest darling', L 60–1. 'I find it', Pears to the Princess of Hesse, 1
Nov. 1975. 'I've lost Ben', HCI. 'something playful', HCI.

570 'the best brought-up', HCI. 'on one of Peter's', HCI. 'I don't care', HCI.
'has been the subject', *Times*, 31 Dec. 1974.

571 'I am very', to Paul Reding, 3 Dec. 1974. 'My dear Michael', to Sir Michael
Tippett, 10 Jan. 1975. 'to ask me', HCI.

572 'I wouldn't have', HCI. 'With two new', *Daily Telegraph*, 22 June 1975.
'macabre nonchalance', Evans 449. 'I have to-day', to Donald and Kathleen Mitchell, 29 June 1975.

573 'I want to', HCI. 'a variation on', quoted in Hamilton 291. 'heavy,
hollow', Vishnevskaya 377. 'chord [of] consummation, BC 410.

574 'He himself sat', RB 174. 'Britten completed', RB 177. 'Bill and Pat', HCI. 'we were going', HCI. 'the whole place', HCI.

575 'We cannot but', BC 391. 'I want the work', RB 179. 'obsessive . . . frenetic', Evans 345. 'Just back', to Bettina Ehrlich, n.d. [Nov. 1975]. 'Ben was in', RB 179. 'We used to have', HCI. 'I am in bed', to William and Patricia Servaes, n.d. [Jan. 1976].

576 'Ben has stood', Rita Thomson to Donald and Kathleen Mitchell, 27 Dec. 1975 (B–PL). 'an occasional', to Oliver Knussen, 21 Jan. 1976. 'a slowly progressive', Ian Tait to the author, 24 April 1991. 'progressive heart', Michael Petch to the author, 6 Nov. 1991. 'Very much undermined', Ian Tait to the author, 24 April 1991. '*Paul Bunyan*'s tone', *Times Literary Supplement*, 20 Feb. 1976.

577 'Ben was profoundly', HCI. 'sanguine about', notes by Isador Caplan on first draft of Headington, *Pears*. 'continued to judge', HCI. 'Try and keep', notes by Isador Caplan on first draft of Headington, *Pears*.

578 'represented the publishing', HCI. 'Glad you find', to Donald Mitchell, n.d. [summer 1976]. 'I want you', HCI. 'The word "gay"', ATTW. 'took a lot', HCI. 'a fairly complex', Ian Tait to the author, 24 April 1991. 'lucky', HCI. 'a young man's', HCI. 'an emotional moment', BC 67. 'The way he', *Evening Standard*, 17 June 1976.

579 'It is certainly', to Colin Graham, 27 Nov. 1974. 'He was really', *Guardian*, 15 June 1974. 'BENJAMIN BRITTEN MADE', *Times*, 12 June 1976. 'He'd been offered', HCI. 'He got there', HCI. 'curiously unnecessary', Harewood 147. 'Somehow it didn't', HCI.

580 'saved energy', HCI. 'Ben said to', HCI. 'Ben didn't mind', HCI. 'traumatic in', to Donald Mitchell, n.d. [July 1976]. 'began the score', RB 181. 'We arranged', HCI.

581 'It was supposed', HCI. 'We sat on', HCI.

582 'a long-distance', *Toronto Globe & Mail*, 12 Nov. 1976. 'I felt Ben', HCI. 'until Peter came', HCI. 'very ill but', Pears to Michael Sells, 29 Nov. 1977. 'I broke the', ATTW. 'he'd really been', HCI.

583 'so direct and', Pears to Michael Sells, 29 Nov. 1977. 'You know, we', ATTW. 'he asked what', HCI. 'on one occasion', ATTW. 'largely because', Ian Tait to the author, 24 April 1991. 'I don't think he', ATTW. 'Ben, having had', Pears to Oliver Holt, n.d. [25 Nov. 1976].

584 'Ben was very', *Observer*, 27 Nov. 1977. 'Ben is slowly', Pears to Philip Ledger, n.d. (Nov. or Dec. 1976]. 'In fact he', HCI.

585 'He died in', ATTW. 'His hand was', Pears to Michael Sells, n.d. [late 1976 or early 1977]. 'Ben asked me', IHD 29 Sep. 1952. 'a private message', *Observer*, 5 Dec. 1976. 'It's a recognition', HCI. 'Benjamin Britten, the', *Daily Telegraph*, 6 Dec. 1976. 'Ben will like', Headington 144. 'weird sense of', HCI.

586 'a fearful task', Pears to Michael Sells, n.d. [late 1976 or early 1977]. 'socially . . . ideally', *Times*, 6 Dec. 1976. 'I've always rather', *Advocate*,

12 June 1979. 'I think he'd', HCI. 'I think he dabbled', HCI. 'passionately devoted', *Observer*, 30 March 1980. 'I'm particularly', ATTW.

587 'But I wouldn't', HCI. 'There was this', Berkeley. 'I must retire', Headington, *Pears*, 286. 'he couldn't let go', Berkeley. 'He couldn't stop', HCI.

588 'When Ben died', HCI. 'Peter did not', Headington, *Pears* 291. 'Peter wasn't an', HCI.

589 'Though outwardly', Wren 121. 'Everything went on', HCI. 'We support', HCI.

590 'It's such a strange', HCI. 'a phenomenal', HCI. 'swung back', HCI. 'I've heard', HCI. 'he was a *good*', Pears to Michael Sells, n.d. [late 1976 or early 1977].

591 'Ben Britten was', ATTW. 'I want to say', *Listener*, 16 Dec. 1976. 'If I had been', *Observer*, 27 Oct. 1946. 'could have been', HCI. 'That's a silly', HCI.

Acknowledgements

I have already written in the Preface of Donald Mitchell's generosity in stepping aside, at least for the moment, from his role as Britten's biographer, and encouraging and helping me with the book. To this I must add my gratitude to him and his wife Kathleen for their friendship and hospitality in London and Suffolk. In Aldeburgh, I was given tireless support and help, and the frequent use of her spare bedroom, by Rosamund Strode, a great encourager and friend. Rita Thomson kindly made me equally welcome as her guest on several occasions at the Red House.

The team at the Britten–Pears Library provided endless help. My thanks to Philip Reed, staff musicologist and Donald Mitchell's co-editor of Britten's letters; to Paul Banks, the librarian; to Sylvia Rush and Jennifer McGough in the office; and to Pamela Wheeler, who with her colleague Anne Surfling kindly guided me through a mass of press cuttings and recordings, and provided photographs (expertly copied by Nigel Luckhurst) from the wonderfully stocked archives. In London, Donald Mitchell's assistants Eileen Bell and Judy Young helped me patiently.

Among Donald Mitchell's fellow Trustees of the Britten–Pears Foundation, Isador Caplan, Marion Thorpe, Colin Matthews, Noel Periton, Peter Carter and Sir John Tooley individually gave generously of their time and helped in many crucial ways to pilot the biography on its course. At Faber and Faber, I was encouraged and helped by Matthew Evans (who, as I have written, first suggested the book), John Bodley and Mary Hill. Fabers' kindly allowed me my own choice of editor and copy-editor. I asked Candida Brazil, whose skills I had encountered on a previous project, to undertake these jobs, which she did with sensitivity and wisdom.

Among Britten and Pears's associates, friends, and acquaintances, other than those already mentioned, I must particularly single out Eric and Nancy Crozier (Nancy Evans), Myfanwy Piper, and Stephen Reiss for help, friendship and support, and for reading and commenting on my typescript. Eric Crozier was especially generous in allowing me to quote from his unpublished writings. But in a sense it is unfair to pick out individual names, since virtually everyone whom I approached for help responded generously and patiently, writing to me at length, giving me recorded interviews, providing hospitality, and answering endless questions. In alphabetical order, the others were:

John Alston, John Amis, Don Bachardy, Dame Janet Baker, Adrian Beers, Steuart Bedford, Jim Berrow, Freda Lady Berkeley, Michael Berkeley, T. A. Blanco White, James Bowman, Alan Britten, Marjorie Britten, Billy Burrell, Catherine Butler, Richard Butt, Keith Cable, Pamela Cadogan, Joan Caplan, Reg Close, Basil Coleman, Ludmilla Cooper, Jean Cowan, Fidelity Lady Cranbrook, Joan Cross, Gordon Crosse, Jeremy Cullum, Meredith Davies, Norman and Pauline Del Mar, Basil Douglas, Ralph Downes, John Drummond, Roger Duncan, Rose Marie Duncan, Peter and Mollie du Sautoy, Valerie Eliot, Graham Elliott, Osian Ellis, D. J. Enright, Sir Geraint Evans, John Evans, Howard Ferguson, the late John Francis, Jonathan Gathorne-Hardy, Samuel Gathorne-Hardy, Letty Gifford, Sir John Gielgud, Lord Goodman, Colin Graham, Keith Grant, David Green, Edward Greenfield, Jeremy Greenwod, Basil Handford, the Earl of Harewood, Heather Harper, David Hemmings, Thomas Hemsley, HRH the Princess of Hesse and the Rhine, Jack Hewitt, Derek Hill, Susan Hill, John Hope-Simpson, Emanuel Hurwitz, Graham Johnson, Oliver Knussen, Briony Lawson, David Layton, Philip Ledger, Iris Lemare, Raymond Leppard, Ethel Little, Norman Lumsden, Sir Charles Mackerras, Neil Mackie, Anne Macnaghten, Ronan Magill, George Malcolm, the Hon. Humphrey Maud, Sir Yehudi Menuhin, Graham Nicholson, Patricia Nicholson, Sir Sidney Nolan, Bayan Northcott, Arthur Oldham, Tony Palmer, Michael Petch, Sue and Jack Phipps, Anna Pollak, Julian and Valerie Potter, John Pounder, Lady Redcliffe-Maud (Jean Maud), Basil Reeve, Eric Reeve, H. J. R. Reeve, Beth Reiss, Basil Robarts, Mstislav Rostropovich, Beata Sauerlander, Robert Saxton, William and Patricia Servaes, Donald Sewell, Desmond Shawe-Taylor, John Shirley-Quirk, Sir Stephen Spender, David Spenser, Ursula Strebi, Derek Sugden, Peter Summers, Elizabeth Sweeting, Ian and Janet Tait, Charles Tait, Robert Tear, Stephen Terry, Adrian Thompson, Alan Thompson, Leonard Thompson, John Thwaites, Sir Michael Tippett, Jeremy Thorpe, Waltheof Tooth, Peggy Lady Trevelyan, Galina Vishnevskaya, the late Marian Walker, Susie Walton, Sebastian Welford, Anne Wood and John Woolford.

I am also grateful to the following for information, assistance and advice: Meirion Bowen, Hugo Brunner, Simon Collier, Michael Cox, Richard Drakeford, Barbara Dunkerley, Sara Forman, Colin Good, William Hetherington (Peace Pledge Union), Julie Kavanagh, Martin Kingsbury (Faber Music), Ian McEwan, Michael Morley, Cathy Nelson (London Symphony Orchestra), Piers Nye, Andrew Potter (Oxford University Press), Libby Purves, Anthony Storr, Kathleen Tynan, Gordon Walker and Colin Watson.

The Bibliography (Appendix B) acknowledges previous books on Britten which have been indispensable to me. I must particularly single out Peter Evans's *The Music of Benjamin Britten*, without which I could have achieved little in the way of musical commentary. Michael Kennedy, another Britten author, has kindly given me encouragement, while Clifford Hindley has generously made available to me his recent research into Britten's operas. Christopher Headington, author of a previous short biography of Britten, and an old friend of mine, took enormous trouble, while writing the official biography of Peter Pears, to help me in every possible way from his large store of Britten lore. I am very grateful to the Earl of Harewood for permission to quote from *The Tongs and the Bones*, and to the Estate of Ronald Duncan for permission to quote from *Working with Britten*. Edward Mendelson and Sir Rupert Hart-Davis, in their capacities as literary executors of W. H. Auden and William Plomer respectively, kindly gave me permission to quote from unpublished letters by those writers. Mstislav Rostropovich generously allowed me to print excerpts from his letters to Britten.

While every effort has been made to trace the owners of copyrights of photographs printed in this book, it has not always proved possible to do so, and any such owner should contact the publishers with regard to this matter. I am very grateful to the Trustees of the Britten–Pears Foundation for allowing me to print photographs of which they are the copyright owners.

Though the Britten–Pears Library at Aldeburgh was able to supply most of my needs, I am also grateful to the staff of the music reading room in the Bodleian Library, and to the staff of Blackwell's Music Shop, Oxford, for dealing expertly with my emergency wants.

The Index, which follows these acknowledgements, was compiled with great skill by yet another Britten expert, Jill Burrows.

General Index

Index of Britten's Works